For a SHORT TIME ONLY

TUESDAY, APRIL 1, 1788.   THE   VOLUME VII. NUMBER 718.

INDEPENDENT GAZETTEER;
OR, THE
CHRONICLE OF FREEDOM.

That the People have a Right to Freedom of Speech, and of writing, and publishing their Sentiments; therefore the Freedom of the Press ought not to be restrained. —Pennsylvania Bill of Rights.
Let it be impressed upon your Minds, let it be instilled into your Children, that the Liberty of the Press is the PALLADIUM *of all the civil, political, and religious Rights of Freemen.* —Junius.

THIS EVENING,
The first of April, 1788,
At the usual place of performance in the Northern Liberties,
SIGNOR FALCONI,
Will exhibit several new INGENIOUS
EXPERIMENTS.
In one of which will be
An AUTOMATON

REPRESENTING an Indian, who will shoot an arrow into any number (which will be fixed in a frame) he is desired by any of the company, placed at the distance of twelve feet. In the same manner he will answer any question that may be made him.

As the mechanism of this piece has been much admired by the connoisseurs in every part it has been exhibited; Sig. Falconi hopes it will meet with the same success in this city.

By particular desire, will be repeated Letour of the ring, which by its complication will be unknown to them who saw it before.

⁂ Tickets to be had at the place of performance.

BOXES, Half a Dollar; PIT, Two and Six-pence; GALLERY, One Quarter Dollar.

The Ladies and Gentlemen that would wish to engage boxes, are requested to send their servants soon.

⁂ *The doors to be opened at five, and to begin at seven o'clock.*

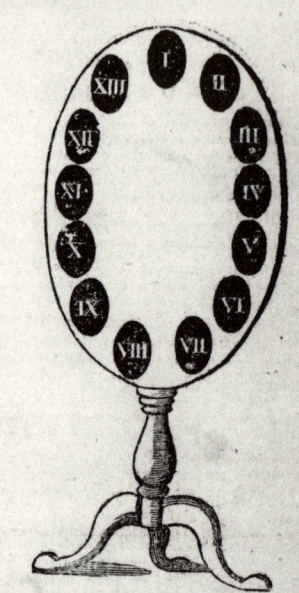

 For Charleston and Savannah
(IN GEORGIA)
The Brig PHŒBE,
DAVID M'CULLOUGH, Master,
LYING at Walnut-street wharf; will sail the 6th of April, wind and weather permitting. For freight or passage apply to the Master on board.
Philadelphia, March 26, 1788.   tdf

To be Sold at Public Auction,
ON FRIDAY,
The 18th day of April next, at 12 o'clock, at the Merchant's Coffee house in the city of New-York,
The Mills and Farm,
At Patamus, in Bergen county, state of New-Jersey, now

For a SHORT TIME ONLY

*Itinerants and the
Resurgence of Popular Culture
in Early America*

Peter Benes

University of Massachusetts Press
AMHERST AND BOSTON

Copyright © 2016 by University of Massachusetts Press
All rights reserved
Printed in the United States of America

ISBN 978-1-62534-199-0

Designed by Dennis Anderson
Set in Adobe Garamond Pro by House of Equations, Inc.
Printed and bound by Sheridan Books, Inc.
Cover design by Jack Harrison
Cover art: Illustration of, "Mr. HARRINGTON, the slack-wire walker," from
William Pinchbeck, *Witchcraft; or, The Art of Fortune-Telling Unveiled.*
Boston: Privately printed, 1805.
Courtesy, American Antiquarian Society.

Library of Congress Cataloging-in-Publication Data
Names: Benes, Peter, author.
Title: For a short time only : itinerants and the resurgence of popular
culture in early America / Peter Benes.
Description: Amherst : University of Massachusetts Press, 2016. |
Includes bibliographical references and index.
Identifiers: LCCN 2016012902 |
ISBN 9781625341990 (jacketed cloth : alk. paper)
Subjects: LCSH: Sideshows—North America—History—18th century. |
Sideshows—North America—History—19th century. |
Itinerant entertainers—North America—History—18th century. |
Itinerant entertainers—North America—History—19th century. |
Popular culture—North America—History—18th century. |
Popular culture—North America—History—19th century.
Classification: LCC GV1835.56.N67 B46 2016 | DDC 791.3/50709033—dc23
LC record available at https://lccn.loc.gov/2016012902

British Library Cataloguing-in-Publication Data
A catalogue record for this book is available from the British Library.

Frontispiece: "THIS EVENING, *The first of April,* 1788, Signor FALCONI, *Will exhibit several new* INGENIOUS EXPERIMENTS." Advertisement showing an "Indian" automaton about to shoot an arrow at one of thirteen locations on a target from a distance of eight feet. Relief engraving for an entertainment by Joseph Falconi (fl. 1785–1819) at Philadelphia's Northern Liberties district. Philadelphia *Independent Gazetteer,* 1 April 1788. Courtesy, American Antiquarian Society.

To Emilie, Parvaneh, Alice, Taraneh, and Michael

Contents

✥

Introduction   1

PART I. THE TRADITION-BEARERS

1. Itinerants and Popular Culture   17
2. Travel Routes and Circuits   36
3. A Legacy of Diversity, a Reputation for Distrust   51
4. Establishing a Public Presence   68
5. Acquiring Skills   85
6. The Impact of Images   99

PART II. SOME EARLY STROLLING PRACTICES

7. Street Performers   127
8. Tavern Entertainers I: Magic Lanternists   156
9. Tavern Entertainers II: Puppeteers, Ropedancers, Conjurers   172

PART III. ITINERANTS ASSUME SCHOOLED AND MANNERED CALLINGS

10. Art of Psalmody   199
11. Musical Life   212
12. Pantomime Entertainment   225
13. A Time to Dance   237
14. Confronting the Professions   248

PART IV. POPULAR CULTURE FLOURISHES IN AMERICA, 1780–1825

15	Waxwork Museums	271
16	Public Painters	288
17	Taking Faces I: The Itinerant Portraitist	300
18	Taking Faces II: The Physiognotrace	314
19	The World of Automatons	329
20	Penmanship Schools	345

Conclusion: America Comes of Age	355
Part 1. Fading Carnival Texts in American Popular Culture	355
Part 2. Itinerancy in the Antebellum Period	365
Part 3. The Itinerant Legacy	369
Notes	385
Bibliography	453
Acknowledgments	479
Photo Credits	481
Index	483

Supplementary materials are available online at
http://scholarworks.umass.edu/umpress_short_time_only/

For a
SHORT TIME
ONLY

Introduction

ITINERANT OR "strolling" entertainers, artists, and healers have an enduring history in the English-speaking world. London's St. Bartholomew district, the oldest of the fairgrounds in that city, hosted traveling miracle plays, jugglers, mountebanks, and animal shows as early as the twelfth century. By the seventeenth century this type of annual event had spread over two adjoining parishes with competing fairs at Southwark, St. James's, and Tottenham Court; others took place at Stourbridge, near Cambridge.[1] The men, women, and children who set up temporary booths and stalls at these sites included puppet showmen like John Harris, who used "Figures as large as Children two years old" to enact drolls, or puppet-plays, of Fair Rosamond, the "merry Humors of Punchinello," and the famous history of Friar Bungay and Friar Bacon.[2] These fairs were celebrated by playwright Ben Jonson and chronicled by diarist Samuel Pepys, who sometimes described these events as bacchanalian but acknowledged that they attracted a mixed audience of onlookers from all parts of the English realm. "Moveable Fairs" were so well attended in England's seventeenth and eighteenth centuries that publishers sold manuals for use by chapmen and promoters that listed towns alphabetically, the holidays on which fairs were held, and the distance of each town from London.[3] There was a marketing element to this fairground activity too. The "cries" of London street tradesmen were transcribed as early as the fifteenth century; hawkers' chants and songs, with their music, found their way into Elizabethan masques and musical fancies and were republished well into the nineteenth century.[4]

In British North America, especially in New England and portions of the Hudson and Chesapeake River Valleys, a geographically dispersed population diffused but did not extinguish popular culture as it was traditionally practiced in English and European festivals. The mountebank healers, peep showmen, musicians, ropedancers, acrobats, and animal exhibitors who for generations had congregated in Europe's markets, village centers, and town piazzas gradually reappeared along North American byways and commons, in its taverns and long rooms, and in its theaters and dance halls.[5] As the colonies prospered and won independence, these initial entrepreneurs were followed by a second immigrant group made up of more sophisticated "professionals" that included specialized physicians, balloonists, singing teachers, and strolling theater companies who saw in federal and early national America an unprecedented opportunity to reach new clients and audiences.

By 1800 transient entrepreneurs were the driving force behind the reshaping of many aspects of American popular culture. Itinerants not only provided traditional indoor and outdoor entertainments but served as transmitters of eighteenth- and early nineteenth-century traditions governing leisure, health, and religious practices that had been virtually abandoned in the face of the perils and uncertainties of the transatlantic passage. Because they employed similar marketing strategies, frequented the same taverns and public halls, and were themselves highly adaptable, itinerants developed a subculture whose lifestyle defined them more clearly than a specific vocation or occupation. They occupied (or shared) the same beds at the neighborhood tavern; they cultivated the same newspaper publishers; they carried with them specially made woodcuts to use again and again in their newspaper advertisements and broadsides. At the height of this movement, between 1790 and 1825, educated and trained portrait painters, science lecturers, dancing-masters, and language teachers traveled about the country in company with street musicians, animal handlers, acrobatic performers, and mountebanks. The fundamental strategy of advertising limited engagements was so widespread that warnings such as "For two nights only," "One week longer," or "For a short time only" became their most common advertising refrain.[6]

Many of the transient activities described in these pages lasted only as long as the country was young, undereducated, underpopulated, and moving westward. But even as some professionals established permanent ties in cities and towns, their place was taken over by a new generation of itinerants whose ranks included painters of "moving" panoramas, daguerreotypists, decorative stencilers and fresco artists, phrenology lecturers, and cart peddlers. Itinerants were now remembered principally by genre painters and fiction writers reflecting on a nostalgic and romantic vision based on their childhoods. Chief among the painters was Charles Bird King (1785–1862), whose domestic scene *The Itinerant Artist* depicts a portraitist grandly taking a likeness in a rural farmhouse surrounded by admiring women and young girls, while the men and young boys whittle and play with their dogs or leave the house to hunt game (fig. I.1).[7]

This nostalgia also permeates some of the most widely read classics in American literature. In a well-known exchange between two Mississippi River characters in Mark Twain's *Huckleberry Finn,* one confidence man meets another for

Figure I.1. *The Itinerant Artist* by Charles Bird King (1785–1862), showing a storybook view of this difficult occupation. Circa 1850. Oil on canvas, 44¾ by 57 inches. American. Courtesy, Fenimore Art Museum, Cooperstown, New York. Museum Purchase, N-537.67.

the first time in the presence of Huck and Jim. The "Duke" and the "Dauphin" (as they are later called by their enthralled hosts) share their mutual expertise in the fields of religion, acting, medicine, and fortune telling. The Dauphin is about seventy years old; the younger Duke is about thirty:

> [The Dauphin:] "What your line—mainly?"
> [The Duke:] "Jour printer by trade; do a little in patent medicines; theater-actor—tragedy, you know; take a turn at mesmerism and phrenology when there's a chance; teach singing-geography school for a change; sling a lecture sometimes—oh, I do lots of things—most anything that comes handy, so it ain't work. What's your lay?"
> [The Dauphin:] "I've done considerable in the doctoring way in my time. Layin' on o' hands is my best holt—for cancer and paralysis, and sich things; and I k'n tell a fortune pretty good when I've got somebody along

to find out the facts for me. Preachin's my line, too, and workin' camp-meetin's, and missionaryin' around."[8]

Pooling their resources, the two men lead Huck and Jim as they proceed farther south along the Mississippi River, touching at small towns where each demonstrates his skill and ending with an outrageous scene from *Romeo and Juliet*. Although the Duke and the Dauphin are eventually discovered by a revengeful mob and tarred and feathered for their pains, Huck and Jim develop a warm friendship with them and are sorry to see them caught. According to his autobiography, Twain modeled his characters on a pair of Englishmen who passed through Hannibal, Missouri, when he was a schoolboy. He recalled that "one day they [the actors] got themselves up in cheap royal finery and did the Richard III sword-fight with maniac energy and prodigious powwow, in the presence of the village boys."[9]

It was in reminiscences, biographies, and fictional accounts like these that itinerant stereotypes evolved—shrewd, irresponsible, shiftless, inebriated, incompetent, and self-serving—formed at a time when some entrepreneurs were still active in rural areas. While these characterizations may in some instances have been valid, on the whole they are inaccurate. The men, women, and children described in this study were often more knowledgeable and talented than they have been given credit for, and they were as committed to their families and the welfare of their colleagues as any other American or American guest. Moreover, they were essential to the growth of this country's appreciation of popular culture at a time when the combined impact of immigration, a reformed religious calendar, and a need to survive in a hostile wilderness obscured the memory of an earlier and perhaps in some respects richer way of life.

When Edmund Rising traveled from London in 1743 to exhibit his optical experiments to audiences in provincial Pennsylvania and Massachusetts, he found a disciplined, religious, and task-oriented sedentary population whose prime concerns remained taming "the wilderness"; surviving against French, Spanish, and Native American incursions; finding cheap labor to run their plantations; and preparing for their own expansion westward. Slavery of Africans was rampant; the majority of people were still attempting to imitate English, Spanish, German, or French upper classes and spent much of their spare time going to funerals, observing fasts, listening to lectures and ordinations, performing road maintenance, serving on training days and militia musters, attending Election Week, and observing Pope Night. What remaining leisure time was available was given over to attending executions and punishments, playing lotteries, and participating in sporting events. A few public pleasures were enjoyed at taverns by mariners and soldiers who passed their time with drinking, gaming, card playing, and dancing (when a fiddler could be located). Others played billiards and backgammon and went freshwater fishing. Sports often involved animals—like horseracing (first advertised in the *Boston Weekly News-Letter* of 29 August 1715), bear and wolf baiting (both with dogs), and marksmanship.[10]

Beyond this, however, most Americans who had not traveled or lived abroad faced a provincial wasteland. Except for those who received private schooling in Europe, almost no one knew how to dance in the "accepted" fashion enjoyed in Europe before 1715; some dancing-masters who taught in Massachusetts were arrested and forced to leave the province. Few people could read music or play an instrument. No one had seen a waxwork exhibition before 1733, a conjurer or a magic-lantern showman before 1743, or a trapeze artist before 1767. No one had been formally taught to draw or paint; few had attended a musical concert or had seen a play or a puppet show. The majority of Americans could do little more than read about these events in the newspapers. "Culturally experienced" Englishmen were sometimes withering in their comments—for instance, John Rowe (1715–1787), a London merchant living in Boston in the 1760s, stated that the model of Jerusalem exhibited in a tavern "was a great imposition on the publick." Rowe was equally patronizing about the Boston stage: "Went in the evening over to Gardner's to see the Orphan acted, which was miserable performed; about 210 persons there. . . . Went in the evening to the Concert Hall to hear Mr. Joan read the Beggars Opera and sing the songs; he read but indifferently."[11]

The people who brought these "missing" cultural elements to America stunned as many people as they offended. Eighteenth- and early nineteenth-century sedentary residents of Boston, New York, and Philadelphia were offered a way of learning current styles of dancing. They were taught shorthand, ornamental penmanship, and flower-making. They tried out electrical cures and listened to clockwork music. They witnessed exhibitions of Italian shades and experiments with solar microscopes and kaleidoscopes. They saw for the first time exotic animals, entered for the first time into a circular panorama, heard for the first time a ventriloquist and the music of theatrical harlequinades, and experienced the thrill of seeing five fireworks pigeons fighting each other "with their natural noise." While some of these innovations were handed down from the upper classes, the majority appear to have been introduced by individual teachers, artists, entertainers, and performers working from the "bottom" up against high odds, one client at a time, in the larger arena of public demand.

WHILE ITINERANCY forms the core of this book, it is organized around a larger and fundamentally more elusive concept. Popular culture has been described as a "melting pot of confused and contradictory meanings" or simply as a "horrendous" concept.[12] In this volume, the term *popular culture* encompasses the British cultural historian Peter Burke's non-elite system of "shared meanings, attitudes, and values, and the symbolic forms (performances, artifacts) in which they are expressed or embodied." In early America this principally means amusements and the "minor" arts—watching or participating in puppetry, acrobatics, wirewalking, balloon flights, street music, street demonstrations, tavern dancing, theatrical side events, and exhibitions of show animals, prizefighting, fireworks, profile taking, waxworks, and large-scale panorama displays. But, as the historian Tim Harris suggests, popular culture (like other anthropological terms such as *material culture* and *visual culture*) touches on and sometimes includes a broader domain unrelated to entertainment.[13] Formal portrait painting, psalm singing, and peddling—subjects that form important segments of the present volume—were pursued by itinerants, but of course none was intended to amuse. These activities—viewed here as composing *mannered* or *schooled culture*—were often introduced by itinerant teachers, singers, and artists in an informal environment variously driven by affordability, access, public visibility, and impermanence. Other "schooled" activities—among them penmanship, foreign language lessons, and electrical demonstrations—were popular because they were usually inexpensive and available to everyday people. Alternative medical treatments and religious proselytizing were popular because they were generally provided in plain sight of others and sometimes in a tavern or an open street. Performances by mountebanks were popular because they employed acrobats and Merry-Andrews (or clowns) to attract crowds, and Harlequin pantomimes because they represented the crowd-pleasing, bawdy, and unwritten elements of the theatrical and circus arts. Even ephemeral events, such as the exhibition of transparencies celebrating the repeal of the 1765 Stamp Act—now known only from a Paul Revere imprint—were popular because these were designed for temporary public consumption.

The work that follows examines the rise of early American popular culture—viewed in its larger sense—as seen through the perspective of itinerants who circulated in British North America and the United States over a period of about 150 years, from roughly 1675 to 1825. Contradictory meanings of course obscure the world of strollers and itinerants just as they obscure the larger world of popular culture. Much of maritime life is entirely excluded from this discussion, as is much of military service. And runaway servants and slaves, key sources of data for music and show people, were not itinerant by choice even as they readily fit into itinerants' surreptitious lifestyle. These omissions notwithstanding, studying itinerants and itinerant "thinking" can expand our understanding of "the world we have lost" and produce new models and approaches for those aspects of events whose origins are now unavailable. We know much about the ballad "Springfield Mountain" because versions of it survived in the Connecticut Valley when collected there by folklorist Phillips Barry in the early twentieth century, but we know very little about how the song spread from one community to another and who communicated it.[14] Ironically, it is the very ephemerality of this itinerant subculture that actually provides this opportunity. While balladeers, street musicians, and acrobats attracted audiences simply by performing, most other itinerant entrepreneurs were obliged to promote themselves by repeated exposure through printed media. Even as they remained personally elusive, they left a substantive trail of advertisements, broadsides, and handbills whose paths we can follow with the help of occasional eyewitnesses (mostly clergymen, lawyers, and plantation owners—and their families) who left diaries, letters, and other recollections.

A related line of inquiry is whether a given entertainment or practice was traditional or innovative. Animal shows, acrobatic exhibitions, puppetry, and trick horseback riding can all be traced to Europe's medieval period, if not earlier, and were shared by most Western, Mediterranean, and Asian cultures. The primary purpose of these traditional entertainments was to attract crowds regardless of the audience's ability to pay; the showmen's cohorts and colleagues found other ways of remuneration such as hawking medicines and pharmaceuticals, pulling teeth, performing eye operations, and selling sewing notions, books, and pamphlets. But transients who exhibited recently conceived European practices or inventions—among them electrical devices, hot air balloons, and music-making machines—found they could attract large numbers of paying admissions. This distinction was important because it helped determine how quickly a given occupation left its place of origin in Europe, who comprised its initial American audiences, and whether semiprofessional entrepreneurs could readily join the ranks of the professionals.

A reliance on itinerants necessarily excludes or glosses over elements that make up the broader world of traditional folk culture and everyday life—colloquialisms, slang, witchcraft, regional dress, sports, balladry, and chapbook and broadside literature, to name just a few. And it does not genuinely address some of the more flamboyant street scenarios of the eighteenth century. No one can tell us, for example, which English immigrants brought with them knowledge of the Fifth of November Pope Night—the practice of mounting a wooden image of the Catholic prelate and the devil on an old wagon and parading them through the streets before burning the wagon in a bonfire. This custom was common in England after 1678, but it was not initially communicated to the English-speaking New World either by printed handbooks or by the deliberate movement of entrepreneurs.[15] Nor is itinerancy always synonymous with popular culture. Most early theater productions and miniature painters—both highly dependent on itinerancy for their American existence—appealed to the same privileged classes in England, France, and Italy where they had originated. And in some instances itinerants saw themselves as formal teachers and not as "tradition bearers." Choral music education in early America—usually pursued by transient but highly trained singers and choristers—confronted a hesitant public who were generally content to stay with their "traditional" or untaught manner of psalmody. In response, many of these teachers adopted itinerant marketing tactics, founded multiple schools, and issued publications—methods also employed extensively by penmanship teachers, fencing-masters, and drawing teachers.

This approach, however, does help us narrow our focus on those individuals whom the Swedish folklorist Carl W. von Sydow describes as the "active bearers" of popular culture and whom Peter Burke calls "tradition-bearers" or "carriers," whose efforts kept alive old practices and introduced new ones among their relatively "passive" audiences.[16] These were the professional and semiprofessional show people, artists, and healers—commonly called charlatans, Bohemians, comedians, mountebanks, tumblers, fools, jugglers, Merry-Andrews, wire dancers, and seventh-sons, but later increasingly known by their specific occupations, such as dancing-masters, fireworks artificers, actors, actresses, ventriloquists, balloonists, phrenologists, and oculists.[17] They provided a direct means of transmitting old and new activities to everyday family life in America and were responsible for much of the transfer of what we are calling popular culture from the Old World to the New. Equally important, this approach allows us to see how American itinerants intersected with other cultural practices that had the benefit of written and taught histories going back for centuries—especially those in singing, music, theater, and dancing.

The preparation of this volume has been guided by three main objectives. The first involves a return to a deeper and more nuanced meaning of popular culture in an early American setting. Most historians of entertainment and popular culture equate the emergence of these genres with the growth of an urbanized working class operating in a capitalistic economy. They essentially point out that "popular culture in the United States . . . did not exist until the nineteenth century."[18] Leroy Ashby, for example, sees popular culture as a nineteenth-century phenomenon that emerged from the American Revolution and was led by "ruffians" in league with large theater owners. Ashby cites the daredevil fall in 1829 by Sam Patch, who plunged 125 feet into the waters at the foot of Genesee Falls in New York, as the beginning of "a turbulent new era" in American showmanship. But evidence reveals that "popular reading" of European imprints had begun decades earlier and that scores of daredevil acrobats, rope flyers, and legerdemain entertainers had crossed the Atlantic more than a hundred years before that date and pursued their vocations—indications that agents of popular culture had made their presence felt much earlier than has been generally thought. In fact, the first puppet master and animal showman in America—Edward Burlesson, born in Suffield, Connecticut, in 1686—had already retired and was teaching school fifty years before American chapbooks came into their prime and eighty-three years before Sam Patch took his plunge.[19] And entertainments of this type were already crowded. Besides Burlesson, there were nineteen professional or semiprofessional puppeteers trying to make a living in British North America before 1775; twenty-three "tumblers," posture-masters, or ropedancers; and at least thirty-seven conjurers or sleight-of-hand show people.

The second objective has been to examine whether the transmission models developed by historians of early modern Europe can apply to circumstances in North America. Where did American popular practices originate? In his *Popular Culture in Early Modern Europe,* Peter Burke devotes an entire chapter to the key role of itinerancy in the movement of popular culture in early Europe, distinguishing between professionals and amateurs. Elsewhere Burke builds on Robert Redfield's 1930 thesis that there were two strands of culture in early modern European life. One was the "great culture" of the classical educated tradition carried on by schools, universities, and organized religious groups; these shared a common language, Latin. The second was the "little culture" of the farmhouse, fairground, street, and tavern—the culture that produced ballads, mystery plays, broadsides, chapbooks, waxworks, and festivals.[20] Burke suggests that the upper classes that pursued the great culture also participated in the little culture, which was open to all, but that the reverse was not true. He further postulates that these two strands were in conflict with each other and that eventually the taught or "reformed" tradition overcame the peasant tradition during the Enlightenment and Industrial Revolution. Scholars have warmly debated the source of popular culture, espousing primarily two views on the subject. On the one hand, Jonathan Swift stated in 1708 that "Opinions [are] like Fashions . . . always descending from those of Quality to the middle Sort, and thence to the Vulgar, where at length they are dropt and vanish."[21] On the other hand, the brothers Wilhelm Karl and Jacob Ludwig Grimm, who collected hundreds of traditional tales among German speakers, claimed in 1812 that popular culture comes from common people: "*Das Volk dichtet*" (The people create).[22] They compared their stories to trees—only those that grew within the larger Indo-European context—which accounts for the stories' many variations. While this appraisal of the Grimms' work has changed over time as more has become known of their collecting stratagems and the role played by a storyteller called "Die Frau Viehmännin," it serves as a starting point for understanding one element in the movement of popular culture in a colonial setting.[23]

In North America, however, Redfield's thesis in a sense may have been reversed. "Great culture"—instituted on the back of an indentured and slave-holding society—established itself as an outpost of "civilized" Europe in what was otherwise an "uncivil wilderness." Harvard College was teaching Latin at least one or two generations before the first conjurers began performing in Boston taverns; the College of William and Mary was teaching classics two generations before the first mountebank physicians are known to have visited Virginia; Pennsylvania College was teaching the Greek language a generation before the first magic-lantern operators began to exhibit to tavern crowds in Philadelphia. By contrast, the "little culture" of the fairground and tavern—the one stimulated by occasional fairs and calendar holidays—followed decades later as colonial and early American society in a sense caught up with its own past.

The work of later historians, including Keith Thomas, Carlo Ginzburg, and Philip Butterworth, whose scholarship straddles the medieval and early modern worlds, also contributes to this picture, as do David Gentilcore (*Medical Charlatanism in Early Modern Italy,* 2006) and M. A. Katritzky (*Women, Medicine, and Theatre,* 2007), which sum up the role of mountebanks and itinerant women as health providers in the period from 1500 to 1750. There are no American studies comparable to these, but writers do address the problem. Authors such as James Deetz state that English folkways, like the English language, were resurrected in an American setting regardless of the background or circumstances of individual families. In his study of early American archaeology, *In Small Things Forgotten,* Deetz sees Americans reworking the "English tradition" in the British colonies. He also finds that the essence of early American life was contained in the "rural tiller[s] of the land" and not in its urban middle class.[24] David D. Hall in turn argues that immigrants came fully equipped with a particular point of view. "The people of seventeenth-century New England," he writes in *Worlds of Wonder, Days of Judgment,* "lived in an enchanted universe. Theirs was a world of wonders. Ghosts came to people in the night, and trumpets blared, though no one saw the trumpeters. Nor could people see the lines of force that made a 'long staff dance up and down the chimney' of William Morse's house in Newbury."[25]

How, when, and where American society reestablished and developed its "little culture" or its "world of wonders" forms the core of this study. Did these practices originate from the mannered upper stratum—meaning the merchants, wealthy planters, officer classes, and religious and civic professionals—"trickling down" to the masses? Or did they originate within the lower social strata—mariners, servants, slaves, soldiers, laborers, and tavern-haunters—gradually expanding into acceptance by the majority of Americans? By focusing on itinerants, we see that the transfer of popular culture was a mixed process that selected some practices but ignored others. Many ideas and tastes that had been deeply imbedded in English life failed to materialize in the New World because the culture "carriers" or "active bearers" of these customs had not joined the emigration. We look in vain for masked festivals such as "The World Turned Upside Down" or the "Lord of Misrule," the appearance of "Savage Men" and London's "City giants," or stories about the cat-woman "Grimalkin." We look in vain for blood sports like the practice of cockfighting or "throwing at cocks," or bull-baiting.[26] Indeed, a review of early works on popular culture—among them

Henry Bourne's *Antiquities of the Common People* (1725), Joseph Strutt's *Sports and Pastimes of the People of England* (1801), and Jehoshaphat Aspin's *A Picture of the Manners, Customs, Sports and Pastimes of the Inhabitants of England* (1825)—shows that fewer than a third of the sports and pastimes found in eighteenth-century English life were actually carried at any point into Britain's American colonies. Other practices grew out of obscure common memories of English traditions such as Pope Night and Punch's Opera. Still others appeared through shared interests and curiosity: horseracing, exotic animals, puppetry shows. A few were initiated by wealthy families when they imported viewing machines, microscopes, and music machines, which later became street attractions. This selective thesis is addressed by Carl von Sydow when considering the movement of culture from Norway to Iceland, which began in the initial immigration of Norwegians in the ninth century: "The bearers of tradition who had thus emigrated, did not, however, represent all the traditions of the whole of Norway not even those of Western Norway. . . . The whole of the stock of tradition that was carried to Iceland by the early settlers must thus have been considerably smaller and poorer than the stock left in Norway."[27]

Finally, this study strives to fill in the scholarship of nineteenth- and twentieth-century historians of early American popular lore and tavern culture such as Alice M. Earle, Harriette M. Forbes, R. W. G. Vail, and Richardson L. Wright, who address some of the same subjects but who worked outside of an academic framework and did little to annotate their research. It especially hopes to reinvigorate Wright's three books, *Hawkers and Walkers in Early America* (1927), *Revels in Jamaica* (1937), and *Grandfather Was Queer: Early American Wags and Eccentrics from Colonial Times to the Civil War* (1939), all of which attempt to define itinerancy as an important component of American culture. A New York City gardener and magazine editor (*House Beautiful*) who enjoyed access to the collections at the New-York Historical Society, Wright viewed America as a collector of eccentric characters and their "stories." His insights, however, are filled with the undiluted marrow of American history. This study also hopes to reinforce more recent investigations of American-based itinerancy undertaken for example by Kate Van Winkle Keller, whose *Dance and Its Music in America, 1528–1789* (2007) stands as an important study of dancing-masters active in eastern America. David Jaffee's ground-breaking investigation of "Peddlers of Progress," published in the *American Historical Journal* in 1991, was followed by an acclaimed larger work in 2010; and John A. Hodgson, whose comprehensive investigation of the itinerant careers of James and John Rannie and the relationship of these two entertainers to Richard Potter will soon become available under the title "Ventriloquism Becomes American." Other historians include Milbourne Christopher, Paul McPharlin, James W. Barriskill, Norman A. Benson, Kym S. Rice, Barbara Lambert, Nym Cooke, Donna-Belle Garvin and James L. Garvin, and Alan Clark Buechner, who have written extensively on itinerant entertainers, psalmody teachers, musicians, dancing-masters, singing-masters, and early American tavern life.

In terms of research sources, this study is based first of all on diary accounts, reminiscences, and household and shop inventories. Chief among the diaries are those of Samuel Pepys of London, England; Joshua Hempstead of New London, Connecticut; the several Holyoke family members of Salem, Massachusetts; as well as the diaries of Reverend Ebenezer Parkman of Westborough, Massachusetts, of Samuel Sewall of Boston, and Reverend William Bentley of Salem. Other diarists include Reverend Ezra Stiles, Reverend John Ballantine, William Pynchon, Nathaniel Ames, and William Byrd. These are supplemented by reminiscences—for example, those of dancer John Durang, profile taker James Guild, portrait painter Chester Harding, and actor John Bernard.

At the same time, because itinerants disseminated their ideas through promotional documents, an important research avenue has been the systematic examination of newspaper advertisements issued in eastern America between 1700 and 1825 and of handbills, broadsides, and other printed announcements in American historical collections and libraries. Beginning with the *Boston Weekly News-Letter* in 1704, almost two hundred newspapers were published in early America, many of them coming out twice a week or even daily. While the study gives particular emphasis to announcements by itinerant portrait painters, limners, and profile takers, these sources also generate unusual discoveries about individuals. The central role of showman Richard Brickell in the 1740s and 1750s is derived entirely from newspapers. The knowledge that John Templeman the surgeon-dentist and John Templeman the acrobat were the same individual (a key link that bridges medieval and modern points of view) is based on two brief postings, one in the *Pennsylvania Evening Gazette* on 6 March 1780 and the other in the *Providence Gazette* on 10 February 1781; it was confirmed by the reminiscence of William Wirt of Maryland, who remembered meeting the well-dressed but corpulent acrobat as a land-dealer in Washington, D.C. And the fact that the French balloonist Jean-Pierre Blanchard hired a black band of musicians (a clue to the larger role of blacks as street musicians) comes from a single notice he issued in the *Massachusetts Mercury* on 21 July 1795 apologizing to his backers. The extensive use of newspaper sources has led to a fundamental geographical bias that concentrates the argument on the American Northeast. Readex's "Early American Newspapers, 1690–1922"—the digital source for much of the advertising considered here—more fully represents newspapers published in Boston, New York, and Philadelphia than those published in Charleston, Williamsburg, Annapolis, and Fredericksburg.[28] To some extent a close reading of compilations and histories whose authors did have access to the early sources can sometimes offset this. We know this from Milbourne Christopher's work on conjurers in Maryland and from Kate Keller's *Dance and Its Music in America,* which found dancing-masters widely active in South Carolina, Virginia, Maryland, and Georgia in the 1720s and 1730s long before they became common in New England. But it is a bias nonetheless.

We are indebted to earlier historians for many of the names that resonate throughout the book. Some of the most promising insights were discovered (often serendipitously) by writers and compilers whose notes and sources have been lost. The identification of Edward Burlesson was occasioned by a now-missing paper "at the City Clerk's office" in Boston cited by editor Justin Winsor in his four-volume history of that city. (This information was fortunately confirmed by entries in the diary of Reverend Ebenezer Parkman, which were kindly provided by Ross W. Beales, Jr.) The identification of Dr. Anthony Yeldall was drawn from a typescript copy of a diary kept by Reverend John Ballantine, whose original manuscript is now illegible. (Yeldall's role was substantiated by the diary of Elizabeth Phelps, who lived in an adjacent town in the Connecticut River Valley.) Finally, we are grateful for the tireless efforts of antiquarians and librarians who collected and bound old newspapers, as well as for the photographic and digital technology that eventually made them available to scholars and the general public.

Part I

THE
TRADITION-BEARERS

Chapter 1
Itinerants and Popular Culture

IN 1687, at a critical moment in New England's history, when the Massachusetts Bay Colony was still struggling with the revocation of its charter, a Boston tavern owner and artillery captain named John Wing twice came to the attention of the town's authorities. Jurist Samuel Sewall (1652-1730) recounted in his diary that in April, two English soldiers dressed in red-and-white livery paraded in the town with naked swords followed by a boisterous crowd; they later fought a duel before Wing's Castle Tavern. The winner, who wounded his opponent, left Dock Square shouting in triumph accompanied by a drummer. Sewall let the incident pass, although it seemed to bother him. The following December, however, John Wing allowed a showman the use of his long room for an exhibition. This time Sewall acted. Joined by other members of the Third Church of Boston, Sewall accosted Captain Wing and held him accountable. An entry in Samuel Sewall's diary described the outcome. "Sabbath, December 4," he wrote,

> In the Evening Capt. Eliot, Frary, Williams and Self, Treat with Brother Wing about his Letting a Room in his House for a man to shew Tricks in. He saith, seeing 'tis offensive, he will remedy it. It seems the Room is fitted with Seats. I read what Dr. Ames saith of Callings, and Spake as I could, from this Principle, that the Man's Practice was unlawfull, and therefore Capt. Wing could not lawfully give him an accomodation for it. Sung the 90th Psalm from the 12th v. to the end. Broke up.

In response to Sewall's request, Wing, who like Sewall was a member of the Third Church, quietly obliged his colleagues. Acknowledging that the man's practice was "offensive," he sent the entertainer away.[1]

The church's discipline of Brother Wing was not the first time that religious authorities had censured popular entertainers in the seventeenth-century

Western world. Peter Burke tells us in *Popular Culture in Early Modern Europe* that the Catholic curé in Nanterre, France, came across a group of wandering stage players in 1637 and "tore the mask from the face of the leading actor . . . [and] took the fiddle away from the man who was playing and broke it." He directed the officers accompanying him to overturn the stage. Burke also reports that in Russia when Archpriest Avvakum Petrovich came across dancing bears led by a clown in the 1640s, he took the time to break "the buffoon's mask and the drums" and to take the bears to the open country where he let them go.[2]

But the event in Wing's tavern does mark the beginning of an important but little-known American experience. While we do not know the name of the man who "shew[ed] Tricks" in Castle Tavern, his entertainment is one of the first documented examples of popular culture in early America and probably the first example of an entertainer in North America performing in a room "fitted with seats" in front of a paying audience. Because the English-speaking colonies were still disparately inhabited and basically unformed, this conjurer—as comedians were sometimes termed in England—was obliged to range far and wide in the New World and possibly well beyond to find audiences. Was he the same unidentified "jester" encountered by Huguenot exile Durand of Dauphiné on the banks of Virginia's Potomac River just before Christmas in 1686? This jester was accompanied by three fiddlers, a tightrope dancer, and an acrobat.[3] If they followed the paths of other show people in this early period, many originated from Italy, Germany, and England and had already made stops in London, Dublin, Rome, Paris, and other capital cities as well as most of "the country[side]" in every sovereign state in Europe. In the New World they probably stopped in British, French, and Spanish possessions of the West Indies; in Central and South America; in Virginia and the Carolinas; and in Boston.[4] Their careers were typical of scores of strolling entertainers and related specialty performers and teachers—not all so intriguing and controversial as conjurers—who circulated in the North American colonies while depending on itinerancy for their survival. Others include a "famous German Artist" who performed "Dexterities of Hand" in a New York City bakeshop in 1734; a Connecticut-born "cripple" exhibiting puppets in a tavern in Westborough, Massachusetts, in 1739; and a London entertainer projecting images of Noah's Ark in a barn in Ipswich, Massachusetts, in 1794. The list encompasses healers, dancing-masters, musicians, peddlers, and prizefighters. Many lived in the same rooming houses, boarding houses, taverns, inns, and hotels. They traveled about on foot, on horseback, on stage wagons, and in packet boats. In terms of their ages, the Rannie brothers were in their twenties when they began their unprecedented conjuring tour of North America; the puppeteer Samuel Jameson Maginnis, also known as James Maginnis, was twenty-three; animal trainer William F. Pinchbeck was probably in his early thirties; and penmanship teacher James Guild was twenty-one. But they were all familiar with the same newspaper editors and printers who published their advertisements and sold them printed matter. And they considered a positive letter of reference more important than a good meal.

Cultural transmission through the medium of international itinerants of course had been going on in England and continental Europe at least since the late medieval period if not earlier. Philip Butterworth's study of magic on the early English stage indicates that Italian and Hungarian jugglers and tumblers readily infiltrated late sixteenth-century Elizabethan society, as did French, Turkish, and Dutch ropedancers and vaulters. One rope flyer performing in London in 1547 was "a Native of Arragon"; others in 1698 were a "*Morocco* Woman, two *German* Maidens, and the Danish Woman and her Company."[5] The number of foreign-based or foreign-trained itinerants entering North America may have equaled those in England or have been even higher (see tables 1.1 and 1.2 at the end of this chapter). Allowing for exaggerations and reporting errors, out of an estimated 4,200 professional and semiprofessional itinerants or tradition-bearers known to have been working in North America before 1825, between half and two-thirds were European-born. Stage professionals and dancing-masters were the most common, but there were also large numbers of musicians, portrait painters, circus people, and language teachers. Their activities seem to have been concentrated wherever population density was highest: in New England, New York City, and contiguous areas of New Jersey, eastern Pennsylvania, and the Hudson River Valley; in the middle and southern Atlantic colonies of Maryland and Virginia; and in the southern ports of entry of Charleston and Savannah, as well as in Mississippi and Louisiana. Most were recent arrivals in the New World, but some were Americans who had learned their skills in Europe. About one out of ten traveled with a married partner or companion. Successful strolling actors, for example, almost always toured as couples, many of them with children. Acrobats worked and performed as families; musicians and singers frequently designed their acts around their children, some as young as three. And at least one mother accompanied her artistically talented son.[6] The ranks of itinerants included former military officers, newspaper publishers, college graduates, and educated as well as self-trained physicians. Two were blind or half-blind (a Scottish lecturer and an English keyboardist); several others were physically handicapped or deaf.[7] One child whose parents had lately perished in a shipwreck toured North America as an independent thirteen-year-old acrobat.[8] Some were self-employed, unattached women. And a few were runaway slaves or former slaves, both African American and Native American.

While these figures all but disappear in a 1790 census population of approximately 4 million people, traveling entrepreneurs made their presence felt well beyond their relatively small numbers. They were critical to the resurgence of popular culture in a North American landscape where these practices had been neglected or absent for several generations. During the 1750s and 1760s—shortly after a company of strolling players and musicians formerly touring the West Indies landed in Yorktown, Virginia—a steady stream of transient English and continental European alternative healers, apothecaries, surgeon-dentists, portrait painters, dancing-masters, fencing masters, equestrians, tavern entertainers, language instructors, japanners, and decorative arts teachers began arriving in the seaports of North America looking for opportunities and careers. This influx represented an unprecedented cultural invasion of the North American provinces, and it came to a head in the vital provincial prerevolutionary period from 1765 to 1775 when at least twenty dancing-masters and fencing teachers, all of them newly from England and France, and many with experience as musicians and language teachers, began holding schools in New England, New York City, Philadelphia, and Charleston. About twenty itinerant healers entered the colonies and about twice that number of tavern entertainers. Overall, for every known or presumed transient entrepreneur operating in British North America in the period prior to 1750, thirty years later there were three or four times that number.

When they resumed their activities after the American Revolution, traveling entrepreneurs met greater acceptance and broadened tastes, especially in the fields of language instruction and the polite arts (dancing, fencing, etiquette). Acrobats for the first time performed before paying audiences "by permission" of the authorities. Plays and operatic and pantomime pieces began to be staged on a regular basis in coastal cities such as Philadelphia, New York, and Baltimore. After the French Revolution and the uprising in the French West Indies the number of expatriate dancing-masters again doubled, and new forms of entrepreneurship appeared in the form of art exhibitions, balloon flights, fireworks displays, and ventriloquy acts. The majority of itinerants were foreign born as before, but they were increasingly diverse. Ireland, Spain, Italy, Holland, and Germany became as commonly represented as countries of origin as England and France.

Reverend William Bentley (1759–1819), minister of the Third Church in Salem, Massachusetts, noted these changes after reading through the advertising columns of the town's leading newspaper on 25 May 1798. The *Salem Gazette,* he wrote in his diary,

> never had so many advertisements of the same kind as at this day. The Theater for this Evening at Washington Hall. Ibrahim Adam Ben Ali, a Quack Doctor, cures all. A new stage to run from Boston. We have two from Salem already. P. A. Von Haegen, jun: on the Forte Piano. 5D. entrance. 6D. for 8 lessons. Mr and Mrs Rosier's Concert on 1 June. Mrs Solomon, an Actress, to teach Tambouring. Besides these we have Hotels, French dancing Masters, French

Grammar Master exclusively of Am[erican] Dancing Master, & many private Schools. The Pig of Knowlege has left the Town. The Dog went before him. Such is the change since I have been in Salem.[9]

As many varieties of itinerancy existed as there were occupations. At one end of the spectrum was Enoch Noble, a black healer who in 1777 strolled about central Massachusetts "pretending to practise Physick" and selling medicinal wares. Noble spent at least some time in Reverend Ebenezer Parkman's parsonage in Westborough where he was sent by a neighbor concerned about the failing health of Parkman's daughter Hannah. Parkman learned about a month later that Noble was a runaway, that his real name was Constant, and that he was eventually recaptured by his master, who visited Westborough in search of him.[10] Noble was one of a long succession of healers, exhorters, and wild animal keepers traveling through rural North America—whose open spaces in effect served as the provincial equivalent of London's street fairs. He and others like him appear and disappear in the pages of clergymen's and inn keepers' diaries as they made what may have been systematic rounds in search of meals and overnight lodgings. As soon as these itinerants had exhausted their livelihood in one community, they moved on to the next.

At the other end of the spectrum was John Griffiths (fl. 1783–1810), the experienced and socially well-connected, French-speaking dancing-master listed in the *Boston Directory* of 1789. Griffiths began his professional career in 1783 as a French teacher in Albany.[11] In his role as a dancing-master his popularity was so great and his methods so widely imitated that his schools virtually defined the profession at the close of the eighteenth century. As he traveled in New York and New England, he published five dance manuals. The first was issued in 1786 with printer Daniel Bowen, who was in New Haven when Griffiths opened a dancing school there. Griffiths named a few dances after himself, such as "Griffith's Fancy." But, like composers of psalm tunes and hymns, he titled many after locations where he had taught school: "The Pleasures of Providence," "Greenfield Assembly," and "The Humors of Boston."[12] He seems to have been traveling with his family, possibly a wife and four children (two boys and two girls); he was the owner of a fourteen-year-old slave named Rachael (who ran away from her new owner in 1786), and his periodic stays in cities such as New Haven, Boston, and New York were advanced by introductions to the "best families" and affidavits from previous clients and other dancing-masters attesting to his integrity and competence.[13] In Boston, Griffiths arranged to hold classes at Concert-Hall from owner William Turner. In the Connecticut River Valley, Griffiths is mentioned in the diary of Elizabeth Porter Phelps (1747–1817) of Hadley, Massachusetts, who sent two daughters, Thankful and Betsy, to his school across the river in Northampton.[14] But like Enoch Noble, he was subject to the same market forces that kept both of them on the move. Noble relocated on a daily or weekly basis; Griffiths, about once every two or three years. Despite his financial ability to purchase or lease a home, Griffiths's attraction in a given community hinged on his having just arrived from a desirable center of fashion like New York City, Philadelphia, or Boston. Once his appeal was expended, he was obliged to pull up stakes, arrange for a new round of referrals and letters of recommendation, and move to a new venue.

Two chief characteristics distinguish itinerants' callings. First, their travel was speculative and dependent on circumstances over which they had little control. Although they constantly moved about in order to increase the likelihood of finding clients, there was no guarantee that removal to another tavern, town, or region would bring them employment. In 1819, when playwright William Dunlap (1766–1839) was working as a portrait painter in Norfolk, Virginia, he encountered Allison Wrifford supplementing his income as an itinerant penmanship teacher by giving evening lectures on chirography. Dunlap reported that Wrifford lectured to an almost empty hall.[15] And despite Benjamin Trott's success as a protégé of and copyist for painter Gilbert Stuart, his career as a miniaturist—and those of many others—is best summed up in Dunlap's haunting remark: "Trott . . . is starving in Phila."[16] Dunlap had himself encountered a similar problem. Leaving New York City on his way to Boston in 1813, he spent a few days in Providence. But "finding no employment for an itinerant painter," he "pushed on."[17]

The second characteristic was versatility. Bearers of cultural traditions working in early America seemingly took on new occupations as easily as they changed their clothes. They were so facile in this regard that, for a majority, their ability to move from place to place was itself a calling, and their choice of a particular trade was determined by a marketplace that they themselves helped fashion and create. This opportunistic mentality was a hallmark of American itinerancy in the eighteenth and early nineteenth centuries and in a sense was a holdover from a medieval definition of callings. It also gave a degree of unity to a group of transient artists and tradespeople marked by an otherwise overwhelming diversity of backgrounds and talents.

Most multiple callings fell within logical parameters. James Joan or Juhan (d. 1797), a French or Italian singer and musician, landed in Boston in 1768 with the three regiments of British troops and officers newly assigned from Halifax, Nova Scotia, to help reinforce the customs officer assigned to the town after the Stamp Act disturbances. To support himself Joan relied on his profession as an instrumentalist and his background as a cultivated European, holding schools for dancing, learning French, and musical instruction. He also made and sold stringed instruments and screw bows, gave concerts, and performed musical theater. There were many others like him. Samuel Jameson Maginnis

(c. 1772–1805), a Scottish-born puppeteer and mechanic who showed up one year in Newburyport, Massachusetts, took his "Artificial Wax-Work Commedians" over the next ten years to every major city between Albany and Charleston. But halfway through this excursion Maginnis unexpectedly shifted his emphasis and offered his audiences a medley of songs and recitations, followed by "philosophical experiments," such as card shuffling, tricks with pistols, magic acts, and deceptions with broken watches. It is clear that he was an experienced conjurer and "stand-up" showman besides a maker of automatons.[18]

At other times the combination of careers among itinerants was so unlikely it defies understanding. There were electrical healers like Martin Howe who took up profile painting, hairdressers and bootblacks like Peter Choice who became profile makers, museum proprietors like Philip Woods who administered electrical treatments, waxwork specialists like Joseph Chiappi who removed cataracts, tavern showmen like Joseph Falconi who gave lectures on science, optical specialists like Edmund Rising who entertained in public taverns, and acrobatic performers like John Brenon, who cured "the Tooth-Ach without drawing" after completing his ropedancing routines.

At least one itinerant merged a career as a gymnast with top-level occupations as a dental surgeon, securities broker, and real estate dealer—doing all four with equal success. Identifying himself with the cachet "late from Europe," Virginia-born John Templeman (fl. 1779–1818) performed in the late 1770s and early 1780s as a wirewalker, wire dancer, and fireworks artist in Maryland, Philadelphia, and Providence. A reminiscence of Templeman by William Wirt (who was about six years old at the time he saw him) in Bladensburg, Maryland, provides one of the earliest close-up descriptions of a strolling eighteenth-century ropedancer performing in North America:

> We got there at early candle-light. The room was brilliantly lighted. A large wire fastened at each end of the room, near the ceiling, hung in a curve, the middle of it within twelve or fifteen inches of the floor. . . . The entrée of Templeman—a tall man, superbly attired in a fanciful dress; of a military air, with a drum hung over his shoulder by a scarlet scarf. . . . Saluting the company with dignity, he placed himself upon the wire; then giving a hand to his attendant, he was drawn to one side of the room, and, being let go, swung at ease,—beating the drum like a professional performer. He performed all the usual exploits, balancing hoops, swords, &c.—and, to crown the whole, danced what I had never seen before, a hornpipe, in superior style;—his spangled shoes, in the rapidity of his steps, producing upon me a most brilliant effect.[19]

In Philadelphia, Templeman was seen by aspiring stage dancer John Durang (1768–1822), son of French Huguenot parents, who left a manuscript reminiscence of his formative years that describes the circumstances under which he assumed his occupation as a stage dancer and trick rider. He described Templeman as the "most compleat in the art" of slack-wire dancing, playing before crowded audiences.[20] When he reached Boston, Templeman hoped to continue his acrobatic career, and in a document cosigned by many Boston inhabitants, he requested permission from the town's selectmen. Despite a second visit to the selectmen, Templeman's petition was never acted on. But apparently relying on European training in which acrobats still pursued what Peter Burke calls the "extremely old" combination of healing and entertainment, he began advertising in Boston as a surgeon.[21] Templeman was so skilled at this profession that the same year he applied to Boston's selectmen, his methods in dental surgery won approval from the Boston Medical Society. Later that year he was one of thirteen original medical subscribers to the clandestine anatomical lectures held in Boston in 1780. Templeman continued to reside in that town as a practicing dental surgeon, seeking to buy live teeth for transplants.[22] It was only a matter of the selectmen's choice that forty-five-year-old Mary Vial Holyoke (1737–1802), second wife of physician Edward Augustus Holyoke of Salem and one of many patients in Massachusetts whose teeth were "set" (meaning straightened) by Templeman in July 1782, did not see her surgeon-dentist entertain in Boston on the slack wire dressed "in representation of Mercury."[23] Seven years later in 1789, Templeman was back in Boston working as a financial broker and lottery manager.[24] Eleven years after that, John Durang ran into Templeman a second time in Georgetown, Maryland, where Durang found the performer "a very rich man, a tall well handsome made." Templeman kindly procured a tobacco barn for Durang and his colleagues for their circus performance.[25]

Behind these characteristics were clear-cut patterns of behavior that helped determine which practices were likely to succeed and which would probably fail in an American setting. One pattern relied on centuries-old traditions—as exemplified by a pharmacist based in Philadelphia and active before and during the American Revolution. We learn most about Dr. Anthony Yeldall (fl. 1770–1799) from an eighteenth-century Massachusetts eyewitness, a Westfield clergyman named John Ballantine (1716–1776). In the summer of 1773, Ballantine saw something on the town's common so astonishing that he went home to document it in his diary. "Doct. Anthony Yeldal," he noted on Tuesday, 10 August, "set up a stage, on it 2 lads entertained spectators by walking on their hands & by various feats of activity. The Doctor harangues on what he can do, the terms on which he doth anything, the way he goes on in. He harangues on the virtues of certain Medicines he hath to sell. There was not a large collection of people. He is to appear on 5 Tuesdays."[26]

While we do not know how close Reverend John Ballantine's residence was to the Westfield Common, he nevertheless obligingly tracked Yeldall's visits. On Tuesday, 17 August, one week later, the clergyman reported, "Doct. Yeldal set up his stage, a great concours," and a week after that he related, "Stage set up. New feats," and on Tuesday, 31 August, "Stage set up." Finally, on Tuesday, 7 September, Ballantine observed, "The stage set up. Walk on wires, many spectators."[27] Nor was Ballantine the only Massachusetts diarist following Yeldall's appearances. Elizabeth Porter Phelps, who lived nearby with her husband at Forty Acres, wrote that on 2 September 1773, a Thursday, "Esq. Chaunceys son, Daughter here." She continued, "Mr. Phelps and I and they went into town to see Mountabank Doct. play his tricks etc."[28]

Two points stand out here. First, Yeldall was a peddler of pharmaceutical goods, a common but virtually unstudied occupation in early America.[29] Second, John Ballantine's and Elizabeth Phelps's eyewitness descriptions recognize him as a haranguing mountebank, a curiously relict post-medieval figure seemingly out of place in provincial eighteenth-century American society, which for the most part had left behind popular "nostrums," platform healers, and medical and sexual quacks in the marketplaces, bedrooms, and fairgrounds of Europe. His two "lads"—later identified as John McDonald, the "tumbling" journeyman, and Michael Handley, the apprentice—were professional entertainers who, as with Yeldall, were likely to have been recent immigrants from England and may have come over with him. (They were also known by their stage names "Mr. Merryman" and "Mr. Quicksilver.") Yeldall and his assistants probably devoted at least five weeks to canvassing this area of the Connecticut River Valley, setting up their stage in Westfield and Hadley on alternating Tuesdays and Thursdays. He may have scheduled stops in other local towns on the remaining days of the week. But soon they were back on the road. By October 1773 they had reached New London, Connecticut. And early the following year they returned home to Philadelphia.[30]

Trained as a surgeon, Yeldall was known by his critics as an adventurous "stroller" but by his friends and family as a "distinguished physician." According to his own account, he toured eastern North America observing "the different diseases incident to each climate"—and his visits to Westfield and Hadley were presumably part of this initial learning process.[31] A wealthy member of the English middle class, he apparently came to North America in 1770, arriving in Philadelphia in September and taking lodgings on Fourth Street, near the Old First Reformed Church. He laid out a schedule in Philadelphia and four nearby towns where he attended on a weekly basis. He also set up a small pharmaceutical factory, advertising that he cured a variety of conditions such as dullness in hearing and *morbus Gallicus* or French Disease (the same one the French called "the English Disease"). He couched cataracts, removed wens and cancers, and addressed problems like harelip and persistent coughs.[32]

Once established, he brought over from England his wife, Esther, and five children, the oldest of whom was Anthony, Jr. He purchased a four-story brick house on the north side of Chestnut Street, which consisted of six rooms (exclusive of the parlor and shop), each twenty feet deep with a fireplace, two garrets, a commodious kitchen under the house, a cellar for provisions, and a large underground vault that ran to the middle of the street, "sufficient to contain wood for the winter."[33] He bought several rural properties and acquired a nineteen-year-old black indentured servant named Prince (who ran away from Yeldall in August 1774). A devoted member of the Church of England, Yeldall donated a silver cup to St. James's Church of New London in 1773 in celebration of the sacrament by the first Protestant Episcopal bishop in America, Samuel Seabury.[34]

In his capacity as a peddler, Yeldall toured parts of New York, New Jersey, Pennsylvania, Delaware, Maryland, and Massachusetts as well as all of Connecticut—an area of over 160,000 square miles. He seems to have focused his efforts on communities that lay within a day's ride of one another. An incident in Brooklyn, New York, in August 1771 reveals the conditions under which Yeldall worked. According to a newspaper account, he was exhibiting his "Harangues, the odd Tricks of his Merry-Andrew, and the surprising Feats of Activity of his little Boy" to audiences coming across the water by ferryboats from New York City. After the show, when the spectators were returning to New York, too many people got into the first boat, which left without waiting for the ferryman. It soon ran onto a rock that shattered the rudder and damaged the bottom, threatening the lives of 110 men, women, and children. At first the passengers' consternation was taken to be the "effects of Mirth and Jollity" occasioned by Yeldall's show, but when water was seen rising above their knees, other boats finally came to their assistance. The newspaper noted that a "strong lasting Impression" was made on all who were present. William Dunlap, who was five years old at the time, recalled this incident when writing *History of New York for Schools* in 1837. He also remembered that Yeldall used to come to Perth Amboy once a year to sell his pharmaceuticals, and that John McDonald was charged in New York for killing a farmer during a robbery.[35]

With the advent of the American Revolution, Yeldall spent less time on the road and more time selling medicine chests to British and American troops stationed around New York and Philadelphia. It was this involvement that proved his undoing. A staunch backer of the English crown, Yeldall was recruited by the British Army in 1778 to identify supporters of the American cause so that it could confiscate contraband and war supplies.[36] When the British left Philadelphia, this act of disloyalty led to his attainder for high treason. In 1780, his house was taken and auctioned, and sales were made of his forfeited estates. At that point Yeldall removed to New York City; Esther was obliged to follow him after an order was issued confining Loyalist wives to the workhouse until they gave security to leave the state and not return. The following year in New York he advertised a lecture at City Hall addressed "To the Curious" on the subject of the five senses; he used a waxwork body illustrating the path of the nerves and a large waxwork eye showing the retina.[37]

Yeldall was a consummate traditionalist, keeping alive centuries-old selling methods. By contrast, a second immigrant Englishman, William Frederick Pinchbeck (fl. 1795–1819) represents a culture bearer employing a more innovative approach. Pinchbeck—the same showman who brought "The Pig of Knowledge" to William Bentley's attention in Salem in 1798—was a restless, secretive, and relatively obscure figure, but his twenty-four-year career in Philadelphia, New York City, New England, the southern states, and possibly the West Indies as an author, animal trainer, showman, and perhaps designer and maker of automatons (clock-driven mechanical figures) can be traced with some accuracy.[38] Despite his apparent fabrications and intermittent periods of anonymity, he promoted himself with such zeal—performing on the stage, treating longstanding medical disorders, and soliciting subscriptions for a manned balloon ascension—that he has become something of an itinerant archetype.

Descended from three generations of London clockmakers, Pinchbeck attracted the attention of the American public in the summer of 1795 as an unidentified entrepreneur who arrived in Philadelphia with an automaton writer that could inscribe anyone's name. About a year later, Pinchbeck—operating under his own name—promoted the automaton writer and the "Grimacer" at a Mr. Kerr's new building in December 1796, and the "Learned Pig" at a Mr. Cook's house in June 1797. He hailed the pig as a "scientific" achievement because it could read, spell, tell time, and distinguish colors. In August 1797, he showed the animal in New York City. Reaching Boston in January 1798, Pinchbeck called himself a "Philosophic experimenter" and took a four-week lease on the hall below the Columbian Museum located at the head of the Mall (a tree-lined avenue on the west end of Boston Common).[39] He was soon performing with a different trained pig, the "Pig of Knowledge," which he took on a long tour of eastern New England seaports.[40] This time the animal could read "print or writing" and answer "any questions in the four first rules of Arithmetic." An engraving of the pig depicts the animal with five cards on the ground in front of him spelling "BOSTO"—and holding in his mouth the final letter "N" (fig. 1.1). A second illustration, dating to 1802, shows the pig holding a card (nine of diamonds?) at an event at Lewis Farmer's Inn, sign of the Connestoga Waggon, Market Street, Philadelphia (fig. 1.2).

William Pinchbeck always displayed a superb sense of publicity. He claimed in Philadelphia that his "Learned Pig" was going to take over as editor of a local newspaper *and* increase its circulation—to better mislead the "swinish multitudes" that made up its readers. In New England he pretended to squelch ongoing rumors that the pig was a mechanical object. "The Pig," he declared,

Figure 1.1. The PIG of KNOWLEDGE!! Frontispiece from William Frederick Pinchbeck (fl. 1795–1819), *The Expositor; or, Many Mysteries Unravelled,* illustrating the Pig of Knowledge spelling "BOSTO . . . N" with alphabet cards. Engraved cut attributed to James Akin (1773–1846), Newburyport, Massachusetts. Boston: Privately printed, 1805. Courtesy, American Antiquarian Society.

"is not an automaton, but a living animal." And in 1802, Pinchbeck circulated a report of the untimely end of the "Pig of Knowledge" during its recent tour of the West Indies. While performing in Cuba, its handler incurred the wrath of suspicious Spanish audiences. "Not being able to divine how such an animal could perform such mysterious tricks," the authorities "thought there was something supernatural in it, and in consequence seized the man and his pig, tied the harmless animal to a stake, and burned him to ashes, then threw the man into the Holy Inquisition, where he is doomed to end his existence." There were many who were prepared to believe these stories.[41]

Pinchbeck also experimented in electricity, invented an acoustical deception, and began a publishing venture.[42] In 1805, he issued the first of his two conjuring manuals. *The Expositor; or, Many Mysteries Unraveled* begins by outlining the method with which an animal handler can train a pig or a dog to the "sapient" state: by withholding food. Pinchbeck then went on to expose the secrets of the "Invisible Lady," detail the working secrets of the "miniature theater" (meaning puppetry) of James Maginnis, and explain the ventriloquy acts of the Scottish brothers John and James Rannie, who were then appearing in Boston. The book's style is epistolary, being an exchange of letters between himself, "WFP," and "AB," probably Abel Bowen (1790–1850), a young nephew of Daniel Bowen. The second manual, *Witchcraft; or, The Art of Fortune-Telling Unveiled*, was issued later in the same year and describes the steps in the fabrication of air and fire balloons and the method of preparing gas.

No sooner were these in print than Pinchbeck promoted on 24 July 1805 an "Aerial Excursion" that would not disappoint the public (fig. 1.3). "Mr. Pinchbeck," he wrote, "intends a visit to the upper Atmosphere. This orbicular is calculated to contain no less than 1100 yards of silk, inflammable air, injecting apparatus, car, balloon."[43] In September 1807, Pinchbeck was in Boston again

Figure 1.2. "A CURIOSITY, *In which the public will not be disappointed.* The Learned Pig." Illustration for an animal show at Lewis Farmer's Inn, sign of the Connestoga Waggon, Market Street, Philadelphia. While the proprietor is not cited, both the advertising text and the offer to return money suggest it was William F. Pinchbeck. Philadelphia *Poulson's American Daily Advertiser*, 5 May 1802. Courtesy, The Library Company of Philadelphia.

with the "Sapient Dog," which illuminated the hall at the beginning of the act and fired a cannon (fig. 1.4). Pinchbeck concluded the show by extinguishing the lights and revealing "Mons. Rien de Tout, a Shadow," dancing a hornpipe on the tightrope, a lantern exhibit. This may have been one of his last public performances in North America.[44]

The careers of Yeldall and Pinchbeck illustrate contrasting examples of how popular culture was being transferred from the Old World to the New. Yeldall carried with him a centuries-old European, Mediterranean, and Asian tradition of alternative healing that attracted audiences and clients with performing clowns. While educated American colonists like John Ballantine and Elizabeth Phelps readily recognized him as a mountebank and had a general sense of what this meant, few of their neighbors had ever heard the term. To the majority of his audiences Yeldall was a fascinating curiosity, and after watching his acrobats perform, at least some people patronized him. That Yeldall was eventually banished from Philadelphia as a Tory (and his home and properties confiscated) is less important than his role as a bearer of traditional if already outmoded

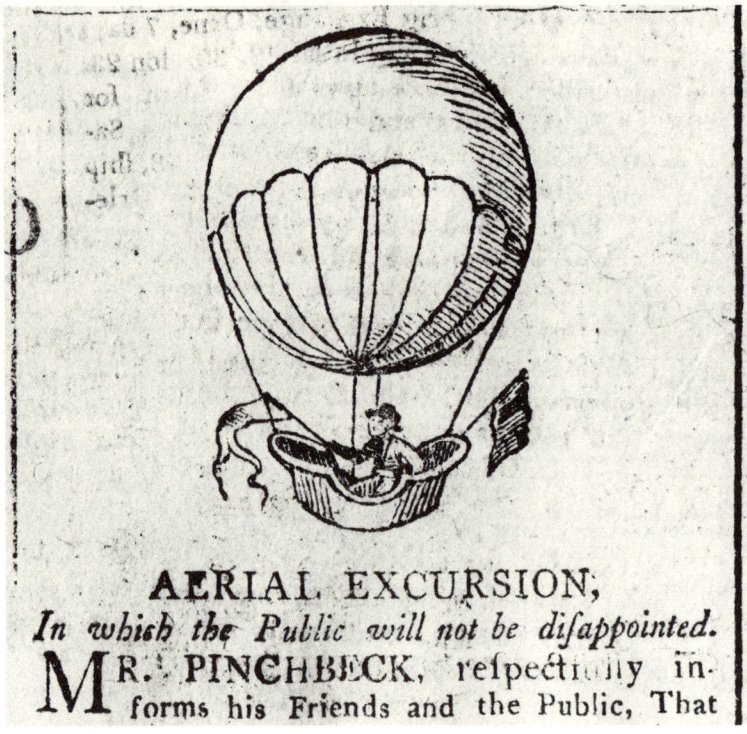

Figure 1.3 "AERIAL EXCURSION, *In which the Public will not be disappointed*. Mr. Pinchbeck, . . . [proposes] a Visit to the Upper Atmosphere." Flushed with the success of his two conjuring books, William F. Pinchbeck announced a subscription in Boston for four thousand dollars for a proposed balloon ascension that would take him, a load of ballast, a car, and an anchor to the upper atmosphere. Relief engraving attributed to James Akin (1773–1846). Boston *Columbian Centinel,* 24 July 1805. Courtesy, American Antiquarian Society.

Figure 1.4 "TRULY CURIOUS & INTERESTING. In which the publick will not be disappointed." Advertisement for William F. Pinchbeck's Sapient Dog showing the animal discovering a card drawn by a spectator at Turrell's Long-Room in Boston. This was the last "Canine Performer" that Pinchbeck trained. Relief engraving signed by James Akin (1773–1846), Newburyport, Massachusetts, 1807. Boston *New-England Palladium,* 4 September 1807. Courtesy, American Antiquarian Society.

European practices. Pinchbeck, on the other hand, was representative of showmen bearing newer European technologies augmented for their popular appeal. He introduced eighteenth-century mechanical and stage innovations not previously seen in North America: he created machines that could write names and balloons that (if subscribers paid for them) could presumably fly Pinchbeck or anyone else into the "upper Atmosphere." But he also carried traditional knowledge. His "educated" pigs and dogs were trained with English and European strategies published as early as 1584.[45]

The careers of both men underscore Carl W. von Sydow's theory of Norway's ninth-century colonization of Iceland that postulates that some cultural practices were transferred and others left behind. Since many of the ethnic and rustic traditions that made possible Yeldall's successes in England did not reach the New World, he basically failed to import his style of mountebank healing to the British colonies where medicine was characteristically in the hands of educated or apprenticed physicians as well as clergy and independent male and female midwives. By the same token, the novelty of Pinchbeck's mechanical genius and ability with animals dazzled New World audiences and inspired imitators. At least one individual purchased a pig from Pinchbeck and became a showman himself; another repeated Pinchbeck's attempt to ascend in a balloon. These differences may help explain why Yeldall ultimately faltered as a cultural carrier and Pinchbeck by and large succeeded.

Nevertheless, both men's styles of itinerancy had been in circulation in the western world for centuries and were quintessentially European in their makeup. We get a sense of the variety and prevalence of these vocations in England from the legal notices posted against unlicensed strollers that were inserted in several early eighteenth-century papers cautioning Londoners to be on the lookout for them. Appearing in 1715 and 1720, these announcements warned against "Stage-Players, Mountebanks, Rope-Dancers, Prize-Players, Poppet-Showers, and several other Show Keepers, of wild Beasts, moving Pictures, musical Clocks, &. Horse Doctors, and others on Foot, and many persons that make Show of Motions and Strange Sights, as Activity of Body, Dexterity of Hand, spinning of Glass, and many others, who are strolling and wandring up and down the Countries within the Kingdom of Great Britain." The notice was signed, among others, by the "Gent[leman] Master and Comptroller of the Revels" who urged constables and officials to prosecute those who were acting unlawfully in these "Employments."[46]

Ninety years later, comparable itinerants were inundating America. Just focusing on Boston during the decade that followed George Washington's triumphal two-month tour of New England in 1789 reveals that Americans called on European culture bearers again and again to define the way they spent free time, how they amused themselves, their perceptions toward alternative health care, and their sense of history. British, Irish, French, Italian, German, Dutch, and Scandinavian men and women dominated most of Boston's tavern entertainments, concert life, specialized teaching professions, and many vocations in theatrical and visual arts. In the flurry of activity that swept through the town in the 1790s and early 1800s, an Irish slack-wire acrobat rented space at George's Tavern at Boston Neck, a Swedish circus impresario leased a ring and viewing stands at the bottom of the Mall, and an English horseman built a riding amphitheater with covered boxes and seats in west Boston. Not far away on Orange Tree Lane, an English artist displayed giant, circular, panoramic views of the city of London and Westminster District; nearby, an Irishman challenged another prizefighter in West Boston's Military School and a pugilistic instructor, formerly an English actor, demonstrated the "attitudes" of the English prizefighters Richard Humphries and Daniel Mendoza. In the town's taverns and warehouses, a Frenchman was trying to raise money for a balloon ascension, an Englishman entertained crowds with a trained pig that spelled "Boston," a German-speaking Dutchman diverted audiences with a trained dog dressed as a fortune-teller, an Italian was showing electrical experiments using Alessandro Volta's discoveries, a second Italian (and his wife) were staging spectacular fireworks exhibitions, and a third Italian amazed crowds by walking a tightrope strung from chimney to chimney dressed in women's clothing. It was little wonder, then, that when English actor John Bernard wrote his *Retrospections of America* for English readers in 1811, he called the genteel society of the town of Boston, formerly the seat of the American Revolution and still one of the significant metropolitan areas in the new country, indistinguishable from that of London.[47]

Table 1.1. Thirty-five occupations commonly pursued by itinerants in North America before 1826, divided into twenty-five-year intervals. Approximately one out of every ten itinerants appears in more than one occupational category (or about 460 out of a total of 4,664).

Occupation	Before 1751	1751–1775	1776–1799	1800–1825	Total
Acoustical showmen	0	0	12	24	36
Acrobats, tumblers, ropedancers	11	14	35	57	117
Animal handlers	12	11	36	51	110
Automaton showmen	0	0	14	36	50
Balloonists	0	0	21	27	48
Circus professionals	0	0	39	110	149
Conjurers, mimics, ventriloquists	13	24	27	31	95
Dancing-masters	42	62	119	193	416
Drawing teachers	1	6	46	76	129
Electric lecturers	5	11	14	15	45
Electrical healers	2	1	17	45	65
Equestrian performers	0	6	11	15	32
Fencing teachers	3	20	37	54	114
Fireworks artists	0	5	18	33	56
Language teachers	4	24	61	83	172
Lantern showmen	6	7	37	22	72
Menagerie proprietors	0	0	0	40	40
Miniature painters	0	6	73	76	155
Mountebanks/alternative healers	11	54	33	30	128
Music-machine operators	5	9	11	20	45
Music teachers	3	24	61	142	230
Musicians for dances and schools	21	54	60	11	146
Panorama artists	0	0	6	33	39
Peddlers	15	51	9	57	132
Penmanship teachers	0	0	11	168	179
Portrait painters	2	17	59	138	216
Prizefighters	0	0	9	16	25
Profile takers	0	0	16	123	139
Proprietors of "curious" devices	11	11	12	46	80
Psalmody teachers	9	25	47	145	226
Public artists	0	1	1	36	38
Puppeteers	7	13	16	9	45
Stage professionals	0	110	280	443	833
Street exhorters	13	15	25	27	80
Waxwork proprietors	4	7	19	152	182
Total	200	588	1,292	2,584	4,664

Sources: Diaries, newspaper advertisements, handbills, and posters. Additional data for tables 1.1 and 1.2 were obtained from Barriskill, "Newburyport Theatre"; Belknap, *Artists and Craftsmen of Essex County*; Benson, "Itinerant Dancing and Music Masters"; Cooke, "Itinerant Yankee Singing Masters"; Corry, Keller, and Keller, "Performing Arts in Colonial American Newspapers"; Dow, *Arts and Crafts*; Dunlap, *History of the Rise and Progress*; Flint, "Early-Nineteenth-Century Circus"; Garvin and Garvin, *On the Road North of Boston*; Gottesman, *Arts and Crafts*; Groce and Wallace, *Dictionary of Artists in America*; Guerra, *American Medical Bibliography*; Hill, "In Search of Early Massachusetts Itinerant Artists"; Hodgson, "An Other Voice"; Hodgson, personal communication; Jackson, *Silhouette*; Johnson and Burling, *Colonial American Stage*; Keller, *Dance and Its Music*; Lambert, comp., "Music Masters in Colonial Boston"; Little, "Itinerant Painting in America"; McPharlin, *Puppet Theatre in America*; Nash, *American Penmanship*; Odell, *Annals of the New York Stage*; Rosenfeld, "An Index of Miniaturists and Silhouettists"; Rutledge, "Artists in the Life of Charleston"; Seilhamer, *History of the American Theatre*; Sonneck, *Early Concert-Life*; Sonneck, *Early Opera in America*; and Vail, "Random Notes."

Table 1.2. Known or presumed national origins of thirty-five occupations commonly practiced by itinerants in North America before 1826. Approximately one out of every ten appears in more than one occupational category (or about 460 out of a total of 4,664). For sources, see table 1.1.

Occupation	Known American	Known English	Anglo/American (surname)	Irish, Scottish, Welsh	French	Italian	African, African American, or Native American	Other European or Asian	Unidentified	Total
Acoustical showmen	9	2	2	0	2	1	0	1	19	36
Acrobats, tumblers, ropedancers	8	10	15	11	9	14	8	15	27	117
Animal handlers	24	2	1	0	1	0	2	3	77	110
Automaton showmen	6	1	2	4	9	5	0	9	14	50
Balloonists	4	3	2	1	15	0	0	3	20	48
Circus professionals	8	4	47	7	25	7	2	9	40	149
Conjurers, mimics, ventriloquists	11	13	18	12	11	2	4	4	20	95
Dancing-masters	31	105	29	32	165	14	2	15	23	416
Drawing teachers	16	5	25	6	37	6	0	4	30	129
Electric lecturers	20	4	7	1	1	2	0	0	10	45
Electrical healers	17	4	9	0	1	3	0	2	29	65
Equestrian performers	4	9	3	1	4	2	0	0	9	32
Fencing teachers	4	9	10	6	74	1	0	1	9	114
Fireworks artists	6	2	6	0	17	7	0	3	15	56
Language teachers	1	4	17	0	111	18	0	6	15	172
Lantern showmen	7	20	3	3	5	5	0	2	27	72
Menagerie proprietors	4	0	0	0	0	0	0	0	36	40
Miniature painters	20	12	30	6	35	8	1	7	36	155
Mountebanks/alternative healers	30	15	20	2	13	2	12	17	17	128
Music-machine operators	8	3	2	0	1	6	0	4	21	45
Music teachers	10	35	44	1	42	21	0	27	50	230
Musicians for dances and schools	0	0	0	1	0	0	112	5	28	146
Panorama artists	7	4	0	1	0	1	0	0	26	39
Peddlers	5	2	33	38	0	1	1	9	43	132
Penmanship teachers	169	2	0	1	1	0	0	0	6	179
Portrait painters	55	25	55	4	22	2	0	7	46	216
Prizefighters	4	7	0	2	1	0	0	1	9	25
Profile takers	33	5	38	4	15	1	1	2	40	139
Proprietors of "curious" devices	26	8	1	0	5	0	0	2	38	80
Psalmody teachers	128	6	60	0	0	0	0	0	32	226
Public artists	14	1	1	0	4	0	0	0	18	38
Puppeteers	3	16	6	2	6	2	0	0	10	45
Stage professionals	2	761	0	5	60	2	0	3	0	833
Street exhorters	6	1	22	3	0	0	31	2	15	80
Waxwork proprietors	98	5	5	0	5	5	0	3	61	182
Totals	798	1,105	513	154	697	138	177	166	916	4,664

Chapter 2

Travel Routes and Circuits

BECAUSE MOVEMENT lay at the heart of their marketing strategy, the transportation available to itinerants had considerable influence on the distances they traveled, the destinations they chose, and the nature of their clients and audiences. As a mountebank, Anthony Yeldall was obliged to "set up a stage" each time he and his two clowns harangued the public. He probably used a large horse-drawn carriage fitted with hinged planks, which, when lowered, served as a platform—the same equipage probably housed his pharmaceutical stock and stage equipment. All three men may have also cooked and slept in it as circumstances dictated. Their remote destinations in Delaware, New Jersey, Massachusetts, Connecticut, and central Pennsylvania suggest they mainly traveled on rural roads. William Pinchbeck, on the other hand, who toured alone with a trained pig (or a trained dog), may have made his connections using a commercial stage especially since he is known to have lived and worked at rooming houses and taverns along readily accessible routes between Boston and Portland, but he also may have used sailing packets when traveling from Newport, Rhode Island, to Savannah. After 1800, however, when the "Learned Pig" went from Alexandria to Frankfort, Kentucky, Pinchbeck (or perhaps Pinchbeck's replacement or understudy) may have traveled and possibly lived in a carriage.

In any case, both scenarios posed difficulties. At its best, travel in the eighteenth and early nineteenth centuries was time-consuming, expensive, hazardous, uncomfortable, and disorienting. With little to encourage it and much to discourage it, establishments serving travelers in most areas were either underpatronized or overcrowded on specific occasions such as cattle drives, militia meetings, and college commencements. Travelers frequently shared the same bed, and there were usually many beds in a single room. Maryland diarist Dr. Alexander Hamilton (1712–1756) noted in 1744 that when he stayed overnight in Bohemia (now Maryland City), Maryland, he "went to bed at nine at night; my landlord, his wife, daughters, and I lay all in one room."[1] Kym S. Rice points out in her study of early American taverns that one woman traveling in North Carolina, Elizabeth Trist, was required in 1784 to share a bed with her female servant in a small room also containing a bed with two male transients; the floor around them accommodated a hog driver, his son and daughter, a black woman, and several children. And facilities were often poorly maintained. A woman journeying alone through the Spuyten Duyvil section of New York in 1778 was handed a pair of sheets that were not only filled with "Dirt" but had been "Iron'd on, until they were Dark Brown."[2] At the same time, many peddlers, tinkers, and beggars expected to be housed wherever they solicited work or charity. Reverend Ebenezer Parkman was alarmed one night by a beggar "of ill behaviour" who insisted on having overnight lodging; Parkman wanted to oblige him, but his wife and daughter refused, and Parkman offered the man use of the barn. The beggar, however, left "high and Mal[a]pert."[3] Reverend John Ballantine's household, however, may have been more hospitable to passing tradesmen and beggars; Ballantine noted in 1763 that his "Rasors [were] ground by a man who had an apparatus for grinding on a Wheelbarrow," very likely an itinerant stopping in Westfield as he proceeded along the Connecticut Valley.[4]

When embarking from Europe for any major American port, transatlantic travelers in the eighteenth century had to plan on passages of weeks or months. Ships headed west from the British Isles faced contrary currents and winds on a voyage lasting four to ten weeks or more. Portrait painter Ralph Earl spent four weeks on his return from London to Boston in 1785, a relatively short trip, but he had enough time on his hands to paint a group portrait of the ship's captain and family. John Rowe, whose business as a Boston-based London merchant put him in daily touch with Atlantic schedules, pointed out that sailing times between English ports and Boston ranged from five to eight weeks. But Rowe also cited a Captain Bruce, who made the run from London to Boston in twenty-six days, calling it "the shortest passage ever known."[5] Bassoonist William Priest, who came to Philadelphia to join a theater band, was nine weeks in transit on his voyage from England to America in 1793, and five and a half weeks on his return to England in 1797. Those traveling between the northern colonies and the West Indies set aside three and a half to four weeks to reach their destinations.[6] Travel time was often prolonged by inclement weather. In 1821, H. A. Wells's and H. C. Breslaw's circus troupe made the trip from Savannah to New York in a period of bitter cold: "The *Telegraph* [the name of a passenger-carrying brig] has experienced heavy gales since the 5th, and is loaded with ice."[7]

Once travelers arrived on the North American mainland, the most common means of moving about was by packets—also called "water stages" or "stage boats." These were shallow-draft vessels, usually sloop-rigged, designed for transporting goods and people relatively short distances across bays, sounds, and up and down navigable rivers. Most packets observed strict schedules. A sloop working the Connecticut River and Long Island Sound in 1767 left Middletown on the first and third Wednesday of each month; the vessel touched at Saybrook and crossed the sound to Oyster Pond, Long Island. The trip took two days, and the charge was one dollar for a man and horse. A similar vessel between New London and Long Island left every Friday and cost eight shillings in New York currency for a man and horse.[8] Berthings and meals were usually supplied on even the shortest passages, and vessels remained underway night and day—a major advantage for voyages requiring days or weeks to complete. Richard Smith (1735–1803), a New Jersey Continental Congressman and attorney who sailed up the Hudson (or North) River in 1769, found packets much to his liking: "These Albany Sloops contain very convenient Cabins. We eat from a regular Table accommodated with Plates, Knives & Forks & enjoyed our Tea in the Afternoon. We had laid in some Provision at N.York & the Capt. some more, so that we lived very well. Our Commander is very jocose & good company."[9]

But not all packet connections resulted in a convenient or direct trip. When singing-master Daniel Read (1757–1836) took the packet *Maria* from New Haven to New York in 1798, he left New Haven at eight in the evening on 22 May. Upon embarkation he learned the vessel was "full of passengers" and that only fourteen lodging berths were available for fourteen men and four women. Lots were cast by the men, and Read drew a blank, obliging him to sleep on the deck. Winds being contrary, the sloop arrived in New York at about sunset on Thursday, 24 May, after an elapsed time of forty-eight hours. His return on the packet *Juno,* however, which had the benefit of trailing winds, took only thirteen hours.[10]

Packets provided the most direct route between New York City and Boston. The custom was to board a packet sailing between Hellsgate and any of several towns in southern Rhode Island, and then to complete the distance to Boston by stage. This avoided a long sea voyage around Cape Cod as well as overnight accommodations at a roadside inn. The popularity of this combined mode of transit was noticed by English author Edward Augustus Kendall (1776?–1842) when touring New England in 1808: "Newport is a town of much notoriety, for which it is partly indebted to its situation, between New York City and Boston; the common mode of traveling being that of passing by one of the packets, (of which there are several, with the best accommodations), between New York City and Newport, and thence, for the remainder of the distance, by land."[11] The Newport connection was so frequently used that special shallow draft vessels were employed to further reduce the distance traversed on land. Two men ran a packet between Newport and Swansea, Massachusetts, in 1769, advising travelers reaching Rhode Island that the distance from Swansea to Boston is "10 or fifteen miles nearer than from Providence to Boston." Once arrived in Swansea, passengers were taken overland to Boston.[12]

Nevertheless, water transport was not always the desired means of conveyance, especially in winter months. When the Old American Company ended its theatrical season in Boston in the middle of the winter season 1795–96, stage dancer John Durang reported that the greater part of the company returned to New York City by water. He hesitated to join them: "A heavey snow came on. I hired a slay with a coach body on the runner to take my family comfortable to New York all the way on the snow, thro Providence, New Haven, and several other towns, putting up every night in comfortable lodgings. . . . We arrived the first and safe to New York, while those who went by water where frose in near two week."[13]

Travelers not wishing to take water packets were obliged to ride scheduled stages (fig. 2.1). Horse-drawn "stage waggons" ran regardless of the weather (blizzard conditions excepted), and their schedules were affected only by the status of bridges, fords, and ferries—or equipment breakdown. They usually

Figure 2.1 Hartford and New Haven turnpike tickets showing fees ranging from twenty-five cents (for a carriage drawn by two horses) to five mills (for a sheep or a pig). Uncut blanks. Hartford, Connecticut: N.p., c. 1790. Courtesy, The Connecticut Historical Society.

made good time. The Boston to New York City stage wagons ran three times a week in 1786; the connection required four days, with rest stops about every twenty miles, and three overnight layovers of about eight hours.[14] Scheduled routes were sometimes unreliable. Dancing-master Mr. Baconais had to cancel his Hagerstown, Maryland, school in 1799 because "the Winchester stage being stopped."[15] Unscheduled stage trips, which required bargaining or negotiating for each leg, were not only unreliable but slower. William Dunlap's journey from Boston to New York City, undertaken in the middle of the winter in 1797, was typical of what travelers had to endure. Dunlap left Boston on 14 December at about half past ten in the morning, stopping to "dine" in Walpole and spending the night at Attleboro. He pulled into Providence in heavy rain on the morning of the fifteenth for a late breakfast but was prevented from going farther by poor roads. He then negotiated with the mail stage leaving Scituate, Rhode Island, and continued to Norwich, Connecticut, arriving on the sixteenth. Since the mail did not run on Sunday, he "bargained with the Innkeeper" for a private chaise to New London, which he reached on the seventeenth. He arrived at New Haven on the evening of the eighteenth; at Rye, New York, on the evening of the nineteenth; and at his home in New York City, about noontime, on the twentieth—a journey of seven days.[16]

Many itinerants preferred to ride horseback, but it was both expensive and risky. Penmanship teacher and profile artist James Guild got about on foot for more than three years in upstate New York before he could afford to acquire a horse. It was a heavy investment, and his first horse was stolen from him; another threw him repeatedly before he succeeded in breaking the animal. But he admitted he was not entirely prepared for riding, and the experience made him tired. The value of horses to singing-masters was recognized by Andrew Law (1749–1821), the Connecticut psalmodist and publisher who distributed his own imprints to teachers venturing into the southern states. "I wish all who come would get Horses there," he wrote to his brother in 1791. "It lays them under great disadvantage not to have a horse, and it is a great disadvantage to us, for they cannot teach so many schools nor go into distant parts where they would sell most books."[17]

Travel by horse-drawn, covered conveyances of a kind popularized by peddlers and daguerreotypists in the middle and late nineteenth century was apparently still rare in the eighteenth and early nineteenth centuries. Nevertheless, they were used occasionally. The "cabbin" by which puppeteer Edward Burlesson went to Westborough, Massachusetts, in 1739 is an early example. This vehicle may have incorporated a small stage for his shows and most likely provided Burlesson's sleeping and cooking arrangements. At the end of the century, James Sharples (ca. 1751–1811), an itinerant English pastel artist, toured with his family throughout eastern coastal America in a horse-drawn cabin that he designed and built himself. An inventor and "mechanician," he was led to this expedient after a harrowing incident in which one of his children was put in peril by a runaway stagecoach.[18]

While ocean voyages posed the greatest physical dangers, overland travel into interior and northern regions engendered the greatest frustration. Travelers making the trip overland from New York City to Quebec City or Montreal (trying to avoid a lengthy sea passage up the St. Lawrence) ran into constant difficulties. In 1797, English equestrian John Bill Ricketts (ca. 1767–1800) followed a circuitous route to reach Montreal via a combination of river sloops, ferries, stages, and open wagons. Ricketts was accompanied by a staff of five showmen, grooms, and musicians—one of them John Durang—and six performing horses, which required specially built stalls on the ferries and riverboats. The party's route took them from New York City to Albany on a sailing packet that made six overnight anchorages. They continued overland to Whitehall, New York, at the lowermost extremity of Lake Champlain. Here they traveled the length of the lake with the horses on a flatboat ferry, while forwarding their baggage and equipment on a packet to St. John's, Quebec. The company covered the remaining distance by horseback, hiring horse-drawn wagons and flat-bottom ferries. At one location Ricketts's party had to rebuild a bridge that they found impassable; at another they were obliged to clean the stables before using them. They often had to travel at night, and where the road dwindled to a path, the party had to enlist "pilots" or guides. To get from Albany to Montreal took them two weeks; another week elapsed before they gave their first performance.[19]

Reaching Lower Canada from Boston was even more difficult because it required considerable overland travel. Variety actor John Bernard, his wife, their infant child, and a servant made a trip from Boston to Montreal in 1810. The party traversed the distance across Massachusetts, New Hampshire, and Vermont to Rutland by scheduled stages, and the distance from Rutland to Whitehall by hired wagon. Bernard described the wagon as an "oblong, unpainted box, with three seats nailed across, and without springs or cushions." At Whitehall they switched to a packet to St. John's where they continued to La Prairie by a "diligence." There they crossed the St. Lawrence by ferry to reach Montreal. The party was approximately six days en route, but they spent an additional five days waiting for the packet to take them from Whitehall to St. John's.[20]

John Bernard was pleasantly surprised to find that the Champlain packet was powered by steam. (His only annoyance was having to listen to a lady passenger who was naming all the recent instances of exploding boilers.) Experienced travelers came to prefer steam power. After fielding a succession of separate schools in Albany, Pittsfield, and other locations in western Massachusetts and in Schenectady and Hudson Counties, one dancing-master, a Mr. Johnson, found it advantageous to place advertisements on two days of the week. His decision coincided with the addition in 1814 of the *Fulton* to the steam packets working the Hudson River, which enabled him to teach Mondays and Tuesdays in Albany, and Thursdays and Fridays in Hudson, thirty-two miles south. By the following year river and coastal vessels were running so efficiently that a Signor Pucci, an Italian instrumental and vocal soloist touring New England, gave a "grand" concert at Mr. Baird's Eagle Tavern in Albany on 15 July 1815 and repeated the same concert, completely rested, at Aldrich's Hall, Providence, eight days later on 23 July, a distance of three hundred miles.[21]

Railway lines made reliable travel even faster. In a long career serving eastern Massachusetts and southern New Hampshire, Boston dancing-master Lovet Stimson was able to double both the distance he traveled and the number of schools he taught simultaneously as a result of newly introduced steam-powered vessels and trains. In 1811, he was taking stagecoaches to four schools in Boston, Dedham, Taunton, and Providence. By 1839, however, Stimson had increased the number of his concurrent schools to seven and was using new railway connections to extend his range of weekly circuits to include Boston, South Boston, Cambridge, Charlestown, Salem, and Lowell, Massachusetts, and Nashua, New Hampshire. The speed and reliability of the railroads was unprecedented. On Tuesdays Stimson taught a class at 9 a.m. in Lowell and at 3 p.m. in Nashua. No longer simply a traveler, Stimson had become a commuter.[22]

Some itinerants concentrated on a specific geographic area where they made repeat visits and gained a local reputation. John Griffiths, for example, began teaching dance at Alexandre Quesnay's Academy of Polite Arts in New York City in 1784. (He later named one of his dance compositions after Quesnay.) Once on the road, Griffiths set up his schools fairly close together so that he could keep two classes going at the same time, each meeting two to three times per week. After completing his schools, he would go on to another community, telling his former pupils when he would return. This defined the region where Griffiths was known and patronized. One such circuit extended into Connecticut and included Hartford, Wethersfield, New Haven, Norwich, and New London. A second originated in Boston and extended to Medford, Newburyport, and Providence, Rhode Island. A third area centered in Albany and in Massachusetts towns such as Northampton, Deerfield, and Stockbridge. Each of these areas was anywhere from fifty to eighty miles wide, and while these distances were small compared to the length of the eastern seaboard, two or three full days' travel time was still required to journey from one end to the other. By limiting his movements, Griffiths was able to center his attention on his classes and publications. While teaching in Boston, he would advertise in Providence, telling pupils he would be in town once a week to hold classes at a Mr. Rice's long room, giving "two Lessons while he is here; the Evening for the young Gentlemen, and the Morning for the Ladies."[23]

Much the same pattern was followed by John C. Devero (1774–after 1840), a dancing-master who replaced Griffiths in southeastern New England in the late 1790s. Devero immigrated to America as a dispossessed Irish Catholic landowner who had fled his homeland to escape England's repressive policies. He entered the economic mainstream of his newly adopted country by holding a series of schools that capitalized on his genteel training, privileged upbringing, and musical talents to teach dancing and polite address to children and young men and women in towns and villages in southern New England—this while his extended family in County Wexford joined an open rebellion against the English that culminated in a series of military defeats for Irish nationalists in 1799.[24] Like Griffiths, Devero was a meticulous advertiser. He, too, concentrated on a patronage zone of about eighty by thirty miles. In February 1798, Devero advertised concurrent schools at Jewett City, Plainfield, and Canterbury, Connecticut; in August 1799, at Hebron, Middletown, and Glastonbury; and in January 1802, having "nearly completed schools in Middletown and East Haddam," he proposed new ones in New London, Montville, and Bozrah.[25] Over the years Devero made a habit of returning to the same establishments. In Newport he leased a Mrs. Penrose's (formerly Mary Cowley's) assembly room; in Providence, he used Ammidon's Golden Ball Inn (also known as James Hidden's Tavern). He rented the courthouse at Norwich and a tavern ballroom at Norwich Landing. When running simultaneous schools, Devero typically selected locations about ten to twelve miles from each other and held classes on three different days of the week spaced a day apart. In December 1799, for example, he began one in Hebron on the fifteenth, in Middletown on the eighteenth, and in Glastonbury on the twentieth. While his range of movement was slightly smaller than Griffiths's, Devero's efforts gained him the "very decisive preference, pleasing patronage, and unbounded confidence" of his Connecticut and Rhode Island clients.[26]

The regions served by Griffiths and Devero were similar in more than just their geographic size; they also formed a distinctive travel and information zone. Griffiths's routes through New York City, Connecticut, Rhode Island, and eastern Massachusetts were linked not only by highroads and turnpikes but by the continuing traffic of coasters and packets sailing from Boston and New York City. Devero's stopping places, in turn, were connected by packet and stage lines reaching the length of Long Island Sound and Narragansett Bay as well as the Connecticut River. Each was served by half a dozen or more weekly or biweekly newspapers with overlapping readerships. In Griffiths's area, besides the core group of Boston newspapers led by the biweekly *New-England Palladium* and *Columbian Centinel,* there were two newspapers in Salem, three in Newburyport, one each in Haverhill and Exeter, two in Portsmouth, three in Portland, and one in both Newport and Providence. Devero's section of Connecticut and

Rhode Island included newspapers such as the *Connecticut Gazette,* the *Norwich Packet,* the *Providence Gazette,* and the *Newport Mercury.*

As they made the decisions that defined their respective careers, both dancing-masters must have been aware that the internal characteristics of their circuits were critical to their professional viability. Approximately eighty miles of networked newspaper readers provided an area compact enough that each could reach clients while still being populous enough to sustain them financially. Both made optimum use of simultaneous scheduling and return trips. There were, of course, important differences in how long they remained in a given community. Griffiths could stay for several years in one of his districts; Devero usually taught a "quarter" of eight to twelve weeks. But regardless of their lengths of stay, both men kept to a pattern just emerging among itinerants at the beginning of the nineteenth century—spacing visits to allow time to regenerate interest in the services provided while still discouraging competitors.

Eventually, John Griffiths and John Devero went on to other things. Griffiths moved to Northampton, Massachusetts, managing a reduced schedule of classes. His novelty as a teacher in Boston at that time may have been diminished by the cultural fatigue that dancing-masters seem to have encountered after two or three years in a given circuit. After completing a school in Williamstown, Massachusetts, and Albany in 1796, he eventually returned to New York City. Devero left southern New England in 1802 and taught at least one quarter in Albany before moving to upstate New York. He had prospered so well that he sent for his brothers Walter and Francis and other members of his family to join him. Devero's place in Providence was taken in 1802 by William H. Smith, who told readers of the *Providence Gazette* that he hoped to find encouragement now that "Mr. Devero . . . [has] relinquished his intentions."[27]

Few entrepreneurs kept up the focused itineraries maintained by Griffiths and Devero. Nevertheless, routes and cycles analogous to theirs were common enough to reveal a distinct pattern that applied not only to dancing-masters but to most other itinerants operating in North America. Itinerants who were contemporaries with Griffiths and Devero—be they portrait painters, animal showmen, profile takers, or medical electricians—seem to have cultivated a standard three-day, three-year travel area. As an artist, Ethan Allen Greenwood (1779–1856) normally kept within a forty-mile radius of his home in Hubbardston, Massachusetts, painting families in central Massachusetts and southern New Hampshire. After leaving New York City, Ralph Earl by and large stayed in central Connecticut, taking advantage of packets serving the Connecticut River and Long Island Sound. But the same demographic forces that channeled their movements worked over time to shorten the distances that they needed to traverse and to reduce the intervals at which they returned to the same sitters, pupils, and patrons. In this larger equation, the roughly eighty-mile circuits cultivated by Griffiths and Devero represented a transition between a well-defined beginning and end. Fifty years before their time, itinerants were moving from colony to colony along North America's eastern seaboard and often visiting the islands of the British West Indies. Fifty years after their time, most were taking what were essentially suburban routes. In other words, the circuits had significantly shortened over a hundred-year period.

The principal influence shaping this reduction was the lucrative patronage area in the eastern coastal United States. Entrepreneurs naturally gravitated toward clients with leisure, money, and a willingness to spend it. In the eighteenth century such consumers were centered in relatively small pockets—chiefly the older ports of entry such as New York City, Albany, New Haven, Newport, Providence, Boston, Salem, Portsmouth, and Portland in the northern colonies; Baltimore, Annapolis, Philadelphia, and Trenton in the middle colonies; and Savannah, Charleston, Norfolk, Alexandria, Williamsburg, and Richmond in the southern colonies. Few itinerants ventured above Albany on the Hudson River, above Windsor Falls (just north of Hartford) on the Connecticut River, or above Amesbury and Haverhill on the Merrimack River. In Pennsylvania similar cutting-off points existed on the Schuylkill and Trenton Rivers and farther south on the Susquehanna, Potomac, and James Rivers.

During Griffiths's and Devero's time these profitable pockets expanded as elite tastes reached the new urban middle classes and the "upwardly mobile" strata of smaller and secondary seaports, whaling centers, and estuary towns. Accelerating or retarding this process was a combination of settlement and migration patterns, the existence of impassable terrain or bodies of water, the opening of canals into the western territories, and relict zones of genealogical cohesion. But the overall results were the same. The gradual broadening of coastal consumer pockets formed a fulcrum around which Americans came face to face with an international, itinerant-carried popular culture during the critical decades that created the birth and flowering of a new nation.

This fulcrum was further divided by geophysical, religious, and ethnic boundaries. Cape Cod, the sandy peninsula surrounded by a treacherous sea passage and long known and feared for its shipwrecks, divided New England into two sections. In eastern New England the principal path of movement consisted of seaports and estuaries to the north and east of Massachusetts Bay that stretched from Boston to Portland and in which Haverhill, Exeter, Hallowell, Gardiner, Bath, Augusta, St. John (New Brunswick), and Halifax (Nova Scotia) emerged as secondary connections or extensions. Although populous, these ports accommodated only one-fifth of the inhabitants in their respective areas, but they furnished one-half to three-quarters of its mercantile, maritime, and artisanal resources. So lucrative was the eastern route that showmen passed back and forth along it time and again in full confidence that they would attract new audiences.

When actors John Bernard and Thomas Caulfield took their program of readings and recitations into eastern New England, they stopped in Portsmouth where they met with the French consul. They then progressed to Portland, Brunswick, and Wiscasset, Maine, and subsequently to Bath, where they learned to their delight that the town "had never been visited by any amusement whatever of our kind." Returning, they traced the same track: "We . . . turned our horses' heads homeward, and lecturing again at Portland, Portsmouth, and Newburyport, as we passed through them, arrived in Boston, about $500 in pocket from our excursion."[28] Bernard became renowned between Wiscasset and Boston because he toured the area almost every summer.[29]

An equivalent route to the west of Cape Cod developed in southern and western New England and contiguous portions of eastern New York State, extending from Newport to New York City and north to Albany. Here, too, the population of the southwestern ports of entry represented a relatively small proportion of southern New England and eastern New York State inhabitants, but again it was the residents of the seaport communities (especially New York City) who were most inclined to spend money on itinerants. Like their eastern New England equivalents, the passages to the west of Cape Cod were principally geared around water transportation. In the three decades from 1787 to 1817, at least sixteen passenger or cargo sloops sailed the three-hundred-mile distance between points in southeastern New England and Albany, usually on a posted schedule of about four trips a year. The full extent of this route is illustrated by the movements of Maryland-born Ralph Letton (1778–c. 1836), a profile taker and waxwork proprietor. Letton, who had previously advertised in Canada, was at Thomas Pool's coffeehouse in Keene, New Hampshire, in March 1806; in New London, Connecticut, in April 1806; at a Mr. Hubbard's in New Haven in early 1807; at Middletown in March 1807; again at New London in April 1807; and in Pittsfield, Massachusetts, in September 1807. A year later he traveled with a waxwork collection through Hartford and Wethersfield on his way to Providence. He founded a museum in Albany in January 1809, but by December 1810 he had returned to Providence where he opened a museum with a Dr. Hall, a male midwife. Over a five-year period Letton had touched the outermost ends of the Providence/Albany corridor and stopped at most of the secondary seaports in between. He may have used packet connections extensively, particularly when transporting his wax figures.[30]

Farther south, Philadelphia's dominance of the middle and southern states marked another corridor defined by the movement of ships and packets and by the circulation of newspapers. The routes among Philadelphia, southern New Jersey, Delaware, Maryland, Virginia, the Carolinas, and Georgia stand out, for example, in the itineraries of portrait painters. Raphaelle and Rembrandt Peale were "lately arrived from Philadelphia" when they came to Charleston in 1795.[31]

The same link shows up in the Georgetown advertisements of painter William Williams, who "arrived from Philadelphia" in 1797; he continued south toward New Bern and Charleston.[32] It comes up in the advertisements of limners such as Charles P. Polk and Samuel Folwell, who cited their Philadelphia credentials in southern cities.[33] (Folwell additionally told Charleston residents that his drawings on silk and satin were "done agreeable to the newest fashions in the first schools in Philadelphia."[34]) Similar ties served profile takers moving south in 1798—among them F. Duvivier and Son, who came to Baltimore "from Philadelphia"[35]—and patent holders of John I. Hawkins's physiognotrace (a mechanical profile machine), who went from Charles Willson Peale's Philadelphia museum into the neighboring states of Maryland, Virginia, and South Carolina from 1803 to 1804. Many profile takers advertising in Charleston stated or implied they had just left Philadelphia—among them John I. Hawkins, J. Paul, and Augustus Day.[36]

Comparable links benefited dancing-masters. Philadelphia-based teachers typically targeted large southern ports, some returning north after several seasons. James Robardet was "lately from Philadelphia" when he got to Annapolis in 1792, although he had spent much of his time previously in New England, as was dancing-master Gaspard Cenas in Baltimore in 1786. Thomas Turner in 1790 said he "improved himself under Monsieur Sicard, . . . professor of dancing in Philadelphia" when he opened a school in Charleston. A Mr. Lancon, an instructor in Philadelphia in 1797 was teaching in Savannah in 1800.[37] These examples demonstrate that Philadelphia was distinctly visible on the extremity of Charleston's and Savannah's artistic and cultural horizons, and that a city located more than seven hundred miles away was still one of the gateways to accomplished southern living—connected as Philadelphia was to Baltimore, Alexandria, Richmond, Charleston, and Savannah by packets running close to the eastern waters of Maryland, Virginia, the Carolinas, and Georgia.

As they moved in and out of these corridors, itinerants sometimes shifted the base of their advertising appeal. Portrait and miniature painter N. Wheeler, for example, assumed no fewer than three personae as he traveled east from Boston along the New England coastline during 1809 and 1810, each apparently triggered by a different assessment of his potential audience. In Boston he formally addressed his notices "to Amateurs and Patrons of the Fine Arts" and cited his experience painting portraits in the principal cities of Virginia and North Carolina. He characterized his miniature style as "masterly." In Newburyport and Portsmouth (where he called himself "from Boston") he simply offered to paint miniature likenesses, adding the customary guarantee: "No likeness no pay." In Exeter, New Hampshire, however, he recast himself as a "profile" artist and highlighted his use of a patent tracing machine and his elegant style of "shading." The word "miniature" did not even appear in his Exeter announcement. Clearly,

Wheeler was aware of the limited marketability of expensive, formal miniatures in the more remote coastal locations and adjusted his language accordingly.[38]

A similar shift took place in the language of Riyt Rosee as he proceeded eastward along the Connecticut shoreline toward Newport. A miniature painter and teacher of French language and fencing, Rosee was one of many recent émigrés to travel along this corridor in the 1790s and early 1800s as they fanned out from their embarkation point in New York City. Rosee was in Norwich on 11 December 1794; eighteen days later he was advertising in Newport, and two weeks after that he reached New Bedford, Massachusetts. There he changed his name to "Mr. Rose" and limited his publicity to French language teaching with no mention of fencing or miniature painting. He, too, had passed a cultural divide that called for a different entrepreneurial tactic. Situated about twenty-five miles due east of Newport (about half a day's sail), New Bedford was a rapidly growing but relatively young whaling and trading center, and until 1787 had been the waterside parish of the older town of Dartmouth. Although its population was about equal to that of Norwich, the seaport, like rural Dartmouth itself, remained outside the usual travel routes since most eastbound coasters and packets went directly to Providence and Bristol after reaching Newport. Rosee, whose short-lived notices indicate he found little work either in Norwich or Newport, may have hoped that New Bedford's clerks and supercargoes would consider French as useful to the new mercantile houses and the families of the traders themselves. In any case, like so many other émigrés fleeing the French Revolution, "Mr. Rose" vanished thereafter without leaving a trace.[39]

Residual ethnic or cultural influences may have also affected itinerants seeking work in New York State. The upriver towns of the Hudson River, especially Albany and neighboring Troy, Schenectady, and Hudson, were the northern terminus points of the longest and most heavily used inland waterway in the American Northeast. But because of the dynamics of their geography and their Dutch settlement history, Albany and its environs were seemingly insulated not only from most entrepreneurs active in the contiguous portions of northern and central New England (Berkshire and Hampshire Counties of Massachusetts and western Connecticut) but also to some degree from those approaching from New York City. Characterized by a patroon land-tenure system, by overlapping and conflicting English/Dutch homelife traditions, and by competing and partial mixing of two or more languages, the Hudson Valley exhibited a cultural imprint all its own. The process of Anglicization and Americanization was somewhat tentative, and in the period from 1780 to 1830, some areas had progressed further than others. Advertisements for runaway servants distinguished their ability to speak English from "high Dutch" or "low Dutch." Unlike New York City, where English language and culture formed a template shaping new arrivals from Europe, the Albany enclave sustained pockets of Dutch culture that remained estranged from more Anglicized regions of New York State and New England. Even after 1800, when much of the Hudson River area had adopted English language and social customs, gentry or patroon families such as the Van Rensselaers, Schuylers, Philipses, and Van Cortlandts still inhabited manors of hundreds of square miles and lived from the rents of their tenants. The "underside" of the patroon system was the continued prevalence of peasant customs.[40]

English-speaking itinerants who traveled up and down the Albany corridor sometimes found themselves in unfamiliar circumstances. When Noah Webster returned to New England after a tour of the southern states in 1786, he took what in effect was a detour to give his philology lectures in Albany and its environs before continuing home to New Haven. But Webster was unable to attract audiences in towns such as Lansingburgh, Troy, and Schenectady. When he did manage to gather listeners, as in Albany in 1786, he found them "dull." As he left the district, he told himself that "the Dutch have no taste for the English language."[41]

Those itinerants who taught culturally sensitive subjects—such as portraiture, dancing, and polite manners—may have found that encouraging a "Dutch" perspective helped their business in the Albany corridor. Gerrit Schipper (1775–c. 1830), a pastel artist working his way from Charleston to upper New York State between 1802 and 1805, sometimes called himself "a painter from Germany." But when he reached Albany, for the first time he was candid about his actual country of origin. "Correct Likenesses," his 1805 notice reads, "G. Schipper, from Holland."[42] A more pointed example is found with Mr. J. Johnson (or Johnston; fl. 1799–1818), a dancing-master who also began his teaching career in the South in Savannah and gradually wandered northward. A decade later, when he arrived in Albany, he leased a former boarding academy and founded a school along the lines of the old cultivated or polite-arts academies championed by Alexandre Quesnay in New York City and the Huletts, who established themselves as musicians and dancing teachers in New York City and Hartford. Johnson hired a Mr. Smith, a graduate of Williams College, to teach languages and English grammar. He recruited a Miss Johnson (perhaps a family member or his own daughter) to teach drawing and embroidery. Like many dancing-masters before him, he stressed that "genteel deportment and ease and elegance in their manners" were helpful to children. But, in a notice in 1814, he also added that "the elementary principles of Dancing, and also the rudiments of Politeness will be taught agreeable to the celebrated Mr. Ver Beck's method of teaching."[43]

While neither Ver Beck nor his method has been identified, there is every likelihood his system contained an ethnic Dutch dimension that caught the attention of the parents of Johnson's pupils. Over time, he prospered where others failed. He took his school to a succession of hotels, taverns, assembly rooms, and ballrooms in Albany itself, as well as in nearby Hudson and New Lebanon and in

Pittsfield, Massachusetts, remaining in the Albany enclave for at least a decade.[44] By contrast, other dancing-masters active in eastern and southern New England, New York City, and Philadelphia seldom found permanent work in the Albany area where the fashionable cotillions and contra dances of London, Paris, and Philadelphia may not have interested Anglo-Dutch families.

Chapter 3
A Legacy of Diversity, a Reputation for Distrust

J. Johnson's stated willingness to teach "the celebrated Mr. Ver Beck's method" in the Albany enclave suggests that itinerants were well aware of where they fit in the American milieu. Almost always, they were outsiders attempting to survive in an unfamiliar, mixed-ethnic environment. This was true of London physician Dr. Sharp, the mountebank, who three times in October 1720 admitted to his Boston readers, "he is a Stranger," meaning that he was not a resident of the town. It was also true of Dr. Isaac Calcott, who came to Rhode Island in 1769 as a "Seventh Son of a Seventh Son" to cure a variety of disorders.[1] In all likelihood, these erstwhile physicians, like most itinerants, spoke English with an ethnically or regionally discernible accent. Distinguishing traits of spoken language were always paramount in early America. Accounts of Dutch, German, and French accents mixing into the common English or English/European idiom were prevalent—eighteenth-century runaway servants were recognized because they spoke "low" or "high" Dutch, with a "German dialect," or "pretty good English, only in the French Dialect, and has a bold Look." Irishmen were noted for "having a brogue on his Tongue" or for having the "*Irish* Brogue pretty strong." In the British Isles English itself was broadly classed into districts—such as Scottish, northern Irish, and Welsh dialects. These were further divided into regions (West Country and North Country dialects) and counties (Staffordshire, Yorkshire, and Kentish), as well as into larger cities such as Worcester in the English midlands and Bristol in southwest England. These accents were widely noticed and their peculiarities were advertised. "Hopping Peg," a (limping) indentured servant woman who ran away from a Virginia household, "talks West Country, and pretty much through her nose." One teenaged Pennsylvania servant who had spent time with Native Americans even pretended "to talk Indian."[2]

The known or presumed national origins of the itinerant occupations summarized in tables 1.1 and 1.2 suggest that about 26 percent of the culture carriers identified between 1686 and 1825 were American born—among them Virginia-born acrobat John Templeman, Massachusetts-born profilist William King, and Vermont-born penmanship teacher Allison Wrifford. By contrast, approximately 68 percent were European expatriates looking for new career opportunities or fleeing from political or social turmoil, most coming from England, Scotland, Ireland, France, Italy, Holland, and Germany. The same data also reveal an unusual degree of gender and social diversity. Itinerant occupations attracted marginalized people of all types: loners, single women; the handicapped; and people of African, African American, and Native American backgrounds. While this diversity reflects the high level of individual skill and talent required for success in the fields of entertainment and the arts, an inherent separation nevertheless existed between "strollers" and the "conventional" American society in which they operated. Itinerants were conspicuous not only because they were strangers but because they were personally suspect or disadvantaged to begin with. It was no coincidence that balloonist Jean-Pierre Blanchard had just been expelled by the revolutionary French government, that dancing-master Monsieur O. Duhigg was an exiled plantation owner fleeing the racial tension in Santo Domingo, that the mountebank doctress "Charles" Hamilton was a former British felon, and that puppeteer Samuel Jameson Maginnis was a deserter from the English army. Even those who were American born fit this "suspect" category. They include Edward Burlesson, the "crippled" puppeteer from Connecticut; the unidentified Abenaki woman who was one of the first "documented" American alternative healers; and Richard Potter, the biracial son of an African American slave from Hopkinton, Massachusetts, and a local white patriarch, who was the first American-born ventriloquist (fig. 3.1).

Expanding on this data, we find that three identified trained animal showmen coming to America in the eighteenth century were from northern Europe. Bernard Clements, a German, traveled in British America in the 1730s with a dog and a horse named "Hans." His act was seen in December 1739 by Joshua Hempstead of New London, Connecticut, who noted that the dog "Ride[s] on him about the house Sitting up on the Sadle."[3] Clements drew on a horse-training tradition in Europe that developed after the remarkable exploits of William Banks and his horse Marocco, active in England and France in the late sixteenth and early seventeenth centuries.[4] A bird trainer named Mr. Willman, who performed in Boston and New York City in 1786 and 1788 and later in Jamaica, was born in Augsburg, Germany.[5] Animal trainer Gabriel Salenka was from northern, German-speaking Netherlands. He carried a trained card-playing dog with him in 1797 and 1798, and finished his acts with "Slight of hand" tricks and a program of German songs.[6]

VENTRILOQUISM.

Mr. & Mrs. POTTER,

Beg leave most respectfully to inform the Ladies and Gentlemen of that they will give

An Evening's Brush to sweep away Care; Or,

A MEDLEY TO PLEASE.

At Mr. Ball Room, on

day Evening,

In the course of the evening will be offered upwards of

100 Curious, but Mysterious Experiments.

PART FIRST.

Mr. Potter will commence the Performance with the *Automaton Dance*, to be followed by a number of Philosophical Experiments, a few of which are here detailed.

Mr. P. will fire from a gun, any lady's or gentleman's ring, and cause a dove immediately to appear, in whose bill the ring will be found. He will allow any lady or gentleman to cut their gown or handkerchief and will unite it in such a manner that the most discriminating eye cannot discover the least blemish. He will break a number of gentlemen's Watches with a large hammer and restore them to their regular form again. He will allow any gentleman to draw a Card, and make the same apparently to have the appearance of life, and move across the room. These are but few of the Experiments that will be offered in the course of the evening.

Mr. P. flatters himself that his Performances have been so well known, in various parts of the Country, as not to require the aid of a pompous advertisement; but will only inform the ladies and gentlemen, that may wish to honor him with their company, that this Bill can give but a faint idea of the Performance.

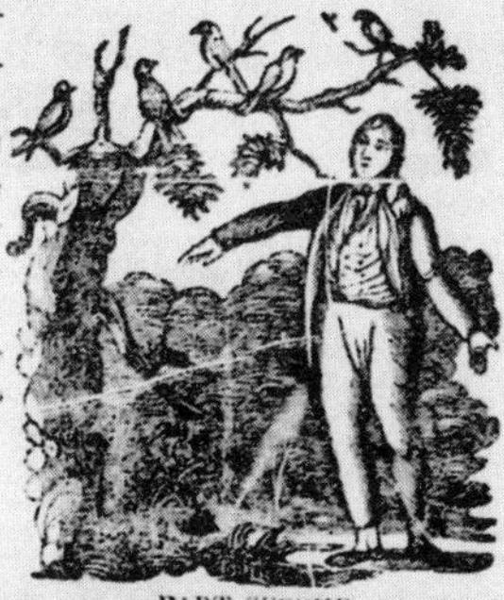

A SONG, by Mr. Potter.

PART SECOND.

VENTRILOQUISM.

Mr. P. will display his wonderful but laborious powers of Ventriloquism. He throws his voice into many dif-ferent parts of the Room, and into Gentlemen's Hats, Trunks, &c. &c. Imitates all kinds of Birds and Beasts, so that few or none will be able to distinguish his Imitations from the reality. This part of the performance has never failed of exciting the surprize of the learned and well informed, as the conveyance of Sounds is allowed to be one of the greatest curiosities in nature.

AFTER WHICH WILL BE SUNG

THE FAVORITE SONG of by Mr. *Potter*.

PART THIRD.

WILL BE PERFORMED THE FOURTH SCENE OF THE REVIEW, OR THE

Wag of Windsor,

(WRITTEN BY COLEMAN, JUN.)

Phoebe, or the disguised Captain, with a Song, - - - - Mrs. *Potter*.
Caleb Quotem, with a Day's Work and Song, - - - - Mr. *Potter*.

TO WHICH WILL BE ADDED THE PANTOMIMICAL PIECE, CALLED THE

Agreeable Surprise, *or the Wonderful Little Giant*,

GIANT, - - - - - - - - - - - - - Mrs. *Potter*.

Mr. POTTER will add to the diversion of the Entertainment in his representation of the Comic Scenes of the **CLOWN**, and close with a favorite Song in the Character of TIMOTHY NORPOST.

Tickets 25 Cents, to be had at the place of performance. **Performance to commence at early candle-light. The public may rest assured that the Room will be in ample order for the reception of Visitors, handsomely illuminated, with good music during the Interludes.** Ladies or **Gentlemen** desirous of having seats reserved for them, are requested to send timely notice.

True & Rowe, Printers, 75, State-street, Boston

Figure 3.1. "*VENTRILOQUISM . . . An Evening's Brush to sweep away Care.*" Illustrated announcement of songs, deceptions, and ventriloquism performances by Richard Potter (1783–1835) and Sally Harris Potter (c. 1785–1836) in Northampton, Massachusetts, September 1818. Richard Potter was already looking back on nine years' experience as an American entertainer in a career that began with a Mr. Johnson in Portsmouth, New Hampshire, in 1809. Potter's wife joined him in his acts as a singer in 1811. Boston: True and Rowe, 1815. Paper, 23 by 18 inches. Courtesy, Historic Northampton, Massachusetts. Acc. no. 57.227.

Other entertainment occupations, however, were drawn primarily from England or France. Nine of twenty-three identified trick horseback riders whose origins are known before 1826 came from London or Yorkshire County, England; four were American but only two of these, Christopher H. Gardner and Thomas Pool, disclosed their town of origin in their advertising. Out of thirty-five identified puppeteers active in North America and the Caribbean, sixteen were English or had learned their trade in London fairgrounds, six were French, two were Italian, and two were Irish or Welsh. Only three puppeteers were American born—chief among them Edward Burlesson, the first touring showman in early America. Virtually all of the large number of identified stage professionals entering the country after 1790 were recruited from London and Parisian theaters, as most actors, actresses, singers, musicians, and composers had previously played at Drury Lane, Covent Garden, or the King's Theatre in London or at the Académie de Musique or the Comédie-Française in Paris.

Frenchmen in turn dominated the worlds of fencing, fireworks, and balloon ascensions. No fewer than 74 of 109 identified fencing-masters active in North America before 1826 were previous members of the French Army or had trained in Paris or some part of France. (Twenty-three of these also took the time to give dancing lessons.) Seventeen of the forty-one known fireworks exhibitors performing in North America before 1826 were French, including Citizen Ambroise Varinot, who made a business of supplying fireworks to other parties in Philadelphia. Seven were Italian, beginning with Felix Fissour and his brother, who billed themselves as "Engineers to the King of Sardinia."[7] Other Italians included Laurent Spinacuta, a Mr. Codet, Nicholas Baschia, a Mr. Dusolla, and a Signor Gatty. Only six were American born. Of twenty-eight balloonists seeking subscriptions for manned "ascensions" on hot air or hydrogen gas, fifteen were French and three English, though only two Frenchmen (Jean-Pierre Blanchard and Louis Guille) were successful in raising money and actually getting aloft. Frenchmen also seemed to have dominated polite dance. Of 416 dancing-masters who advertised schools in North America between 1673 and 1825, 165 were French or had French surnames, and many who were not—like John Griffiths—constantly referred to their French connections as a way of defining or promoting themselves. Dancing-master Lawrence D'Obleville arrived in Salem in 1755 "from Paris." Dancing-masters named Du Poke and de St. Pry identified themselves as French in 1775. At the same time, the French connection to polite dance became an Anglo-American caricature—so much so that the "French dancing school" became a standing joke among newspaper editors when calculating the most pressing expense of every household.[8] By contrast a much smaller number of dancing-masters (134) were known to have been Englishmen or had Anglo-American surnames. And other European countries were also represented. Italian dancing-master Jonn Baptist Tioli opened a school in Providence for "Minuet, Double Minuet . . . of the newest Figures" "near Mr. Richard Olney's" in 1768. Christopher deGraffenried, a native of Switzerland, for years kept a school in Williamsburg in the 1730s and 1740s—as did his son Tscharner. Francis Christian, a German, ran schools in eastern Virginia in the 1760s, and a Williamsburg diarist reported he was still in the area in 1774.[9]

Diversity among showmen, tavern entertainers, and healers was even greater. Of the seventy-five identified conjurers, jugglers, or ventriloquists performing in America before 1826, most were evenly divided among French, English, Irish, Scottish, and northern European backgrounds. Two were African Americans, two were Italian, and two were German. Few Americans seem to have supported themselves in this demanding field—Richard Potter, the African American who began his career in Portsmouth, New Hampshire in 1809, was probably the first to do so, and he too is said to have learned his skills in Europe.[10] Out of ninety identified ropewalkers, slack-wire dancers, and tumblers who entertained in America before 1826, fourteen came from Italy; eleven from Ireland or Scotland—among them John Bradley and John Brenon—ten from England; nine from France; and eight from Mediterranean Africa or African American families. Of the eight identified American acrobats, at least three learned their trade in Europe, including John Templeton and a Mr. Bennett, the "American Balance-Master."[11]

Among the estimated 111 alternative healers circulating in North America, most had English, French, or German backgrounds. Mountebanks like Dr. Sharp and Anthony Yeldall were English. Dr. Lawrence Stork, an oculist who worked in Connecticut in the 1780s, was from Germany. Dr. Joseph Sabbe, who advertised remedies for jaundice and ague in Williamsburg, Virginia, in 1774, pointed to his prior thriving practice "in France." Dr. John Sals, advertising in New York in 1775, was "from Paris." At least five others, including Dr. Louis, Dr. Boduin, Dr. Blouin, Dr. Dubuke, and Dr. Dastuge (who may all have been the same person), stated they had come from France.[12] As the century came to a close, the influx of northern European alternative physicians began to decline and was superseded by those with Mediterranean, Ottoman, and even Asian backgrounds. Ibraham Adam Ben Ali, from Constantinople, promoted his style of "Algerine Medicine" in Boston for three weeks in February and March 1795. Ali pointed to his cures in "Dublin, Liverpool, Greenock, Glasgow, Edinburgh," and was last heard from in Baltimore. Dr. F. Cadete called himself "Vice President of the . . . Physical Faculty at Salamanca," Spain, and "lately from Providence" in Boston and Salem in 1799. That same year, John Howard began styling himself as a "Chinese Doctor" in Harrisburg, Pennsylvania, dispensing a variety of treatments for cancer, gout, and dropsy using herbs and roots that he had brought with him from Canton; he eventually relocated to Carlisle and Philadelphia. A Dr. Angelis in Philadelphia had previously practiced in "hot climates" in Italy and Portugal.[13]

Africans and African Americans were involved in many of these occupations. At least one early miniature painter was an English-trained African, a "Negro man whose extraordinary Genius has been assisted by one of the best Masters in *London*." He put "specimens of his performances" at the watch-making shop of John McLean on King Street in Boston in January 1773 and remained in town for about ten months.[14] Blacks, however, were much more active as street and tavern musicians and as violinists working for dancing-masters. Kate Van Winkle Keller's work on dance musicians indicates that a preponderance of violin players active before 1783 were African American slaves, former slaves, and descendants of slaves. They were performing in the seventeenth century when Caesar Wheeler accompanied an English dancing-master to Boston in 1678, and they were performing more than a hundred years later when balloonist Jean-Pierre Blanchard hired "men of color" in Boston in 1795.[15]

At least eight people of color gained prominence as acrobats, beginning with the unidentified "young *Negro Boy*" who accompanied Anthony Joseph Dugee on the "Stiff-Rope" at Denberg's Garden in New York in 1753.[16] Likewise, the "Baltimorean Boy" entertained local crowds with feats of jumping and tumbling in Louis Roussell's Maryland ballroom in 1787. His advertisements describe him as an "incomparable African" who played four musical instruments on the slack wire, and it seems likely he was the first independent black acrobat to perform for money before an American audience.[17] The next year "Signora Africana ... twenty years of age" appeared with a tumbling group at Corre's City Tavern in New York City.[18] William Nesbet, a "black Man," demonstrated a similar set of feats at a Mr. Slater's Tavern in Baltimore in 1794; like other acrobats he promised to dance the Spanish fandango blindfolded over fifteen eggs "and break none."[19] In Charleston in 1803, one Mr. Church, "an Aboriginal [Native American] from the Province of Lower Canada," teamed with trick rider John Ricketts to put on a slack-wire and tumbling show.[20] Another black acrobat, Othello, "the grand African," played on the slack wire in Maginnis's company in New York in 1804. Known also as the "Venetian Moor," Othello was termed a "pupil of Don Carlos" and recognized for his ability to hold his body out straight like a "Weather Cock."[21]

Othello's mentor, Don Carlos, more commonly called Donegani, was himself an African and probably the best-known acrobat in North America during this period. Active from 1788 through 1801, Donegani seems to have changed his name almost as often as he changed his nationality and place of origin. He began his American career in a partnership as "Carli and Donegani"—one of two "Celebrated Italian Balance Masters" who exhibited in Corre's City Tavern in 1788. As "Peter Cloris, the African," in Boston in June 1789, he presented feats of agility on the wire and acts of tumbling and slack-rope dancing that involved his walking through a hoop and balancing a dog on his nose. As the "Celebrated Italian Balance Master Donegani," he walked with two flags and balanced three swords on his nose at Salem's Concert-Hall (fig. 3.2) in 1789. As "Peter Clores, the Principal Performer of Mr. Donegani's Company," he played the French horn, violin, and castanets in New York in 1792. As "Don Peter Clores" he partnered with acrobat Mr. Martin (the "Little Devil") in "Mr. Walker's large

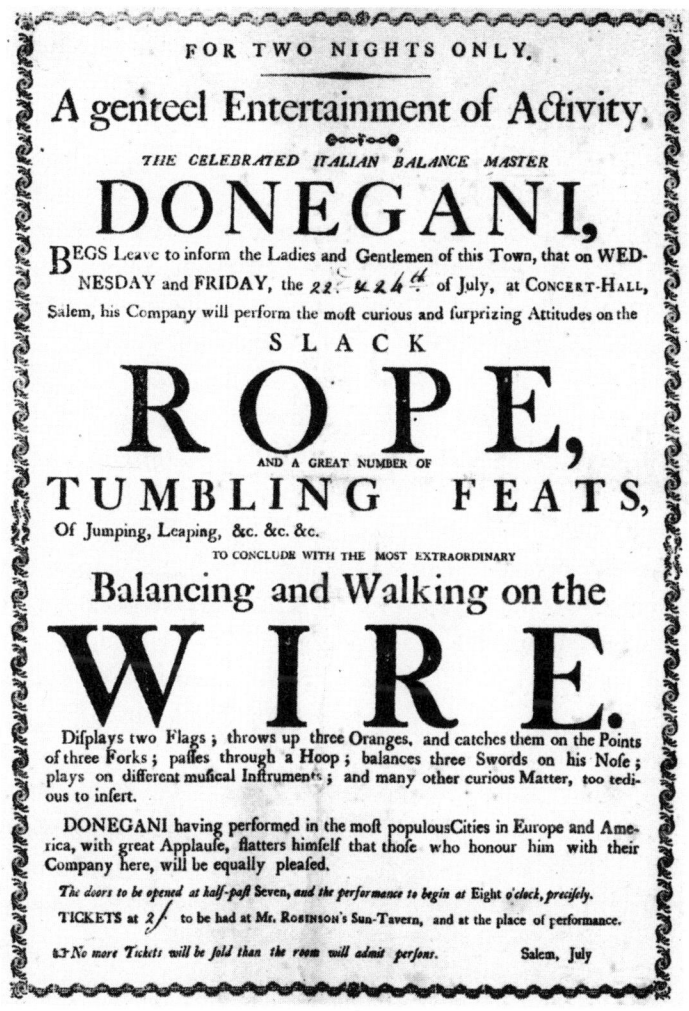

Figure 3.2. "FOR TWO NIGHTS ONLY. A genteel Entertainment of Activity. The Celebrated Italian Balance Master DONEGANI, Begs Leave to Inform the Ladies and Gentlemen of This Town." Broadside announcing an exhibition by Donegani (or Peter Cloris) at Concert-Hall, Salem, Massachusetts, July 1789. Variously identifying himself as an "Italian," "African," or "from Italy," Donegani reigned supreme among high-wire and tumbling artists in America in the period 1788–1801. Printed area: 12½ by 10¼ inches. Courtesy, Peabody Essex Museum, Salem, Massachusetts.

ball ally" on Great-George Street in New York City in 1793. As "Donegani's Co. From Italy" he tumbled, balanced, and sang at Salem's Washington Hall in 1794. After touring New York, Philadelphia, and other parts of the United States, he returned to Connecticut and eastern New England—this time as "Don Pedro Cloris, known in general by the name of Donegani"; he went again to Portsmouth and Portland in 1796 and 1797. He appeared a final time in New England in 1801 at Salem's Washington Hall and at Portland's Mechanics Hall.[22] Donegani's racial profile was never publicly mentioned, but he found that his shows were restricted to white audiences. With unintended irony, the proprietor of Portland's New Assembly Room on Water Street, where Donegani played on 9 March 1801, announced that since there were "no seats appropriate for people of colour, they cannot possibly be admitted."[23]

Finally, a significant number of itinerants were women. An estimated 10 percent of strollers in North America were composed of spouses and families. The most outstanding example is the Sharples family of portrait painters active in New England, New York, and the Mid-Atlantic in the decade after 1798. James Sharples; his third wife, Ellen Sharples; and children Rolinda, James, Jr., and Felix—all of them artists—visited virtually every town of importance in America producing pastel likenesses of "distinguished" men and women.[24] Acrobats and actors often traveled with their wives and children, who participated in their shows. James and Mrs. Maginnis, well-known puppeteers, were one of many actor-actress couples that performed harlequinades, burlettas, and programs of songs. Other pairs included John and Mary Durang, Laurent and Signora Spinacuta, and Alexandre and Madame Placide.[25]

Some women appear to have traveled alone. The earliest professional acrobat in North America was the unidentified "Woman" who in 1724 obtained permission from Governor William Keith to perform "Roap-Dancing" at Philadelphia's "New Booth on Society Hill." She was accompanied by a seven-year-old boy who "dances and capers" with her. She also danced with "baskets" and "Iron fetters" on her leg and pushed a wheelbarrow before her.[26] At least four unaccompanied women promoted miniatures in New York City in the period from 1801 to 1818. They included Miss Goudal, "Paintress from Paris," who advertised in 1801; Mademoiselle Beze, who arrived from Bordeaux, France, in 1804; Mary Way, who traveled alone and toured parts of Connecticut and New York City in 1812; and Madame Jacot, who "lately arrived from Neuchatel, in Switzerland," in 1818. Other female portrait and miniature painters included Madame Riviere "from France," who displayed samples of her miniatures in Boston in 1787, and "Mrs. Harris," who advertised in Charleston in 1819 and in Augusta, Georgia, in 1826.[27] Several dancing-mistresses traveled alone, like Louise Gervaise, who taught classes in Hartford and Middletown, Connecticut, between 1807 and 1810. And in 1826, Susanna Paine, calling herself "Miss S. Paine," took a room at a Mrs. Robinson's in Portland, Maine, to begin a decades-long trek through eastern New England and central Connecticut painting portraits at a very "reduced price," a career that she later recollected in her volume *Roses and Thorns,* published in 1854.[28]

Up to one-third of the alternative healers circulating in North America during the eighteenth and early nineteenth centuries were women. Using techniques that were either self-taught or learned from Native American practitioners, they cast themselves in opposition to "regular-bred" physicians and acquired a public following. In the North their history dates at least to 1769, when the *Essex Gazette* in Salem published a letter from a clergyman in Maine about a "certain Squaw" who resided in Brunswick and was going about extracting cancers without the use of "charm[s]" by administering both internal and external medicines. "Herbs and roots, manufactured in her own way, are her only remedies." The minister described her practice as being of some years' standing and added that she "never undertakes any cure without four Dollars in hand: if she fails of effecting it, she voluntarily returns the Fee." Regrettably we do not know this woman's name, but she may have been a member of one the Passamaquoddy or Abenaki tribes living in that area.[29] In the South at least two out of five rural practitioners advertising non-surgical cures for cancers in Virginia were females.

These women had urban counterparts. The leading cancer-curer in Boston at the end of the eighteenth century was Hannah Raymer Pope (1743–1805), the matriarch of the Pope family of alternative healers. She earned enough notice to be published in the city's directory as a "Cancer doctress" between 1798 and 1803 at three different addresses, the only cancer-curer of either sex listed in Boston in those years.[30] Recently widowed, she was a member of the Society of Friends; she died in her sixty-first year at her dwelling-house at 63 Newbury Street. Like other Pope family members, she followed the practices articulated by her husband, John Pope (1740–1796), who was recorded in the Boston Directory of 1789 as a "school-master and self-taught surgeon, particularly a curer of cancers and malignant ulcers." While not an itinerant, John Pope made himself available to patients in outlying towns such as Barnstable, Massachusetts.[31]

Single women also practiced the "cunning" trades. Living in rural enclaves and called "walk-abouts" by their nineteenth-century clients, they supported themselves through a variety of peddling, healing, and predictive occupations. According to contemporary William Bentley and other later historians, several early nineteenth-century families of mixed Algonkian and African American heritage residing in the barren hills overlooking the Malden and Woburn turnpikes told fortunes, exhibited rattlesnakes, grew and sold herbs, and made and peddled baskets. Sal Magos, a biracial "Indian" herb seller and fortune-teller living in Malden, was born about 1778, the daughter of an African American Revolutionary War soldier. Likewise, Deb Saco or Sawco, who died in 1839, was portrayed as a servant and "illegitimate daughter" of a colonial collector of customs in Salem. A warrant taken out in 1786 against "Deborah Sawco a Negro Woman (Daughter to Cuffe Sawco of Medford)" warned her to leave Malden and return to Salem. Saco's range of travel normally extended from Salem to Cambridge, but she sometimes remained on the road "for months." She was so widely known and admired that her character and clothing were imitated by women attending nineteenth-century social balls and other events at local ladies' fairs.[32]

ACCOMPANYING THIS diversity was a reputation for criminality. North American distrust of outsiders was no doubt grounded in age-old social instincts, but it was exacerbated by a deeply entrenched parochialism. Most Americans in the eighteenth and early nineteenth centuries lived, married, and died in an encapsulated world made up of several adjoining parishes or precincts of about one to three thousand individuals, approximately one-fifth of them heads of households. They knew their townspeople by sight; they prayed and sang together once or twice a week at the same meetinghouse; they were united by kinship and marriage, and tied by a network of labor-sharing indenture agreements, promissory notes, and account book debts and credits that bound the social fabric into a single unit. These financial obligations were kept up to date and crossed off when discharged; some remained in force for years until cleared by the process of inventory-taking and probate review.

This parochialism is evident in the forty-seven-year diary kept by Joshua Hempstead (1678–1758) of New London. In it he took note of any outsiders or "Transient persons" interacting with his community as he chronicled everyday events in this port of entry on Long Island Sound.[33] Hempstead's work as a surveyor, gravestone cutter, and justice of the peace regularly took him to Groton, Stonington, and Norwich, but his immediate domain encompassed three contiguous New London parishes whose meetinghouses he attended on a rotating basis and whose marriages, births, and deaths he faithfully documented in his diary—most likely as a memory aid. (The diary has been indexed with approximately six thousand names.) Some of the strangers mentioned in Hempstead's diary were recent European immigrants: the "Saylor Spanyard or Porteguee Newly arrived from the Wine Islands," the "Stranger . . . [an Irishman] that came Lately over from Jamaica," and an "Old England man." But they also included a "Stranger named Jon[a]t[han] Lawrence . . . who belonged to Providence," a stranger named "Barnard or Barnee. Born att Rehoboth tis said," and a "stranger belonging to Glouster—a Town on the Cape"—in short anyone living outside Hempstead's immediate circle. It goes without saying that these people were subject to a different set of rules. As the printer of the *Hudson*

Balance expressed it, "Advance pay for advertising will always be exacted from strangers, or persons living at a distance from Hudson."[34]

Deserved or not, distrust of itinerants was based on well-publicized cases of drunkenness, criminality, and profligacy perpetrated by itinerants taking advantage of America's provincial reputation for gullibility. The worst was expected of outsiders—and they sometimes obliged. Alternative healer Dr. Isaac Calcott was found in a drunken stupor in the streets of Middletown, Connecticut, in 1770.[35] Itinerant engraver Richard Brunton (d. 1832) was confined to Connecticut's Old Newgate Prison after he was found guilty of counterfeiting money. (Brunton did some of his best engravings there; fig. 3.3). Acrobat Alexandre

Figure 3.3. *A Prospective View Of Old Newgate Connecticut's State Prison.* Engraving attributed to Richard Brunton (d. 1832), probably done while Brunton was jailed at Newgate Prison for counterfeiting. Circa 1799–1801. Ink on paper with line engraving. Courtesy, The Connecticut Historical Society.

Placide (fl. 1791–1812), known as the "first rope dancer to the King of France," ran off in 1796 with Charlotte S. Wrighten, daughter of actress Mrs. Mary Ann Wrighten Pownall (1751–1796); theater historian George O. Seilhamer reported that Mrs. Pownall died of heartbreak.[36] A Mr. Martin, an acrobatic colleague of both Donegani and Placide, ran into a different sort of trouble. An accomplished Harlequin actor who later played the lead in the *Birth of Harlequin* and the *Restoration of Harlequin* in New York City, Martin was also skilled in producing indoor and outdoor fireworks and in giving lantern presentations. After giving a phantasmagoria show in Boston's Columbian Museum in 1807, he was careless in putting away his lighting equipment, and the museum caught fire and was reduced to rubble. Six young bystanders were crushed to death when a wall gave way.[37]

But these episodes were relatively infrequent and do not represent patterns of behavior. The two most common forms of criminality were actually financial: absconding with tuition advances or leaving town with unpaid debts. Both seem to have been failings among itinerants who were unable to resist the temptations of their status. A textbook case took place in Portsmouth, New Hampshire, in August 1773 during a busy and confusing summer when an unprecedented number of stage plays, pantomimes, and musical concerts were being promoted by a company of strolling English players who had come to that town with impresario William Sampson Morgan. One of Morgan's musicians, William Crosby, announced in the *New-Hampshire Gazette* that he would teach "Music, Theor[et]ical, Rudimental, and Practical," specifically a curriculum of psalmody, airs, duets, solos, and dialogues composed by Henry Purcell, George F. Handel, and others. He was to open his school at the assembly room with a public dissertation on music and hold class three times weekly either by month or quarter.[38]

Within four weeks, however, the following advertisement ran in the same paper: "SIX PENCE O.T. REWARD. Last Sunday Evening our Professor of Music, Theor[et]ical, Rudimental and Practical has absconded. . . . As the damage the public must sustain by his unexpected Retreat, will be very great, the above reward of SIX PENCE O.T. is offered to any person who will apprehend W C[_]sby Professor of Music aforesaid, and convey him to this Town, before the Fifth day of November next." It was signed by "The Sufferers." The notice concludes by observing that Crosby had on "when he went away a green coat, a white waistcoat and breeches" and was noticeable for a "peculiar Mark which Time will ne'er deface"—possibly a birthmark or more likely a scar left by a branding.[39] Almost a year later, William Crosby—after having "boasted" of his intimate knowledge of classics, music, dancing, and fencing in southern newspapers—was being sought by authorities in Fredericksburg, Virginia, for absconding with a silver watch, a chestnut mare, and a new well-sprung carriage painted green.[40]

Much the same set of circumstances surrounded a known mountebank working in North America named Dr. Louis, whose notoriety in the 1770s did little to help the tarnished reputations of foreigners generally and of Frenchmen in particular. Louis seems to have practiced under at least two other names, Dr. Boduin and Dr. Dubuke, and may have partnered with (or assumed the identity of) at least two other mountebanks—usually identifying himself as an "oculist and dentist" from Paris or "Old France." He comes to our attention first in March 1774, when Philadelphia inn keeper Susanna Cryder twice put up a reward of thirteen pounds for the arrest of "the noted Doctor Louis" and the return of her horse. She alleged he had stolen a gold watch and a roan-colored horse from her establishment, describing him as a "well-made" man, dressed "gentlemen-like" with a "smooth and full face," wearing his own hair curled up on both sides of his head and tied behind. He carried several French books on physic and surgery and a "fine" set of surgical instruments. She added he had traveled through Germany, Spain, France, Italy, and England and that he understood some German, Spanish, and Italian, but spoke Latin very well.[41]

Despite the size of this reward, Dr. Louis was still using his own name when he turned up in Newport and Providence a month later—indicating, among other things, that Philadelphia papers apparently went unread in Rhode Island. Three weeks later he was advertising in Boston and Salem as "Dr. Louis" and still claiming his medical prowess had "given sight to 27 persons in Philadelphia, 7 in Baltimore, and 5 in New-York." But he could not evade the law. The *Boston Post-Boy* related in July 1774 "that the well known Quack, Dr. Louis late from the Southern Colonies" was committed to a Boston jail for "burglariously" entering a dwelling house in Cambridge. For about a year nothing was heard of him. His story resumes in August 1775, when Louis reappeared in New London and in New Haven. He was now calling himself Dr. L. Boduin. But newspaper editors continued to pursue him, and in September 1775, New Haven's *Connecticut Journal* warned that "Dr. Boduin, who has advertised in this paper . . . has been detected in stealing from an apothecary's shop here. . . . He is the same person who advertised in the last New London paper, by the name of Louis; he is supposed to be an old offender, and will change his name wherever he goes."[42]

Dr. Louis next worked in New York where he apparently practiced under a new name, "Dr. Dubuke," residing at a tavern on Dock Street. The extent of his professional activity during his stay in New York is not known, but his patients could take little solace in a report published in the New York *Constitutional Gazette* of 9 March 1776, which stated that "the famous Dr. Dubuke, a Frenchman, who was branded here last January term, for stealing indigo &c. departed to Phila. He professes himself a dentist and has traveled under various names."[43] Here his story apparently ends, but it is entirely possible that Dr. Louis continued practicing as Dr. Blouin or Dr. Dastuge, both from "old France" and "from Paris," whose advertisements, claims, and counter-claims filled New York's papers in the period after 1775.[44]

Some American editors took extra pains to point out itinerant transgressions. In 1824, Boston's *New-England Galaxy* reported on the fate of John Montaes (who was also known as Jerome or J. Montas), a young French or Italian dancing-master who had begun his American career by offering his compliments to residents of Nashville in 1820. (His was the first school to teach polite manners in the newly acquired territory of Tennessee.) Montaes apparently did well in this region. But about four years later he advertised a dancing school in Providence, received advance pay of twenty dollars from his scholars, accepted a number of loans (amounting to two hundred dollars), and then absconded well before the term was up. The paper mockingly lamented that Montaes "slipped his cable and danced off to the tune of 'over the hills and far away' leaving his scholars to take such steps as they thought proper, with regard to his French leave, and his musicians to whistle for their pay." He was tried for the same violation in New York City, where he was defended by three lawyers "in the very teeth of strong circumstantial testimony"—and got off. But when he reached Philadelphia, he was charged with stealing two pistols and a Masonic medal from the trunk of a sea captain and pawning them. Montaes was apprehended when he tried to leave by boat and given a one-year sentence in the Philadelphia jail where "any Providence scholars can find him at his lodgings corner of Walnut and Sixth Streets where he will always be at home." His fate (titled "A New Step") was reprinted almost verbatim in seven other newspapers ranging from Haverhill, Massachusetts, to Easton, Maryland.[45]

Criminality among itinerants of course was not confined to immigrants. The most egregious case may be that of William King (1754–after 1825), who was born in Salem. A New Englander with an established trade and family background, King possessed multiple talents and indefatigable energy, but he left a tarnished record. In a far-ranging career he trained as a cabinetmaker and ivory turner but later turned to profile making and medical electricity. King seems to have been driven to vagabonding by intemperance and an open disregard for his own family. Both he and his wife were members of Reverend William Bentley's East Parish in Salem; the clergyman called him "very capricious" and occasionally recounted the twists and turns of King's career.[46] Bentley began by noting that King returned to Salem in 1785 "after having been long absent in the West Indies." Two years after King's marriage to Rebecca Phippen in March 1785, he left her a letter stating his intention to abscond, stole a sulky and horse, and disappeared. He was later apprehended near East Haven, Connecticut, and obliged to pay sixteen pounds in damages. He was then the father of a one-year-old daughter and prospective father of a second child. Again settling down in Salem from 1789 to 1792, he maintained an ivory turning shop near the East

Schoolhouse, selling items such as canes, fifes, dice, dice boxes, backgammon boards, and billiard balls. He also made cabinet furniture—labeled examples of which were catalogued and photographed by antiquarian Homer E. Keyes in the 1920s.[47]

In 1794, William King removed with his family to New York City where he once more advertised himself as an "Ivory and Wood Turner," but not for long. In June 1796, Bentley recorded in his diary news from Philadelphia that "Wm. King, belonging to a good family in this Town, after having dragged his family from Town to Town, left a note that he meant to drown himself and disappeared. It is supposed that he means to ramble unincumbered. The family are to return to Salem."[48]

Thenceforth King remained permanently "unincumbered," making money with a profile-taking machine (fig. 3.4) apparently of his own invention. King's travels now covered much of eastern coastal New England and parts of Canada in a regular circuit that brought him to Newburyport in December 1804, Portsmouth and Portland in 1805, and to Hanover, New Hampshire, in 1806. In the meantime he had trained his seventeen-year-old second child, William, Jr., to take profiles, and the two of them virtually dominated the trade in eastern New England in 1805.[49] At some point he boarded a packet to Halifax, Nova Scotia,

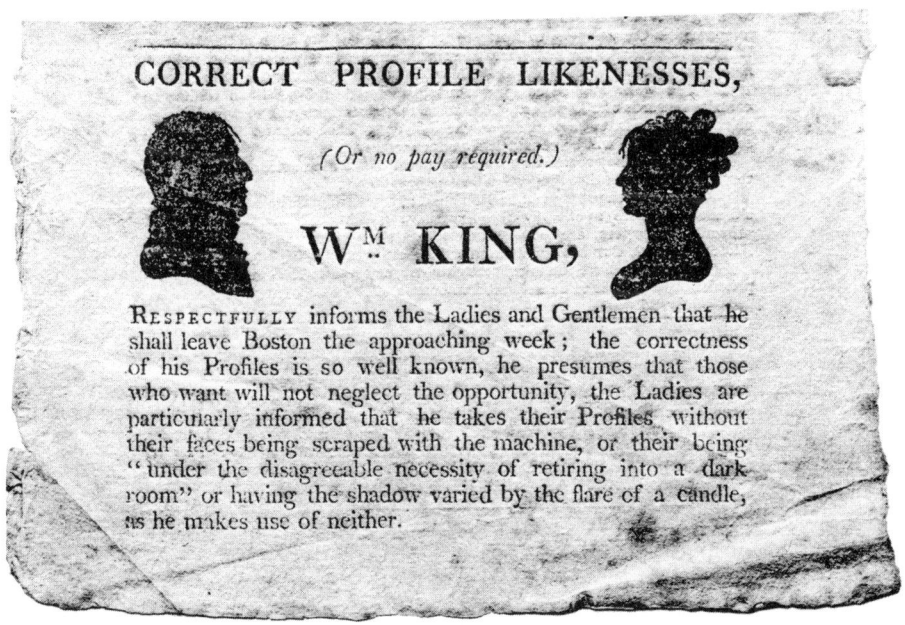

Figure 3.4. "CORRECT PROFILE LIKENESSES, *(Or no pay required.)* WM KING." Handbill indicating that profile maker William King (1754–after 1825) would leave Boston "the approaching week." King's appeal emphasized that his machine made correct profiles without clients' "faces being scraped" or their having to retire "into a dark room." Boston: N.p., c. 1806. Courtesy, American Antiquarian Society.

and sold profiles in that town. When he returned to Salem, he again caught the attention of William Bentley: "Mr. King has a panorama still in Salem. It is the siege of Tripoli. The Ships are done by Corné, formerly living in this town & introduced by E. H. Derby from Naples."[50]

King came to Bentley's attention a final time in November 1809, when the Salem clergyman learned of the death of William King, Jr., at Martinique, an island in the Lesser Antilles.[51] According to Bentley, "The father a Wanderer. An ingenious mechanic but full of projects, & what he gains from one, he loses in another. The Father is now upon his pilgrimages & [the] family at Salem. The Son, an amiable youth, was sent with a machine for portraits upon an adventure to Martinoco & died in that climate about 20 years of age."[52]

Unknown to Bentley, William King was then on the road as a scientific demonstrator, calling himself a "Philosophical and Medical Electrician." King advertised exhibitions in Norwich and New London, Connecticut, in 1809, and the next year at the house of Joseph Wheeler in Kingston, New York—all the time expanding the scope of medical complaints he could cure into a two-paragraph catalogue that included toothaches and "hysterics and diseases peculiar to women." At this point his showman's routine involved simulating lightning strikes on a small house, driving gold leaf into glass so it could not be rubbed off, experimenting with a "Leyden Phial" and an "Electrical Battery," and illuminating the name *Washington* with "electrical fluid."[53] When a second son, Nathaniel Phippen King, died in 1819, Rebecca King was appointed administrator of the estate. In a petition to the probate court, she noted that her husband "about ten years ago left this part of the country and went to the Southern States, and has not been heard of since to our knowledge."[54]

In the end, the risks faced by transients, the demonstrated criminal behavior of a few, and the overall uncertainties and questions regarding their methods so discredited the term *itinerant* that many culture carriers tried their best to distance themselves from it. In several pointed exchanges itinerant surgeon-dentist Richard C. Skinner parried unexpected competition in Albany in 1814 from two men. For years Skinner had treated patients in New York City, New Haven, Hartford, and Albany and areas between, but he was called up for military service during the War of 1812. After his discharge, he found that two surgeon-dentists had taken over his territory. In a sharply worded series of advertisements he rhetorically asked whether a regularly bred operator (meaning himself) with twenty-four years' approved practice was not preferable over "itinerant or self-taught surgeon-dentists, who too often assume the practice of a delicate profession, which they have neither studied the theory of, nor experienced the practice necessary to establish a professional reputation."[55] Elsewhere a few portrait painters characterized themselves as "itinerant" in the privacy of their diaries (among them William Dunlap), but they seem to have done so reluctantly.

Others used the term as a sign of opprobrium. Ethan Allen Greenwood, himself an itinerant painter for many years, noted that "various itinerant & vagabond exhibitions" arrived in Boston in 1823, cutting down on the patrons that came to his museum.[56] And when American portrait painter Chester Harding was compiling his memoirs in the 1860s, he recalled how he learned English grammar while struggling to build a career as painter in new communities in the Ohio and Mississippi Valleys: "It was here [St. Louis] that I obtained a perfect knowledge of the English language: at least I was assured by an itinerant professor that he could make me a thorough grammarian in twelve lessons, and as I took the required number of lessons, if I am not all that he promised me, it must be his fault and not mine."[57] Harding had reduced his "itinerant professor" into a caricature.

By the turn of the nineteenth century, town officials, newspapers editors, and newspaper readers were using the terms *strolling, vagrant,* and *itinerant* with derision. In 1796, Baltimore passed an ordinance that required constables to list "every" common prostitute, vagrant, wanderer, juggler, fortune-teller, stroller, and gambler in his jurisdiction and make it available to the court. And the same year, a writer in South Carolina deplored the "itinerant habits" of a local politician who had recently inflamed the public mind.[58] Even educated itinerants were fair game. When Dr. Elisha Perkins and his son John D. Perkins were promoting and selling their stroking "Metallic Points" in New England in 1797, an editor in Litchfield, Connecticut, reported that a critic of these "itinerant geniuses" conducted a test case to see if the points really worked: "A person present, having a rheumatic pain in his shoulder, (who had ridiculed the quackery) immediately drew off his coat, and submitted to the experiment—a few moments application upon the skin relieved the complaint, and carried off the inflammation. On the man's confessing himself *made whole,* the *chap* produced the wonderful *stroker*—when lo' a Corn Cob, and not the points, had wrought the prodigy."[59]

The unmistakable liability of the term was corroborated by another surgeon-dentist who publicized the opening of a new office over a variety store in Hartford in 1827. He assured his readers that "as he is not fond of the character of an Itinerant he will remain 'at home' and hopes that the success of his workmanship in Hartford and its vicinity will gain him that patronage which he merits."[60]

Chapter 4

Establishing a Public Presence

FACING DISTRUST and suspicion from all sides, strollers and itinerants characteristically relied on a wide range of promotions to attract audiences and clients and to overcome the considerable disadvantage of working as strangers and foreigners. To do this they called on a centuries-old repertory of personal charisma, testimonials, claims, exaggerations, promises, and diversions described in some detail by contemporary observers like William F. Pinchbeck in 1805 and more recently by cultural historians like Peter Burke, who used terms such as *mountebank, saltimbanco, merry Andrew, quacksalver,* and *juggler* to describe them. But there was an important American difference. Whereas traveling singers, healers, and entertainers in early modern Europe literally mounted platforms and wooden stages in crowded town squares, their counterparts in America called attention to themselves primarily by advertising in a rapidly expanding network of newspapers, broadsides, and placards.

This may explain why itinerants who prospered in early America were almost always those who most effectively promoted themselves through their skill in writing. John Bonnin, for example, publicized a "diagonal mirror" in New York City in 1748, saying that his perspective views of London were so "*insensibly*" attractive, that unless an "Embargo . . . on all Vessels bound for England or an Act made to forbid the *Ladies, especially,* from leaving this colony, by next summer there will be but few of the Fair Sex left in it."[1] Much the same exaggerated rhetoric was raised by showmen like John Maison, writing-masters like Allison Wrifford, alternative healers like James Graham, and conjurers like Joseph Falconi, who enhanced their prospects through the acuity and magnification of their verbal arguments. A great deal, of course, depended on the availability of local newspapers. In America, papers were not published in the seventeenth century, but after 1700 this changed quickly. Beginning with a single paper issued in Boston in 1704, the number of weekly or biweekly editions in the American colonies jumped from 4 in 1720 to 18 in 1750, to almost 80 by 1780; by 1800 the overall figure had risen to over 450.[2] Their "advertisement pages" circulated a common language, mutual recognition, and shared expectations that became central to the survivability of scores of teachers, showmen, artists, and other bearers of popular culture.

In part this American reorientation of popular culture to the printed page was a function of the "spaciousness" of the colonial and early American setting—meaning its lower population densities and greater distances relative to those in Europe. The likelihood of finding receptive audiences anywhere in North America was always limited. Crowds might sometimes materialize in cities such as Philadelphia, New York, and Boston, but for much of the seventeenth and eighteenth centuries, Boston, the single most important of these population centers, was constrained by its Sabbath culture. In general, New Englanders came together to celebrate royal anniversaries, witness executions, oversee punishments, listen to preaching evangelists, attend college commencements and bridge-openings, and gather for militia trainings. Diarist Joshua Hempstead wrote that ten thousand people "of all sexes & Nations" assembled in New London, Connecticut, to watch the 1753 hanging of Sarah Bramble, who had murdered her "bastard child."[3] The throngs that witnessed the opening of the Charles River Bridge in Boston in 1782 were composed of, in the words of diarist John Tudor, "Sutch a Concourse of people, Carriages &c I never Saw at one Time before."[4] Outside of New England, crowds were attracted by sports events (bull-baiting, horseracing) and Masonic parades. But these occasions did not always lend themselves to mountebank benches, open-air plays, and street entertainments.

These limits were consolidated by the reforms introduced by immigrant Englishmen who put an end to the traditional religious calendars and the succession of holidays that Europeans had long been accustomed to celebrating. In England, fairs, festivals, carnivals, and sports days were tied to local customs and history, and were typically held on a town's feast day.[5] Stages and booths were erected in fields adjacent to churchyards, and market activities were mingled with plays, puppetry entertainments, and acrobatic feats. Essex County, England, was the site of seventy such venues in the seventeenth century. In London alone, four annual fairs were held at Mayfair, Tottenham Court, Bartholomew, and Southwark. Although some were suppressed on moral grounds at end of the eighteenth century, others persisted and became the pleasure fairs of the nineteenth century.[6] In colonial America, however, few such festivals or feast days existed in a society in which even agricultural fairs were sometimes discouraged. An almanac published in 1721 by Titan Leeds (1699–1738) of New York City reveals that the year's monthly rotating agricultural fairs began at Cohansie, New York, in April and ended in Amboy, New Jersey, with events at Chester, Philadelphia, New Castle, New York City, and Providence. There were no equivalent circuits in Massachusetts, Connecticut, or New Hampshire until the late eighteenth century. Horseraces with substantial purses were still being held at Perth Amboy, New Jersey, in the 1760s, but as diarist Noah Webster noted somewhat ruefully in 1785, none was held in Connecticut.[7]

Restrained by a reformed calendar, an almost universal suspicion of strangers, and a dearth of festive audiences, culture carriers in North America turned to a self-initiated world of inflated postures, finely tuned promotions, and subscription schemes designed to transform public uncertainty into sources of appeal and public suspicion into buyer confidence. The first step generally taken by a newly arrived itinerant was to contact the informal networks that stood to gain from his or her presence. In almost every American community—be it a city, town, parish, or hamlet—could be found a tavern, an inn, a meeting lodge, or even a neighborhood where a leisure mentality and an acceptance of strangers were quietly tolerated or even encouraged. These sites have been extensively studied by historians, among them Donna-Belle Garvin and James L. Garvin (New Hampshire), Kym S. Rice (New York), Bruce C. Daniels (New England), who all agree that these establishments were usually centrally or strategically situated and served as a point of focus for popular culture and specialty trafficking, some of it probably illegal. In Boston it was Wing's Lane near the lower end of King Street and adjacent to Long Wharf and the Town Dock—a teeming waterfront area that housed taverns, schools, boarding houses, storehouses, butcheries, physician's offices, and dye-houses. This was the neighborhood where Samuel Sewall put an end to a man's "Tricks" in 1687; where George Brownell taught "ciphering," dancing, and the violin, as early as 1712; where the Deblois family organized the first musical concerts in America in their "great Room" in 1732. (Next door was a boardinghouse patronized by itinerant music teachers.)[8] Thomas Brooks, a shopkeeper, maintained a waxwork museum here with his wife, Sarah Briggs, in 1739. George Mason, the first London-based itinerant limner to advertise likenesses in Boston in 1765, stayed at a Mrs. Coffin's Seven Stars coffeehouse at the bottom of King Street.[9] Dr. William Clark and his family—best known for their trepanning operations—lived for years in a dwelling house on Wing's Lane. One of the last mountebank physicians traveling in North America, F. Cadete, lived in a rooming house in Wing's Lane in 1800.[10] Elsewhere in the colonies, Abraham Van Dyck's inn was located on New York's Broadway near St. Paul's Church. Jacob Jacobs's long room at "No. 33, on the Bay" in Charleston was the venue for public auctions. Other taverns were built at crossroads, like Isaac Woodruff's in Springfield, New Jersey, where church lotteries were held. Positioned at the juncture of the main thoroughfare from

Elizabethtown to Morris and the road going from Newark to New Brunswick, it provided easy access to four central New Jersey communities.[11]

Rather than looking on itinerants with a mixture of curiosity and trepidation, proprietors of these establishments often knew them by person or reputation, and they certainly stood to make money from itinerants' activities. They welcomed itinerants for the same reason they sold newspapers, coffee, and alcoholic beverages and invited lottery drawings, estate auctions, and meetings of hunt clubs and slavery abolition societies to their premises. Captain Frederick Bull, who kept one of the largest taverns in late eighteenth-century Hartford, catered to an entourage of entertainers passing through central Connecticut—the acrobatic team of John Brenon and his wife, Hannah; the ropedancer Mr. Bennett; and an unidentified showman with two Arabian camels. Bull most likely knew about them from the proprietors of other taverns in nearby Middletown, Goshen, and Litchfield, who also accommodated them with the same economic motivation.[12] In Boston, "The Sign of the Green Dragon"—first on Middle Street and later on Union Street—was a site for auctions, "outcrys," horseracing wagers, and fire-fighting clubs that also served Boston for years as a place of entertainment for acrobats, dancing-masters, and wild animals in captivity, and for displays of unusual items such as a scale model of Jerusalem. (Later the Green Dragon was known for its use as a boarding school during the American Revolution.) In New York, a Mr. Vandewater's long room and a Mr. Corre's assembly room hosted John Brenon's slack-wire acts in 1774 and Joseph Falconi's electrical experiments in 1787.[13] In Philadelphia, the Barracks presented fireworks in 1769, and the Bunch of Grapes Tavern was where Hyman Saunders exhibited his dexterity in 1772 and Daniel Bowen opened a waxwork museum in 1790. In Baltimore, a Mr. Grant's tavern offered a school by dancing-master Gaspard Cenas in 1793. In Charleston, Williams's long room hosted Thomas Turner's dancing school in 1796. In Savannah, Alexander Crighton's tavern was where members of the "Ugly Club" met before their festivities and the Society of St. Andrew gathered to celebrate their "Day."[14]

By encouraging itinerants, tavern proprietors played out the time-honored role of the impresario or agent, supplying overnight lodgings, a long room or assembly hall for audiences, a staff to prepare drinks and food, and stables and fodder for horses. They also provided access to printing services, newspaper readerships, and the public respectability that enabled entrepreneurs to abandon the strategy of door-to-door marketing. And they were there in numbers. One study by Daniels estimates 3,000 taverns served New England by 1790. Research by Nancy L. Struna identifies 100 taverns in Philadelphia in 1731, and 120 in the 1750s when the town's population was 18,000. New York City counted about 100 with a population smaller than Philadelphia. Struna estimates that each of these cities had one legal drinking establishment for every one hundred citizens.[15]

Collectively these taverns created a commercial milieu that was governed by established rules of conduct, a recognized promotional vocabulary, mutual expectations, and shared advantages. Habits and old memories kept alive the drawing power of these establishments even as they passed to the hands of successive proprietors and leaseholders who may or may not have shared the professional interests of their predecessors. In the 1760s and 1770s, Mary Cowley ran a dancing academy, boarding house, and coffeehouse in her establishment on Church Lane in Newport, Rhode Island, in a neighborhood of several meetinghouses and a synagogue. Cowley was a ready friend and hostess for traveling entrepreneurs—among them the proprietor of a clockwork cuckold drummer (and his clockwork wife) from "the King of Prussia's Army" in 1764, stage singer and theatrical impresario David Douglass in 1769, and French surgeon-dentist Michael Poree on his way from Philadelphia and New York City in 1773.[16] After the Revolutionary War, Cowley entertained George Washington, the Comte de Rochambeau, and other officers of the American and French armies at a grand ball held in March 1781. Following her retirement, her premises temporarily became a rehearsal hall for dancing schools during 1784 and 1785 while also functioning as a boardinghouse. But in the 1790s, the former home of Mary Cowley again emerged as a site for lectures and subscription schools—this time as "the assembly room at Church Lane" or as "Mrs. Penrose's Assembly Room," named after its new proprietress.[17] In the next decade the location continued to be leased by a series of Connecticut-based dancing-masters and was still serving as an assembly hall in the first decade of the nineteenth century.[18]

Some entrepreneurs found it helpful to link up with other itinerants or recent immigrants. These connections occasionally produced curious crossovers in the fields of medicine, puppetry, language teaching, balloon-making, and music. While sometimes defying our attempts to reconcile them, they seem to have been important for those entering a community for the first time. Joseph Gibbes, an English puppeteer traveling through Massachusetts in 1768, gave his shows at the house of John Moore, a Boston wine merchant newly arrived from Lisbon.[19] In Charleston in 1793, an unidentified "gentleman Planter in Hispaniola," lately fled from the violence on that island, sought to teach violin and published the name of Peter Henri, a miniature painter on George Street, as his contact.[20] George Keisselbach, a physician and oculist briefly practicing in Boston in 1795, gave Monsieur Nadau's dancing academy as his. Nadau, a Frenchman, was well known in Boston by then, having served as a dancing instructor for several seasons.[21] French language and flageolet teacher Louis Boquet in turn made his services available in 1809 "at T. Parsons's Dentist," a recent English immigrant and traveling surgeon.[22] Itinerants also received encouragement from doctors, apothecaries, retired military officers, and sea captains (and their widows) who saw themselves as artistic or cultural patrons. In the year that pharmacist William Stearns of Salem provided housing and a painting room for portraitist John Brewster, Jr., Stearns let the same room to a man who was touring with a caged leopard from Bengal.[23]

After 1790, however, many itinerants began to receive their greatest support from the country's newly built theaters and amphitheaters. Among all strollers, theatrical professionals and related equestrian and tightrope entertainers together constituted the most prolific of the Europeans crossing the Atlantic. Beginning with the Old American Company, which was active in the Mid-Atlantic colonies between 1750 and 1773, and Yorkshire trick riders arriving in the 1770s, stage and equestrian organizers increased about sixfold by the 1790s with the founding of permanent theaters and amphitheaters in Boston, New York, Philadelphia, Baltimore, Alexandria, Williamsburg, and Charleston. By the next decade this number had almost doubled. The demand for actors, actresses, and skilled horse riders was so great that managers were obliged to recruit scores of candidates who literally came over by the boatload. An estimated six hundred theater and music professionals and one hundred circus professionals had entered the country from England and France by 1810. Each new permanent theater provided opportunities for acrobats, ropewalkers, ropedancers, balloonists, conjurers, tumblers, and animal trainers.

The most clear-cut example of theatrical interdependency is Jean-Pierre Blanchard's use in 1793 of an open-air rotunda that John B. Ricketts had recently raised for his equestrian team on Market Street near Philadelphia's artillery ground. Advertising the event as an experimental "Parachute or Falling Screen," Blanchard claimed it was the first ever made on the "Continent of America" and promised that if it rained or the wind was too high, he would postpone it until the next day. By sandwiching himself in among Ricketts's horsemanship performances, Blanchard solved his immediate problem of charging admission for something that American crowds were still basically unwilling to pay for (balloon flights) but that he hoped would help him raise money for a second ascension. (Blanchard was warmly appreciated by the circus-crowds, but he failed to raise the required money.)[24]

More important, this concentration of theatrical activity brought a whole new generation of foreign-born players, singers, dancers, musicians, mechanics, and stage painters into cities where it flourished. Of the fifty-one stage professionals and members of the band who signed with the Federal Street Theatre in Boston in June 1796, all except the prompter were recently from Europe.[25] Eighteen were "late of the theaters of" Covent Garden, Drury Lane, Exeter, or Bath; the two principal dancers and essentially all the musicians were immigrants from Paris and London, and its chief scenery painter and mechanic was a portraitist from Denmark. To bring home the point, the manager concluded his list of cast members by noting that "a confidential messenger is dispatched to Europe to complete the other engagements." That same year, their rival, the Haymarket Theatre, hired virtually all its employees from Europe including its manager, bandleader, scenery painter, and stage designer. Manager James A. Dickinson (whose English name was Dixon or Dickson) reportedly crossed the Atlantic forty times in search of talent.[26] This reputation of theatrical productions was so prevalent that theater opponents and polemicists gained considerable strength from prevailing anti-foreign and anti-British sentiment. As one New York commentator advised in 1785, if the theater was to open, "let it not be . . . by a set who, one or two excepted, are *British strangers.*"[27]

But even as they generated opportunities, theater managers were frequently abandoned by their new recruits once they had fulfilled their contractual obligations. Many if not most actors, actresses, and musicians continued their careers independently once they left the theater. Beginning with violinist William C. Hulett, who established a dancing academy after leaving Lewis Hallam's American Company in New York City in the 1760s, an entire generation of performers, band members, and scenery painters left the stage to work as concert musicians, music teachers, dance instructors, teachers of elocution, fencing-masters, fireworks artists, puppeteers, needlework preceptresses, and house decorators.[28] In Boston nearly the entire Federal Street cast and musicians abandoned the theater: vocalist Mrs. Solomon resumed her solo singing engagements, vocalist Mr. Legé organized a dancing school, bandleaders Mr. and Mrs. Gottlieb Graupner opened a music store, actress and author Susanna Rowson founded a finishing school, band member John H. Ives taught a circuit of music schools, actor William Bates launched a career as a showman, composer Trille Labarre started a music academy in Newburyport, and pianist R. Leaumont put together a series of French language and dancing schools.[29]

ONCE LOCATED in a community, itinerants had to come up with strategies to make their offerings appealing. The most effective and immediate means to dispel a negative image was to provide free services to the poor or donate financial resources to local charitable causes such as prison inmates or orphanages. These gestures helped allay the public perception that all transients engaged in quackery and posturing while also placing an apparent value on an entrepreneur's services, regardless of their actual worth. When performing in New York in 1767, showmen Mr. Bayly and Henry Hymes gave the proceeds of their first Punch comedy "for the Benefit of the Prisoners."[30] Itinerant physicians usually gave advice "to the poor gratis," and some, like Dr. Anthony Yeldall, made the gesture so frequently it is unclear how they had the time for their paying patients. Dr. James Graham, "Oculist and Aurist," limited his generosity to the poor "who apply, properly recommended." Presumably, indigent patients without documentation were turned away.[31] John Griffiths began his long and lucrative career as a dancing-master by making "One Hundred and Fifty Cords of Wood" available to New York's poor, requesting that the aldermen recommend such persons as "they may think proper objects."[32]

Although improving public perception was the primary motive, the aid proffered to charities and victims of catastrophes was real and sometimes substantial. According to Boston records, actors Joseph Harper and Alexandre Placide turned over fifty-three pounds seven shillings to the selectmen in September 1792 following a theater benefit at the New Exhibition Room—a gift that no doubt worked in their favor less than four months later when Harper was arrested for violating the state's anti-theater laws. But it also assisted the poor in seven wards of the town, each receiving between six and seven pounds. And the truth was that those who gave a benefit one evening might themselves need similar help the next. A week after Daniel Bowen set aside a day's receipts for the victims of the 1803 conflagration in Portsmouth, his own Columbian Museum in Boston was itself gutted by fire. During the following year, fundraisers held by Bowen's friends and colleagues were an important means by which he reclaimed his losses and rebuilt his museum.[33]

The promise of a short stay was another means of ensuring success—a strategy that instantaneously turned itinerants' disadvantage as outsiders into an effective marketing incentive. Few things triggered the impulse to patronize an unknown stroller as surely as the prospect of forever missing the opportunity to do so. We see this tactic early in the eighteenth century when the unidentified female acrobat who rope-danced at Philadelphia's Society Hill in 1724 was "to begin on *Thursday* next, being the last day of *April* and to continue Acting, the Term of *Twenty Days* and no longer."[34] Showman and musician Richard Brickell—believed to be from England—who brought puppets, waxworks, electrical machines, and posture-masters to New York, Philadelphia, and Charleston audiences between 1742 and 1756 had five different ways of telling readers that his time in each city "will be but very short," each designed to urge "speedy Attendance" to his spectacles.[35] The son of English mechanic Henry Bridges cautioned in 1755 that his father's musical clock would remain in Philadelphia only until "the 8th of March, being obliged to be in New-York." In fact none of these show people and demonstrators may have followed through with their promises. The 1724 acrobats apparently lingered in Philadelphia only briefly; Brickell usually ran his advertisements about two weeks and then left, and Bridges departed for New York in early February.[36]

Over time itinerants developed a simple rule of thumb: the greater the anticipated difficulty of attracting clients, the more emphasis was put on an early departure. Portrait painters, limners, and miniature painters, who always found it hard to win commissions, led all entrepreneurs in announcing short stopovers, sometimes specifying the exact number of days. J. A. De Florat, who advertised miniatures painting on 5 January 1784 in Burlington, New Jersey, told readers he "does not expect to continue in this place longer than till the first of April next." Ralph Letton, the profile taker, advertised in Keene, New Hampshire, on 15 March 1806 that he "will stay in town [until] Friday the 21st and no longer." Portraitist Frederick Mayhew publicized in New Bedford, Massachusetts, in 1815 that he would stop at Barney Cory's coffeehouse "for [only] a few days."[37] But dancing-masters, psalmody teachers, and penmanship instructors, who had a greater expectation of finding pupils, were less time conscious. And waxwork showmen, ventriloquists, and animal handlers, who commonly attracted large crowds, hardly mentioned time at all. Many notices left blanks that could be filled out. When Letton added some of what may have been Daniel Bowen's waxworks to his tour, he made up a new handbill that left two spaces on the printed sheet. Each time he started a new venue, he filled one out with the date and place of the exhibition, and the second with the number of days it would remain (fig. 4.1).[38]

When it seemed advantageous to prolong a stay, convenient formulas enabled graceful extensions of time: to assist victims of recent fires, to help the family of an indigent performer, and (most commonly) to remain in response to the repeated entreaties of unidentified "gentlemen of the town." What really mattered of course was that their announcements made itinerants seem as if they were *about* to leave.[39] The African acrobat Donegani worked this approach with considerable skill. During his initial engagement in Boston, he held the region in thrall with his promises to leave. He began in Boston's Concert-Hall with an evening exhibition on 30 May 1789. On 20 June—three weeks after his opening—he regretfully advised audiences it was the "Last week!" of his act. On 27 June he again proclaimed his "Last night!" But on 4 July he was still there, stating this time that 11 July was "positively" the end. Four days later, in response to what he described as the entreaties of a "considerable number of strangers whom the commencement [at Harvard] has brought to town," he once more extended his engagement. At this point by any calculation Donegani had spent twice the time leaving Concert-Hall as first performing there, the benchmark of spectacular success. It comes as no surprise that when he actually did leave on 16 September, he made no mention of it. Boston audiences were so enchanted by him, it is entirely possible Donegani would have remained through the fall and winter seasons had not the impending October visit of George Washington and his entourage presented a more compelling diversion.[40]

Strollers who offered healing services counted on personal references to convince prospective patients of their professional qualifications—especially if they were controversial. To show her good intentions, an unidentified female Indian healer who extracted cancers in Brunswick, Maine, in 1769 consumed a portion of the medicines she prescribed.[41] Other providers made use of more formal testimonials that read like legal documents—no doubt a carryover from much earlier English and continental European practices. In a printed broadside issued in 1793, alternative cancer-healer John Pope of Boston published three letters praising his treatments. Two letters were witnessed by local justices of the peace and attested to their public "duty" to challenge "prevailing opinion." One, by a witness who lived in Bristol, Rhode Island, named the physicians and surgeons whose efforts had been ineffective—singling out Dr. John Warren (1753–1815) of Boston, brother of the revolutionary hero Joseph Warren, as having told him he

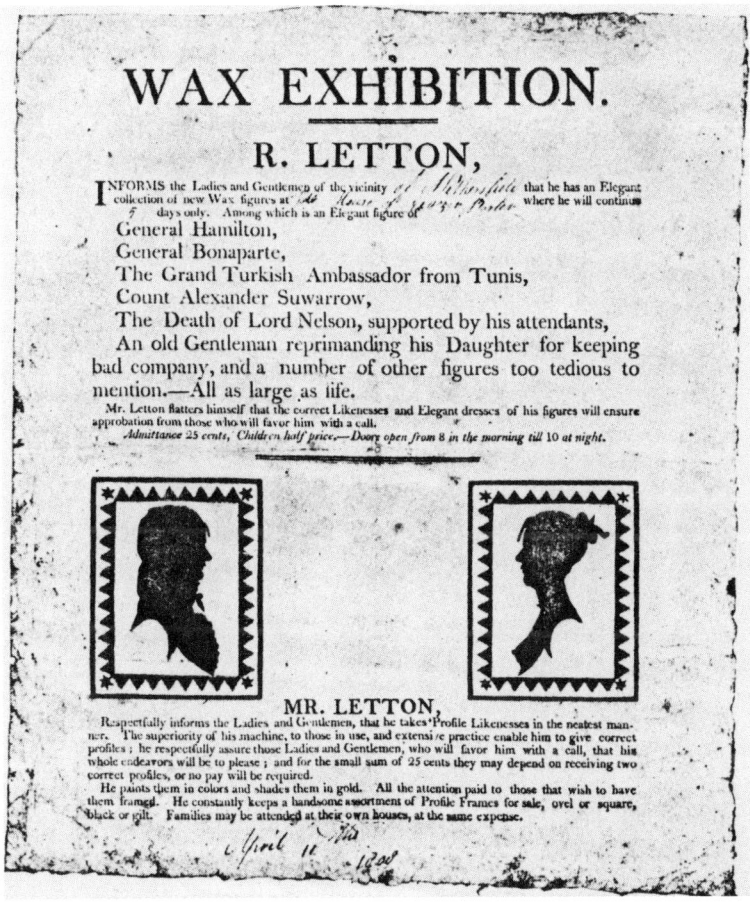

Figure 4.1. "WAX EXHIBITION. R. LETTON." Announcement for an exhibition of wax figures at Eleazer Porter's house, Wethersfield, Connecticut, 11 April 1808. Not known as a waxwork artist, Ralph Letton may have borrowed or purchased the figures of "Alexander Suwarrow," Lord Nelson, and the "old Gentleman reprimanding his Daughter" from Daniel Bowen, who had exhibited these at the Columbian Museum in Boston. Printer unknown. From Carrick, *Shades of Our Ancestors,* opp. 118, photographed from an original formerly owned by George D. Seymour, Letton's grandson. Courtesy, Widener Library, Harvard University, US 42505.475.

was past all remedy. Other affidavit authors simply noted that "Doctors, gentlemen of the Faculty" had tried and given up on them.[42]

Penmanship teachers, dancing-masters, and theatrical troupes were also dependent on references. Penmanship teachers published long lists of people who sanctioned their methods; dancing-masters traveled with letters from prominent families in the towns where they had just taught. Theater professionals commonly sought out testimonials and letters of reference and presented them as circumstances dictated. When David Douglass's company of comedians entreated the civil authorities in Newport for permission to exhibit a play in 1761, their petition was endorsed by the governor of Virginia and one hundred principal gentlemen of the colony who had seen and approved of their performances. The signatories may be the longest list of "references" ever compiled by aspiring actors in North America.[43]

The strategy that most challenged both itinerants and the public was the warranty. Despite the miasma of exaggeration and seeming charlatanry that surrounded them, most strollers ostensibly provided safety nets for those willing to take risks with them. The simplest was a vow to decline remuneration unless a client was indeed satisfied. Artists and miniature painters used this tactic so much they concluded their advertisements with phrases that became mantras: "No likeness no pay," "Warranted likenesses," or "Warranted to be striking." Some showmen even promised to refund or postpone the price of admission. William Pinchbeck notified newspaper readers that "any person doubting the merit of this [Learned Pig] Exhibition may be at liberty to pay after they have seen [it]."[44]

Teachers were often adept with guarantees. Mr. J. and Mrs. D. White, who taught flower-making in New England, developed a felicitous fee schedule during their brief stay in Newport in 1809, where they outfitted their rented Thames Street apartment as a gallery, teaching studio, painting and japanning room, and residence. Their main source of income was the sale of "Artificial Flowers set in Pots" designed for use as ornaments in drawing rooms and bedchambers. To this purpose they put their collection on public display and offered to make flowers for any customer "to pattern or order" at an agreed upon price. For their school, however, they charged seventy-five cents for "each different Flower when Perfect," or a total of seven dollars for twelve different flowers, with the pupils having the privilege of "keeping the last Flower of each sort they might have made, so as to form a handsome cabinet." In short, they only charged for those flowers the pupil had mastered—a warranty that was essentially foolproof.[45] A more straightforward assurance was the one extended by Pietro Ancora, a recently arrived Italian drawing-master who opened a school in Philadelphia in 1808 to teach figures, landscapes, and flowers "after the same method by which he was taught in Rome." Keeping separate hours for girls and boys, Ancora promised that "after using his best exertions, in case he discovers in any of his pupils no inclination for the task, [he will] send them back to their respective parents, without requiring any compensation for his trouble."[46]

The entrepreneurs who needed to give the most advantageous guarantees were usually in the worst position to do so. Popular healers had to be highly inventive because they advertised warranties while also telling potential patients to act quickly because they were about to leave town. Few mountebanks or alternative healers could produce instantaneous cures, and even if they were successful, specialized treatments generally required weeks and months stretching long past the times that most healers remained in a community. This did not deter them, however. Correctly judging that the mere phrasing of not accepting "pay" helped build the image of a dedicated professional, healers frequently made this claim. One surgeon in 1772 worded his guarantee in a succinct manner virtually identical to those of artists: "No Cure No Pay"—a pledge used by scores of itinerant surgeons, physicians, and pharmacists practicing in America between 1768 and 1825.[47] A variant plan was to divide payment into installments. Dr. Ibrahim Adam Ben Ali, for example, proposed in 1799 an agreement with each patient by which half his fee was to be paid at the time of treatment and half when the cure was effected.[48]

Some strollers endeavored to protect their interests as well as those of their clients. So-called books or subscription papers—by which clients collectively promised their support for an itinerant school or event—stipulated that if the proposed activity were to take place at all, the number of subscribers had to meet a specified minimum. This method put the burden on those who wanted the event most to persuade others to patronize it. Some subscriptions required a deposit of money against expenses or as advances on tuitions; these were sometimes held by third parties. But the advantages actually worked both ways. Entrepreneurs knew beforehand whether it was financially worth their while to remain in town; prospective clients could tell at a glance who else in the community had signed up.

Instructors of dancing, penmanship, and foreign languages frequently used subscription papers to promote their businesses. One sign of the surfeit of teachers in a given field was their willingness to fix low subscription rates before beginning a school. One Mr. Kimberly, for example, who advertised a dancing school in Pittsfield and adjacent Massachusetts towns in 1798, indicated he would "open his school as soon as there are ten subscribers." In addition he said he would "provide a Musician" and offer a "Scholars Ball" every three weeks. His terms, one dollar at entrance and three at the expiration of the quarter, may hardly have covered his expenses.[49] Of the many hundreds of short-term schools profitably run by penmanship teachers in the period from 1800 to 1830, at least half and perhaps as many as three-quarters were undertaken through subscriptions.

A typical sign-up sheet was the one prepared by writing master Daniel H. Leonard (1783–1837) for a course of lessons to be held in the morning from 5:00 a.m. to 7:00 a.m. It reads in part: "We [the undersigned] severally promise to furnish the number of scholars affixed to our names."[50] Teachers usually distributed these sheets at taverns, boarding houses, or coffeehouses—often in two or more of these locations simultaneously—any one of which might serve as the site of the proposed school. They also left them with printers or at bookstores that sold their imprints. When two dancing-masters publicized a school to teach country dances and cotillions in Portsmouth in 1797, they asked readers of the *New-Hampshire Gazette* to apply to the *Gazette*'s printer, "who has lodged with him a subscription paper." When E. Harrington advertised a dancing school in rural Brattleboro, Vermont, in 1816, he requested "those that wish to attend will please to leave their names at Mr. Dickinson's tavern." Dickinson's long room was probably the only one in the village, and no doubt Harrington planned to rent it if he reached his subscription count. Similar arrangements were made by Massachusetts singing teacher Samuel Adams Holyoke (1762–1820), who left his subscription papers at the principal bookstores in Newburyport and Haverhill that regularly stocked his musical publications. Both bookstores stood to gain if Holyoke organized a school.[51] Later, when he submitted a bill to the parishes that hired him, Holyoke listed the names of all "Schollars" who attended (see fig. 10.1).

Subscription papers also benefited balloon makers. Joseph Deeker enticed a substantial number of New York City's male residents to underwrite the launching of a hundred-foot balloon designed to fly him over upper Manhattan in 1789. Four years later Jean-Pierre Blanchard employed this method to fund his first U.S. ascension in Philadelphia on 9 January 1793. Again, there was no certainty. Having succeeded in Philadelphia, Blanchard spent the next four years in New York, Boston, Salem, Providence, Baltimore, and Charleston trying to find backing for a second manned ascension. He was unable to raise a similar sum.[52]

When other expedients failed, itinerants sought clients during those rare occasions when potential buyers and audiences gathered in one location. Agricultural events sometimes afforded this opportunity, and strollers took maximum advantage of them. In 1816, Philip Woods brought his museum of waxworks and an old panorama to Nantucket during the second week in June when the island's sheep were rounded up for marketing and fleece clipping. He told islanders that the exhibition would "remain till after shearing."[53] But the occasions that attracted the greatest variety of transient entrepreneurs—and the only events that in any way matched the cultural ambiance of traditional European fairs and calendar festivals—were the annual commencements at local colleges. These generally took place in the late summer or early fall and drew scores of graduates, parents, and guests for a week or more of ceremonies and festivities.[54] Exhibitions, balls, and entertainments accompanied them. Among the first entrepreneurs to recognize their potential was Daniel Bowen. In late August 1788, just after he acquired Patience Wright's collection, Bowen carried an exhibition of wax figures from its usual location at 100 Water Street, New York, to the house of Thomas Sabin in Providence with the caveat it would "be removed from hence immediately after commencement" at nearby College of Rhode Island (now Brown University). Reuben Moulthrop (1763–1814) similarly timed the 1793 opening of his first waxwork exhibition in New Haven to coincide with Yale's commencement exercises, usually held the second Wednesday in September. Moulthrop featured a replica of Louis XVI under the guillotine and expressed hope it would "prove a valuable Addition to the Entertainments" of that week.[55]

Commencements at Harvard College, whose officers encouraged or at least countenanced these practices for years, tended to attract curiosities not normally seen in nearby Boston. Captain Crowninshield's elephant—the first one in the country—came up from Providence to attend the school's exercises in July 1797, as did Calvin Phillips, the twenty-six-inch "living dwarf child" from Bridgewater, Massachusetts, who was being toured in New England by his relatives.[56] A devotee of college commencements, Reverend William Bentley took the time at the July 1800 Harvard exercises to walk "over to the Common to see the several amusements & to observe the Merry Andrews, federal wheel [Ferris wheel], &c." The next day he visited a cassowary on display at a Mrs. Hilliard's tavern. On tour in New England, the same cassowary appeared in Salem in August (see fig. 6.26) and just missed commencement at New Haven. In 1804, Bentley arrived late to Harvard's commencement but found to his delight that "many sights" still remained. Among these were Charles Packard's version of the "Invisible Lady" acoustical exhibition, Daniel Bowen's two ostriches (fig. 4.2) lately imported from Africa, an ichneumon (mongoose), and a "Genet" (civet cat).[57]

The amusements Bentley witnessed on Cambridge Common testify to the growing popularity of itinerant-carried culture, especially those aspects that lifted the veil of provincial life and put people in touch with far-off places and distant marvels. To compete in a society where they were viewed as strangers, most itinerants immersed themselves in a mountebank's aura of charisma and success. Relying on the traditional language of promises and beguilements, itinerants aspired to satisfy the public's most cherished desires at a cheap price. This was a language guaranteeing clients "no likeness no pay" and promising their patients "no cure no pay." It assured good penmanship, good grammar, and a "French Ear" after twenty lessons. It was a language short on time ("twenty days and no longer") but long on social benefits ("for the poor gratis"). It boasted magical arts: John Maison's installing artificial beings with the "gift of speech"; acrobat John Childs's "flying" from the highest steeple in Boston; William Pinchbeck's training animals to master difficult multiplication tables. It heralded exalted audiences: Jacob Bates's performing on horseback "before the Emperor of Germany" and engineer Felix Fissour's illuminating his fireworks before the Royal Family of Spain.[58]

Was this simply a web of make-believe fabricated by an early American advertising language long in place before the dawn of industrialization? It certainly encompassed as much deceit as honesty, as much subterfuge as openness—designed (as critics pointed out) "to draw from children and other weak minds, the product of their labor [and] giving them in return no intrinsic value."[59] This duplicity may help explain the unarticulated collaboration between the "Albiness" and an itinerant profilist named Mr. Hervé during their three-year visit to North America between 1817 and 1820. Hailed in the American news-

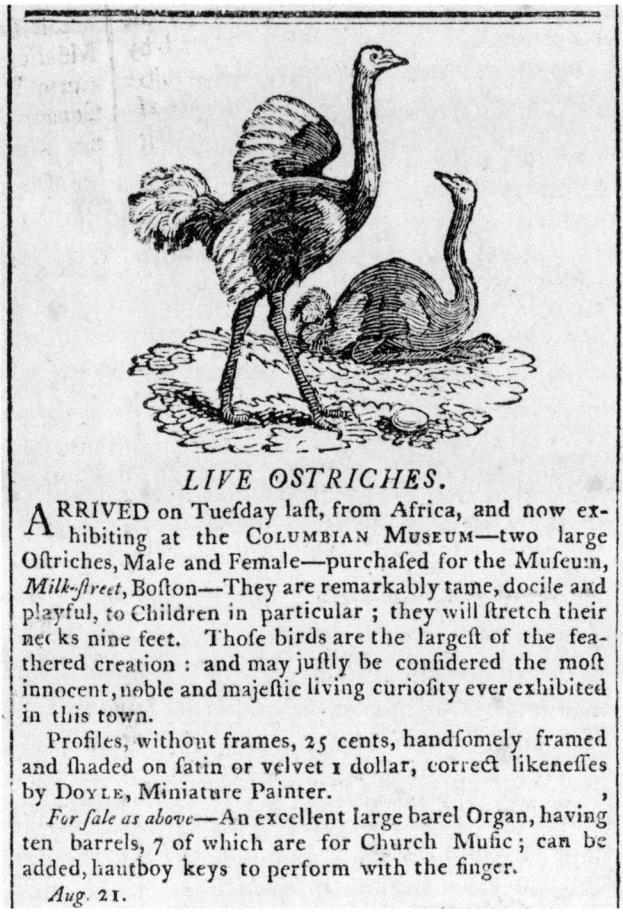

Figure 4.2. *"LIVE OSTRICHES."* Purchased in New York by Daniel Bowen, these birds were seen by Reverend William Bentley at Harvard College's commencement on 24 August 1804 along with a "Genet, Ichneumon, [and] stuffed Lyon." The next day Bowen advertised that he had put the ostriches on exhibition at Boston's Columbian Museum. *Boston Democrat,* 25 August 1804. Courtesy, American Antiquarian Society.

papers as the most astonishing phenomenon ever known, the Albiness, who was also called Miss Elizabeth Hervey (fl. 1813–20) arrived in Boston in August 1818 after brief visits to Quebec, Albany, and New York City. Born in Essex, England, this "Celebrated Female" captivated her audiences with her pure white complexion, long white hair, and pink-colored eyes. She may have come with a reputation that any pregnant woman who saw her would bear a child with similar features. Within three weeks proprietor William M. S. Doyle (1769–1828) of the Columbian Museum had created a waxwork of her "from life" and placed it next to "the beautiful Mrs. O'Neal of the London Theater." August turned into September and still the Albiness remained. Finally, in October 1818, Hervey resumed her New England tour, making her way east to Salem and Portland, Maine, whose newspapers promoted her arrival with similar hyperbole. From there she turned toward the middle and southern states where the climate was warmer.[60]

Although few newspaper readers may have noticed it at the time, Elizabeth Hervey's advertisements were often accompanied by a second notice, sometimes discreetly separated from hers, detailing the services of Henry Hervé, an English miniature and profile painter who came to America in 1817.[61] The paired notifications first surfaced in Quebec City newspapers in the summer of 1817; they next appeared in Albany in December 1817, where Hervé was described as an artist "from Cheapside, London." The promotions were published in Norfolk, Baltimore, Salem, and Portland. Both always gave identical addresses: in Quebec City the pair was at Malhiot's Hotel, St. John's Street; in Albany, at Hazard's Hotel, 199 North Market Street. She hired rooms to receive visitors, and he rented a room to paint miniatures and take profiles.[62]

Their juxtaposition was, of course, no coincidence. Henry Hervé, a virtual unknown in the United States, faced overwhelming competition from established miniature painters and profile takers who produced likenesses within a matter of minutes. He traveled with the Albiness at least partly because she generated business. While Hervey attracted throngs to her popular parlor exhibitions, Hervé sold a range of miniatures, small-scale likenesses, and reverse-glass and cut profiles to those who waited for her audience. It was the best approximation he could find in America to the multitudes normally passing his Cheapside studio in London. More important, the Albiness was likely to fascinate persons who could afford Hervé's prices for miniature paintings executed on ivory, which ranged from "$30 on upwards."[63] No examples of Hervé's American portraits have been discovered, nor has any substantial information emerged to offer a clear explanation of their relationship or the meaning of the similar surnames. But the journey taken by the pair in North America eventually had two positive outcomes. The first was that miniaturist Margaret G. Doyle (fl. 1820–1830), daughter of museum proprietor William Doyle, painted "The Albiness" for an exhibition at the Boston Athenaeum Gallery.⁶⁴ The second was personal. On 13 January 1820—the last time that either Hervé or Hervey was heard from within the United States—a paper in Savannah, Georgia, announced, "Married . . . Mr. H. Herve, to Miss Elizabeth Hervey."⁶⁵

Chapter 5

Acquiring Skills

IF CARRIERS of European popular culture like William Pinchbeck and Henry Hervé found themselves outside the ordered mercantile, agrarian, and maritime society of eighteenth- and early nineteenth-century America, the reverse was equally true. Few things characterized itinerants' subculture as much as the difficulty of outsiders' becoming part of it. This was true despite the fact that the very purpose of itinerants' marketing strategy was to spread their appeal rapidly from individual to individual and place to place. Even as strollers attracted enthusiastic street crowds and packed tavern halls, statehouses, and theaters, they continually sought additional audiences to pay the bills. They did not want imitators or competitors, however, who inevitably cut down on their share of paying clients. This standoff between performers and inquisitive audience members was inevitable.

How, then, did early Americans gain enough knowledge and experience to become "carriers of culture" themselves? When John Schaffer, for example, deserted from the military garrison at Norfolk, Virginia, in 1801, he was identified in a Charleston paper as of "Dutch descent, born at Reading in the state of Pennsylvania, [and] has some knowledge of drawing and portrait painting."[1] But how did someone like this twenty-six-year-old man obtain these skills? We seldom have a good answer. Regrettably the written agreements for most agricultural, mercantile, and craft occupations normally kept on file by county and town officials rarely exist for itinerants' trades.[2] Virtually no schools or internships were available for musicians, actors, artists, or conjurers during this period. Cunning people, fortune-tellers, and most alternative healers worked on the periphery of the law and avoided leaving records or attracting public scrutiny altogether. In the absence of guilds and art academies—or any system of regulated apprenticeships and indenturing arrangements—the knowledge and skills necessary to pursue many of these trades were publicly unobtainable.

Nevertheless, some apprenticeships or schools—or informal versions of them—did occur. In the 1790s, Italian showman Joseph Falconi twice advertised in the newspapers for a boy to be indentured and travel with him. In the Charleston *City Gazette* for 20 July 1793, he posted, "Signor Falconi intending shortly for Europe, he would wish to have a boy, either white or colored, who could be well recommended, to be indented." Two years later, in the *New York Daily Advertiser* for 15 July 1795, he sought "a boy, between twelve and thirteen, to be indentured for the above business." Falconi's openly citing his "business" was a major admission by the leader of one of the most demanding trades in the litany of itinerant employments. He was also looking for a boy who was either "white or colored"—a tacit admission that ability and talent rather than race or ethnic background were the principal criteria he was seeking.

At least three itinerant portrait and landscape painters placed notices for apprentices in the newspapers. An unidentified artist inserted such a request in 1772 in the *New-York Gazette* for a boy "of a promising Genius" aged between ten and thirteen. He expected the child would accompany his trips to neighboring colonies but said that "Nothing but the Youth is required"—meaning no apprenticeship fee was necessary.[3] Jacob Wicker, a landscape painter in Northampton, Massachusetts, who previously had teamed with Ralph Earl in painting Niagara Falls, took out an advertisement in 1806 looking for "two boys of 14 and 15 years of age" to serve as apprentices.[4] One year later in 1807, Moses Dupre Cole, a French-born painter in Newburyport, Massachusetts, recently arrived from Martinique, posted between 26 May and 23 June 1807 for "an apprentice to the Painting, Glazing, and Gilding business." His notice sought "A Lad 14 or 15 years old [who] will meet with good encouragement."[5]

A few stage showmen acknowledged a system of masters and pupils. Three informants (correspondents for the *New-York Journal* in 1771 and the *Pennsylvania Chronicle* in 1773, and William Dunlap in 1837) identify Michael Handley, the younger of Yeldall's acrobats, as an "auxiliary" or "apprentice" to John McDonald, who was a journeyman. At least one semiprofessional conjurer in New York City attempted to initiate a school: Camou Meyere, known as the proprietor of the "Invisible Woman," issued a call to teach juggling, card tricks, and the "magic inkhorn," proposing in 1801 to initiate a class of "25 subscribers at 20 dollars each." He added, "50 dollars for single one."[6]

These notices are unusual because they seek an assistant whose indenture had a future, with several promising the applicant would be "initiated" or receive "good encouragement." But as we examine itinerants' lives more closely, we find that like so much else in the preindustrial economies of Europe and North America, skills were often acquired through relatives—husbands, wives, sons, daughters, uncles, nephews, stepparents—as well as from immediate neighbors. William F. Pinchbeck learned to build and repair automatons from two earlier generations of English clockmakers and metalworkers. His grandfather, Christopher Pinchbeck, Sr. (1669–1732), had given his name to a gold-like alloy commonly used for watchcases and jewelry. Christopher's sons Christopher Pinchbeck, Jr. (1709–1783), and Edward Pinchbeck (1713?–1766) made astronomical and musical clocks, and musical automatons, some of them fabricating the voices of birds or playing tunes for country dances and the singing of psalms—activities favored by royal patronage. Edward Pinchbeck also kept a conjuring, waxwork, and puppet booth at Southwark's and Bartholomew's Fairs in the 1730s.[7] And William grew up just three doors down from Philip Breslaw's home on Cockspur Street in London.[8] Breslaw, a conjurer who kept a playhouse of his exhibitions and "Deceptions," sold tickets at the Pinchbeck household. (That not all may have been smooth among Pinchbeck family members is implied by a story that William F. Pinchbeck's father, Christopher, left a will instructing that "one guinea per week to be paid to my undutiful and afflicting son Will Pinchbeck whom I am unhappy to say has never done a single thing to oblige me since his infancy.") William Pinchbeck had also learned to train horses and other animals, such as dogs, cats, and pigs, from professional animal handlers who were colleagues of his relatives. Samuel Bisset (1721–1783), who worked with Pinchbeck's father, taught young William an act during his stay in London in the 1770s in which three cats played a dulcimer. Bisset later turned to other animals, teaching a hare to stand on its hind legs, twelve turkeys to demonstrate a country dance, and a tortoise to spell its name on the floor.[9]

By the same token, to be a circus acrobat usually meant being part of a family of performers. As early as 1753, John McDonald, who ran away from his shoemaking employer in Charlestown, Maryland, was described as "an Irish boy, an apprentice of Thomas Pryer's. He was bred to tumbling, slight of hand, &c. and acquainted in Philadelphia."[10] The "famous Saxon" who rope-danced in Savannah in 1790 introduced his seven-year-old son, "the young Saxon," to his audiences.[11] Elsewhere, Master Jones, son of acrobat and singer J. Jones, "being but three years and a half old," sang "A Little Merry He" at a benefit held for his family at the Charleston Theater in 1796.[12] At Lailson's Circus in Philadelphia acrobat Matthew Sully presented his three children, calling them "Natives of Philadelphia—the youngest but 4 years old," performing some "astonishing" equilibriums.[13] And Don José Vilallave's company of acrobats employed as many members of his family as were available—some of them apparently adopted. In their early routines in 1814, the cast consisted of Vilallave, his wife, and a supporting staff of three youths—a young Roman, a young "Spaniolet," and "the Little Chinese." Also assisting were three of his children: a son of twelve, a daughter of five, and a boy of six, "who will execute some of the most difficult feats every night of the performance."[14] By 1828 the Vilallaves had increased their family by two more children and promptly incorporated them into their

Figure 5.1. "JEFFERSON-HALL. For a Few Nights. . . . Mr. VILLALAVE . . . has just arrived from Boston, Salem and Newburyport." Two details showing a barrel-related springboard act and young children performing on an elevated table for Don José Vilallave's circus in New England. Portsmouth, New Hampshire, 11 July 1827. Paper, 28 by 21 inches. Courtesy, New Hampshire Historical Society, S 1997.533.25.

acts. "Miss Vilallave, only 7 years of age," and Master Vilallave accomplished feats that were "wonderful" for children of their age (fig. 5.1).[15] The next year the troupe played in Augusta, Georgia, and Saratoga, New York, and then headed for New Orleans.[16] Similarly young children were prominent in Godeau and Blanchard's Circus, which featured Elizabeth Blanchard (aged six) as a singer and slack-wire dancer and Master George Blanchard (aged about eight) as a balancer. The circus manager, Mr. W. Blanchard, included "one of his *infant daughters*" in the same exhibition.[17]

Alternative healers also acquired skills from family members. Besides training his wife, Hannah, self-taught cancer-curer John Pope passed along the details of his healing methods to three of his sons, who continued his work as itinerant physicians in Massachusetts, Rhode Island, and Connecticut well into the nineteenth century. One son, John Pope, Jr. (1769–1806), described himself as "fully acquainted with the Practice of his Father, the noted John Pope of . . . Boston," and practiced in Providence, living at the homes of local schoolmasters. Samuel Pope (1781–after 1831) practiced in Hartford, Boston, and Providence, calling himself "the Brother and formerly the Partner of the late Dr. John Pope [Jr]." Benjamin Pope (1783–1811), who also said he learned cures "from his father, and his brother," taught in Providence; he died at the age of twenty-nine, leaving a wife and two children.[18] Nevertheless, while the elder Pope was willing to discuss his techniques with regularly trained physicians, he stopped short of passing his formulas to them. The diary of Reverend Ezra Stiles (1727–1795) provides a brief, if secondhand, history of one of John Pope, Sr.'s cures administered when Pope was still in his thirties:

> This Afternoon [11 January 1773] the hon. Judge Oliver came to drink Tea with me and spent the Evening at my house. . . . The Judge told us that his Wife had been last year cured of a Cancer in her Neck of 30 years stand[in]g by a young man Mr. Pope of Boston. . . . His remedy is a secret, but he explained the operation of it to Mr. Oliver in a Philosophical Manner, though Mr. Pope is not a man of Letters nor does he make pretension to any other part of Medicine or Surgery.[19]

After his death, Pope was termed a "Physician" in a 1796 probate document.[20]

For those who did not have a family network to learn from, aspiring healers were obliged to go elsewhere. Henry Tufts (1748–1831), a New Hampshire–born army deserter, horse thief, preacher, and bigamist, learned many of his skills by accident. Tufts's *Narrative of the Life, Adventures, Travels and Sufferings of Henry Tufts* (1807)—a wordy and boastful document filling more than three hundred pages—may have been written by an enterprising lawyer when Tufts was under a death sentence, but it does shed light on the transient underworld of which he was a part, as well as on the several legitimate street occupations by which he supported himself and (sometimes) his family during his long periods of absence from his farm in Lee, New Hampshire. He was in his early twenties, in about 1771, when he "came across a man, who was in possession of a set of pictures, called shows, which were viewed by looking through magnifying glasses, artificially disposed for that purpose. I was so much enamoured with the sight of these rarities, that I purchased them of the showman . . . and the principal business I followed for one winter, was carrying about those insignificant trifles, which I exhibited with great ostentation, at about a groat [four pence] a sight."[21]

Tufts became interested in herbal and Native American healing techniques in the years 1772 to 1775 in an attempt to overcome a physically debilitating knife wound. Finding a closely knit group of Abenaki Indians living in the borderland between Canada and America, he joined a village of about three hundred residents near Lake Memphremagog, in an area called "Sudbury Canada," learning the language and living with them for three years. To gain knowledge about eighteenth-century Abenaki practices in botany and physic, he observed the tribe's chief herbal practitioner, Molly Occut, or Ockett, and others when they collected plant material: "Frequently was I inquisitive with Molly Occut, old Philips, Sabattus and other professed doctors to learn the names and virtues of their medicines. In general they were explicit in communication, still I thought them in possession of secrets they cared not to reveal."[22]

To secure their cooperation Tufts procured shipments of rum sent in from English settlements, and to further dispel suspicion as to his real purpose, he courted Polly Susap, a niece of a leading Abenaki elder.[23] As soon as he had obtained all the medical knowledge he needed, however, Tufts abandoned both her and the village and returned to a life of vagrancy. Years later, while traveling through Vermont in company with his companion, a "mistress Nabby," he put his experience to use. In the words of his *Autobiography,* "This place [Pownal], I made my home, for a number of months, and or the support of myself and family, practiced Physic the whole time, gadding about quack like, far and near, in the character of a Indian doctor."[24] Indian healing may have been one of the few professions he practiced with some integrity.[25]

Short of being born or marrying into a profession, an aspiring stroller might try to become a "follower" with no guarantee of learning the essentials of the trade he or she sought. As a teenager in the 1780s, dancer and trick rider John Durang was fascinated with all aspects of the stage, circus, and amphitheater and spent much of his time at the theater on Philadelphia's South Street. At one point he came across a dancing-master named Louis Roussell, a Frenchman, who could perform the "pigeon wing," a step in which a dancer jumped up and struck his legs together. "I contrived to get Mr. Rusell to board at my father's house that I might have the opportunity to dance more correct then I had been used to. I learned the correct stile of dancing a hornpipe in the French stile, an allemande, and steps for a country dance. Except the pigeon [wing] was the only difficulty I had to encounter."[26]

Receiving little encouragement from his family, Durang ran away from home at the age of fifteen in company with a magic-lantern showman who was on his way to Boston. There he befriended a student of dancing instructor William Turner and mastered his earliest professional dance steps. Durang had his first stage experience with Lewis Hallam, then manager of the Old American Company of Philadelphia, where he picked up pantomime roles; shortly thereafter he began dancing harlequinades with Hallam's company. Durang subsequently learned horsemanship from Matthew Sully, Jr., son of Matthew Sully, Sr., and joined John Ricketts's circus troupe.

Over time, Durang developed the stage routines by which he became widely known. One of them was a solo dance, now called "Durang's Hornpipe," for which a Mr. Hoffmaster composed music. Others are illustrated in Durang's watercolor self-portraits that embellish his manuscripts. In one he wears a sailor's costume and dances a hornpipe with a cane (fig. 5.2). In another, called "Dwarf Metamorphosed" (fig. 5.3), he plays two simultaneous roles without changing clothes. He first dances as a woman wearing a full skirt and a heavy apron. By raising and joining his arms over his head, he reveals a larger painted head and a pair of dangling arms (almost reaching the floor), which make him appear dwarflike—an act he performed at the Federal Street Theatre in Boston in 1795 and later in Charleston in 1816 and Alexandria in 1818.[27] Durang often took

Figures 5.2 and 5.3. *John Durang in Character of a Hornpipe* and *Mr. Jno Durang in character of The Dwarf Metamorphosed.* Self-portraits by John Durang (1768–1822), illustrating two of the stage routines by which he became widely known. Watercolors bound in a manuscript diary and reminiscence. Philadelphia, 1800–1822. Courtesy, York County Heritage Trust, York, Pennsylvania.

his family with him on longer acting tours, including a visit to Newport with a sister and his wife, Mary McEwen Durang, who also played in Harlequin pantomimes. John Durang was so successful in his diverse employments that he purchased a lot in Philadelphia and built a substantial house. His three sons and two daughters all became actors and dancers. His eldest son, Charles Durang (1796–1870), was a nationally known actor and dance instructor and the first historian of the early Philadelphia stage; his second son, Ferdinand (c. 1785–1831), is said to have helped Francis Scott Key select music for the poem that became America's national anthem.[28]

Durang was fortunate because he found teachers and employers who profited from his talent and encouraged him. But most established strollers held tightly to their crafts, a position that annoyed aspiring portrait painter Chester Harding (1792–1866), who found it hard to cross the threshold into the art world as he traveled in the newly opened states and territories of the Ohio River Valley. In a rambling autobiography written after he attained standing as a painter, he described his early frustration trying to acquire a vocation that had no teachers. The son of a New York State farmer, Harding began his career as a peddler selling patent spinning wheel heads in Connecticut. After marrying and going into business independently as a tavern keeper, he abandoned this trade and went on the road with his wife, finding work as a sign painter, clarinet player, and museum hawker, occasionally riding the river on a raft. He eventually "fell in" with a portrait painter named Nelson, "one of the primitive sort," who took likenesses of Harding and his wife for ten dollars each but who refused to permit Harding to watch him paint. After Harding finally attempted a likeness of his wife on his own, he "became frantic with delight; it was like the discovery of a new sense." But when he showed Nelson his work, his mentor "declared it to be no more like his wife than like him" and told him he would be ten years mastering the trade. Harding persevered and turned out to be a rapid and facile learner. He found his way with his family from Pittsburgh down the Ohio River to Lexington, Kentucky. "Here . . . I took a room, and painted the portrait of a very popular young man, and made a decided hit. In six months from that time, I had painted nearly one hundred portraits, at twenty-five dollars a head."[29]

The picaresque early career of Vermont-born James Guild (1797–1844) represents a similar struggle to obtain the secrets of profile taking, miniature painting, and penmanship teaching. James Guild's early life is known from a document now called a journal but which (like Durang's) was probably a series of reminiscences written near the end of his extended travels in America before going to Europe for art instruction. Guild's narrative looks back over the years when he was experimenting with vocations before he found his career in art. His odyssey began on 9 July 1818 in his twenty-first year when he was freed from an apprenticeship as a "farmer boy" in Tunbridge, Vermont. He had seventy dollars in a note and no inclination to continue as a farmer. After trying work as a peddler, tinker, and animal handler (he took care of a bison in exchange for one-quarter of the gate), Guild taught himself to be a penmanship instructor by taking a few classes in Royalton. When he returned home to his relatives eighteen months later, Guild had mastered an impressive range of mercantile and ornamental hands and said he could teach any pupil a good "running hand" in twelve days' time.[30]

Taking to the road again, Guild learned to cut profiles while working for the proprietor of the Albany Museum, who had hired him to beat a tambourine to attract crowds. As he continued his travels, he purchased a diamond to make glasses for frames, paying for it by cutting profiles; he then sold it for three hundred frames to put his likenesses in. In Casanova, New York, he met a fortune-teller who predicted he would "learn to paint likenesses [and] that I should go into a painters shop an[d] my profiles would look so mean . . . that I should give them a small sum to learn me to paint." When Guild reached Canadaigua, he saw his chance. He went into the shop of Edwin Weyburn Goodwin, an upstate New York painter of watercolor portraits on paper. Guild found that his profiles indeed did look so "mean" that he "asked him . . . [if] he would show me [how to paint] . . . how to distinguish the coulers & he said $5, and I consented to it and began to paint." He then took a sample of Goodwin's painting and went looking for a subject:

> I put up at a tavern and told a Young Lady if she would wash my shirt, I would draw her likeness. Now then I was to exert my skill in painting. I opperated once on her but it looked so like a rech I throwed it away and tried again. The poor Girl sat niped up so prim and look so smileing it makes me smile when I think of while I was daubing on paint on a piece of paper, it could not be caled painting, for it looked more like a strangle cat than it did like her.

Guild persisted, stopping at every house to inquire if they wanted any profile likenesses taken, and "if I could not get but a trifle, I would paint for the sake of learning. In about 3 day I was quite a painter."[31]

Hoping to paint miniatures on ivory, Guild went to Albany and "dashed about in this Citty and to gain information in painting, I visited all the different painters and learnt all I could." Even after spending a promising year as a painter of miniatures and small-scale watercolor portraits (figs. 5.4 and 5.5), he found he "lacked very much for instruction" and determined to go to New York City to receive direction from the best artists. "I gave Mr. Inman a very fine miniature Painter $30 to paint my likeness that I might see him [do it]." The portrait by Henry Inman (1801–1846) shows him with quill in hand and the inscription "James Guild / Penmanship" (fig. 5.6).[32]

Acquiring a calling through outright partnership was probably more dependable. One of the earliest postings for a partnership was taken by the German

Figures 5.4 and 5.5. *Janette McArthur Bailey* (1791–1839) and *Reverend Phinehas Bailey* (1787–1861), by James Guild (1797–1844). Inscribed "J Bailey 1819 By James Guild" and "P Baily 1819 By James Guild." These portraits were painted in Berkshire, Vermont, early in the artist's career before he went to New York City and Europe for instruction. Watercolor, each 3 by 4 inches. Courtesy, Collection of Arthur B. and Sybil B. Kern.

Figure 5.6. *James Guild* (1797–1844), attributed to Henry Inman (1801–1846), New York City, circa 1823. As a young man, Guild taught himself to be a penmanship instructor by taking a few classes in Middlebury, Vermont. Oil on panel, 18 by 14 inches. Courtesy, Collection of Arthur B. and Sybil B. Kern. Photograph by Nina Fletcher Little, former owner.

mountebank physician Dr. Isaac Calcott when he arrived in the colonies in 1769. He noted that "any Gentleman willing to enter into Partnership with Mr. Calcott, may treat with him at his lodgings above mentioned."[33] Probably Calcott's motive was merely practical since it was likely to have been his first visit to this part of the world. Although he claimed to have practiced previously in London, his command of English may have been imperfect.

Purchase agreements were also known. While showing his pig during his initial stay in Boston, William Pinchbeck informed the public in April 1798 that business obligations required him to return to Europe immediately. Under the heading "A Good Chance for a Spec!" he promised to sell the "Learned Pig" if someone applied to him within the week.[34] We do not know the price, but within days a Mr. Brigshaw began a tour with what may have been one of Pinchbeck's old animals in Rhode Island and Connecticut while Pinchbeck took a newly trained pig to Salem, Newburyport, Dover, and Portland. Pinchbeck apparently reserved the right to compete with Brigshaw because he notified newspaper readers in Providence in September 1798 that "the public were lately much imposed upon by a Mr. Brigshaw, who attempted to show Something for the Learned Pig, that was not by any Means competent to what was advertised."[35] Other animal handlers also advertised their charges for sale. Elisha Norcross, who toured an eight-month-old leopard in 1809, apparently decided he had had enough of transient life and marketed the animal for five hundred dollars in a Boston paper. The new proprietor took possession of the leopard at Harvard's commencement in August 1810 and then headed for the state of New York.[36]

Electrical lecturers, puppeteers, and sometimes miniature painters sold the equipment on which their vocations depended. Although not a demonstrator herself, Rebecca Clagget, widow of clockmaker William Claggett of Newport, put his "famous Electrical Machine" up for sale for an unspecified sum in 1749. Her language shows she was well aware of its potential to entertain: "most suprizing Effects of Electricity *viz* The wonderful Phenomena of Electrical Attraction, Repulsion, and Flamatick Force, particularly the new Method of electerizing several Persons at the same Time, so that Fire shall dart from all Parts of their Bodies."[37] Within months electrical machines were being operated by storekeepers in Boston and Salem.

Among puppeteers, Jacob Henninger, an understudy to the showman Mr. Bayly (also known as "Doctor Bailey"), who in 1783 had apparently inherited Bayly's "apparatus," offered it for sale, for "cash only." This not only included a company of artificial comedians (puppets) four feet high, but the "complete machinery" of Bayly's table-tricks as well as fifty magic lantern figures representing the various nations of the earth.[38] After deciding to retire, J. Manly, a miniature painter and engraver working in Boston, New York, and Philadelphia as the "European Artist," tried on two occasions to sell his optical equipment to other painters. The first time was on 7 August 1793 when he compiled what amounted to an inventory of his "colours," "ivories," and "glasses" for use by miniature painters and hair-workers. He claimed these items were "valuable and rare" and that for one week, "he will instruct at a moderate price how to use these glasses." He seems to have had limited success, however. In December of the next year, he put what was left up for auction.[39]

Sales of waxwork figures were routine among museum proprietors, who soon realized they had dated material on their hands. In 1822, just after he had purchased the contents of Philip Woods's Boston Museum, Ethan Allen Greenwood recorded two transactions regarding some of the wax figures he had bought:

> Sept. 4th. Mr. [ ] of Worcester called concerning sale of Wax figures & proposed to buy 12 at $700 for travelling exhibition. . . .
>
> 7th. Sold a man from Montreal 7 wax figures & an Alligator from the B[oston] M[useum] for $200.[40]

Panoramas that had exhausted their local appeal (and the buildings that housed them) were also sold. A Mr. Lang put up for sale the Edinburg artist Robert Barker's forty-by-twenty-foot *View of London and Westminster* in New York in July 1795; a second proprietor in Baltimore advertised this painting, or a copy of it, for sale in 1796 as well as the rotunda "in which the Elephant has been seen."[41]

Finally, at least some itinerants entered into franchising agreements. They may have cost less, but they too could prove to be restrictive. James Brown's arrangement with penmanship teacher Daniel H. Leonard of Sharon, Vermont, severely limited Brown's movements. According to the articles of agreement signed between the two men on 5 March 1813, Leonard was to spend three days instructing Brown "in the principles of teaching the art of Writing" at the time of signing and to teach him further in the spring or summer. In return Brown was to devote himself full-time to using Leonard's "system" until 1 June 1814, to keep strict accounts, and to pay Leonard one-quarter of all money (or in-kind payments) he received. Brown was to confine himself to Windsor County, Vermont, for the present and after that "to teach in such part of the Country as . . . Leonard shall direct."[42] Because Leonard was a disciplined and competent instructor, James Brown no doubt learned penmanship teaching from a well-qualified source, but the contract, if fulfilled to the letter, was plainly stifling.

Apprenticeships, partnerships, purchases, and franchises aside, the transfer of most examples of early American popular culture inevitably came down to an individual practitioner relaying skills and information to another. While it is hard to document them, we get a sense of how these chains might have worked in the seventeenth century from a commonplace entry kept by a university student. David D. Hall describes a section in Edward Taylor's notebook recording the details of a conjuring performance that had been passed along by teachers and students at Harvard College. According to this story, Taylor was told of "magical performances by a juggler" by Jonathan Mitchel, "the young minister in Cambridge, who learned it as a student ('during recitation') from Henry Dunster, then the president of Harvard. Dunster had it from the Reverend John Wilson of Boston—and here the chain comes to an end."[43]

Sometimes these transfers of skills can be traced within Europe before crossing the Atlantic. Professional or semiprofessional mimes and mimics were active in London taverns and theaters at least by the early eighteenth century. We begin, for example, with a Mr. Clinch (or Clench), a native of the Barnet district in the north part of London, who in 1706 used his voice to simulate the flute, the organ, and the horn. He also imitated a horseman and his hounds, a "sham-Doctor," a "Drunken-Man," and "Bells." Clinch's last performance was in 1711.[44] Next was Herr Von Eeckenberg, a German performer in London who imitated "the Lark, Thrush, Blackbird, Goldfinch, Canary-bird, Flagelot and German Flute" in 1743.[45] Then came Signor Gaetano Rossignol (fl. 1774–1800), a professional mimic from Naples who in the 1770s counterfeited at London's Covent Garden Theater "all kinds of singing birds" and finished his act by playing a concerto on a "stringless" violin, reproducing its sounds with his voice.[46] Rossignol—a stage name taken from the French term for *nightingale*—dominated the world of mimicking in London theaters over the next several decades and inspired at least five performers who cited his name (and imitated his style) between 1777 and 1805.[47]

Gradually mimicking skills reappeared in North America. One of the first may have been a "Mr. Wendall, a young gentleman from Boston," a nonprofessional encountered by diarist Alexander Hamilton at a dinner party at a Mrs. Hogg's tavern in New York City in 1744. Wendall used his voice to imitate the sounds of "several beasts, as dogs, cats, horses, and cows, and the cackling of poultry"—all the while playing a violin. (Hamilton said the tavern proprietor and her staff were so transfixed they were turned to "statues" who had seen a "Gorgon's head").[48] After 1790, professional mimics imitating Rossignol found their way to eastern American cities. These included an unidentified "Clown" who accompanied a Mr. Martin and Donegani in New York City in 1793 by mimicking "the French Horn, Clarinet, Bassoon, &c."[49] William Patridge in the character of a Merryman mimicked different instruments and played a "Mock Solo Concerto on the violin" in Portland, Maine, in 1797.[50] A Mr. Robinson or Robertson, a colleague of James Maginnis, performed in Boston in 1800 "Rosenall's wonderful imitation of Birds," choosing "the Chicken, Duck, Blackbird, Thrush, American Robin, Sky-Lark, and Nightingale," and later whistled a grand overture, accompanied by the band.[51] And finally an unidentified amateur gave an imitation of "the Lark, the Nightengale, Thrush, Black Bird and American Robin" at a musical concert by the Old American Company in Albany in 1803.[52]

While as many gaps as links exist in this chain of imitations, there are two commonalities. First, six performers in England and America publicized an association between themselves and Rossignol, some even duplicating Rossignol's concluding mock-violin performance. One imitated birds "à la Rossignol"; another called himself "the English Rossignol"; still another said he would perform "Rosenald's wonderful imitation." Second, the contemporary literature confirms some of these connections. Joseph Strutt's *Sports and Pastimes of the People of England* (1801) identified "Clench," who imitated horses and hounds and a flute in London during the reign of Queen Anne, as well as an unidentified competitor called the "whistling man," who simulated bird songs. Strutt described Rossignol's entry onto the London scene in the 1770s with Breslaw's conjuring and juggling troupe.[53] When Rossignol's imitators, like Patridge and Robinson, began playing in New York, Baltimore, Boston, and Portland in the 1790s, the American connection became complete.[54] An entertainment form that had been thriving in London and its suburbs since the reign of Queen Anne but that had not accompanied the early and mid-eighteenth-century migration of English families to North America finally arrived with professional itinerants entering the country in the 1790s, about eighty years after Clench's early productions. As shown in later chapters, additional instances of this type of delayed transmission and its reliance on an Atlantic transit system can readily be found elsewhere.

Chapter 6
The Impact of Images

❖

NOT MENTIONED in the discussion so far is the extensive use of images that routinely appeared in newspapers, broadsides, and handbills—the daily and weekly documents that cultural carriers and printers liked to call "Advertisements" and "Bills of the Day." When inn keeper Abraham Van Dyck publicized a leopard for public viewing in the *New-York Gazette* in 1768, he used a crude but effective drawing about 2½ inches wide that displayed the animal's "black and white spots," its "large sparkling Eyes," its "long Whiskers," and a characteristic stance testifying to its unusual "leaping" ability (fig. 6.1).[1] One of the earliest illustrated advertisements in America's newspapers, Van Dyck's

Figure 6.1 "JUST ARRIVED, and to be seen at Abraham Van Dyck's . . . The LEOPARD." Detail of an advertisement taken in New York City announcing that the leopard and "several other Animals" could be seen at Van Dyck's Inn on Broadway. Woodcut. *New-York Gazette,* 1 August 1768. Courtesy, American Antiquarian Society.

image—a woodcut—was a bold stroke. The proprietor was so confident of success he charged New York residents one shilling admission per person to see the animal. Almost four decades later, a comparable image illustrated a handbill circulated by Christopher Newel in Providence, Rhode Island (fig. 6.2), announcing another leopard "Lately imported from Bengal" to be shown at James Hidden's Tavern near the statehouse. Here, too, the proprietor alluded to its power and ferocity but added the animal was confined in an iron cage to "quiet the apprehension of the most timid." Newell charged only nine pence because leopards had become more common.

First seen in New York City's papers in the 1750s, images began appearing regularly in American newspapers and broadsides throughout the country in the postrevolutionary period.[2] They initially called attention to items such as balloon ascensions, acrobatic performances on the slack wire, and exotic animals like camels and dromedaries (fig. 6.3), but they were also used for a host of more mundane and legal events such as lotteries, sales of farms and mansions, and escapes of slaves or servants. With what seems to have been little artistic training, engravers produced thousands of images on wood or in metal that were used

Figure 6.2 "To the Curious. A LEOPARD, Lately imported from Bengal . . . is supposed to be the first ever shewn in the *United States* . . . secured in an iron Cage." Handbill announcement by an unidentified proprietor that a leopard would be exhibited at J. Hidden's Tavern in Providence. On verso: "Christopher Newel's leopard." Woodcut. Boston?: N.p., 1802? Courtesy, American Antiquarian Society.

Figure 6.3 "TO BE SEEN, . . . A DROMEDARY." The animal was shown in 1811 at the house of Richard Lewis, on King Street in Alexandria, Virginia, where the proprietor also had a "general assortment of Jewellery" for sale. Lewis operated a tavern in that location between 1797 and 1812. *Alexandria Gazette,* 8 May 1811. Courtesy, American Antiquarian Society.

for mastheads, borders, and special characters as well as for highlighting scheduled departure and arrival dates of sailing vessels, packet boats, steamboats, and horse-drawn stages. Despite their small size, these images distinguished among three-masted ships, brigs, sloops, and schooners. They offered representations of portraits and miniatures, frames, coats of arms, and civic and national emblems. They showed women spinning flax and men fencing with one another or conversing with automatons. Northern papers created merchandizing logos for umbrellas, toothbrushes, shoes, boots, and distilleries; southern newspapers centered their cuts around farm animals: studding opportunities, strayed or stolen horses, prancing horses, saddles for sale, and stables for hire. Images differentiated runaway Irish servants from black slaves, the latter characteristically carrying staffs. Some papers devised special icons for fugitive women. And most of these were reproduced in quantity. In 1803 Boston's *New-England Palladium* ran between ten and seventeen ship cuts announcing departures on each advertising page; the *New-York Daily Advertiser* in 1795 had thirty-eight such cuts.[3]

A typical grouping of images used by itinerants was that depicting the second elephant shown in the United States, a female named "Betts" or "Old Bett," who toured eastern America with her Bengali and later her black handler between 1804 and 1816.[4] Old Bett was first illustrated in Richmond, Virginia, on 24 December 1805, when she was shown in the Washington Tavern for twenty-five cents. The original image (fig. 6.4) shows a side view of the elephant facing right; it is delicately made, possibly by an engraver working for the *Richmond Enquirer* or the Charleston *City Gazette*. Over the next few years Old Bett, her handler, and the image visited places like Utica, New York, in 1806; Charleston, Easton, and Philadelphia in 1807; and New York City in 1808. After visiting Lexington, Kentucky, in the winter of 1808–9, the animal disappeared from the record for more than two years. In 1812, however, still accompanied by its original cut, Old Bett reappeared in New Bern, North Carolina, where she was exhibited at Jones's Tavern, then moving on to Alexandria and other southern locations.[5] When the

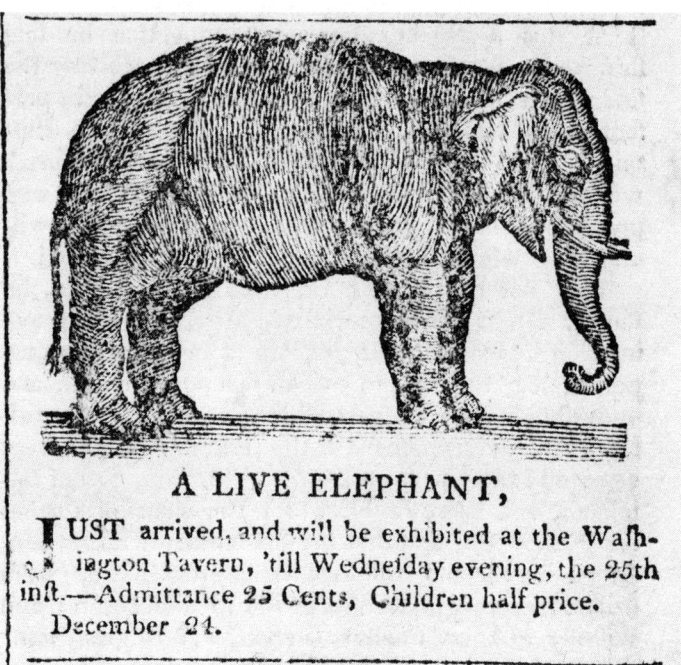

Figure 6.4 "A LIVE ELEPHANT, Just arrived, and will be exhibited at the Washington Tavern." Named "Old Bett," the elephant arrived in Boston in 1804 and was shown in New England and New York City for about nine months before reaching Richmond, Virginia, in 1805. During her subsequent career as a touring animal in eastern North America, Old Bett was illustrated by four different images. In the first, prepared in Virginia, the elephant looks right and stands on plain earth. *Richmond Enquirer,* 24 December 1805. Courtesy, American Antiquarian Society.

Figure 6.5 "NOW OR NEVER. *A FEMALE* ELEPHANT, TO be seen . . . in Portland." Copy of the original image of Old Bett reversing its format. The animal now stands in a field of grass and looks left. Initially made for the *New-York Gazette* when the animal was shown in New York City in 1812, the cut was subsequently added to the proprietor's portfolio. *Portland Gazette*, 21 May 1812. Courtesy, American Antiquarian Society.

animal reached New York City in June 1812, local engravers created two additional images because her advertisements were now appearing in three newspapers simultaneously. One image was reversed so that the elephant faced left (fig. 6.5); the second added what may have been the bottle out of which the elephant drank (fig. 6.6); a third (fig. 6.7) with the elephant facing right was created in Hudson, New York. These three images toured with the animal as it continued its journey through Pittsfield, Massachusetts, in 1812; Cooperstown and Albany, New York, in 1813; and Dover, New Hampshire, in 1815. We know it is the same elephant because the printed descriptions show her getting older every year (four years old in 1804, seven in 1807, twelve in 1812, fifteen in 1815) and because her weight increased from 4,700 to 6,000 pounds. Her length and girth also increased, and she was always described as uncorking and drinking from a bottle.[6]

The twelve-year saga of Old Bett's tour constitutes only one episode in a larger advertising campaign just beginning to transform American merchandising in the years 1780 to 1825. The campaign represented the coming together of cheap,

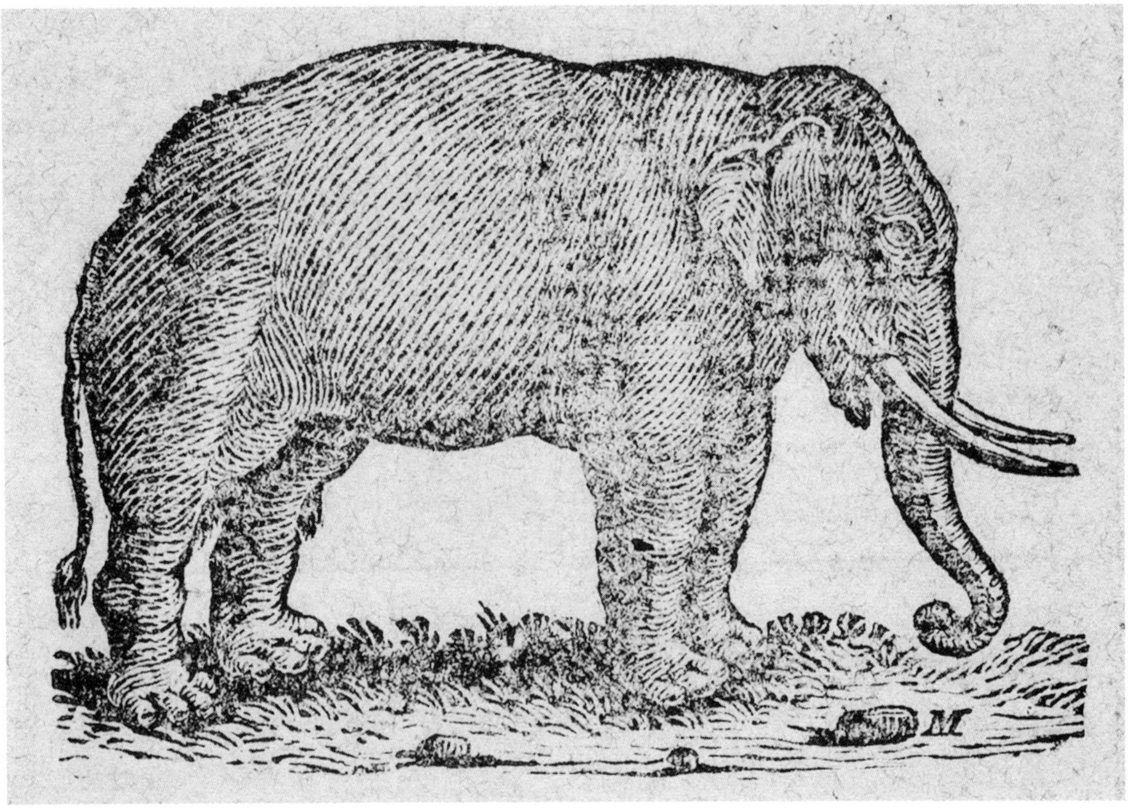

NOW OR NEVER!!!

JUST arrived, and to be seen at No. 324 Broadway, near the head of Pearl-street, till Saturday, the 13th instant.

A FEMALE ELEPHANT,

Twelve years old, upwards of eight feet high, and weighing more than 4700 lbs.

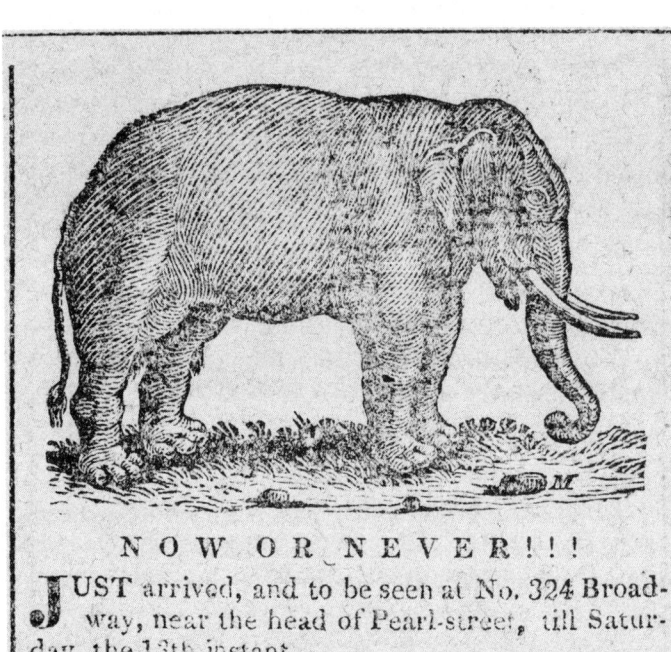

Figure 6.6 "NOW OR NEVER!!! JUST arrived, . . . A FEMALE ELEPHANT." Second copy of the original image of Old Bett, also showing her standing on grass. Prepared for the *New-York Evening Post* in June 1812, it was possibly made by Peter Maverick (1780–1831) or a member of his family. Signed with the initial "M" in the lower right-hand side of the foreground. It too was acquired by the animal's proprietor and later used in Pennsylvania and upstate New York. *New-York Evening Post,* 9 June 1812. Courtesy, American Antiquarian Society.

The Impact of Images

print-based images; a growing number of engravers to produce them; and an expanding newspaper readership. We can begin to understand its relationship to itinerants by asking who actually produced these pictures. Out of the many thousands of images designed for newspapers in this period, only one is known to have been signed. William Pinchbeck's *Sapient Dog* (see fig. 1.4) was inscribed "J Akin" in the lower right-hand corner by engraver James Akin (1773–1846), still living in Newburyport, Massachusetts, in 1807. Akin may have been responsible for Pinchbeck's *Pig of Knowledge,* his *Learned Pig,* as well as his balloon "excursion" (see figs. 1.1, 1.2, and 1.3). A second engraver may have identified himself through the initial "M," which appears in the lower right-hand corner of Old Bett's redrawn image in 1812 (see fig. 6.6). This may have been Peter Maverick

Figure 6.7 "Now or Never! A female ELEPHANT, 12 years old." Third copy of the original image of Old Bett, which appeared in Hudson, New York, in September 1812. Quickly made, the image had the virtue of emphasizing the animal's bulk by means of the converging lines. Hudson *Northern Whig,* 21 September 1812. Courtesy, New-York Historical Society, neg. no. 90793d.

(1780–1831), who lived and worked in New York City.[7] The name of at least one other artist is known, though not from a signature. Alexander Anderson of New York City created a cut of Peter Blancan's *Theatre Pitoresque and Mechanique* (see fig. 9.6)—a French-based puppet theater taken throughout eastern North America from 1808 to 1809—leaving a copy now preserved among the Anderson Papers at the New York Public Library.[8] The figure on the right is the hunchbacked Punch, or Polichinelle; the one on the left with the oversized sleeves is Pierrot.

Determining who actually commissioned the cuts, however, is not always easy. Ample evidence exists that newspaper printers ordered and owned everyday images—meaning those that depicted departing ships, homes for sale, and runaways. Presumably these cuts were equivalent to type and belonged to the paper. But individual entrepreneurs—rather than newspaper editors or publishers—may have owned and controlled many of the cuts they used in their advertising. This is suggested by the several specialized images posted by Joseph Falconi, the well-known Italian showman active intermittently in North America over a period of three decades between 1787 and 1819. Falconi traveled with images of an "Indian" automaton and its accompanying target (a table), which he first illustrated in a Philadelphia advertisement in 1788 (frontispiece). Because this entertainer had an established reputation in Europe, the West Indies, and Mexico before his arrival in America, it is possible both cuts were made in France or Italy and not by English or American engravers. Six years later, in 1794, he used the Indian image in his advertisement in Norfolk, Virginia, and again in 1796 at the Providence Theatre—though both times without the target.[9] Since the automaton was unique to Falconi, it is clear he controlled these cuts and carried them with him because no other performer could have used them. Much the same might be said about the relief cuts run by ventriloquists John and James Rannie, balloonist Jean-Pierre Blanchard, animal showman "Citizen" Cressin, and acoustical impresario Charles Packard, all of whom employed highly personalized illustrations.

Some newspaper printers, however, might also have routinely acquired special images as part of their way of doing business. Horatio Bigelow, who helped found the *Boston Daily Advertiser* on 3 March 1813, frequently ran unusual visual items in the advertisements he printed—among them images of steamboats, whales, patent liquor cocks, quill pens, and overshoes. In 1818, when Italian Antonio Cannata advertised a school for the art of fencing, Bigelow's engraver made a cut of two fencers sparring with short swords. Neither fencer wears a mask, but both have protective garments strapped with suspenders and hooks to their upper bodies. Two years later, when a Mr. Gras, a Frenchman, opened a fencing school in the same neighborhood of Merchants' Hall, Bigelow used an identical image (though clearly not the same cut) to illustrate his advertisement, choosing an earlier printed version as a model. In other words he may have recut it for a different client.[10]

Newspaper publishers also had a say as to how and where these cuts were placed. Since the expense of advertising was in part a function of the space the image occupied in the newspaper, an editor could position it in a way that reduced its cost to the client. As a profile taker making rounds in Connecticut, Ralph Letton apparently permitted his New London printer to tilt his profile sample ninety degrees, most likely because that was less expensive.[11] These layout decisions led to bizarre outcomes which not only indicate that showmen and artists and their printers were trying to save money but also reveal the relationship between newspaper images and printed broadsides and chapbooks. Large cuts originally prepared for broadsides and handbills—many of them obviously unable to fit a standard newspaper column width of about 2½ inches—were repositioned for publication. A broadside for two camels, male and female, exhibited in New Haven used a handsome relief cut—approximately 3½ inches in width—when the camels stayed at Major Leavenworth's stable in that town in June 1789 (see fig. 7.1). The same cut, placed vertically, accompanied a newspaper advertisement in New Haven's *Connecticut Journal* of 3 June 1789 allowing the proprietor to fit the image into a narrow space (see fig. 7.2). As the animals moved from town to town, some editors faced the animal down, while others faced it up, and when they had room they placed the image into a more natural position.[12] But the exchange between newspaper and broadside cuts was reciprocal. The likeness of Gabriel Salenka's trained dog (fig. 6.8), which illustrated that performer's advertisements in New York City, was the same as the one found on a broadside published in Philadelphia. On the broadside the cut is so small relative to the size of the document that a casual reader would barely see it.[13]

A critical question concerns the standard by which untaught engravers judged their work. For example, some cuts prepared for itinerants working in Philadelphia, New York, and Charleston generally started out ambitiously but deteriorated over time because they were used repeatedly and replaced by poorly designed copies. The several images of the so-called Crowninshield elephant (named after the American captain, Jacob Crowninshield, who brought this animal from India) illustrate the several stages of this progressive degeneration. The original image was part of a "sophisticated" broadside publicizing the animal when it came to Newburyport in 1797. Later copies and re-engravings that appeared in newspapers in Alexandria and Charleston degraded the figure or made it into a caricature (figs. 6.9, 6.10, and 6.11), sometimes reversing the image in the process.

This tendency to alter drawings is seen even more clearly in the sequence of eight images prepared for the "beautiful African Lion," a young "dun-colored"

GABRIEL SALENKA,

Lately arrived from Europe; presents his respectful compliments to the Ladies and Gentlemen of the city of New-York, and informs them he will in future exhibit the feats of sagacity, performed by his surprizing

DOG,

in private families, at any house they may request from 9 o'clock in the morning till 10 at night.

Mr. Salenka has performed in the presence of the king of Prussia and in most of the genteel families of Europe, to their satisfaction, and he doubts not but he will be able to afford an equal degree of satisfaction to the Ladies and Gentlemen of this polite metropolis.

As it would be too lengthy so it would be useless to mention the number of astonishing tricks which his DOG can perform. The price of each person in company will be 4s small children excepted. The smallest number he will perform for, must be 10 persons.

N B. The public may find him at no. 78, Wall street, the 6th door below the Tontine Coffee house, at any hour of the day.

March 2   4t.

Figure 6.8 "GABRIEL SALENKA, Lately arrived from Europe." Advertisement for a trained performing dog in New York City, *American Minerva,* 2 March 1796. Besides showing trained dogs, Salenka was a skilled conjurer, singer, musician, and fireworks showman whose evening entertainments sometimes continued for three hours. Courtesy, American Antiquarian Society.

Figures 6.9, 6.10, and 6.11. Three details of the Jacob Crowninshield elephant, which toured in America between 1796 and 1799, showing the progressive deterioration of the image. Top: "THE ELEPHANT." Copy made after the original 1797 broadside (fig. 21.5) by an Alexandria, Virginia, printer in 1798. *Alexandria Times,* 15 October 1798. Library of Congress. Center: *"The ELEPHANT."* Copy of the Alexandria image by a Charleston, South Carolina, printer in May 1799. *Charleston City Gazette and Daily Advertiser,* 29 May 1799. Charleston Library Society, Charleston, S.C. Bottom: "FINAL NOTICE. *THE ELEPHANT."* Copy by a second Charleston printer on 1 June 1799, *South-Carolina State Gazette.* Courtesy, Charleston Library Society, Charleston, S.C.

Figure 6.12. "TO THE CURIOUS. A beautiful African LION, . . . *at the sign of the Rising Sun.*" Woodcut from Philadelphia *Claypoole's,* 2 April 1792. This rampant lion, first published on 26 March 1792 to draw attention to its arrival in that city, is possibly the most accomplished image published in American newspapers before 1825. Courtesy, American Antiquarian Society.

male caught on Gorée Island that toured the eastern United States, New Orleans, and Havana in the last decade of the eighteenth century and the first decade of the nineteenth. Brought to New York City as a whelp in 1791, the lion was taken the next year to Philadelphia. Between 1792 and 1807 the animal toured America with its proprietor making long stops in New York City, Boston, Baltimore, and Albany. He visited Salem, Newburyport, Portsmouth, and Portland as a five-year-old; New London and other portions of Connecticut and New Hampshire as an eleven-year-old; Charleston and Baltimore at the ages of twelve and thirteen; and Albany at the age of fifteen. During this period the lion's height grew from three to four feet, his length increased from seven to nine feet, and his weight reached six hundred pounds. How he was transported is not known.[14]

This animal was illustrated for the first time in a Philadelphia newspaper on 26 March 1792. The image shows a rampant lion (fig. 6.12)—three columns' wide—dominating the advertising text headed by the caption "To the Curious."[15] Published in *Claypoole's,* this cut was so artistically competent it may have been supplied by a member of the Charles Willson Peale family or even by a London publisher who had prepared it for another purpose. When the lion moved to Baltimore, the cut came with him and occupied virtually the entire front page of the 1 August 1792 *Baltimore Evening Post.* The image was tilted ninety degrees to fit (fig. 6.13). But when the lion reached Salem, Massachusetts, in 1795, the

The Baltimore Evening Post
AND DAILY ADVERTISER.

(Price, Four-pence.)   WEDNESDAY, AUGUST 1, 1792.   (No. 17.)

BALTIMORE: Printed (daily) by PHILIP EDWARDS, in Market-street, seven doors West of Gay-street.

A BEAUTIFUL AFRICAN LION,

To be seen every day in the week, Sundays excepted, during his continuance in town, at Mr. Thomas Dewitt's, at the sign of the Black Horse, opposite the Centre-Market.

THIS noble animal is upwards of three feet high, measures seven feet from nostrils to tail; is of a beautiful dun colour, and uncommonly strong built: His legs and tail are as thick as those of a common-sized ox: He was caught in the woods of Goree, in Africa, when a whelp: He is as tame as any domestic animal whatever, and is really worth the contemplation of the curious.

☞ Price of admittance *One Eight of a Dollar*, and half price for children.

The stay of this sovereign of animals, in this place, will be but short; the proprietor intending to exhibit him throughout the United States.

Baltimore, July 31, 1792.

CHARLES WARD,

At his Warehouse, on Bowly's Wharf, has for SALE,

A Parcel of good Sugars, in Barrels; Loaf & Lump ditto, by the Hundred or smaller Quantity; Molasses; old French Brandy, well flavoured; Jamaica Spirits; West-India and New-England Rum; Gin; Cherry-Bounce; Tea; Coffee; Pimento; Essence of Spruce, in small Pots; Castor-Oil, in Boxes, containing 12 Bottles; Candles; Cheese; Two-Bushel Bags; a few Pieces of coarse and fine Linens; cheap Hair Ribbon, by the Piece; Writing and Wrapping Paper, by the Ream; Women's Satin and Stuff Shoes; Men's Leather ditto; Beef and Pork, in Barrels; Flax; a Quantity of Wool; Lampblack; Naval Stores; Burlington saltpetre; Hams, cured in the very best Manner, and in prime Order, for shipping, in Tierces; Fifty Barrels of Philadelphia Porter, containing three Dozen Bottles each, warranted equal to any shipped from that Place; Fifteen Hundred Bushels of sound Corn; Fourteen Thousand Weight, of good Virginia Bacon, well cured, and in prime Order. The Public may rely on being furnished with the above Articles cheap, particularly the Bacon.

He has just received, from BARBADOS,

A Quantity of excellent TAMARINDS, in Cags and small Stone Pots;

Also, a few Hundreds of COCOA-NUTS.

JAMES STEWART,

WATCH and CLOCK MAKER, COPPER-PLATE ENGRAVER, SEAL CUTTER, and GILDER,

At Mr. James Bull's Shoe and Boot Manufactory, near Tripolet's Alley, Market street, Baltimore,

RETURNS the gentlemen of Baltimore and the public in general, his sincere thanks for their kind encouragement since his commencement in business, which he will constantly pay unremitted attention to—

Watches & Clocks.

Said Stewart informs the gentlemen and ladies of Baltimore and its vicinity, that he purposes importing from Europe, horizontal, striking, and repeating watches, patent second, stop and plain watches, which may be depended on as they will be of the first quality, and made by the first workmen in London or Dublin, and chosen on the spot by a brother of said Stewart's, who is perfect master of the business.

He further requests that the gentlemen and ladies who wish to embrace this opportunity, may come forward on or before *Saturday* the 4th August, to give their directions (which they may depend being attended to) whether they will have their own name or the makers on the watch, the figure of the dial plate, if the cases are to be gold or silver, or if they wish to have them made in London or Dublin.

☞ Those gentlemen who would wish to have their stone seals cut either in cypher or arms, may have them done in an elegant manner, as the subscriber is well acquainted with a person of that trade in London.

July 27, 1792.

FLAX of a superior quality well cleaned, to be sold by the subscriber—Who has on hand at his store on Bowley's Wharf

Muscovado sugar of the 1st and 2d quality.	Wool and cotton cards
Loaf ditto	Nails
French Brandy	Iron shovels and spades
New England Rum	Dutch ovens
Madeira Wine	Tea kettles
Carcavilla ditto	Turks Island, Lisbon and French salt
Wine and cider vinegar	Window glass
London Porter	Copperas
Beef	Allum
Pork	Russia cordage assorted
Dry Cod Fish	Anchors
Pickled ditto	Oars
Pickled Salmon	Plaister of Paris, ground & unground
Mackrell	
Mould and dipped candles	Clover seed
Tanners Oil	Timothy seed
Sole Leather	Raisins in casks
Mens and womens shoes	

Which will be disposed of on reasonable terms for cash or produce

JOSEPH WILLIAMS.

☞ CASH given for BEES WAX, and WHITE OAK STAVES.

Baltimore, July 24, 1792.

FOR SALE,

THE time or servitude of a young healthy GIRL, who has three years and ten months to serve. For further particulars, enquire of the Printer.

Baltimore, July 18, 1792.

WANTED IMMEDIATELY,

A Journeyman Compositor,

To whom generous wages and constant employ will be given.

Two Apprentices, of good Character & Abilities, wanted by the Printer hereof.

MADDOX ANDREW,

At the GOLDEN SCALE, and EAGLE, on the North side of Market-street, and seventh door above Gay-street, and opposite the New Printing-Office,

HAS FOR SALE,

A very general Assortment of European and India

GOODS,

Just come to hand, which will be worthy the attention of those inclinable to purchase.

HE most earnestly returns his sincere thanks to the citizens of Baltimore, and his neighbouring acquaintance, for their encouragement since his short commencement, and hopes still to continue to merit their further favors, as it shall be his object to please.

HE HAS ON HAND,

Federal jeans, fustians, royal ribbs, ribbed jeans, cotton stripe and linsey, all for cash only, as no credit will be given.

Baltimore, July 13, 1792.

Brandywine Writing Paper and Paste-Boards.

THE subscriber has just received a fresh supply of Brandy-wine paper, and good pasteboards, hatters trimmings, &c. which, together with his usual assortment of brushes of his own manufacture, he will dispose of on the most reasonable terms.

JOHN FISHER, Brush Maker.

JUST RECEIVED, AND FOR SALE BY CHARLES WARD, EXCELLENT NEW ENGLAND CHEESE.

James Buchanan and William Robb Have for SALE at their STORE in COMMERCE STREET,

WEST-India Rum
Muscavado Sugar in Hhds
Coffee in Barrels
Carolina Pork
6-8 7-9 8-10 11-13 Window Glass
London, particular Madeira Wine, very old and mellow
Nankeens
Gin in Cases
Hyson and Souchong Tea
Pork in Barrels
Hogs Lard in do.

Figure 6.13. "A BEAUTIFUL AFRICAN LION, *To be seen every day in the week, Sundays excepted.*" Front page of the *Baltimore Evening Post*, 1 August 1792, showing the lion on exhibit at the Sign of the Black Horse, opposite the Centre-Market in Baltimore. The image dominates the front page of the newspaper. Courtesy, American Antiquarian Society.

animal's proprietor or handler was using a smaller, "anthropomorphic" version of it (fig. 6.14), much less artistically competent, which served as a model for several that followed. In its first imprints, the Salem representation seems relatively pristine. But during the next two years as the lion toured Maine, New Hampshire, Massachusetts, Rhode Island, and New York City, the Salem image gradually deteriorated. Each time a cut appeared in a paper, it required between four to eight hundred impressions, and many advertisements ran for weeks on end. Improper or repeated cleaning of the old, half-dried ink may have left deposits or loosened small sections of wood, reducing its clarity. Worn cuts on wood also tended to split along the grain lines, further compromising the image. At some point, engravers began to copy the Salem version. Not all were successful. One remake that appeared in the 1795 *Amherst Journal* in New Hampshire looks more like a bulldog (fig. 6.15) than it does a lion. (The editors quickly replaced it with a better image.) Another remake (fig. 6.16) that showed up in Boston and Salem advertisements in 1802 seems strikingly similar to the Salem original with the only difference being the clumps of grass growing in front. A third remake (fig. 6.17), which appeared in New York in 1802, shows the same pose but emphasizes the animal's ferocity, especially its enlarged claws. And, finally, one engraver in Albany reversed the image so that the lion faced left and its hair assumed a tufted appearance (fig. 6.18). By now the lion had become so popular, newspapers apparently were creating their own cuts when they needed them. Looking very much like caricatures, these later versions tend to be much cruder than their predecessors.

What has happened here? The public conception of the lion was gradually being shaped under the influence of printers and editors, who were furnishing their own figures and keeping an archive of them for future use. Introduced in print in Philadelphia as a rampant lion, the animal was redrawn by a Massachusetts artist and then altered into successive regional variants on the same theme: a Boston lion, a New York lion, and an Albany lion. By then the animal itself may have been less important than the visual portrayal of it. Over time, the advertising shelf life of the old lion expired, and by 1815 a new "lion image" took its place—one with character in his expression and doll-like eyes (fig. 6.19). It too had its own variations, such as the mournful lion that came through Providence in 1823. These sorrowful types became as common as the earlier ones, and some artists adopted the same doll-like look when illustrating tigers and large cats.[16]

Engravers' use of what might be construed as a sorrowful expression again raises the larger question of realism. Confined to a column width of a little more than two inches, engravers found little opportunity for accuracy. Always pressed for time, artists, editors, and entrepreneurs readily made compromises, and if a client wanted a dog, any dog would do. The trained dog that Gabriel Salenka relied on to do four levels of arithmetic is a short-haired mastiff on his Philadelphia

Figure 6.14. "TO THE CURIOUS. A BEAUTIFUL AFRICAN LION, . . . caught in the woods of Goree." Detail of an advertisement taken in Salem, Massachusetts, of the same rampant lion (now more subdued) at a Mr. Webb's Sun-Tavern, Essex Street. This image was widely copied by engravers as the animal toured America between 1795 and 1808. Woodcut. *Salem Gazette,* 14 April 1795. Courtesy, American Antiquarian Society.

Figure 6.15. "To the CURIOUS. A beautiful African LION, To be seen at Doc. S. Curtis', At the Sign of the Pestle and Mortar." Rural imitation of the Salem lion by a printer in Amherst, New Hampshire, in 1795. The editors quickly replaced this with the original image, which apparently had been unavailable at the time the newspaper went to press. *Amherst Journal,* 10 October 1795.

Figure 6.16. *"TO THE CURIOUS. A beautiful African LION, . . . at Capt. WEBB's."* New England imitations of the Salem lion were fashioned for use in advertisements published in Massachusetts, New Hampshire, Connecticut, and Maryland. Showing clumps of tufted grass below the lion, the image closely resembles the original and may have involved a new reproduction process. *Salem Gazette,* 19 March 1802. Courtesy, Collections of Maine Historical Society.

Figure 6.17. "THE KING OF BEASTS." New York City imitation of the Salem lion. This new image enhances its savage appearance by showing enlarged claws, a more bestial demeanor, and an intent face. *New-York Evening Post,* 13 November 1802. Courtesy, New-York Historical Society, neg. no. 90792d.

Figure 6.18. "*Just Arrived,* AND TO BE SEEN, . . . THE AFRICAN LION." Albany imitation of the Salem lion to be seen "at the lower end of Hudson-street." The Albany version of the lion was engraved when the animal was fifteen years old; the image made caricatures of its eyes, and the animal faced left. Albany *Republican Crisis,* 9 March 1807. Courtesy, American Antiquarian Society.

handbill and in his New York newspaper advertisements, but in Charleston, the animal appears as a hunting spaniel—a cut presumably owned by the printer of the Charleston *City Gazette* to advertise lost or stolen dogs.[17] Nevertheless, other evidence suggests engravers sometimes did provide accurate depictions of their subjects. We learn from Falconi's 1788 woodcut that the thirteen numbers aimed at by his Indian automaton ran clockwise on a raised oval card table supported with a tripod leg, that the arrows probably entered and stuck into it, and that the arrows were powered by a bow about half the size of a standard one. Gabriel Salenka's image informs us that his "surprising" dog performed on top of a similar oval table, manipulating the playing cards laid out in front of him.

A sense that we are dealing with relatively accurate figures is suggested by the relief cuts employed by a pair of ventriloquists and acrobats who toured eastern North America between 1801 and 1811.[18] Members of a Scottish family of entertainers, James Rannie and his younger brother John immigrated to America in their twenties. As pointed out by historian John Hodgson in 1999, the images depicting their acts provide one of the few proofs they used a mechanical doll now known as a *dummy*—a small stuffed figure that seemingly held a conversation with the ventriloquist or his audience. The Rannies called it "Tommy," and it was probably the first time a device like this was employed by an entertainer on the American stage. The showman would ask a question, and Tommy would answer in its own (presumably childish or idiosyncratic) voice, a routine touched on in some detail in William Pinchbeck's *Expositor*.[19] The Rannies also kept Tommys on their knees or hidden under their coats as they conversed or answered questions. They may also have pretended a Tommy was hidden in the pockets or scarves of their audiences. Several relief cuts of these figures are known, and they reveal three important facts: first, the dolls were stiff but capable of some movement through jointed limbs; second, they were dressed in a

Figure 6.19. "NAKED TRUTHS.—TO THE CURIOUS." A red lion exhibited at 122 Duane Street, New York City. Shown with its tail lowered and its eyes mournful, the animal was now part of a small menagerie that included a royal tiger, an orangutan, and an African ape. *New-York Evening Post*, 4 April 1817. Courtesy, American Antiquarian Society.

child's costume; and third, they varied considerably in size. Large Tommys, estimated at two and a half feet high, were balanced above them on a cane (fig. 6.20) or on an outstretched hand (figs. 6.21 and 6.22). Smaller Tommys, about one foot high or less, stood on the speaker's outstretched index finger (fig. 6.23).

Figure 6.20. "SEE AND BELIEVE!, . . . At the Assembly Room." James Rannie shown balancing a large "Tommy" (the Rannies' name for their hand-held ventriloquist's doll or dummy) on his chin while swinging on the slack wire in a Broadway performance in New York City. The Tommy is dressed in a child's costume and is approximately two and a half feet tall. *New-York Evening Post,* 23 April 1804. Courtesy, New-York Historical Society, neg. no. 90791d.

Figure 6.21. "Mr. RANNIE RESPECTFULLY informs the Ladies and Gentlemen of George-Town, and its vicinity, that he will exhibit his various entertainments." John Rannie shown holding a large Tommy in the palm of his hand during a ventriloquy exhibition in Georgetown, Maryland. This Tommy also wears children's clothing (pants and boots) and sports a tufted hat. *Georgetown Olio,* 19 May 1803. Courtesy, American Antiquarian Society.

Figure 6.22. "TO MORROW EVENING, MAY 5, At the Assembly Room, Broadway." James Rannie shown holding a large Tommy in a performance on Broadway, New York City, in 1804. The image is a better version of the one shown in fig. 6.21; the Tommy's boots are more prominently designed and his hat decoration more explicitly revealed. *New York Morning Chronicle,* 4 May 1804. Courtesy, New-York Historical Society, neg. no. 90793d.

Like many strollers the Rannies used the same images in their newspaper advertising and on their placards. Two images publicizing James Rannie's slack wire and Tommy performances on New York City's Broadway in 1804 are the same ones that later appeared in an 1811 poster made for an event by him in New Bedford, Massachusetts (see fig. 9.8). That the Rannies themselves were not the engravers of these images is suggested by another pair of cuts, prepared respectively for an 1802 performance John gave in Fredericktown, Maryland, and for an 1804 Broadway production James gave in New York City (see figs. 6.21 and 6.22).[20] Both illustrate the same staged scene: a half-dead tree with four branches, with three crows or jackdaws sitting on it, and a Tommy, wearing a patterned or serrated collar and a flower-decorated hat, standing on his hand. But the Maryland image made for John in his southern tour is cruder and seemingly the work of a "lesser" artist than the one created in New York City for James.

Other images used by the Rannies provide what may be accurate illustrations of their costumes. When John Rannie played in Charleston at 7 p.m. on 28 February 1807, it was the dead of winter and already dark out as he began his routine.[21] Figure 6.24 shows him wearing a heavily embroidered jacket complete with epaulettes and a neck stock, and standing next to a pair of candles. He plays a tambourine with about a dozen jingles. Figure 6.25 in turn shows James Rannie in formal attire as he fires a gun and balances on the slack rope. Like John Templeman's "fanciful" and "military" dress from the 1780s, these costumes may have been the uniform of a turn-of-the-century conjurer or showman whose success was closely dependent on his appearance—in this case generated by white-lined frock coats, pin-striped pants, open collars, and occasional neck-covering stocks. This once again raises the question whether European showmen still wore identifying clothing or "motley"—such as that worn by Harlequin. If so, this was a tradition that went back for centuries. Philip Butterworth's research suggests that as early as 1592 English jugglers wore jerkins "of leather," "cloakes of three coulers," and hose "pain[te]d with yellow drawn out with blew" as opposed to the "Civill sutes" of his audience.[22] The Rannies—just like the African lion—had become "emblematized," identified by the key visual emblems of their acts, their costumes, and their Tommys.

In the end, the question of images all came down to matters of persuasion. Old Bett's newspaper announcements make it very likely the animal's proprietors were honest about the elephant's age, length, and weight (and her stage appearances in *Alexander the Great, Blue Beard,* and *Forty Thieves*). Americans knew their animals and owners had to be forthright. Nevertheless, like the "harangues" of mountebanks and the affidavits of lanternists and public painters, most printed images were ultimately misleading or counterfactual. If Van Dyck had wanted to be entirely straightforward, he would have captured the leopard's wild, aggressive nature and not shown the docile, smiling animal seen in his woodcut. The Rannie brothers would have revealed the positioning holes by which they "balanced" their Tommy as they swung on the slack rope. And Pinchbeck would have depicted the semi-starved condition he kept his "Sapient Dog" in so that the animal would "read" letters by responding to his hidden hand signals. While all four itinerants knew that the images they used were deceptive, they also knew these methods were effective in appealing to a provincial American public. By contrast, London-based advertising prototypes were aimed at the top end of a stratified and educated society. The advertising columns of English papers seldom presented anything like the 1789 vision of an "Ourang

Figure 6.23. "Mr. *RANNIE's EXHIBITION.*" A small Tommy was used by James Rannie in a program given at the Union Hall, Newburyport, Massachusetts, in October 1804. The doll appears to be about ten inches high and is balanced on the end of the performer's index finger. Like the others, it wears a child's costume, although this one is designed as a jumpsuit. *Newburyport Herald,* 12 October 1804. Courtesy, American Antiquarian Society.

Figure 6.24. "*VENTRILOQUISM.* MR. RANNIE. *FROM JOHNNY GROT'S HOUSE.*" John Rannie balancing two pipes and playing a tambourine while suspended on a slack wire at a performance in Charleston, South Carolina. His richly embroidered coat and epaulettes provide evidence that proper costuming was essential for conjuring performances. *Charleston Courier,* 27 February 1807. Courtesy, American Antiquarian Society.

Figure 6.25. "☞ The inclemency of the weather on Tuesday evening last having prevented a great number of ladies and gentlemen from attending the performances of Mr. RANNIE." James Rannie, mounted on the slack wire, discharges a gun while balancing a wine cup, a card, a coin standing on end, a sword, and a plate. This image provides a closer view of a showman's costume consisting of an open frock coat, waistcoat, pantaloons, and neck stock. Advertisement in the *New York Morning Chronicle,* 24 May 1804. Courtesy, Library of Congress.

Outang: or, Wild Man of the Woods"[23]; enticed their readers with a child riding a cassowary (fig. 6.26); beguiled their readers with a horse of knowledge called "Spottee" (fig. 6.27); or advertised a "Mammoth Hog" (fig. 6.28). These were Americanisms, pure and simple. Only when English engravers tackled American subjects—such as the two rattlesnakes displayed in a coffeehouse in London in 1729—did a similar sense of artistic ingenuity materialize.[24]

The American visual artfulness witnessed here argues that the huckster stratagems which for centuries had governed the larger European experience of culture bearers were still at work guiding the entry of these traditions into North America and producing a culture that thrived in an American environment. The peddlers, animal handlers, show people, conjurers, healers, profile artists, and wirewalkers—the very same itinerant entrepreneurs who were commissioning these cuts in America in the late eighteenth and early nineteenth centuries—promised much and proposed more but in the end provided only enough to stay in business. Multiethnic and multinational, these enduring methods extended from Europe to the Mediterranean and from North Africa into Asia and flourished in North America because colonial and early federal America was still a relatively unformed society. To survive in their respective occupations, strollers had to project an exaggerated notion of themselves and one that was highly inviting. In this climate a portrait painter like Moses Cole announced his arrival in

Figure 6.26. "NATURAL CURIOSITY. *To be seen at Washington Hall, for this day only,* THE CASSOWARY, *A Bird, from the East Indies.*" This was the same cassowary Reverend William Bentley visited following commencement exercises at Harvard College on 18 July 1800. *Salem Gazette,* 12 August 1800. Courtesy, American Antiquarian Society.

Hallowell, Maine, in 1818 by calculating the exact date he was leaving town (fifteen days). A showman like "Citizen" Cressin, who displayed trained monkeys in New York and other eastern cities in 1795, vowed he would no longer "paste up [handbills] at the corners of the streets" because they attracted "unruly boys" and prevented respectable persons from attending.[25] Profile artists like William King pledged they would refuse to accept money if their work failed to please a client: "Correct Profile Likenesses (or no pay required)." All three promises, liberally reinforced with cuts and devices, of course, were half-truths. Cole could leave in an instant if he failed to get any clients; Cressin no doubt spread his handbills in order to attract, not dispel, unruly boys; most profile takers, including King, "warranted" their profiles but never expected to return any fees. But these images did attract business by providing a visual medium for an itinerant's claims. Like the upbeat jargon of their advertisements, they helped augment and perpetuate itinerants' uncertain livelihoods.

Figure 6.27. "EXHIBITION. The Famous African Horse *SPOTTEE,* Has Just Arrived from New York, . . . *The Real Horse* of Knowledge, *Will be exhibited every day.*" This was one of many varieties of "educated animals" that entertained Americans in the eighteenth and nineteenth centuries. This notice led readers to the Sign of the Black Horse on Market Street, Philadelphia, in 1807. Philadelphia *Poulson's,* 12 March 1807. Courtesy, American Antiquarian Society.

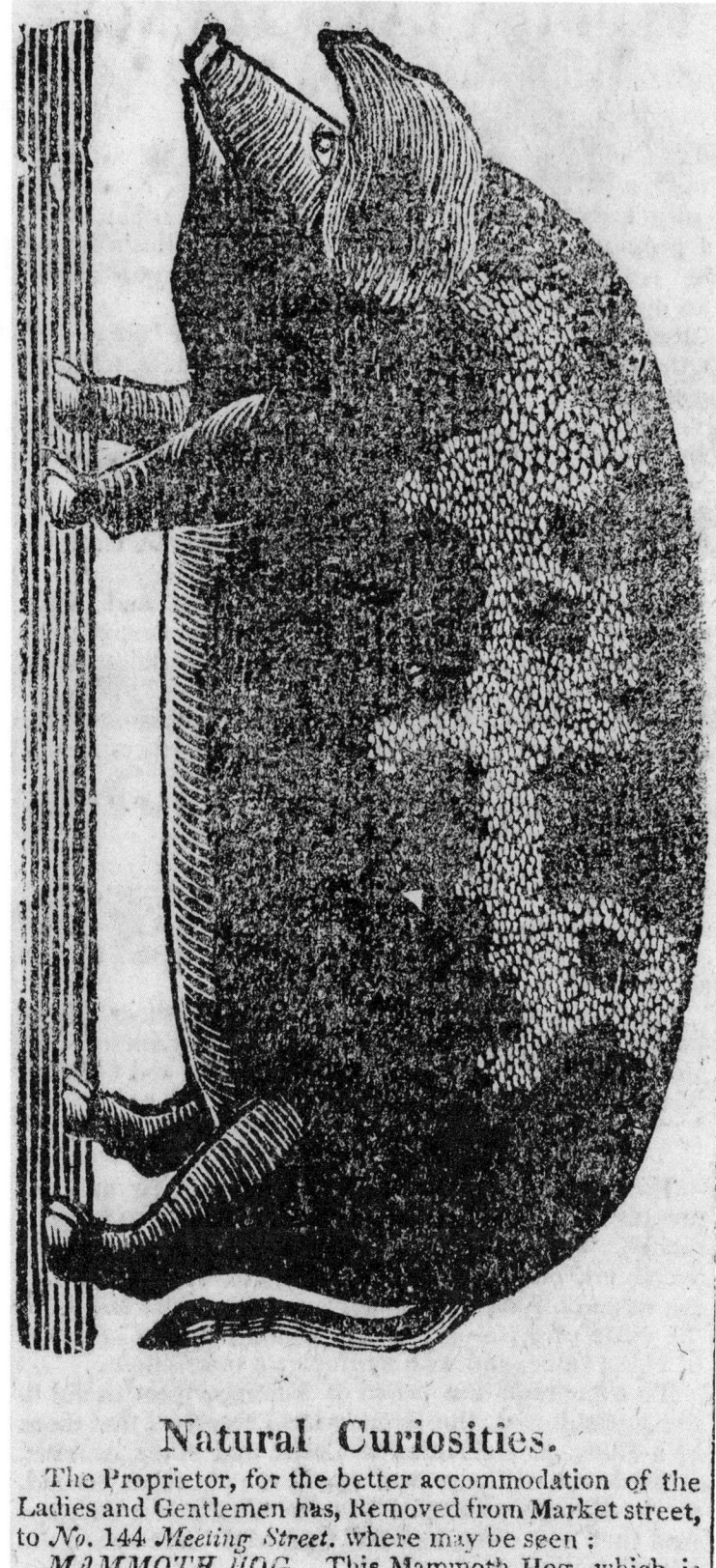

Figure 6.28. "Natural Curiosities. [The] MAMMOTH HOG." Detail of an advertisement for a two-year-old hog weighing 1,260 pounds exhibited in Charleston, South Carolina. This is one of many examples of huge animals (and people) that toured North America in the early nineteenth century. Charleston *City Gazette*, 19 January 1822. Courtesy, Charleston Library Society, Charleston.

Part II
SOME EARLY STROLLING PRACTICES

Chapter 7
Street Performers

OUTDOOR SPACES in early America—be it a street corner, a sidewalk, a field, a public common, or a semi-enclosed setting such as a backyard or a prison yard—provided an opportunity for impromptu and anonymous crowds to congregate and disperse easily. Many spectators in these settings were there by accident and probably included apprentices and servants, off-duty sailors, militia men, and everyday householders and their children who presumably stole time from their workday assignments to look at exotic animals, watch daredevil leaps of rope flyers, and delight in the performances of fireworks artists and balloonists. The itinerants who catered to them were mostly professional and semiprofessional entertainers fresh from European careers and in search of new audiences. To most Americans who spent their entire lives working in shops or restrained by the demands of homesteading, farming, fishing, and housekeeping, the careers of the men and women pursuing these occupations must have seemed baffling and improbable. What did people think of Joseph Broome, the German conjurer who performed "Wonders of the World by Dexterity of Hand" for New York City audiences at Charles Sleigh's baking establishment in 1734; Felix Fissour, from Turin, Italy (but most recently from London), who exhibited blazing "tornants" (turning fireworks) and "fixed suns" for Boston street crowds in 1768; or Mr. Victorani, the Italian acrobat who walked from chimney to chimney in Boston, Massachusetts, in 1810 while wearing shackles on his feet? We seldom have the answer, but it comes as no surprise that despite their popularity early entertainers often faced an uphill fight finding acceptance in an American setting.[1]

Animal Handlers

The earliest successful show people in America were handlers of exotic animals.[2] On a cold December day in 1726, a first-year divinity student at Harvard College was walking on Boston's waterfront when he saw an unusual cargo being taken on board the *Phoenix,* a merchant vessel lying at the town's busiest wharf. Jacob Eliot (1700–1766) stopped long enough to watch as the cage was hoisted, lowered, and securely tied in a location protected from the weather. Later that evening he noted in his diary: "The Lyon [was] convoyed on Board a Ship at the Long Wharf to go off to Barbadoes." A familiar sight to the waterfront residents of this provincial British seaport, the lion was first shown in Boston in 1716 at the Brattle Square home of Captain Arthur Savage, a merchant mariner. In 1718, it was taken to London but brought back two years later and was exhibited at the home of Martha Adams, who supplemented her publicity in the *Boston Gazette* with a sign on her front door informing passersby that "the Lion King of Beasts is to be seen here." After shipping to the West Indies in 1726, the animal was taken to Philadelphia in 1727 and to New York City and New Jersey in 1728. It was last documented in the diary of Joshua Hempstead in April 1729. "Fry[day]," he reported in New London, Connecticut, "Misty & Some Rain. . . . I went to Mill to see the Lyon in Madm Winthrops Stable who was brot here yesterday in a Wagon drawn by 4 oxen. came from towards Lyme & Saybrook & hath been all winter in the Western Towns & at Long Island, N.York ye Jerseys & Albany last fall." The next day, a Saturday, Hempstead "Carryed Joshua [his grandson] to See the Lyon."[3]

Although Savage was the original proprietor of this lion, there is a good possibility the animal at some juncture was acquired by the Connecticut-born showman Edward Burlesson (1686–after 1746). According to a document at the Boston City Clerk's office cited by Justin Winsor, editor of the *Memorial History of Boston* in 1880, Burlesson along with "his puppets" was warned out of town in 1735 by selectman Edward Bromfield, who denied him permission to exhibit them. The showman had earlier argued that the "Lyon, the black and whight bare, and the Lanechtskipt were shown by me that had their . . . [times] as long as they pleased." Burlesson's "Lyon" was very likely the one seen by Jacob Eliot, Joshua Hempstead, and his grandson. And the "whight bare" was almost certainly "Ursa Major, or the great White Bear," advertised in Boston in 1733 by an unknown handler, again probably Burlesson. Newspaper notices that year termed the bear "a Sight far preferable to the Lion in the Judgment of all Persons who have seen them both," and in a "Farewell Speech" published in the *Boston Weekly News-Letter,* the bear remarked that he had satisfied his curiosity about America, thanked New Englanders for their many civilities to him, and was preparing to sail for Europe "in the first ship."[4] The third animal, "the Lanechtskipt," may have been a camel or dromedary described by a metaphorical Dutch phrase "langnek schip van de woestijn" ("long-necked ship of the desert") and presumably sold to Burlesson in Boston by a Dutch sea captain sometime between 1726 and 1733.[5]

If this identification is correct, Burlesson was by this time a well-traveled animal entrepreneur who habitually visited the major cities of British North America as well as the West Indian islands—one of over a hundred such individuals circulating in North America before 1825. His occupation as an animal proprietor had real advantages over other itinerant professions in that period. Demonstrations of wild animals in captivity, trained animals, and unusual examples of domesticated or farm animals were an accepted form of public diversion in North America and the one least subject to regulation. Initially these curiosities were the joint enterprises of sea captains and tavern owners. Later, individual or pairs of animals or small menageries were extensively toured by professional handlers, who exhibited them on street corners or in barns, theaters, museums, hotels, taverns, or coffeehouses. They were also frequently taken to college commencements. Unencumbered by either cultural or religious constraints, handlers rapidly traversed eastern North America by following the simplest and most direct routes between population centers. These teams almost always traveled on foot, though some animals like the lion were hauled about in ox carts or transported by boat. The price of viewing was as little as twelve and a half cents or as much as one dollar (for season tickets).

Many of these animals were native to the eastern American seaboard. A nine-foot "Sea Lion" (actually a walrus with six-inch tusks), taken from Monument Pond near Plymouth, Massachusetts, was displayed in 1734 for sixpence in Boston's Dock Square, the first of many sea lions, sea dogs, sea tigers, and sea elephants presented in that town. A possum from Carolina, "of the Female Kind," was exhibited with eight young ones at the house of Boston tanner George Hewes. A three-month-old catamount was shown for one shilling at a tavern in Roxbury in 1741—again the first of many. This catamount was described as "exceedingly ravenous" and capable of jumping thirty feet. A four-month-old moose from Halifax, with ears eight to ten inches long, was stabled below the Granary in Boston in 1749, "tame as a Lamb." Later in the century North American elk, moose, rattlesnakes, and bison (commonly known as buffalo) were repeatedly exhibited, usually in the backs of taverns or barns, though sometimes in museums.[6]

Not surprisingly, foreign species continued to excite the most attention. The seven-foot camel, "just arrived from Africa," was shown at the bottom of Cold Lane in Boston for at least four weeks in 1721. Another camel (or perhaps the same one at a more advanced age) made its way in 1739 from Boston to Stonington and thence to New York City and Philadelphia the following year. It was seen by Reverend Ebenezer Parkman of Westborough, Massachusetts, in Boston in February 1739 and by Joshua Hempstead in Stonington, Connecticut, at Hobart's Tavern in July 1739.[7] In 1743, Boston encountered its second large cat: "Just arrived from Barbary, on the coast of Africa, a beautiful LEOPARD, about

13 months old; the first that was ever seen in this Country—It is to be seen at Mr. Seth Cushing's in Royal Exchange Lane." The price of admission was a shilling in old tenor and half price for children.[8] That same year Philadelphia met its first kangaroo. New York welcomed its first leopard in 1768; Newburyport, its first cassowary in 1800; and Portland, its first zebra in 1805.[9]

Organized animal showmanship in America began with the arrival of a pair of Arabian camels in New York City. On 14 August 1787 inn keeper Mr. Stephens announced that two camels, male and female, had recently arrived from Madeira (via the West Indies) in the Brigantine *Olive Branch* and could be seen for one shilling at his livery stable.[10] During the next five years, the two camels were extensively promoted with illustrated broadsides (fig 7.1) and newspaper advertisements (fig. 7.2) making it possible to retrace their movements with some accuracy. According to Ezra Stiles's diary, they walked north from New York City through Vermont and the Lake Champlain area in 1787 and 1788; they wintered in Boston in 1788–89 where they were kept warm with a stove.[11] The following year the pair stopped in Dedham, Massachusetts, where they were seen by Dr. Nathaniel Ames (1741–1822), son of almanac publisher and physician Nathaniel Ames: "2 Camels here exhibited 9d sight the 9th." The animals so impressed a

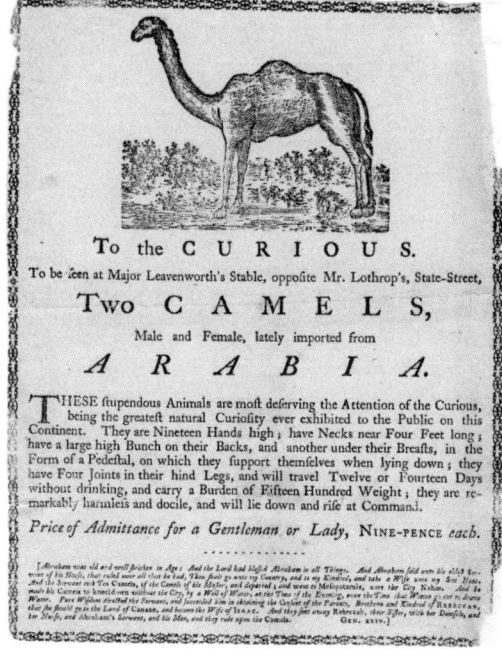

Figure 7.1. "To the CURIOUS. To be seen at Major Leavenworth's Stable, opposite Mr. Lothrop's, State-Street, Two CAMELS, Male and Female, lately imported from *ARABIA*." This relief cut for the first organized animal exhibition in North America was also used in newspaper advertisements (see fig. 7.2). Broadside with relief cut. 8¼ by 16½ inches. New Haven, c. 1–15 June 1789. Courtesy, American Antiquarian Society.

Figure 7.2. "To the CURIOUS. To be seen at Major Leavenworth's Stable, opposite Mr. Lothrop's, State-Street, Two CAMELS, Male and Female, lately imported from ARABIA." Newspaper version of the same advertisement seen in fig. 7.1. New Haven *Connecticut Journal,* 3 June 1789. Courtesy, The New Haven Museum.

family in neighboring Hingham that they retained a tuft of camel hair from one of them—the souvenir eventually finding its way into the collection of a New England museum.[12] The camels continued to Connecticut, New Hampshire, and eastern Massachusetts, and after spending a second winter in Boston, visited Hartford in 1790 and Litchfield and New London in 1791. It is possible that the surviving male was shown in Lancaster, Pennsylvania, in February 1793; in Hagerstown, Maryland, in May 1793; and again in York, Pennsylvania, in June 1796.[13]

A similar, well-publicized trek was made by "Old Bett," the female elephant who walked back and forth across the United States six times while wintering in relatively warm climates (see figs. 6.4–6.7). While most of her appearances involved short stays of one or two nights at a local inn or tavern, she also appeared in about twenty stage productions in Boston, Charleston, New York City, and Philadelphia of the plays *Blue Beard, Forty Thieves,* and *Alexander the Great*.[14]

Behind every exhibition animal was an entrepreneur who exposed himself to considerable financial risk. Stiles reported that the 1787 male and female camels were purchased in New York City for "200 Half Joes or 1600 Doll[ars]." Tickets for admittance for the pair were sold at nine pence each, or one-eighth of a dollar, with half-price for children. To recover their purchase price the owners needed to attract almost thirteen thousand paying adults, and to meet the expenses of feed, winter housing and heat, stable and barn rentals, printing and advertising, and a stable boy or handler required half again as many spectators. There was no guarantee either animal would survive in a northern climate for the four or five years it took to reach those numbers.[15] The importer of the first elephant in the United States, Captain Jacob Crowninshield (1770–1808) of Salem, Massachusetts, bought the animal in 1796 in Bengal for $450 and sold her on his arrival in New York for $10,000.[16] The elephant was never named, but William Bentley noted in his diary that the animal was a "female" and that she took bread "out of the pockets of spectators . . . drank porter & drew the cork." Her new owner, a Mr. Owen of Philadelphia, at first set admission at a half a dollar; later he reduced it to a quarter for adults and one-eighth of a dollar for children—or twice the admission cost of the pair of 1789 camels. At this rate forty thousand adult spectators were necessary in order to reimburse Owen for the purchase of the elephant. But Owen soon found other sources of revenue. When actor Thomas Cooper realized that all the seats were not taken for his benefit in Philadelphia in 1797, he hired the Crowninshield elephant for sixty dollars to appear on the stage with him. According to William Dunlap, the house was "filled . . . to overflowing."[17]

To make ends meet, proprietors and handlers put themselves through a grueling drill. In 1809 and 1810, Elisha Norcross singlehandedly toured his eight-month-old, four-foot Bengal leopard in eastern New England. The animal had been recently imported from Calcutta and was confined in a three-by-six-foot wooden cage with round bars. The schedule that Norcross followed would have taxed even the most disciplined handler. Beginning in January 1809, he showed the animal twelve hours each day as he moved from the "chamber over Dr. Stearns store" in Salem; to Mechanics Row near Market Square in Newburyport; to Colonel Gain's woodhouse, near the Bell Tavern in Portsmouth; to Dr. Coffin's brick building, opposite Mr. Graffam's tavern in Portland. His only day off was Sunday. The elapsed duration of his journey through eastern New England

Figure 7.3. *The Buffallo.* North American bison were commonly exhibited in taverns and barns in the late eighteenth century. Engraved print from "Account of the Buffalo, illustrated with a Plate," *Massachusetts Magazine* 4, no. 4, April 1792, 219. Copperplate engraving; artist and engraver unknown. Courtesy, American Antiquarian Society.

was a little more than nineteen weeks (10 January–25 May 1810), suggesting that in addition to several long stays in the large coastal centers, Norcross made numerous stops at small rural and coastal communities.[18]

Nevertheless, for some proprietors animal showmanship was their sole means of support. Samuel Dean, who made his way with a female bison through Newport, Providence, and Salem in 1795, was a disabled veteran of America's war with the Shawnee and Miami tribal confederations in the Northwest Territory. He described the animal as coming "from the Miame [Miami] Indian Village"— possibly the same bison (fig. 7.3) pictured in the *Massachusetts Magazine* in April 1792. Dean said it was upward of fifteen hands high and bearded like a goat, and that it possessed long, bushy hair on its head resembling a "Lady's Crape Cushion." Dean then went on to speak briefly about himself: "As the Proprietor is totally disabled from bodily Labour, by Reason of the Wounds he received at Gen St. Clair's Defeat, Nov. 4, 1791, and having no other Means of Subsistence, humbly hopes for the Assistance and Encouragement of the Public." Since the bison originated from the site of Arthur St. Clair's disastrous engagement in what later became Indiana and Ohio, Dean presumably brought the animal home with him after he recovered from his wounds.[19]

Animal showmanship also attracted Africans, African Americans, and Native Americans both as handlers and as proprietors. The unidentified "Negro at the

Gate" who escorted each person visiting the lion on display at Arthur Savage's Boston home in 1718 may have been Sharper, Savage's personal slave who was inventoried in his estate in 1735.[20] (Savage may not have entirely trusted him since he publicized the six pence admittance price in advance to prevent "all disputes," that is, the keeper's charging a higher rate and pocketing the difference.) In Baltimore in 1800, a man, possibly a Native American identifying himself as "Robert Wilson, alias Whistling Bor," purchased a young female panther from the Northwest Territory that had been advertised for sale earlier in the year. Whistling Bor put the animal on exhibit at the town's marketplace for one-eighth of a dollar. At least one African American—Othello Pollard—became a proprietor of a leopard and displayed it in February 1802 for twenty-five cents' admission (fig. 7.4) at his hotel and restaurant next to Daniel Bowen's Columbian Museum in Boston. His newspaper advertisements listed his name

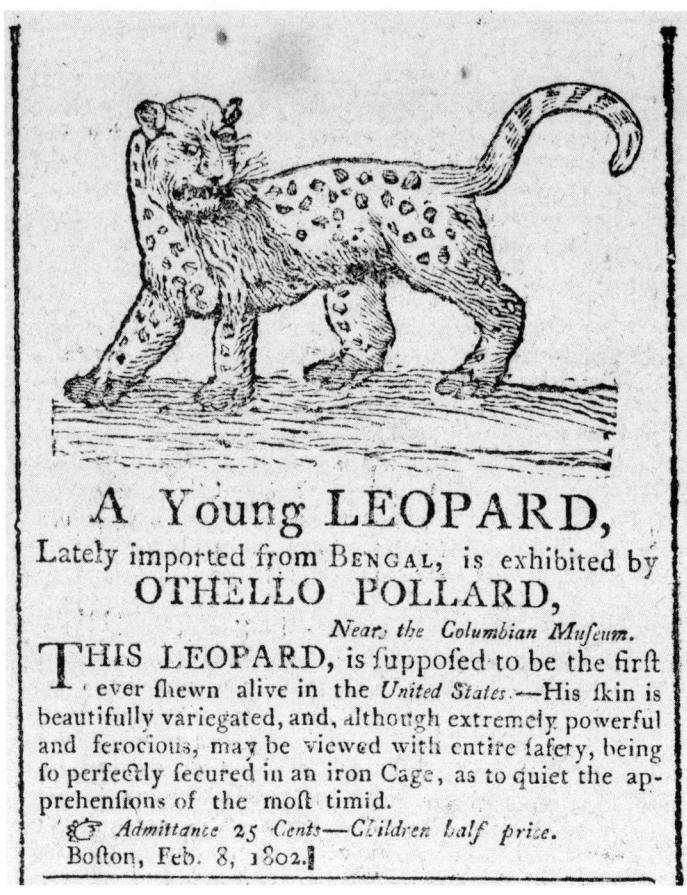

Figure 7.4. "A Young LEOPARD, Lately Imported from BENGAL." Othello Pollard, a black entrepreneur in early nineteenth-century Boston, announced the exhibition of an exotic animal near the Columbian Museum. Boston *Independent Chronicle*, 8 February 1802. Courtesy, American Antiquarian Society.

prominently, and like other proprietors of large cats he declared the animal was "secured in an iron Cage" and was "supposed to be the first ever shewn alive in the *United States.*" Pollard, a highly motivated entrepreneur in Boston and Cambridge, married Eupha, or Upkah, Brown in 1799 at which time both were identified as "blacks" in the marriage record; Pollard was also described as a "man of Color" in a warning he received against issuing private bills in 1804. He may have been a relation of a Boston tavern proprietor named A. Pollard who later exhibited a white Greenland sea bear. Othello Pollard's establishment burned during the fire that consumed Bowen's museum in 1803.[21]

Owners and handlers of performing animals may have undertaken even more exacting regimens. The first "high-rider" circulating in the British colonies was probably John Sharp, who in November 1771 performed equestrian tricks at the King's Arms Tavern on the neck in Boston. He called himself "late from England." A month later a Mr. Faulks put on a show of trick riding in an "inclos'd Piece of Ground" behind the windmill in New York City, making it likely that one performer had heard about the positive reception of the other.[22] Their sudden success may have been occasioned by the increasing English military personnel stationed in Boston and the colonies in that decade. These performers, in turn, were followed by Jacob Bates, a professional showman with a long history of exhibitions before European royalty. Bates may have had an easier time of it than most animal handlers because he traveled with assistants to help care for his three trained horses. But he had other problems. In 1773, he was obliged to secure a gated field with guards to prevent spectators who lacked tickets from watching his act free of charge and to hire carpenters to prepare "seats" appropriate for ladies. He also had to persuade "gentlemen" not to bring their dogs—no doubt much more easily said than done.[23] Bates eventually retired to a horse farm outside Philadelphia in 1789 where he sold "covering" rights until 1791.[24]

Wirewalkers, Posture-Masters, Rope Flyers

Unlike animal handlers, most acrobats in early America teamed with a colleague or assistants. The tightrope dancer seen by Durand of Dauphiné in Virginia in 1686 was accompanied by a jester and three violinists. In New England in 1712, Judge Samuel Sewall wrote of seeing a sailor playing "Tricks on a Rope" aboard an anchored British warship in Boston Harbor. He stopped to watch the stunts and later mentioned them in his diary.[25] A month later diarist William Byrd of Westover, Virginia, observed a similar diversion, again one associated with anchored ships: "One of Captain M-r-l's seamen showed us some feats of tumbling."[26] These sailors were continuing a tradition of ropedancing and tumbling that flourished in London in the late 1660s—witnessed by Samuel Pepys during a visit to Southwark Fair.[27] By 1724 ropedancers were charging admission in

North America, beginning with the unidentified woman and seven-year-old boy who played at "the New Booth on Society Hill in Philadelphia." (The term *booth* of course implies an open-air setting, perhaps a space behind a high fence.) A "Pickle Herring" or clown was part of her show, and she charged three shillings "upon the Stage," two shillings in the pit, and one shilling and six pence for the gallery. In September 1734, John Bradley requested permission to entertain Boston audiences on the "tort rope" (tightrope), boldly arguing for preferential treatment as a "Protestant dissenter from the Kirk of Scotland." But Bradley was turned down. When he repeated his petition a month later, asking to "shew and exercise the Diversion of Rope Dancing, Tumbling, and Posturing with Swords," he again was disallowed.[28] Four years later, in 1738, a troupe of four acrobats showed up in Williamsburg, Virginia. Made up of a "man and his wife, and with them two children," they performed "the agility of body, by various sorts of postures, tumbling, and sword dancing, to greater perfection than has been known in these parts for many years, if ever."[29]

At least one rope flyer visiting the colonies took his act directly to the people. On 12 September 1757 a curious and boastful declaration appeared in the *Boston Gazette*. "This is to give notice," it read, "that John Childs has flewn off of most of the highest steeples in Old-England, and off of the monument by the Duke of Cumberland's Desire, and does intend this Day, and two Days following, to fly off of Dr. Cutler's Church, where he hopes to give full Satisfaction to all Spectators."[30] Not unexpectedly, a large crowd assembled at Reverend Timothy Cutler's Christ Church in Boston's north end to watch. Perhaps some people (like twentieth-century storyteller Edward R. Snow) actually expected Childs to strap on a pair of wings like Icarus of the Greek legend and flutter his way down to the ground.[31] Although Childs's exploit was nothing so dramatic as this, he did achieve some distance. He attached a rope from the top of Cutler's 190-foot-high steeple and executed a spectacularly long slide to a point on the ground 700 feet away at the base of North Street near the ferry to Charlestown. In his descent he passed over rooftops and trees, remaining in the air an estimated sixteen to eighteen seconds. On the following day, Childs performed the feat two more times, once carrying a pair of loaded pistols; he fired one and cocked and snapped the other twice before reaching the ground.[32]

While no woodcut images illustrated the newspaper reports of Childs's flight, his technique can be readily understood from a detail in William Hogarth's 1735 *Southwark Fair* (fig. 7.5) in which a rope flyer descends headfirst from a bell tower. These acrobats strapped a flat board with a groove running down its center across their chests. The principal requirement for the feat was staying balanced using one's arms and legs; feather mattresses may have cushioned the landing. Exactly how common rope flyers were in North America is not known. Hannah Andrews Breck (1747–1830) of Boston, who watched Childs's act as a

Figure 7.5. Two details of William Hogarth's *Southwark Fair* showing a rope flyer performing behind a temporary puppetry stand at Southwark, England, in September 1733. John Childs's 1757 flights from the steeple of Boston's Christ Church may have been executed in the same manner. From an etching and engraving by William Hogarth (1697–1764). London, 1734. Sheet: 16¼ by 21⁷⁄₁₆ inches. Courtesy, The Metropolitan Museum of Art, Gift of Sarah Lazarus, 1891, Acc. no. 91.1.72, www.metmuseum.org.

ten-year-old, told her son Samuel many years later that "a man from England entertained [us] . . . with an extraordinary feat at the North Episcopal church." Another onlooker may have been Reverend David McClure (1748–1820) of East Windsor, Connecticut, who remembered having imitated him as a child in his neighbor's yard.[33]

Childs's undeniable achievement in gathering crowds in Boston like few other episodes in early American entertainment history demonstrates the extent to which the ports of call bordering the North Atlantic seaboard had remained part of an international community. Europe and the Mediterranean seldom seem so close to North America as they do in Childs's announcement—a characteristic of acrobats and other outdoor performers whose vocations were often dominated by northern Europeans (primarily Irish and Scots), Italians, and northern Africans.

Another showman who marshaled outdoor crowds was a Mr. Victorani (also known as Mr. Victorian). He first turned up in Charleston in 1808 as a partner in Messrs. Berry and Victorian's company of Italian ropedancers and wire dancers, balancers, tumblers, and pantomimists who played at Mr. Sollee's "theatre" on Church Street. Victorani came with impressive credentials, calling himself a pupil of the "celebrated Cortez" and "formerly belonging to the Great Company of Mr. Franconi, the most celebrated [acrobat] in Europe." He specialized in dressing and undressing himself on the tightrope and in partaking of a "collation" spread on a table. He frequently joined and rejoined other acrobatic and entertainment companies, playing alternately with the Rannie brothers and Mr. Bell, or teaming with his Italian compatriot, a Mr. Manfredi, to perform what they called a double ropedance. He also teamed with a Mr. Codet in a "Leap over Four Horses" in an appearance in New York City in 1809. When acrobatic business declined in 1810, Victorani began to promote himself by walking between buildings in the medieval tradition. In Boston he crossed Newbury Street (now Washington Street) at the White Horse Tavern on a rope extended from "Chimney to Chimney." In Salem he "walk[ed] the rope . . . across the streets a little above Frye's Tavern," first forward then backward, then with shackles on his feet, and a fourth time blindfolded. In Newburyport, he traversed a rope stretched above State Street between the Clement House and the Wolfe Tavern, a stunt remembered many years later by Newburyport nonagenarian Sarah Smith Emery. (After two performances, the town's selectmen belatedly banned Victorani and his "mountebank's tricks.") He was last seen in Massachusetts walking chimney to chimney across the main square in Charlestown "attired in a woman's dress," but in November of that year a Rhode Island paper reported that he attempted to dance across a rope spanning the Providence River. Although Victorani failed, the feat nevertheless attracted a vast concourse of people.[34]

After tightrope walkers formed companies for entertaining in theaters and amphitheaters, individual acrobats still found opportunities to play before assembled street audiences. French ropedancer Monsieur Godeau introduced himself to Americans in 1820 when he joined with a Mademoiselle Adolphe from Paris to perform a few nights at the Anthony Street Theatre in New York City. By July 1821 he had formed his own company, and as he moved south, he reverted to outdoor exhibitions, astonishing street crowds in Richmond in September 1821 by traversing a rope stretched between porticoes of the Eagle Tavern to the city's main hotel some fifty or sixty feet off the ground—a feat celebrated in that city for years.[35] In the end he probably regretted his American visit, however. On a sea passage from Norfolk to New Orleans in January 1822, Godeau was shipwrecked and lost his wife and child—and what was described as his life savings ($10,000 in gold). He returned to Baltimore hoping to recoup his losses but was greeted by an empty house. Later that year in New York City he fell from a rope twenty feet in the air and "was very much injured." Attempting to recover from this fall, he took his show to Canada, where in 1823, he announced in the *Montreal Advertiser* he would "dance on the shoulders of Mother Ango, *ninety* years old, from Paris."[36]

Fireworks Artists

Pyrotechnical artists also attracted outside crowds, although it took many years before they were well known. In 1749, eight months after peace was signed among France, England, and Holland, one New York City entrepreneur showed an etching of the plan for the London fireworks celebrating the event on a "diagonal mirror" set up in a store front (fig. 7.6). A full description of the memorable occasion was available in a handout. Among fireworks specialists who traversed North America in the 1760s were Italian brothers from Turin named Fissour who heralded themselves as "Engineers to the King of Sardinia." These men devised a program of rockets, wheels, and globes in New York City in May 1768, with music "proper for the entertainment." The following month they joined instrumentalists and vocalists from the New York theater for a combined concert and fireworks demonstration at Ranelagh Gardens, one of two concert gardens in New York City. The pair mounted a concluding exhibition at Vauxhall Gardens in June 1769.[37] Later that year Felix Fissour came to Boston to stage a set of sixteen fireworks celebrating the coronation day of George III. Fissour contracted to build a large platform and gallery on Boston Neck and sold admission for three shillings for the gallery seats and two shillings for platform seats. He held two events, with music between acts, and a third by subscription on Boston Common.[38]

After the American Revolution, fireworks displays were greatly expanded, with at least fifty individuals traveling town to town preparing them before 1826. These events were typically associated with the birthdays of French royalty,

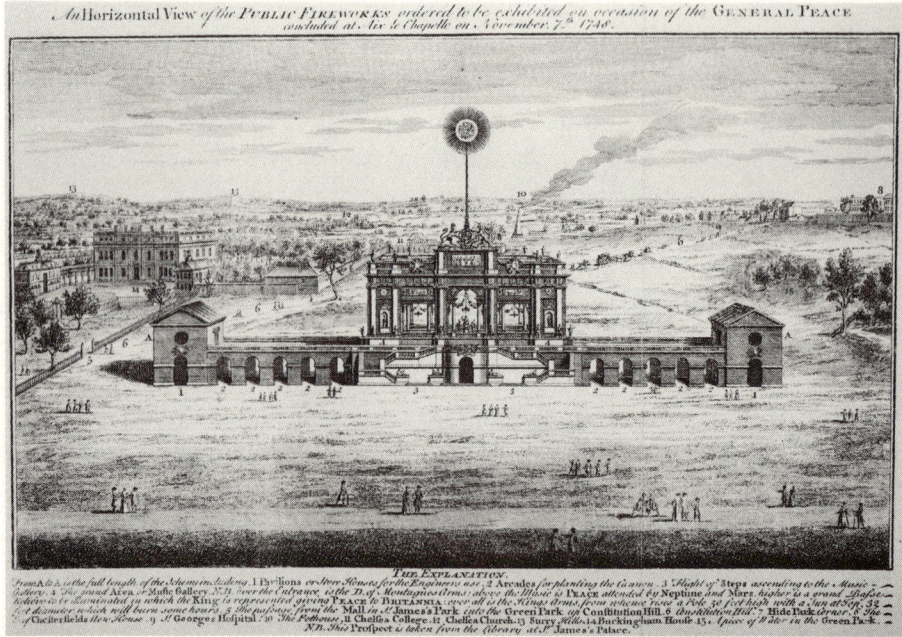

Figure 7.6. *An Horizontal View of the Public Fireworks Ordered to Be Exhibited on Occasion of the General Peace.* Etching of the fireworks design for the celebration of the Peace of Aix-la-Chapelle at Green Park, London, on 27 April 1749, shown by James Shaw on the "diagonal mirror" in New York City on 19 June 1749. Artist and engraver unknown. Ink on paper. England, 1748, 7 1/16 by 10 7/8 inches. Courtesy, The Metropolitan Museum of Art, The Elisha Whittelsey Collection, The Elisha Whittelsey Fund, 1956, Acc. no. 56.586.9.

displays of horsemanship and acrobatics, and the new Fourth of July celebrations. One of the first to market this expertise was "Citizen Ambroise," also known as Ambroise Varinot, of Philadelphia, who set up and staffed a fireworks factory on Mulberry Street. A Frenchman, he supplied or organized many of the celebrations in that city as well as in New York (fig. 7.7), Alexandria, and Fredericksburg, Virginia. He was alternately termed a "fireworker" or "celebrated fire-worker" in the advertisements for his displays; he was so renowned that other fireworks entrepreneurs claimed theirs were "in the stile of the celebrated Ambrose, whose fame, as a Pyrotechnical Artist, is well known throughout the continent."[39]

Laurent Spinacuta, a former French plantation owner, was a fireworks innovator who fled the revolution in Santo Domingo in 1793 and with his wife joined John Ricketts and the Haymarket Theatre in Boston as dancers and tightrope walkers. In August 1796, when Ricketts was competing with Philip Lailson's troupe in Boston, Spinacuta prepared ten "Chinese" fireworks that began with "American Independence" and illuminated architectural motifs such as "Church of St. Sophia in Constantinople" and "St. Paul's Church, London." He closed his spectacles with the "Arms of the United States."[40] Many in his audience must have been seeing thematic fireworks for the first time. In August 1797, Spinacuta advertised simultaneous subscriptions in Portsmouth and Boston for what he promised would be dual exhibitions of "brilliant fire-works" prepared with the help of an unidentified "military gentleman of Boston." Plans called for building a stage in each town twelve feet from the ground for good viewing. The admission price was half a dollar. Although both events had to be postponed (subscriptions were slow in coming, and Portsmouth was running low on gunpowder), when they finally happened their displays were so sensational they were immediately met with calls for more. In response, in the fall of 1797, Spinacuta used Ricketts's old amphitheater in West Boston to mount the most grandiose fireworks yet seen in that town. The three-part program, given at the amphitheater on 28 October, was accompanied by a band and consisted of cascades, wheels, windmills, suns, and gerbs (sparkling fireworks); a tableaux of the Temple of Liberty supported by Generals George Washington and Joseph Warren; and a moving tableaux of the frigate *Constitution*. The extravaganza culminated in a launch of skyrockets.[41]

By the second decade of the nineteenth century, fireworks events were held in "gardens" at Boston, Providence, and New York City every Fourth of July. Some were designed by French and Italian pyrotechnical artists like a Mr. Codet, a pupil of the "famous Mr. Rudgery [Ruggieri]" of Paris, who was attached to

Figure 7.7. "Mr. AMBROISE, Patentee from several kingdoms of Europe, and celebrated FIRE-WORKER . . . will exhibit THIS EVENING." This woodcut of Ambroise Varinot's exhibition at the New Theatre in Alexandria, Virginia, may be the earliest image of a fireworks display that was designed, executed, and printed in America. Two standing wheels with a pinnacle assembly in the center. *The Times and Alexandria Advertiser,* 30 November 1797. Courtesy, Library of Congress, vol. 1546.

circus owner and trick rider Jean Baptiste Breschard's equestrians, and a Mr. Dusolla, who toured with the Cayetano troupe.[42] Others were created by Americans such as T. Patrick and James Dench (both of New York City) and a Mr. Brown (of Philadelphia), who produced elaborate fireworks displays in Boston, Providence, Newport, New York City, and New Haven. Patrick normally selected sites on the slope of hills that could be cordoned off. Patrick, who presented "the grand falls of Niagara," ignited his in Providence on the Federal Hill property of Colonel J. B. Wood, charging twenty-five cents per ticket. The first occasion may have proven unruly: at a second performance Patrick arranged for an enclosing fence fourteen feet high, and at the third showing he added police supervision.[43]

Not all pyrotechnical artists were connected with the theater or equestrian troupes. Two specialists in the repair of musical instruments, F. Fontaine and L. Boucherie, "lately from Europe," arrived in July 1808 in Newport where they made their customary plea to tune and repair pianofortes and organs. After posting the same request in the *Providence Gazette,* they prepared to hold a "Grand Fire-Works" on two successive Fridays—taking advantage of the open space and covered seating around the amphitheater used by traveling circuses. Their twelve-piece repertory was relatively simple, composed mostly of skyrockets, suns, double suns, Roman candles, spirals, and the "explosion of a bomb shell." One unidentified incendiary device was called "the great Coombe, a mechanical piece very much admired." Making no mention of fireworks, in early November Fontaine and Boucherie were in Boston seeking to teach harp, pianoforte, and singing, and to tune and repair organs and pianofortes; their contact was Graupner's music store on Franklin Street.[44]

Balloonists

The most arresting of the outside entertainments were balloon launches, which, like fireworks, were performed with the accompaniment of musical "bands" and elaborate costuming. About fifty individuals were engaged in this activity in America before 1826. Initially the leaders of American ballooning were private citizens in Maryland, South Carolina, and Georgia who learned—apparently from published accounts—European hot-air balloon technology and attempted trial flights in the early months of 1784. Peter Carnes, a tavern keeper from Bladensburg, Maryland, found he was too heavy and instead put his thirteen-year-old assistant on board. (The balloon rose ten feet before the young occupant fell.) Carnes tried again in Philadelphia, with uncertain results.[45] In the meantime, European mechanics, principally French- and Englishmen, soon came to dominate the field by virtue of their financial backers and specialized training not yet available to North Americans. Charles Busselot, a young French officer who had served in the guard of Louis XVI and was introduced into Philadelphia and New York City society by the Marquis de Lafayette, staged in 1784 and 1785 demonstrations of hot-air balloons—the first attempted in the United States. Because his expenses were considerable, Busselot was obliged to collect advance payments from spectators, but—given the universal visibility of an ascending balloon—he was always in a poor position to do so. His balloons were small (twenty-four feet high, fifty-five feet in circumference), and they were not without danger. His first effort struck a nearby prison wall as it rose, and when about one mile high the balloon disintegrated and released a lighted woodstove above the city. After two attempts, Busselot did not try again, remaining in Philadelphia as a fencing teacher and showman. He later married Catharine Durang, the older sister of stage and pantomime dancer John Durang, and helped Durang make puppets and "grandes ombres Chinoises" in Philadelphia and New York.[46]

Other European balloonists recognized considerable potential in North America and struggled to overcome Busselot's problems. Joseph Deeker, a professional aeronaut and mechanic from Bristol and London who had recently flown forty miles in an English ascent, used a succession of illustrated handbills and advertisements to find supporters in New York City. Deeker sold subscriptions for two twelve-foot balloons in the summer of 1789 in an attempt to underwrite a larger balloon one hundred feet in circumference designed to carry a manned flight. Both smaller launches were successful. Deeker further helped meet costs by selling tickets to examine the larger balloon before its ascent and to view an acoustic exhibition installed in his rooms at 14 William Street. One of Deeker's visitors was Reverend Ezra Stiles, who absented himself from his responsibilities as president of Yale College to see "the Balloon thirty feet Diam. at Mr. Deckers." The following afternoon, Stiles was one of "Ten or 12 Thous[an]d Spectators in the Fields No[rth] of the City" (an estimated two-thirds of the population of New York City) who had come to watch the takeoff. Only those who had purchased subscriptions were permitted to observe its inflation. Finally, at four o'clock, Deeker tried to make his ascent. Stiles reported that the balloon immediately "collapsed after inflation & took fire on the ground." This failure ended Deeker's efforts in New York but not before he had dipped "into the purses of the generous and disappointed spectators."[47]

The stage was now set for serious launchings. The first manned balloon flight in North America was performed in 1793 in Philadelphia by Jean-Pierre Blanchard, the French inventor and mechanic who had previously ascended forty-four times in the principal capitals of Europe. (He was forced to flee with his family to the United States after he was accused of spreading revolutionary propaganda.) Blanchard advanced balloon technology to a new level in North America, using chemically generated hydrogen gas instead of the usual hot air. He reached Philadelphia with 4,100 pounds of acid, enough for one inflation.

A band playing a "slow movement" marked the balloon's inflation. When it was ready, Blanchard, dressed in a plain blue suit and wearing a cocked hat with white feathers, stepped into his "boat" (painted "blue and spangled") and gave the signal. He ascended without incident on 9 January 1793, waving American and French flags, and landed forty-six minutes later near Woodbury, New Jersey. Blanchard published an account of his triumphal flight and later visited several southern cities including Baltimore and Charleston, each time trying to accumulate enough subscriptions for what he hoped would be his forty-sixth ascension. To cover daily expenses he and his partners raised small- and medium-sized hot-air balloons, but sufficient subscriptions for another manned attempt never materialized.[48]

Blanchard subsequently headed to New England, and in 1795, he leased a barn and workshop on Greene's Lane, located in the undeveloped west end of Boston. Here he began work on a balloon of the same dimensions (requiring one thousand French ells of silk) that had carried Dr. John Jeffries and Blanchard from Dover to Calais. Subscriptions again were slow in coming. Although spectators were willing to pay a small admission price to see him work on the half-completed balloon, Boston residents expected to witness the flight itself gratis. A standoff ensued between the promoter and potential subscribers that dragged on for months. While waiting, Blanchard kept busy at his Greene's Lane workshop building the "Wonderful Woman." In the end Blanchard once more had to abandon his plans, and he settled for a less expensive "aerostatical experiment" based on the Montgolfier principle (hot air) during which several live animals were dropped from a balloon by parachute (fig. 7.8). After a final aerial exhibition on 20 November 1795, Blanchard moved on to Salem and later to Providence, Portsmouth, and Portland, hoping to find the generosity he had failed to garner in Boston. But the result was the same.[49]

Amid widespread recriminations by promoters that Americans were willing to watch but not pay for manned ascensions, flights of large-scale balloons were replaced by smaller and even indoor ones, many of them fabricated by stage mechanics and scene painters associated with theater companies. A Mr. Duval, "a gentleman from France" traveling through New Haven in 1811, raised a balloon at John Mix's Columbian Gardens carrying a live cat, which parachuted from three or four hundred feet (fig. 7.9). Actor James West, who toured with Joseph Harper's company in Providence in 1803, posted a subscription at fifty cents per spectator; purchasers could bring one lady and their children for free. Actor Andrew Allen of the Boston Theatre released three balloons on Boston Common "near the Gun-House." They were said to be "embellished with the Portraits of the immortal Washington, Warren, &c," executed by scenery painters; for his balloon launching in Providence in November 1809, Allen hired the theater band to play a sendoff.[50]

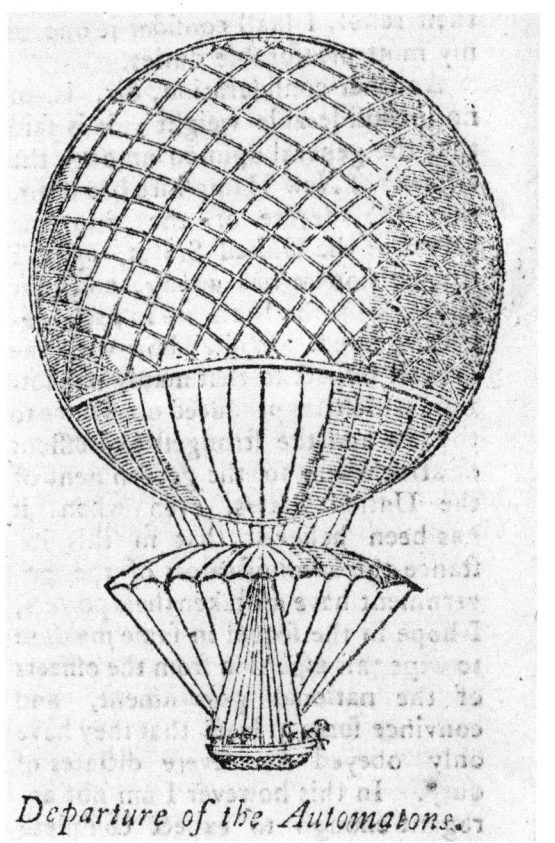 

Figure 7.8. "*Departure of the Automatons. Mademoiselle Moderate, Mr. Aristocrat and The citizen Democrat.*" While waiting to raise money for another flight, French inventor and mechanic Jean-Pierre Blanchard (1753–1809) designed and created automatons while also building smaller balloons that raised dogs (looking to the right) and other small animals and then released them with a parachute. Blanchard advanced balloon technology in America using chemically generated hydrogen gas instead of hot air. *New-Hampshire Gazette,* 6 February 1796. Courtesy, American Antiquarian Society.

Figure 7.9. "[A] BALLOON . . . of More than 100 Feet in circumference, will be raised in Mr. Mix's Columbian Gardens on the 12th Day of September Next, the day after Commencement." Advertisement taken by the Frenchman Mr. Duval in New Haven, Connecticut. Duval intended to release an attached small "boat" carrying a live cat with a parachute from a height of three or four hundred feet. Woodcut. *Connecticut Journal,* 5 September 1811. Courtesy, American Antiquarian Society.

Outdoor Audiences

Who made up the crowds watching outdoor entertainment? Diaries establish that just about everyone went to see wild animals, many on multiple occasions. Nathaniel Ames, for example, returned for a second look at the Crowninshield elephant, which stopped in his town in 1797:

> 15 [July 1797] View'd a female Elephant 4 years old, larger than an Ox at Gay's Stable in Dedham

17 [July 1797] resort to see the Elephant, who goes at Night to Cambridge.⁵¹

Some handlers aimed their notices at attracting young people. A Mr. Cressin took his "Little African Theatre" from New York City to Elizabethtown, New Jersey, to Newburyport, Massachusetts, claiming that "children that see this performance will ever remember Coco and Gibonne"—the two trained monkeys (fig. 7.10) that walked a tightrope, operated a printing press, and jumped over a "pyramid of fire."⁵² Another of Cressin's broadsides (fig. 7.11) was aimed at guests "with their families." But political figures and the privileged were intrigued as well. One of the first identified visitors of the Crowninshield elephant was George Washington, whose account book indicates a payment "for [him] to see [the] Elephant" in 1796.⁵³ Thirty-year-old Margaret Holyoke related that she "Saw the [Crowninshield] Elephant" on 20 July 1797 after the animal had left Cambridge and gone on to Salem.⁵⁴ Reverend William Bentley, who glimpsed this elephant ten days later at the Market House, complained that the event was

Figure 7.10. "INNOCENT *AMUSEMENT. Mr. Cressin,* Natural Philosopher . . . proposes to commence his Exhibitions." The image shows Coco, Mr. Cressin's trained monkey, on the tightrope with a balancing pole. This advertisement, sometimes titled "Little African Theatre," appeared in Newburyport, Massachusetts, in 1797, one of many aimed at attracting parents and their children. Newburyport *Impartial Herald,* 10 March 1797. Courtesy, American Antiquarian Society.

Figure 7.11. "INNOCENT AMUSEMENT. Mr. CRESSIN." Broadside for an exhibition of Coco and other trained monkeys by Mr. Cressin at the store of Joseph Davis, Newburyport, Massachusetts. Advertised tricks include riding a dog (center), sleeping and flag-waving on the tightrope (left panels), and sword play and balancing acts (right panels). Newburyport, March 1797. Courtesy, New York Public Library.

so well attended that the "crowd of spectators forbad me any but a general & superficial view."[55] Neither Holyoke nor Bentley, however, made any mention of "William," the attendant who took care of the elephant during her New England tour in 1797 and ensuing trip to the middle and southern states. The attendant apparently had so much leeway in handling the animal that her owner issued a warning in Providence in July 1797: "The public are hereby cautioned against trusting William, the black Man attending the Elephant, as the Proprietor will not pay any debt of his contracting."[56]

Years later both Salem diarists viewed Old Bett when she stayed in Salem in 1816. This time Bentley went early in the morning so that he could examine her "without any of the tricks . . . [she] has been taught to play." Although he perceived "nothing pleasing in the form," he was impressed by the animal's "surprising volume."[57] In 1821, Abner Sanger saw an elephant in Keene, New Hampshire, where it was stabled for two days. He noted the price of admission—"9 [shillings] per sight for grown persons."[58]

Other diarists and their families visited animals. Reverend Ebenezer Parkman saw a captive jackal in Westborough, Massachusetts, in 1750; Parkman was entranced, calling it an "Entertaining sight." The next day he returned with his wife to look at "him and his pranks," but "so many resort there to see this Strange Creature that I am doubtful what the Event will be."[59] Reverend John Ballantine observed a "She Lyon," very likely a catamount, at "Landlord Fowler's" in Westfield, Massachusetts, in 1764.[60] Margaret Holyoke noted that she went with "Papa and Mama to see a Cat of Mount," part of Mr. Harrington's acrobatic and lantern tour of eastern Massachusetts in 1793.[61] Clearly animals were a great favorite, though not everyone was impressed. Alice Tucker (1751–1808) of Newbury, Massachusetts, who kept her own diary, related in 1790 that "Just after dinner a Traveler call'd to show us a Porcupine—All the family assembled in the kitchen to look at it, but we were not at all pleased with its appearance, it is an ill formed stupid looking creature."[62]

Trained animal acts and feats of horsemanship also found audiences because American editors filled their newspapers with gossipy information about English riders and trainers. Three years before John Sharp and Mr. Faulks began their careers as "high-rider[s]" in 1771, the *New-York Gazette* reprinted "as a curiosity" an advertisement taken from an English paper in 1768 of an exhibition at the Southwark Fair by a Mr. Wolton, describing in some detail ten of Wolton's rides and training exercises.[63] Much the same happened when Gabriel Salenka and William Pinchbeck started showing their trained dogs and pigs. In their case it was the announced death of Samuel Bisset in Chester, England (reported in New Hampshire, Massachusetts, and South Carolina papers in 1785), which alluded to Bisset's ability to get cats to play the dulcimer. This was followed by a flurry of articles on several trained pigs circulating in England and Ireland and the growing popularity of a comic song sung in theaters called "The Learned Pig."[64] A decade later, when Salenka and Pinchbeck advertised their first shows in Philadelphia in 1796 and 1797, they had a ready audience waiting for them.[65]

Most people watched the tumblers, rope flyers, and high-wire walkers, and servants and children in particular seemingly imitated them. A want advertisement in the Pennsylvania papers in 1740 describes a runaway named James Cosway as being "bare-footed, and can play several Tumbler's Tricks."[66] Another runaway, Ebenezer Woodbury, was termed in 1797 "a native of Greenland, near Portsmouth, New-Hampshire . . . a juggler by profession, is fond of entertaining people by swallowing live cats and sharp knives and forks."[67] Tricks like John Childs's flying acts were remembered not only in the families of Hannah Andrews Breck and David McLure but were common enough to irritate William Bentley, who considered these exploits a bad example. During the spring and summer of 1792 when theater companies were touring Boston and Salem, Bentley feared that the recent arrival of actors and actresses in town would by their example inevitably take a similar toll on Salem's youth: "The fact puts in mind of the effect from the Rope flyers, who visited N. England, after whose feats the children of seven were sliding down the fences & wounding themselves in every quarter." Eighteen years later Bentley again recalled the practice: "This day we had rope flying across the road entering Salem & in the evening we had Recitations from the servants of the theater."[68]

And people from all walks of life also watched balloon launchings, not only those by professional aeronauts but those by amateurs as well. On the way to South Carolina in May 1785, Noah Webster went through New Haven and saw "a Balloon ascend—ingenuity of Mr Meigs. It rises several Hundred feet."[69] This was likely Josiah Meigs, New Haven's city clerk, who had just joined proprietors Daniel Bowen and Eleutheros Dana as printers of the *New Haven Gazette.* When Webster returned to Hartford in 1790, he observed another: "Balloon ascends, takes fire & falls."[70] The William Pynchon family of Salem followed balloon ascensions closely. "I have a letter from R. Lechmere, Taunton [England]," Pynchon wrote in his diary in 1785, telling of "the balloon news from Blanchard and Jeffries tour from Dover to Calais."[71] Their neighbors, the Holyoke family, witnessed balloon flights in 1784 and 1790—Margaret Holyoke stated "went to see the Balloon" on 22 November 1790.[72] William Bentley apparently chose not to attend this launching, but his diary entry for that day provides additional details: "A Baloon Driver, Wire dancer, & Legerdemain Irishman and wife are to exhibit this day at 1/6, & /9 for children. The Baloon passed overhead at three o'clock towards the Harbour into which it dropped."[73] Bentley also reported on Blanchard's 1795 animal launching in Salem: "The Balloon ascended & continued at the same height for a long time . . . the Parachute with the animals fell while it was at its greatest height just beginning to fall." A forty-year-old carpenter named Thomas B. Hazard, then visiting Newport, watched a Blanchard animal launch on 19 May 1796: "Blanchard Rose A Abbeloon [balloon] with aCat and Dogg at 10 O.Clock this morning. I saw it Rice."[74]

Thomas Hazard's easy access to this event explains why fireworks and balloon professionals seemed more concerned about excluding non-paying spectators than guaranteeing public safety. Many outdoor spectators tried to avoid admission costs by climbing on rooftops, poking holes through surrounding fences, or watching from afar. Laurent Spinacuta staged his last fireworks in Charleston from a location "in the College Yard."[75] Peter Carnes addressed the problem by releasing his balloon from the "New Workhouse Yard" in Philadelphia; Busselot, from the city's public jail yard; Blanchard, from the courtyard of the city's Walnut Street Prison.[76] But curious crowds were always trying to get a free show. In Boston in 1796, a group of onlookers who had climbed onto the roof of Philip Lailson's equestrian amphitheater caused a sensation when the structure collapsed and injured spectators below them. When this happened again to Lailson in Philadelphia, a Boston paper commented, "Experience is lost upon him."[77] John Durang, who traveled with John Ricketts to Canada in 1797, said of Albany crowds that "there were about twice the number of people out side of the building [as inside] some boring holes thro' the boards to get a peep."[78]

Warnings from town officials also speak to the nature of outdoor crowds. When Boston's selectmen denied a petition to allow John Bradley's ropedancing in 1734, they feared that "the said Divertisement may tend to promote Idleness in the Town, and great Mispence of time"—an indication that large numbers of Boston's servants and working people were prepared to drop everything and watch. In 1757, John Childs's acrobatic feats persuaded the selectmen that they "led many People from their Business," and he was forbidden from "flying any more in the Town." Later, when acrobat Victorani was ropewalking from building to building in Newburyport, Sarah Smith Emery complained that his act worked "to the detriment of many more, who were called from their avocations to see this mountebank's tricks." After Newburyport's selectmen prohibited him from undertaking further attempts, Victorani left without paying his bills.[79]

Horseracing may have attracted some fringe elements as well as middle- and upper-class audiences. One runaway in Pennsylvania named Richard Gamble was described in 1745 as an English servant aged twenty-six who was "mostly us'd to Horse-Racing . . . and can play many Tricks in Legerdemain, or Hocus Pocus."[80] Sometimes a discerning level of appreciation was seen in spectators who knew something about equestrian sports—perhaps having spent time in England or Europe. English-born merchant John Rowe was impressed in 1771 when he saw a trick rider from England performing in Boston: "After dinner we went over to Bracket's and see a Yorkshire man stand upon a horse's back and gallop him full speed, afterwards upon two horses, and after that on three; he endeavored to make all them gallop as fast as he could; then he mounted a single horse and run him full speed, and while running he jumped off and on three several times."[81] Rowe also admired stunt rider Jacob Bates. He reported in 1773 that a "great many People attended him," observing that Bates was "a smart active & strong man, & does every thing to General Acceptance." Nathaniel Ames praised Bates too and made a special trip from Dedham to Boston on the same day in 1773 to see him.[82]

But trick riders and wirewalkers also fueled old prejudices and animosities. One citizen in Boston was so provoked by Bates that he privately published a pamphlet titled *Mr. Bates and His Horses Weighed in the Balance*—sold in Boston on 5 October 1773—which argues Bates's exhibitions were "impoverishing, disgraceful to human nature, and downright Breaches of the 6th commandment."[83] At least one contemporary newspaper reader agreed. After watching Jacob Bates ride in Newport, this critic added his own handwritten assessment of Bates's advertisement in the *Newport Mercury*. To Bates's list of emperors and kings who had previously seen him perform, he penned, "and the Devil"—stating that Bates had a received a certificate of acceptance "from the High Court of Pandemonium."[84]

Some acts of vandalism against itinerants appeared to have been gratuitous and not ideologically motivated. After noting that his equestrian company had been prompt to donate relief to the victims of fire at Cape François and the poor of the city of Charleston, John B. Ricketts bitterly complained about audience misconduct in Boston in 1796 when he charged that "on several Exhibitions Evening[s] his Amphitheater has been violently attacked by Boys, and he is sorry to say, even *Men,* who have materially injured a building, considerably expensive in its erection, and no ways immoral in it use."[85]

Ricketts returned to this theme after his amphitheater was burned down in Philadelphia in 1799: "Whereas it has been intimated to mr. Ricketts that from the circumstance of the part of the roof that was first observed by the spectators in the street, that it is extremely probable the act was perpetrated by some incendiary on the outside of said roof, the access to which was not difficult." Rickets offered a one thousand dollar reward for the person or persons who committed this crime.[86]

Latent hostility at these events seems to have been a fact of life. John Templeman assured the Philadelphia public in 1780 that his balancing act would be well illuminated and the audience entertained with good music. He also informed them that his exhibition "will likewise be guarded inside and outside."[87] Felix Fissour advised New York City spectators that "there were [so] many squibs thrown at the last fire works, to the great fright of the Ladies, Constables will be placed there to prevent it." Fissour had to repeat this reassurance at least once.[88] In some instances audiences took their revenge on failed performers. In 1819, a Philadelphia mob pelted stones at a Monsieur Michel, a partner of Louis Guille, because his planned ascent proved slower than anticipated. When a guard hired to protect the balloon injured a boy trying to get a better look, the crowd flew into a rage, tore apart the balloon, stole Michel's money, and burned the pavilion where the event was taking place. Four arrests were made.[89]

Rise of Entertainment Groups

Over time, most outdoor entertainers and showmen began to gather into cohesive units. Except for one or two "educated" bears or dromedaries, animal acts generally coalesced into traveling menageries organized by museum proprietors and animal handlers to increase their profit. These groups were financed by investors and governed by timetables and commitments. Gardiner Baker in New York, a colleague of Daniel Bowen, was the first to offer in 1794 a "Menage of Living Animals, and Birds," consisting of a Kentucky panther, a wildcat from Virginia, and rattlesnakes. Bowen in Boston promptly followed with his. Before long, menagerie showmen added exotic species such as large cats and elephants and began to travel with as many as forty or more animals at one time. The "Museum of Living Animals" and "Grand Caravan of Living Animals" toured New York and Connecticut in the period from 1815 through the 1820s. These caravans were composed of monkeys, tigers, Asiatic and red lions, and a host of "minor" animals, many of them sporting popular names: "Saucy Jack," "Dandy Jack," "Tippoo Sultan," or "Nero."[90] In some instances simians were gaily costumed and were taught to ride the other animals (fig. 7.12).

Figure 7.12. "A Caravan of LIVING ANIMALS." Dandy Jack, in costume, riding the spotted llama from the coast of Peru. Detail of an advertisement for a procession of animals, consisting of an African lion, a llama, a "Mammoth" ox, two large bears, a baboon, and an ichneumon, that passed through Salem, Massachusetts, and other New England towns in 1824. *Salem Gazette,* 24 February 1824. Courtesy, American Antiquarian Society.

Individual tumblers, ropedancers, and wirewalkers in turn coalesced into acrobatic theaters. Performers like Joseph Curtis, José Vilallave, and Monsieur Godeau—frequently accompanied by spouses and using their own sons and daughters as assistants—learned they were more theatrically acceptable as "families" or "companies" than they were as solo players. Mr. and Mrs. Manfredi and their daughters, Louisa and Catherina, entertained with "ground" tumbling in Charleston, New York City, Philadelphia, and Washington. Mr. Van Antwarp and company performed "lofty" tumbling in Alexandria. Mr. Dumoulain's company presented slack-rope and tightrope balancing at the theater in Philadelphia's Northern-Liberties.[91]

Finally, equestrian shows and trick riders merged with other outdoor exhibitions and performed in newly constructed open-air amphitheaters. John Partridge, who built a riding rink in Charleston for his horsemanship events in April 1786, included a "Drunken Sailor with a Song" to his repertory as well as backward "Riding Taylor" and a "Gentleman from Dublin who will dance a Hornpipe." He also engaged tightrope artist Signor Plasidora. This meant he added a musical band and drums. With the doors opening at 3:30 p.m. and the performance beginning at 4:00, most of the horsemanship and tumbling was performed before sunset; as the show progressed into the evening, however, he must have lighted torches and flares.[92]

But it was probably John Bill Ricketts (fig. 7.13) who was the first to combine horsemanship, pantomimes, music, fireworks, balloons, and acrobatics all under one roof and on one program. A former pupil of equestrian entertainer Philip Astley in England, John Ricketts went north to join the Edinburgh Equestrian Circus where he worked under George Jones and slack-wire performers such as Laurent Spinacuta, Matthew Sully, and Master MacDonald who later joined him in America. Ricketts began his American career in 1792 when he formed a riding school in Philadelphia. His first performance consisted of "equestrian exercises" with a group that included "Master Ricketts" (presumed to be his younger brother Francis) and Spinacuta. After 1793 the company went on the road, bringing the "Equestrian Pantheon" to New York City, Boston, Hartford, and Providence. When John Ricketts returned to Philadelphia and New York City in 1795, he leased an oval raceway, one end of which was enclosed by a roof and furnished with elevated seats and raised galleries. In August 1796, Ricketts played twelve nights at a large new enclosed amphitheater at the base of Beacon Hill. With Francis Ricketts and himself as the principal riders and Mr. and Mrs. Laurent Spinacuta on the tightrope, he assembled an evening of entertainments along with Sully and one "Master Hutchins" that featured a "Grand Moresque or Cannibal Dance," pony races, flag dances, a peasants' frolic, aerial tumbling, and Francis Ricketts riding "on his head." The entertainments concluded with an

"Epilogue" during which Sully, in the character of Harlequin, took a "flying leap thro' a Balloon, surrounded by Fire Works."⁹³

After profitable seasons in 1797 and 1798 in the eastern United States (fig. 7.14) and Canada, the Ricketts clan suffered disastrous fires at amphitheaters in New York City and Philadelphia. The next year Francis Ricketts was captured by pirates, and John Ricketts himself was lost at sea on his return to England.⁹⁴ But the family had left a legacy. Traveling equestrian exhibitions, trick riding, acrobatic feats, and pantomime theater were now being actively toured by Philip Lailson, a Mr. Langley, a Signor Francisquy, and Mr. Manfredi; within a decade they were joined by many others who

Figure 7.13. *John Bill Ricketts* (c. 1767–1800), by Gilbert Stuart (1755–1828). Portrait known at one time as *Breschard, the Circus Rider*. The artist probably lived in New York City when Ricketts and his circus performed there in August 1793. The painting remained with his brother Francis Ricketts and was later owned by George Francis Riggs. Oil on canvas. Overall: 29⅜ by 24³⁄₁₆ inches. Circa 1793 to 1795. Courtesy, National Gallery of Art, Washington, D.C. Gift of Mrs. Robert B. Noyes in memory of Elisha Riggs. 1942.14.1.

Figure 7.14. "Ricketts's Circus, Lower End of Greene-Street. On Friday, August the 4th, 1797, A Great Variety of EQUESTRIAN EXERCISES, *By Mr. RICKETTS and his COMPANY*." John Bill Ricketts was probably the first to combine horsemanship, pantomimes, music, fireworks, balloons, and acrobatics in one program. Illustrated broadside. Albany, New York, 1797. Courtesy, Harvard Theatre Collection, 002302677, Houghton Library, Harvard University.

were inspired by Ricketts's success. With these shows a new term emerged in American usage. As Margaret Holyoke wrote in her Salem diary on 22 August 1796, "We were at Lilson's [Lailson's] Circus."[95] An element of popular culture had finally left the anonymity of the street and blossomed as a recognized entertainment.

Chapter 8
Tavern Entertainers I: Magic Lanternists

LONG BEFORE riding circuses and their amphitheaters had begun to animate daily life in North America in the 1790s, other elements of European popular culture had begun to infiltrate neighborhood taverns and, in some instances, literally take them over. Inns and taverns were not simply places to have a meal, consume spirituous drinks, or read newspapers. They provided ready settings for sales of property and slaves, auctions of estates, social levees and dancing parties, and meeting places for fraternities—all these typically situated in a tavern's long room or an adjoining barn or stable. Among the entertainers working in taverns were lantern performers, ropedancers, sleight-of-hand artists, puppeteers, stage singers, fencing-masters, peddlers, profile-takers, penmanship and drawing teachers, translators, and language teachers. Musical events were sometimes held in taverns, such as the "Ode on Masonry," which was performed by instrumentalists and vocalists at the New Exchange in New York City in 1755.[1] In 1801, at a public house in Exeter, New Hampshire, diarist William Bentley ran across a miniature painter named Mr. [Nathaniel] Hancock, who normally worked from his studios in Boston and Salem.[2] And in a Reading, Massachusetts, tavern in 1813, Bentley encountered a "Sweating Doctor" celebrated for his healing skills.[3] Scores of taverns between Savannah and Montreal accommodated waxwork museums such as those prepared by Daniel Bowen and Reuben Moulthrop. Many taverns hosted electrical experimenters; others supplied sites for proprietors to demonstrate small-scale models of famous cities like Jerusalem or Malaga, Spain; fortresses such as the Bastille or St. Helena; or a Caribbean sugar plantation. Tavern patrons never knew what to expect next.

The richness of eighteenth-century tavern life is captured in two entries in the journal of inn holder Samuel Adams of Ipswich, Massachusetts. Adams, who had only lately acquired ownership of his inn, found he had inherited a local reputation for attracting entertainers, and he obligingly documented them. On 4 December 1793 Adams wrote of a visit by a London performer named Mr. Harrington (fig. 8.1), who traveled about New England with a small troupe and a panther recently caught in New Hampshire: "Many people Came to see the

Figure 8.1. "Mr. HARRINGTON, the slack-wire walker," conducted scores of lantern shows as he traveled in North America between 1793 and 1802, many of them featuring animals with "moving" eyes and scenes of Noah's Ark. From William Pinchbeck, *Witchcraft; or, The Art of Fortune-Telling Unveiled*. Boston: Privately printed, 1805. Courtesy, American Antiquarian Society.

Catamount &c—and in the evening, our Hall was crowded with people to see Mr. Neventon [Harrington] perform many feats of activity such as walking &c on the Slack wire & Slack rope—Balancing swords (illeg.) together with many representations of Animals with the Magic Lanthern &c." Two weeks later so many spectators turned up Adams had to relocate them outside: "Neventon & wife Mr. Todd performed in the evening in my Barn for want of a Suitable room any where else—the Italian shades—Shewed the Magic lanthern—performed on the sheet. . . . had about 100 spectators." The following year other strollers stopped by. "Some Puppet Show man dined here & would have tarried and gave me a taste of their office if I would have kept them for about nothing." This time Dr. Adams declined and the showmen moved on.[4]

But because tavern space was always limited, many of these diversions required some form of miniaturization or compartmentalization. Actors, singers, dancers, and conjurers toured in small groups that involved a minimum number of musicians and instrumentalists. Stanchions for holding slack ropes were made low enough so that dancers would not hit their heads on the ceiling. Theatrical "olios" replaced full plays, and a dulcimer and flute player substituted for an orchestra. And, as always, actors and show people whose multifarious talents were put to the test rose to the occasion. For example, Richard Brickell seems to have had his hand in virtually all tavern entertainments from sleight of hand to waxworks to puppetry as he moved from Philadelphia to New York City and Charleston, revealing himself as one of the first multitalented entertainers active in early America. Besides giving lantern and Punch puppet shows, he toured a musical clock, played a dulcimer and violin, gave (or sponsored) legerdemain and posture exhibitions, delivered lectures and demonstrations on electricity and multiple-firing military ordnance, and exhibited views of buildings and gardens in England, Scotland, France, and Italy.[5] Because he (and others) told and retold the same stories through different mediums, it is sometimes impossible to ascertain today whether Brickell's audiences were looking at "optic tragedies" (lantern slides), "artificial figures" (puppet shows), "Chinese shades" (shadow puppets), or mechanical automatons.[6] Much the same was true of many other eighteenth-century entertainers.

At the heart of this miniaturizing process was a European optical machine—the so-called magic lantern—a portable device that projected life-size or larger transparent "representations" against the wall of a darkened room. The magic lantern was optically similar to the solar microscope, but instead of using the sun's reflection, the magic lantern produced its own light. Both devices required a darkened room, the "camera" where the audience sat and in which the image was projected.[7] Initially brought to America by itinerant showmen in the 1740s, the magic lantern was central to the rise of the tavern as a place of entertainment because it created a crowd-pleasing and carnivalesque atmosphere while being small enough to carry. Virtually every performer, acrobat, ropedancer, or conjurer who pursued a career in North America ended his or her act with a vivid and colorful display of English and European folklore, tavern humor, bawdy songs, tragic ballads, or even images of the creation of the world—bringing an unending source of popular culture to hungry audiences. Almost simultaneously, however, itinerant lecturers and opticians began to use lantern images to present more serious subjects such as battlefield history, maritime engagements, and foreign costumes and customs, as well as to illustrate academic talks on geography and astronomy—often in the same long room used by entertainers. While these applications do not always fit into easily defined cultural categories, they were nevertheless as important as printing and print-making in the rapid rise of an American consciousness during the eighteenth century. From the viewpoint of popular culture, these machines probably represented the single greatest technological advance that differentiated everyday life of mid-eighteenth-century residents from the generations that preceded them.

The North American story of this machine began in December 1742 when two Philadelphia tavern proprietors almost simultaneously hosted a London-based entertainer at their establishments. The first, who operated the Coach-and-Horses Tavern on Chestnut Street near the Statehouse, featured a strolling puppeteer performing comedies and tragedies "by changeable Figures of two Feet high." He ended his show with a lantern entertainment titled "A Sight of Sea and Ships" followed by a "merry Dialogue between Punch and *Joan* his Wife." Front-row seats cost two shillings, middle seats eighteen pence, and back seats six pence. About a month later, when a nearby competitor moved to a new place of business on Second Street, he apparently hired the same entertainer (or entertainers) hoping to attract new customers, as well as to keep his old ones. This time the anonymous showman promised to use the "Magick Lanthorn" every evening to display "upwards of 30 humorous and curious Figures, Larger than Life" and described the device as one "by which Friar Bacon, and other famous men performed such wonderful curiosities, as made the ignorant believe it was done by magic, conjuration, or witchcraft"—a favorite theme by which strolling entertainers attracted their audiences. The show continued for three hours, from six to nine in the evening. The proprietor charged each spectator six pence.[8] Scheduling events seems to have been difficult, and one group was obliged to reduce the number of times they played. While unidentified, these performers were most likely Richard Brickell and Richard Mosely, who posted notices with similar wording in Philadelphia and New York City in 1743, 1746, and 1747.[9]

These two events taking place within walking distance in the same Philadelphia neighborhood may have been the first time in colonial America that image-based theatrical amusements were publicized in the newspapers. By the end of the year, however, other competitors using lantern technology had entered the colonies. On 12 December 1743, John Dabney, a London-trained mathematical instrument maker, opened in Boston what he called an "Entertainment of the Curious, the Magic Lanthorn, an Optick Machine, which exhibits a great Number of wonderful and surprising Figures, prodigious large, and vivid."[10] On the very next night, and most likely in conjunction with Dabney, the London optician Edmund Rising unveiled a "Camera Obscura"—his own term for a magic lantern—to illustrate scenes from a recent European battle. This was the same Edmund Rising of London who had had come to Boston to set up a solar microscope to project a live image of a common louse, pointing out "the pulse of the Heart, [and] the moving of the bowels, the veins and arteries." Rising's price was much higher: five shillings per person, or more than ten times the price charged by Joseph Barber.[11]

By juxtaposing these two basic uses of this machine—Brickell's and Mosely's as entertainers and Rising's as a formal lecturer—we can view the process by which an itinerant-carried tavern entertainment was transformed into a communications icon a hundred years later. Crude as they were, magic lanterns were capable of projecting large and small objects with a certain amount of clarity and shifting rapidly between one scene and another. The manufacture of the small, hand-painted "glasses," which the lanterns projected on a screen or darkened wall, drew on the expertise of post-Renaissance miniature transparency painting, much of it the work of Italian artists.[12] To provide illumination, magic lanterns burned whale oil; they are often shown in period illustrations with smoke coming out of a small chimney mounted at the top of the apparatus. A conventional fixture in European popular entertainments from the late seventeenth to the early nineteenth century, these projectors were typically carried around by show people who sometimes employed a barrel organ or monkey to attract attention (fig. 8.2).

Perfected in Europe in the hundred years between the mid-seventeenth and mid-eighteenth centuries, this invention was still poorly understood by Americans in the 1740s. "Friar Bacon," cited by the anonymous showman in his 1742 advertisement, was Roger Bacon (ca. 1214–1292), an English Franciscan and student of optics who was widely said to have invented the magic lantern in the year 1252—allegedly to amuse his young Oxford students.[13] The veracity of this story, however, has always been questioned. More recently, the invention has been credited to Christiaan Huygens (1629–1695), a seventeenth-century Dutch astronomer and mathematician; to Thomas Walgenstein (1622–1701), a Danish mathematician; and to Athanasius Kircher (1602–1680), a German Jesuit priest who published several noted images of magic lanterns (fig. 8.3).[14] We know from Samuel Pepys's diary that a London telescope maker named Richard Reeves was selling these devices in the 1660s. Samuel Pepys invited Reeves to his house in August 1666 to deliver one.[15]

Most period descriptions of magic-lantern entertainments are brief. In Boston Dabney promised "a great Number of wonderfull and surprising Figures, prodigious large, and vivid." Presumably he had purchased sets of slides created by "Italian" artists that were available in European cities. We learn a little more from Brickell's advertisements in the 1740s in Philadelphia and New York City that appealed to "curious" adults and children. According to Brickell, his "30 humorous and entertaining Figures" were "larger than Men or Women," and involved scenes "such as the Rising Sun, the Friendly Travellers, the Pot Companions, the blind Beggar of Gednal Green and his Boy, the meery Piper dancing a Jigg, to his own dumb Music, the courageous Fencing Master, the Italian Mountebank, or

Figure 8.2. *Lorgue de Barbarie.* Eighteenth-century French street musician carrying a magic lantern and hand organ to attract attention. Etching with some engraving by Anne Claude Philippe de Tubières, comte de Caylus (1692–1765), after Edmé Bouchardon (1698–1762). Originally published in *Études prises dans le bas peuple; ou, Les cris de Paris.* Paris: Fessard, 1737. Illustration from George Hirth, *Kulturgeschichtliches Bilderbuch aus drei Jahrhunderten.* Leipzig: Privately printed, 1881–1890. Courtesy, Picture Collection, New York Public Library, Astor, Lenox and Tilden Foundations.

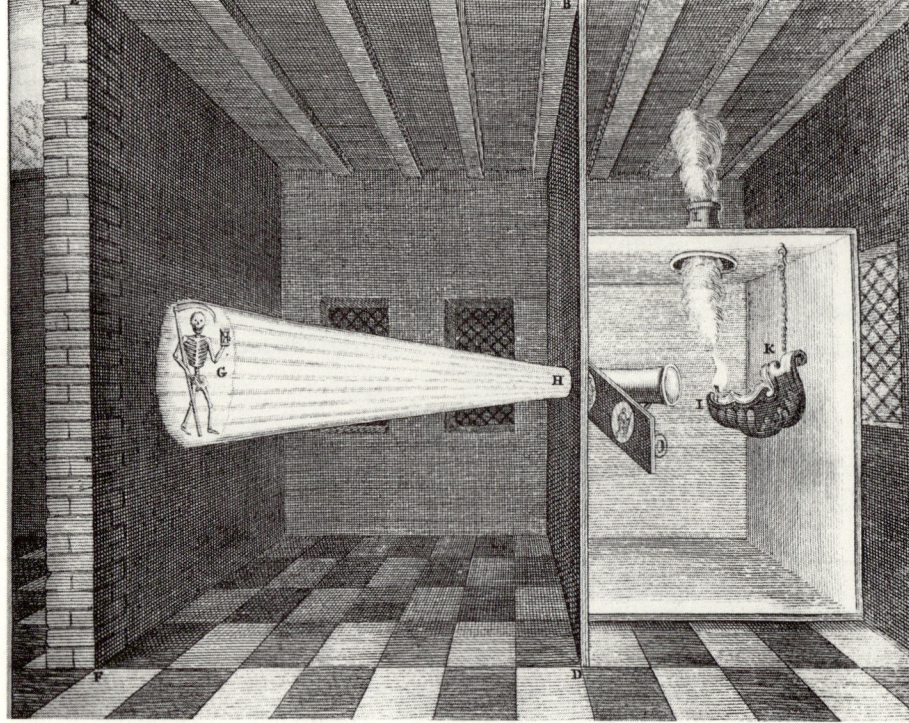

Figure 8.3. Athanasius Kircher's illustration of the magic lantern. A German priest, Kircher (1602–1680) is one of several people credited with inventing the magic lantern. This may be one of the earliest depictions of it. From *Ars Magna Lucis et Umbrae*. Amsterdam: Janssonium à Waesberge, 1671. Courtesy, Houghton Library, Harvard University, f GC6 K6323 645ab (A).

famous infallible Quack, the Man riding on a Pig, with his Face toward the Tail, the Dutchman scating on the Ice in the midst of Summer, with a great Variety of other Figures, equally diverting and curious, too tedious here to mention."[16]

Each one of these stories was part of a popular litany of mid-eighteenth-century character sketches. Some, like the "Italian Mountebank" and the "blind beggar of Gednal [Bednal] Green," came from centuries-old children's literature, handed down through English, Italian, and German storytellers, as well as through ballads, chapbooks, and living memory. Others entailed carnival or sporting characters, such as a man riding on a pig facing its tail and the skating Dutchman in "the midst of Summer"—meaning he was enjoying his sport in July or August through the "magic" of the lantern.[17]

Early lantern shows were often accompanied by instrumental music and music machines. Brickell, for example, offered New York City and Charleston audiences the "best pieces of Music" played on a violin and dulcimer. Others combined projected images with ballads and songs. In 1749, when James Wyatt with his Punch's Company of Comedians was exhibiting puppets and waxworks in New York City, he concluded his program with an "Optic Tragedy" (meaning a lantern show) that accompanied a popular English ballad, "Babes in the Wood."[18] This story—also called "The Children in the Wood" or "The Norfolk Tragedy"—begins with the death of a mother and father who had entrusted their children to the care of an uncle. In order to acquire their inheritance, the uncle pays two ruffians to take them into the woods to be killed; these men end up fighting and abandon the children, who subsequently die and are covered up by a passing robin. It ends with the fate of the uncle, who is found out and jailed. As he projected the images, Wyatt or his partner alternately sang or read the ballad and was accompanied by a musician.[19]

Other performances at the same time addressed historical and biblical subjects. Edmund Rising, for example, showed his Boston audiences scenes from the Battle of Dettingen, fought just six months earlier on 27 June 1743 between a combined English-Austrian force against the French.[20] The same paper that printed his advertisement also provided a detailed account of this conflict, which marked the last time in English history that a reigning monarch (George II) personally led his troops. Rising in effect was giving a firsthand report on the battle. In all likelihood he used "representation[s]" displayed earlier in London that came out about a month after the battle. One London show by a Mr. Phillips was to exhibit "the taking of the [French] White Household Standard by the Scots Greys, and Blowing up of the Bridge, Destroying and Drowning most Part of the French Army"—key moments in the Dettingen engagement. A second, by a Mr. Wright, was given at Sadler's Wells showing "the English Forces in Camp, and a Prospect of the Town at a Distance." A third depicted "the Battle between the English (commanded by his Majesty) and French on the Bridge, where the French was defeated." While we do not know whether any of these English scenes were projected as sequences, they were advertised as *representations*—the same term used by Rising for magic lantern images. Rising also projected several "Italian Landskips, representing Armies, both Horse and Foot, going through their Exercise at the Word of Command," reflecting the English description that "both Armies, Horse and Foot, are now cloath'd, with all other Accoutrements, as Drums, Kettle-Drum, Trumpets, Hautboys, French Horns, and Cannons."[21]

In 1755, religious subjects from England were shown to Philadelphia audiences depicting "in the largest and plainest Manner, the Creation of the World; the full Scenes of Paradise; . . . with sundry other Representations, too tedious to mention."[22] The proprietor called his machine a "Venetian Globe," and it was viewed in the dancing room formerly owned by a Mr. Quin on Second Street. In 1769, an unidentified operator of "Machinery" in Philadelphia presented "Adam and Eve" followed by Queen Charlotte in the state coach "with a view of the horse and foot guards exercising" and the king of Prussia hunting "in a most lively manner."[23] Not to be outdone, Henry Hymes diverted his audiences in Newport, Boston, and New York in 1767 with what amounted to a traveling encyclopedia of the human race. Hymes's "Magick Lanthorn" projected images "near six Feet high" of "all manner of different Sorts of Persons,—grand Cities, Palaces, the Sun, Moon, Stars, and Sky with all Manner of Birds and Beasts, Soldiers marching, Ships sailing on the Ocean."[24]

Once magic lanterns became better known, their numbers multiplied. At least fifty-nine transient showmen, entertainers, or lecturers advertised lantern programs in American newspapers before 1826, the bulk of them between 1780 and 1800. But Americans' unfamiliarity with the machine engenders ambiguity for later historians because the devices and their slides were known by many different names. While some early projectionists simply called their instruments by their seventeenth-century European names—the "magic lantern" or "camera obscura"—others spoke of showing "representations of the sea," "shades representing wild beasts," or the "Brilliances of Peru in twelve different representations."[25] Still others spoke blithely of presenting "optic tragedies," "Venetian Globes," or "magic pieces," or they stressed the origin of the art, calling them "curious pieces of Machinery, Representing the Italian shades" or "Curious Italian machinery which presents against the Wall all Manner of different Sorts of Persons."[26] A few projectionists devised laboriously convoluted phrases in what may have been an attempt to mislead: "Catoptric Machine," "Megalographic Apparatuses," "an Optical Piece of Apparatus," or even "a curious Philosophical Optical Machine, properly adapted to the Philosophical System of Sir Isaac Newton's Opticks."[27] Three entertainers in 1798 alluded to the diaphanous nature of the images. One, working in Newport, Rhode Island, called them "Transparent Figures." A second, Gabriel Salenka, who stopped in Savannah, called them "Transparent Pantomime[s]," apparently because sequences of images told stories. A third called them "Transparencies." These names eventually coalesced around common terms like *Italian shades* or *Les Grandes ombres,* especially after the old term, *magic lantern,* had become commonplace. Until that happened, however, lantern shows sometimes remained indistinguishable from puppet shows, backlighted imaging devices, front-lighted opaque instruments like diagonal mirrors, and even movable theatrical flats and large-scale transparencies.[28]

In the decades after the American Revolution the number of titles rapidly increased. Americans were eager for entertainment, and audiences were quick to embrace what was then being called "Ombres Italianes" or "Italian Shades," particularly if they incorporated traditional coarse country humor. The "Broken Bridge," for example, was based on an old French song recounting a mocking dialogue between a traveler trying to get across a bridge and a carpenter who was repairing it. After a long singing match in which the carpenter brazenly bares his backside, the traveler finally rows across the river and gives the workman the beating he presumably deserves. (A c. 1785 print [fig. 8.4] by L. Wilhelm

Figure 8.4. *Les Ombres chinoises. He! l'Ami! . . . quelle heure est-il?* The "Broken Bridge" being shown as a shadow play to a German audience circa 1785 using the tune of an old French folksong, "Le Pont Cassé." Between 1786 and 1811 this indelicate European variation was played and sung in most American cities with the exception of Boston where it was apparently not permitted. The piece was variously staged with live actors, artificial comedians (puppets), transparencies (magic lanterns), Chinese shades (shadow puppets), and unspecified machinery—all supported by a small group of singers. Copy of an engraving by L. Wilhelm Chodowiecki (1765–1805). Courtesy, Harvard Theatre Collection (Ms Thr 959), Popular Entertainments and Prints, Houghton Library, Harvard University.

Chodowiecki shows a well-dressed German audience enjoying this scene told with movable shadow puppets and a six-piece orchestra.)[29]

The "Broken Bridge" was introduced to the American stage in June 1786 when James Godwin and a Mr. Kidd, managers of the American Company of Comedians, selected it as an "interlude" for theatrical audiences in Charleston. Godwin and Kidd then moved to nearby Louisburgh "without the city" and sang the "Broken Bridge" as a skit. The diversion next appeared in 1789 as a lantern show exhibiting "The Grotesque Scene of The Broken Bridge and Drunken

Carpenter" at the conclusion of an evening program of plays given by the Old American Company in New York City. These performances precipitated a flood of imitations in taverns and theaters in New York City and Philadelphia, and the interlude was soon seen regularly in Newburyport, Salem, Portsmouth, Providence, Baltimore, Alexandria, and Norfolk.[30] Some showmen presented the sketch as "Shades" (movable shadow puppets) or a "new invented transparency." Story variations cast the carpenter as a stonecutter and the traveler as a "macaroni" (a dandy or fop), and at times the carpenter was simply insulting instead of drunken. Between 1786 and 1811 the "Broken Bridge"—sung to the tune of an old French folksong, "Le Pont Cassé"—became one of the favorite entertainments in America, repeatedly presented by John Durang, James Maginnis, Joseph Falconi, George Esterly, Peter Blancan, and Richard Potter along with scores of unidentified showmen moving up and down the eastern seaboard from Charleston to Portsmouth. And the tradition persisted. Music for this song was published in England in the 1780s; cut-outs illustrating the story were printed in America for children in the nineteenth century.[31]

Other lantern show people told stories about conjurers, mermaids, duck hunters, stag hunters, and millers and their jackasses. "Sportsmen" were shown with their faithful dogs, seamen whose boats were swallowed by whales, and "unfortunate" beggarmen being scolded by a housewife. Inn holder George Esterly, who in 1791 was managing a concert garden in Philadelphia called Harrowgate, was a master of this type of amusement, offering "Les Grandes Ombres Italianes; Or, Large Italian Shades" depicting "a Grotesque and entertaining Scene between the Tooth-Drawer and his Landlady; after which he turns Doctor and cuts off a Man's Head."[32] Later Esterly titles included the "Merry Coblers [and] Barbers," a "Cooper, a Taylor and the most Humourous Shoemaker," and "Shades of the Likely Family, in Grotesque Characters."[33]

Theater and concert managers soon began to insert lantern exhibitions or "glasses" between acts in order to provide time to reset the stage, sometimes accompanying them with songs "in character." These were almost always described as "laughable scenes," "comic figures and forms," or "Droll." In Charleston in 1797, a traveling theater company introduced the "Comic Scenes of the Dentist, and two Gamblers, and a Man that grows from 5 feet to 15 in the course of a few seconds."[34] In Savannah, between his dog acts in 1798, Gabriel Salenka's transparent pantomimes enacted scenes such as "The Wonderful Barber," "The Droll Doctor curing a sick person," and "The Droll Gamblers, who will be taken by the Devil."[35]

Some showmen specialized in animals, especially scenes of Noah's Ark. James Maginnis projected "the Birds and Beasts entering the Ark, a striking representation of the Elephant. The wild Hyenna which never can be tamed. The large Bengal Tyger. Also an exact likeness of the large Russia Bear"—all "rolling their eyes." Elsewhere in 1796, Maginnis selected a "curious Magic Piece": "From Rome, in Italy, wherein will be displayed . . . a beautiful View of a Stag Hunt. The surprising German County Dance as natural as Life. Mercury, with Fame and Venus, Likewise Bell and the Dragon, ascending and descending. The grand Procession of Bacchus in his Car, drawn by two Lion Tygers, attended with Gods and Goddesses."[36]

Mr. Harrington twice took lantern slides of Noah's Ark into rural eastern Massachusetts and Rhode Island. These also depicted the "Wild Hyena, the Lyon, the Elephant, the Tyger, the Bear," which "rolled their eyes as they pass, natural as life."[37] In Maryland, a Mr. Duff presented "a procession of Birds and Beasts, viz. The Hyena, the Lyon, The Elephant, the Tyger, the Bear &c.—They all roll their eyes as they pass, natural as life."[38] These similarities again indicate that Maginnis, Harrington, and Duff were purchasing packaged sets—perhaps even made by the same manufacturer—that showed the "rolling eye" through magic-lantern glasses that created animation with mechanical sliders.

Lanternists frequently selected subjects that were inaccessible to the public, especially those involving maritime encounters: sequential slides of fleets engaging one another, sinking vessels, or being blown up in the water. This allowed spectators to follow each step of the battle, although these images were often mixed with fanciful views. A Mr. Patridge in 1780 capped off his puppetry exhibition with a Mrs. May in New York City "with a representation of the besieging and taking of the Havana. In which will be a lively appearance of ships, sailing on the water, engaging the castle and batteries." Patridge finished with pictures of "sea horses, dolphins, [and] mermaids," descriptions again suggesting showmen were using manufactured sets of painted glasses.[39] Elsewhere, a theater company playing in Charleston concluded its program in 1796 by projecting pictures of "A Naval Engagement, between the famous Spanish Armada and the British Fleet."[40]

In the years after the French Revolution one unidentified proprietor showed a "Curious Optical Machine" in Philadelphia that projected the terrors that took place "in the dungeons of the Bastille when it was taken." He promised to present the story of "the Count Delorges, 70 years old brought to life after 31 years imprisonment, the Governor seized by the people, the iron cage, &c." He repeated these scenes as he moved to Baltimore and Charleston in 1797 and 1798.[41] Another unidentified proprietor from Europe illustrated Lord Nelson burning Admiral Bruyeux's flagship *L'Orient*, a scene "taken by a gentleman of genius on an English man of war." At this point even traveling waxwork proprietors were carrying with them "large Camera Obscura" or "large Magnifying Glasses" to show views of faraway places—country seats, palaces in England, and the city of London.[42] And in 1807, a Mr. Banks—who had just come from Italy—ended a puppet show in Charleston with "a beautiful projected representation of the bombardment of Tripoli," a subject lately in the news because of American involvement in the burning of the captured frigate *Philadelphia* in Tripoli Harbor.[43]

A few lanternists managed to intersperse serious subjects with humorous ones. In 1816, an unidentified lecturer in Salem, Massachusetts, designed a program to exhibit "The Lord Mayors Show—Peace with the United States and England—Harlequin and Columbine—English and American Frigates—Mad Bull knocking the Taylor into the air—Country Ghost—Hamlet and Ghost—French Cavalry and Cossacks—Battle of Trafalgar—Lawyer and Taylor—Dartmoor Prison—John Bull, Bonaparte, and Oyster Wench."[44] About half his subjects were designed to appeal to a country still trying to recover from a disastrous war with England—combat between English and American frigates, and Dartmoor Prison, the scene of a massacre of American prisoners. But others like "Harlequin and Columbine" and "Oyster Wench" were character sketches no different from the "Italian Mountebank" advertised by entertainer Richard Brickell in New York City seventy years earlier or the "Droll Doctor" shown by Gabriel Salenka in Savannah in 1798.[45]

Soon teachers and academicians began to utilize projection devices. Ebenezer Kinnersley, who continued to give a course of electrical talks at the college in Philadelphia, stated in his 1767 prospectus that his experiments would exhibit "some curious Representations with the Magick Lantern"—one of the earliest such implementations in a formal academic lecture. Before long these projectors turned up in other schools. Reverend John Prince (1751–1836), for example, sold instruments to numerous New England colleges. Harvard University still owns one of the few eighteenth-century magic lanterns with a documented history (fig. 8.5), donated in 1766 to the college along with a solar microscope by Robert Hale of Beverly, Massachusetts, after the 1764 fire that destroyed the Harvard Library. This one may have replaced an earlier model. An inventory of scientific instruments taken in 1779 records that there were two magic lanterns in the college's collection, along with "18 painted glasses, two of them broken." The inventory also lists twelve "painted slides." In 2009, the curator of the collection described them as pedagogical, mostly dealing with astronomical and geographic subjects.[46] By the second decade of the nineteenth century, speakers were customarily using lantern projectors to augment travelogues, communicate current events, and illustrate talks on architecture, landscape, biology, and history.[47] Kimball Union Academy in Meriden, New Hampshire, bought a magic lantern with "astronomical slides" in 1837 "for illustrating the principles of the sciences"; the next year, a lecturer was presenting the "History of Babylon" with slides in Portsmouth, New Hampshire.[48]

Even as these trends were playing out in popular and academic realms, retail sales were turning projection devices into a product of early consumerism—

marketed especially for children and juveniles. Initially, opticians and stationers sold magic lanterns in North America to individual collectors who aspired to own examples of "philosophical" or scientific apparatuses. In 1754, Gilbert and Lewis Deblois's shop in Boston advertised "A Magick Lanthorn, with three Dozen Pictures" and a microscope with a "solar apparatus."[49] James Rivington, a New York bookseller and stationer, carried "surveyor's instruments, reading glasses, burning glasses, and the magick Lanthorn" in 1762.[50] A "Magic Lantern, With a Dozen curious Slips containing grotesque groupes of figures," was put up for sale in New York City in 1779.[51] William P. and Lemuel Blake publicized

Figure 8.5. Magic lantern used at Harvard College in the eighteenth century. One of two inventoried in 1779 and donated, along with a solar microscope, to the college in 1766 by Robert Hale of Beverly, Massachusetts, after the 1764 fire that destroyed Harvard's library. Height: 41 inches. Courtesy, Collection of Historical Scientific Instruments, Harvard University.

"a complete Lucernal Microscope, with Magic Lanthorne and two patent lamps" in 1798.[52] In each instance the advertisement cited one or two machines.

But by the opening of the nineteenth century the emphasis was on quantity. Inexpensive magic lanterns were being sold to shops by the case and were often incorporated into their lists of children's toys. Margaret Newman, a Boston importer and retailer of toys, announced in September 1817 that a case of German toys she had just received contained "100 boxes of magnetical tin toys [and] 50 Magical Lanthorns with drawings."[53] The same year John Langdon in New York was selling off his stock of toys "at reduced prices" that included "Magic Lanthorns . . . magnetic Fish [and] Ducks . . . Cities, Gardens, Encampments, Noah's Arks and the Sea Serpent in miniature, which will move in any direction by the least touch, having joints throughout its body."[54] By 1819 W. B. Gilley, a prolific publisher of children's books about foreign lands from about 1814 to 1830, publicized in New York that he had for sale a "Magic Lantern—96 glasses—upward of 250 subjects—Ancient and Modern History from the creation to 1806."[55]

These numbers tell us that the use of lanterns had become so widespread that they were functioning as a medium which influenced the American imagination as closely as newspapers, campaign events, and chapbooks. The excesses of the French Revolution (and droll stories such as "Harlequin creeping into a bottle") were now only as far away as the nearest oil lamp and an experienced speaker.[56] As always, lantern operators combined several occupations in one person—a characteristic that not only identified Brickell's first use of it in Philadelphia but scores of itinerants working after him: lanternists like Dabney, Rising, and Cesar Cossa were also opticians; Hymes, Mr. Bayly, Patridge, and Charles Burton were showmen and singers; a Mr. Duff was a slackwire dancer and actor; Mr. Cressin was an animal handler; Daniel Salter was a musician; Durang was a stage dancer; Lewis Mera was a glass-spinner. Each one introduced magic lanterns into his routine.

But more than that, these numbers reveal the time it took to bring lantern devices to North America. Samuel Pepys purchased in London "a lanthorn, with pictures in glass, to make strange things appear on a wall" in 1666.[57] Its first American use was in a Philadelphia tavern 1743. What accounts for this delay? Hundreds of ships arrived from European ports each year, but none seemingly carried an entertainment as simple as a magic lantern. Was the time lag driven by transatlantic distances, economics, or colonial or imperial demands? We might also ask why it took ten years for another highly popular entertainment, the "Broken Bridge," to leave the Great Room in London's Hay-Market District in 1776 before finally appearing as an "interlude" in Charleston in 1786. There is no ready answer.

Of course once audiences became used to these kinds of stories, they lost no time in showing their "sophistication." Cesar Cossa, "lately arrived from Italy," advertised himself as a glassblower, electrical healer, and electrical entrepreneur as he traveled through the Mid-Atlantic states and Connecticut in the period 1804 through 1807. Like his fellow compatriot Joseph Falconi, he repaired and made optical machines, sold barometers, demonstrated a Leiden jar, set fire to the spirits of wine by electrical fire, rang bells without any communication—all the while projecting entertainments on his "Catroptic Machine" featuring "300 different figures in bright colours, dancing, marching, and fighting with correctness equal to life itself."[58] Like Falconi, he claimed to have studied under Alessandro Volta, "Professor of Physic at the University of Pavia." But unlike his rival, who preferred big crowds, Cossa stuck primarily to small-scale venues—usually small taverns—"at the Sign of the Spread Eagle" in Fredericktown, Maryland; "at the sign of the Horse" in Newark; "at Mr. Bloomfield's Assembly-Room" in New Haven. Cossa's medley of entertainments did well until he reached Connecticut. There, however, an audience member at Bloomfield's Assembly Room persuaded a young boy to pretend he was electrocuted during one of Cossa's experiments involving electrical discharges. When the boy fell "lifeless" at his feet, Cossa turned "pale as ashes." As a doctor stepped in to help, the boy sprang up and made his escape, leaving the showman "on the floor . . . while laughter made the old Hall roar." Cossa then moved on to Hartford where he leased the old City Hall for his final exhibition.[59]

Chapter 9

Tavern Entertainers II: Puppeteers, Ropedancers, Conjurers

THE TIME lag that defined the entry of lantern shows into British North America also appears to have characterized other forms of early tavern entertainment. Virtually no evidence of puppetry—one of the most readily compartmentalized and portable of tavern entertainments—exists in seventeenth-century diaries, town documents, or court files. Mention of tumbling, balancing, ropedancing, and conjuring acts is found in only two occasions before 1700. The example in Virginia was private entertainment; the other, in Massachusetts, was quietly suppressed by Boston's Third Church. Nevertheless, these entertainments drew big crowds in the booths and stalls of London's fairs, and artists like William Hogarth made a career of depicting them and their audiences. While carriers of these performances were not part of the initial emigrations, many Americans had heard about them. In 1732, the *Boston Weekly Rehearsal* told readers that a "Rope-Dancer at Sadler's Wells" had the misfortune of slipping and breaking his leg. Two years later the *New-England Weekly Journal* reported that "the poor Punchinello in the Puppet Shew at St. Laurence's Fair" had been arrested in Paris for what amounted to treason.[1] By 1750, however, most of these activities were being circulated by individual performers in North America, and they form an important part of the itinerant story.

Early Puppeteers

Animated puppetry in the northern hemisphere of the New World dates at least to the early decades of the eighteenth century. In his *British Empire in America* (1708), John Oldmixon described a "Company of Poppet Strollers . . . from England" who came to Barbados and "set up their Fairy Drama at the Bridge. . . . From thence they went to the Leeward Islands, and thence home."

While Oldmixon's "Strollers" apparently never reached the mainland, the American beginning of the genre may have occurred in New England in the 1730s. According to two entries in the diary of Reverend Ebenezer Parkman, a man showed up at Ensign John Maynard's tavern in Westborough, Massachusetts, who attracted considerable attention. On Tuesday, 14 August 1739, Parkman had spent much of that day supervising the plowing and mowing of his fields and noted that "Neighbor Hezekiah How came with his Team and got in Two Turns and somewhat more." Then as an afterthought he added, "N.B. a Puppett show at Ensign Maynards at Eve." No doubt Parkman, his neighbors, and the entire Westborough parish were delighted by this unusual turn of events. Probably the first puppets ever seen in this rural Massachusetts town, they may have been the only ones circulating in North America during the 1730s. Before he left the town on Friday morning, the puppeteer stopped at Parkman's home: "[Friday 17 August 1739] Mr. Edward Burley Son [Burlesson] came to my House in his Cabbin with his Puppetts, etc. there in. N.B. I had my Self Seen them in some measure my self Yesterday just at Evening."[2]

Parkman's second entry confirms that the puppeteer was none other than Edward Burlesson, Jr., the animal handler who previously had taken "the Lyon, the black and whight bare, and the Lanechtskipt" to Boston.[3] This was the same individual who had been warned out of that city by its selectmen, and his appearance in Westborough once again indicates that strolling cultural carriers—figures entirely out of keeping with what is commonly believed about New England or early America—were wandering the region in the early eighteenth century. He was an old-world character thriving in a provincial setting.

The facts concerning Edward Burlesson, Jr., are sparse but suggestive. One of five children of Edward Burlesson (or Burleson), Sr., of Suffield, Connecticut, the son grew up with an unknown handicap. Soon after his father died in 1698, he was placed under the supervision of his mother. The following year the town of Suffield voted to "take care for the maintenance of Edward Burleson ye Decripit youth; and allsoe for his cure, if it be attainable." He was then thirteen. In 1700, the town again assumed his maintenance and voted to "treat and agree with a Doctour, in order to [obtain] a cure for him if it may be obtained." Three years later the town decided "to put out Burles, the cripple, upon tryall to Goodman Smith, of Hadley . . . to make experiment, whether he be capable of learning his trade."[4]

Whatever his physical handicap, Burlesson seems to have overcome it. Two surviving letters signed by him, now in the Kent Memorial Library in Suffield, reveal not only that his writing was legible but that his spelling was excellent—indications he had an above-average education. In 1720, at age thirty-four, he proposed marriage to Elizabeth Jesse of Suffield, but the union was stopped jointly by her mother and stepfather, Joseph King. According to court documents, Burlesson was the plaintiff in a 1721 legal action against King and a Suffield constable who had entered Burlesson's home and broken into his chest and "looked over many of the Pltfs [plaintiff's] writings that were in sd chest." (The jury awarded Burlesson two pounds and thirteen shillings for court costs.) In these documents he is identified as a tailor, possibly the vocation "Goodman Smith" had taught him. Four years later, he was composing, illustrating, and selling broadsides and was the author of a verse (fig. 9.1) mourning fifty victims of a fatal epidemic in Hartford.[5]

By this time, Burlesson seems to have been permanently employed both as a puppeteer and animal proprietor. A Salem diary entry records that an unidentified showman, presumably Burlesson, gave a nighttime "poppet show" there on 20 March 1733.[6] He was absent from Suffield so much that he apparently leased the house he had inherited from his mother. This arrangement may have again led to some difficulty with the King family. In January 1733, Burlesson wrote from Springfield, Massachusetts, to Thomas King, who was living in his house in Suffield, assuring him that neither King nor "Blogget & James" need leave the house regardless of "the Noise or talk of Neighbours."[7]

When Burlesson was warned out of Boston in 1735, he was almost fifty years old. In May 1736, Burlesson again wrote to his tenant, Thomas King, this time from Hartford. He told King and his brother John he had heard in Boston of the death of Thomas King's son and encouraged them and their families to live in the house as "Christian Brothers." Three years later Burlesson emerged as a puppeteer in the journal of Reverend Ebenezer Parkman; he was then living

Figure 9.1. Detail from "A Lamentation in Memory of the Distressing Sickness in Hartford, from *November* 5th. 1724. to *February* 20th, 1724,5." Illustrated broadside verse from a document signed "E. Burlesson." This is the only known example of Edward Burlesson's art. Woodcut. New London, Connecticut: Timothy Green, 1725. Courtesy, The Connecticut Historical Society.

and possibly showing his puppets in a "cabbin," likely a horse-drawn covered vehicle.[8]

Despite his uncertain past, Edward Burlesson occupies a critical place in American entertainment history. He marks a turning point not only as the earliest puppeteer in North America—one of about forty-three active between 1730 and 1825—but also as the first American-born showman this country has produced. We know enough about Burlesson to put him in Boston, Westborough, and perhaps Salem. But nothing from this short history establishes what he looked like or the size or costumes of his puppets. We know that one eighteenth-century American performer named William Philips was "very remarkable for his thick Legs (a Shewman) and had on a striped red and white Jacket, old Shoes, with Brass Buckles and Speaks much on the Welsh Dialect."[9] Another, Thomas Plant, was "an uncommon short Man, and looks strangely with his Eyes, pretty much deformed in his Limbs, beats the Drum, and plays Legerdemain."[10] Did Burlesson wear a striped jacket? Did he beat a drum? And what about his "apparatus"? Did he use glove puppets? Were his puppets wooden? Did he give voice to the lead characters through a "squeaker"? Or had he already realized (as did "Madame de la Nash" in London in 1748) that the "squeaking of the puppets has been thought disagreeable."[11] Burlesson may have traveled abroad to obtain or exhibit his animals, and he may have spent enough time in London to learn how to project his voice, create stories, and make costumes from known show people who played at booths at Southwark and Bartholomew Fairs. The most likely time period for this training would have been between 1721 and 1724 when there are no records of Burlesson's being active in the colonies. Perhaps he served as an apprentice in what was then an extremely active London puppetry circuit under showmen such as John Harris (fl. 1700–1726), Martin Powell (d. 1725), Isaac Fawkes (1675–1732), Mr. Yeates (fl. after 1725), or Martin Powell, Jr. (fl. 1725–1726). Martin Powell himself is believed to have been a "cripple" and is pictured as a hunchback in a 1715 English publication (fig. 9.2).[12]

Equally intriguing is Burlesson's cabin. Did it house a stage so that he could perform outside? Was there room enough to contain the equivalent of the "forty dressed and eight undressed figures" inventoried among the possessions of John Harris when his goods were confiscated at the Southwark Fair in 1723?[13] What characters was Burlesson portraying? They were not likely to have been puppets guilty of "abusing the Puritans," as recounted in the diary of Samuel Pepys in London in 1668 or the axe-wielding "beheading puppets" described by historians of the London fairs in the early eighteenth century.[14] More plausibly they were "Punch comedians," meaning the unruly characters derived from the Italian commedia dell'arte tradition, such as Harlequin, Punch, and Joan, which delighted crowds in Europe by mercilessly satirizing English and French royalty. Regrettably there is no evidence Burlesson benefited from a London apprenticeship or even that he owned traditional European character puppets.[15]

Puppeteers and Showmen in Mid-Eighteenth-Century America

The earliest known use of Punch character puppets in North America is documented to 1742, when an unidentified Philadelphia showman (presumably Richard Brickell) gave evening productions of "An agreeable Comedy or Tragedy, by changeable figures of two Feet high"—language suggesting dimensional puppets suspended by strings or wires or held up by stiff construction.[16] We assume he was a professional entertainer because he charged four separate ticket prices (from two shillings to as low as a sixpence) and because the show remained in Philadelphia at the same location for more than two months. Five years later Richard Brickell, this time accompanied by Richard Mosely and calling themselves "late from Philadelphia," employed "a Set of lively Figures" in a rendition of "Punch's Opera" in New York City, enacting the German folktale "Bateman, or the Unhappy Marriage" followed by a dialogue between Punch and his wife. They too advertised four prices "according to situation," but this time they remained only two weeks.[17]

Figure 9.2. *Martin Powell* (d. 1725), English puppeteer. Frontispiece to Thomas Burnet, *A Second Tale of a Tub; or, The History of Robert Powel, the Puppet-Show-Man.* London: J. Roberts, 1715. If Edward Burlesson learned puppetry in London, he would most likely have been affiliated with Powell or one of his understudies. Courtesy, Houghton Library, Harvard University, Br 2115.25.

Tavern Entertainers II: Puppeteers, Ropedancers, Conjurers   177

Figure 9.3. Three puppets from "Mr. Punch's Celebrated Company of Comedians, Formerly Mrs. Charke's," announcing a play during the time of Bartholomew Fair in 1740. Harlequin is on the left; the hunchback Punch is the center figure; on the right is the Spanish pirate Don Pistole. The raised position of their arms suggests these were stringed puppets. The original cut comes from the London *Daily Post*, 21–27 August 1740. Facsimile image engraved in 1842 by Thomas Gilks for George Daniel's *Merrie England* (2:137) under the title "The Three Scaramouches." It is one of the few puppet images that have survived from the mid-eighteenth century. Courtesy, Widener Library, Harvard University, Br 3504.5.

What did Brickell's and Mosely's puppets look like? They certainly did not resemble the amiable Punch and Judy figures seen by children in the nineteenth and early twentieth centuries. The eighteenth-century Punch was physically repulsive and uncompromisingly abrasive both toward the royal family and his wife.[18] The same detail of William Hogarth's 1734 engraving of Southwark Fair that depicts a rope flyer (see fig. 7.5) also reveals a booth for drolleries by live actors (*The Siege of Troy*) and puppet performances called "Punches Opera," where a banner shows Punch, distinguished by a distended belly and humpback, trundling his wife, Joan (later called Judy), into the fiery mouth of Hell in a wheelbarrow. The puppets appear to be about three feet in height. Hell is the head of a huge monster with flames shooting out of its mouth. Above them is a placard for *Creation of the World*, also called *Adam and Eve in the Garden of Eden*, a well-known puppet play. Below them are two assistants, one riding a cockhorse and a second wearing a Harlequin costume. Another contemporary view of English Punch occurs in a woodcut of three figures in "antick" costumes that illustrated an advertisement in the *Daily Post* of London for a show at Bartholomew Fair in August 1740 (fig. 9.3). This image of an event that took place at "Fawkes, Pinchbeck, and Terwin's Great Theatrical Booth" is one of the few that have survived from this period. It depicts three "Comedians"— meaning masked puppets—about three feet in height and part of "Mr. Punch's

Celebrated Company." On the left is the bat-carrying Harlequin; in the center, the hunchbacked Mr. Punch; and on the right, the thieving Spanish "pyrate" Don Pistole.[19]

Nothing is known about Mosely after 1747. But Brickell remained active and was the first in a series of show persons, conjurers, balancers, and acrobats who performed in New York City, Philadelphia, northern Maryland, and Charleston in the period from 1742 through 1774, most of them manipulating Punch characters, performing slack-wire acts, displaying wax effigies of the royal family, and showing perspectives of European castles and cities. These entertainers appear to have derived their stories from London performers like Isaac Fawkes, a Mr. Yeates and his son, John Harris, and "Madame de la Nash" (now believed by some scholars to have been the novelist Henry Fielding), who drew inspiration from English legendary tales taken from ballads and chapbooks.[20] James Wyatt used his "Punch's Company of Comedians" to stage a curious mixture of history and buffoonery in a large, specially built theatrical room next to the Sign of the Dolphin Privateer in New York City from July through October 1749. Wyatt may have previously worked with the "Incomparable Yeates," because one of Wyatt's puppet titles, "the whole play of Princess Elizabeth, or the rise of Judge Punch . . . Showing the cruelty of Queen Mary and the intrigues of Bishop Gardiner," reads almost the same as a Yeates title. This was the story of English prelate Stephen Gardiner and his efforts to traduce the Protestant Elizabeth in order to keep the Catholic Mary on the throne. Punch played "Lord Judge of the Inquisition." Wyatt also produced "Whittington and his Catt, shewing how he was rise from a poor Sculling Boy, to be lord Mayor of London, with the cruel Usage he received from Marg. the Cook Maid when sculling under her." Wyatt gave puppet and waxwork shows at the Dolphin Privateer for four months and then he disappears from the record; little is known of him.[21] Was he the seafaring trumpet player who worked for four years under English puppeteer James Churchill and later wrote *The Life and Surprizing Adventures of James Wyatt*, which describes his Moorish captivity after being taken by Spaniards in 1741?[22] We do not know.

Other New York puppeteers included the showman Mr. Bayly who entertained with "Drolls and Burlettas" using "Punch and his merry family" at the Sign of the Orange Tree on Golden Hill in 1767. His "artificial comedians" were "near 3 feet high."[23] That same year Mr. Bayly and a Mr. Tea together produced a Punch diversion, "Particularly a new Farce called An Enchanted Lady of the Grove." William Patridge began a Punch series in a commodious room in New York City on 24 December 1770. He promised to delight the audience with "Mr. Punch and his Merry Family with new Alterations every evening," and later Patridge teamed with a Mrs. May to put on "St. George and the Dragon," in which "Mr. Punch Intends to do himself the pleasure to make his appearance and promises on his honor to behave with decency"—the usual sign he was going to insult everybody.[24]

In Maryland in 1769, Mary Chapman performed with an "Apparatus of a Puppet Show." Her name appeared in the paper when she complained that a "Punch Head, remarkably large" had been stolen from her by two men.[25] These entertainers were followed in 1770 by Hyman Saunders, who had "just arrived from Europe." One of the few strollers whose name actually can be traced to England's entertainment world, Saunders offered his American audiences grand deceptions that would "deceive the eye of the nicest observer, and appear in a manner supernatural."[26] A band of music played between acts. Beginning in New York City in 1770, Saunders went on to Philadelphia, Annapolis, Baltimore, Chester, and Charleston, all the time claiming to have been "honoured with the greatest applause . . . in Europe, America, and the West Indies."[27]

Up to this point, most Punch puppeteers and showmen had prospered in urban areas and major port towns in the American colonies where there was always a strong royalist component. By the late 1760s at least one of these entertainers came to Boston. Joseph Gibbes, who is otherwise unidentified, arrived there in 1768 with "a compleat sett of Artificial Figures Representing divers Masquerade characters." This is the first known use of the term *masquerade* in American newspapers—designating the customary commedia dell'arte characters whose faces were always masked. Gibbes gave his shows "at the house of Mr. John Moore," the wine merchant recently arrived from Lisbon, and he noted that "any Gentleman or Ladies that chuse to have a private night, are desired to apply."[28] Gibbes's visit to the community coincided with those of other English actors and musicians seeking the patronage of English officers and their families then living in Boston.[29]

Puppeteers also turned south to Maryland, Virginia, and the Carolinas. Peter Gardiner took a set of four-foot puppets to Alexandria, Annapolis, and Williamsburg in the years 1769 to 1772 to act out *Babes in the Wood, Dick Wittington and His Cat,* and *Bateman and His Ghost.*[30] An unidentified puppeteer and ropedancer—perhaps Gardiner—played for a week during the annual fair held in Fredericksburg, Virginia, in 1774.[31] Curiously, both Gibbes and Gardiner chose traditional English stories for their repertoire, leaving unchanged the titles introduced more than two decades earlier by Brickell and Wyatt.

Postrevolutionary Puppeteers

In the heady postrevolutionary decades of the 1780s and 1790s, at least four puppeteers were active in Massachusetts despite the efforts of selectmen who tried to suppress them. One was Mr. Harrington; the second was Richard Hoyt; a third and fourth were unknown puppet show people performing in Boston and

Salem. In the middle states Mr. Bayly (or Bailey), who had lost his equipment and clothes (and his wife) during the revolution, began playing in Baltimore in 1782 and 1783; he now called himself "the noted Old Artist." In 1783, Jacob Henninger, one of Bayly's assistants, introduced his "richly dressed" artificial comedians before the same audiences; a surviving playbill describes Henninger's puppets as four feet high and headed by "Seignior Punchinello."[32] In the South the French partnership of Tessie and Goichon brought "the pleasant tricks of Polichinel[le]" (the French Pulcinell or Punch) to Charleston in 1794 (fig. 9.4). Dominic Jonotty, an Italian, introduced "Mr. Punch and his merry family" to New Haven in 1795; he later visited Salem, Newburyport, and Portland with his balancing acts, Chinese shades, and machinery that created fireworks "without any fire."[33]

Figure 9.4. "Polichinelle," also called Pulcinell or Punchinello, was brought to Charleston, South Carolina, by the puppeteers Tessie and Goichon in 1794. This character was the French equivalent of Punch and was "armed" with a pincher and a grill. Taken from Nicolas Bonnart (1637–1717), *Recueil des modes de la coeur de France*. France, circa 1678–1693. Volume of hand-colored engravings by several artists, bound 1703–4. Sheet 14⅜ by 9½ inches. Courtesy, Los Angeles County Museum of Art, www.lacma.org, acc. no. M. 2002.57.159.

One of the most innovative puppeteers of this new generation was Samuel Jameson Maginnis, whose advertisements sometimes identify him as from Edinburgh but who, according to John Durang, was one of four military runaways arriving in Boston from British Canada in 1795, all former musicians in a regimental band. In Boston Maginnis sponsored (sometimes with Durang's help) a series of mechanical and optical shows at Dearborn's long room that featured "a grand set of Artificial Wax-Work Commedians from Rome, in Italy."[34] These were marionettes, controlled from above by means of strings and wires or from the side by revolving crossbars. In the course of an active, ten-year career that also involved lantern exhibitions and "philosophical" entertainments, Maginnis took his marionettes throughout the northern and some southern states. In 1798, he performed in Newfane, Vermont, the seat of Windham County, then consisting of little more than two small hamlets located a dozen miles upriver from Brattleboro. Maginnis frequently billed himself "from Sadler's Wells" and termed his marionettes "Prussian Fantoccini," "Italian Fantoccini," or simply "Automaton figures" (meaning they imitated clockwork mechanical automatons). They were jointed wood and waxwork likenesses three-and-a-half feet high portraying a wide range of characters, such as the "Babes in the Wood," those in the "Ancient Court of Alexander the Great," "The American Tar," "The Italian Scaramouch," and the "Black Queen of Morocco," all of them dancing jigs, hornpipes, and fandangos. Sometimes Maginnis named his puppets after the wood from which they were carved ("Mr. Cedar," "Mr. Maple").[35]

A consummate performer, Maginnis seems to have had an eye on helping other struggling puppeteers and conjurers around him. When he reached Baltimore in 1797, he handed over his figures to an understudy or apprentice named Mr. Hackley, who then advertised a complete Maginnis show in what amounted to an outdoor venue at "Porter's enclosure, near the Observatory"—perhaps alluding to W. Hackley, who had an earlier history as a sleight-of-hand and magic lantern showman in Albany in 1790. The words "By Permission" that began Hackley's advertisement may actually have meant by *Maginnis's* permission.[36] Years later in 1804, Maginnis decided to sell off his "group of artificial comedians," which had formed the core of his performances over the past decade. He inserted a notice in the Washington *National Intelligencer* saying, "Mr. Maginnis shortly Intending to sail for Europe, wishes to dispose of the whole of his Apparatus." Like others, he added that he "will instruct the purchaser." (Maginnis in fact may have been terminally ill since his death was announced in Leonard-Town, Maryland, about ten months later.)[37]

Aside from his occasional descriptions, we have little idea of what Maginnis's marionettes actually looked like. But because they were passed from showman to showman it is sometimes possible to trace them and even find an image of them. In 1807, some of them likely appeared in a "Grand Exhibition" given by a Mr. Banks, a puppeteer and lantern performer working in Charleston during his stay at Wood's long room. Banks's performances included Maginnis standbys such as the "Norfolk Tragedy; or, The Children of the Woods," and the "Grand Italian Fantaccina, from Rome in Italy—by a wonderful group of Artificial commedians, three feet and a half high, effecting by the power of mechanism, the exact movements of life." Other highlights were the "Old Man marrying a Young Wife," and the "Bombardment of Tripoli." But after several weeks Mr. Banks, too, offered the marionettes for sale, seeking "to dispose of all his Apparatus, or part of them."[38] We do not have all the details, but four years later a new entertainer, a Mr. Barton, gave a show on Sullivan's Island in Charleston Harbor using the same equipment, this time calling it "Phantisena; or, The Animated Figures." His figures again virtually duplicate Maginnis's: "1st. The Court of Alexander—2nd. A Hornpipe by an American Tar. 3d Jack Junk and Susan. 4th the Prince and Princess of Morocco—5th Scaramouch, who will place his body in different position; with a number of Figures too numerous to describe. The whole to conclude with Jolly Dick, His Merry Wife and Mock Doctor."[39] Barton's advertisement comes with a picture of an animated tumbler (fig. 9.5) turning round and round on a crossbar—the only visual link we have to Maginnis's inventive genius.

Other Postrevolutionary Entertainments

Throughout the postrevolutionary period the usual variety prevailed. In addition to puppets, strollers brought sleight-of-hand deceptions, marionettes, moving figures, shadow puppets, transparencies, clockwork figures, lantern

Figure 9.5. "Grand Exhibition, *At the Theatre on Sullivan's Island.*" Image of a tumbling, spring-driven puppet designed and made by Samuel Jameson Maginnis (c. 1772–1805) and used by the showman Mr. Barton in Charleston, South Carolina, in 1811. Barton had purchased many of Maginnis's figures from a Mr. Banks who had received them from Maginnis. Estimated height of figure: 3½ feet. *Charleston Courier,* 27 July 1811. Courtesy, American Antiquarian Society.

shows, "Petites Ombres Chinoises," and "wax-work Commedians" to virtually every major tavern throughout the eastern seaboard. Figures danced to music played by instrumentalists; they narrated droll sequences and simulated a "Court of Foreign Kings, Queens, and Princesses." The list is long and complex. Joseph Pouyard took his "Shew named the Fantoxing Italiano" to a Mr. Paillolet's new tavern in Baltimore in 1786. John Brenon brought his slack-wire acts, his feats of dexterity, and his wife's singing performances to long rooms in New York's City Tavern in 1787. W. Hackley demonstrated "Slight of Hand" and the "Magic Lantern" to audiences at Cavenough's Inn in Albany in 1790. John Durang presented the "Doctor and the Landlady," the "Barber and Cobler," the "celebrated Tooth Drawer," and the "Glutton" at an improvised theater in Newport, Rhode Island, in 1790.[40] An unidentified entertainer told stories of a conjurer, a beggar, a robbery, and a stag hunt at a Mr. Teel's tavern in Norwich, Connecticut, in 1794. A Mr. Bellisarius and his company (he boastingly called himself a student of the "great Italian Painter and Architect" Ambrosio St. Verico) staged "The Dialogue between the Miller and the Sportsman" at the Church-Street Theatre in Charleston in 1800. A Mr. Elliott, a "Citizen of America and resident of Richmond," brought his agility of hand to the long room of the Exchange Coffee House in Providence in 1803. Mr. Green produced his "surprising Deceptions" (patterned after the manner of the celebrated Breslaw), his magic sheet, and his "Punch's Opera" at the Union Hall in Newburyport in 1807.[41] Variety was always present. When Peter Blancan along with young Miss Blancan and a Miss Thomas took the "Theatre Pitoresque & Mechanique" to the Vauxhall Garden in Charleston in 1808 and New York City's Broadway (fig. 9.6) in 1809, they based their amusements on four styles of communication. One consisted of suspended puppets controlled by wires or strings ("fantoccini"); a second was heavily ornamented, painted, and presumably backlighted scenery ("faux arabesques"); a third was stories and songs like the "Broken Bridge" based on lantern images ("ombres chinoises"); and a fourth consisted of traditional moving pictures ("tableaux animes").[42]

Although we know little about most of these entertainers, we learn something about the private life of one of them owing to a lost animal, an unexpected marriage announcement, and two citations in William Bentley's diary. John Brenon (fl. 1773–1790), the strolling Irish entertainer, made at least three transatlantic crossings to the English colonies or the United States. He first appeared in Virginia in 1773, when he left a cryptic notice in the *Virginia Gazette* saying he had lost a flying squirrel on the road between the Gloucester courthouse and Kingston that was formerly the property of a legerdemain performer named Phillips. Brenon offered a five-shilling reward for the animal's return and noted his wife's grief was "almost insupportable."[43] He turned up next as an acrobat in 1774 at Hampden Hall near the Upper Barracks showground in New York City teaming with a Mr. Johnston. The pair pronounced themselves "from England." But after the revolution in 1786, when Brenon returned to Philadelphia at Peter Duplessis's Long Room and to New York City at Corre's City Tavern, he called himself "from Dublin" and was accompanied by his enterprising wife, Mary Brenon, an accomplished singer, actor, and conjurer.[44] Experienced show people, they demonstrated feats of dexterity and staged a Harlequin comedy called *The Vagaries; or, Harlequin Triumphant* with John Brenon taking the role of Harlequin and Mary Brenon, Columbine. A colleague, a Mr. Sullivan, played the Irish bagpipes and danced a hornpipe.[45] Leaving New York City, Brenon's troupe embarked on an extended tour of New England, occasionally promoting themselves in newspapers or by releasing hot-air balloons.[46] Their advertisements (fig. 9.7) emphasize Brenon's membership in the Brotherhood of Masons, a connection he possibly capitalized on to avoid his company's arrest as vagabonds. They performed at Mr. Woart's Free Mason Hall, Green Dragon, in November and December 1788. Two years later, on 22 November 1790, Reverend Bentley observed his publicity balloon fall into Salem harbor.[47]

Figure 9.6. *Theatre Pitoresque & Mechanique*. Peter Blancan brought French versions of traditional European puppet figures to audiences in Charleston and New York City through the medium of Italian "Fantoccini," or stand-up mechanisms. Relief engraving by Alexander Anderson of New York City. *New-York Commercial Advertiser*, 14 December 1808. Courtesy, New-York Historical Society, neg. no. 90794d.

Tavern Entertainers II: Puppeteers, Ropedancers, Conjurers 185

Figure 9.7. "At Mr. Nichol's Long Room . . . the Surprising PERFORMANCES of the celebrated JOHN BRENON, from Dublin." Announcement by John Brenon and Hannah Etridge Brenon for an acrobatic exhibition at Nichol's Long Room, Middletown, Connecticut. Mrs. Brenon, called the "American Lady" in the advertisement, is shown walking on the slack wire below a Masonic emblem. *Middlesex Gazette*, 19 December 1789. Courtesy, American Antiquarian Society.

In June 1788, Mary Brenon reputedly ran off with another man. Undeterred, Brenon declared he would no longer be responsible for her debts, and he found another wife—the "amiable" Hannah Etridge of Hartford, Connecticut, whose marriage to him was announced in a Boston paper on 9 September 1788 and a Worcester paper on 16 October 1788.[48] During their visit to London in 1789, Brenon took the opportunity to train her, and on their return to North America he began performing with her. In an April exhibition in New York City in 1790, she gave a demonstration of "the curious and ingenious art of dancing on the

Slack Wire" without a balance pole and was described "as a Native of New England."[49] John Brenon was last mentioned in 1792 when the *Windham Herald* passed along to its readers a story that he had been arrested for violating laws in Maine against "itinerant stage players and wire dancers." He was fined twenty shillings but was excused when he offered the judge free admission to his next performance.[50]

The Rannies

With the arrival of the young Rannie brothers in 1801, North Americans experienced a conjuring activity that was just gaining prominence in Europe (fig. 9.8).[51] These two entertainers had grown up around Scottish and English fairgrounds during the late eighteenth century and were probably looking back on less than five years' experience on the European stage. John Rannie (c. 1775–after 1811) came first, identifying himself as a ventriloquist from Edinburgh, Glasgow, and Aberdeen at a Mr. Francis's dancing room in Philadelphia on 6 May 1801.[52] John had recently been found guilty with two other persons of "meal mobbing" (harassing strangers for food) in Aberdeen and was subsequently banished from Scotland for seven years.[53] When his older brother James (1772–1812) arrived in Boston in November of that year, the two began to demonstrate the ambiguity and posturing that seemed instinctive to them as itinerating showmen. They seldom used their first names but, depending on the circumstances, the older was sometimes known as Mr. Rannie the elder or Mr. Rannie, Sr., while the younger was known as Mr. Rannie, Jr. But despite the help of over two hundred newspaper advertisements, handbills, journal entries, and mail notices, their careers are difficult to pin down. After 1805, when one of the brothers apparently left the United States, it is sometimes not entirely clear which brother remained.

Their initial move was to stage simultaneous "first" exhibitions in New York City and Boston. On 4 December 1801 John Rannie, calling himself "Mr. Rannie lately from Europe," announced an exhibition of ventriloquism at Lovet's Hotel, New York, for that evening, a Tuesday. He claimed that his performance had never been "attempted or done by any person in America but himself." Voices were to issue from closets, presses, the floor, or audience members' pockets or shoes. On the following evening, however, James Rannie, who called himself a European ventriloquist, publicized *his* "first appearance in *America*" at Boston's Concert-Hall. He too called himself "the only one alive in the known world, who possesses . . . the ability of making any object to speak," and promised to project his voice from clothes, under chairs, and the ceiling of the room.[54] Neither performer mentioned the presence of the other.

James Rannie took a calculated risk by playing in Boston because the town's selectmen were still actively monitoring and banning entertainments. But his

At *The Newbedford Hotell* HOUSE,

On *Monday Evening April 1st 1811*

EVENING,
WILL BE DISPLAYED THE

Neficos Box,

Rope Dancing, Wire Walking, and 100 deceptions: Also, *imitations* of all kind of Birds, Ducks, Chickens, Cats, Dogs, and Hogs.

TO WHICH WILL BE ADDED,

An Imitation of a Bagpiper, and a BRITISH OFFICER.

The whole to Conclude with the Surprising Powers of the

VENTRILOQUIST,

He possesses by *nature* the *power* of causing a voice to be heard in all Parts of the Room ;---also, from the adjoining Rooms and Closets. HE CAUSES THE VOICE OF A CHILD TO BE HEARD IN A TEA-POT, and exclaim, " Let Me Out, Let Me Out, or I Shall Smother ;" the same Voice will be heard in any Gentleman SNUFF BOX, or in a Ladies' THIMBLE. Mr. R. will throw his Voice into a COD-FISH, which will immediately make a noise like that of a Hog. He will cause an OYSTER to imitate a number of BIRDS : To give a minute detail of this Exhibition would fill Volumes.

Doors opened at half past Six, the Performance to begin at Seven o'clock ;—Admittance Fifty Cents.

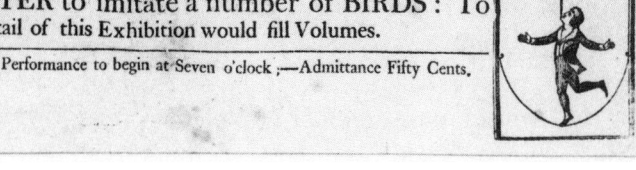

Figure 9.8. "At [The Newbedford Hotell] House, On [Monday April 1st 1811] EVENING, will be displayed the NEFICOS BOX, Rope Dancing, Wire Walking, and 100 Deceptions." Illustrated broadside announcing James Rannie's engagement in New Bedford, Massachusetts, on 1 April 1811. This event took place shortly before the Rannies revealed their retirement in Boston. Three of the relief cuts seen here had appeared earlier in newspaper advertisements. 14 by 9 inches. Printer unknown. Courtesy, The Whaling Museum. New Bedford, Massachusetts.

timing was right. Despite the high admission price (one dollar for front seats and fifty cents for rear ones), his acts so astonished Boston audiences that the selectmen took no action against him during his long engagement there. By January 1802 James had moved to Salem's Washington Hall where John Rannie joined him so they could perform together: "The Brothers will unite their respective talents, to render their entertainments more attractive and gratifying." After returning briefly to Boston, the pair headed for New York City where James leased the Tontine Assembly Room, which could seat five hundred spectators. According to his own calculations, James claimed he appeared "forty-six nights" at Boston, though this may have been an exaggeration since he said the same of his time in New York when he played later that year in Philadelphia.[55] Meanwhile John continued south to Baltimore. What followed was a coursing romp through eastern America that took them from Savannah, Georgia, to Lexington, Kentucky, to Portland, Maine. Playing one entertainment off against another, the two sometimes worked together, sometimes independently; they shared publicity woodcuts, rumors, ventriloquy stories, automatons, musicians, "domestics," and stage accessories. On occasion, they seemed to argue with one another. James told New York audiences in 1802 he was "*not the Rannie who performed here lately*" and insisted all his acts were new. John, in turn, claimed that his older brother paid most of the profits to himself and failed to pay debts. At some point in 1803, James sailed to the West Indies.[56] When he returned to New York City from Jamaica on the schooner *Echo*, he brought with him a new portfolio of images that probably made them the most heavily advertised showmen in America. After stopovers in Salem, Newburyport, and Portsmouth, James apparently headed for Quebec in 1805. Then, either James or John went on to New Orleans, Natchez, and Charleston, remaining in North America until his retirement in 1811. A Boston obituary reports James's death in Puerto Rico in 1812 at the age of thirty-nine.[57]

Like most showmen, the Rannies were as clever at generating publicity as they were at entertaining on the stage. They told a story of a farmer stopping in the street and unloading his carts, looking for the speaker of the voice emanating from within it; of a small child caught in a snuff box who was "distinctly" heard to exclaim, "Let me out, let me out, or I shall smother." They also informed their audiences that they were the ones who convinced a hotel manager a guest was bringing a live pig into his establishment, causing him to examine the man's luggage. Like the proprietors of Old Bett, the Rannies often told their audiences they were never coming back. But the final retirement of the remaining Rannie had some of the melodrama of their initial entry. Just before actually leaving America in 1811, he staged a finale in Boston's Concert-Hall with all of the bravado and flair of their 1801 premiere. This time, however, he called the show "Light!" and set about to reveal all his own and his brother's secrets. First he issued a sweeping denial that anyone had discerned their methods. "The publications," he wrote, "concerning Rannie's deceptions, circulated by Boaz, Breslau, Catterfelta, and Pinchback, are all fake . . . which will clearly appear at Concert-Hall this evening." He then went through and explained "fifty-one deceptions" or illusions on which he and his brother had built their reputation. This, of course, was his way of bidding farewell to their American audiences (somewhat in the style of Prospero in *The Tempest*). Equally important, it prevented potential imitators from copying their acts. All future showmen in the genre were obliged to devise their own.[58]

Tavern and Assembly-Hall Audiences

We know very little about who made up the eighteenth- and early nineteenth-century tavern audiences. Edward Burlesson's only documented performance as a puppeteer was the one in 1739 at Ensign Maynard's tavern in Westborough—a community located about ten miles east of Worcester and a little more than midway between Burlesson's home in Suffield and the port of Boston. The one member of his audience whom we can identify was the Westborough minister himself, Reverend Ebenezer Parkman. It is revealing that Parkman mentioned "Eve" or "just at Evening" twice in his reporting of Burlesson's events (meaning when the workday had drawn to a close) and that he remained in Westborough three nights, and it is interesting that Parkman did not mention Burlesson's handicap (as he did with many other strollers and beggars).[59] We have to assume that this puppeteer was familiar with other taverns that lay on the upper post road between Boston and New York City and may have served as principal sources of his income.

We can only speculate that it was also Burlesson who gave a puppet show at a private home in Salem in March 1732. Burlesson was warned out of Boston with his puppets just three years later, and four years after that he showed up with his puppets in Westborough. In other words, the timing was right. Either way, however, the Salem diary entry tells us where the puppet show was given, the time of day it was performed, and the social and family circumstances that preceded it. The writer was Benjamin Lynde, Jr., son of Judge Benjamin Lynde, Sr., of Salem, and like his father he was a Salem justice. "Fair," he wrote. "Town meeting; disappointed; at Mr. Plaisted's; the poppet show there at night." Plaisted was Major Ichabod Plaisted, Lynde's cousin and a man highly placed in Salem's social life and involved in its militia; he served in the 1756 expedition against Ticonderoga and was promoted to colonel before his death in 1762. "A dear friend" to Lynde, they often dined together.[60] "Night" implies the puppet show began around six or seven o'clock. That Lynde described it as "*the* poppet show" implies the show was already known locally and had appeared elsewhere on previous nights.

The audiences enjoying puppeteers in the next decade apparently were concentrated in America's major cities. The site where an unidentified 1742–43 puppeteer or puppeteers gave shows was located in the heart of Philadelphia: "At the Sign of the Coach-and-Horses against the State-House, in Chestnut Street." Brickell and Mosely were exhibiting puppets, music machines, and acrobatic shows "at the house of Mr. Hamilton Hewetson, at the Sign of the Spread-Eagle, near White-Hall Slip" on the waterfront in New York City in 1747. Perhaps the pair counted on a seafaring clientele. Brickell continued to choose locations near or at taverns along the New York waterfront—near the "Weigh House" (1748), "at Mr. Beekman's, at the Spring-Garden" (1752), and "at the Sign of the Blue-Anchor at Peck's Slip" (1756). In Charleston, Brickell played at Mr. Doughty's long room.[61] Puppeteers and waxwork proprietors, such as James Wyatt, Mr. Bayly, and William Patridge, did the same: Wyatt, at the "Sign of the Dolphin Privateer, near the Work-House" (1749); Bayly, at the "sign of the Orange tree, on Golden-Hill" (1767); and Patridge, "at the sign of Lord John Murray, in Orange-street, Golden Hill" (1770).[62] As is true earlier in the century, little information exists as to who actually sat in showmen's audiences during this period. The only identified prerevolutionary woman to have seen an acrobatic entertainment was Ann Manigault, wife of the Charleston merchant Gabriel Manigault, who went "to see" Mr. Sturgess perform on the slack wire at Gordon's Tavern in 1754.[63] The only identified man was the Boston merchant John Rowe, who watched legerdemain and tumbling demonstrations with his friends in 1767: "Capt Clark a Stranger diverted us much in playing the slight of hand."[64] Rowe incidentally found some entertainers better than others. When balance-master Henry Hymes performed at Samuel Blodget's tavern in that town the same year, Rowe was unimpressed: "He is but a clumsey Hand."[65]

As we approach the postrevolutionary and early national periods, however, more members of the "best" families and additional prominent professionals attended these entertainments. On 2 September 1783 three of Mary Vial Holyoke's children (Margaret, twenty years old; Betsy, twelve years old; and Judy, nine years old) "went in the Evng to the Puppet Show." Two days later Mary noted, "*We* went to the Puppet Show."[66] The Holyoke family of Salem included a college president and several physicians; they regularly attended balls and assemblies, patronized miniature painters and portraitists, and sent their children to leading Boston and Salem dancing-masters. Others must have joined them because Boston's selectmen became so incensed by the numerous puppet shows in the town in 1785 they ordered that anyone staging them should "desist from such exhibitions" or face prosecution.[67] In the 1790s, William Bentley kept track of John Brenon's activities in Salem, even if he may not always have bought a ticket to his performances. Bentley called Brenon a "Legerdemain Irishman." Noah Webster reported in New York: "I attend the Slack Wire Dancing" on the same day that Brenon advertised there.⁶⁸ At least some educated men were watching ropedancers.

The Holyoke family was also busy patronizing the automaton and ventriloquy shows passing through Boston and Salem. Two members of the family, Susanna Holyoke Ward and her mother, Mary Vial Holyoke, saw Blanchard's automatons on different occasions in 1795. On 31 April when visiting Boston sometime before her marriage to her neighbor, sixteen-year-old Susanna Holyoke wrote, "I at the Automatons with Joshua Ward."⁶⁹ In December 1795, she and her mother went to see Blanchard's figures when they were being toured by John Maison: "Evng at the Atomata."⁷⁰ Susanna and Margaret visited Washington Hall in Salem on 7 September 1796, "at Falcon[i]'s exhibition," witnessing "The Sagacious Mermaid," an automaton that executed several experiments with a sword.⁷¹ Several years later, on 13 January 1802, Margaret and her father, Edward A. Holyoke, took in the third of James Rannie's four performances in Salem: "Went to see the ventriloquist with my Papa." And William Bentley, even though he may not have sat in the audience, carefully monitored the public's reception and attendance of the evening shows given by "Raynier, the Ventriloquist," whose opening night attracted a "select & small company" in Salem but later was attended by a "great concourse" when the admission was cut in half.⁷² James Rannie's exhibitions continued to interest people from the "highest social circles." In the spring of 1802, on 14 May after dining with several colleagues including Captain Meriwether Lewis, Mahlon Dickerson (who later became governor of New Jersey, a U.S. senator, and secretary of the navy) saw him perform in Philadelphia. Dickerson was "much pleased" with "Rannie's deceptions."⁷³

If we are often uncertain about the gender, background, and education of audience members, we can be more definitive about where these entertainments were taking place. In spite of their impressive skills most prerevolutionary entertainers like Burlesson, Brickell, Wyatt, Bayly, and Saunders were defined by a tavern ambiance. Even after the revolution, entertainers generally kept to taverns. Out of fourteen venues advertised by John Brenon in the period between 1774 and 1792, ten were in long rooms. Only three of his locations were formal assembly rooms in New York City, Salem, and Portsmouth; one was a storefront in Philadelphia.⁷⁴ By contrast, younger men like Mr. Bennett, whose repertoire of slack-wire balancing and conjuring almost duplicated that of Brenon, increasingly took advantage of public buildings—among them the Rhode Island Statehouse, the Free Schoolhouse in New London, and the Courthouse in Burlington, New Jersey—as well as three private assembly halls (fig. 9.9). Of the twenty-two venues advertised by showman Joseph Falconi, only two were in taverns; all the rest were in theaters, courthouses, and major assembly rooms. It was the same with the Rannies, who performed at only eight tavern long rooms

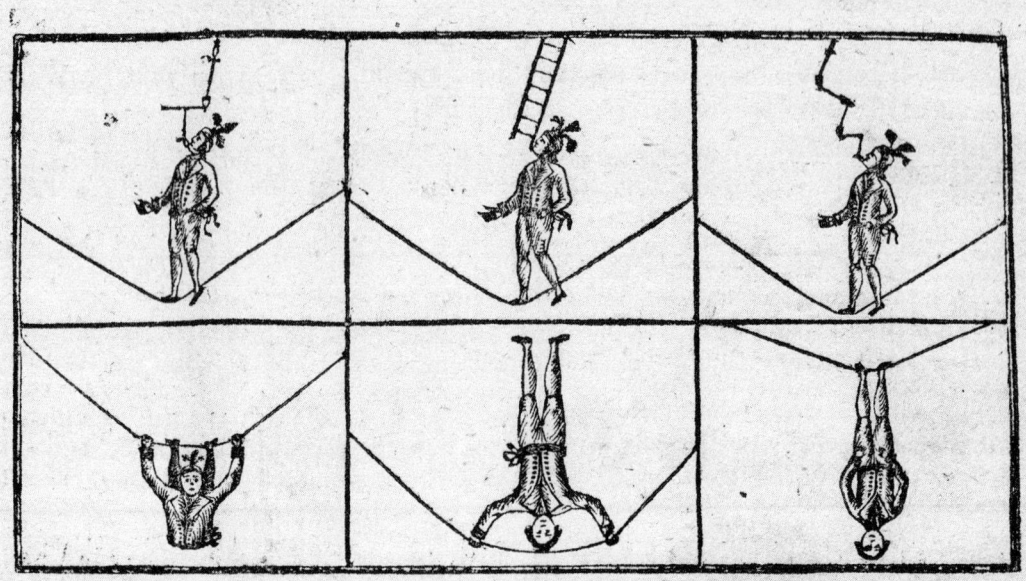

Figure 9.9. *"FOR THE LAST TIME, POSITIVELY!"* Mr. Bennett's advertisement for an acrobatic exhibition in Portsmouth, New Hampshire, proudly proclaiming in 1790 he was "From London and Italy." In other notices, however, he called himself an "American Balance-Master" or "the noted balance master from Canada but originally from Sadler's Wells, London." Portsmouth *Osborne's New-Hampshire Spy,* 3 February 1790. Courtesy, New-York Historical Society, neg. no. 90789d.

or large rooms in tavern settings during their ten-year American sojourn—most of them in Maryland, Richmond, and Charleston. Everywhere else they leased concert halls, assembly rooms, coffeehouses, formal gardens, theaters, Masons' halls, ballrooms, dance halls, hotels, and inns.

The move from taverns to public buildings follows the steady buildup of popular culture in the American colonies. George Speaight's research uncovered about twenty puppeteers active in England before 1660, another thirteen between 1661 and 1700, and another forty in the period 1700 to 1775. By contrast, during the seven years that Burlesson ostensibly circulated his puppets in New England between 1732 and 1739, he may have been the only puppeteer in North America. The same can be said with other early showmen and -women. Richard Brickell, who brought legerdemain, the magic lantern, and tumbling to New York City, Philadelphia, and Charleston, essentially worked alone during this time, as did John Brenon and Hyman Saunders in the 1770s when they brought ropedancing and other entertainments to New England, Philadelphia, New York City, and southern audiences. By 1790, however, a rush of puppeteers and show people had invaded all major centers of population.

At the same time, we have to remember that this expansion cut both ways. Whereas outdoor entertainments such as exotic animals, fireworks, balloon ascensions, and wirewalking feats tapped into a universally shared passion or interest, many tavern entertainments increasingly relied on a particular "cultural memory" or even a European "education" to be fully enjoyed. For most performers, this prior knowledge was not there initially. We find evidence of its gradual emergence, however, in some early New York City and Philadelphia conjuring advertisements. When Mr. Bayly presented his "dexterity" at the Orange Tree Tavern in New York, he claimed his tricks were done "without the use of Pockets, Bags, or Sleeves."[75] A few years later, in 1772, Hyman Saunders—then teaming with Abraham Benjamin, a balancer—described himself as a "most astonishing proficient in the art of clean conveyance" and promised to entertain his audiences "without descending to the low tricks of cups and balls, ribbons, &c." Both conjurers were now using technical terminology as part of their advertising appeal. "Pockets, Bags, or Sleeves" were the first things the audience looked for in order to discover the source of Bayly's tricks. The term *conveyance* was jargon long used by conjurers to transfer objects openly from one location to another without the spectators' being aware of it. *Clean conveyance* usually meant the conjurer had an assistant helping him.[76] Bayly and Saunders were sharing with their audiences what in effect were relatively advanced techniques.

If the concept of "cultural memory" is valid, it suggests the existence of a growing divide facing strollers as they attempted to pursue their North American careers. Most showmen faced naive audiences unaccustomed to the degree of sophistication and learning found in Philadelphia and New York City. Did Boston residents recognize "Margaret, Countess of Heininburg, who had 365 Children at one Birth?" This waxwork was exhibited in that town in 1733 after being housed for many years at a Mrs. Salmon's establishment in London, but it is unclear whether the work was subsequently taken to other cities. Were waterfront audiences in New York City familiar with "Fair Rosamond," the puppet story that James Wyatt presented in 1749? And Wyatt is not known to have traveled to Philadelphia, Annapolis, or Charleston. Did theatergoers know about "The Miller Deceived" or "Harlequin and Columbine" when commedia dell'arte afterpieces were first staged in New York City in 1753? Harlequin pantomimes do not appear to have been understood or appreciated by American audiences until well after the revolution. Yet thirty or forty years later, these same stories had become familiar enough to the American public at large that strollers no longer had to compromise or de-Europeanize their productions.[77]

Regardless of our inability to pinpoint who actually was watching or fully understanding the performances, it seems that most eighteenth-century American consumers of tavern-based culture were commoners who had somehow retained a memory or acquired a knowledge of popular culture as it was known in Europe. Again we can see hints of this when servants, deserters, and other disenfranchised Americans were imitating or replicating itinerants' entertainments—a process that helps consolidate our earlier hypothesis regarding the uneven dissemination of these practices in North America. In Pennsylvania alone between 1740 and 1780, dozens of runaway servants displayed a working knowledge of tricks and feats of dexterity demonstrated by strollers. Margaret Philips, a runaway servant of about thirty years of age, was described as "of middle size . . . [who] can sing well, and dance the ropes, with many other tricks." The notice adds, "She calls herself Mary Smith, she has a brindle dog with her, . . . [which] is known by the name of Bellanamony."[78] William Pennel, another English servant, was "much addicted to swear[ing] and get[ting] drunk, plays a great many antick tricks, such as making a piece of silver dance in a glass full of water, and filling a little tin cup full of wheat with one grain, which he used to call his bushel and bell."[79] Samuel Alsford, a forty-year-old deserter from the 34th Regiment in Philadelphia, was "famous for shewing the dexterity of hand, when he generally takes the name of Ford."[80]

Elsewhere, Samuel Salter, a convict servant who had absconded in 1745 from his master in Baltimore, was "dextrous in showing slight of hand tricks."[81] John Robison, an Irish servant boy from Winchester, Virginia, was said to "play cards, dance, and tell fortunes by the cards."[82] John Willmot of South Hadley, Massachusetts, a revolutionary enlistee who had fled with his bounty in 1777, was described as "artful in playing tricks with cards, and before the time of his enlisting had with him an artificial snake, which he has since left behind to prevent being discovered."[83] Labe Galand, who had masqueraded as a priest on board a French ship lying in New London, Connecticut, in 1778, had "a good Notion of Slight of Hand."[84]

Making a piece of silver dance in a glass full of water? An artificial snake? Philip Butterworth's study of English magic practices tells us that water tricks and artificial vipers (or real but nonvenomous snakes) served as accessories in sixteenth- and early seventeenth-century passion plays dealing with the reputed powers of Saint Paul.[85] We have no evidence that either William Pennel or John Willmot (or any of these runaways) had watched tumbling, juggling, ropewalking, ropedancing, or conjuring acts such as those given in 1728 in Philadelphia, or New York in 1734, Charleston in 1770, or Halifax, North Carolina, in 1778. Some servants may have grown up and presumably learned their trade (and their tricks) in England, Scotland, or Ireland. But this trend does suggest that Philadelphia, New York City, and Boston to the north, and Annapolis, Baltimore, Williamsburg, and Charleston to the south, may have formed an axis about which key elements of tavern-oriented popular culture in mid-eighteenth-century America emerged. While still inconclusive, this much is clear: the runaways who had honed these skills enough to be recognized by them received their ideas from somewhere, and imitating tavern-based itinerant cultural carriers presents one distinct possibility.

Part III

ITINERANTS ASSUME SCHOOLED AND MANNERED CALLINGS

Chapter 10

Art of Psalmody

THAT EIGHTEENTH-CENTURY runaway servants, apprentices, and military deserters may have frequented itinerant entertainments should come as no surprise. The activities pursued by strollers were designed to be fascinating, and they often captivated the attention of America's rank and file. But this was by no means true for the population as a whole. At this point in American history, the act of itinerancy itself—the process that carried people like Richard Brickell, John Brenon, and the Rannies to Boston, New York, and Philadelphia in the first place—was still a relatively aberrant notion to most genteel inhabitants in the English-speaking Atlantic world. This was especially true for those in the American Northeast, who continued to regard itinerant business ventures as controversial, unethical, or suspect. When much of New York City's male population went out of their way to witness Joseph Deeker's balloon ascension—even when a majority of them suspected the shell might catch fire—the event highlighted an important distinction between popular and schooled culture. Balloon flights were exciting and attracted thousands of people, but they were likely to fail. The importation of European theater and concert life was less exciting and attracted fewer people, but musicians and actors had at least a chance for long-range employment.

We see the same divisions in other occupations as an itinerant "mentality" and even an itinerant lifestyle began to suffuse additional strands of culture arriving from Europe. Much of the early sustainability of these ventures depended on an itinerant's ability to read accurately what the American public wanted and what it could afford because adaptability was a principal factor in the transmission of popular culture from the Old World to the new. As tradition-bearers assumed an "American" perspective, they were obliged to reassess what best induced clients to take an interest in them. Not all itinerants made this transatlantic passage readily. Tumblers and trick riders had a much easier time of it than miniature painters because virtually all Americans enjoyed watching demonstrations of acrobatics and horsemanship, whereas only a minority could afford the luxury of miniatures and jeweled portraits. Miniatures never became a ubiquitous or common item even though most miniature painters were itinerants.

For many inhabitants of North America the first socially acceptable form of itinerancy may have involved schools designed to improve Congregational and Anglican singing practices. This may explain why the teaching of psalmody—a practice long used by Christian denominations—occupies a central place in the roster of callings that worked to further Europeanize and bring mannered discipline to early American provincial life. Congregational New Englanders particularly, who praised the Lord with psalms and hymns on every Sabbath, for years had viewed their music as an integral part of their Protestant worship and had sustained it by musically untrained deacons or choristers who relied on their memories of tunes. But some members of these New England churches aspired to praise the Lord more harmoniously, just as they sought to own the latest styles of English furniture, plate, and domestic architecture, and they constantly discussed and argued the issues raised by musical training. When a talented clergyman organized a singing group that performed in public at the Brattle Square Meetinghouse in Boston in the 1720s, the congregation and town residents were enthralled, and many became filled with a desire for change. They were aided by those New Englanders dissatisfied with the current state of psalm singing who supported setting up "singing schools" staffed in part by transient teachers.

Few people understood this need as well as Samuel Sewall. After serving almost two and a half decades as precentor (or chorister) for the Third Church in Boston, Sewall knew his voice was failing in 1718 when he "set" the psalm for York tune (one of half a dozen commonly known melodies) and the congregation, relying on its memory, "fell" into St. David's during the second verse.[1] It was a discouraging experience for Sewall, who just three weeks earlier had listened helplessly as singers in the gallery had done the same thing during the afternoon exercises.[2] For years Sewall had been aware of his shortcomings as a singer, and in both these instances, instead of following the tune Sewall had selected (as they properly should have done), the strongest singers in the congregation responded unknowingly or knowingly with one of their own choosing.

Another difficulty was that Sewall himself was sometimes unaware which tune he intended (or was carrying), and as a result his efforts worked at cross-purposes. After a wedding in 1700, he set York tune "not intending it." On other occasions he "intended Windsor, and fell into High-Dutch" or "try'd to set Low-Dutch . . . [but] fell into the tune of the 119th Psalm." And he had as much trouble recognizing tunes as his congregation. "I would have assisted Capt. Frary but scarce knew what Tune he design'd; and the Tune I guess'd at, was in so high a Key that I could not reach it." A devoted singer who frequently led psalmody at weddings, fasts, and private prayer meetings, Sewall regarded his weakness as a signal that it was time to hand his duties over to someone else. He went to his minister to ask that he be replaced as singing leader—only to be urged by Reverend Thomas Prince (1687–1758) to "do it six years longer," which he did.[3]

Sewall's problem with identifying tunes reflected the prevailing low state of musical literacy in New England in the opening decades of the eighteenth century. He and other precentors in the Third Church congregation might have recognized about a dozen tunes printed in the ninth (1698) edition of the Bay Psalm Book. But neither Sewall nor the others were likely to have been able to lead in singing more than six. These traditional English psalm tunes were what remained of the thirty-nine tunes printed in Henry Ainsworth's *Book of Psalmes* (1612) and the forty-two "common" tunes printed in Thomas Sternhold and John Hopkins's *The Whole Booke of Psalmes* (1562), the two psalters brought to North America by first-generation Englishmen. Many had been printed in woodcut musical notation in later editions of the Bay Psalm Book and in Nahum Tate and Nicholas Brady's *New Version of the Psalms of David,* recently issued in London (1696).[4] But given the reduced state of musical training after three generations, tunes had been sustained principally through oral tradition and had been somewhat simplified and changed in the process. Reverend Thomas Walter (1696–1725) complained he had heard three different melodies sung as Oxford tune in three different churches; he added that to a "good Judge," there might be five hundred different tunes in a single melody. Walter called for a reform of the "Depravations and Debasements our Psalmody labours under." Reverend Cotton Mather (1663–1728) complained that singing in his congregation had "degenerated into a odd noise, that has more of what we want a name for, than any Regular Singing in it." Others characterized church singing as "jarring" or remembered it as "drawling" and "quavering."[5]

This was the state of congregational singing in New England when the first attempts were made by singing teachers to reintroduce musical literacy into parish life. Beginning with fundamentals such as scales and the names of notes, instructors emphasized musical notation, accurate pitch, and harmony; they also encouraged continuous singing instead of reciprocal psalmody (meaning deacon-led recitations or chanting of individual lines) and the founding of singing schools and musical societies. The teaching of psalmody gained its initial impetus from the writings and sermons of a few early eighteenth-century Massachusetts clergymen. Reverend John Tufts (1689–1750) of Newbury, Massachusetts, issued his *Introduction to the Singing of Psalm-Tunes In a Plain and Easy Method* in 1712. Reverend Thomas Symmes (1678–1725), a clergyman from nearby Bradford, authored *The Reasonableness of Regular Singing; or, Singing by Note* (1720). Both publications took to task the arguments that musical training was "popish," that the names of notes were "bawdy" or "blasphemous," and that practice sessions were indecent and disorderly.⁶ In time their efforts led to the founding of formal singing societies essentially dedicated to the eradication of a form of popular culture that had been actually carried over from England but which through neglect and lack of training had achieved a provincial status that many found undesirable. The center of this new effort was Boston. Samuel Sewall's diary records that "Great singing" took place in the Court Chamber on the night of 15 March 1721. The following evening, Mather preached in the schoolhouse to "the young Musicians." The "House was full," Sewall wrote, "and the Singing extraordinarily Excellent, such as has hardly been heard before in Boston. Sung four times out of Tate and Brady."⁷

Within weeks comparable societies gathered in surrounding towns. One of the first was led by Reverend Richard Brown, Jr. (1675–1732), who preached a singing lecture at his Reading, Massachusetts, meetinghouse on 15 March 1722 accompanied by a three-part singing group of about fifty people including some from "Towns adjacent." The effect of these lectures was related by Brown in the records of the First Church of Reading, Massachusetts, for the year 1722: "Several publick Lettrs [Lectures] wr had to promote him [regular singing], ye 1, preacht by myselfe, 2nd by Mr Symes, ye 3d by Mr Fish we much ws Sd to encourage it & in each of we yy Sang 4 time exact by ye rule no man opposing a School ws set up, may [many] both men & women learnt some indeed wr not so clear in it (as by mistake) concieving it popery but at lenght having been encouraged . . . 4 of his family, attended ye Schools."⁸

The 1722 Reading "school" is the first known instance of parish-sponsored musical training held in New England. The music-master who conducted it is unidentified, but strong circumstantial evidence points to Reverend Thomas Walter, whose education at Harvard College encompassed music theory and part-singing and who was instrumental in founding Boston's Society for Promoting Regular Singing in 1721 where he served as the principal musician and choirmaster. The society's singers, who may have numbered up to one hundred, seem to have been gathered from musically talented parishioners in the Cambridge and Boston congregations, some of them possibly Walter's classmates who had received comparable training at the college or pupils of one of several secular music masters newly arrived in Boston.⁹

As singing demonstrations and schools proliferated, votes were taken by many towns and parishes in the Boston area to abandon the "old" or usual way of singing and promote the new. One contemporary account indicates that by 1723 regular singing had been instituted in eleven local communities.¹⁰ Three years later the singing issue had spread beyond eastern Massachusetts Bay to communities in rural Massachusetts and Connecticut. Barnstable voted on the matter in 1726, Beverly in 1730, and Southbury in 1734.¹¹ As in Boston, the musically educated clergy led the way. The ministers of the General Association of

Hartford County voted their recommendations for singing reform at a meeting held on 12 May 1727; the North Association in the county of Hartford took this one step further by voting in 1727 "that persons may well Improve their Time in taking pains to be Instructed . . . [in the] Singing of Psalms."[12] In Farmington, Connecticut, in 1727, the question was proposed whether to approve "the way of singing of Psalms which is recommended by the Reverend Ministers of Boston." Some votes tied regular singing to the use of psalm books with "prickt notes"; some limited the number of tunes (citing them by name) that choristers were allowed to call; many votes were simply postponements or compromises allowing congregations to sing half the time in the new way and half the time in the old.[13]

The first evidence of traveling psalmodists holding these schools is found in the Connecticut River Valley. Little is known of George Beale (1675–1760) and his son Matthew Beale (1715–after 1797), who have been described as the first itinerant singing-masters active in the American colonies. English immigrants who arrived in Willington, Connecticut, in 1725, they appear in clergymen's diaries and the ledgers of the Connecticut River religious societies voting to hire them between the years 1727 and 1758. In a sequence of entries continuing over several months, Reverend Timothy Edwards (1669–1758) of the second or south society of Windsor noted that George and Matthew began to teach regular singing in his parish on 13 March 1727. Their efforts met with approbation because a vote taken by the parish a month and a half later, on 22 May 1727, resolved that the congregation would sing "according to the rule . . . taught us by Mr. Beall." They were also active in other parishes. According to Edwards's diary, Beale and his son lived Friday through Monday at Windsor and Tuesday through Thursday at Hartford. Typically they spent as much time traveling as they did teaching:

> March 13 [1727]. Mr. George Beale and his son Matthew came to my house at noon, and went that day to Dinner, both of them, and at night to Supper, and Lay here that night and went to breakfast and dinner the next day: in the afternoon went to Hartford. . . .
>
> March 17. They both came again on Friday and Supped and Lodged here, and continued here until the next Tuesday after dinner and then went again in the afternoon to Hartford. . . .
>
> March 31. They came again on Friday evening and continued here till Tuesday after dinner as before.

During the five months the Beales taught in Hartford and South Windsor, they also made appearances across the river in Windsor's first parish, in Springfield, and in Willington. Their names were very much alive in the memory of Windsor's south society nine years later when the town again debated "whether they would sing [the old way or] the way taught by Mr. Beal, commonly called singing by rule." Both men probably taught at the school for Native Americans at

Stockbridge in 1753 as well as at Woodbury and New Milford, Connecticut. And Matthew Beale may still have been active five years later when the new third society in Windsor voted in 1758 eight pounds "to hire Mr. Beal" to teach them how to sing.[14]

While slow in building momentum, the itinerant singing school eventually became one of America's most popular educational institutions, second only to the dancing academy and the one-room schoolhouse. At least 226 choristers, singers, composers, and compilers from all walks of life found musical vocations open to them as singing-masters before 1826; of these about 145 were transients active in New England, eastern New York, New Jersey, and Philadelphia. This may be well below their actual numbers; music historians like Nym Cooke estimate the number of psalmodists or "Yankee tunesmiths" (as they were later known) ranged between 750 and 1,200.[15] These teachers rented space in schoolrooms, courthouses, and meetinghouses and set up a schedule to accommodate simultaneous schools. The field was dominated by white, Anglo-American males, the majority of them members of large musical families in New England.

The work of teaching psalmody could be grueling. In 1809, Amos Holbrook, an associate of Connecticut publisher Andrew Law, reported to Law he was "worn out" trying to teach grammar in New Jersey while also maintaining a weekly circuit of four singing classes undertaken in schools in surrounding towns: "During the short days in winter, [I] sleep six hours, then ride 2, 7, 10 or 22 miles, & sing three or four hours, & afterwards return to my school. All this has employed all my hours; indeed after I could not find time to eat, or sleep, drink, nor smoak." A comparably rigorous schedule was kept by Amzi Chapin (1768–1835), a Springfield, Massachusetts, singing-master, composer, and instrument maker who taught in Virginia, North Carolina, Kentucky, and Pennsylvania. Chapin sometimes held schools in three or four locations simultaneously, each school lasting a full quarter, or three months. He was often required to travel between schools at night. In order to spare his horse he walked the shorter distances, and he was constantly having to shoe the animal.[16]

Nevertheless, psalmody teachers enjoyed several advantages over other transients. The chief of these was the widespread acceptance of religious music. Singing the Lord's praise was sanctioned everywhere, and it gave singing-masters an easy entry into communities that supported an organized church, as most did. Singing-masters were welcomed in the homes of their clients, usually reform-minded clergymen, deacons, and laymen, and they conducted their schools in meetinghouses, schoolhouses, parish halls, and grammar schools provided by the religious society that hired them or by the many private individuals who wished to improve parish singing. The more enterprising singing-masters sold their publications in the communities where they held schools, or they franchised other singing teachers to distribute them. Some even printed their own music sheets. Concluding almost all singing schools was a public performance given at the meetinghouse, and it was sometimes a combined effort by several singing schools from neighboring towns and parishes.[17]

The late 1760s and early 1770s saw a considerable increase in the number of singing-masters. They seem to have come in waves. Newport was approached by as many as three singing-masters in two years, from 1770 to 1772, one of them employing the town's brick Market House.[18] Four psalmodists taught in Salem from 1772 to 1774, variously using the town's assembly hall, schoolhouse, and a meetinghouse.[19] Four more appeared in close succession in Boston from 1769 to 1773, one located at an auction house in Dock Square.[20] At least some schools were organized by subscription lists, which drew momentum from parents who signed up their offspring. One teacher in Salem divided his singing school into classes for children at five in the afternoon and for young gentlemen and ladies at seven in the evening. He left subscription "papers" at the Salem printing office. And where space was not readily available, teachers rented public halls. Jonathan Nichols taught in the county courthouse in Newark in 1797; A. Coburn made use of a courthouse in Elizabethtown, Maryland, in 1803.[21]

One of the most influential of the new psalmodists was a Boston leather worker named William Billings (1746–1800). In October 1769, Billings and John Barry advertised a singing school near the Old South Meetinghouse. Both were members of the New South Church where Barry was also singing-master, and they proposed to hold school at night. Billings followed this with a succession of singing schools in towns to the south of Boston, the first in 1771: "W. Billings began his Singing School in Weymouth, boards here at Mr. Smith's." In 1774, he held other schools in nearby Stoughton and in Providence. After the evacuation of Boston he resumed classes at the Old South and Brattle Square Meetinghouses. A self-taught composer, Billings supported himself as a full-time tanner and as Boston's inspector of leather. Shortly after opening his initial school in Boston, he issued in 1770 the first of seven publications containing psalm and hymn tunes as well as some secular songs on patriotic and musical subjects. *The New England Psalm-Singer; or, American Chorister* was the first American tunebook, with many compositions named after Boston churches and neighboring towns associated with Billings's music schools and his Boston tan yard.[22] His *Psalm-Singer's Amusement* contained "fuguing" tunes and anthems (another first), which imitated the structure but not the style of European counterpoint. Few of his contemporaries recognized his contribution to New England music, but one who did was Reverend William Bentley, who two days after Billings's death in 1800 observed that "this self-taught man . . . may justly be considered as the father of our New England music." Bentley continued, "Many who have imitated have excelled him, but none of them had better original power. . . . He was a singular man, of moderate size, short of one leg, with one eye, without any address, and with uncommon negligence of person. Still he spake and sung and thought as a man above the common abilities. He died poor and neglected and perhaps did too much neglect himself."[23]

Other singing-masters began to follow Billings's style of teaching. In Westborough, for example, Reverend Ebenezer Parkman, who had received some musical training (and dancing lessons) while a student at Harvard College, learned that an itinerant singing-master named Lemuel Badcock had been invited to come to Westborough to teach four singing schools.[24] Badcock, a cousin of singing-master and composer Samuel Babcock, was related by marriage to Jacob and Edward French, well-known musical brothers.[25] Lemuel's first school began on 12 January 1778 and convened every day for a month at the home of a Deacon Woods. His "singing Scholars" numbered forty-six, of which thirty-four were males and twelve were females. He charged two dollars per pupil. As the school progressed, changes in Westborough's Sunday service became visible: "Mr. Badcock and his Singers sat in the Front [gallery], on the Women's Side & rose up to Sing." A week after the close of the school, Parkman ordered a shipment of unbound Tate and Brady's psalmbooks; Parkman's sons (and others) were soon engaged in binding them and "pricking out Tunes."[26]

In mid-March Badcock returned to hold a second school, this time for two weeks, at a charge of "another Dollar" per pupil. Again the school was conducted at Deacon Woods's and ended when Badcock returned to Wrentham on 2 April 1778.[27] He began a third school in October 1778 that lasted for about eight weeks. More innovations crept in. According to Parkman, "The Singers more generally sat today in the Front, and some no. stood up. Mr. Lemuel Badcock was among them. . . . Mr. Badcock and his Scholars sang a number of good Tunes, in Parts." Badcock started his fourth school on 18 January 1779 at Barnabas Newton's home, ending 10 February 1779 when Parkman noted, "This is Mr. Badcock's last Day." It was during his final school that changes in singing came rapidly. "Anthems and Tunes" were added to the religious exercises. The singers were given permission to sit permanently in the front gallery and to stand when they sang. Selected "good Tunes" were sung in harmonic parts. In 1780, or about a year after Badcock's visits, Parkman observed that singing on the Sabbath was conducted for the first time "without Reading *lineally*," meaning the congregation had given up the old practice of reciprocal reading and singing of the first verse led by the deacon.[28]

These reforms exacted a special cost to the social unity of the Westborough parish. On one occasion Parkman was obliged to take a Mr. Batherick aside and talk to him "about his holding down his Head" when the congregation was singing triple-time tunes—presumably Batherick's way of showing his disapproval. The task of choristers had become so controversial that eventually all four of them resigned. A small minority of parishioners walked out of the meetinghouse anytime that Tate and Brady was sung or discussed. Parkman suspected that some were "disgusted" at the sight of singers standing in the gallery; he was told by others that they thought the singers' behavior was "abominable" when they stood to sing.[29]

Although some members of the Westborough parish criticized Badcock, the emergence of a new generation of teachers like him in the Connecticut Valley and central Massachusetts was the first sign that New England was becoming a regional center for innovative psalmody. A hint of this is present in the announcement made by Hartford-based singing-master Amos Bull (1745–1825), who left subscription lists in New York City in 1774 telling prospective scholars he had taught for many years "in several parts of New England."[30] Almost identical language was used by a Mr. Fuller, "lately from New-England," when publicizing a school of psalmody in New York City in 1784.[31] But the perception emerges more clearly in the diary of Noah Webster, who conducted a series of singing schools during his tour of the southern states in 1785. In Charleston where he arranged his initial schools, Webster recorded, "I go to the White Meeting & hear a little New England singing." The region's psalmody, like its thanksgiving days, was progressing "Southward."[32]

Some singing teachers targeted specific regions. Ishmael Spicer, for example, focused on the Hudson Valley. Spicer was born in Norwich, Connecticut, and lived (and married) in nearby Bozrah. By his own estimate he conducted 106 singing schools in the eastern United States during a 31-year period from 1793 to 1824. The "whole number of scholars" in his schools totaled 4,880, and he earned $3,394.26 for his efforts. Many of these schools were concentrated in eighteen Hudson River Valley communities extending from Kingston, New York, about seventy miles north to Balston Spa. As some dancing-masters did, Spicer seems to have taught concurrent schools in towns located about ten miles apart, very likely on different days of the week. In 1805, he held schools in Castleton, Schodack, and Nassau, three contiguous towns in Rensselaer County ten miles southeast of Albany; in 1806, he taught in Hudson and Claverack using "Mr. Schwartz's room" at the City Tavern. He also returned at regular intervals to the same communities. Curiously, he kept out of larger localities such as Troy, Albany, Poughkeepsie, and New York City. Rather, he appealed to smaller parishes whose populations favored music in public worship. Although few details of Spicer's travels are known, he returned each spring and summer season to Bozrah.[33]

Besides covering long distances, psalmody teachers faced other challenges, the most important being the seasonal nature of their profession. Singing schools were almost always gathered in midwinter when the agricultural cycle was at its lowest ebb and members of the congregation and their children had time to practice during the long evenings. This was especially true of rural areas where farm labor was in short supply during the spring, summer, and early fall. This model is reflected in the movements of Brattleboro, Vermont, singing-master Levi Redfield (1745–1838), who ran schools in northern and central New England from 1786 to 1796. Redfield's 1798 autobiography, compiled to promote his career as a singing-master, claims he had taught seventy-one schools and "in the whole, 3785 pupils." He always held schools in the winter months and always at two communities fairly close to one another—presumably negotiating the second while teaching the first. In October 1785, he began a ten-week course in Mason, New Hampshire, and followed it with a three-month school in nearby Hollis beginning in January 1786. The next winter he was ten weeks at Groton, Massachusetts, and eight weeks at neighboring Shirley. In subsequent years he held winter schools at Lunenburg and Harvard, Massachusetts; Chesterfield and Washington, New Hampshire; and Rockingham and Chester, Vermont. Each time he returned to his family and homestead in Brattleboro for the spring, summer, and early fall agricultural seasons.[34]

To supplement their income, some psalmodists took up work as sacred music compilers and as music printers, publishers, and retailers. William Billings was an innovator in these fields, although they were never enough to support him. Billings not only posted a subscription list at Levi Hall's in Providence but left his "singing books to be sold by said Hall." Singing-master Samuel Adams Holyoke frequently coordinated his schools with the distribution and sale of his musical texts. Holyoke's notice in Newburyport for a subscription singing school to commence on a Monday in December 1797 coincided with Edmund M. Blunt's selling Holyoke's texts at his bookstore; in return, Holyoke kept his subscription list there. Later, on 17 February 1804, when he called for a singing school in Salem, he asked subscribers to sign up at Cushing and Appleton's bookstore. In a receipt for payment on 23 April 1804, he listed thirteen women and thirteen men who received lessons (fig. 10.1).[35] Isaac Lane, a "celebrated Master and instructor of Sacred Music," was more circumspect. When advertising his Portsmouth school, he promised that "any singing book will answer the purpose of the first evening." But that he, too, was looking for opportunities to hawk his *Anthem Suitable to be Performed at an Ordination* is suggested by William Bentley's observation in 1797: "A Curious Mr. Lane from Bedford in Town to sell Anthems." Daniel Read may actually have undertaken schools primarily as a way of promoting and selling copies of his hymn and anthem collections and music texts because part-singing and other advanced forms of psalmody obligated choirs to use multiple copies of tunebooks.[36]

By the second decade of the nineteenth century, psalmody teachers increasingly traveled deeper into southern and mid-western states. William Wood, of Newburyport and compiler of *Harmonia Evangelica,* opened a singing school in Alexandria, Virginia, in the spring of 1815; by September he announced he would teach a second quarter. Thomas Essom, whose place he had taken in Alexandria, moved west to Charles Town, Virginia, where he began a singing school at the Zoar Meeting House, located on the way to Shepherd's Town. Ezekiel Simonds, who had taught a number of years at Hudson, New York, moved in 1815 to Baltimore where he opened two schools for vocal music, one at St. Peter's Academy on Mondays and Thursdays, and a second at the Jerusalem Church on Wednesdays and Saturdays.[37] Nevertheless, the welcoming environment that had met psalmody instruction since the early eighteenth century still prevailed. Singing schools became so common in rural areas that special halls were designated for their use. Hallowell, Maine, established a "Singing School room" opposite the meetinghouse in 1820; the same year Middlebury, Vermont, had a "Singing School Room" near its meetinghouse where scholars who had lost or misplaced clothing could come to claim it.[38]

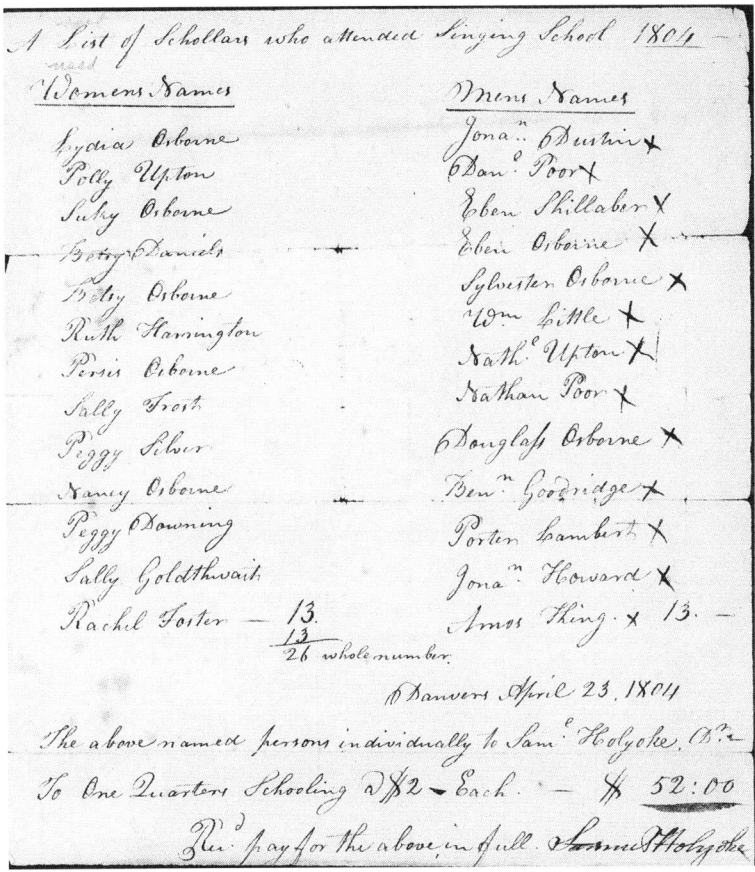

Figure 10.1. "A List of Schollars who attended Singing School 1804." Manuscript. Receipt signed by the singing-master Samuel Adams Holyoke (1762–1820). Danvers, Massachusetts, 23 April 1804. The course instructed thirteen men and thirteen women for one quarter's schooling at two dollars each. Courtesy, Peabody Essex Museum, Salem, Massachusetts.

While the field never achieved racial diversity, at least one singing-master was born in Africa. Occramer Marycoo (1746–1826), also known as Newport Gardner, arrived as a fourteen-year-old slave in 1760 at the Rhode Island home of Caleb Gardner, a prominent Newport merchant. Possessing a "remarkably strong and clear" voice, Marycoo attended a singing school given in 1783 by Connecticut-born psalmodist Andrew Law and readily learned to read and write music. He soon founded a music school on Newport's High Street where his owner was one of his students. By 1791 his school was so profitable that Marycoo was able to buy his freedom and those of some family members. He composed numerous hymns and dance tunes, and one of his melodies ("Crook'd Shanks") appeared in Uri K. Hill's *A Number of Original Airs, Duetto's and Trio's,* published in 1803 in Northampton, Massachusetts. Other compositions were sung for years in African American congregations, and at least one, an anthem named "Promise," was still being sung in Boston in the 1940s.[39] He did not take his school on the road as did so many of his musical contemporaries. Instead, he remained in Newport, joining Reverend Samuel Hopkins's abolitionist First Congregational Church. In 1826, he returned to Africa to help found Liberia.[40]

For the most part, however, psalmody teachers active after 1770 were white Americans, and primarily second- and third-generation New Englanders. This set them apart from most other eighteenth- and nineteenth-century itinerants whose origins were predominantly European. Moreover, they generally espoused a "teaching" and learned tradition (rather than a populist one) in an effort to improve and unify a dispersed English singing culture "misremembered" by many Congregational, Presbyterian, Baptist, and Anglican churches. They took full advantage of known itinerant teaching methods not because they enjoyed the freedom of unfettered travel but because they worked. In the few short years that George Beale and his son Matthew taught "Regular Singing" in the Connecticut Valley, they accomplished what dancing-masters, rope dancers, tavern showmen, and alternative healers had so far been unable to achieve. They won enough acceptance in provincial and rural communities to put a good face on their transiency—thereby opening the way for other itinerants such as the dancing-masters, violin teachers, language teachers, and puppeteers who followed them.

While singing-masters continued to struggle financially throughout the eighteenth century, they did help raise musical proficiency. Ishmael Spicer and Amzi Chapin ran concurrent schools; Levi Redfield established interconnected corridors of movement; Samuel Holyoke arranged subscription schools; Lemuel Badcock taught his students to sing in parts; Andrew Law, Isaac Lane, and William Billings published and sold their own compositions and anthems. Each one of these actions was an early benchmark in the steady merging of mannered and popular culture in eighteenth- and early nineteenth-century America that later influenced penmanship, language schools, music instruction, and English grammar. And every once in a while a respected American singing-master even found himself branching out. Shortly after Uri Hill announced in Boston in December 1805 that "Musick, Vocal and Instrumental, will be taught in Devonshire street, a few rods south of the Post Office," he passed along a second notice. "At the same place," he informed his readers, "Profile Likenesses will be elegantly taken in gold on glass for seven dollars each, or cut in paper for fifty cents for eight of the same person; by means of Hawkins' Patent Physiognotrace, which is universally allowed to excel all others for accuracy."[41] Historian Peter Burke's "little culture" was now thriving in the heart of Hill's mannered singing school.

Chapter 11

Musical Life

SINGING-MASTER Uri Hill's decision to make, sell, and frame "Hawkins" profiles during his brief stay in Boston was precipitated as much by the surplus of singing teachers in that town in 1805 as by the cultural divide that seems to have been pervading America. Like everyone, Hill was obliged to support himself. In fact, he may have fared rather well, especially when we consider the circumstances then surrounding the larger sphere of secular music. The schooled or mannered tastes that were brought over by immigrant English and French musicians competed against those of hundreds of self-taught musicians, ethnic musicians, stage singers, military bands, and hired or enslaved accompanists who were essentially oblivious to what was being composed and played in the refined circles of Vienna, London, Stockholm, Rome, and Paris. This competition took place within a provincial North American society unaccustomed to the social differences that in Europe encouraged aristocratic families and church institutions to patronize professional musicians. Discerning audiences were limited in early America and could only support a few professional musicians; the skills, talents, and repertories that had maintained them in England and Europe were all but unmarketable to the generally sedentary public in the New World.

The story of the Salter family is telling. On Sunday, 20 December 1795, Daniel Salter (fl. 1791–1818) took his usual place at the organ during the service at New Haven's Episcopal Trinity Church. A partially blind keyboardist and violinist recently arrived from England, Salter had just been hired by the vestry at a salary of twenty guineas per year.[1] His employment capped the purchase of Trinity's organ in England by a group of wealthy New Haven subscribers ten years earlier at a cost of £125. A spinet had also been acquired by the church for the purpose of "instructing" keyboardists in the organ's use. Salter worked hard in his new position. He began a music school in New Haven, giving lessons on the harpsichord, violin, guitar, German flute, and pianoforte.[2] He brokered musical instruments and advised buyers in the southern Connecticut area. Enjoying a close relationship with New Haven violinist John H. Ives, he was also a friend of Daniel Read, a composer and compiler already known locally and nationally for his sacred music compositions and publications.[3]

But Trinity Church was only one side of Daniel Salter's musical life. On the Wednesday immediately following the service at Trinity—one night before Christmas Eve—he and one of his older children went to Ebenezer Parmelee's large hall in New Haven where they encountered an entirely different audience. Salter's and Reuben Moulthrop's "Waxwork and Musick" opened that evening with life-size "striking likenesses" in wax of President George Washington and the late Reverend Ezra Stiles. Next to them, also in wax, was a Native American with a tomahawk rushing on a wounded General Richard Butler. Then followed Louis XVI of France, just decapitated, with a grim Republican executioner holding his head aloft for the crowd to see. In a corner huddled the lovers Palemon and Lavinia from the epic poem *The Seasons* by James Thompson. Elsewhere stood wax representations of "Polygamy, or the man with two wives"; a barber shaving an old hermit; two drunken sailors; a mother chiding her daughter; and Caroline, one of the celebrated beauties of nearby Litchfield. At regular intervals Cleaveland Salter, Daniel's nine-year-old son, played a program of airs, marches, and minuets on the pianoforte, sometimes accompanied on the violin by his father. Daniel Salter succeeded him on the pianoforte with František Koczwara's wildly acclaimed sonata "The Battle of Prague" along with other compositions.[4]

Salter and Moulthrop remained at Parmelee's for several weeks. Then Moulthrop advertised for a "light covered Waggon" to take them to Middletown and Hartford.[5] But their liaison did not last. By the time the show left Hartford's city hall, Moulthrop had acquired a pedal organ and hired a less distinguished keyboardist and continued east along the Connecticut shoreline, eventually reaching Providence. Salter and his son returned to New Haven where the father resumed his position at Trinity. But his income was still insufficient to support his family, and neither the increase of his stipend to thirty pounds nor the several benefit concerts arranged for him by Read and Ives provided an answer.[6] Within a year the Salters were back on the road, this time on their own as a "Musical Family." Daniel and Cleaveland Salter, together with Cleaveland's sister Rebecca, a child of seven, played songs and cotillion dances along with airs, marches, and minuets. Concluding each evening's presentation was a lantern show titled "A Sea Engagement," illustrating two fleets locked in a fanciful battle. Salter's newspaper announcements gently nudged hesitating patrons. "Having the misfortune to be afflicted with weakness of sight," he hoped his program would "claim the attention of the Public."[7]

After several 1797 engagements in Norwich, New London, and other Connecticut locations, Salter and his family set out in 1798 for the middle and southern states, appearing first in New Jersey at the Courthouse in Newark, at Mr. Sutton's tavern in New Brunswick, and at the City Hotel in Trenton. They then traveled farther south in 1799 to Alexandria, Richmond, and Fredericksburg, Virginia, and on to Savannah and Augusta, Georgia. In 1800, they returned to Charleston where they briefly joined the performers from the St. Cecilia Society for a concert of vocal and instrumental music. Georgetown, Maryland, was their next stop. By this time Salter's failing eyesight incapacitated him as a music teacher, and again he solicited patronage from "a generous and humane public to enable him to support a wife and three young children." New Haven's Trinity Church, in the meantime, was obliged to hire dancing-master and musician John Ives to play on the Sabbath "in the absence of Salter."[8]

The experiences of the Salter family must have taught them a hard lesson about American musical values. Simply put, Salter's keyboard artistry was worth more as musical background to the horror, pathos, and fascination of a waxwork display than as a means of raising and refining the religious sentiments of the oldest and arguably most prestigious Episcopal congregation in Connecticut. It was not only a matter of being caught between the conflicting domains of sacred and secular musical performances but also a question of discovering the underlying contours of musical priorities in a provincial society. Salter learned why his colleague Read pursued a mercantile career as a dry goods retailer and publisher and why Ives kept a dancing school. The Salters faced this harsh dilemma as the family struggled to earn a competence in a society where the few who aspired to European musical values were separated from its powerful, patronizing aristocracy. Whatever their previous training and whatever their artistic preferences, once the Salters had cast their lot for North America, they were dependent for their living on public entertainments and not on public piety. Granted they performed works by recognized contemporary European composers, but they were obliged to make themselves more crowd pleasing by showing magic-lantern slides of fictitious naval engagements and including comical elements in their acts. Master Salter at age thirteen spoke a "humorous Piece" and danced a hornpipe "in the Character of an American Sailor"; Miss Salter at age nine sang songs and exhibited a "humorous Dance in Character of a Dwarf."[9]

In the end, fate was relatively kind to the Salters. The family returned to New Haven in 1802 where Daniel Salter was restored to his part-time position as organist at Trinity Church. In spite of earlier misgivings about his deteriorating eyesight, he resumed giving private music lessons.[10] For its part, the vestry at Trinity thanked him by providing several amenities including a new seat, a screen, a "handsome frontispiece" for the organ, and an enclosed space "for the Boy who blows the Bellows." Daniel Salter continued to play the organ at Trinity until 1816 when Cleaveland Salter took over; he in turn was replaced by Rebecca Salter in 1832.[11]

The Salters' reliance on a traveling waxworks and catchy dances was endemic to professional concert life in America in the 1790s. Like many European-trained musicians in North America, Salter was doing what he had to in order to survive in a region where music had always been socially fragmented and ecclesiastically defined. At the opening of the nineteenth century, musical life in America encompassed a wide range of performers that included not only instrumentalists and singers but theatrical band members, dance musicians, proprietors of music machines, and street musicians—not to mention music theorists and teachers of instrumental and secular vocal music. These musicians ranged from accomplished European composers, such as cellist John George Schetky and keyboardists Charles Theodore Pachelbel and Peter Pelham, to "common fiddlers" hired for sleigh rides, enslaved violinists directed to play at dance halls, and bassoonists engaged to accompany trained animals.[12]

At the same time, when they were needed, professional musicians were often hard to find. Virtually all North American church organists like Daniel Salter were recruited in London; part of their contract was passage across the Atlantic and the liberty to teach privately. Professional musicians were so rare in early America that when Charleston's St. Cecilia Society in 1771 sought two violinists, two hautboy (or oboe) players, and a bassoonist for engagements lasting up to three years, it placed notices in newspapers as far north as Newport, Rhode Island.[13] And judging by the number of amateurs who were recruited for subscription concerts, part-time performers outnumbered full-time musicians by a ratio of ten to one, a much higher ratio for example than in the theatrical profession. At Pachelbel's harpsichord concert in New York City in 1736, the accompanying "Songs, Violins, and German Flutes" were played by "private Hands." Almost a hundred years later musician Gottlieb Graupner was obliged to recruit his nine-year-old daughter and several "amateurs of the town" to put together a concert for audiences in New Bedford in 1833.[14]

Many musicians who rose to prominence were compelled to rely on itinerancy. In New England, concert life centered around the Van Hagen, the Graupner, and the Hewitt families. Peter Albrecht Van Hagen, Sr. (ca. 1755–1803); his wife, Elizabeth Van Hagen (1750–c. 1809); and his son Peter Albertus Van Hagen, Jr. (1781–1837), were originally from the Netherlands. They moved to Boston in 1796 after periods of residence in London, Charleston, and New York City. From their "Musical Magazine and Warehouse" at 3 Cornhill, the Van Hagens retailed and repaired musical instruments and sold and published sheet music. Concurrently they conducted circuit schools locally and in eastern New England. As organist at Boston's Trinity Church in the years from 1801 to 1809, Van Hagen, Sr., practiced a purposeful style of itinerancy that put him in touch with music lovers throughout eastern New England. For many years he kept a weekly teaching schedule among finishing schools accessible within half a day's ride of Boston—principally in Dorchester, Milton, Dedham, Newton, Watertown, and Cambridge.[15] Elizabeth Van Hagen taught voice and pianoforte in Boston and twice a week at Susanna Rowson's Academy in Medford.[16] Beginning in 1798, Peter Van Hagen, Jr., annually opened spring and fall schools in Salem for instrumental and vocal music, making weekly visitations to that town.[17]

Johann Graupner (c. 1767–1836); his wife, the English singer Catherine Comerford Hillier Graupner (1773–1821); and their seven children were also career musicians. Johann, a German-born oboist, was well known to the larger music audience in New England. In 1798, he founded the first musical academy in Boston with Italian composer Filippo Trajetta and French musician François Mallet; Graupner also maintained a store at 6 Franklin Street where he sold and published music and imported Clementi pianos.[18] He wrote and published his own pianoforte instruction manual. The Graupners, too, regularly organized and performed concerts, composed and published their own compositions, and taught music at Rowson's Academy and other schools in eastern Massachusetts. Catherine Graupner is said to have sung the first minstrel melody, "The Negro Boy," in Boston on 21 December 1799, at a performance of *Oroonoko; or, The Royal Slave*.[19]

For his part, Englishman James Hewitt (1770–1827) was more closely aligned to theatrical music. Hewitt began his career with Philip Astley's circus in England and immigrated to North America when he was hired to lead the band for New York City's Park Theatre in 1792. He remained at the center of concert life in New York City, Boston, and Providence for almost four decades as a performer, conductor, composer, church organist, and music teacher.[20] In 1798 Hewitt was hired as a bandleader by theater manager William Dunlap.[21] Playing in concerts and orchestras in eastern New England and the Atlantic seaboard, he went as far south as Charleston, South Carolina, and Augusta, Georgia. A compiler and publisher, he also taught vocal and instrumental music during stays in Boston, Salem, and Providence. His wife gave music and French language lessons; their six children and three grandchildren also pursued musical careers. Prominent among them was Sophia Hewitt Ostinelli (b. 1799), known for her vocal and instrumental performances as well as for being a concert impresario.[22]

The events that brought these musicians together were subscription concerts. Usually impromptu affairs, they were made possible by the availability of local amateur musicians, variations in the theater season, or the presence of a celebrated vocalist or instrumentalist. The subscription concerts planned by James Hewitt at the New Assembly Room in New York City in February and May 1795 featured three stage singers employed at the Park Street Theatre, the entire theater band for which he was director, and the organist at New York's Trinity Church (Peter Albrecht Van Hagen, Sr.). Hewitt's concert at the City Hotel, New York, in 1804 was undertaken with Charles Berault, who for years sponsored dancing schools and annual exhibition balls at Washington and Tammany Halls in the city.²³

Just how improvised a subscription concert could be is exemplified by the program organized in 1798 in Salem by Gottlieb Graupner. He told readers of the *Salem Gazette* on 8 May 1798 that twelve of the "best musicians from Boston" planned to hold a concert of vocal and instrumental music in Salem at a date to be announced. What he failed to mention was that the six-week theatrical season at Washington Hall, arranged by managers Charles Powell and James Dickinson, had recently begun, bringing to Salem sufficient singers and musicians to perform symphonic and choral pieces. Among them were instrumentalists François Mallet and R. Leaumont and male vocalists Mr. Granger, Mr. Collins, and Mr. Shield, who had just ended a season at the Federal-Street Theater in Boston. Three female vocalists, a Mrs. Solomon, Miss Solomon, and Catherine Graupner, had also begun a three-week engagement in eastern Massachusetts, and two instrumentalists, a Mr. and Mrs. Rosier, were coming for a performance in Salem later in the month. A third instrumentalist, Peter Van Hagen, Jr., was in Salem teaching pianoforte lessons. Graupner saw his chance, organized the concert, and reduced the price of tickets from six shillings to three while also selling a new round of tickets through the same outlets as well as from his boardinghouse. The entire hall was rapidly sold out and the concert fixed for the following week on May 15.²⁴

Nevertheless, for the overwhelming majority of musicians outside the immediate circle of a few entrepreneurial families, opportunities for concert work were found under less advantageous circumstances, if at all. Some were fortunate enough to gain employment in theater bands. Trille Labarre (1758–1797), a recent emigrant from Paris who for years sponsored music schools in Boston and Newburyport specializing in voice, pianoforte, and flute, in the last year of his life was appointed "composer" to the Federal-Street Theater at a salary of sixteen dollars for the 1797 season. It was meager, but it was better than that of the remaining fourteen musicians who made up the orchestra.²⁵ Other musicians combined concert work with subscription balls. When the well-known instrumentalist and teacher Horatio Garnet advertised a concert in Portsmouth in 1789, he added the incentive that "should sufficient number of subscribers apply, there will be given a ball immediately after the concert." Keyboardist and violinist (and "professor" of music) J. H. Smith employed this format with dancing-master John H. Ives in Hartford in 1798. Smith, who later performed in Newburyport and Portsmouth, played concert pieces such as the "Battle of Prague" and the "Taking of the Bastille," and several popular songs before turning the evening over to dancing.²⁶

Other musicians, like the Salters, depended on waxwork shows, slack-wire and fireworks exhibitions, and animal acts for employment. For every waxwork collection touring the region, there was a keyboardist playing "music on an organ," usually shortened versions of familiar works by European composers. Peter Dolliver (1777–1816) for years played a pedal organ and pianoforte at Daniel Bowen's and William Doyle's waxwork rooms in Boston's Columbian Museum. Dolliver found occasional concert work for himself; for his younger brother, Charles Saunders Dolliver (b. 1779); and his sisters, Caroline (b. 1783) and Amelia (b. 1784). But much of his musical life was spent accompanying individual stage artists like "The Infant Roscius" or traveling with Bowen's waxwork lessees like Charles Packard and Philip Woods in eastern New England.[27] Fireworks promoters hired "Fidlers" to entertain those of the company who remained after the program.[28] Animal showmen and puppeteers promised to delight their audiences with the "best Music." A trio (two violinists and an oboist) appeared with a Mr. Cressin's "Comical and Experimental" exhibitions of trained monkeys and dogs in Providence in 1796 (fig. 11.1). "Two tolerable fiddlers" played for puppeteer Signor Jonotty in New York City in November 1795—"one a degree better; and now and then a tune from a hand-organ by one of the managers of the entertainment."[29]

Most lantern showmen enhanced their performances with music—notably Richard Brickell in 1752, Henry Hymes in Boston in 1767, Bayly and Tea in New York in 1767, and Joseph Pouyard in Baltimore in 1786.[30] Even relatively crude versions of these shows involved musicians—such as the backlighted exhibitions (Chinese shades or "Ombres Chinoises") shown by James Maginnis and Joseph Falconi.[31] The presence of musical instruments (and warm fires) seems to have differentiated shows prepared for "Ladies and Gentlemen" from everyday tavern entertainments. In the L. Wilhelm Chodowiecki print cited earlier (*Les Ombres chinoises*), six musicians (two violinists, a flute player, a bassist, and two oboe players—each one attired in a two- or three-cornered hat) accompany the backlighted shadow puppets manipulated by showmen behind a screen. The hats of the first row of the audience are visible just in front of the musicians (see fig. 8.4).

Instrumentalists also found work at the spontaneous frolics, sleigh rides, and dances that flourished in federal America. To supply music for country dances in 1797, David Shepard of Murrayfield hired the musicians who had played for a puppet show at his father's house. English bassoonist William Priest, who spent four years in North America as a member of theater bands, reported in 1802 that "to have a sleighing frolic in style in America, it is necessary to provide a fiddler, who is placed at the head of a sleigh and plays all the way. At every inn they meet with them on the road, the company alight and have a dance."[32]

Who were these impromptu fiddlers? Some seem to have been professional musicians who specialized by playing for dancing academies. Shortly after Mary Vial Holyoke of Salem enrolled her children in John White's dancing school in 1783, she "paid James Noland the fidler for Instructing [them]." Noland was not

EXHIBITIONS,
Comic and Experimental.
At Mr. JOHN THURBER's Tavern, Weſt Side of the Bridge.
This Evening, for the firſt Time,
A Chineſe Automaton Figure
Will perform ſeveral Feats on the Rope.
To-Morrow, for the *laſt Time*,
Mr. CRESSIN will begin his Performance at 3 o'Clock, P. M. and finiſh by Sunſet.
 As there are four different Chambers which communicate with his Place of Performance, by which Means Ladies or ſelect Companies will be leſs incommoded, he will take Care to have a Fire in each of thoſe Chambers, for the Convenience of the Spectators.
 A civil Officer will attend, to keep good Order.
 Tickets for Sale at the Place of Performance, and at Mr. Todd's Book-Store. Price, a Quarter of a Dollar, Children Half Price.
Providence, November 18, 1796.

Figure 11.1. "EXHIBITIONS, Comic and Experimental . . . Mr. CRESSIN will begin his Performance at 3 o'Clock, P.M. and finish by Sunset." Handbill for Mr. Cressin's exhibition of his two trained monkeys at John Thurber's Tavern in Providence, Rhode Island, 18 November 1796. Printer unknown. Courtesy, Rhode Island Historical Society, RHi X3 1399.

a Salem resident and most likely was a transient hired by dancing-masters such as White.[33] In Connecticut, Samuel Dibble, a runaway who broke out of jail in 1799, was described as living with his family in Wallingford and playing "on the violin for the dancing school at East-Haddam, and in sundry other towns in this state, and in Massachusetts."[34] Their services were always in demand. In November 1787, Salem lawyer William Pynchon twice provided lodging and meals for an unidentified fiddler who traveled through Salem on his way to Gloucester. This violinist may have been Horatio Garnet, who went with Pynchon's son John to visit friends in Marblehead in 1789.[35]

Hired violinists were also competing against a substantial number of instrumentalists of color. African Americans and Native Americans formed an important subset of dance musicians in North America. While few were "itinerant" in the sense that they were free to travel of their own volition, many were runaways who were obliged to operate like itinerants in order to survive. Surprisingly, their overall number may have been greater than musicians of European American backgrounds. Appearing as early as 1678 when Ceaser Wheeler, the "servant fiddler," accompanied dancing-master Charles Clete from Virginia to Boston, black instrumentalists played a pivotal role in providing music to American life. In 1750, at least one black musician in Boston touted his services. "Any Gentlemen or Ladies," he wrote, "that may have Occasion for a Person that can play well upon the Violin for Dancing, by enquiring at Mr. Stone's, Tavern-keeper near the Court-House, will be waited on by a Black Man, that equals if not excels any in Boston."[36] In Williamsburg, William Fearson put out a notice in 1769 in the *Virginia Gazette* that he "wanted, to buy or to hire, an orderly Negro or Mulatto man, who can play well on the violin."[37]

The most compelling evidence of African American and Native American involvement in musical life, however, is found in want advertisements. Of ninety-three instrumentalists listed by Kate Van Winkle Keller before 1790 who were described as "excellent" or "extremely good," approximately seventy were black slaves or household servants.[38] Jack, a runaway from Gloucester County, Virginia, "is fond of the violin, and has taken with him a new one, which his master lately gave him. He is well acquainted in Williamsburg and Gloucester, and in many other places in this colony."[39] Similar ratios exist for Keller's lists of runaways in Georgia, South Carolina, North Carolina, and Maryland—data suggesting that southern dancing was almost always accompanied by black fiddlers. Knowledge of music sometimes became a determining factor in slaves' recovery. One Maryland slaveholder indicated that Ned (the runaway) plays extremely well on the violin, and has been "accustomed from his infancy to wait in a house, and always very much indulged."[40] In New England and New York it may have been much the same, although not so dramatic. At least three Native American and African American slaves were advertised in Boston in the mid-eighteenth century, some carrying their instruments. They included Covy, a Native American manservant from Exeter, New Hampshire, who was characterized in 1737 as being able to read and write and to play "on a Viol," and a seventeen-year-old Native American named Pallas Worrison, who carried "a good Fiddle on which he delights to play."[41] Similar notices surfaced in New York State towns (black runaways Har, aged twenty-two, in 1801, and Cuff, aged twenty-five, in Hudson in 1802)" and in New York City in 1768, "Ishmael, a Negro Fellow, . . . is a great Fidler, and often shewing slight of Hand Tricks; has a Squaw for a Wife."[42]

That musicians of color were performing in organized groups during this period is evidenced by a note in William Pynchon's diary in 1788 that two blacks were involved in leading dances in Essex County: "30 [May] Friday. The carousing, musick, etc., etc., go on with spirit in Northfield and in Southfield, at Danvers and Marblehead. Titus and Primus and attendants are getting money apace."[43] Titus, or Titus Cabot, was a black slave in Mrs. John Cabot's household in Salem. Often dressed in "cloth shoes, ruffled shirts, silk breeches and stockings," he was apparently partial to dancing "minuets at Commencement."[44] Primus Grant was a servant, possibly a slave, in Pynchon's household. Pynchon's entry implies that both Titus and Primus had special "privileges," paid involvement with music being one of them. Less than seven years later balloonist Jean-Pierre Blanchard punctuated his stay in Boston in 1795 with an apology to his patrons: "Having been informed that the music performed by the men of color had been disagreeable to some ladies, . . . [he] has changed it." Blanchard had hired this group to accompany an exhibition of his automatons while he was attempting to raise funds for a proposed ascension.[45]

Black musicians may also have been playing to black audiences. In 1740, one Boston slave owner noted that he went to a nearby town to look for a runaway and reported finding "about a Dozen black Gentry, He's an She's in a Room, in a very merry Humor, singing and dancing, having a Violin, and Store of Wine and Punch before them. They all belonged to Gentlemen in this Town; and 'tis much to be wondred at, how they can absent from their respective Families without their Masters Knowledge."[46]

A 1799 New York City notice offered a reward for finding "a Mulatto Boy named Peter, about 18 years of age, 5 feet 7 inches high, strong made" and "remarkably active, and a great dancer, well known in the neighborhood of Lumber street, and in the negro dancing cellars in Banker street, by the appellation of *Hazard's Peet,* having lately belonged to Capt. John Hazard."[47]

In 1806, William Bentley recorded a black's funeral in Salem where "members of the African Society appeared with their music," adding that the procession was long and everything well conducted.[48] And by the 1830s black musicians were sometimes in the forefront. Christopher C. Baldwin, librarian at the American Antiquarian Society, shared a stage ride in 1831 from Worcester,

Massachusetts, to nearby Templeton in company with John Field, a multiracial ventriloquist on his way to perform in Vermont. When Baldwin noticed Field had a violin, he persuaded him to "pull it from his bag and scrape away, which he does after much solicitation, and he fiddles all the way to Templeton greatly to my edification."[49]

Finally, professionally trained as well as self-trained white and African American musicians were competing for audiences with a growing number of music machine operators—primarily of hand organs and street hurdy-gurdies. One of the earliest of these was the "Microcosm" built by London clockmaker and mechanic Henry Bridges, which toured theaters, courthouses, and private homes in Virginia, the middle colonies, and New York and Boston in 1755 and 1756 (fig. 11.2). Bridges's son James Bridges, who exhibited it, claimed the music was created by 1,200 revolving wheels and pinions. After two years the Microcosm returned to London. Other instruments were less complex. Henry Hymes played music "on a new invented Instrument made by himself" when he accompanied his lantern images in Boston in 1767.[50] Several unidentified "Hurdy Gurdy women" drew crowds at Yammacraw, a district in Savannah, in 1785. Elsewhere, a Mr. Champion, living at Monsieur Adancourt's house in Newport in 1792, carried about a hand organ "lately imported from France."[51] A similar instrument (or perhaps a hurdy-gurdy) seems to have been owned by two Italian showmen who were entertaining in towns along the Connecticut River Valley a few years later. Their performance on 26 April 1795 captivated the impressionable religious imagination of fifty-six-year-old Rebecca Dickinson (1738–1815?), a seamstress who kept a diary of weekly events in Hatfield between the years 1787 and 1802:

> This Day there is two forrenners here from Europe from itterly [Italy] with Shows and musick an organ which was so charming that it Drew tears from my eyes.
>
> How terefick Some musick is but how short of heavenly Strains. Count over all the joys of Sence. Their sounds are of no account.

Neither of these Italian showmen has been identified. Nor is it certain that their "terefick" but "no account" music was generated from a hand-cranked organ. Nevertheless, it is possible they were the same Italians who eight years later parted company in Boston. In that incident, Francisco Albares, a street musician who was then residing in Boston, advertised a reward for the arrest of Peter Barrell, "an Italian." Barrell had allegedly absconded in an easterly direction toward Maine with Albares's hand organ. Barrell was described as "a tall man of a dark complexion, black hair, has a small mole under his right eye, on his arm is the mark of an anchor made with India ink."[52]

What we do know, however, is that these two Italians represented one side of the great American divide in the appreciation of music. At one end was a group of musically proficient families of professionals and semiprofessionals who supported themselves primarily by teaching, composing, selling music, working in theaters, and performing for religious societies and subscription concerts. Among their ranks were the Hewitts, Graupners, and Van Hagens—as well as the visually impaired keyboardist Salter who visited six states in a failing attempt to support his "musical family." At the other end were the "popularizers," the fiddlers, dance musicians, entertainers, drummers, tavern and cellar musicians, and street organists who played for the crowds. John Hill Hewitt, the eldest son of James Hewitt, took due note of this disconnect when he informed his father about his experiences at the theater in Augusta, Georgia. "Waltzes, and

Figure 11.2. *The Microcosm*. Engraving of a music machine made by Henry Bridges (1697–1754) that was shown in North America in 1755 and 1756 by his son James Bridges after Henry's death. The image shows the portraits of Henry Bridges (on right) and Isaac Newton (on left), who is said to have checked the mechanism. Artist unknown; engraver unknown. London, 1744. © The British Library Board, 04/10/2015. Evan. 9205.

quadrilles," he wrote in 1823, "were the favorites of the public, who, at that period, were not refined enough to comprehend the great masters. An 'overture' was rather beyond their comprehension, but 'dance music' they understood thoroughly—and Washington's March was sure to be greeted by the denizens of the pit with a rhythmic stamp of the foot, which also kept pace with the quick measure of Yankee Doodle, which usually followed."[53] It was a divide between mannered and popular culture that survives to this day.

Chapter 12

Pantomime Entertainment

As JOHN HILL HEWITT headed toward an uncertain musical future, yet another cultural interaction had been unfolding between the strolling theater professionals just beginning to appear in large numbers in New York City, Philadelphia, and Charleston and their new American audiences. In this case the bearers of tradition were the estimated eight hundred stage people and musicians who had acquired their skills in England (primarily London's Haymarket, Drury-Lane, and Covent Garden Theaters) and who had begun to intersect with inexperienced American theatergoers just learning to appreciate the art of the stage. These professionals brought with them a theatrical domain of written plays and operas already well established in Europe but whose ancillary or supporting elements—musical pantomimes and harlequinades—were still very much in flux as theater managers adjusted to their new, American circumstances. Consisting of brief drolls, dance exhibitions, and masquerade performances (described by Sybil M. Rosenfeld in her 1960 study *The Theatre of the London Fairs in the Eighteenth Century*), these ancillary elements were part of players' and musicians' training, and were brought over by actors, actresses, dancers, composers, prompters, writers, and instrumentalists who had memorized these routines in England, France, and Italy. Although some professionals had access to written scripts and produced what amounted to familiar stories, most comic (or "grotesque") versions of these pantomimes were improvised, even if they were rehearsed. Their audiences were the same as those who came for serious theater, but pantomimes were introduced to provide comic relief. The result was a core program of schooled or mannered English and French theater—tragedies, light comedies, and comic operas widely available in published form—around which a spontaneous pantomime culture thrived in the form of afterpieces.

The character of Harlequin appeared in America as early as the 1730s when dancing-master Henry Holt staged *The Adventures of Harlequin and Scaramouch; or, The Spaniard Trick'd* for audiences in Charleston in 1735 and New York City in 1738, presumably with the help of his pupils. Holt described the piece as "A New Pantomime Entertainment in Grotesque Characters," probably meaning that his students wore masks and Renaissance costumes. This production has been said to derive from the comic parts of Lewis Theobald and Johann Ernst Galliard's *Perseus and Andromeda* and was calculated to demonstrate his pupils' newly acquired dancing expertise.[1] When the first professional London theater companies reached Yorktown, Virginia, in the 1750s under the direction of Lewis Hallam (1714–1756) and David Douglass (1720–1786), they brought with them a repertory of twenty-nine plays and farces that had proved successful in England. They performed in major seaports and colony capitals including Williamsburg, Charleston, Philadelphia, Annapolis, and Alexandria as well as in the West Indies. New York City soon became a focal point of theatrical entertainment, and in the winter season of 1753 and 1754, Hallam's and Douglass's "Company of Comedians from London" spent the better part of six months staging plays at a new theater on Nassau Street before relocating to Philadelphia. In the 1760s, the American Company, as it was now called, ventured north into Newport, Providence, and Albany, its advertising copy replete with disingenuous euphemisms that did not mask its intentions.[2] In Newport in 1761, the company promoted its productions by calling them "Moral Dialogues"—a technically correct designation since the lines were spoken or sung by actors and taught lessons about the human condition.[3] According to Harvard student Nathaniel Ames, "Boston People flock up to Newport to see the Play's by the English Actors."[4] The next summer, when the company opened at the new schoolhouse in Providence, Douglass publicized the event in the Boston papers as a "Concert of Musick" accompanied by a tragedy. Ames, who lived with his father in Dedham, Massachusetts, was among those attending. An amateur actor and experienced theatergoer of student performances, he watched John Home's *Douglas* on one evening and Ambrose Philips's *The Distressed Mother* on the next.[5]

Like their London counterparts, the managers of the American Company added comic afterpieces and pantomimes to their programs based on English, French, and Italian comic entertainments such as the one produced earlier by Henry Holt in Charleston and New York. Designed to express meaning through dance, mime, gesture, costume, and "feats," these routines evolved from a theatrical tradition already several generations old in London and Paris. Music for these pantomimes was orally transmitted from theater to theater and was devoted in large part to accompanying stage tricks, costume changes, and masking. Actors learned the roles of internationally known commedia dell'arte characters such as Harlequin, Scaramouch, and Columbine—the same ones puppet players and lanternists used to create figures like Punchinello (Punch) and his wife, Joan—and generated a repertoire of pantomimes that soon became a staple of American theater. While never approaching high drama, these comic interludes brought to the provincial American stage the very latest in biting London and Parisian satire. They also introduced a domain of sixteenth- and seventeenth-century Italian make-believe that, like other elements of popular culture, connected North Americans with their European past.[6] Typically they combined pantomimes with operatic pieces and epic tragedies. In New York City one company that presented *The Beggar's Opera* in 1751 inserted a "Harlequin Dance" after the first act, a "Pier[r]ot Dance" after the second, and ended the evening with "the Drunken Peasant." In 1754, the same company put on Nicholas Rowe's *Jane Shore*, a play based on the concubine of Edward IV, and followed it with a pantomime called *Harlequin Skeleton; or, The Miller Deceived*. The first known pantomime in New England was produced by David Douglass during one of his company's infrequent trips north.[7] About two decades later William Sampson Morgan took a small group of traveling dancers and musicians to try out Harlequin comedies in Portsmouth, New Hampshire; the run proved highly successful until the authorities intervened.[8]

Initially these pantomimes must have alternately confused and overwhelmed their American audiences. The scenarios, however ridiculous and improbable, were compelling. Characters turned into skeletons and then back into themselves again; actors were metamorphosed into pictures and motionless statues, all the time interrupting each scene with dancing, singing, and acrobatics. The net result was the proliferation of a musical entertainment form that at its height in the years from 1795 to 1815 saw an estimated two hundred separately choreographed arrangements performed on the American stage.

Because so few were scripted, most pantomimes are shrouded in obscurity.[9] A leading English pantomime player, John Rich (1692–1761) or "Mr. Lun" (fig. 12.1), is said to have made up his story as he acted, bringing improvisation to a new height. Nor is it always evident what "acting" consisted of in these pieces. The actors sang, danced, and performed acrobatics, but it is not clear if they ever had speaking lines. Rich is said never to have spoken. It is likewise not known if they ever used facial expressions, with some actors perhaps portraying life-size puppets like Joseph Gibbes's "masquerade characters." Episodes and storylines can to some extent be reconstructed from titles, cast lists, and promotional descriptions printed in theater bills and newspaper advertisements, but these can be misleading.[10] Other contemporary sources offer little more. Critics, diarists, letter writers, and travelers usually took these entertainments for granted—like Nathaniel Ames, who reported he "saw Douglass [the play] acted [along] wth Harlequin."[11] But Ames never told us if he understood the pantomime; he certainly did not describe it.

As is often the case with other popular entertainments, English sources help to reconstruct American pantomimes. According to eighteenth-century accounts from London's Covent Garden and Drury Lane Theatres, English audiences knew the masked and diamond-patch costumed Harlequin by the tightly choreographed movements he made with his hat and wooden bat, by a fast-stepping dance in which he executed three hundred paces while advancing only ten yards, and by the "snap rhythm" of the music that accompanied his entrances and solos.[12] At least one comic tune associated with the character has been identified: "The Birth of Harlequin," attributed to Johann Ernst Galliard (c. 1687–1749), a composer employed by John Rich when he was serving as a theater manager. The character thus conceived and choreographed was a theatrical type rather than a particular individual. Two Harlequins might perform on the stage simultaneously, or a dance might take place "between a Harlequin man and Harlequin woman." Scaramouch in turn always wore a prominent ruffle, a broad hat, and an over-shirt girdled at the waist; his movements were developed around the "long, unformed" steps or *pas de Scaramouch* danced to a slower, more punctuated "Scaramouch air." He, too, was a generic stage figure. A routine might consist of a dance between two Scaramouches, or between a large Scaramouch and two dwarf ones, or between two Punches and a Scaramouch.[13]

The Harlequin tradition in England had a long and sometimes off-color history in the booths of London's Bartholomew and Southwark Fairs. In a 1704 arrangement, a grimacing actor squatted on the stage and reenacted Harlequin's and Scaramouch's "Monstrous Birth" as puppies.[14] But the birth stories were also capable of inspired entertainment. In one of the best-known scenes played

FIGURE 12.1. Photolithograph of the actor-manager John Rich (1692–1761), also known as "Mr. Lun," playing Harlequin and carrying his slapstick, a device that helped him move stage props during his acts. From an 1818 engraving based on the small colored drawing *Arlequin Rich,* dated 1753, in the collection of the Garrick Club, London. A copy is in the Victoria and Albert Museum.

by John Rich, the actor dramatized Harlequin's birth by hatching himself from a gigantic egg. A short description of this scene was published in 1793 in an obscure history of the Scottish stage: "From the first chipping of the egg, his receiving of motion, his feeling of the ground, his standing upright, to his quick harlequin trip round the empty shell, through the whole progression, every limn has its tongue, and every motion a voice."[15]

Rich's enormous success in this field inspired critics. One "speaking" pantomime is a short three-act play written by the Shakespearean actor David Garrick (1717–1779) called *Harlequin's Invasion* (1759). It recounts Harlequin's incursions into Shakespeare's territory of "Parnassus," Harlequin's expulsion from the play, and the triumph of poetry and drama over pantomime. Minor characters include Joe Snip, who clad in armor goes after Harlequin's head, and Dolly Snip, who has a love affair with Harlequin. *Harlequin's Invasion* was performed about a dozen times in theaters in Philadelphia, New York, Charleston, and Boston between 1786 and 1801; it was not well received, possibly because Shakespeare did not yet have the following in America that he had in London.[16]

In the 1780s and 1790s, many English pantomimes took their cue from a scenario that began with non-magical characters, some of whom were transformed into magical ones in order to resolve the plot. Before William Bates and James A. Dickinson left the London stage in the 1790s to seek careers in Boston and New York City, they collaborated with composer William Reeve on a "pantomimical entertainment in two acts" titled *Harlequin Mungo; or, A Peep into the Tower*. In this pantomime the principal character is modeled after Don Diego's manservant Mungo in Charles Dibdin's play *The Padlock*. The first act takes place in the West Indies, where Mungo (Harlequin) has been purchased as a slave. When he learns the master's daughter (Columbine) has been promised to a wealthy Chinese gentleman visiting the island, he frustrates the plan by confining the Chinese gentlemen in a trick chair, assuming his identity, and marrying Columbine himself. The second act is set in the Tower of London and is composed of a succession of escapes and transformations as the couple attempts to get away from the Chinese gentleman and his servants. The final scene takes place in a fanciful grand palace of flowers where a wizard pronounces Harlequin his son and seals the happiness of the lovers.[17]

Although *The Padlock* appeared numerous times in Philadelphia and New York theaters, the pantomime *Harlequin Mungo* was never staged. Nevertheless, it typifies many harlequinades produced in America whose plots were similar, some written by Bates or by Dickinson or perhaps by both.[18] Each presumably began with an initial "serious" character, such as a balloonist, fisherman, gardener, or lottery player, who was transformed into the costumed dancer Harlequin in order to thwart Columbine's forced marriage and elope with her. One two-act pantomime titled *Harlequin Ranger* (presented by Dickinson in

Portland in 1803) opens with a storm at sea and a burning shipwreck, after which "Harlequin is seen floating on the Waves, pursued by a Dolphin." In the ensuing chase by the evil characters (Clown, Carlos, and Don Testy), Harlequin becomes entangled in magical chairs and tables. And in an enchanted tomb, Columbine "change[s] . . . into an object of horror."[19]

Absent from this picture, however, are the many pantomimes in which American managers and actors put aside the layered or satirical roles of the genre (the ones which so delighted sophisticated English theatergoers) and presented Harlequin and other commedia dell'arte characters as primary players. Out of approximately two hundred known pantomime titles, the most common are generic stories in which Harlequin plays the central character in a fantasy world inhabited by magicians, furies, fairies, dragons, witches, and emblematic characters. These stories seemingly derived from early popular dance routines as well as from a bawdy stage tradition in England satirizing the French taste for Italian theater. They repeated a stock repertoire of scenarios centering on escapes, mistaken identities, births, deaths, and reanimation scenes, as well as Harlequin's romance with Columbine and his elevation to theatrical immortality. The episodes were regularly cited in handbills and advertisements and were so fixed in the minds of the players and their audiences that there was little call for them to be described in any detail.[20]

While no evidence has surfaced that off-color themes played a role in the American stage, at least two and possibly three variants of Harlequin's birth were enacted in theaters in eastern American cities. One, titled *Birth of Harlequin; or, The Enchanted Cauldron,* which was staged in Newport in 1796 and Boston in 1799, suggests that the Harlequin's birth was represented by his rising out of a boiling cauldron surrounded by witches. Another, produced in Providence in 1807 under the title *Mother Goose; or, The Birth and Adventures of Harlequin,* involves a "Golden Egg"—reminiscent of John Rich's performance in which Harlequin was hatched from an egg. A third, *Birth of Harlequin,* given in Philadelphia in 1791, features an "Enchanter" and an "Airy Spirit" as magical characters as well as a "Harlequin Pigmy"—indicating that the birth may have entailed a change in size.[21]

The celebrated "Dying" and "Restoration" scenes and their many variations are also relatively common. The concept was derived from the celebrated skeleton scene in *The Royal Chase; or, Merlin's Cave,* introduced at Bartholomew Fair in 1739; these scenarios were produced under titles such as *Harlequin Skeleton* (Philadelphia, 1790) and *Life and Death of Harlequin* (Boston, 1800) in which Harlequin apparently falls lifeless and turns into a skeleton (only to be resurrected and surprise his rivals). Staging them required quick changes of tight-fitting costumes alternately representing a skeleton and a live Harlequin, or two different actors playing Harlequin. And, like the birth scenes, they may have had a common ancestry in the crowd-pleasing "lazzi"—the stage tricks, poses, costume camouflage, and trompe l'oeil devices that originated in sixteenth-century Italy.[22]

Harlequin's "statue scene" and "Gladiator scene"—repeated more times than any of the others—seem to have centered on a sustained motionless pose (fig. 12.2) broken by his suddenly coming to life. Other stock openings and escapes—like Harlequin's disentanglement from an "Enchanted Tree" (*Triumph of Mirth*, Boston, 1795), his leap from within a split rock (*American Volunteers*, Boston, 1800), and his disappearance into chests and chairs (*Harlequin Mungo*)—are now known only from short descriptive phrases. They were executed by costume camouflage, scenery changes, and fairly complex stage machinery. Still others sequences, such as his escapes through walls, mirrors, or "animated pictures," necessitated doubles serving as mirror reflections or as temporary stand-ins.[23] In some instances the episodes followed hard on one another. *Harlequin Restored*

Figure 12.2. *Mr. J. Durang in Character of Harlequin, Animation Scene, In Five Positions.* Self-portrait by John Durang as he holds a motionless stage pose as a statue. Watercolor bound in a manuscript diary. Philadelphia, 1800–1822. Courtesy, York County Heritage Trust, York, Pennsylvania.

(Hartford, 1795) begins with Harlequin's magical release from an enchanted tree and progresses to his combat with a gladiator, his leap into a lion's mouth, and his escape from the Clown "on the prongs of a pitchfork."[24]

Over time the settings and plots of pantomimes produced in North America became locally inspired. While no script or libretto has survived for *Harlequin's Tour through the Continent of North America* (New York, 1787) or *Plymouth Rock; or, Harlequin Released from Bondage* (Portsmouth, 1796), such titles indicate that arrangers worked these Italian "grotesque characters" into typically American narratives.[25] Managers introduced settings and emblems drawn from neighboring landmarks, fauna, and history. Transformation scenes presented in Massachusetts theaters found Harlequin being turned into a lobster; pursuits involved the Boston glass factory and the Massachusetts Statehouse. Some scenes have a patriotic flavor: the "Temple of Liberty" in *Harlequin's Release* (Boston, 1804) has the number of pillars (twenty) corresponding to the number of states in the union.[26] Produced in Baltimore in 1795 and Philadelphia in 1796, *Harlequin Shipwreck'd; or, The Grateful Lion* may have been inspired by the "African Lion from Goree" that was currently touring the eastern states. Other roles cast the "Indian Chief," the "Savage Princess," and a "Genius of Liberty."[27]

American Harlequin productions also developed a distinct shift in theatrical emphasis. For one, the acrobatic feats performed by Harlequin were intensified at the expense of choreographed dance. Although acrobatics were always part of the Italian, French, and English Harlequin traditions, stage feats, stage machinery, and trompe l'oeil transformations seem to have received proportionately more attention in North America as the popularity of the genre reached its height in the period just after 1805. In a crescendo that began with William Bates's "leap through the Window of a Post-Chaise," Harlequin variously fired himself into the air from the mouth of a mortar, dropped limb to limb after an exalted hanging, sprang into a red-hot bake oven, and took a grand trampoline leap sixteen feet high.[28] Alexandre Placide's and Laurent Spinacuta's company of actors and acrobats playing in Charleston complemented the opera *Two Hunters, and the Milk Maid* with the pantomime *Harlequin Balloonist; or, Pierrot in the Clouds,* which entailed an air balloon, a "magic chamber," a mechanical bird, and a view of the "palace of Cupid."[29]

For another, the Harlequin lore was recast to serve American goals. At a relatively late point in the evolution of the genre (1800–1810), political and nationalist motifs began to color pantomimes. In Boston in 1800, *American Volunteers* (a renamed and reworked version of *Harlequin Restored*) ended with a "Dance of Mount Vernon" in honor of George Washington's Virginia home. The same year, Catherine Graupner, in the unlikely costume of Helen of Troy, concluded *Harlequin Dr. Faustus* by singing "Columbia's Bold Eagle" to a tune composed by her husband. And halfway through the main scene of *Harlequin's Release,* stage singer Mr. Darley, evocatively dressed either as a Renaissance scholar or a clown, sang the patriotic air "Hail Liberty Supreme Delight."[30] Whatever else might be said, American pantomime forms had been impressed to serve the cause of republican America.

The emergence of a new generation of Harlequin actors underscored these shifts. In New England John Worrall (c. 1783–1825) became the leading arranger and player of Harlequin pantomimes. At this point in his life Worrall had no known on-stage experience, having been employed for years by the Federal Street and Haymarket Theatres in Boston as a chief mechanic, scenery designer, and stage painter. (This was the same John Worrall who had painted the acclaimed scenic backdrops for theaters in Providence and Portland and who was so highly regarded for his theatrical scenery and transparent paintings he was given benefit nights as frequently as lead actors.) Starting in 1808, however, James Dickinson cast Worrall as Harlequin in a new routine prepared by Worrall himself. Thereafter he played the lead in virtually all Harlequin pantomimes produced in Boston and Providence, sometimes joined by a member of his family. His leaps "through a butt of Porter, 12 feet high" in 1809 became as famous as his stage paintings, and his stage tricks became increasingly complex. In one production "a dog kennel changed to a Dove House," a bower of roses into a fruit tree, and skeleton figures into the pillars of a "Temple of Virtue." In another, two rose trees "change to Pedestals with Columbine and Punch on them."[31]

In Charleston the foremost Harlequin actor was Matthew Sully, Jr., son of English comedian Matthew Sully, Sr., one of six siblings who immigrated with their parents to Richmond in 1792. Sully, Jr., in 1794 began his epilogues in the character of Harlequin rising in a balloon "8 feet high" and surrounded on all sides "with Fire Works."[32] Not to be outdone, in 1796, his colleague J. Jones inaugurated his extraordinary acrobatics, traversing the theater "in the Character of Harlequin." As explained in the *Columbian Herald,* Jones "will fly from the back of the Stage, to the extent of the gallery, and down again."[33] In Alexandria, Virginia, James Warrell—not to be confused with the Boston actor—presided over a magic apple tree "which changes to a Giant Eight Foot High."[34] Like John Worrall, none of these performers was principally a dancer; each relied on "whimsical" changes or "odd" metamorphoses, leaps, and tricks.

By 1810 Harlequin was everywhere. An icon of traditional European popular culture was thriving in America in part because it helped serve national aspirations but also in part because a formal structure (established theater) was there to hold it together. The character surfaced in theater productions ranging from Savannah, Georgia, to Lexington, Kentucky, to major eastern cities such as Philadelphia, New York, and Boston. Harlequin appeared in "grotesque" or "masquerade" entertainments presented by equestrian circuses and in those staged by acrobatic companies in amphitheaters; he appeared in events and shows staged by puppeteers, sleight-of-hand artists, and magic lanternists.[35] He and his cohorts also found their way into waxwork exhibitions, children's books, and decorative ceramics.[36] During the two decades of their greatest popularity, Harlequin pantomimes were the most commonly enjoyed musical entertainment in America's eastern cities, and Harlequin and Columbine the most widely recognized stage characters by people of all ages and backgrounds.

Nevertheless, as quickly as it had blossomed, this new generation of pantomimists faded away. John Worrall's acting career inexplicably ended after four years. He performed his first Harlequin role in *Harlequin's Choice* in March 1808 and his last in *Hurry-Scurry* in March 1812, a piece that culminated in his customary leap through a blazing star into the "Garden of Pleasure." Worrall then resumed his more mundane vocation of scenery painting.[37] In the meantime, Boston's theatre managers again looked to England for new pantomime talent. They specifically wanted actors who had learned to play the Clown (another commedia dell'arte character), especially as interpreted by Joseph Grimaldi (1778–1837), son of an Italian actor, who was just beginning to bring this role to the English stage. When Boston Theatre manager Mr. Entwistle advertised *Harlequin Salamander; or, The Humors of the Clown* in April 1812, he informed the public "that this Pantomime is prepared in order [to feature the] . . . celebrated Clown from Saddlers Wells London being his first appearance here." The actor is unidentified but was most likely an understudy or imitator of Grimaldi familiar with the dimensions he gave to the part. Entwistle's announcement fell on deaf ears. Nothing further is heard of the "celebrated Clown" either in Boston or elsewhere in New England.[38] The event may represent the first time that a successful English theatrical formula did not immediately take root in America. In fact, Harlequin comedies were rarely performed in Boston after that date, and the unknown actor who was cast as the Clown apparently returned home. Commedia dell'arte entertainments entirely disappeared from New England after 1815 (and eventually from eastern America altogether) at the very moment that both the stage and puppet versions of the Harlequin genre began their remarkable rise to popularity in England. Harlequin had died in Boston, and this time there was no one there to resurrect him.

John Worrall's experience may have been as much an artistic miscalculation as it was a divergence of theatrical values. Boston managers and arrangers neglected the element that had made Italian-style pantomimes preeminent since the sixteenth century: choreographic virtuosity. The routines of the early leading "grotesque" characters are revealed by the backgrounds of the actors who played them. A Mr. and Mrs. Val, Alexandre Placide, a Mr. Francisquy, and Anna Gardie were all professional stage dancers; several were also dance teachers and choreographers. Mr. Legé, who performed in Charleston, was a ballet-master. John Durang was a gifted stage dancer, acrobat, and equestrian. By contrast,

John Worrall and James Warrell were primarily theatrical mechanics and painters, and Matthew Sully and J. Jones were stage acrobats. Nor was the decline of pantomimes simply a case of anti-British emotions influencing popular theatrical tastes, although this seems to have been a contributing factor. The latest London plays and musicals continued to open in Boston and New York City in the war years of 1812 and 1813 as if no conflict existed. Rather, it had a deeper catalyst. Separated from their traditional satiric and romantic plots, their comic tunes, and their tightly disciplined dances, the masquerade characters of the Italian Renaissance that had evoked laughter as "zannies" were poorly suited to double as singing and dancing patriots.[39]

Two things can be learned from these events. First is the larger question of timing. Newspaper readers in Boston and New York first heard about Harlequin when the execution at Tyburn, England, of John Sheppard, a housebreaker, was announced in the *New England Courant.* They were told that "Mr. Lun" (actor John Rich) "not doubting but to make as much of him as he has done of Dr. Faustus," was rehearsing a new pantomime called *John Sheppard; or, Harlequin in Newgate* on Sheppard's notorious career.[40] This was in 1725, when only a handful of American editors and readers might have been familiar with Sheppard's name and almost no one understood what a theatrical pantomime entailed or how writers, actors, dancers, and musicians could find humor in the event. This collective disregard continued for another sixty years. While some Harlequin productions were performed by London-based companies as they toured Pennsylvania, Virginia, and Rhode Island, it was not until the blossoming of the American theater in the 1780s and 1790s that Harlequin afterpieces entered the popular scene. This gives us yet another working measure of the extended cultural silence facing players and their audiences in Britain's colonial and early American worlds. In this case the wait lasted for two generations.

Second was how easily European theatrical afterpieces could be adopted and dismissed. Worrall's four-year career was paralleled by a decline of pantomimes among most American theater productions. With audiences unresponsive to innovations then emerging from the London stage, the Harlequin genre essentially disappeared from the American scene after 1815. Theater managers began to hire acrobatic troupes like those led by Mr. Manfredi, Mr. Dumoulain, and Don Pedro Cloris to help divert the crowds with their "Feats of Activity" and to relegate afterpieces to a lesser role. These tended to be one-act "patriotic effusions" and "allegorical entertainments." *Constitution and Guerriere* (October 1812); *American Tars; or, Huzza for the Navy* (December 1812); and *Genius of America* (October 1814) celebrated America's new victories on the high seas in a period when American patriotism was still in question.[41] More coherent musically than the earlier pantomimes, their replacements drew on a repertoire of favorite songs, duets, and choruses sung against changing painted backgrounds of sea engagements. But their pantomimic origins are manifest. What used to be Harlequin's "grand palace of flowers" became "a grand marine palace" where the entirety of the back stage was flooded with "Real Water." What used to be a "Pavilion of Pleasure and Temple of Delight" was now a tableau of columns, transparencies, ships' paintings, and portraits glorifying the exploits of naval commanders.[42] Theatrical afterpieces were putting America first.

Chapter 13

A Time to Dance

THE STROLLING occupation that brought mannered and popular culture much closer together was the teaching of "mixt" dancing, meaning involving men and women dancing simultaneously. Several contradictions characterized this evolution. One was that dancing-masters—the sophisticated and experienced Europeans who came to the New World to teach these skills—quickly learned they were seen in the New World as controversial culture bearers. Many were literally ignored or repelled by suspicious colonial authorities. But they persevered, and in the end dancing instruction seems to have attracted more teachers and pupils than any other itinerant profession in the country. A second contradiction was that the same urban communities that most vehemently discouraged these schools were the first ones to patronize them in overwhelming numbers. The teaching of dancing in Boston, for example, was made illegal in that town for decades. This policy changed, however, and by 1780 Boston led the rest of eastern North America in the number and variety of its dancing schools, practice rooms, assemblies, public dances (or "publics"), and balls. A third was the major incompatibility that governed its rationale. The most common justification cited by teachers to prospective parents (that is, the education of manners for the young) was framed in an aristocratic tradition of polite behavior derived from English, French, and Italian court society—the very set of values most Americans ostensibly rejected at the time of the revolution.

The documentation of social dance instruction began in North America in 1678 when Charles Clete, "Dancing Master," arrived in Boston from Virginia accompanied by his servant fiddler Ceaser Wheeler. Like other newcomers, Clete petitioned the town's selectmen to become an inhabitant. Unfortunately for Clete, it was an unsettled time in Massachusetts and the British colonies generally. New England had recently concluded hostilities in a two-year rebellion by local Narragansetts and Wampanoags under Metacomet, or "King Philip." (The suggestion had been made by clergymen that the war and other calamities, such as pestilences and droughts, were visited on the region as punishment for its worldliness and religious declension.) A similar Native American uprising had just taken place in Virginia and may in fact have prompted Clete's removal north. Not unexpectedly, Boston's selectmen informed Clete on 19 July 1678 that he and Wheeler were to return to the vessel in which they had arrived and to remain on board until it left.[1]

This was just the start of a political minuet between dancing-masters and New England authorities that lasted for a hundred years or more and was choreographed with moves at least as subtle and poised as those that Charles Clete proposed to teach. In 1681, another dancing-master, Henry Sherlot, entered the town. A shadowy character whose prospective tenure in Boston was even less promising than Clete's, Sherlot was discovered to be "a frenchman yt is newly come into this Towne as he saijth a Dancing master"—an early reference to what became a stereotype broadly shared in England and British North America. A court of assistants hearing his case additionally determined that Sherlot was "a person very insolent & of ill fame that raves and scoffes at Reliton [religion] of a Turbulent spirit no way fitt to be tollerated to live in this place." When the selectmen learned that Sherlot had been prosecuted for rape in Ireland, he was judged unfit to be a resident, and he too was required to leave.[2]

Next came Francis Stepney, a dancing-master who took advantage of an increasingly uncertain political standoff in the colony to actually open a school for dancing in Boston in 1685. When ordered to close it, he challenged the judgment in court, and when he broke a temporary injunction, he was arrested and placed under a one-hundred-pound bond. Stepney appealed. He offered as sureties Lieutenant Colonel Samuel Shrimpton and Captain Humphrey Luscombe—the former, the most successful Boston merchant of the seventeenth century, and the latter, a wealthy founder of the Anglican King's Chapel. In the ensuing court proceedings, Judge Samuel Sewall noted that Stepney's school was held on "Lecture-Day," or every Thursday. When Stepney rashly claimed that with "one Play he could teach more Divinity than Mr. [Samuel] Willard or the Old Testament," the town's clergymen were consulted and Reverend Joshua Moodey spoke for all when he declared that it "was not a time for N.E. to dance." Increase Mather and several colleagues put an end to the debate with a sermon "against mixt Dances" published in 1686 under the title *An Arrow against Profane and Promiscuous Dancing. Drawn out of the Quiver of the Scriptures*.[3]

At least three other dancing-masters who attempted to found schools in Boston over the next several decades were treated with similar disdain. Finally, with the increasing size of Anglican congregations, the climate began to improve. While working as an organist for King's Chapel under Church of England patronage, Edward Enstone managed to establish a school in 1716 because of his position. But when Enstone announced a ball, Governor Samuel Shute was induced not to attend. Another school was opened surreptitiously by Boston schoolmaster Samuel Grainger, who occasionally gave dancing classes in 1719. So much pressure was put on him, however, that he was obliged to pay for an advertisement claiming that despite "newly reviv'd" reports, the "dancing Phaenomena's" had never been seen or heard of in his schoolhouse.[4]

In time opposition to dancing-masters sufficiently waned in Boston to allow dancing to take place in public on a regular basis. In Boston in 1713, the same year that Thomas Brattle gave an organ to the "Manifesto" Church on Brattle Street (and the same year that Reverend John Tufts issued *An Introduction to the Singing of Psalm Tunes*), George Brownell (fl. 1703–after 1750) opened an academy of manners and polite arts whose curriculum addressed music and genteel address.[5] A school master and musician, Brownell had formerly been a resident of Charleston. Over a period of time his academy (located in Dock Square near the former tavern of John Wing) evolved into the town's first permanent dancing school. Brownell prospered in Boston and attracted considerable notice, including that of the young Benjamin Franklin, who afterward remembered Brownell as "very successful in his Profession." By August 1716 Brownell had lowered his fees ("dancing cheaper than ever was taught in Boston"). Two years earlier his bill for dancing lessons on 16 July 1714 submitted to thirty-four-year-old Elizabeth Shrimpton Stoddard (then in her second marriage) provides the earliest financial record of this teaching profession in New England.[6]

Elsewhere in New England the arguments raised both for and against prospective dancing schools were less vehement but no less serious. In Providence the debate surfaced in 1763 when an anonymous advertiser let it be known in the *Providence Gazette* that "very good Encouragement will be given to any Person who understands Fencing, Dancing, and the Violin, who will come and set up a school." The very next issue of the paper contained a lengthy letter from "a Lover of Virtue" expressing the belief that Providence no more needed a dancing school than it did a "public Stew or Brothel" and hoping instead for a "spinning or working School." Letters that followed designated dancing schools dens of "Idleness, Lewdness, and Debauchery." Nevertheless, when Italian dancing-master John Baptist Tioli finally opened a school for "Minuet, Double Minuet . . . of the newest Figure" at Hacker's Assembly Room in 1768, he was treated with such deference that he was reluctant to leave when his school was over. In New Haven Reverend Ezra Stiles observed that the prospect of a dancing school caused such "a great Noise" and "Dissatisfaction" in the town in March 1782 that the selectmen and civil authorities were summoned to a meeting to deal with it. Nevertheless, Stiles noted that his own children, Ruth, Polly, and Isaac, "went to the Dancing School." And six years later, when grammarian Noah Webster attended Yale's commencement ball in September 1788, he commented that the event attracted "120 Ladies."[7]

With the immigration to North America of experienced professional dancing-masters after 1750, the pool of available teachers began to grow. Approximately two hundred full-time instructors were active in New England and eastern parts of New York in the period from 1685 through 1825. An equal number worked from Albany south to Philadelphia and to Baltimore, Charleston, and Savannah. The total of over 416 was unprecedented in an occupation essentially dependent on itinerancy for its survival. Most were recent French, English, and Italian immigrants who were also skilled as fencing and foreign language teachers. The profession attracted at least a dozen working husbands and wives, several fathers and sons or fathers and daughters, and many partnerships among siblings and between colleagues. Among them were the wayward son of a Boxford, Massachusetts, shoemaker; a former plantation owner in the French West Indies; a clergyman in the Dutch Reformed Church; a young Salem medical student; and a freed household slave born in Africa who had learned to fiddle and call while still living with his owners in Malden, Massachusetts.[8] At least six women organized schools—notable among them was Mademoiselle Louise Gervais, an accomplished musician who sometimes traveled alone between New York City, Hartford, and Providence or in company with one of two French-speaking associates. While approximately one-third of all dancing-masters were men of recent French extraction, the "French dancing-master" was more than a stereotype inherited from English cultural prejudices. It was a reality. As Frances Trollope discovered in 1827, they were in America in "abundance."[9]

The leading dancing instructors were skillful managers of their resources. They compiled publications, maintained ties to the theatrical world, obtained recommendations from established families, and promoted their access to new dances straight from the royal courts and drawing rooms of Europe. Besides John Griffiths, dancing-master John C. Devero maintained a succession of schools in Connecticut and Rhode Island bringing his upper-class Irish background into populated cities (and isolated hamlets). He later moved to Albany and upstate New York. There were many others. Former theatrical musician William C. Hulett with his sons, John Hamilton and David, for years dominated New York City. James Robardet, a Frenchman, taught in every important city in New England, New York, Pennsylvania, and Maryland. George Labottiere, another Frenchman, ran schools for fencing and dancing and served communities from Portland to Providence and New York, and Francis D. Nichols, author of *A Guide to Politeness,* taught for many years in Boston.

The best known dancing-masters in eastern Massachusetts were members of the Turner family, whose dancing classes and balls were patronized by three generations of socially prominent families in Boston, Salem, Newport, Newburyport, and Portsmouth. Ephraim Turner (1709–1765) (fig. 13.1), a former inn holder, opened his school of politeness in 1738 at Thomas Brownell's former residence on Boston's Tremont Street. (Dancing-master Thomas Brownell had taken over from George Brownell when the latter removed to Philadelphia.) In 1742, Edward Holyoke, then president of Harvard College, paid "Mr. Turner" 40 shillings to secure Margaret Holyoke's place in his dancing school, with a promise to pay three pounds for the quarter. While a student at Harvard College in 1760, nineteen-year-old Nathaniel Ames took a series of lessons from Turner, who thrived financially in his new career.[10]

Ephraim Turner's son William Turner, Sr. (1745–1792), a member of Boston's new Trinity Church, took over his father's schools after 1765. Two years later he married Ann Dumaresq (b. 1747), daughter of an affluent Huguenot merchant. After visiting England, William Turner began teaching concurrent schools in Boston and Salem, reserving Wednesday and Thursday mornings for his Boston scholars at Concert-Hall, and Monday and Friday afternoons for his Salem

Figure 13.1. *Ephraim Turner* (1709–1765), by John Greenwood. Signed and dated "J.G.pinx 1749." Ephraim Turner; his sons, William, Sr., and Thomas; and grandson William, Jr., dominated dancing schools in Boston, Salem, and Charlestown, Massachusetts, for over two generations. Oil on canvas, 30 by 25 inches. Courtesy, New England Historic Genealogical Society.

pupils at the new assembly room there. His seasonal balls were a particular favorite of Salem's young people. According to William Pynchon, Turner's decision to retire in 1788 left his Salem pupils "in tears." He was presumably in ill health since this was the same year John Griffiths took over Turner's dancing school at Concert-Hall in Boston.[11]

Captain Thomas Turner (1754–1809), half-brother of William Turner, Sr., also taught in eastern Massachusetts and New Hampshire, publicizing on 28 July 1801 simultaneous schools in Newburyport and Portsmouth. Captain Turner kept up this schedule for nine years, working alternately at Davenport's Wolfe Tavern in Newburyport and Whidden's Assembly Room in Portsmouth. He later taught in Charleston. He was remembered by a younger family member as a tall man who came "north in the summer and made it very merry—played the violin and flute. Resembled his father."[12] In the 1790s, a third-generation namesake, William Turner, Jr. (1769–1828), linked himself to a prominent Salem family by marrying Judith Holyoke (1774–1841), daughter of Salem physician Edward Augustus Holyoke and granddaughter of Harvard's Edward Holyoke. He opened a dancing school in Concert-Hall in Boston and also founded a school in Salem, setting aside Mondays and Fridays for Boston and Wednesdays and Thursdays for Salem—the reverse of his father's schedule—maintaining this arrangement through 1820.[13]

Prejudices against dancing schools nonetheless persisted. Even in the last decade of the eighteenth century, when Boston was supporting up to nine full-time academies every season, dancing schools occasioned a setting for tragic fictional characters. In *The Coquette; or, The History of Eliza Wharton,* a fashionable novel published in Boston in 1797, author Hannah Webster Foster (1759–1840) contrived "a party of pleasure at Mr. Frazier" where the unfortunate heroine, Eliza, first meets her seducer, Peter Sanford. Although the encounter is set in Connecticut, "Frazier" is undoubtedly Ignatius Curley Frazier (fl. 1797–1814), a French language teacher, translator, and dancing-master whose school had lately opened in Boston's north end. In Foster's fiction, Sanford's machinations eventually lead to the death of Eliza, who perishes with her stillborn child. Frazier's schools, however, continued in Boston, Hartford, New London, and New York City at least until 1807.[14]

As with any itinerant profession suddenly top heavy with teachers, dancing instructors after 1790 encountered considerable competition. For every John Griffiths or John C. Devero there were dozens of others whose success was transitory. Typical is the checkered career of Henry Paul Nugent (fl. 1795–1813), a graduate of the University of Paris and a former principal dancer at theaters in Philadelphia and New York City who wandered throughout the United States to sustain his career. He started in Boston in 1795, proposing in the *Columbian Centinel* "to remain in town and to take over the dancing classes of M. Nadau," who had just retired. The next year Nugent was at Benjamin Dearborn's academy where he taught French and did translations; six months later, in May 1796, Nugent was living in Providence providing afternoon dance classes to young women at a Mrs. Butler's boarding school. In October he was giving French language lessons at a Mr. Osborn's house in Newport and promising to hold a dancing school as soon as he had obtained a subscription of ten pupils. By April 1797 Nugent had removed to southeastern Vermont where he taught in Bennington and nearby Williamstown, Massachusetts, on alternate days. He followed this by stints at Worcester and Lancaster for "two successive days of the week" in each town. In spite of his best efforts, Nugent seems to have run only three schools. He then tried his luck in the Ohio River Valley and in 1805 advertised a "dancing school at Mr. Bradley's New Rooms" in Lexington, Kentucky, before retiring to Albany where "Mr. and Mrs. Nugent" founded a boarding academy in 1813.[15]

Another émigré instructor who traveled extensively was O. Duhigg (fl. 1792–1804), an expatriate Frenchman who had fled the insurrection in Santo Domingo and tried his luck as an itinerant dancing-master in the United States. Duhigg (newspapers sometimes Irishized his name to "O'DuHigg") first advertised as a dancing-master in Baltimore in 1792, initially alluding to having lost his estate in the West Indies. Thenceforth he leased a room and got to work. He removed to Fredericksburg, Maryland, in 1793 where he partnered with a Mr. Large. He relocated to Georgetown in 1795 and taught alone there. To survive, he occasionally sold off remaining portions of his estate. A slave owner, he advertised in Savannah, Georgia, in 1799 the sale of "Eight Heads of Negroes in a single family," presumably "personal property" he had taken with him when he fled the Caribbean. In 1803, in New York City he joined another expatriate, a musician named Berault; one year later he moved to Albany where he advertised a French school; and in 1805, he was advertising a school in New Orleans.[16]

A further sign of the unsettled status of this profession is the decreasing length of time that a dancing-master could prosper in a given community. Like many itinerants, transient dancing teachers were subject to built-in obsolescence—in part produced by their own success—which obliged them to move about constantly to find paying students. For dancing-masters it amounted to a game of musical chairs. As a dancing instructor's novelty waned in one location, his subscribers dropped off and a new and fashionable competitor appeared in town to take his place. John Griffiths's schools in Connecticut and Rhode Island, for example, usually lasted about six to eight quarters (two years); thereafter public interest in him dissipated. His longest tenure was a four-year period from 1788 through 1792 in Boston. Griffiths returned intermittently to Providence where he conducted concurrent schools, but he did not revisit Hartford, Norwich, New Haven, or Northampton once he had completed his instruction there.[17]

Griffiths's two- to three-year tenures were remarkably similar to those of John C. Devero as he circulated between eastern Connecticut in 1798 and Albany in 1802. They also paralleled those of James Robardet (fl. 1784–1812), a French dancing-master who taught a succession of schools in western Connecticut, eastern New York State, the Albany area, Philadelphia, and Maryland in the years from 1784 to 1812. (Robardet and Griffiths virtually dovetailed their arrivals and departures in New Haven in 1785. The same issue of the *New Haven Gazette* announcing Griffiths's intention to organize a dancing school published a note from Robardet requesting that his creditors call on him promptly because he was "designing to leave this city in order to open a new school in Litchfield.") As Griffiths journeyed eastward to Hartford and Norwich in the ensuing years, Robardet was moving at about the same rate northward and westward through Connecticut and the Hudson River Valley, usually at intervals of two years. After completing his term in Litchfield in 1787, Robardet removed to Albany, Lansingburgh, and Schenectady, where he held schools in 1787 and 1788. In 1789, after he had "taught in Albany upward of two years," he conducted classes at Fraunces Tavern in New York City. Two years later in 1791, Robardet was in Philadelphia, and two years after that he surfaced in Baltimore where he called himself "Citizen" Robardet. In 1810, he taught in Hagerstown, Maryland, and in 1812, in Charles Town, Virginia.[18]

As educators of young people, dancing-masters emphasized their role as teachers of correct manners and polite behavior, instructing children and young adults in the rudiments of posture, strength of body and limbs, and appropriate address. Louis J. Guey (fl. 1800–1808) and Calvin Richardson were two among many who pledged to give particular attention not only to dancing but "to morals and manners" or to the "morals and polite behaviour" of their pupils, upholding a pedigreed tradition that had begun in Europe and reached its greatest audience in North America through dancing teachers.[19] Their selection of dances also emphasized good breeding. At the heart of their training were stylized court performances like the minuet and related dances such as the Louvre, la maletete, the gavotte, and the Devonshire. These required posture and control—elevation on the toes, obeisances, and coordinated movements and gestures that helped develop the goal of respectful manners and decorum. The many variations of the minuet included the "English," or plain or common, minuet; Minuet Grave; the Minuet Congo; and the Duo-Minuet. John Griffiths taught "four different Minuets" in Boston in 1789, among them the Cotillion-Minuet and Solo Minuet. When Griffiths returned to New York City after a ten-year tour of New England, he announced he would teach the "plain Minuet, Mr. de Fierville's Minuet, and Mr. Southern's."[20]

Dances designed for rows or opposed couples had broad appeal. Country dances, or "longways dances for as many as will," in which a row of men faced a row of women, were the most common. Cotillions arranged for sets of four facing couples were often presented by a select, pre-rehearsed group at formal balls and assemblies.²¹ The curriculum also entailed stage dances or dances primarily designed to impress spectators, usually minuets; other choreographed dances for two, three, or more dancers; and hornpipes. A Mr. Drummond, who held a dancing school in the ballroom of Moody's Tavern in Albany in 1814, taught a *pas seul*, a *pas de deux*, a *pas de trois*, and a hornpipe, all of them involving the complexities of baroque dance. While not all movements of individually choreographed hornpipes have been identified, a description of "Durang's Hornpipe" has survived and suggests an early form of tap dance performed in soft slippers. Pantomime, fancy, or character dances—including George Labottiere's "*Pas de deux de caractaire*" as well as garland or flag dances—were demonstrated for parents at school exhibitions.²²

Ultimately, parents' strongest motivation to pay tuition was a dancing-master's European connections. Pandering to a prevailing cultural royalism, dancing-masters flaunted their courtly credentials. When he founded his dancing school in New York City in 1739, Henry Holt informed his prospective clients that "he had served his time to Mr. [John] Essex, jun, one of the most celebrated masters in England, and danc'd a considerable Time at the Theatre Royal in Drury Lane." When William C. Hulett advertised a school in New York City in 1753, he introduced himself as the "late apprentice to Mr. Grenier of the City of London, Dancing-Master." William S. Morgan, a dancing-master, musical entrepreneur, and actor who ran academies for "Musick and Dancing" in New England from 1771 to 1773, proclaimed himself in Portsmouth a pupil of Signor Giardini (leader of the band at London's Hay-Market Theater, Covent Garden). Even when royalism became increasingly residual after 1770, W. Birchall Tetley told New York newspaper readers in 1774 and 1775 that he had been an assistant under Maximilien Gardel (1741–1787), "dancing-master to the present King and Dauphine."²³ And only three years after a treaty was signed ending the American Revolution, John H. Hulett resurrected in 1786 his late father's dancing school in New York City by "thank[ing] the parents of all his father's schollars who most kindly have declared their adherence to the *Old School*."²⁴

Dancing-masters were so keen to demonstrate their immediate access to royalist Europe that they repeatedly emphasized the origins of their dancing styles (almost always from France) and the short lengths of time these had been in transmission from Europe to America. When John Griffiths moved his school from Providence to Boston in 1789, he posted in the *Massachusetts Centinel* that he "teaches new cotillions, which have been but four months since invented in Paris." Dancing-master Mr. Ruggles "has by the favor of a friend in France, received five sets of cotillions, composed, adapted to music, and arranged in sets by some of the first masters there." Louis Arnal promised to implement the celebrated Gavotte dance, which "was the mode in Paris last winter." And where access to the latest European dancing styles was beyond reach, dancing-masters had to improvise. George Labottiere, himself a recent French émigré, reassured Boston readers of the *New-England Palladium* in 1809 that, although he "cannot boast of receiving the new cotillions from Paris," his own talents would offer a "sufficient variety of Dances for the improvement of his Pupils, which he hopes will be equally satisfactory to them, without the need of *foreign aid.*"[25] Another Frenchman, a Monsieur Armour, active in New York and Connecticut in the period from 1801 to 1807, claimed that the styles he adopted "are a near resemblance to those of Mr. Duport," a teacher with impeccable French connections.[26]

With much of this publicity directed toward parents, dancing pupils themselves may have focused instead on a burgeoning undercurrent of popular dance and its music. When twenty-one-year-old Elizabeth Bancroft returned from the assembly that culminated Mr. Oleves's 1794 dancing school in Groton, Massachusetts, she first remarked on the music: "Eve 8 clock. Mr. Moor came to wait upon us to the Ball—such sweet musick I never before heard, flute, violin and a drum." But she also remembered the names of the dances: "Soldiers Joy, Sirrah, Flowers of Edenburg, Germans Spaw."[27] These were American variations of English country dances, which had become favorites and now predominated in ballrooms in eastern Massachusetts. Adults who joined in the fun gave it little thought. Noah Webster noted in New York that on 15 January 1788 he attended a ball given by John H. Hulett: "At a hellkicking at Mr. Huletts Public."[28]

Looking back on their profession in 1820, men and women like John C. Devero and Louise Gervais could take pride in the number of their colleagues, in the gender equity they represented, and the myriad of new dancing schools that had emerged in the region. At the height of the profession in the years from 1795 to 1815, Boston was supporting eight subscription dancing schools every season as well as one or two practice sessions. Two or three such schools were held each quarter in Salem, Portsmouth, Portland, Newport, and Providence. Interspersed between classes were weekly, monthly, or quarterly assemblies; school exhibitions and performances; and subscription and charitable balls, usually arranged by the same individuals who were teaching subscription schools. And this was only in the major cities. Most dancing-masters or -mistresses had assistants who covered one or more circuits in outlying towns. Boston teachers led schools in Roxbury, Milton, Dedham, Cambridge, Watertown, and Charlestown; instructors in Portsmouth worked in Newburyport, Haverhill, and Exeter; dancing-masters in Hartford serviced Windsor, Suffield, and Wethersfield.[29] Counting those held within private academies, the number of subscription dancing schools active in a given season in the larger New England and eastern New York region ranged anywhere from fifty to seventy-five.

Dancing instruction proliferated in other cities as well. In Philadelphia alone, at least eleven dancing-masters taught between 1780 and 1800. Six full-time dance instructors—Mr. Sicard, Alexandre Quesnet, Gaspard Cenas, Mr. Byrne, Mr. Francis, and John Dozol—advertised in Philadelphia's *Aurora General Advertiser* on the same day (8 December 1797), each one citing considerable European experience. That evening Mr. Byrne gave the first ball of the fall season. Philadelphia dancing-masters were so acclaimed they typically found supplemental work in southern cities such as Baltimore, Alexandria, Richmond, and Charleston. In Georgia and other southern states, much the same transpired except on a smaller scale. Ten dancing teachers served Savannah before 1799 including John Revear, Timothy Cronin, Charles F. Chevalier, and Mr. Francis; another two joined them after 1800. Augusta, Georgia, employed three more: a Mr. Cadusch and Mr. and Mrs. Ker.[30]

But more than just appealing to legions of pupils, the dancing business and the itinerants who pursued it also cut across professions and social classes. In Boston's *New-England Palladium* in 1811, Francis D. Nichols frequently pointed out that he taught in a new style conceived by the "celebrated Italian master Mr. Pouchon." Nevertheless, he composed his notices in plain language to help broaden his reach. Addressing himself to the young merchants of Boston, he invited them to a "Charitable Ball" to benefit the sufferers of the 31 May Newburyport fire. And in August he called for a "Printers' Ball," asking support for the same cause from the journeymen and master printers of the town. He opened up his summer classes to the "Carpenters, Masons, and Painters of Boston who have families" to help their children acquire "correct" and fashionable dancing, saying he was also willing to accept country pay "received in their line of business, one year from this date."[31] Nichols's announcements suggest that carriers of a European dance culture derived in part from court assemblies and drawing rooms were now extending their embrace to an emerging American middle class. It may have even touched the country's immigrant workers. One of the early unidentified owners of Nichols's 1810 manual on politeness, now in the Theatre Collection at Harvard College Library, carefully recorded inside the back wrapper the title of an ethnic tune—"Irish Washwoman"—a theatrical melody from the 1790s that has maintained its popularity with the Irish diaspora for more than two centuries.[32]

Chapter 14

Confronting the Professions

DESPITE THE proliferation of itinerant-based livelihoods in music and dancing, some elements of English and European popular culture fell short of gaining a solid foundation in America. Prospective itinerants whose vocations seemed relatively secure in Europe's rural areas or crowded cities sometimes ran into a wall of ideological and societal impediments—as well as a certain militancy—that stymied their activities and made it impossible to align themselves with existing schooled and mannered influences. At times these American restrictions were so serious they led to the banishment or arrest and jailing of those who ignored them. Others occasioned fatal consequences.

American opposition was particularly evident toward itinerants whose occupations raised public suspicion, and it was often intensified by mainstream competitors. Itinerants who exhibited "electrical fire" and other phenomena were distrusted by some members of the general public. Peddlers importing foreign and domestic goods were faced with an incessant drumbeat of opposition by local merchants and clergymen—critics even making a political issue of their presence during the revolution because they sold British goods such as tea. "Itinerant preachers" quickly gained the worst reputation, one fueled by established clergymen and clerical associations trying to keep at bay religious proselytizers who challenged their Protestant style of Christianity. "Strolling Doctors" and "medical quacks" in turn were so exposed by the medical establishment and newspaper editors that few of them ever prospered. But whatever their faults, the men and women pursuing these controversial vocations were among the most widely celebrated. While only a minority of New England and New York residents had ever heard of or seen the puppeteer Edward Burlesson or the animal handler William F. Pinchbeck, it is likely that a majority of householders in eastern North America were familiar with the name of Ebenezer Kinnersley, the man who first introduced "Mr. Muschenbroek's wonderful Bottle" to his audiences. Most American women probably knew the seller of silks, pins, and printed tracts who periodically showed up at their door. Most people had heard of the "great itinerant" George Whitefield and his early nineteenth-century successor Lorenzo Dow, whose assemblies gathered audiences at least as large as those of the most spectacular public hangings.[1] A lesser but still sizable number had even heard about the "famous" itinerant Dr. William Stork, the oculist who introduced the earliest cataract surgery into the American colonies.[2]

Electrical Fire

An early cultural collision involved the discovery of "electrical fire." In the 1740s, when table-mounted electrostatic generators were first publicized in London, these machines were still rare and interest was largely confined to professional opticians.[3] English men and women presumably regarded electricity as a branch of university-taught "philosophy," and the subject aroused little street interest. In America, however, these items were big news and itinerants soon saw their economic potential. Among the first demonstrations were those in Boston and Salem where operators used what appear to have been American-made electrical machines. On 3 March 1746 a Boston paper reported that William Claggett (1696–1749) had built an electrical machine and duplicated several electrical experiments.[4] A Newport, Rhode Island, clockmaker and organ mechanic, Claggett was already known to Boston residents as the musical instrument maker who had installed an organ at Christ Church.[5] In December 1746, the papers reported that Claggett employed electricity to "set fire to the Spirits of Wine, the most satisfactory and difficult [experiment] of all."[6] The following year, on 24 August 1747, Claggett advertised a series of "curious Experiments of the most surprising Effects of Electricity" at the King Street house of Captain John Williams, a Boston merchant and importer. Claggett promised to demonstrate attraction, repulsion, and "flamific Force," particularly "the New Way of Electrifying several Persons at the same Time so that Fire shall Dart from all parts of their Bodies; as has lately been exhibited, to the Satisfaction of the Curious in all Parts of Europe."[7]

After four weeks Claggett informed readers of the *Boston Evening-Post* that his clock business would "not suffer him to make any long Stay here," and that he would be returning to Newport. But before leaving he taught his host to replicate his experiments and apparently gave or sold him a machine. Williams, who also advertised two others (a "curious Musical Machine" and a "Posture Boy") as well as a "Tyger-Lyon" (possibly a bobcat), claimed all four items would not stay in town for long. In addition, Claggett sold a machine to David Mason, a japanner on Boston's Wing's Lane, and one to Daniel King of Salem. By the time Claggett reached home, King was giving demonstrations in Salem. Williams and Mason continued exhibiting out of their Boston homes.[8] Williams, who was termed a shopkeeper in Boston records, died the following year in 1748 and among his inventoried possessions was "an Electrical Machine" valued at eighty pounds—unquestionably the same one that Claggett had provided him.[9] King, a shopkeeper like Williams, operated Claggett's apparatus in that town for several years.

The first itinerant known to carry about an electrical machine, however, may have been Richard Brickell, the puppeteer and musician then entertaining New York City and Philadelphia audiences. Brickell began giving electrical presentations in New York City in 1748. His announcement in the *Weekly Journal* in May of that year promised "the most surprising Effects or Phenominas on Electricity of Attracting, Repelling, & Flemmies Force"—language almost identical to Claggett's—making himself available for electrical experiments twelve hours a day provided the weather remained favorable.[10] While Claggett and Brickell both may have lifted text from the same printed instruction pamphlet, the timing implies that Brickell acquired one of Claggett's electrical generators. Recognizing the fascination of electricity, Brickell advised readers, "This Machine is but a short Time in this Town." His whereabouts are unknown between May 1748 and April 1752—excepting a possible waxwork appearance in New London, Connecticut, in 1751. It is entirely possible he was touring electrical shows in the southern and middle colonies during that period.[11]

The first traveling lecturer on electrical fire was Ebenezer Kinnersley (1711–1788), a Philadelphian who came to Boston in September 1751 to demonstrate at Faneuil Hall "Electrified Money" and a curious machine that played bells. This was his second stop in an extended lecture tour of the North American colonies and the West Indies, said to be the first tour of its kind in Europe or America. A neighbor and colleague of Benjamin Franklin, Kinnersley made important discoveries in electrical experimentation, among them positive and negative forces, the conductive property of water, and the protection of buildings and barns through conductive rods. Kinnersley's format was a "course" of two lectures, the first delivering "Some account" of "Electricity in General," including the discovery of the phenomenon, and the second a demonstration of its many properties. Although Kinnersley won acclaim as a researcher, his lectures entertained audiences by animating artificial spiders, passing electricity through "a number of Bodies at the same Instant," causing electricity to dart out of a woman's lips and eyes, and making fish seemingly swim in the air.[12] After his Boston lectures Kinnersley went to Newport, New York City, and the middle and southern states. Like Claggett, he left in his wake others who carried out the same experiments. One Kinnersley imitator was Benjamin Bates, who showed "the newly discovered electrical fire" to the curious in Providence in 1752. Another was a Boston jeweler named Joseph Hiller, who cited Kinnersley in his notices during the winter season of 1754.[13] And like John Williams and

Richard Brickell, Joseph Hiller and his wife, Abigail (who ran a school for polite arts), sponsored other popular exhibitions and entertainments in 1751 and 1756, among them life-size waxwork collections of "Kings, Queens, &c" that were making the rounds among entrepreneurs in Boston, New London, and New York City.[14]

Altogether about forty-five individuals gave electrical lectures and demonstrations before 1826. Most were American-born though a few were English- or Italian-born. Those who followed Kinnersley still heralded the "newly discovered electrical fire" despite its being more than two or three decades old. William Johnson's "Course of Experiments" in electrical fire and natural philosophy in New York City in 1763 and 1764 copied Kinnersley's two-day format and repeated almost the same content (electricity as a "subtle fluid," melting metals, killing small animals). Johnson's presentations in Philadelphia and at the courthouses in Newport and Providence in 1764, and his successful application to Boston's selectmen to carry out his experiments "in the Electrical Way" indicate he made a practice of working the Atlantic seaports.[15] David Mason, the son of upholsterer David Mason, also combined his experiments with theoretical lectures. He maintained a shop in Boston, delivered lectures at his Boston home in 1765, and demonstrated "Mr. Muschenbroek's wonderful Bottle" at Zachariah Foss's tavern in Portsmouth in 1766 and at the Assembly Hall in Salem in 1771.[16]

Several entertainers got into the business of showing electrical experiments. Joseph Falconi, the Italian conjurer and student of Alessandro Volta, made a name for himself in America demonstrating miniature thunderstorms. He particularly liked to characterize his performances as always being one step ahead of the current knowledge of electricity. In 1785, when he was still working in the West Indies, he persuaded one member of his audience to write to his colleague: "I have just received a letter from the Cape assuring me that Animal Magnetism, in the cure of diseases, actually does subsist, and that Signor Falconi had given proofs of his being in possession of the secret." Years later, when he returned to New York City in 1817 to sell off his "apparatus," Falconi again alluded to his knowledge: "[I] will bring forward such novelty in Mechanism, Magnetism, Catoptrics, Optics, and a number of Electrical Experiments, (which the exhibitor flatters himself are *yet unknown* to Electricians) as have astonished the learned world, and drawn crowded houses in most of the principal cities in Europe and America, and in this some 20 years back."[17]

As showmen and museum proprietors increasingly made these experiments available to their guests and audiences, it becomes difficult to separate entertainers like Joseph Falconi and Isaac Greenwood from serious lecturers like Ebenezer Kinnersley. In spite of advances made to protect buildings with lightning rods, "Electrical Fire" was for years better known as the subject of common levity. Two brothers—both medical students—who took their female friends on a visit to

Gardiner Baker's American Museum in New York in 1796 reported an incident that may have been typical. Following their visit, Alexander Anderson recalled he "had the pleasure of waiting upon Miss N who was much delighted with the Experiments in Electricity—My Brother's attempts to kiss Miss Jane while insulated excited no small mirth, when they were separated by the fire flying from their noses."[18]

Hawkers and Peddlers

By contrast, the collision between storekeepers and peddlers involved a wholly different set of issues. While little has been written about early American peddling, newspaper announcements tell us that the hawking of goods was one of the most dangerous civilian occupations in early America. Out of approximately 130 instances where this occupation was identified before 1826, no fewer than 16 peddlers or "Petty Chapmen" were murdered in North America—most between 1753 and 1809—almost always by persons who encountered them on the road or by householders or tavern keepers where peddlers sought shelter or food for their horses. The motive was to steal merchandise and money. The actual number of such murders may have been in the hundreds. News of these crimes raced across the countryside as editors reprinted each other's notices. One of the most notorious was the unidentified "Old German pedlar" who was attacked and killed by John Coulton and his "doxey" in York County, Pennsylvania, in 1768. According to the testimony of the female accomplice, Coulton knocked down the peddler and she cut his throat with a razor. Another well-known case was that of Jost Folhaber, a peddler murdered in 1798 on the road to Catawissa, Pennsylvania, by a perpetrator who claimed a local tavern keeper had done it; prior to his execution, the culprit confessed his guilt. In 1808, the country was shocked to learn that two women in western Virginia who had fed a New England peddler's horse and invited him in for refreshment calmly cut his throat to get access to his "plunder."[19] That same year the traveling bookseller William Edwards, who had taken a sailing packet from Boston to Castine, Maine, was killed by two local men who determined that he was deranged and discharged a musket at him when he stooped and seemed to be about to throw a stone. The newspapers termed it a homicide.[20]

Another ten peddlers are known to have been assaulted and robbed during the same period by "footpads" and "Highway" men—many organized into gangs. John Woodside was attacked by two Philadelphia men in 1762; heavily wounded, he was stripped of sixty pounds in cash and eighty pounds in merchandise, which the robbers sold to another peddler.[21] A few peddlers suffered indignities from marauding "Indians" and police officers. An additional eleven in this period died due to accidents or poor traveling conditions (drowning, falls, crossing rivers on ice). It was a stressful occupation, and many were incapacitated by unexpected medical conditions on the road.

But sometimes peddlers were themselves the aggressor. Just after the American Revolution an unidentified peddler of "Yankee notions" passed through East Hampton, Long Island, showing obvious symptoms of measles. He nevertheless attended church one Sunday to advertise his wares; the congregation became enraged, and a group of young men followed him out of town, seized him, tied him to a rail, and ducked him in the town pond. Nearly one hundred people came down with the disease, and two died.[22] The act of hawking goods at individual households served as a convenient cover for entering homes, passing fraudulent notes, counterfeiting money, and affecting skills in other occupations. Between 1705 and 1825 twenty-three reports indicate that a peddler had committed some form of felony including theft of merchandise belonging to other peddlers.[23]

These challenges attracted a group who were among the toughest and most motivated of early American itinerants. The pronounced concentration of peddlers with Scottish and Irish backgrounds—a popular identity that is both supported and contradicted by the existing evidence—argues that it was helpful to be Caucasian, preferably with a Celtic background. Out of ninety-eight peddlers whose background information is known, nine were identified as Scotsmen, fifteen as Irishmen, and an additional fourteen had known Irish or Scottish surnames and had presumably just emigrated. Some Scots-Irish were inclined toward "impudence" and inebriation, and the term "drunken peddler" became common in American speech—even entering into the vocabulary of Reverend Ebenezer Parkman, who bitterly complained about them.[24] Other peddlers were Native Americans, Italians, and French Canadians, with a few of Jewish backgrounds. Isaac Jacobs and Emanuel Lyon, both Germans, were called "Jew Peddlers" in a wanted advertisement in Philadelphia in 1772. A sizable reward ($500) was offered for their apprehension on charges of fraud. One peddler of children's toys in New York City who was suspected of breaking into houses when there was no response to his knocks was identified as a "Jew Pedlar" in 1776. Native American peddlers (primarily women) tended to travel in groups, such as the "7 or 8 Injons Squaws" that passed through Shirley, Massachusetts, in 1771 selling household goods. And at least one Anglo-American woman became a peddler. When she died at the age of ninety in Ipswich, Massachusetts, in 1739, widow Sarah Abbot was mourned as a "Notable Pedlar in Goods through the Course of many Years in that and the Neighboring Towns."[25] Like Abbot, most peddlers (well over a majority) had Anglo-American surnames, including several who were known to have come from London.

Peddlers tried to counter opposition to their occupation by directing sales at new brides and established households. While the commodities carried by foot peddlers were generally those that took up the least space in their "budget" (an archaic term for a leather bag) or their "pack," they chose goods that appealed to women.[26] One of the earliest peddling inventories was listed in an indictment handed down in the district of Maine in 1721 against William Moore, said to be an Irish "Pedler or Petty Chapman." Among the materials that he was accused of "exposing" for sale were "Lase for a Cap," "Stuff for handcarchiefs," muslin, fine thread, black silk, garters and a "Poke mantle," "firritting," and other "smole trifeles." Moore's goods were confiscated, and he was fined twenty pounds, one-third of which was given to the man who informed against him.[27] Another early peddler operating in the 1760s in New Jersey and Philadelphia carried "Calicoes, Cottons, Chintzes, printed linen, long, clear and flowered Lawns, sundry Sorts of Silk and Linen Handkerchiefs, Satin, Pelong, solid Silver Buttons," as well as "a Variety of other goods." Still others sold Irish linens, thimbles, pins, needles, ribbons, garters, laces, fans, and printed tracts. Silk was a major staple of peddlers' goods and may have been bought and sold at high prices. A peddler passing through Hampton, New Hampshire, in 1781 sold farmer and surveyor Samuel Lane a "Silk Gownd . . . Cost 1500 paper Dollars, Equal to about 10 Silver Dollars." Lane later noted the gown (and its source) in an account of his daughters' dowries.[28] A few peddlers concentrated on table knives and forks, clasp knives, and buckles, while others carried earrings, ballads, and broadsides.

By 1750 some peddlers owned push-carts and carried their wares in "boxes" that could be locked like trunks. With a cart, especially those pulled by one or two horses, peddlers expanded their stock; besides the usual tinware cooking and eating utensils, they began to carry wooden ware, pewter, textiles in bulk, and small items of furniture, while also taking broken metal items in trade. Again, these goods were aimed at households. When Connecticut clockmakers started to produce cheap timepieces after 1830, successful peddlers often acquired wagons pulled by two horses and were commonly known as "clock" peddlers.[29]

Even as peddlers fought off weekly assaults from highwaymen and unscrupulous tavern keepers, they were routinely harassed by a network of clerical and civilian criticism. Yale President Timothy Dwight, who encountered numerous peddlers on his tour of New England and New York before 1817, flatly observed that "no course of life tends more rapidly or more effectually to eradicate every moral feeling."[30] Virtually everyone agreed with him, and even foreign visitors joined them. Thomas Hamilton, an English writer visiting the United States in 1833, judged that "the whole race of Yankee pedlars, in particular, are proverbial for dishonesty. They go forth annually in the thousands to lie, cog, cheat swindle, in short to get possession of their neighbors property in any manner it can be done with impunity."[31] Throughout the eighteenth century and well into the early nineteenth, most colonies and states followed the English precedent of requiring peddlers' licensure. Some states expressly prohibited them from operating. The New Hampshire and Massachusetts legislatures passed laws against "hawkers, peddlers, and petty chapmen," and Connecticut approved a similar restriction because peddlers were bringing wares in from Long Island.[32] In 1738, the city of New York banned the sale of any goods except through markets and shops, expressly forbidding "Hawkers or Pedlars" from carrying merchandise on the streets.[33] The next year the province of New York required all hawkers and peddlers to be licensed. Similar laws were passed at various times in South Carolina, New Jersey, Pennsylvania, Connecticut, Virginia, Kentucky Territory, and Rhode Island.[34] Tin plate peddlers were seen as a nuisance in Boston's marketplace in 1800.[35] Even as late as 1816, New Hampshire considered a petition against the "class of men denominated peddlers, [which] consists principally of those who are either too idle to live by honest industry, or too vitious to remain in security at home."[36]

Street Exhorters

Most religious proselytizers faced similar hostile circumstances. In his diary of 1726, Harvard student Jacob Eliot noted that "An Evangel" was active in Boston, possibly an outdoor preacher.[37] But it was not until the Great Awakening revival that street exhorters appeared in North American communities when the revival received the support of Reverend George Whitefield (1714–1770), who began at Newport, Rhode Island, a six-week tour of New England, the Connecticut River Valley, and western Connecticut in 1740 (fig. 14.1). An ordained minister in the Church of England, Whitefield was ostensibly fundraising for an orphanage in Georgia, but his sermons drew five thousand listeners on Boston Common and eight thousand listeners in the streets outside Boston's Old Brick Meetinghouse.[38] By the time he left New England, the region's parish discipline (and at least one of Boston's meetinghouse galleries) was in shambles.

Whitefield attracted scores of clergymen who embarked on similar pilgrimages. One of the most extreme was James Davenport (1716–1755), who abandoned his pastorate in Southold, Long Island, to undertake a tumultuous, twenty-four-month odyssey with two assistants to awaken what they called "sleeping" congregations. In Boston, Davenport stood on a joiner's stool and sang psalms to elicit people's attention and then accused the Boston ministry of being unconverted. An opponent to the movement, diarist Nathan Bowen recorded on 4 August 1742 that he had attended a meeting in Charlestown where Davenport "held forth under an apple tree." Bowen continued, "He is now gone eastward and preached this week at Ipswich in the Meeting House, which I believe is the first into which he has been admitted since he came to Boston & I wish it may be the last."[39] Davenport's journey collapsed in a book-burning incident in 1743 in New London, Connecticut, and the next year he gave a public recantation.

Nevertheless, as the Great Awakening spread, it enticed converts from all segments of New England society. Characteristically, they experienced public distress (often expressed by outcries and sobbing) and found relief in a Christian conversion. In the words of one commentator, exhorters suddenly "sprung up under [us] . . . like Mushrooms in a Night."[40] In time, most people expressed their dislike for these conversions. Reverend Charles Chauncy, a clergyman opposed to the revival, judged that the majority of converts were "raw, illiterate, weak and conceited young Men, or Lads . . . [who] take upon them what they imagine is the Business of preaching."[41] Nathan Bowen observed that in Marblehead exhorters were so common that "even carters, coblers, & the meanest labourers leave their honest employments & turn Teachers." He added, almost incredulously, that a "woman's meeting is on foot."[42] A correspondent to the

Figure 14.1. *Reverend George Whitefield* (1714–1770). An itinerant preacher, Whitefield drew thousands of listeners during his six-week tour of New England in 1740. Attributed to Joseph Badger (1708–1765), Charlestown, Massachusetts. Oil on canvas, 41^{15}⁄$_{16}$ by 32⅞ inches. Boston, circa 1745. Courtesy, Harvard Art Museums / Fogg Museum, Harvard University Portrait Collection, Gift of Mrs. H. P. (Sarah H.) Oliver to Harvard College, 1852, H27.

Boston Weekly News-Letter proffered a solution: "[Since there is] a very wholesome Law of the Province to discourage Pedlars in Trade," he wrote, "[it is now] Time to enact something for the Discouragement of Pedlars in Divinity."[43]

Who were these "Pedlars in Divinity"? Did they hope to nourish a "popular religion" among New Englanders? Like singing-masters they were overwhelmingly homegrown—in contrast to the large number of itinerants of European origins in other areas of popular culture. Many were inexperienced students, unattached or married women, alcoholics, and children. Some were seen as disaffected and sullen like Elisha Paine, who was jailed in Worcester in 1743 for "Publishing or Uttering Mock Sermons in Imitation or in Mimicking preaching and other parts of Divine Worship." A few were "enthusiastic" women like Bathsheba Kingsley, the "brawling" housewife in the Connecticut River Valley, who, after receiving "immediate revelations from heaven" in 1741, stole her husband's horse and began to ride from town to town preaching the gospel. She was examined by several ecclesiastic councils and was urged to remain in Westfield, Massachusetts, and preach privately.[44]

But many also came from alienated classes of society, especially blacks, former slaves and slave runaways, and Native Americans, who joined with women and took it upon themselves "to exhort their Betters even in [the] pulpit before large assemblies"—the usual signs of a popular religion.[45] Contemporary diaries and newspapers are replete with examples. Pallas Worrison, a runaway, is described in a Boston advertisement in 1740 as "a pretty handsome Indian Man . . . about 17 years of age [who] speaks good English, gets in drink and then affects to be a scholar, and to talk Religion, and to preach."[46] "Webster's Caeser," a black slave in Lebanon, Connecticut, who is mentioned in the 1742 diary of Reverend Jacob Eliot, spent a day exhorting at "Smiths" (a Lebanon tavern) and then attempted that night "to lie with an Indian woman telling her . . . that Hell was not so dreadful a place as had been described."[47] Still others were servants in New England households. Flora Negro (born 1723), a slave of Thomas Choate of Ipswich, Massachusetts, is said to have served as an itinerant minister among her fellow slaves and was one of four servants who joined the newly formed separate church in that town in 1746.[48] Eliot reported that in central Connecticut religious excitement was so strong in 1742 that "young men and Indians" regularly went about from parish to parish interrupting the service. Eliot waited an entire month before he could write in his diary that there were "No Exhorters at meeting."[49]

There is occasional evidence that some street exhorters were drawn from America's land-owning middle class. Reverend Ebenezer Parkman's diary reveals that he commonly sheltered destitute or ill men, women, and children passing through his central Massachusetts parish of Westborough. He typically gave these transients a meal and a place on the floor in front of the fire; usually they would leave the next morning. Parkman took in such a drifter, who arrived on horseback, on Monday evening, 3 January 1774. According to Parkman, Ichabod Jones (as this individual called himself) was an "old and miserable man . . . a poor distempered, rheumatic, Object" laid low by an exhausting mid-winter ride from Dorchester to Westborough, a distance of forty miles.[50]

It turned out, however, that Jones was different from most other vagabonds who sought Parkman's hospitality. The following day, Parkman learned to his great surprise that Jones not only went "about as a Vagrant," but "Sings, makes Verses and is sometime Crazy." Worse yet for Parkman, Jones had gained so much attention with his religious talk at an estate vendue in Westborough that he received an invitation to preach on Wednesday evening at a private home. Parkman immediately called on his parishioner to prohibit it and advised him of "the sin and folly" of inviting an unknown exhorter to preach; Parkman also summoned his deacon to learn why he had endorsed the idea.

But it was too late. What transpired during the next ten days tested not only Parkman's patience but the loyalty and discipline of his most trusted parishioners. On 5 January 1774, despite inclement weather and Parkman's explicit objection, Ichabod Jones preached to a large crowd. The gathering was enthralled by his presentation, and Jones began living at the deacon's home. On Saturday, 8 January, Jones preached from another house in Westborough, and on that Sunday, from still another. At this juncture Parkman reversed his strategy and tried his best to ignore this intrusion into his parish. To those who would listen, he pointed out that the proceedings were "irregular" and that it was disorderly for Jones, a "preaching stranger," to thrust himself into the neighborhood without consulting the minister. But Jones had tapped into the same religious convictions that preserved Parkman's own status in the community, and Parkman was obliged to wait and hope that Jones's audiences would tire of his verses before Parkman's own support crumbled.

Fortunately for Parkman, he did not have to wait long. To the clergyman's great relief, Jones took up his "bundle" and departed on foot for Providence ten days after arriving in Westborough—apparently leaving behind his horse. Jones was not seen again in the parish, and after Parkman made enquiries, he learned from Reverend John Cushing in the neighboring town of Ashburnham that "Crazy Isaac Jones" had precipitated similar encounters in his parish.[51] Parkman may have also heard from Reverend John Ballantine, who in December 1770, three years earlier—almost to the day—had given Jones lodging at Ballantine's parsonage in Westfield, only to face his barrage of verses and exhorting. Ballantine recorded in his diary that Jones "rides about the country, lives on the charity of the people, says he is sick but travels in all weathers." Ballantine also noted that although there was "an appearance of religion," Jones had a considerable estate that he neglected.[52] It is also possible, however, there was a darker side to this story. According to a notification originally placed in the 28 November 1769 *Essex Gazette* in Salem, Massachusetts, an itinerant preacher named Dr. John Jones "Pretends he is craz'd at Times," claimed he owned land and lived variously at Westfield and Granville, "makes and sings off-a-hand, Songs on various subjects" (apparently for money), and had publicly loitered during the Provincial courts meeting at Concord and Newburyport during the previous seven or eight months. The informant is not named, but he did issue a warning that Jones was a "filthy Vagrant" who destroyed the health of a number of hopeful young men that he slept with.[53] There is every possibility that Ichabod or Isaac Jones also went by the name of Dr. John Jones.

The opening of the nineteenth century gave rise to a new generation of religious itinerants—chief among them Baptists and Methodists—whose preaching was institutionalized in camp meetings and whose tenets made proselytizing a duty of every believer. These meetings began in Kentucky in 1801 and spread to Virginia in 1803 and 1804 but soon expanded north into New Jersey, New York, and New England. Among these preachers was the Methodist Lorenzo Dow (1777–1834), born in Coventry, Connecticut. His talent for organizing weeklong assemblies fueled for years an itinerant lifestyle that took him to Canada, Ireland, and most parts of the United States. Dow advertised camp meetings in Virginia in 1803, and in Kentucky, eastern Connecticut, and Massachusetts in 1805. He typically provided pasturage for horses but no lodging or board. These gatherings were open to people of all denominations.[54]

After 1820, camp meetings became a widespread American institution. Many involved extensive preparations. For example, an 1824 advertisement for a weeklong meeting in Falmouth, Massachusetts, on Cape Cod informed readers in nearby New Bedford that a vessel had been engaged to convey passengers to and from the meeting.[55] But these assemblies were not without their critics. In their heyday in the American South and Midwest, camp meetings came under the shrewd eye of Frances Trollope. She described one she attended in Indiana that was led by a Methodist who preached "in a low nasal tone" and whose eloquence induced "above a hundred persons, nearly all females," to come forward, "uttering howlings and groans . . . [they] were soon all lying on the ground in an indescribable confusions of heads and legs."[56] According to Trollope, these meetings were fixtures in Presbyterian, Methodist, and Baptist denominations; the itinerants themselves were "for the most part lodged in the houses of their respective followers." Trollope was merciless in her assessment of her hostess, who was "fortunate enough to have secured a favourite Itinerant for her meeting."[57] Later, while visiting Philadelphia, Trollope was told a story her mantua-maker had witnessed as a young woman living with her father, a widower, and her two sisters:

> An itinerant preacher came to the city who contrived to obtain an intimate footing in many respectable families. Her father's was one of these, and his influence and authority were great with all the sisters but particularly the youngest. The young girl's feelings for him seem to have been a curious mixture of spiritual awe and earthly affection. . . . At length the father remarked the sort of covert passion that gleamed through the eyes of his godly visitor, and he saw too, the pallid anxious look which had settled on the brow of his daughter; either this, or some rumours he had heard abroad, or both together led him to forbid this man his house. . . . The preacher withdrew, and was never heard of in Philadelphia afterwards.

"In due course of time," Trollope concluded, "no less than seven unfortunate girls produced living proofs of the wisdom of my informant's worthy father."[58]

Alternative Healers

At the time of the initial seventeenth-century European migrations to North America, popular or traditional healers still occupied a legitimate place in European everyday life. According to the classic twentieth-century study on European mountebanks by Grete de Francesco, not only did alternative healers exist side by side with "university educated physicians" but they probably treated nine out of every ten patients receiving care.[59] There is no evidence that mountebanks joined the first migrations; public health care—so far as it was available—was provided by clergymen trained in medicine, self-taught midwives, women, and a few professionally schooled physicians. Nevertheless, when popular healers did arrive in America in the early eighteenth century, they came in large numbers. Over 120 alternative practitioners emerged in North America, hoping to relieve the frustrations of patients who had experienced the inadequacies of educated physicians. But a more compelling reason was economic: large segments of the population had previously been unable to afford medical treatment of any kind.

The first practicing mountebank circulating in British North America appears to have been a Dr. Sharp, a London physician who was criticized for charlatanism in an English paper in 1719 along with other transient healers.[60] Sharp stopped in Boston on his way home to England from Jamaica in October 1720. He took lodgings at Lablond's tavern and began to advertise. An accomplished promoter, Sharp did what countless alternative healers had done before him in England and continental Europe, openly acknowledging and addressing his circumstances as an outsider. In several postings in the *Boston Gazette* and the *Boston Weekly News-Letter* listing the disorders for which he was willing to provide immediate relief, among them scurvy, leprosy, and scrofula (the King's Evil), he advised readers that "he is a Stranger" and that he intended to "stay but a few Weeks in this Country." He also promised that if he "miscarries of curing (if such a thing should happen) . . . he will take no money." Sharp ran notices for approximately four weeks. In each he reminded his readers he was "of London."[61]

No evidence has surfaced concerning Dr. Sharp's patients, if indeed he had any. But he probably found at least some business because he remained in eastern New England for a little over a year, not simply a few weeks—a relatively long time for any alternative healer. Possibly his landlady, Anne Lablond, received care from him. A recent widow, she managed her late husband's tavern and boarding house on Tremont Street at a time when the street was fast becoming one of the principal thoroughfares in the town's south end. By mid-November Sharp had left Boston. He reappeared in January 1721 while living at a Madam Story's house in "Piscataqua" (Portsmouth) in the province of New Hampshire. There he announced his forthcoming publication of a treatise on cancer treatments, "designed purely for the benefit of the People in New-England," which relied on "Sanative and Gradual" applications rather than the "common, but cruel practice of manual Operation [surgery]."[62] How long he remained in Portsmouth is not known, but within a year some old habits may have caught up with him. When an anonymous correspondent warned New Hampshire readers of the Boston *New-England Courant* against the "immoderate Pursuit of gaming," he mentioned "the famous Mountebank who lives there, [who] has lately lost his Watch, Diamond Ring, Peruke, &c. at that Exercise." Very likely this letter, dated December 1721, is referring to Dr. Sharp.[63]

The most volatile of the early mountebanks was Charles Hamilton, a convicted felon and indentured servant who seems to have assumed several identities. A notification issued in Chester, Pennsylvania, in 1752 discloses that local authorities had arrested a person attempting to sell "sundry medicines for different Disorders." According to a preliminary statement, this physician was trained under "Doctor Green, a noted Mountebank in England, and that he embarked on board a Brigantine, at Topham, in England, last Fall for Philadelphia, but was cast away at the latter End of January on the Coast of North-Carolina; . . . But it being suspected that the Doctor was a Woman in Mens Cloaths, was taken up, examined and found to be a Woman. . . . She says now her Name is *Charlotte Hamilton*." The account goes on to say that Charles or Charlotte had confessed to using that disguise for several years, making her about forty years old.[64] That Hamilton had done well is suggested by the blue camlet coat with silver buttons that she was wearing.

We learn a little more about Charlotte seven months later when a Virginia plantation owner offered two gold pistols for the apprehension of a "convict servant woman" going by the name of Sarah Knox, who claimed she was born in Yorkshire and had been in the army for several years. He alluded to the Chester report saying, "She may pretend to be a dancing mistress; will make a great many courtesies, and is a very deceitful, bold, insinuating woman, and a great liar." He concluded he had "reason to believe that she is the very servant who belongs to me." As an after note he added, "This Sarah Knox was imported from Whitehaven, in the Duke of Cumberland, with other convicts, among whom was one William Forrester, who, I have heard her say, was sometime with the above Dr. Green."[65]

In the late 1760s and early 1770s, a wave of more specialized mountebanks (usually calling themselves oculists, aurists, or surgeons) began working the principal American seaports. Coming variously from England, France, or Germany, this group may have had better luck than their predecessors because some brought techniques unfamiliar to many American physicians. Dr. William Stork, whose advertisements call him "Surgeon and Oculist to her Royal Highness the Princess Dowager of Wales," was first heard from in Jamaica in 1760 when he published an advertisement in the *Kingston Journal* claiming to restore failing eyesight.[66] He arrived in eastern Pennsylvania in 1761 and continued on to Philadelphia, Annapolis, New York City, Jamaica (Long Island), Hartford, New Haven, New London, Newport, Providence, Dedham, Boston, and Portsmouth—all the while paving his way with glowing testimonials about himself. Even as he showed characteristics of a committed mountebank, he also may have been a pioneer in the medical field and the first person to advertise cataract surgery openly in North America. A recent study by the physician Christopher Leffler and his colleagues not only indicates that "Occulist. William Storck, MD" was included among the attendants at the princess dowager of Wales's court in 1752, but that Stork's steady progress in America over a period of four years suggests he had a measure of professional success.[67] Dr. Nathaniel Ames reported in June 1764 that "Dr. Stork famous Occulist [was] here [in Dedham]"; Ames then followed Stork's progress. On 16 June Ames recorded that "Mr. Ellis's Eyes [were] couch'd for a Cataract." On 23 June "Saml. Fullers Eyes [were] couch'd." On 25 June "Mrs. White's Eyes [were] couched." More than a month later on 30 July "Dr. Stork couch'd Mrs. White's Eyes again."[68] Stork was obviously making follow-up visits and undertaking difficult procedures that may have been beyond the capability (or daring) of local physicians, or outside the means of most of their patients. Although Stork never used his first name in his American advertisements, two letters waiting at the Boston post office in 1765 belonged to "Stork William Doctor," the same William Stork of London who published a geographic treatise on East Florida in 1766. He is reported to have "died with the fright" during an insurrection of indentured servants in Florida in August 1768.[69]

Another healer who garnered considerable notice was Dr. Isaac Calcott of London, who initially took up lodgings at an obscure tavern in the village of Little Compton, Rhode Island. Like Stork, Calcott glibly announced he possessed "the Art of curing" and named thirty disorders that he could treat "if curable." He worked in Newport and Providence for six weeks, and over the next several years practiced in New London, Hartford, New York City, and Boston. He ran his last posting in Portsmouth in July 1773. Like all mountebanks, Calcott moved about constantly. According to his own reckoning, he attended patients at no fewer than six taverns in six days in the Hartford area in early October 1769: "Any of my medicines may be had of me, on Monday, at Mr. Samuel Easton's at East Hartford; on Tuesday at Mr. Porter's Tavern at East Windsor; on Wednesday, at Mr. Buck's tavern at Wethersfield; on Thursday at Mr. Pomeroy's tavern in Rock Hill; on Friday, at the Wid. Shaylor's tavern in Middletown; and on Saturday at Mr. Hale's tavern in Glastenbury."[70]

And like Stork, Calcott was credited with some medical competence. An unusually detailed account of one of his cures in Wethersfield, Connecticut, in 1770 was recorded many years later by Reverend Ezra Stiles. The patient's name was Elizur Belden, a child of six when Calcott treated him, who had suffered from blindness, lameness, and abdominal swelling since his infancy. When Belden, as a student at Yale College, died in 1786 at the age of twenty-three, Stiles recorded the parents' recollection of what Calcott had done for their son: "Mrs. Belden holding the Child in his Lap, Dr. Calcott . . . licked the Eyes, first putting his Tongue into one Eye & then into the other Eye of the Child—it was soon done,—and instantly the Child saw, & ever after continued to see well." Calcott was remembered by Stiles's informant as "decently dressed," about thirty years old, but suffering from alcoholism.[71]

The watchfulness of American newspapers may have persuaded some mountebanks to return to Europe. Among them was "Dr. Graham, the Oculist and Aurist" who toured North America from 1771 to 1773, writing flamboyant advertisements and promising to cure blindness and treat the poor "gratis." Graham's route took him to Williamsburg, Baltimore, Philadelphia, and New York, where he lectured extensively on the "Eye."[72] Dr. Graham was none other than Scottish-born James Graham (1745–94), more popularly known as the "Emperor of Quacks." On his return to England in 1776, Graham launched a career as one of the most outrageous and affluent medical impostors in English history. He purchased a mansion house in a fashionable district of London, hired a retinue of young girls and servants, and opened a "Grand Temple of Health and Hymen," whose showpiece was a resplendent bed impregnated with scents, sounds, and sights guaranteed to make couples fertile. Graham's excesses eventually led to his ruin, and he died in poverty and under suspicion of insanity.[73]

The response of the press may also be why Yale-educated Dr. Elisha Perkins (1741–1799), inventor of "Patent Metallic Instruments" or "Metallic Tractors," became famous in North America and why his practice essentially failed after two or three years of intense publicity (fig. 14.2). Perkins's treatment consisted of rods that were applied to afflicted body parts with a downward stroking motion. Claiming they cured epilepsy, rheumatism, and convulsions, he sold patent rights to their distribution, supplied free treatments to the poor, and toured the country giving demonstrations.[74] But—like Dr. John Pope in Boston—he kept his manufacturing formulas a secret within his own family in order to franchise his devices and ensure maximum profits, sending his son John D. Perkins to Charleston to sell them along with "a Pamphlet of evidences from many of the most respectable characters in New-England." Another son, Benjamin D. Perkins, took a shipment of "tractors" to England where he found they were much better received than in America.[75] Perkins himself seems to have followed epidemics, though it is unclear whether he had the best or worst of motives. In 1798, he took lodgings in Boston at a Mr. Clark's boarding house in the middle of a yellow fever epidemic, saying the outbreak was the same one that then raged in Philadelphia, New York City, and New London. After declaring that repeated

Figure 14.2. *Dr. Elisha Perkins* (1741–1799), inventor of "Patent Metallic Instruments" or "Metallic Tractors," which cured pains, swellings, and inflammatory tumors. Attributed to Dr. Perkins's daughter Sarah Perkins (1771–1831). Plainfield, Connecticut, circa 1787–88. Pastel on paper, 19 by 16 inches. Courtesy, The Connecticut Historical Society, 1980.89.1.

experiments demonstrated the disease could be eradicated by a "simple means, easily obtained," he went to New York City in an attempt to work his cures. Ironically, four weeks after his arrival, he died of the fever himself.

Stung by persistent criticism, alternative healers who continued to reside in North America were obliged to adopt more locally acceptable methods—principally those offered by electrical machines and Native American pharmaceutical suppliers. The idea that electrical treatments could alleviate persistent illnesses had received some early acceptance when an unidentified "gentleman" traveling through Maryland in 1749 used "electrical experiments . . . in curing the toothach, pain in the head, deafness, pain in all the limbs." In August 1749, he was in Suffolk, Virginia, and on his way to Norfolk, Hampton, York, and Williamsburg, where he planned to remain while the general court was in session. He has not been identified but may have been Richard Brickell or one of his understudies.[76] In New England, one of the earliest practitioners was a neighbor of diarist Ebenezer Parkman, who had heard in February 1779 about an "Electrical Machine" owned in Grafton. Parkman twice rode there to see it. Although the owner, a Mr. Grosvenor, was not at home, he persuaded his wife to have it demonstrated. "I dined there," Parkman wrote, "and she sent her son Obadiah to call Mr. Henstick, the Baptist minister, to show me the said Machine. Mr. Grosvenor had by this time returned from Sutton, and came to me and kindly assisted Mr. Henstick in the Electrical Operations, which were wonderful. I was electrized a number of times, the rather as it was said to be a Remedy against the Cramp, which I am much subject to."[77]

Over time electrotherapeutic remedies became commercially available by itinerants in major cities such as Providence, New York, Boston, Baltimore, and Charleston. For example, surgeon-dentist Isaac Greenwood (1730–1803) proclaimed himself "ready to electerize" his patients in 1786. Dr. Hornby, a surgeon-dentist, promoted his "short" stay in New York in 1787 with the announcement that "the Doctor's Medical Electrical apparatus [was available] as usual."[78] With at least sixty-five electrical therapists known to have practicing in North America before 1826, medical electricians were common enough to be found in every city and large town in America. Their numbers were split about evenly between long-term itinerants and local practitioners associated with museums.

"Indian" physicians and pharmaceutical suppliers assumed a comparable profile. While few people took Henry Tufts's approach of living with and marrying into a tribe to learn their secrets, physicians and nurses did make arrangements to serve as agents for Native American pharmaceuticals. Eli Starr, of Stoneham, Massachusetts, made himself available at Eager's Tavern in Boston in 1805 to administer a remedy for an unnamed "fashionable disease" that he had purchased from an Indian doctor about thirty years earlier. To help his patients, Starr installed himself every Thursday in a convenient tavern near the Charlestown bridge, but after about three years he moved on. Two promoters, J. P. Hall and Charity Shaw, set up a dispensary in Boston that promised "immediate relief obtained from the Indian Medicine" in 1805. The following year, Shaw extended her distribution of "Indian Medicine" to West Boston and sent her products to Newark, Bennington, and New Orleans in an elaborately publicized scheme extolling and justifying her Native American treatments for consumption, dysentery, and scurvy. Over the next five years Shaw remarried and lived in New York City as Mrs. Charity Long with contacts in Philadelphia, Utica, Troy, and Albany, though by then she was retailing her wares as "Botannical Medicines."[79] A later healer, Edward Lockwood, for years practiced Indian medicine in Baltimore "in the Seneca manner by roots, herbs, barks, seeds, and flowers"—locating his shop near the circus, one of the last vestiges in North America of the medieval alignment between showmanship and healing.[80] By the time that Reverend Peter Smith (1753–1816) published his *Indian Doctor's Dispensatory* in 1813, much of this empirical knowledge had entered the public domain, and the skills that had previously been limited to those who had access to, or who feigned access to, Native Americans now became available to anyone who could read.[81]

OVER TIME, itinerants in three of the four professions considered here succeeded in neutralizing criticism directed at them and became accepted in antebellum nineteenth-century American life. Electrical healers proliferated; peddlers and their horse-carts became as familiar and convenient as the general store; religious exhorters gradually escaped the "itinerant" stigma and flourished under the leadership of nineteenth-century leaders of "camp meetings" like Lorenzo Dow. But public opinion basically defeated the transfer of most traditional healing and mountebank practices. Generally more cautious than European and English peasant-based societies, North Americans on the whole remained inhospitable to alternative medical techniques.

Not surprisingly, however, we find that many strollers who practiced one of these challenging professions also pursued some form of the other three—much like the fictional Duke and Dauphin in Mark Twain's *Huckleberry Finn*. This tradition can be seen in the mid-eighteenth century when Johannes H. Fretzel, a runaway Dutch servant in Philadelphia, alternately served his 1746 clients as a "doctor of physick" or a "preacher." In 1764, Dr. William Stork gave up his medical profession and returned to America as an agent of Florida real estate. Dr. Anthony Yeldall seems to have been a pharmaceutical peddler and medical supplier long before he became a mountebank. In 1787, Dr. James Graham, who found himself destitute after his great London triumph, took up Methodist preaching. There were many others: Moses Hale cured diseases in 1818 Connecticut by "immediate revelation"—apparently he repeated texts of scripture to ensure his treatments worked. James Hamilton (alias John R. Bedford and G. Gallop) variously identified himself in 1823 as a physician, an Episcopal clergyman, and a peddler—all the while conveniently changing his name to cover his true motive as an imposter.[82]

These cross-purposes may explain a certain unity of language and style among itinerants who pursued controversial vocations. The verbal fluency shown by peddlers John Day and James McIntire (both were described as "talkative" in 1772) matches the verbal persuasiveness of religious exhorters like Ichabod Jones ("makes Verses and is sometime[s] Crazy") and the brilliant medical advertising of Dr. James Graham ("no cure, no pay"). Elsewhere, aspiring healers may have learned to smooth up their potential followers with a peddler's "palaber" or with a "budget of doggrel rhyme" based on an ingeniously created language.[83] Or, for that matter, preachers themselves could have learned their religious cant from the unflinching certainty of mountebank physicians like Dr. Isaac Calcott ("I cure if curable") or the self-reliance of a peddler like John Jackson, who in 1758 played a bagpipe while his "lusty" wife sang Scottish songs.[84]

These interlocking relationships of course mirror the larger strategic mentality of itinerants and strollers who found that success was bestowed on those providing the most compelling verbal message. In all likelihood many transient "professionals" were imposters first and carriers of European (or Native American) culture second. The most diverse and multitalented among them were the medical electricians, who incorporated forms of showmanship, artistic acumen, mechanical ability, and museum competence in their appeal. Claiming that electrical machines were both "medical" and "divertive," they frequently crossed the line between therapy and entertainment to make sure their voices were heard.[85] At least nine museum proprietors, seven tavern showmen, four profilists or miniature makers, four electrical mechanics, three waxwork proprietors, one itinerant painter, and one pharmaceutical seller routinely advertised electrical machines for medical purposes.[86] Philip Woods (1774–1828), founder of the Boston Museum, gave small shocks and cured ailments while touring Daniel Bowen's waxwork figures and a naval panorama by Michele Felice Corné. Woods owned a Nairne patent device (fig. 14.3), but he also manufactured and repaired electrical machines at his workshop in the Boston Museum.[87] William King, the former furniture maker, treated rheumatism and deafness with a "galvanic" machine in Portsmouth, New Hampshire (possibly one of his own construction), setting the stage for his subsequent career in Rhode Island, Connecticut, New York, and Virginia promoting the effects of electrical fluid. Henry Williams, a respected Boston wax artist and miniaturist, got into the business of teaching electricity to future physicians while also making wax models for them. Signor Joseph Falconi, the professional conjurer, boasted of his ties to Alessandro Volta.[88] Even serious portrait painters utilized "electrical fire" for their purposes. Cephas Thompson, active in Massachusetts and South Carolina, not only

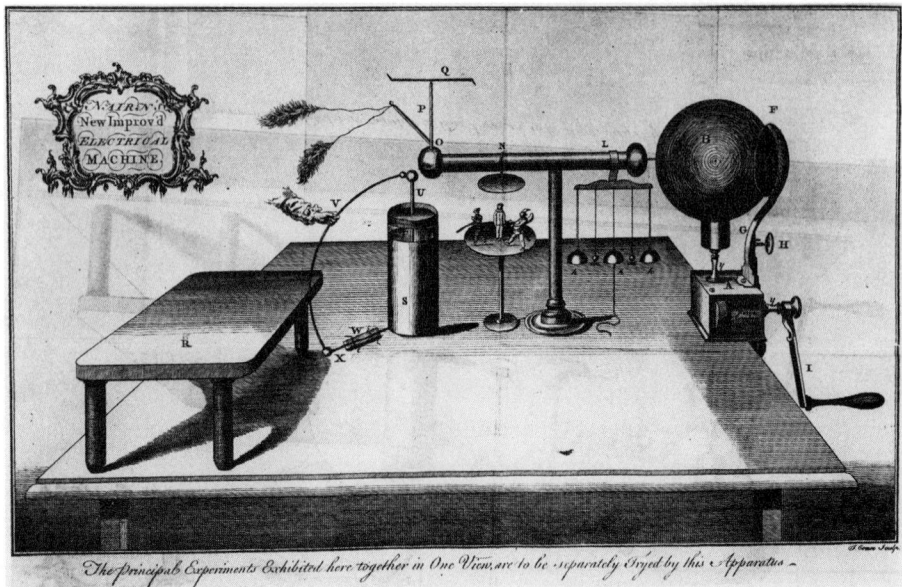

Figure 14.3. Schematic illustration of *Nairn's New Improv'd Electrical Machine* used by Philip Woods (1774–1828) to cure ailments at the Boston Museum. Folded plate from *Directions for Using the Electrical Machine as Made and Sold by E. Nairne* showing the handle to turn the crank and the variety of experiments, toys, bells, and condensers to store electricity. J. Couse, sculptor. London: N.p., 1773. Courtesy, Huntington Library, San Marino, California, RB 710613.

invented his own electerizing machine but tried it on his wife and neighbors.[89] And in some instances, medical electrical applications were exploited for their entrepreneurial and entertainment value. One healer, practicing in Richmond in 1801, requested that those coming for therapy "will please to provide a person to keep the machine in motion."[90] Another, working in Boston, gave treatments in medical electricity while providing help "drawing Deeds, Wills, Indentures and all kinds of Conveyances," all at a reasonable price.[91] Anthony Cross, visiting Boston and Newburyport with a galvanic machine in 1804, unwittingly clarified his "therapeutic" goals when he assured readers of the *Eastern Argus* in Portland, Maine, that spectators would "be supplied with Tickets" at Thomas Clark's bookstore on Fifth Street. Nor was he alone. Cross was one of three operators in the American northeast who cited "Hours for Spectators" or "Tickets of Admission"—customarily making them available through local book and music stores.[92] This was medical electricity with a distinctively American touch.

Part IV

POPULAR CULTURE FLOURISHES IN AMERICA, 1780–1825

Chapter 15

Waxwork Museums

POPULAR CULTURE in America virtually exploded during the early federal and national periods, dramatically altering social attitudes and behavior patterns, revising old ways of thinking, and enriching common vocabularies. Part of a massive upheaval that accompanied the establishment of individual states, the signing of the Articles of Confederation, and the adoption of a new federal Constitution, the earlier divisions between mannered and popular culture were ignored, overwhelmed, or reversed. What was "elite" became "popular," and what was popular became elite. This was the period of "the American, this new man," as J. Hector St. John de Crèvecoeur phrased it in 1782.[1] It was an environment in which everything seemed possible. For the first time itinerants encountered unambiguous signs of welcome, unmistakable indications of financial profitability, and a profusion of invigorated clients, pupils, and audiences. Together these changes gave both itinerants and their patrons a perspective and self-confidence they had seldom enjoyed before.

Traveling exhibitions of waxworks, a traditional art form that dated to the Greek and Roman civilizations, became widely popular in America after 1790. Like broadsides and chapbooks, the "striking Likenesses" of traveling wax museums brought the outside world directly to the threshold of everyday people.[2] Featuring music on an organ, occasional live animals, and up to fifty authentically costumed and well-documented wax representations, these exhibitions animated biblical scenes, European royalty, beautiful women, and Native Americans so realistically that proprietors had to post signs asking their audiences not to touch them.[3] They also mirrored incidents of domestic violence, the outcome of revolutions, multiple births, famous actresses, and emblematic compositions that lay close to the hearts of most Americans. The numbers and dissemination of their work were impressive. Altogether, over 182 waxwork museum proprietors, agents, or partnerships toured eastern North America, Lower Canada, and the Ohio Valley between 1733 and 1825, the majority of them between 1800 and 1820 and most of them American-born. They were supported by about twenty professional wax sculptors, seamstresses, and decorators—again primarily American but with increasing Italian, French, and English participation. Their exhibitions not only focused on major cities but penetrated rural areas where they were often the only form of itinerant-based culture available.

How did waxwork museums suddenly rise to this level of importance? The likely answer is that American audiences were curious and the art was timely. Shortly after the combined Russian and Austrian armies under General Alexander Suvorov-Rymnikski (1730–1800) defeated the French expeditionary forces in Italy in early July 1799, a Viennese artist named Joseph Kreutzinger took several sketches of the victorious general as he prepared to paint Suvorov-Rymnikski's portrait (fig. 15.1). Kreutzinger sent one of his illustrations to Florence where it was engraved as the frontispiece for a history of the campaign already in preparation. He sent a second to London to be engraved by James Anthony Minasi and then published it as a portrait print by a Mrs. Bovi at 207 Piccadilly on 16 July 1799 and by J. Wright on 1 September 1799. Five and a half months later, a waxwork representation of the Russian commander-in-chief based on Minasi's likeness was advertised as an addition to the main hall of a leading Boston museum. The six-foot standing form of the medallioned Russian general joined about fifty other wax figures—among them those of President John Adams, the inventor Benjamin Franklin, the English boxers Humphreys and Mendoza, a famed "Boston Beauty," and the king of France under the guillotine.[4]

By late eighteenth-century standards, the five-and-a-half months that had elapsed between Kreutzinger's sketching Suvorov-Rymnikski and Daniel Bowen's announcement that a new figure was available at his Columbian Museum was relatively short. Although events were rapidly reshaping continental Europe, the general's July 1799 victory was still major news in Boston the following December, and Boston museum visitors were examining "Suwarrow's" features months before they had the opportunity to read the first book-length account of his campaign in English. How long Suvorov-Rymnikski's waxwork likeness remained at the Columbian Museum is not known. If the figure survived the two successive fires that gutted the museum in 1803 and 1807, it was probably sold or traded to a competitor. Ralph Letton carried a "Count Alexander Suwarrow"—possibly Bowen's—on his trip through Connecticut and Rhode Island in 1808. This was eight years after Suvorov-Rymnikski had left the historical stage. By that time the Russian general, who had never been defeated in a standing battle, was recognized by most people in English-speaking North America only as a style of boot.[5]

Although these displays were later deemed a "barbarous branch of art" by Frances Trollope, they may have been more than just sensational or titillating effigies of eighteenth- and early nineteenth-century "celebrities." The proprietors of these museums succeeded in communicating public history to new American audiences, many of them rural and semiliterate—whetting the appetites of their clients by using the subject's "real" clothes, finding "authentic" personal accessories, employing suggestive labeling, and entertaining them with hours of organ music.[6]

In terms of numbers of displays, approximately 1,500 wax figures or figure groups were exhibited in North America in this period—enough wax people to fill the main floor pews and two tiers of galleries in one of New England's largest meetinghouses. As icons of contemporary and popular history, waxworks gave many Americans their first appreciation of statuary art and their first face-to-face

Figure 15.1. *Field Marshall Count Alexander Suworow Rymnikski. AEtat. 69* (1730–1800). Engraved by James Anthony Minasi after an original drawing by Joseph Kreutzinger (1757–1829) taken in Vienna in July 1799 and published in London by a Mrs. Bovi, 207 Piccadilly, 16 July 1799, and redone by J. Wright, 169 Piccadilly, 1 September 1799. Minasi's engraving was "the late English print" from which Daniel Bowen created Suvorov-Rymnikski's waxwork unveiled in Boston in December 1799. Image height: 5½ inches. Frontispiece from Frederic Anthing, *History of the Campaigns of Count Alexander Suworow Rymnikski*, London, 1799. Courtesy, Houghton Library, Harvard University, Slav 1043.2.

exposure to the stories, traditions, and historical personalities that helped define them as European Americans. Like ballad sellers and authors of chapbooks and broadsides, waxwork proprietors spoke to the values of a society that paid twenty-five cents per person to see their exhibits. Unstudied for years by art critics and historians of material culture because of the flammable nature of the medium (no full-size wax figures, or even fragments of such figures, and almost no images of them survive in American collections), these exhibitions nevertheless produced what authors of religious and moral tracts of the period liked to term a "looking glass" of the American mind. It is a mirror, however ephemeral in nature, which even today furnishes insights into America's racial, political, and personal history.[7]

European waxworks were introduced into North American cities as early as 1733. That year Boston resident John Dyer exhibited a set of figures believed to have been part of a collection shown for years by a Mrs. Salmon at her Fleet Street establishment in London—apparently living out their final years in the American colonies. Another group of effigies, "The Royal Family of England and the Queen of Hungary," were exhibited in 1749 in New York City by James Wyatt, who sometimes companioned them with puppet shows put on by "Punch's Company of Comedians." A third early group "in full proportion . . . in their Hungarian Habits" were shown in New England, Philadelphia, and Charleston in the 1750s by the showman Richard Brickell.[8] Joshua Hempstead saw this group in a tavern in New London in July 1751, recording in his diary that he "Rid into Town to Capt Lees to See the Shows. the Queen of Hungary &c."[9] In Charleston in 1753, Brickell announced that the wax image of the "Queen of Hungary" was "taken from the Life by Gerard van Squartzenger of Vienna," presumably a Dutch or German wax modeler. Brickell and a musician named Mr. Richardson accompanied the exhibit with a dulcimer and perspective views of European cities and castles.[10]

The founders of the American waxwork industry were two widowed sisters from New Jersey, Patience Lovell Wright (1725–1786) (fig. 15.2) and Rachel Lovell Wells (1735–1796), who in 1770 began modeling and exhibiting wax figures to support their large families. The Lovells' achievements in New York City and Philadelphia generated waxwork-making centers founded by their apprentices and coworkers. Among them were the New England museum proprietor Daniel Bowen (fig. 15.3) and Reuben Moulthrop, the New Haven portrait artist. Others included Ralph Letton, a Maryland-born profile artist most recently from Canada; and John Christian Rauschner, a wax modeler from Vienna who made a living specializing in glass-covered wax miniatures. They encouraged a third generation of wax artists and traveling entrepreneurs. Moulthrop recruited his in-laws, some of them sons of local clergyman Reverend Nicholas Street of East Haven. Bowen in turn recruited his Boston neighbors William M. S. Doyle (fig. 15.4), Philip Woods (fig. 15.5), and Charles Packard. Eventually Woods and Packard sold their collections to portrait painter Ethan Allen Greenwood, who founded museums in Boston, Providence, and Portland. These entrepreneurs all knew each other well. They borrowed, traded, and sold wax figures; they purchased each other's collections.[11]

Beyond the need for timeliness, the key to their success was twofold. First was the nature of wax as an artistic medium. So convincingly did dyed beeswax simulate the texture of human flesh that audiences readily imagined they were seeing real people. Reuben Moulthrop promised to replicate "every Circumstance" of

Figure 15.2. *Patience Lovell Wright* (1725–1786). Magazine illustration inscribed "*Portrait of* M:RS WRIGHT, *of New York. The Remarkable Modeller in Wax.*" Wright and her sister Rachel Lovell Wells (1735–1796) founded the American waxwork industry. Second state of an engraving by C. Johnson initially published in the 1 December 1775 issue of the *London Magazine. Wonderful Magazine*, 8 by 5 inches. London, England, 1793–94. Courtesy, Winterthur Museum, Museum Purchase, 1973.199.

Figure 15.3. *D. Bowen* (1760–1856), by Joseph Kyle. Daniel Bowen taught wax sculpting to Reuben Moulthrop while residing in New Haven and also passed the same knowledge to William M. S. Doyle, his neighbor in Boston and assistant at the Columbian Museum. Collection of A. M. Philipps. From William C. Burrage, "Abel Bowen," *Bostonian Society Publications* 1 (1886–88): 33.

the execution of Louis XVI, giving "the Eye of the Spectator a realizing View of that momentous and interesting Event." He literally meant the severed bleeding head of the monarch raised above the gaping crowd; the lifeless, bound body about to be placed in a wicker coffin; and the rows of armed grenadiers surrounding the site.[12] Entrepreneurs liked to play up the trompe l'oeil effect of wax in their advertisements. James Bishop claimed that nine visitors out of ten examining his "Sleeping Beauty" took it for the "original." Similar stories were told of Patience Wright's London museum where an aristocratic visitor was said to have given an order to a wax housemaid. At John Rauschner's studio in New York City, a visiting newspaper correspondent reputedly retreated on tiptoe so as not to disturb a wax mother nursing a wax child.[13]

Second was the aggressive business acumen of the proprietors. Owners of eighteenth- and early nineteenth-century wax museums paraded the pomp and glitter of celebrated actors and actresses, kings and queens, famous explorers, and fictional heroines before their audiences. This alone would have made any American take notice. But proprietors leavened their collections with special favorites—characters from Shakespeare, beautiful women, conversation pieces, emblematic tableaux of American independence and nationhood, as well as figures designed to provoke controversy. One entrepreneur toured with "Polygamy—a man with two wives." Another displayed a professor of anatomy

Figure 15.4. *William M. S. Doyle* (1769–1828). Self-portrait signed and dated "Doyle/April 22/1828" in lower left-hand corner. This image was drawn by Doyle a few weeks before his death. Pastel on paper, 25 by 19 inches. Courtesy, Bostonian Society/Old State House.

Figure 15.5. "Rare Productions of Nature and Art, *from all parts of the world*." Handbill or broadside advertising wax effigies of Charlotte Corday and Daniel Lambert in Philip Woods's museum on the north side of the Market House, Boston. At various points in his career Woods (1774–1828) took his museum to locations such as Portland, Maine; Nantucket Island; and Cincinnati, Ohio. Printer unknown, c. 1810. Woodcut illustrations. Courtesy, New-York Historical Society, neg. no. 233503.

from a medical school showing several specimens. A third, James Bishop, traveled with a wax image of himself under the title "The Welcome Receiver." All were calculated to induce visitors to pay the entrance fee.[14]

About two-thirds of all waxwork figures in this period were historical or biblical. Besides Suvorov-Rymnikski and the execution of Louis XVI, museum proprietors commissioned General James Wolfe expiring on the Plains of Abraham; General Jean Victor Moreau confined to a French prison; the death of Lord Nelson at the Battle of Trafalgar; Muhammad Ali Pacha, the creator of modern Egypt; and Augustín de Iturbide, the founder of Mexico. American subjects included Major General John Butler wounded at Niagara; Lorenzo Dow preaching to his followers; George Washington receiving Lord Cornwallis at Yorktown; and Tecumseh, the Shawnee chief killed in the Battle of the Thames in 1813. Biblical figures tended toward controversial or violent subjects: Judith and her maid with the bleeding head of Holofernes; King Solomon and two harlots; a damsel presenting the head of John the Baptist to the wife of Herodias. Each figure or group was meticulously labeled with hand-lettered sheets attached behind or next to the display: "General Washington receiving the sword of the British general Cornwallis, after the capitulation of Yorktown," or "the late duel between Coms. Decatur and Barron attended by Coms. Rogers and Bainbridge and Capt. Elliot."[15]

Whenever possible, waxwork modelers sought live subjects. Reuben Moulthrop, who had just painted a portrait of Reverend Ezra Stiles (fig. 15.6), persuaded him to have his face and hands sketched for a wax effigy. Once complete, Moulthrop introduced the figure at the long room in Parmelee's Tavern in the fall of 1793, urging local residents to compare the real person with his waxwork duplicate—"the merit of which every citizen of New-Haven can be a perfect judge." Other modelers quoted witnesses who had seen the subject. Philip Woods's "Indian warrior" was a likeness of a Native American who "was in Boston in 1796" and easily remembered by some viewers. A Boston museum advertised a "correct likeness" in wax of Napoleon Bonaparte "procured in Paris by a gentleman who saw the Consul."[16]

Figure 15.6. *The Rev. Ezra Stiles* (1727–1795), by Reuben Moulthrop (1763–1814). New Haven, Connecticut. Moulthrop visited Stiles on four occasions in August 1793 to make a "Picture in Wax." In January 1794, he added Stiles's figure to his wax exhibition at the Sign of the Goddess Iris on State Street. In September of that year Moulthrop returned to paint a portrait of Stiles as well as one of Stiles's wife. Oil on canvas, thought to be a later copy (1812). Courtesy, Redwood Library and Athenaeum, Newport, Rhode Island.

Failing access to firsthand observations, waxwork artists depended on an existing iconography of prints, primarily European but also some American ones. In so doing they served as a critical intermediary—unmatched in any other form of popular art—between their provincial patrons and the world of art and statuary. Besides Kreutzinger's print of Suvorov-Rymnikski, Daniel Bowen worked from engraved scenes of the French Revolution. A print entitled *The Last Interview between Lewis the Sixteenth and His Disconsolate Family in the Temple,* one of 123 prints and paintings on view at his museum in December 1798, was probably the source of his wax group titled *The Late King of France, Taking an Affectionate Leave of His Family.* Beginning with the queen distracted, the king's sister affected, the princess fainting, and the dauphin embracing the king, the poses and emotions of each figure in Bowen's wax composition corresponded to those in the print, itself derived from a 1793 study by the young English painter Charles Benazech (1767–1794) and reproduced by the Italian engraver Luigi Schiavonetti (fig. 15.7).[17] Labels were sometimes detailed enough to name the locations of the prints and paintings being copied. New Haven's James Bishop presented a striking likeness of Napoleon and Ferdinand VII, "from an exact original drawing taken at Bayonne." Nicholas and Elnathan Street exhibited a figure of Christopher Columbus, modeled from an "original print found in the Museum of the duke of Tuscany."[18]

Biblical scenes, particularly, were based on an iconographic lexicon developed centuries earlier by painters from the Renaissance and early modern Europe. If Daniel Bowen's and James Bishop's experiences were typical, the scene of Joseph disengaging himself from Potiphar's wife, shown in a New York City waxwork museum in 1812, may have been inspired by familiar prints taken from paintings by Orazio Gentileschi or Ludovico Cigoli. A waxwork of Sampson and Delilah with her servant shaving his hair, advertised by John Mix in 1807, may have been derived from Peter Paul Rubens. The severed head of John the Baptist likely came from numerous paintings by Michelangelo Merisi da Caravaggio.[19]

The deft timing realized by Daniel Bowen in 1799 with Suvorov-Rymnikski was even more essential when covering local events. New Englanders spent the better part of 1801 monitoring the unfolding prosecution of twenty-year-old Jason Fairbanks of Dedham, Massachusetts, who was tried and condemned to death for the murder of Elizabeth Fales. The case was notorious because Fales was romantically linked to Fairbanks and because after his conviction, he escaped from jail assisted by several friends and supporters. His apprehension was subject to a reward of a thousand dollars, and he was caught shortly afterward in Skeensborough (Whitehall), New York, and returned to Boston. Fairbanks's execution took place at a gallows erected on Dedham Common on 10 September 1801. Printed material was issued in rapid succession. A broadside quoting his dying words was published within days of the event, and his "Solemn

Figure 15.7. *The Last Interview between Lewis the Sixteenth and His Disconsolate Family in the Temple.* After a study by Charles Benazech (1767–1794), engraved by Luigi Schiavonetti (1765–1810). This print, published in London by Colnaghi and Company on 10 March 1794, was displayed in Daniel Bowen's museum in 1798 and may have provided a model for the waxwork exhibited there. Courtesy, Bibliothèque nationale de France.

Declaration" of innocence was available about a month later. Wax modelers followed closely. During Fairbanks's confinement in jail, Reuben Moulthrop traveled from New Haven to Dedham to sketch a likeness of the accused. Soon after Fairbanks's execution, Moulthrop began working on effigies of Fairbanks's head, neck, and hands. Two months later, on 17 November 1801, Moulthrop's two brothers-in-law, Nicholas and Elnathan Street, who had just returned from a tour of major towns along the Hudson River, picked up the new Fairbanks waxwork at Moulthrop's East Haven workshop on their way to Massachusetts. They opened a gallery of thirty-five figures at Salem's Washington Hall—one of them being "a striking likeness of Jason Fairbanks who was executed at Dedham for the murder of Eliza Fales." Fairbanks's unfortunate victim, "the beautiful Eliza Fales," joined Moulthrop's and the Streets' tour about a year later.[20]

Prominent public figures in tragic circumstances were similarly rushed into wax. The duel between Alexander Hamilton and Aaron Burr, which took place in Weehawken, New Jersey, on 11 July 1804, inspired waxwork reenactments within two months. One group was exhibited at Yale's commencement exercises on 6 September 1804; a second, a month later in Northampton, Massachusetts. Each consisted of four figures: "The General [is shown] . . . supported by his Second, after receiving the fatal wound, while the Second of Colonel Burr urges him to retire from the field."[21] But the fastest completion of any waxwork reenactment on record was the ensemble installed in the Columbian Hall of John Mix's museum in New Haven on 27 August 1812. This scene captured the "Cruelties of the Baltimore Mob" on General Henry "Light-Horse" Lee, federalist editor Alexander C. Hanson, and Maryland militiaman James M. Lingan. The episode had taken place in the Baltimore jail on the night of 28 July, leaving Lingan and Lee dead and the editor seriously wounded. The waxwork was unveiled to the public one month less a day after the event.[22]

Above all, historical figures had to exude an aura of authenticity. When Moulthrop came to Dedham to sketch Fairbanks, he apparently arranged to acquire his clothes from the authorities. Two years later, when the partnership of a Mr. Davenport and James Bishop toured Moulthrop's figures in New Jersey and rural Pennsylvania, they made it part of their publicity: Fairbanks "is dressed in the same clothes he wore at the time of his Trial."[23] Entrepreneurs' claims of accurate costuming became a calling card of American waxwork exhibits. Joseph Steward's 1801 effigy of an American who had been a captive in Algiers was clothed "with the dress he wore in his state of servitude." Daniel Bowen's 1793 figure of John S. Hutton (who had lately died in Philadelphia at the age of 103 years and 4 months) was "drest in the same cloaths which he wore when living, with his own cane, pipe, tobacco box &c." Bowen's 1805 effigy of Newburyport merchant Timothy Dexter was bedecked in "an elegant suit of clothes presented by [Dexter] himself"—easily believed given Dexter's penchant for self-aggrandizement.[24]

If costumes were unavailable, proprietors compensated with "genuine" accessories—both physical and verbal—no matter how unusual or bizarre. No fewer than four waxworks of Native Americans held in their belts the "actual" scalps of their victims, including Philip Woods's warrior, which toured in 1799 with "the real scalp of a man . . . taken on the frontiers of America."[25] Two more Native Americans held reputed "scalping knives." And when visitors to James Bishop's exhibition in Portland, Maine, came to see a replica of Uncas splitting open the head of Narragansett chief Miantonomoh, a label informed them that Uncas had exclaimed, "It was sweeter than Englishman's meat"—a paraphrase of a widely known revenge slaying mentioned in John Winthrop's diary but articulated more explicitly in Reverend Benjamin Trumbull's 1797 *The Complete History of Connecticut.*[26]

Not surprisingly, wax museums mirrored other forms of popular history. Virtually any historical or biographical subject that turned up in wax was likely to have appeared in a contemporary chapbook history, broadside, or broadside ballad, with the wax image serving as a visual extension of inexpensive, print-based media. Boston printer Nathaniel Coverly, Jr., alone published broadsides on at least five subjects that were rendered into wax: the Baltimore "mob" attacking James M. Lingan and General Lee; the trial and last words of Ebenezer Mason (another Massachusetts murderer); Calvin, the "American dwarf"; the death of Lord Nelson; and Baron Trenck, the man chained forever in an underground dungeon.[27] Some chapbook publishers advertised wax images on the reverse of title pages, such as one of Ann Moore, an Englishwoman from Tutbury, Staffordshire, who claimed to have lived for three years without food.[28]

Waxworks were even connected to musical pantomimes. In 1792, the same year that French balloonist Jean-Pierre Blanchard spent in New York City vainly looking for subscriptions to his next ascension, he was feted with a waxwork titled "Celebrated Aeronaut" in Gardiner Baker's American Museum. Nearby, the Old American Company was staging *Harlequin Balloonist; or, Pierrot in the Clouds*. After Blanchard got to Boston in 1793, both the waxwork and the pantomime followed him.[29]

Initially waxworks bridged mannered and popular culture. Unlike most popular entertainments, they may have belied Peter Burke's assertion that adherents of the "great culture" of classical education occasionally enjoyed the "little culture" of the London fairs. The first wax museum proprietors in North America actually directed their exhibitions at the colonial urban upper classes. John Dyer, perhaps the earliest wax exhibitor in North America, was a Boston "clothdresser" in the town's north end.[30] Sarah Briggs; her husband, Thomas Brooks; and possibly Sarah's daughter, also Sarah Briggs, all "noted Shop Keepers," kept the "Royal Wax Work" at their stores on Wing's Lane in Boston and in Concord, Massachusetts, between 1739 and 1745.[31] Abigail Hiller, wife of a Boston jeweler, displayed Briggs's and Brooks's wax figures at her finishing school in Boston in 1751, where she taught young women painting on glass, quill-work, feather work, filigree, and tent stitch.[32] Their subjects were almost always aristocratic ("The Princess of Wales," "The Queen of Hungary"). And decades before becoming president, John Adams visited "Dr. Chovet and his skeletons and wax-works" in Philadelphia in 1774, saying these ceroplastic images were "admirable, exquisite representations of the whole animal economy."[33]

Even after the American Revolution, waxworks were tied to the educated elite. Daniel Bowen scheduled his first wax exhibits to coincide with commencements at Yale College and at the College of Rhode Island. Later diary and newspaper accounts attest that George Washington and his wife visited Daniel Bowen's New York and New Haven museums in 1788 and 1789 to see his wax images, including one of Washington himself. (The "Father of his County" was said to have been "exceedingly well pleased.")[34] The Holyoke family visited the same exhibition in Salem in 1791, as did William Bentley, who examined each figure closely, noting them in his diary; later that year he described each one in

Latin. In 1803, Bentley visited Bowen's museum in Boston. He found the waxwork displays "in abundance, & [full of] extravagance," but he evidently could not stay away from them.[35]

But when Bowen and Moulthrop and his in-laws began their entrepreneurial forays into the middle and southern states and to coastal and rural Connecticut and Rhode Island, they employed the same dispersal techniques already long in use by animal and menagerie showmen. They took their shows directly to the people. This translated into a routine of constant travel, repeated packing and unpacking, scheduling short stays, and working in geographic clusters so they could save on the costs of advertisements. Bowen, Moulthrop, Moulthrop's in-laws, relatives, and colleagues sent scores of exhibitions to taverns, inns, and exhibition halls throughout the North American maritime and agricultural heartland as well as to rural taverns along the eastern seaboard and Canada. No fewer than forty tavern long rooms, fourteen ballrooms, twelve meeting halls, eight hotels, and five coffeehouses have been documented as hosting waxwork collections between 1795 and 1825, many displays occupying the site for a couple of days or fewer. After returning from a yearlong journey to towns on the Long Island and Narragansett Sounds in 1796, Moulthrop and Streets' collection of twenty-one presidents, biblical figures, and other celebrities was exhibited in early January 1797 in northwestern Connecticut, beginning with Litchfield and traveling to Goshen, Sharon, Salisbury, Canaan, and Sheffield. The average stay at each tavern was no more than two or three days, each stop being advertised well in advance in the *Litchfield Monitor.* A few weeks later the same twenty-one figures were shown in the Massachusetts communities of Stockbridge, Lenox, and Richmond and in New Lebanon, New York.[36] Other showmen replicated this pattern in the Connecticut, Hudson, and Delaware River Valleys; their reach covered interior Pennsylvania, Maryland, Virginia, South Carolina, and Georgia. Sally Ripley, a bookish, rural schoolgirl in the Connecticut River Valley who kept a diary between 1799 and 1809, recorded her visit to a tavern in Greenfield, Massachusetts: "This afternoon I went with my sister to Mr. Munn's to see a collection of wax figures." She was "much pleased with them."[37]

The tastes shared by political leaders of American society; by villagers of Goshen, Sharon, and Greenfield; and by plantation owners in Charleston and Savannah indicate that most social classes of Americans enjoyed waxwork exhibitions—fulfilling one important definition of popular culture. Waxworks helped many early Americans broaden their cultural outlook and visually "realize" their collective history—bringing to them the world of wonders, traditional folklore, and biblical and historical figures that had inhabited the popular domain in England and continental Europe for centuries. But did waxwork exhibitions ever overcome the "barbarous" reputation ascribed to them by Frances Trollope? As usual, her appraisal was both right and wrong. Supporting her point is the fact that modelers sometimes invented details when they wanted to entice viewers. From an 1812 handbill (see fig. 15.5) advertising Philip Woods's museum in Boston, we know that the waxwork effigy of Charlotte Corday assassinating Jean-Paul Marat shows the victim seated in an armchair with Corday above him plunging a sheath knife into his heart. But Jacques-Louis David's contemporary painting of the scene—like Thomas Carlyle's later description in his history of the French Revolution—puts Marat recovering from an illness in a slipper-bath, not an armchair, and about to sign a document condemning three newly discovered Girondist traitors in southern France.[38]

Furthermore, museum proprietors stopped at nothing to get paying customers in the door. They did this by acquiring wax scenes of multiple births, murderers, human oddities, royalty, and "savage" Native Americans. John Dyer promoted his collection in 1733 as "a lively Representation of Margaret, Countess of Heininburg, who had 365 Children at one Birth, occasioned by the rash Wish of a poor Beggar Woman, who is represented asking her charity." (This thirteenth-century legend is still celebrated with a church plaque and monument in a small village in Holland.) Almost a hundred years later William Doyle set aside a separate room in the Columbian Museum to house "five children delivered at one birth!" (He also added a note saying a "certificate of the attending Physician may be seen at the place of exhibition, should any doubt the fact.")[39] That was just the beginning. Daniel Bowen rigged his Witch of Endor with springs so the figure would jump toward passersby. Bowen's execution of Louis XVI was arranged to "chop off his head every night." Liberty cried "real tears" over the death of President Washington. A barber was even "affrighted by a touch from the Electrical tube," a "hair-raising" experience familiar to spectators who themselves may have been "electerized" on the machines that often accompanied these exhibitions.[40]

Perhaps the best corroboration of Frances Trollope's point of view is the several waxworks of Daniel Lambert (1770–1809), a 739-pound Englishman who emerged as the unofficial centerpiece of the American waxwork industry during its heyday in the first two decades of the nineteenth century. Lambert was the son of a gamekeeper and was depicted by modelers Daniel Bowen, William Doyle, Reuben Moulthrop, and James Bishop as holding four men at arm's length or as seated in an oversized, specially built and reinforced settee. A resident of Leicester, England, Lambert attracted as many visitors in person as his wax replicas did in museums. He gave up his occupation of raising fighting cocks and installed himself in a London apartment where he gained national and international recognition. From the time of his first inclusion in John Mix's New Haven wax collection in 1807 as one of the "wonders of the living world," New Haven and Boston wax modelers expanded his size as his weight increased from 700 pounds at age thirty-six, to 716 at the age of thirty-seven, to 739 pounds at his death in his thirty-ninth year. He then "measured three yards four inches

Figure 15.8. *Daniel Lambert Aged 39 Years, Who Died in Stamfort (England) on the 28th of June 1809. His Coffin Measured, 6 Feet, 4 In. Long. 4 Feet, 4 Inches, Wide, and 2 Feet 4 Inches High. At His Death He Weighed 739, Pounds. He Measured 3 Yards, 4 Inches Round the Body; and 1, Yard, 1, Inch, Round the Leg.* Anne-Marguerite-Henriette Rouillé de Marigny, Baroness Hyde de Neuville (d. 1849). John Mix's Museum, New Haven, Connecticut, 30 August 1813. Watercolor on paper, 8 by 13 inches. Courtesy, New-York Historical Society, 1953.287-B, neg. no. 23503.

Figure 15.9. *Sauvages en cire du museum de M Mix. 1813. 7bre* (Waxwork Indians at Mr. Mix's Museum, 7 September 1813). This sketch suggests the high level of authenticity in some early nineteenth-century waxworks. Anne-Marguerite-Henriette Rouillé de Marigny, Baroness Hyde de Neuville (d. 1849). New Haven, Connecticut, 1813. Pencil and watercolor on paper, 8 by 11 inches. Courtesy, New-York Historical Society, 1953.287-C, neg. no. 51427.

round the body, and one yard one inch round the leg." At his funeral in London in June 1809, Lambert's six-by-four-foot coffin was "rolled to his grave on a car, and the earth cut sloping away to admit it."[41]

On the other hand, wax modelers could also be sensitive artists, contradicting Trollope's point. When French émigré artist Anne-Marguerite-Henriette Rouillé de Marigny, Baroness Hyde de Neuville, visited John Mix's museum in New Haven in 1813, she made a drawing of Lambert's seated image (fig. 15.8) as well as a pair of waxen Puget Sound Native Americans hunting in their canoe (fig. 15.9).[42] Baroness Hyde de Neuville's compelling sketches provide two of the best depictions of American wax figures that have survived. Her sketch of Lambert shows the only graphic evidence of the labels that identified these figures. Almost as high as Lambert himself, the label dutifully specifies his age, the width of his girth, his weight, and the size of his coffin—information that was probably as important to the viewer as the waxwork itself. The detail in her illustration *Sauvages en cire* reveals the care taken by the sculptor to document two human specimens of North American natural history. Their costumes (with woven wicker and furred hats) and personal decorations (earrings, piercings, and tattooing) were likely modeled by the wax artist with the help of notes or diary sketches by an early explorer. Both images suggest that scholarly and artistic representations in this extraordinary medium were as much colored by documents of historical and anthropological relevance as they were by human oddities.

Chapter 16

Public Painters

THE COMPELLING authenticity of early waxwork figures may have influenced other forms of popular art such as large-scale transparencies, genre paintings, landscape views, and circular panoramas. Appearing in most cities of eastern America after 1790, this artwork traveled relatively easily in spite of its massive or cumbersome size. Generally painted on canvas or oiled paper by theatrical or landscape painters, they were rolled up in cylinders and shipped from town to town on sailing packets and in horse-drawn carts. Many were loaned on consignment, though some proprietors kept them in the hands of trusted assistants. They were distinguished by their imposing dimensions (averaging twenty-five to thirty feet in width), captivating subject matter, and dramatic manner of installation. Painted by a new breed of American or English artists whose techniques combined scale and subject matter to achieve spectacular if often impermanent artistic ends, these wall-size and building-size spectacles proliferated just as Hector St. John de Crèvecoeur's "new" American took the limelight. Large-scale paintings of religious subjects, naval engagements, land battles, patriotic allegories, views of natural wonders or disasters, sea monsters, and townscapes as well as memorial portraits—some of them previously known only as folio-size prints—for the first time drew the attention of sizable audiences.

The predecessors of this art form in colonial and early national America were "transparencies," non-opaque images painted on thin cloth or paper that had been soaked in turpentine and hot wax.[1] Most transparencies were affixed to some type of self-standing structure such as a column, huge lantern, obelisk, or pyramid; inside these containers, candles and lanterns provided backlighting for indoor and nighttime outdoor viewing. But some were simply affixed to windows that faced the street; candles and sconces inside the building provided illumination. Transparencies were seen in New England as early as the 1760s when lanterns were added to the wheeled "popes" paraded through the streets (and later burned) on the night of 5 November—the event celebrating

Figure 16.1. *A View of the Obelisk Erected under Liberty-Tree in Boston on the Rejoicings for the Repeal of the _____ Stamp-Act. 1766.* Paul Revere (1735–1818). Signed in lower right "Paul Revere Sculp." The image represents the four sides of a transparent obelisk erected on Boston Common celebrating the English supporters of the repeal. Boston, Massachusetts, 1766. Engraving, 9 by 13 inches. Courtesy, Boston Athenæum, A B64B6 Mo.o.1766.

the discovery of the incendiary plot by Guy Fawkes and his Catholic followers to blow up Parliament in 1605. According to a witness who had seen them as a child, lanterns used on these wagons were formed with hoop poles and covered with oiled paper painted with patriotic inscriptions, portraits, and caricatures. Other transparencies took on political overtones. A self-standing transparency in the form of an obelisk lighted inside by 280 candles was erected by the Sons of Liberty in Boston honoring English supporters of the repeal of the Stamp Act. According to diarist John Rowe, a town meeting was convened on 21 April 1766 "to agree on a method of Rejoicing & Illuminations." Later, on 19 May 1766, Rowe reported, "There was a very grand illumination all over Town. In the Common there was an Obelisk very beautifully Decorated & very Grand fire works were displayed."[2] Paul Revere made a schematic engraving of its four sides (fig. 16.1). The obelisk accidentally caught fire while being transported from the Boston Common to a new location.[3]

Transparencies depicting memorial themes were regularly commissioned by circuses, museums, and theaters. John Ricketts prepared several for his circus in Philadelphia in 1797, bringing a "transparency" of an engagement between American and Algerine vessels showing "Sailors buffeting the Waves—some drowned—others destroyed by Sharks."[4] On 15 February 1802, Daniel Bowen advertised a transparency at the Columbian Museum illustrating the "melancholy" death of Massachusetts Lieutenant Governor Samuel Phillips less than a week after the event. A distinguished jurist and member of the Constitutional Convention of 1779, Phillips had been a longtime patron of the arts and sciences in Boston and no doubt had helped promote Bowen's museum. The transparency may have been the work of Bowen's associate William Doyle, who was summoned to Phillips's home in Andover where he sketched and recorded the death scene. Doyle may also have been responsible for the transparency shown in January 1806 of "a representation of the burning of the Philadelphia Frigate, with a view of the city of Tripoli." Much more common were full-length transparent portraits such as the one Edward Savage installed at his Boylston Hall Museum in 1815 memorializing George Washington. Savage called it "much larger than life"—suggesting a twelve- or fifteen-foot height. In both instances, these transparencies were window installations. Bowen placed Phillips's memorial "in front of the museum"; Savage installed Washington's portrait in the "centre window in the front of the building."[5]

Although transparencies never reached the size of circular panoramas, John Ritto Penniman's *Moscow in Flames,* shown at the Boston Theatre in April 1814, may have had the dimensions of a small curtain drop, or about twelve by fifteen feet. Penniman was then working as a stage and scenery painter, and "painted [the picture] . . . for the late Russian festival" celebrated in Boston marking the defeat of Napoleon's Grand Army. Penniman executed at least one other large-format transparency of a conflagration, a fifteen-by-fifteen-foot view of the burning of Boston's Exchange Coffee House on 3 November 1818 (fig. 16.2). The painting was publicized under the dramatic heading "Fire! Fire!! Fire!!!" and was hung at Greenwood's Gallery of Fine Arts in 1819 with the undisguised intention of drawing viewers from among the many witnesses of the real thing. Nathaniel Ames, located in Dedham more than twelve miles away, noted in his diary, "We saw vast Flame last eve about 8 o'clock[.] Exch[ange] Coffee house burnt."[6] In terms of sheer size, however, the largest transparent painting exhibited in the region was a three-hundred-square-foot historical composition depicting Admiral Lord Exmouth's attack on the Algerine fleet, which appeared in Providence in 1818 and Boston in 1820. It was said to be "brilliantly illuminated," but neither the artist nor the manner of its lighting is known.[7]

More effective in attracting crowds were large-scale landscapes and historical and emblematical compositions painted on cloth. The dimensions of these paintings precluded installations in most galleries, and exhibitions required the joint efforts of the artist and an entrepreneur or institution willing to provide wall space in temporary "painting rooms" or ballrooms that could fit the work. One of the first Americans to attempt this genre was Ralph Earl (1751–1801), who in 1799 sought the assistance of decorative artist Jacob Wicker and cotton goods dealer Hezekiah Hutchens (of Northampton, Massachusetts) in painting a large-scale landscape of Niagara Falls. A well-publicized effort—notices of his plans ran in papers in Northampton, Charleston, Worcester, Albany, and New York, among other places—Earl described the painting as twenty-seven feet wide by fourteen feet high. *The Stupendous Falls of Niagara* first appeared in the Tontine Building in Northampton on 12 March 1800, the newspaper notice praising Earl as "the celebrated pupil of Reynolds, West, and Copley" and promising the artwork would "afford the spectator as just an idea of this stupendous cataract as can be represented on canvas." Six weeks later Wicker and Hutchens displayed the painting at the Statehouse in Philadelphia with a stand of several nights at the Old Theatre on South Street. In the meantime Earl renewed an old partnership with New Haven engraver Amos Doolittle (1754–1832), who announced on 25 June 1800 that Earl's newly renamed *Perspective View of the Falls of Niagara* would be shown that evening at his house on College Street. Admission was nine

Figure 16.2. "Tremendous Fire!! Representation of the Exchange Coffee-House in Flames." Broadside prepared shortly after the destruction of this well-known Boston hotel by fire on 3 November 1818. Woodcut, engraver unknown. Possibly by Abel Bowen (1790–1850), nephew of Daniel Bowen. Boston, 1818. Formerly in the collection of the Wilton Historical Society, Wilton, New Hampshire.

pence—the same price as recently charged to see a pair of camels in the town. The painting may have been hung in a barn or outbuilding, since Doolittle's home was not likely to have had the necessary ceiling height. Perhaps Doolittle planned to engrave and publish a print version of the scene as he had of four views of the Battles of Concord and Lexington taken by Earl twenty-five years earlier; if so, his plans apparently were not realized. The painting is said to have been exhibited in London, remaining there well into the nineteenth century.[8]

Boston stage mechanic and artist John Worrall—the same individual who composed and acted in Harlequin comedies—was another early painter of large-scale perspectives. In 1809, Worrall began work on a twelve-by-twenty-three-foot "Grand Panorama View of the Town of Providence . . . from a correct Drawing taken on the Spot" from Federal Hill. Several playbills from 1812 attributing both the drawing and the painting to Worrall indicate that the latter was used as a drop curtain lowered at the end of a play (fig. 16.3).[9] Other drop scenes by Worrall are known, and it is entirely possible that Worrall customarily prepared them for the theaters where his company gave performances.[10] In 1810, Worrall collaborated with John Rubens Smith (1755–1849) to execute a panorama of Boston and its vicinity "taken from the gallery on the tower of the Old South Meeting-House, in Marlborough-Street." The view was composed of two sections, one facing east and the other west, and it covered a "circuit of upward of 70 miles." Below, members of Boston's Ancient and Honorable Artillery Company paraded up the street.[11]

This large-scale genre is exemplified by the work of Michele F. Corné (1752–1845), who produced a series of views, naval panoramas, and history pieces that fired the imagination of patriotic museum patrons during a period of important American military and maritime engagements. Corné, who fled Napoleon's occupation of Italy in the year 1800, painted an estimated twenty to thirty panoramic perspectives of English and American naval actions.[12] Most if not all of these seem to have been in tempera on paper or cloth and commissioned in response to major victories. Perhaps the best known of his works are of two episodes in America's continuing war with pirates on North Africa's Barbary Coast: the bombardment of Tripoli harbor by Commodore Edward Preble and the nighttime burning at Tripoli of the captured frigate *Philadelphia* by Stephen Decatur. Two months after Corné's Tripoli panoramas opened in Boston in December 1806, William Bentley noted in his diary on 6 February 1807, "Mr. King has a panorama still in Salem. It is the siege of Tripoli. The Ships are done by Corné." William King had either leased or purchased the paintings and was selling admission tickets to them while cutting profiles.[13] On 3 March 1807 the Tripoli panoramas were exhibited in Jefferson Hall, Portsmouth (where King had opened a studio), and by 9 May of that year the panoramas were on display at Mr. Snow's Golden Ball Inn in Providence. King was presumably still

Figure 16.3. *The Old Drop Scene (View of Providence, Rhode Island, Taken from Federal Hill).* John Worrall (c. 1783–1825) was well known as a stage painter and Harlequin actor in New England. The single spire of the First Baptist Meetinghouse is visible on the left; at right center is the twin-towered meetinghouse of the town's First Congregational Church. Oil on canvas, 135 by 288 inches. Providence, circa 1809–1812. Courtesy, Rhode Island Historical Society, 1832.1.1. RHi X3 2570.

with them. A year later museum proprietor Philip Woods was showing Corné's Tripoli paintings in Portland, Maine, in conjunction with his traveling exhibition of thirteen wax figures, "electerizing" treatments, and "philosophical" exhibitions.[14] And a year after that, Corné's paintings were displayed in Charleston at the "house formerly called the Planter's Hotel" under the title "Panorama and Cosmorama."[15] The proprietor, a Mr. John, may have leased them from Woods, who apparently had them again when he visited Nantucket Island and New Bedford, Massachusetts, in 1816. By this time they had lost approximately six feet from wear and tear (or from being mounted in smaller halls) and were being described as fifty-four feet in length.[16] In 1818, at least one Corné panorama accompanied "Robert" Moulthrop's wax exhibit to Alexandria, Virginia, and to nearby Georgetown.[17] The practice of franchising and reuse may explain why, despite their numbers and size, no trace of Corné's panorama paintings has been found. Their likely fate (if not entirely destroyed in the numerous museum fires of the period) was attrition from years of travel. Several smaller copies by Corné have been preserved, however (fig. 16.4).[18]

The celebrity of these painters attracted the attention of other artists. A succession of landscape, historical, narrative, and natural history paintings by English and European artists began appearing in eastern seaboard cities. The most common were scenes of Napoleonic battles: Trafalgar, Leipzig, Waterloo, Paris, Lodi, Alexandria, and Arcola. These were circulated widely from Portland and Boston to Baltimore and Charleston. Views of foreign cities such as Paris, Quebec, Rome, Versailles, Montreal, and Constantinople were interspersed with those of New Haven, Portland, Providence, Charleston, Boston, and New York.[19] American artists soon joined their foreign counterparts. They included James Kidder, the Boston and Philadelphia aquatint and panorama painter who in 1816 collaborated with Daniel Bowen to found the Phenix Museum in Boston.[20] Shortly after the gale of 23 September 1815 destroyed one-quarter of the taxable

Figure 16.4. *The Siege of Tripoli*, by Michele Felice Corné (1752–1845). While smaller copies of Corné's panoramas have survived, no trace of the original painting has been found. Salem or Boston, Massachusetts, circa 1805–1810. Oil on canvas, 33 by 48 inches. Courtesy, Rhode Island Historical Society, 1954.8.1. RHi X3 3035.

Figure 16.5. *A Representation of the Great Storm at Providence, Sept. 23, 1815,* by James Kidder (1776–1852). The gale destroyed one-quarter of the taxable valuation of the town. Kidder used his wall-size panoramas to sell subscriptions to print versions like this one. Providence, 1816. Lithograph. Courtesy, Rhode Island Historical Society. RHi X3 116.

valuation of Providence, Kidder visited Rhode Island and depicted the ravaged city at the height of the storm, no doubt incorporating eyewitness accounts into his composition. Kidder's wall-size view was shown in his and Bowen's new museum in July 1816 for "one month only." After they moved it to Aldrich's Hall in Providence in November 1816, they added panoramas of New York Harbor and Market Street in Philadelphia, both probably based on prints. Kidder used the large-scale exhibition of *The Great Storm* as an occasion to sell subscriptions to print versions of the same scene (fig. 16.5). Another Kidder subject was "an English squadron, with Bonaparte . . . on board the Northumberland, a 74 gun ship," which transported Napoleon to confinement on the island of Saint Helena; this was installed in Boston and Providence in 1816.[21] Daniel Bowen's collaboration with Kidder lasted through 1818 when Bowen arranged a presentation of Kidder's forty-by-nine-foot panorama of New Haven at Aldrich's Hall.[22]

Scenes of wild animal hunts, serpents, snakes, and other "monsters" were particular favorites. *The View of the Tyger Hunt* "in and on the Banks of the Ganges, Bengal, . . . Assisted by Elephants," was one of three anonymous large-scale paintings at the Exchange Coffee House in Boston in 1815. With an area of four hundred square feet, it was hailed as superior in "delineation, coloring, judgment, and novelty."[23] Another was James Ward's "Splendid Painting" of the *Anaconda, Attacking a Horse and Its Rider,* which was shown in New York in April 1817 and was later taken to Philadelphia.[24] The same year, about seven weeks after a 130-foot sea monster or "Kraken" was allegedly spotted sporting off Gloucester, Massachusetts, on 14 August a canvas "about 35 feet by 20" was hung in the ballroom of Washington Hall on Broadway in New York City.[25] It was commissioned by Dr. Nathan Parsons, who had "placed himself at the side of a Painter of acknowledged eminence" to direct his efforts. Parsons, a "celebrated naturalist," had the opportunity at "six different time[s], to approach so near the animal as to see his eyes, teeth, tongue, and the colour of his head and neck distinctly."[26] The next month a copy appeared in John Mix's museum in New Haven, followed by a twenty-four-by-eleven-foot panorama "in oil colours" of the *Monstrous Sea Serpent, Which Lately Appeared in Gloucester Harbour,* which was installed in a second-story room in Merchants' Hall in Boston in 1817 and later in Salem and Brighton.[27] Daniel Bowen displayed a sea serpent in his new museum in Philadelphia, possibly by James Kidder.[28] Other versions came to Charles Willson Peale's Museum (by "R. Pennyman," of Boston) and the Baltimore Museum.[29] One twenty-by-five-foot painting of the sea serpent supplemented the waxwork museum of Hickox and Page in its southern tour of the District of Columbia, Alexandria, and Norfolk.[30] An image of the serpent's "Spawn" and a "satisfactory certificate . . . testifying to the truth and correctness of the representation," together with a report by the Linnaean Society of New England, authenticated these exhibitions.[31] At least two museums mounted the "spawn" itself, a so-called "Young Sea Serpent" taken near Loblolly Cove, Gloucester, where the great sea serpent had frequented.[32] Regrettably we have no firsthand evidence of what any of these monsters looked like. One image published in 1819 Boston newspapers, however, has an uncanny resemblance to an illustration in Erich Pontopiddan's 1747 *Natural History of Norway,* whose snakelike protuberances jut out of the water at even intervals (figs. 16.6 and 16.7). The Pontopiddan image may have been a model for others.

Not everyone was taken in by these reputed monsters or the large-scale art that aggrandized them. Among the skeptics was Dr. Nathaniel Ames, who wrote on 26 August 1817 "that G[reat]. Snake is kill'd at C[ape] Ann. But in the evening contradicted! News mongers say he is very fond of fish." A year later, after a "Sea Serpent 120 feet long was taken at Squam, near C Ann, M[assachusetts]. And is bro't into Boston Harbor for exhibition," Ames noted, "Many people went to see [the] Great Snake, but disappointed! hoax."[33] But the story persisted. Forty-one years after the sightings, Henry D. Thoreau met a man in Lynn, Massachusetts, who remembered the event and provided all the details. Thoreau was skeptical but he jotted them down in his journal.[34]

At least some panoramas were circular and mounted in rotundas. Edward Savage introduced this format in America. In November 1794, Savage publicized in Boston a 2,400-square-foot circular painting of the London boroughs of Westminster, Southwark, and Surrey by the Edinburgh artists Robert Barker

(1739–1806) and his son Henry Aston Barker (1774–1856), who took their perspective from the roof of the Albion Mills. Painted in distemper on canvas, it measured two hundred feet in circumference—requiring Savage to display it in a specially constructed building in Orange Tree Lane. The short length of time it took for the panorama to reach Boston reflects its strong appeal. Completed in 1792 as a semicircular view, the Barkers' painting was first shown in London's Leicester Square. A larger, full-circle version opened in London at the end of 1793, but within a year it had been taken down, transported to America, and reassembled in Boston. Promoted by Savage's energetic advertising ("this painting will never return here again . . ."), its initial four-week stay was extended six months to July 1795. In New York City, the Barkers' panorama was exhibited by Gardiner Baker at a building on Greenwich Street where it remained from August 1795 through December 1797. At least two copies were made by Savage and transported to Pennsylvania and the southern states. Their tour began in Philadelphia in 1797 and ended with Baltimore and Charleston in 1798.[35] Other promoters like John Scudder, John Vanderlyn, and the partnership of Daniel

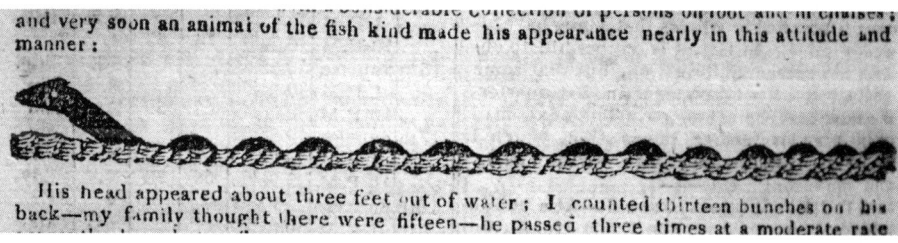

Figures 16.6 and 16.7. Snake-like sea monsters as portrayed in Norway and New England. Above: From Erich Pontoppidan's 1747 *History of Norway* (image reproduced in the *Boston Weekly Messenger*, 2 September 1819). Below: A view taken by James Prince of Nahant, Massachusetts, 16 August 1819 (reproduced in the *Boston Weekly Messenger*, 26 August 1819). Large-scale panoramas of the sea monster were exhibited between 1817 and 1819 in museums and galleries from Boston to Norfolk. Courtesy, Houghton Library, Harvard University.

Bowen and James Kidder followed; many of these ventures were short-lived, and the artwork was eventually auctioned off.

Enchanted by the paintings' size and reputed authenticity, the same audiences that went to see waxwork museums flocked to see the panoramas. Mary Vial Holyoke wrote on 28 April 1795 that she "went to Boston with Burril. Mr. Turner waited on me & Mrs. Minot to the [Barkers'] Panorama."[36] Nineteen years later, in 1814, Margaret Holyoke joined her brother-in-law for a stage ride to Boston "to see the Panorama of Quebec."[37] In the meantime, educated viewers found some elements to criticize but in the end were forgiving. William Bentley noted that the Barkers' circular panorama exhibited in Boston in 1795 was a "catch penny" show but "not without its merit. . . . It encourages better attempts."[38] And when William King took Corné's *Siege of Tripoli* to Salem in 1807, Bentley recorded that "the profits from such exhibitions in Salem are said to be much less than in Marblehead. Few visit in the day time."[39] By 1809 Bentley's artistic critique was less forgiving. He went with Hannah Crowninshield, a Miss H. Hodges, and Mary Williams to see Corné's *Bay of Naples*. This time he discovered it was "only a copy of the Common plates . . . without one stroke of originality. . . . These things seem to speak [to] the infancy of the Arts."[40]

Bentley's comment about originality reminds us that the world of popular culture was primarily an entrepreneurial business rather than a means of disseminating history. Most new ventures after 1790 dealt with visual art, perhaps the easiest form of culture to catch and retain in the public imagination. Lantern shows, optical machines, "artificial" puppet comedians, and waxwork exhibitions brought costumes, architecture, folklore, and historical figures into the public realm. Public painting, in turn, brought to audiences a direct vision of natural history, famous landscapes, and battle scenes buttressed by the "eyewitness accounts" of the sailors and military men who had witnessed or participated in them, by the clothing they wore, and by their celebrity. This led to the usual cycle of itinerants imitating one another, a process that was seemingly unbreakable. One thirty-five-foot canvas of a reputed sea monster rapidly generated five or six others just like it, as well as the monster's "carcass" and "spawn." The Barkers' 1794 panorama produced six imitations, each with its own separate building, eyewitnesses, and printed catalogues. Experienced itinerants—meaning the old "active bearers" and promoters—took full advantage of the physical size and glamor of these spectacles to advance their own careers as proprietors and showmen. William King, Philip Woods, and Edward Savage became "medical electricians" and electrical performers even as they herded audiences in the door to see large-scale paintings and panoramas; Daniel Bowen, John Mix, and John Scudder flourished as cultural magnets in Boston, New Haven, and New York City attracting instant audiences to view worldwide events.

But rampant copying led to a fundamental loss in marketability. Like old waxworks, the value of public paintings became transitory once their celebrity had crested. They were discarded as soon as other attractions took their place. Interest in transparencies—as theater backdrops, memorial pictures, and window adornments—diminished in the years from 1810 to 1820. In the one known instance where a transparency survived more than a decade of use, it was regarded with derision. When an old transparency of George Washington attributed to scenery painter John Worrall, possibly the full-figure version shown in the Boston Theatre in 1820 and 1822, was taken out of storage in 1829 and exhibited in Boston to celebrate the late first president's birthday, an unsympathetic commentator in the *Dramatic Mirror* noted that "the figure of Washington . . . [had] a nose as long as a common man's leg."[41]

Panoramas suffered the same fate. In July 1800, when the firm of Griffen and Glass was auctioning off a panorama at the Tontine Coffeehouse, they stated that "3 large rools [rolls] of paintings of the cities of London, Westminster, and the borough of Southwark, painted by [William] Winstanly, and formerly exhibited at the panorama . . . are in good order, and may be readily prepared for public view." But then they informed prospective buyers: "They will answer very well for floor cloths."[42] And almost two decades later, just after a New York City paper acknowledged that Daniel T. Steel, "proprietor of the Panorama of the Battle of Waterloo," had given "the sum of 81 dollars and 35 cents" to the New-York Institution for the Instruction of the Deaf and Dumb, the same individual was publicly declared "insolvent" by the debtor's office in Philadelphia. Clearly, speculating in out-of-date panoramas had severe financial risks.[43]

Chapter 17

Taking Faces I: The Itinerant Portraitist

WAX MODELERS MAY also have left their mark on early American portrait making. We can understand this probable connection by looking at the responses of Boston museum proprietors to a rare naval triumph in the early part of America's second war with England. On the morning of 15 September 1813, a close military engagement took place on Lake Erie between U.S. and British naval squadrons that ended in a major American victory and produced a new American hero. Twenty-eight-year-old Oliver Hazard Perry (1785–1819), the American commander, signaled the British capitulation by declaring, "We have met the enemy, and they are ours." American sovereignty over the lake was preserved at a critical juncture in the conflict. Five months later almost to the day, on 21 February 1814, an engagement of a different kind was unfolding in Boston. This time it was between two institutional rivals, each vying to attract the large crowds anticipated for Perry's upcoming visit. First, the co-proprietors of the Columbian Museum, Daniel Bowen and William M. S. Doyle, publicized a 1,500-square-foot "Grand" panorama of the battle painted by Michele Felice Corné after topographical drawings by F. Kearney based on Perry's official account and those of the participating American officers. Displayed with it was a life-size wax figure of Commodore Perry "in full Uniform," representing, as Doyle and Bowen were careful to point out, "a perfect Likeness, in form and feature, being made from a Mask taken off of his Face."[1] Not to be outdone, Philip Woods, proprietor of the Boston Museum, located on the north side of the Old Market, advertised a panorama of the battle painted from "a sketch drawn by Com. Perry" along with an "excellent and correct Likeness in Wax of Commodore O. H. Perry . . . elegantly dressed in a full Naval Dress, and the Likeness was taken from life, and is correct."[2] While the painter of the battle panorama is not known, the wax figure was probably done by Henry Williams (1787–1830), who for years kept a studio directly under Woods's museum.³

When Perry visited Boston later that year, he was no doubt moved by an ode read on the occasion by John Pierpont, a young Boston poet on the cusp of a long career as a clergyman of the Hollis Street Church.⁴ He also may have been flattered by the multiple images of his person. Bowen and Doyle hailed him as "the conquering Hero of the Lake"; Woods in turn termed him "The American Naval Hero."⁵ What none of them may have considered, however, is how closely pictorial and historical accuracy had come together in the rapidly evolving values of American portraiture in the early nineteenth century. The parallel language of the two announcements—both as to the details of Perry's appearance (fig. 17.1)

Figure 17.1. *Oliver Hazard Perry* (1785–1819), by Isaac Sanford (d. 1842), after a contemporary New England portrait. The naval career of the twenty-eight-year-old hero inspired battle panoramas, portraits, and waxwork figures reflecting documented historical accuracy and cast wax impressions. From John M. Niles, *The Life of Oliver Hazard Perry* (Hartford: O. D. Cooke, 1821). Courtesy, Houghton Library, Harvard University, US 4936.5.2.

Figure 17.2. *Battle of Erie, 1st View.* The engagement involving the *Lawrence, Detroit,* and *Niagara* took place on 15 September 1813. Reengraving after a contemporary seascape by Isaac Sanford (d. 1842). Based on details provided by the commanding officers, panoramas of Perry's victory were wildly popular. From John M. Niles, *The Life of Oliver Hazard Perry* (Hartford: O. D. Cooke, 1821). Courtesy, Houghton Library, Harvard University, US 4936.5.2.

as well as those of battle accounts (fig. 17.2)—articulates the perceptual and aesthetic dimensions of portrait making in a period of American history when painters, in particular itinerant painters, for the first time were coming into contact with middle-class and rural clients in large numbers. Although portraiture as an act of personal recognition had been prevalent in provincial American aesthetics since the mid-seventeenth century, the shift became literal in the advertisements taken by the more than two hundred itinerant portrait makers advertising in America in the eighteenth and early nineteenth centuries. In one form or another "likenesses" were universally promoted to clients and sitters with a lavish refrain of claims, testimonials, and warranties. The wax "Mask taken off his own face" by William Doyle and the wax portrait "taken from life" possibly by Henry Williams—two examples of what may have been dozens of such images created by these prominent Boston artists—embodied widely shared public expectations that were beginning to extend themselves throughout America.

Their own special circumstances aside, that two leading American painters made simultaneous claims to "documented" accuracy marks something of a turning point. The professional choices made by Williams and Doyle were characteristic of a growing cadre of artists who hoped to advance their appeal through "correct[ness]" and verifiability. In previous decades, because so few sitters could afford their services, most painters were obliged to rely on the usual expediencies to make ends meet: accepting country pay, painting deceased subjects, gratuitously "guaranteeing" likenesses and repainting unacceptable portraits, scheduling short sittings, supplying cheap alternatives, and constantly soliciting commissions from friends, relatives, and landlords. "To paint a likeness of a dead person, whom I never saw while living is such a job I wish to never undertake," wrote Ethan Allen Greenwood in 1808; "it is disagreeable and uncertain."[6] With her usual frankness Frances Trollope captured these circumstances near the end of her stay in the United States from 1827 to 1829. She expressed the opinion that painters in America were much better off than might be expected from the little patronage they received. "The wonder is," she stated, that any individual can be found "with courage enough to devote himself to a profession in which . . . [he has] so little chance of finding a maintenance."[7]

Despite a persistent scarcity of work, itinerant portraitists nevertheless experienced some advantages over other entrepreneurs and considered themselves an elite minority. For one thing, they could travel lightly. In his early years, Greenwood carried his "paint Box &c" on horseback when he rode through central Massachusetts and New Hampshire; at other times he took with him a profile tracing machine, apparently with relative ease, and in some instances he brought along prepared canvases or prepainted wooden panels. Once having finished a commission, he returned to his home in Hubbardston, Massachusetts. But not all artists chose this approach. Susanna Paine, the nineteenth-century portrait painter who worked in cities in Maine, Massachusetts, Rhode Island, and central Connecticut, did not have a permanent home. She traveled with all her "trunks and baggage," that is, all of her possessions. To her, moving to a new location meant relocating her entire life.[8]

Other painters managed to travel with their families. The husband and wife team of Dr. Samuel A. and Ruth W. Shute, both artists, toured widely in New England, often bringing their talents to the same picture. Ralph Earl, who journeyed extensively in Connecticut in the 1790s, was accompanied by his wife and two children on at least one occasion.[9] The five members of the Sharples family, consisting of James; his third wife, Ellen Wallace; their children, James, Jr., and Rolinda; and another child, Felix, from James's second marriage—all of them artists—traversed the eastern seaboard in a horse-drawn covered vehicle. Adept at cultivating ties with socially prominent New Yorkers and other city residents, the Sharpleses drew pastel portraits of "eminent characters," such as Leonard and Johanna Bleecker of New York City (figs. 17.3 and 17.4). Ellen Sharples mentioned one such liaison in her diary for January and February 1810: "Mr. Bleecker dined with us and one or two other gentlemen when sitting for their portraits to Mr. S."[10]

Portrait painters sometimes worked in the homes of their clients—a practice also common among tavern showmen, language teachers, and dancing-masters.[11] This provided privacy for their clients, and each night the artist or teacher returned to his or her own temporary lodgings. Some portrait painters,

Figures 17.3 and 17.4. *Leonard Bleecker* (c. 1755–1844) and *Johanna Abeel Bleecker* (1764–1810), by James Sharples (c. 1751–1811). Sharples and four other members of his family traveled the length of the eastern seaboard drawing pastel portraits of "eminent characters." Pastel on paper, each 9¼ by 7⅜ inches. New York City, circa 1796–1801. Courtesy, New-York Historical Society, object nos. 1940.350 and 1940.351, neg. nos. 8517 and 8510A. Bequest of Mrs. Elizabeth B. Knight, great-granddaughter of the sitters.

however, resided with their sitters until their work was completed. This could go on for days, weeks, or longer—such as the six weeks in 1803 when William Jennys and his dog lived at the home of Jesse and Elizabeth Johnson of Enfield, New Hampshire. According to the account put together by their son George Washington Johnson,

> Father's and Mother's [portraits] were painted about June 1 of this year. Amanda's recollection: Painter Mr. Jennis. He would paint daily from 11 A.M. to 1 P.M. and then chat—he was chatty—and play with his dog. He offered to paint mother with me her in arms for $10 extra but did not. Mother being burdened with a crying child and especially with domestic cares, the new house being built. . . . Jennis painted Mr. Merrill and wife and Uncle John Harris and wife. He was six weeks painting father and mother and boarded in the family. Mother had father's painted first when the painter was fresh.[12]

How often painters actually lodged with their sitters is unclear, but it may have been frequent because references to the custom are often cited in period diaries. Ethan Allen Greenwood, Ammi Phillips, Dr. Samuel Adams, and Isaac

Merrill recorded numerous instances when artists lived and completed their work in the homes of their sitters. On a trip in 1809 to Rockingham and Windsor, Vermont, Greenwood stayed with families who made his life "extremely pleasant." Ammi Phillips "began to board" at a western Massachusetts client's house in October and painted the entire family in 1812.[13] A diary entry written by Dr. Samuel Adams in Bath, Maine, in 1816 documents that Benjamin Greenleaf had settled his board "up to this day—Balance of all accounts." Diarist Isaac W. Merrill of Haverhill, Massachusetts, noted in 1831 that when Samuel Jordan was painting the portraits of his neighbor and his neighbor's wife, he "board[ed] there."[14]

On occasion clients went out of their way to accommodate painters. This is readily seen in the case of John Brewster, Jr. (1766–1854), the deaf artist active in eastern Massachusetts, New Hampshire, and Connecticut. After learning to paint from his Hampton, Connecticut, neighbor Joseph Steward, Brewster made repeated visits to Portland, Saco, Standish, and Kennebunkport, Maine; to Newburyport, Salem, and Boston; and to towns in eastern and coastal Connecticut.[15] He also reached as far afield as Hallowell, Maine; Poughkeepsie, New York; and New Orleans, Louisiana.[16] He learned "to . . . write well & converse by signs" but did not acquire the ability to sign fluently until he went to a school for the deaf at the age of fifty. Brewster lived at the home of his younger brother, Royal Brewster, and instituted a lifelong practice of arranging temporary stays with patrons—some of them philanthropic-minded physicians, merchants, and artisans—painting their portraits, and displaying "specimens" of his work in their homes. Brewster's client James Prince, at whose house he stayed in 1801, served Newburyport as collector of customs. Another sitter was Dr. William Stearns with whom Brewster lived in 1809. A Salem pharmacist and state legislator, Stearns was one of the town's overseers of the poor and was known for his "benevolent feelings." In Boston, Brewster boarded with silversmith Rufus Farnam. Nor did Brewster hesitate to bring his disabilities before the public. In his Boston announcement of 29 December 1802, he asked readers of the *Columbian Centinel* to "favor him in his unfortunate situation" and went on to say he had been "deaf and dumb" at birth. When he returned to Boston two years later, he termed himself "John Brewster. Deaf and dumb miniature and portrait painter." Sometimes he accepted goods instead of money. In Danbury, Connecticut, Brewster received a coat, a pair of stockings, paint brushes, and living supplies from Comfort S. Mygatt for painting his portrait.[17]

In the end it was not artists' circumstances that determined their "American" painting style; it was chiefly their response to popular expectations. We can measure this in the language that artists used in their promotions to convince potential sitters to patronize them. Granted, much of this data comes from unsuccessful or chronically underemployed artists. Prosperous artists, especially those who maintained urban studios located near museums like Henry Williams and William Doyle, advertised much less. Additionally, publicity was often directed at first-time clients whose inexperience may have helped define portrait making as much as the training and gifts of the artists themselves. When Williams assured readers of the *New-England Palladium* in 1806 that his profiles were "to be painted in real flesh colors upon glass," and when Gilbert Haven guaranteed the readers of the *Portsmouth Oracle* in 1809 that his were drawn "with perfect shadows," they were communicating not only to an artistically naive public but to one that saw portraits as a complete novelty.[18]

Advertisements also supply considerable information about artists who needed work badly enough to risk investing their own money in handbills and newspaper announcements. Most of these were the "starving" but entrepreneurial-minded artists about whom historian William Dunlap painstakingly collected information and compiled biographies and whom Frances Trollope doubted could ever find employment in America.[19] Data from approximately 450 advertisements run by itinerant portrait painters, miniature artists, and profile takers in eastern portions of North America between 1765 and 1825 provide an inventory of their reasons for preferment.[20] Listed here in the order of frequency, one hundred thirty-nine portraitists or profile takers promised an accurate likeness—some refusing to accept pay if the client was unsatisfied and others willing to try again. One hundred thirty-seven pointed out that "specimens" of their work were available at their rooms or at other publicly accessible places. One hundred three asserted their European origins or their acceptance in fashionable places. Ninety-two advised readers they would leave town quickly if they failed to attract clients. Sixty offered to give drawing and painting lessons. Forty-two specified some advanced form of optical or machine-assisted drawing technique. Thirty-one were willing to work at clients' houses. Thirty-one promoted greatly reduced prices. Twenty-one guaranteed a speedy sitting or completion, ranging from one-quarter of a minute to three-quarters of an hour. And fifteen promised an elegant or handsome style of painting or drawing.

Other reasons pinpointed incidental benefits. Eight stressed the value of their portraits to families in the event of the "absence or demise of the original." Six painted likenesses from the dead. Five gave credit or accepted "country pay." Two painters drew attention to their physical disabilities or special needs (deafness, impoverishment). And two more informed sitters they could have fashionable hairstyles, one saying that "ladies [could] dress their hair as they wish."[21] One claimed that portraits were the only known household decoration "which keeps pace with the tide of fleeting time."[22] And finally one artist shrewdly declared that portraits were "exempt from taxation"—apparently meaning that portraits were not subject to sale by an estate having to pay its debts by auction. (Some eighteenth-century Boston inventory-takers did not assign values to family portraits because they were deemed to be automatically the personal property of the heirs.)[23]

The language is unmistakable. Beginning with George Mason, who sold "good Likenesses" for two guineas in Boston in 1765, and continuing through announcements by a Signor Rossetti for "striking likenesses" in New York in 1793 and those by Samuel Waldo for "strong Likenesses of their originals" in Charleston in 1804, the schedule of priorities reveals the contours of early American expectations.[24] Measured by the number of times a particular benefit was specified by artists when communicating to their prospective clients, about half the value of any portrait, miniature, or profile was the accuracy of its resemblance or "likeness." The issue of recognition so completely dominated artists' pledges that more than half employed superlatives that went well beyond promising "correct" portraits. Likenesses were to be judged "striking," "perfect," "expressive," "finished to the utmost exactness," or "answer exactly to the original."[25] Some artists—like Raphaelle Peale—touted "Astonishing Likenesses"; others described a "speaking likeness," an apparent allusion to a French opera of this title performed in Newport in 1793.[26] One artist went so far as to encourage "the friends of the person to judge of the likeness, which if not approved, to be returned as soon as possible."[27] Another, T. S. Banton, extended this guarantee to any observer, claiming his profiles "shall be perfect if the sobriety of the person admits, or no pay for them."[28] William J. Weaver told potential clients in Salem that he would expect payment only if his work excelled "in point of resemblance" those of any other portraits executed in the town.[29] Miniature and pastel artist John Roberts summed it up when he assured readers of the *Newburyport Herald* in 1800 that "conscious that a picture is of no value that is not a true resemblance, . . . should they not meet with entire approbation, not the smallest gratuity will be expected."[30]

The idea of creating portraits that were considered "like" their sitters was well known to English-speaking people. In the 1660s, London diarist Samuel Pepys wondered whether the portrait taken of him by London painter John Hale would "be like me." And in 1666, he was delighted that his wife's portrait was "very like" her.[31] Eight decades later, in 1745, New England merchant Thomas Hancock (1703–1764), who had just moved into his newly completed red-stone mansion on Beacon Street, enthusiastically informed his London correspondent Bostonian Christopher Kilby (1705–1771) he had framed and hung Kilby's completed portrait next to others in his home. "Dear Kilby," he wrote,

> My wife & I are drinking your health this morning, 8 o'the Clock, in a Desh of Coffee and under the Shade of your Picture which I rec'd not long since of Mr. Smibert, in which am much Delighted, & have suited it with Frame of the fashion of my other Pictures & fixed it at the Right hand of all, in the keeping-room. Everybody that Sees it thinks it to be Exceedingly like you, as

it really is. I am of Opinion it's as good a Piece as Mr. Smibert has done, and full as Like you as my Father's is Like him, which all mankind allows to be a Compleat Picture."[32]

John Smibert (1688–1751), who came from London to Boston in 1729 after spending three years in Italy and six years painting in the British metropolis, was near the end of his career when he finished Kilby's portrait.[33] He had painted Thomas Hancock's father, Reverend John Hancock, in 1734, and the son's estimation of what constituted a "Compleat Picture" hinged on its being "like" his father. It was the same assessment alluded to by John Singleton Copley in 1767 when he observed that were "it not for preserving resemblance of particular persons, painting would not be known in this place."[34] And it was the same measure that irritated Frances Trollope. "From all the conversations on painting, which I listened to in America," she wrote, "I found that the finish of drapery was considered as the highest excellence, and next to this, the resemblance in a portrait; I do not remember ever to have heard the words *drawing* or *composition* used in any conversation on the subject."[35]

Behind this desire for replication was a limner tradition that went back five hundred years or more and that still formed the core of much of North American portraiture in this period. It, too, was an attempt to achieve resemblance. But its "bizarre neomedievalism" had been driven out of metropolitan England and relegated to the English provinces, including Scotland, North America, and Australia, during the eighteenth and early nineteenth centuries.[36] In America the style was seen as spare, intense, and "liney," and it continued to characterize portraiture despite the best efforts of academic painters to extirpate it.[37] In retrospect a direct line might be drawn between Boston portrait making in the 1670s by the so-called Freake limner to Joseph Badger of Boston, John Durand of New York City (fig. 17.5), Richard and William Jennys in eastern New England, Samuel Broadbent of Hartford, and Ammi Phillips in western Connecticut, to Ruth Whittier Shute, Asahel Powers, and Thomas Ware in northern New York, New Hampshire, and Vermont. All of these painters, excepting Badger, were itinerant.

While some American artists pursued the style with naive abandon, others followed it with discipline and vision. But usually it reflected most sitters' low expectations of a craft whose sophistications they failed to understand. Untrained in the arts, many American sitters presumably preferred a "neomedievalist" style because it made sense to them. When Isaac Merrill first met painter Samuel Jordan (1803–after 1835), he was reluctant to have his portrait taken although he was encouraged to do so by several neighbors. After a few visits to Jordan's painting room—including one when he "had the first impression of a portrait" (meaning he was able to compare the portrait with the sitter)—he finally decided to go ahead. "Sat again today for Mr Jordan, to paint," he wrote on 11 April 1831. When he actually saw the finished work, however, he was again unsure. "Saw Jordan's portrait[s]—dont think they look very natural, or at least most of them."[38] Merrill's experience with Jordan (fig. 17.6) did not prevent him from socializing and playing ball with the painter, nor did it diminish his interest in portraiture. The next year, shortly after he married Lois M. Chase, Merrill met the artist Robert Peckham of Winchester, Massachusetts, who was visiting his clergyman brother in Haverhill. Peckham painted the newly married couple for a fee of twenty dollars. Although Merrill did not record his reaction this time, other people did. Diarist Christopher C. Baldwin of Worcester observed that the portraits by Robert Peckham were "laughable caricatures" and went so far

Figure 17.5. *The Rapalje Children,* by John Durand (1731–1805). Durand's manner of painting faces is an example of the provincial "neomedieval" style of painting. Oil on canvas, 51 by 40 inches. New York City, 1768. Courtesy, New-York Historical Society. Gift of Mrs. Eliza J. Watson in memory of her husband, John Jay Watson. Object number 1946.201, no. 27991.

as to suggest that they were so unlike the sitters that only the name written on them identified the subjects. Baldwin explained that most of Peckham's business was in the countryside.[39]

Some painters were straightforward about recognizing client expectations. In a letter written in 1825 to a young nephew who was considering becoming a painter, John Vanderlyn assured him that "were I to begin life again, I should not hesitate to follow this plan, that is, to paint portraits cheap and slight, for the mass of folks can't judge of the merits of a well finished picture." Vanderlyn's remarks echo Frances Trollope's dismay when an American traveling companion compared England's "immortal" Thomas Lawrence to the "most vile dauber," portrait painter Chester Harding. "The very idea," she wrote, "stuck in my throat."[40] The ideal of "likeness" was also sought by a twenty-two-year-old painter named Abraham G. D. Tuthill (1776–1843), who did two portraits of

Figure 17.6. *Young Man Seated, Possibly Isaac Watts Merrill* (1803–1879), by Samuel Jordan (1803–after 1835). Jordan was arrested on three occasions: for counterfeiting, horse stealing, and burglary. His circumstances after he escaped from jail following his third arrest are unknown. Signed and dated 1831. Oil on canvas, 24 by 19⅞ inches. Courtesy, The Colonial Williamsburg Foundation, Abby Aldrich Rockefeller Folk Art Museum, Museum Purchase, acc. no. 1958.100.38.

his neighbor Reverend Samuel Buell of East Hampton, Long Island, in 1798. Tuthill was apparently dissatisfied with the results and consulted Gilbert Stuart. Following his advice, Tuthill went to Europe to learn how to paint academically. He spent three months in France and eight years in London. His subsequent career as a portrait painter active in northern Vermont, upstate New York, and Ohio and Michigan was marked by bringing to clients in the recently settled areas of the young republic his attempts at the academically exact refinements of English parlor portraiture.[41]

When William Doyle and Henry Williams made their images of Oliver Perry in 1814, they tried to accomplish through technology what Abraham Tuthill had sought by crossing the Atlantic: to provide a "likeness" that the public would readily believe. But unlike more celebrated painters such as Gilbert Stuart and John Wesley Jarvis, who noticeably aggrandized their portraits of Perry, Doyle's and Williams's solution was simple.[42] They had taken a cast "from life" and painted a duplicate. The viewing public had to believe it was accurate because both artists made the process explicit in their advertising. This was not the first time that Doyle had publicly acknowledged using a casting procedure. Six years earlier, in 1808, the Columbian Museum advertised an "exact Likeness" in wax of the late Reverend Dr. Samuel Stillman, minister of the First Baptist Church in Boston: "The Likeness was procured immediately after his decease, by a mask taken from his face, and is finished to the life, by Doyle."[43] (Doyle later sold reduced-size profiles of the clergyman.) That same year he issued a broadside introducing himself to potential sitters: "Doyle takes Likenesses of the Dead, in his own peculiar way, by means of a mask taken immediately from the corps of the deceased, without disfiguring or altering the corps in the least, and preserve the likeness entire, and then paints or makes a profile, as may be wanted, from the same.—Also, any Lady or Gentleman, being at a distance, by taking a shadow of their friend on paper, dead or alive, may have them reduced to any size wanted."[44]

For his part Henry Williams, who had renewed his professional association with Doyle as a portrait and miniature painter in 1811, may have adopted a similar procedure in his life-size portrait of Perry.[45] Williams had previously collaborated with Doyle in selling Stillman's profile, and it is even possible that the two colleagues shared the same plaster cast when painting Perry.[46] Nor was this a temporary expedient for Williams. According to an advertisement in the *Independent Chronicle* in 1825, Williams continued "to paint from the dead in his peculiar manner by masks," as did his widow, who advertised her "long and active practical experience" in making death masks in the *Boston Evening Transcript* in 1832.[47]

Doyle and Williams were reviving a traditional process of making wax and plaster castings that had flourished in England in the seventeenth century. In

1669, Samuel Pepys visited a "plaisterer" and had his face pomaded and covered with plaster for a mold. He returned the next day to see his face, and the result "seemed most admirably like, and I will have another made before I take it away."[48] Other Boston artists, however, may have made a practice of taking masks of people who were expected to die shortly. John Rowe noted on 23 August 1766 that his friend Samuel Wentworth lay "dangerously ill at Roxbury. Mr. Copeland took his Face this afternoon." Three weeks later Rowe attended Wentworth's funeral.[49] Some of Doyle's and Williams's contemporaries were doing likewise. John D. Hoechstaetter, a Baltimore carver and portrait painter, advertised in 1800 "Busts in wax, from the life" in addition to his usual portraits in crayons.[50] Ezra Godfrey, a sculptor who worked briefly in New England in 1792 and again in 1808, used a process that took an impression directly from the sitter's face. Godfrey made likenesses "in Virgin Wax and Alabaster," either by impressing it into a cast or by physical modeling. It is unclear whether the final figures were life-size or reduced to miniatures. No works by Ezra Godfrey have been identified, but he is known from two announcements in which he publicized his services as a sculptor and taker of likenesses. In Salem, in 1792, he stated that he "executes in the various parts of Sculpture, and flatters himself he shall give satisfaction to those that will favor him with their employment." Sixteen years later when stopping in Providence in 1808, he was more specific.

> Likenesses. Taken in Virgin Wax and Alabaster. The Ladies and Gentlemen of Providence, particularly his Friends, and the patrons of the Arts, are respectively informed that Ezra Godfrey takes Likenesses by Impression and by Modelling—Those taken by Modelling relieve the person almost entirely from those Lengths of Sitting required in taking a complete Likeness in any other Way. The likeness taken in this Way is allowed by good Judges to be very striking, and admirably neat and elegant, particularly those taken in Wax. Those who may be pleased to have their own or their children's likenesses taken . . . [will] be waited upon for that purpose at their own houses.[51]

With the advent of a casting procedure came a new way of talking about portraits and portrait making. When George Mason introduced himself as a limner in 1765, he was relying on an old-fashioned but widely understood term for "painter" or "miniature painter." The term was still common in 1789 when "Limners and Portrait Painters" were given their own banner at the parade honoring George Washington's visit to Boston. But when Williams and Doyle advertised their portraits of Perry in 1814, they employed the term *taken,* copying the language of artists who used machines to optically, mechanically, or physically ensure the accuracy of their images. Phrases such as "*taking* likenesses," "*taking* faces," and "*taking* profiles" were now common in newspapers and prevalent in the parlance of Americans, many of whom were having their portraits painted or profiles rendered for the first time. The term has endured and today is preserved in everyday expressions such as "taking photographs."

In the end, it was this concept of likeness that gave authenticity and individual meaning to popular American portraiture. Williams's and Doyle's images—literally "taken" from the faces of their subjects in much the same manner utilized by wax modelists—were designed to create portraits so accurate that they had the authority of an article of the sitter's clothing or personal accessory. This was the aesthetic that led painter Noah North to embellish chairs in his portraits with actual stenciling; that led John Brewster, Jr., to paint the music to "The Silver Moon" within the portrait composition of Sarah Prince; and that led Ruth Henshaw Bascom and Ruth Whittier Shute to employ tinfoil, cut paper, and gilt découpage to fashion spectacles, jewelry, and canary birds on pastel, gouache, and watercolor images.[52] A portrait, miniature, or profile lacking this authenticity—whatever the pretensions or aspirations of its style—could fall short of its intended role as a "family ornament" that kept pace "with the tide of fleeting time."

Chapter 18

Taking Faces II: The Physiognotrace

ENTIRELY MISSING in the careers of itinerant portrait makers is any sense that their work was widely sought by America's rank and file. Few families in the early nineteenth century could afford to patronize these artists. Still a privilege of the upper classes—or of an aspiring middle class—portraits were commissioned by a succession of prosperous generations, often to commemorate events such as a death in the family, a celebrated marriage, or a lucrative business venture. Much the same was true of miniature portraits commissioned as keepsakes or clothing accessories; in some cases miniatures were priced on an even higher scale.

The "physiognotrace"—a drafting technique for making profiles that spread exponentially in the United States after 1803—changed everything. On 11 August 1790, when Reverend Ezra Stiles was in his second decade as president of Yale College, he made a short entry in his diary. "Sat for my Picture to Mr.___ which he took in 2 or 3 minutes by a Delineator or Portable Camera obscura."[1] Apparently Stiles was unable to recall the artist's name, but he did remember that the picture was finished within minutes by use of an optical device. Made up of a lens and darkened box into which the artist inserted a sheet of paper, the mechanism was like a small piece of luggage.

Although unidentified, the artist was likely to have been Joseph Wright (1756–93), son of New Jersey wax modeler Patience Lovell Wright. Joseph is known to have been working with a delineator when he traveled through New York City and eastern New England. A miniaturist and medal-maker formerly based in London (where he grew up), Wright and his partner, Samuel Brooks (fl. 1780–90; fig. 18.1), stopped in Providence on 21 August 1790 (just ten days after Stiles made his diary entry) while en route to Boston. In a handbill printed in Boston on 23 September 1790, these two artists offered "Medals, Miniature, and Profile Painting and Shades . . . and the most correct likenesses in two minutes sitting." ("Shades," named after the manner of tracing the sitter's profile from a shadow image, were profiles.) The pair then left for Charleston. It would have been consistent with their engaging entrepreneurial style for Wright and Brooks to call on Stiles in his position as president of one of New England's leading educational institutions. But the entry is also important to art historians because it is the first indication that a portrait maker was circulating in North America with a drawing device. Carried by transient artists who sold profiles at cheap prices and sometimes even handed them out for free, this contrivance transformed small-scale portraiture in America.[2]

The optical and mechanical technology employed by Wright was neither unique to the English-speaking world nor even to North America. Samuel Pepys referred in 1666 to "the art of drawing pictures by Prince Rupert's rule and machine" as well as to using a "dark roome" and a lens. Pepys also experimented

Figure 18.1. *Thomas Hall.* Miniature. Signed "S. Brooks fecit./1787." Ink inscription on reverse: "Thomas Hall, October 18th—1787." Samuel Brooks was a colleague of Joseph Wright when the two men traveled through New Haven, Connecticut, in 1790. Watercolor, 2 inches. Eastern New England or New York. Private collection.

with a pantograph, calling it a "parallelogram," which enabled him to make smaller or enlarged views of an original.³ In New England, devices that reduced projected images (or enhanced the viewing of prints in artificially illuminated boxes) are known to have been in the hands of private owners by the early eighteenth century as well as in college libraries and instrument collections. Similar items were advertised in Providence and Philadelphia. And there is ample evidence that they were stocked by instrument makers and print and book dealers. In New Haven, optical lens maker Jotham Fenton (who also ran a natural history museum) advertised "glasses for making the Camera Obscura" in 1790. In Boston in the next decade, museum proprietor Daniel Bowen sold "camera lenses" and "Camera Glasses" from his print warehouse under the museum, presumably for better viewing of the prints that he marketed.⁴

At least some of these devices were made for landscape artists.⁵ The unidentified entrepreneur who exhibited a portable camera obscura on Boston Common in May and July 1796 claimed it would "expedit . . . the business of drawing Landscapes in Perspective," adding that "Nature and Art in their utmost perfection and beauty [are offered] . . . in Miniature." No carrying equipment or vehicle was specified in this announcement, but the machine may have been like the "Large Portable Camera obscura, fixed on a carriage with harness complete" put up for sale by an optical store in New York City in April 1797. That one, too, was designed for drawing landscapes.⁶

The first profilist to promote machine-made portraits in North America may have been John Colles, a New York City artist who claimed to have taken the images of "many of the nobility" in England and Ireland. In 1778, 1780, and again in 1783, Colles advertised that "he takes the most Striking Likenesses in Miniature and Profile of any size at so low a price as 2 Dollars each framed and glazed." He also carried "a few machines made on an entirely new plan for reducing Likenesses, &c, which he will sell at 2 guineas each with which he will instruct the purchaser the use of them and the whole art of reducing figures to any size." These machines were almost certainly pantographs.⁷

The 1790s experienced a rapid increase in machine-aided portraiture. Besides the partnership of Wright and Brooks, William Rollinson (1762–1842) worked with an apparatus in New York City in 1790, delivering a "most correct and expressive Likeness in four minutes." He finished these as painted miniatures or crayon sketches. He also produced "family pictures" with from three to a dozen in a frame, and provided sitters the opportunity of seeing each other taken in a few moments. J. Manly, the miniature and profile painter who termed himself the "European Artist," was also using machines for taking pictures. When he reached New England in 1792, he opened an exhibition of two hundred paintings, prints, and hair-work devices in Boston and promised to take "the most correct likenesses in any position of countenance, in four minutes" with what he called "The Polyscophian Delineator, and Physiognometer, which reduces the human countenance or other objects, to any size, and traces it with all lines and shades until painted."[8] When he reached New York City, his four-minute sitting time had been reduced by half: "The delineator reflects the human countenance in a surprising manner, so that a correct likeness may be taken in profile to any small size in two minutes—the phizeognometor reduced the countenance to any size, and preserves the most correct likeness and exact proportions when placed between the object and the painter; and is the greatest assistant that art ever invented to a miniature painter."[9] This was the first time these technical terms appeared in a North America newspaper. Like Wright's and Rollinson's machines, Manly's were probably optical since they captured "any position" of the countenance.[10]

By this time public familiarity with profile taking or shades had increased to the point that amateurs and semiprofessionals were learning how to make them on their own. When Thomas B. Hazard of Rhode Island visited Newport in March 1796, he noted in his diary that "Dockter Man took my Profile last Evaning." Mann was a Newport physician, naturalist, antiquarian, and amateur artist; he may have had at his disposal a profile machine and perhaps an instrument that reduced size, or he may simply have drawn a shadow image.[11] Elsewhere, Sarah Snell Bryant (1768–1847), a physician's wife and mother of William Cullen Bryant, who lived in Cummington, Massachusetts, started furnishing profiles in 1798 and 1799 for family members and neighbors: "Began a shade for Hannah. Cut out one for Mrs. Joy"; "Finished Hannahs shade"; "Drew out a profile for Charity [child of a Bryant family member]."[12] Ruth Henshaw (1772–1848), who became the noted profilist Ruth Henshaw Bascom, began doing profiles when she was working as a school teacher in Leicester, Massachusetts, in 1801: "I spun some and cut out profiles."[13]

Absent so far was any widespread recognition of the merchandising or entrepreneurial potential of these devices. Of the professional artists in the American Northeast using optical and mechanical aids before 1796, only a few either admitted to it or announced it to the public. The real commercial breakthrough in machine-aided portraiture was precipitated by the arrival in America in 1795 and 1796 of several French artists who not only used tracing devices in making portraits but who flamboyantly described their techniques. On 7 November 1796, with a notice headed "Physiognotrace," the engraver J. J. Boudier promised newspaper readers in Philadelphia portraits and likenesses made by an instrument lately invented in Europe that was "both short and infalliable."[14] He employed an Anglicized version of the French term *physionotrace,* which was first used in revolutionary France after 1789. The following February 1797, Thomas Bluget de Valdenuit (1763–1846) and Charles Balthazar Julien Fevret de Saint-Mémin (1770–1852), both former French military officers who had recently fled their homeland, advertised in New York City that they took and engraved portraits "on an improved plan of the celebrated Physiognotrace of Paris."[15] Boudier's, Saint-Mémin's, and Valdenuit's machines were the first tracing or imaging mechanisms in America publicized under the name "physiognotrace." Their instruments were variants of the apparatus invented by the French cellist Gilles-Louis Chrétien which consisted of a large arm chair, an attached tracing frame, a crosshair sighting device, and an offset pencil by which the artist drew a sitter's life-size profile. Saint-Mémin's procedure was to draw an original, full-size sketch in charcoal on a pink watercolor background and to create from this drawing (using a pantograph) a reduced and reversed copperplate engraving. He charged eight dollars for the drawing and seventeen dollars for twelve engraved prints. After a brief partnership with Valdenuit in New York City, Saint-Mémin moved to Philadelphia in 1799, and from 1804 to 1809 he traveled to Baltimore, Annapolis, Washington, Richmond, and Charleston.[16]

Another Saint-Mémin partner, Louis Lemet (c. 1779–1832), advertised in both New York City and Philadelphia large physiognotrace likenesses in chalk on tinted paper for twenty-five dollars and twelve engraved replicas together with the copper plate for twelve dollars. Hemmed in by increasing competition, Lemet went to Albany in 1805 where he remained for fifteen years working as a profile artist, commercial engraver, gilder, and art teacher. Like Saint-Mémin, Lemet originally used a Chrétien-derived tracing and reducing device. But in 1809, he announced that he had "purchased Mr. Jones' correct profile machine" (possibly that of profilist F. P. Jones, who advertised jointly with Lemet and J. Todd in New York City) and sharply reduced his prices, selling four profiles for twenty-five cents.[17]

Saint-Mémin's and Lemet's profitable businesses immediately attracted American imitators. One of the first was John Isaac Hawkins (1772–1855), a thirty-one-year-old English inventor and musical instrument maker then living in Philadelphia, who publicized he had received a patent for a newly designed physiognotrace so simple that likenesses could be taken "in less than a minute."[18] A sketch of the apparatus, with an explanatory index, shows a frame-mounted brass stylus that followed the contours of the sitter's profile; the movement of the stylus was transferred through a pantograph to a pencil that traced a reduced image on a sheet of paper (fig. 18.2). Hawkins sold the rights to the machine to museum proprietor Charles Willson Peale, who began taking profiles at his museum on 1 June 1803.[19] Propelled by a network of similar franchises, Hawkins's invention achieved celebrity status and set in motion what is now called by art historians the "year of the physiognotrace," a period in which Hawkins's and other similar devices were installed in museums and profile cutting rooms in the larger cities of the United States. In December 1803, for example, profile artist Jeremiah Paul Jr. (fl. 1795–1820) advertised in Charleston "faithful likenesses taken by the Physiognotrace invented by Mr. Hawkins." A Hawkins patent made its way into the hands of profilist John Sandford in New York City in 1804. Within a year, two Hawkins operators were active in Boston. The possibilities seemed limitless; although profilists needed to have mechanical ability, they did not have to be artistically talented.[20]

Initially all went smoothly for Hawkins's patentees. Both profilists in Boston had the highest expectations of attracting the windfall business they had found in Philadelphia and the middle and southern states. Raphaelle Peale (1774–1825), son of Charles Willson Peale, took rooms off Newbury Street in September 1804 and composed a grandiose, self-confident advertisement claiming he was the first "to use the Facietrace invented by his Ingenious Friend J. I. Hawkins." Peale emphasized the distances he had covered taking his machine from Philadelphia to Maryland, Virginia, South Carolina, and Georgia. He maintained

Figure 18.2. *Explanation of Mr. Jno. I. Hawkins Physiognotrace,* by Charles Willson Peale (1741–1827). Included in a letter sent 28 January 1803 to Thomas Jefferson explaining the physiognotrace of John Isaac Hawkins (1772–1855). Philadelphia, Pennsylvania. Watercolor drawing. Courtesy, Library of Congress, Jefferson Papers, LCMS-27748 39B 225530.

his instrument drew from four to thirty-two profiles at one sitting, and he cautioned any imitators against "making, using or vending the same without a Right—Such persons who may be guilty of the worst species of Robbery, shall be prosecuted to the utmost right of the Law."[21]

The second Boston operator was Uri K. Hill (1780–1844), the engraver and music compiler (and, according to Hawkins, a "native American genius"), who had taken his Hawkins patent physiognotrace "eastward" from Georgetown and Washington in 1803 to New York City and thence to Boston where he arrived about a year after Peale. Hill leased rooms in December 1805 on Devonshire Street, near the post office, and offered likenesses "elegantly taken in gold on glass" for seven dollars or "wrought on paper" for fifty cents. He, too, proudly boasted that his "Hawkin's Patent Physiognotrace" excelled "all others in accuracy." Apparently to be on the safe side, however, Hill also advertised lessons in vocal and instrumental music.[22]

As it turned out, neither Peale's nor Hill's notices drew much attention. Peale's posting appeared on only four occasions; Hill ran his about nine times. No evidence suggests that either artist found many sitters. Peale returned to Philadelphia to continue an exemplary career as a portrait and historical painter. As for Hill, the public was eventually made aware of his talents as a musician and musical compiler when he published in 1806 a second collection of psalms and hymns (*The Sacred Minstrel, No. 1*). An outstanding musical, engraving, and publishing future awaited him in Philadelphia and New York City.

Raphaelle Peale and Uri K. Hill in Boston had in fact run afoul of the harsh world of pirating, patent infringing, and profiteering that marred the year of the physiognotrace, as competing portraitists, artist-entrepreneurs, and mechanical inventors rushed to take advantage of the popularity of cheap, machine-made profiles. Within a matter of days after Charles Willson Peale had installed a Hawkins machine in his Philadelphia museum in June 1803, six rival devices were being operated in New York City and Boston. On 23 June 1803, John Wesley Jarvis and Joseph Wood made physiognotrace likenesses for two shillings apiece at their New York City drawing academy. Four days later Edward Savage completed a "curious and useful . . . Phisiognotrace" at his New York Museum at 80 Greenwich Street. (It took profiles in half a minute for one penny.) In July 1803, Daniel Bowen gave out free likenesses from a "much admired physiognotrace" to patrons visiting his Columbian Museum in Boston. In September, Edward Savage constructed a second tracing instrument for his "New York Museum" in Boston. In October, a Mr. Morden began using a physiognotrace at the Boston jewelry and fancy goods shop of Dyer and Eddy. And in December, Charles Packard was handing out free profiles taken by "the new invented Physiognotrace" at his Washington Museum at the foot of the Boston Mall. Eight more profilists, including the inventor John Isaac Hawkins, were active between

New Jersey and Georgia. This was just 1803. Within two years, the number of new proprietors in Boston and Charleston had doubled; three years after that, it had doubled again. Profiles were so much in demand that tracing machines were being sold at prices as high as fifty dollars.[23]

Much of this windfall was due to the persuasive rhetoric of merchandising. Almost always the terms *physiognotrace* or *patent physiognotrace* headlined the newspaper appeals. In the rapidly escalating lexicon of profile-selling catch-phrases in post-federal America, old nomenclature such as "delineator," "camera obscura," "facietrace," and "delineating pencil" was swept aside. Together with its second-generation derivatives, *physiognotrace* became the rallying cry of artist-entrepreneurs positioning themselves for public patronage. Hawkins's "Patent Physiognotrace" was rivaled by J. Wood's "Polygraphic Physiognotrace," Edward Savage's "Superior Physiognotrace," William Bache's "Patent Physiognotrace," and J. Fuller's "Best Physiognomy Trace." In time the word also became loosely synonymous with the operators of imaging machines themselves or the quality or appreciation of their work. One artist introduced himself as "John Putnam, Physiognotrace"; profilists T. Nixon and William Bache referred to themselves as "Physiognotrists"; and J. Paul referred to Hawkins's improved version of his machine as producing a "feast to the Physiognomist."[24]

Because a considerable volume of business was essential to keep prices low, most of these early entrepreneurs followed the examples of Peale and Savage and set up machines in museums—or in bathing houses, coffeehouses, taverns, and art galleries. Henry Williams installed a physiognotrace in his rooms under Philip Woods's Boston Museum on the north side of the market, where he took profiles and gave electrical treatments. Dr. Martin Howe of Boston traced profiles at his museum of natural and artificial curiosities (mostly stuffed and mounted animals), located on Common Street near the bottom of the mall where crowds sometimes assembled.[25]

Although described in advertisements as physiognotraces, these devices were not actually licensed under Chrétien's or Hawkins's patents. Experienced inventors, machinists, and museum proprietors like Edward Savage and Daniel Bowen handily circumvented their legal protections (if, indeed, they actually had any) and initiated a series of real or purported improvements, each heralded by language belittling the crudity, inaccuracy, complexity, or discomfort of all prior machines. According to one description of such an improvement (published by William F. Pinchbeck in 1805), the operator placed the sitter in a darkened room and projected the profile against a paper-covered pane of glass by means of a single light source positioned at the far end of a five-foot "trunk" or box. The usual pantograph traced the sitter's shadow, drawing a smaller image on a sheet of paper. The advantage of this design was that it could be assembled by any mechanic from inexpensive components.[26]

A similar instrument was invented by Salem cabinetmaker William King, who worked as a profile cutter in Boston in 1804. King's broadsides and newspaper advertisements apprised readers that he also reduced "from the shadow" but assured prospective sitters that they would "not [be] incommoded with any thing passing over his face, nor detained over six minutes"—a reference to the now infamous Hawkins patent whose brass stylus traced profiles of sitters clamped in a frame.[27] Very likely King continued to make refinements on his own design because his later publicity added, "Ladies are particularly informed that he takes their Profiles without their . . . being 'under the disagreeable necessity of retiring into a dark room' or having the shadow varied by the flare of a candle, as he makes use of neither."[28] King's machines were profitable enough that he franchised them to other operators like John Putnam and James Akin, who purchased or leased King's "patent delineating pencil" and promoted themselves with advertising text identical to King's.[29]

Simplifications and advancements made physiognotraces so lightweight they became more portable. When Raphaelle Peale visited the southern and middle states in the spring and summer of 1804, he carried the Hawkins device attached to the side of a specially modified armchair. But when King undertook his two-year tour of eastern New England and Canada in 1805 and 1806, he packed little more than a lamp and a boxed glass screen. Moses Chapman, who worked in New Bedford and Salem in 1807 and 1808, used a physiognotrace so small it could be tucked under one arm like an artist's easel (figs. 18.3 and 18.4). Chapman's instrument projected a life-size shadow of his sitter's profile onto a screen, which the pantograph reduced to a two-inch pencil image. He could alternately paint his profiles or "neatly cut [them] on a beautiful paper." Unlike King's machine, however, Chapman's was not furnished with a box or enclosure, and he most likely had to work in a darkened room.[30]

The constant travel by profile takers led to widespread diffusion of the technology and propelled it into the public domain. Ethan Allen Greenwood was caught up in this fervor while he was still attending Dartmouth College. On 14 August 1805 he met the New Haven engraver Abel B. Doolittle (1786–1809) and found him "something of a Painter." According to Greenwood's diary, Doolittle introduced him to the art of taking profiles with a physiognotrace, and he may have sold Greenwood one of his machines or at least its key components. Greenwood lost no time. On 6 September 1805, or about three weeks after meeting Doolittle, Greenwood stopped in Haverhill, New Hampshire. Here "I worked on my machine Physiognotrace, brought a lamp & new cloth for transparency & began to take Profiles." Thereafter it was part of Greenwood's permanent portrait-making repertory.[31]

Many profilists found the trade so brisk they concentrated on particular geographical areas. J. Fuller, "Taker of Profile Likenesses," worked along the Con-

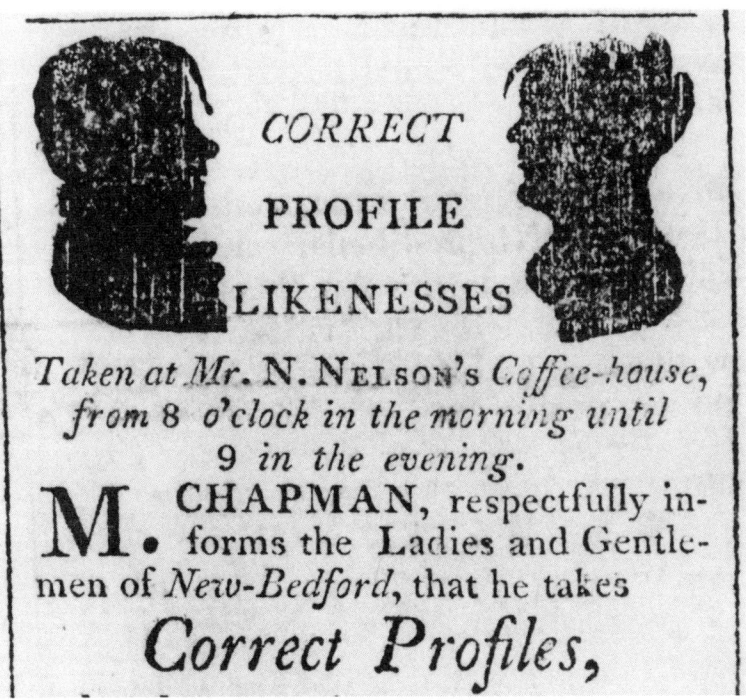

Figure 18.3. *"CORRECT* PROFILE LIKENESSES *Taken at Mr.* N. Nelson's *Coffee-house."* Advertisement by Moses Chapman (1783–1821) in New Bedford, Massachusetts. Chapman alternately painted profiles or cut them from paper and supplied frames. In New Bedford he kept hours from 8 a.m. until 9 p.m. and clearly announced that he would leave the following Tuesday, making it a five-day stopover. *New Bedford Mercury,* 4 December 1807. Courtesy, American Antiquarian Society.

necticut coastline. Gilbert Haven duplicated William King's routes through Newburyport and Portsmouth. John M'Conachie ranged the entire East Coast from Boston to Richmond, while A. Janes covered New York State. William Chamberlain traveled the interior and upland areas of Massachusetts, New Hampshire, and New York.[32] The lure of quick profits for minimum effort was so strong that even accomplished portrait and miniature painters and professional engravers such as Raphaelle Peale and William Jennys set aside or abandoned their usual lines of portrait work and devoted themselves to mass-producing inexpensive profile likenesses. Peale made profiles for twenty-five cents each while neglecting opportunities to paint miniatures for twenty dollars and portraits in oil for thirty dollars. Jennys, who looked back on thirteen years' experience painting portraits in New England and New York, peddled twenty-five-cent physiognotrace likenesses in Concord, New Hampshire, in 1805—apparently under a franchising arrangement with William King.[33] Jennys normally charged twenty-five dollars for a painted portrait and four dollars for a frame. That same year James Akin, who later pursued a career as an engraver and book illustrator, sold cut profiles in Newburyport for six cents each and painted ones for two to four dollars.[34]

During the years from 1790 to 1825 at least seventy professional profilists were retailing inexpensive likenesses taken with optical or mechanical imaging devices in New England and New York. Another sixty-five were working from Philadelphia to Augusta, Georgia, and west to Louisville, Kentucky. While the backgrounds of many are unidentified, a majority were likely American. Most cut profiles from paper, ornamenting the background with minimal suggestions of coiffure and dress by means of pencil touches. The prevailing price for a cut profile was 25 cents for two of the same person, or 12.5 cents each. Higher prices were set for executing a profile image on glass, a process that entailed etching away gold leaf or enameling. Music engraver Uri K. Hill asked seven dollars for a gold on glass profile; D. Melville sold profiles in Newport that were "enamelled on glass" for one dollar.[35] Profiles done in colors on paper brought yet higher

Figure 18.4. Shadowgraph or physiognotrace used by Moses Chapman (1783–1821), active in New England, circa 1807–8. Chapman used this machine to project a life-size shadow of the sitter's profile, which he reduced with a pantograph. Courtesy Metropolitan Museum of Art, gift of Glenn Tilley Morse. Photograph from Alice Van Leer Carrick, *Shades of Our Ancestors,* opp. 6. Courtesy, Widener Library, Harvard University, US 42505.475.

prices. Watercolorist T. Nixon teamed with William Bache to produce machine-imaged profiles "in Miniature style" painted in watercolor for $2.25.[36]

These prices, a fraction of those demanded for painted portraits or pastels, translated into a substantial client base. According to his advertisements, William King took between three and four thousand profiles in Salem and neighboring towns like Marblehead. He may have equaled that output in Newburyport, Portsmouth, Halifax, and central New Hampshire. (William Bentley's comment that King's profile cutting "produced him[self] more [profits?] in Halifax, N.S., than in Salem" suggests that the farther away he traveled the more money he made.)[37] Raphaelle Peale claimed a total of 345,720 profiles after just two years' work in Maryland, Virginia, South Carolina, and Georgia.[38] Granted, Peale may have been counting copies of profiles, not just originals, because the Hawkins patent machine owned by Peale turned out thirty-two profiles at one sitting. But even with this in mind, he may have had up to five thousand clients. And these are just two of an estimated seventy profile takers active in this period.

Like all merchandising strategies, the language of physiognotrace promotion began to lose its effectiveness as soon as everyone started using it. When profilist Gerrit Schipper first came to Boston in October 1803, he faced competition from Edward Savage, a Mr. Morden, William Doyle, and Charles Packard—all vigorously publicizing their physiognotrace-assisted profiles and portraits.[39] Schipper, a Netherlands-born artist, specialized in making reduced profiles in colored "crayons" (meaning pastels). He sold these for about seven dollars.[40] After a period of hesitation, Schipper proclaimed on 6 January 1804 that his "Achromatic Camera Obscura" was now in complete order and was preferable to any other machine "for imitating Nature correctly."[41] Apparently Schipper had been using optical imaging throughout his North American tour but had little incentive previously to draw attention to it. While he did not go so far as to adopt the more popular term *physiognotrace,* he was obliged to respond to others' use of it. A second reason for the physiognotrace's decline was that the active bearers who initially inspired others to imitate them got involved in different pursuits. Charles de Saint-Mémin returned to France to become head of a museum, J. J. Boudier became a professional engraver of bank bills in Pittsburgh, J. I. Hawkins turned his attention to musical instruments, and William King became an electrical lecturer and demonstrator.[42]

The January 1804 date of Schipper's announcement marked the apex of physiognotrace merchandising in the American Northeast. The signs of its advertising demise (but not of the machine itself) began less than two years later when profile artist Joseph Wood omitted the term from his notices. Wood reminded his clients on 9 September 1805 that his profession as a miniature painter afforded him an advantage over profilists relying entirely on machinery because he could revise and correct the finished product, and they could not.[43] The emphasis was no longer on the machines but on the artists themselves, notably handicapped ones and prodigies. Even as profile takers continued to carry their services to every corner of eastern America and Lower Canada, a generation of freehand cutters rose to public prominence. Martha Ann Honeywell (1787–1848), who was born without hands, became one of the most widely touring profile cutters of her generation. In a career spanning about three decades, she used her teeth, toes, and the stump of one arm to create needlework, pinprickings, paintings, watch papers, and profiles—many examples of which survive in historical collections. Sally Rogers (fl. 1806–18), an armless painter and profile cutter who sometimes traveled with Honeywell, marketed her skills in Boston, New York City, and Charleston. In the 1820s, similar engagements were undertaken in the eastern United States by prodigies Master William James Hubard (1807–62) and Master Hanks (fl. 1828), both of whom were children when they began their careers in England.[44] And a decade later William H. Brown (1808–1883), a Charleston-born paper cutting artist, was circuiting the eastern states creating small-scale, full-length profiles in four minutes' time; his visual memory was so good he could replicate likenesses hours after meeting the subject casually in the street.[45]

But before it left the American scene, the physiognotrace dramatically expanded the reach of popular culture. For one thing it allowed servants to enter the field of portrait making. Moses Williams (1777–c. 1825) (fig. 18.5), a mixed-race slave in the household of Charles Willson Peale of Philadelphia, not only learned to operate a Hawkins machine but was so successful at the task that he cut profiles for the major part of Peale's huge patronage base.[46] For another, it greatly expanded popular American interest in the decorative arts. A profile technique that began in 1790 with one or two discerning artists and clients—among them John Colles, Joseph Wright, and Reverend Ezra Stiles—swelled to an estimated ten thousand sittings each year. These numbers were unprecedented both in Europe and America, the product of a new approach in consumer marketing. The "celebrated physiognotrace of Paris," which J. J. Boudier advertised in Philadelphia in 1796 and Thomas de Valdenuit and Charles de Saint-Mémin promoted in New York City in 1798, embodied the daring and inventive spirit of revolutionary-period French artists in the 1790s and was associated with overtones of republicanism, populism, and technology. The term also signified a curious transformation in which the mechanical accuracy of portrait making seemingly eclipsed the aesthetic value of the portrait itself. The profile was not merely a mechanical innovation giving rise to popular patronage of one of the lesser arts of portraiture. It was a mental infatuation—not unlike the "science" of phrenology in the 1830s and 1840s—that rode the entrepreneurial energy of federal and early national America along with ascension balloons, acoustical deception parlors, and "talking" machines. In many cases the same individuals were promoting them. At least six American or Canadian physiognotrace operators kept rooms or establishments where clients could receive "electerizing" shocks during the same visit. Five sold profiles to patrons visiting their acoustical or automaton exhibitions.[47] Three were also balloonists or balloon ascension promoters.[48] A dozen or more were museum and waxwork proprietors who had acquired a physiognotrace to improve their gate.[49]

Unlike their American-based counterparts, English profile takers working in London and outlying towns such as Oxford, Ipswich, and Newcastle, never identified their machines as physiognotraces. These artists may have used the same techniques as Americans to create likenesses, and at least one used Hawkins's patent (running it anonymously).[50] But lacking a French infatuated clientele, they marketed the elegant metal or appearance of their machines: "Silver Instruments," "Silver Plates," "Reflecting Mirrors," or an "Impression Plate Likeness." One English profilist called his studio a "Public Delineatory"

Figure 18.5. *Moses Williams, cutter of profiles*. Recently discovered in the archives of the Library Company of Philadelphia, this profile has been attributed both to Raphaelle Peale and Moses Williams. It may have been made jointly by them because Peale's physiognotrace used a stylus to trace the contours of Williams's face, which required an outside operator. Williams likely cut the profile, however. A biracial slave in the Peale household, Williams worked for several decades creating profiles on the museum's Hawkins-type physiognotrace. After his manumission, he married the Peales' cook. Philadelphia, 1803. White laid paper on black stock, 4 by 5 inches. Courtesy, The Library Company of Philadelphia.

where he "Mathematically reduced" shades for painting. Another employed an "Automaton Artist" which he blithely named *Prosopagraphus*.[51]

Like so much of American popular culture, Boudier's language was transitory. The last profile artist to use the term *physiognotrace* in his advertising may have been William Bache, who was still championing its superiority to residents of Newburyport in 1810. A few months later, however, he merely told newspaper readers in Portland he had been using a device of his own invention for the past seven years. Much had changed by then. William King was on his way to the middle and southern states as an electrical experimenter, showman, and author. William Jennys had given up both profile making and painting and was speculating in Newburyport and Ipswich real estate. Gerrit Schipper had left the United States and was looking for clients in Quebec and Montreal. By 1817, when Henry Hervé brought one of Hawkins's machines from Cheapside, London, for his tour, he was calling it a "patent delineator," a reversion to its older terminology. Although the mechanics and optics for generating profiles persisted over time, and eventually blossomed into photography, the physiognotrace as a merchandising tool had become history.[52]

Chapter 19

The World of Automatons

LIKE PHYSIOGNOTRACES, automatons were brought to America with the spate of European inventions that entered the country from 1790 through 1825. Animated by clockwork mechanisms, by compressed air or in some cases by the power of water, they were programmed to imitate life—simulating human activity such as speaking, writing, "playing" musical instruments, or "competing" in chess matches. They also mimicked the sounds and movements of birds, animals, and fish. The specialty of English, German, French, and Swiss clockmakers since the sixteenth century, automatons were usually designed and made by court-appointed mechanics working exclusively for royal and aristocratic patrons. In England they were created by several generations of the Pinchbeck family—among them Christopher Pinchbeck, Sr., and his sons Christopher Pinchbeck, Jr., and Edward Pinchbeck. In France they were fabricated by Jacques de Vaucanson (1709–1782) and in Switzerland by the Pierre and Henri-Louis Jaquet-Droz and Henri Maillardet families.[1]

Automatons were seldom imported to Britain's North American colonies. Impresarios and showmen simply could not afford to purchase them, and private owners kept them in their families. Attentive readers of American newspapers constantly heard about them, however. One notice, appearing in the *Boston Post-Boy* of 1735, described a "curious Machine-Coach and Horses" that was invented by Corneus of France which mechanically animated a coachman, a pair of horses, a page, and a "Lady" who went through a ritual of arrivals and departures "not to be equal'ed in Europe."[2] Another appeared in the *New York Mercury* of 24 June 1754: "There is shewn at the Hotel of Monaco at Versailles an Automaton of the Figure of a Man, larger than Life, and painted the natural Colour, placed on a Tun; which pronounces most distinctly a considerable Number of Words and Sentences, the Letters of the Alphabet, and the Months of the Year; wishes the Company Good-morrow, &c. To put it in Motion there are required only a Bellows and a Cylinder. This most curious Machine has been seen with Admiration by the whole Court." A month later, a Philadelphia paper reported that "The [French] King sent for the Automaton lately mentioned, that pronounced several Words very distinctly, to examine the Machinery in the Inside, and satisfied himself that there was no Imposition. His Majesty seemed greatly pleased with its Simplicity."[3]

Americans read of a race being held in 1769 from London to Gravesend on the lower part of the Thames by a runner and "Mr. Moore's machine," and that "the bets on Saturday . . . were four to one in favour of the automaton."[4] In 1771, they learned about the chess-playing automaton created by Austro-Hungarian M. Wolfgang von Kempelen (1734–1804), which took the form of a Turk sitting on a cabinet of gears and levers. Before being unmasked as a hoax many decades later, it impressed everyone with its uncanny ability to engage the best chess masters.[5]

The first automaton was brought into the United States in 1787 by Joseph Falconi (fl. 1785–1819), the Italian showman whose electrical and magnetic exhibitions drew considerable notice in American newspapers. Seignior or Signor Falconi, as he liked to call himself, arrived in America after entertaining the courts of Naples, France, and Portugal. He began his tour of the New World in 1785 when he gave an exhibition in Kingston, Jamaica, at a private plantation. Writing to a friend in Spanish-Town, his host described Falconi's programs of "philosophical" experiments and "Magnetism" as being so outstanding they were thought by some to be "wrought by supernatural means."[6] Falconi then continued on to Mexico City and during the next thirty years, he toured most of the major eastern American cities (frontispiece). He started in New York City where he performed his philosophical experiments at Corre's Assembly Room on the evening of 21 June 1787. According to his announcement in the *New-York Weekly Journal,* he placed on a table an automaton figure of a "man in an Indian habit" (Mr. Maccabee) that was armed with a bow and arrow.[7] When instructed to do so by a member of the audience, the automaton would shoot an arrow from a distance of "ten or twelve Feet" into a target painted with thirteen numbers on a table.[8] The effect must have been stunning. The showman invited his audiences to toss dice to select which number Mr. Maccabee was to strike, and the automaton responded by correctly shooting the arrow at the number shown in the throw. The Indian wore a Caribbean-style feathered headdress resembling those seen in the cartouches of eighteenth-century European-made maps.[9] Falconi sometimes demonstrated other automatons such as the "Sagacious Mermaid" (fig. 19.1), which carried out experiments holding a sword in her hand while standing in a bucket of water, and a "Small Figure in a Turkish dress," which played cards with members of the audience and answered questions with hand motions. Since these other machines seldom appeared together on the same evening program, the mechanisms that drove Mr. Maccabee may have been shared with other automatons whose preprogrammed movements were designed to respond to magnetically induced controls.[10]

Finishing his stand in New York City, Falconi took his show to Baltimore in November and to Philadelphia the following year. After spending some time out of the country, Falconi returned to the southern and middle states, entertaining

Figure 19.1. "THIS EVENING, ... *At Washington-Hall*, Salem, Seignior FALCONI, ... will exhibit the *Sagacious* MERMAID." This device, an automaton exhibited by Joseph Falconi in Salem, Massachusetts, in 1796, was the second automaton shown in the United States. The figure knelt in a pail of water and used a sword to answer "every question" proposed by the audience. *Salem Gazette*, 13 September 1796. Courtesy, American Antiquarian Society.

in Charleston in 1793, in New York City in 1795, and Boston in 1796, coming back to America in 1801 and again in 1817. Falconi seldom varied his tricks, although he always claimed to be doing so. He used electrical discharges from a hand-operated generator to create an artificial thunderstorm, a lantern projector to show a battle between an elephant and an orangutan, a duel between "the Doctor and the Quack," and magnetic impulses to cause a watch to stop and go without touching it.[11] Perhaps his most interesting experiment took place in Boston in 1796 where he illuminated the audience hall with an "Electrical and Perpetual Lamp . . . actuated by the ingenious philosophical discovery of Mr. Volta, fully described in Cavello's Treatise on Electricity."[12] This was more than one hundred years before these items became available on the market—and long before the first battery-run electric light bulb was displayed in the United States.

While Falconi likely maintained a matter-of-fact demeanor during his performances, he stimulated publicity by playing on the supernatural. One New York City paper lamented that the devil had "forsaken the confines of Europe, . . . [and] put his cloven foot among his chosen pupils that evening at Corre's"; another editor said he was planning to attend Falconi's show since he was "anxious to see his grim majesty."[13] When Falconi headed north toward Boston, however, the entertainer was a little more circumspect. Like theater manager Joseph Harper, he approached the town by a roundabout route—first making stops at the courthouse in New London in 1795 and then at the theater in Providence in 1796. Finally, nine years almost to the day after he opened his act in New York City—a delay possibly precipitated because automatons, like puppets, may have encroached on the sensitive subjects of idolatry, necromancy, and image making—Falconi presented on 6 June 1796 "A small Automaton In a Turkish Dress" in the Boston Theatre. After exhibiting the "Sagacious Mermaid" and the "Thunder Storm at sea" on 9 and 16, respectively, he unveiled his "Indian Figure armed with a Bow and Arrow" on 20 June along with his usual magic lantern display in which Punchinello, disguised as a beggar, steals a wild boar. All told, Falconi remained in Boston only two weeks.[14] By contrast, he spent the equivalent of seven months in Philadelphia, four and a half months in Charleston, four months in New York City, and three and a half months in Baltimore.[15]

A second itinerant bringing automaton technology to America was balloonist Jean-Pierre Blanchard, who was just initiating his campaign for his forty-sixth ascension when Falconi began his first tour through Charleston in 1793. While Blanchard waited in Boston, New York City, and Providence for subscriptions, he put his skills to work constructing a "self-moving" carriage as well as several "artificial persons of natural size." He programmed these creatures to talk, stand, bow, and dance to music—all in an effort to draw potential supporters to his workshops where he could encourage them to finance his ascensions. Blanchard presented his "Curious Carriage" in the Philadelphia papers in August 1793, saying that it "runs without assistance of Horses, and goes as fast as the best Post-chaise." It was pulled by a wheeled automaton in the shape of an eagle, "chained to the tongue of the Carriage" and "guided by the Traveller who holds the reins in his hands, directs it in every respect." Blanchard claimed that the carriage could easily ascend mountains and drive on any road, and that its distance was "unlimited" since there were no springs in the case that required winding up. He asked gentlemen not to bring hunting dogs with them because they might attack the eagle-like driving mechanism.[16]

Blanchard's artificial persons embodied the political rhetoric of revolutionary Paris. He named the female "Citizen Sans Culottes," presumably clothed in an appropriately lower-class costume. The male was called "Mr. Aristocrat" and was dressed accordingly. Blanchard devised a scenario in which the pair paid obeisance to the audience but refused to dance with one another. Only after he got them to change their minds did the two "agree" to dance. While in Boston Blanchard fabricated a third artificial person, the "Wonderful Woman," as he called her, who stood upright and was capable of "imitating nature in all her actions."[17]

Still hoping to stage his next ascension, Blanchard leased his automatons in 1795 to two of his colleagues. A Mr. Perrette, who identified himself as a "Machinist from Paris" and a "Pensioner to the French Republic," took over Blanchard's "self-moving Carriage" in October 1795, bringing it to Newburyport and Portsmouth and subsequently to New York City.[18] John Maison leased or purchased the three human automatons and began a publicity barrage in the newspapers whose effrontery far exceeded any to have previously assaulted New England. Maison claimed these automatons were the "chef d'oeuvre of the great Blanchard; the result of an infinite series of scientific calculation."[19] And it is here we get the first sense that French-made automatons had the "gift of speech"—the quality that had so intrigued the king of France in 1754. Maison wrote that "the Mechanism of her Body, artificially composed, is so calculated on the invariable basis of the Mathematics, as to make her act in time and measure, and to avoid any false motion. Organized pipes, set into action by a compound and astronomical clock-work, the Trigger of which is let off by a single touch of a Needle, endow that surprising creature with the gift of speech. Her answers to the questions put to her by the Spectators will be pretty well understood." And to ensure her answers suited the questions put to the "Wonderful Woman," Maison had them conveniently printed on a sheet.[20]

As time went on, Maison changed "Citizen Sans Culottes" into "Citizen Democrat" and recast the "Wonderful Woman" as "Mademoiselle Moderate," whose "most amiable" character and artful conversation moderated the "acrimony of the Aristocrat towards the Democrat."[21] He also embellished his announcements with descriptions of previous automatons in history. He cited

Archytas's mechanical pigeon (400 B.C.), Jacques de Vaucanson's flute player (1739), and "M. de Kempelon's" chess player (1771). Always looking to enlarge his audiences, Maison endeavored to refine the automaton's voice, which "is so much improved, that she now speaks as clear and distinct as any real person."[22] Then Maison played his trump card: "To silence certain persons who have given out that those figures were moved by other than mechanical powers, the present proprietor of the Automata hereby declares to such persons as may not know how far art can imitate nature, that any one who will deposit 100 dollars (for the purpose of mending the damage that might be made) that he be at liberty to fire a musket ball through any part of the Automata while in activity."[23] No one reading this could help but feel a pang of sympathy for the imputed live person, if in fact he or she were concealed in there, and no one could fail to be attracted to the entertainment value of a machine that engendered such rumors. There is every likelihood, of course, that the only "person" making these insinuations was Maison himself. In any case, nobody seems to have taken up the challenge.

Soon other promoters saw their opportunity. One unidentified showman (believed to have been William F. Pinchbeck) introduced the "Fair Arithmetician, a writing automaton," and a "Lilliputian Cobler" into Philadelphia in 1795. According to a notice taken in the *Philadelphia Gazette,* the writing automaton represented a seven-year-old schoolboy that was prepared to do arithmetic and inscribe the name of any lady or gentleman in the audience. His companion was the "whispering Fairy," said to be an improvement upon the speaking figure made by the "ingenious Van Wizenfeltz" in London. Pinchbeck may have inherited these automatons from older members of his family—possibly from his grandfather, father, or uncle.[24] Sixteen months later Pinchbeck, exhibiting under his own name, showed the Fair Arithmetician, the Lilliputian Cobler, the "Indian Oracle," and two vaulting and dancing machines at a room in a Mr. Kerr's new building in Philadelphia, along with the "Grimacer," a facial act, possibly a puppet, made famous in London in Astley's Amphitheater.[25]

Once Pinchbeck realized there was a steady demand for trained pigs and dogs, he seems to have taken a diminishing interest in automatons and endeavored to dispose of them at inflated prices when the opportunity arose. (Pinchbeck had already tried to sell two machines in 1795, stating it was his intention "not to travel with them.") In New York City he exhibited the writing figure and the "celebrated" Turk—along with the Learned Pig—at a Mr. Martling's long room at 87 Nassau Street. Eventually Pinchbeck sold most of his machines to Charles Packard, founder of Boston's Washington Museum, who toured them extensively in New England between 1803 and 1805 with a parlor acoustic deception and a large collection of waxworks. According to Packard's text, the "celebrated writing figure" represented a boy of about five years of age that could "actually write the name of any person in the company dotting and crossing the letters I and T, with precision and care."[26] Packard later took them to French-speaking lower Canada.[27]

By 1797 a new automaton was being unveiled in eastern North America almost every month, most often by museum proprietors, acrobats, and showmen trying to boost ticket sales. That year Gardiner Baker, proprietor of the Tammany Museum in New York City, exhibited an automaton birdcage clock, an automaton drummer, an automaton stonecutter and blacksmith's shop, and automatons of Harlequin and Punch that acted out a pantomime.[28] John Paff, who arrived from Germany in 1799, brought several "curious Pieces of Mechanism" to audiences in Savannah. These included fourteen musicians serenading the principals of the Peace of Campo Formio—Napoleon Bonaparte and Philipp von Cobenzl. Elsewhere, Camou Meyere, a physician and professional conjurer, presented "an ingenious and very curious Automaton" in New York City in 1801.[29] And in 1806, a conjurer and fireworks specialist named Mr. Martin began a four-and-a-half-year tour of museum halls, lyceums, assembly rooms, hotels, ballrooms, theaters, academies, gardens, and coffeehouses with a "celebrated" ropedancing automaton. Representing a boy of six years, the automaton ostensibly danced and balanced like the best European acrobats (fig. 19.2) over a table holding Martin's conjuring paraphernalia. Martin's visits to most major towns between Boston and Charleston were dogged by his reputation as an "experimenting" mechanic that caused disastrous fires; he was himself struck by lightning preparing fireworks in Wilmington, South Carolina. He eventually put on sale all his "tools and instruments in part or the whole," along with instructions for their use, in New York City in 1811.[30]

Some automatons played a special role in advancing a showman's public appeal and in a sense became synonymous with their acts. For years James Maginnis showed a group of automaton figures "representing the Ancient Court of Alexander the Great"; another figure took on "the character of an American Tar" that danced a hornpipe and performed a variety of other steps. Not much is known of them, but they may have been clockwork-driven machines that performed tasks and complex dances, not simply puppets.[31] John and James Rannie—possibly coordinating their efforts with Pinchbeck—added an automaton to their repertoire that took advantage of their reputation of having conversed with a codfish being sold at a Scottish market. James went on to explain that he and his brother were the persons "particularized in the Encyclopaedia, who caused the alarm which took place in the fish market at Edinburgh, a few years since, by causing a fish, as it were, to speak to its owner." After the vendor affirmed it was fresh and had just been caught that morning, the fish quickly interjected: "It is false. I am a week older."[32]

Soon after his return from Jamaica in 1804, James (calling himself "Mr. Rannie, the Elder") introduced New York City audiences to what he called a

"Philosophical Fish" (figs. 19.3 and 19.4), an automaton programmed to execute many of his deceptions that was based on this episode. In one performance the fish was given a pen to write out any word that was requested of it, including George Washington's name. In another, the automaton drew from a deck several cards that had been previously selected by the audience, thereby astonishing "the scientific observers of this great curiosity."[33] This automaton became a trademark of their exhibitions.[34]

Other entertainers designed automatons to mimic quadrupeds and arachnids, to serve meals, or to converse with their audiences; some even miniaturized their figures to serve as "animated" models enacting well-known historic events.

Figure 19.2. "THEATRE. Last Night of Performance." In Alexandria, Virginia, Mr. Martin announced the "celebrated rope automaton" representing a boy of six years of age, one of six "mechanical contrivances" he carried to major cities in eastern North America from 1806 through 1811. Other attractions included the "Dutch Landlady," the "Musical Sorcerer," a reversing perpetual motion machine, and fireworks. Martin's events were haunted by mishaps, and he put his "tools" up for sale in New York City in 1811. *Alexandria Gazette,* 10 November 1810. Courtesy, American Antiquarian Society.

Figures 19.3 and 19.4. Two views of James Rannie's "Philosophical Fish," an automaton that played cards with the audience or signed George Washington's and others' names. Rannie selected the design because their trick of "speaking" to fish was described in the *Encyclopedia; or, Dictionary of Arts, Sciences and Miscellaneous Literature,* published in Philadelphia in 1798. Right: "For Two Nights only. MR. RANNIE, THE VENTRILOQUIST, . . . has just arrived from Boston, after finishing sixty nights performances." *Salem Register,* 20 September 1804. Left: "At Washington-Hall, *MR. RANNIE* Will display all the performances introduced on the former evenings." *Salem Gazette,* 25 September 1804. Courtesy, American Antiquarian Society.

F. H. Kallanbach showed audiences in Richmond's coffeehouse in 1818 a mechanical head whose eyes moved "to and fro, with different gesticulations." He also showed a "Mechanical Lizard and Spider, whose formation and movement are so natural that a person not knowing their being mechanical, would take them to be reality."[35] An unidentified proprietor in Charleston in 1820 claimed his figures could dance a hornpipe, play the cudgel, and chase butterflies.[36] Mr. Haddock's "Animated Mechanisms"—or "Androides," as he liked to call them—brought his 1820 audiences in New York City things to eat ("The Fruitery"), made predictions ("The Telegraph"), and served spirits ("The Liquor Merchant"). G. Vogel, a "late Apprentice" to Henri Maillardet, of Neuchâtel, Switzerland, opened an exhibit of clockwork machinery in New York City in 1820 that included his "original Perpetual Motion" display.[37] In Baltimore Charles Duboise—after having worked on it in nearby Fredericktown over a period of four years—showed in 1823 a mechanism called the "Fortunate Lady" (fig. 19.5) that complimented the audience, played checkers and dominoes, demonstrated a love for roses, and circulated a "casket" to collect tips.[38] In 1828, John Maelzel, who later made a name for himself touring Wolfgang von Kempelen's chess-playing automaton, brought to New England his "Conflagration of Moscow," an automaton that employed small moving figures, fireworks to simulate explosions, and some form of incendiary materials to evoke burning. The "Conflagration" was seen by Susanna Holyoke Ward in 1833.[39]

How did these spring-driven and compressed air machines operate? A little can be learned from the woodcuts of Joseph Falconi's "Indian Figure" and "Sagacious Mermaid," both of which are illustrated in his advertisements of 1788, 1794, and 1796. The Indian appears to be just that—a standing figure in the act of drawing back a bowstring with his head lowered slightly to sight the arrow.[40] The automaton seems to have been a three-quarter or half-size figure with most of the operating and driving mechanisms probably housed in its base. Falconi's archer apparently aimed and shot the arrow without the showman's actually touching it—a process possibly triggered by electrical impulses from an assistant. Such intricate actions probably required a complex set of magnetic actuating signals and a battery to store electricity.

Almost nothing is known about the internal parts of Blanchard's artificial beings, especially how they were able to talk and where he kept the drivers and mechanisms of his full-size figures. Maison's promotional texts imply these automatons were free-standing and capable of some kind of untethered movement when they danced. Both feats seem highly improbable. But just five years

Figure 19.5. "GRAND, SUPERB & MAGNIFICENT [a] piece of mechanism, called the *FORTUNATE LADY*." Charles Duboise's automaton was exhibited in Baltimore, Maryland, at a location over the United States Clothing Store. Duboise claimed he invented the machine himself during a four-year residence in nearby Fredericktown. The illustration shows Duboise on the left, the automaton (a life-size woman) on the right; at his bidding, she played checkers, answered questions, and collected money. *Baltimore Patriot,* 9 April 1823. Courtesy, American Antiquarian Society.

earlier, in 1791, von Kempelen had invented a "talking head" in the form of a five-year-old boy that gave answers in a voice that was "soft and agreeable"—suggesting that some kind of voice technology activated by compressed air may have been available by then.[41] And almost nothing is known of the Rannies' fish automaton. Its two modes, one as a writer of famous signatures and the other as a card player, seem incompatible. Images show it suspended in the air, but in all likelihood the fish was supported on the underside by a system of complex driving mechanisms.[42]

Judging from several line cuts illustrating Charles Packard's broadsides and newspaper announcements, the automatons sold or leased to him by Pinchbeck were attached to a box containing the spring-driven clockwork mechanism and system of cams that activated each machine.[43] The "Little Magician . . . of the Turkish type" (fig. 19.6) was mounted on a box equipped with a sliding drawer and what appear to be three bells. (The "wonders" performed by the little magician may have consisted of answering specific questions directed to it by ringing one or another of these bells.) A surviving late eighteenth- or early nineteenth-century European writing automaton, now in the Franklin Institute Science Museum in Philadelphia, follows this basic design in which the base of the figure contains the gears, cams, arms, and pinions that controls its movements (fig. 19.7).[44] The machinery was wound up, an appropriate cam was placed inside, and the automaton was then signaled to respond to specific writing requests.

That some early American automatons were water-driven rather than spring-driven is suggested by contemporary reports circulating in Virginia in the period between 1807 and 1811. According to a local Norfolk historian, an unidentified mechanic installed "an enormous water-powered automaton of figures sawing wood, feeding chickens, and making shoes." The site was one Ducoing's long room, which also exhibited traveling waxworks and Sardi's panharmonicon. While we have no description of this machine or the size of its figures, it may have been modeled after European prototypes such as the water-powered "Mechanical Theatre" installed in a private garden in Salzburg, Austria, about 1750, which moved approximately two hundred figures (each about six inches high) engaged in various occupations.[45]

At the same time, we know that some "speaking" machines were actually acoustical devices relaying the voice of a live operator through concealed tubes. Reputedly conceived by L. Mullert of Germany in the 1780s, these devices had a long history in sixteenth- and early seventeenth-century churches and theaters that allowed "voices" to emanate from wooden or paper religious figures or puppets, or to provide music to inanimate figures celebrating coronations.[46] The only significant improvement consisted of the manufacturer's enhanced skill in hiding the tubes and the speakers behind them. In America these acoustical

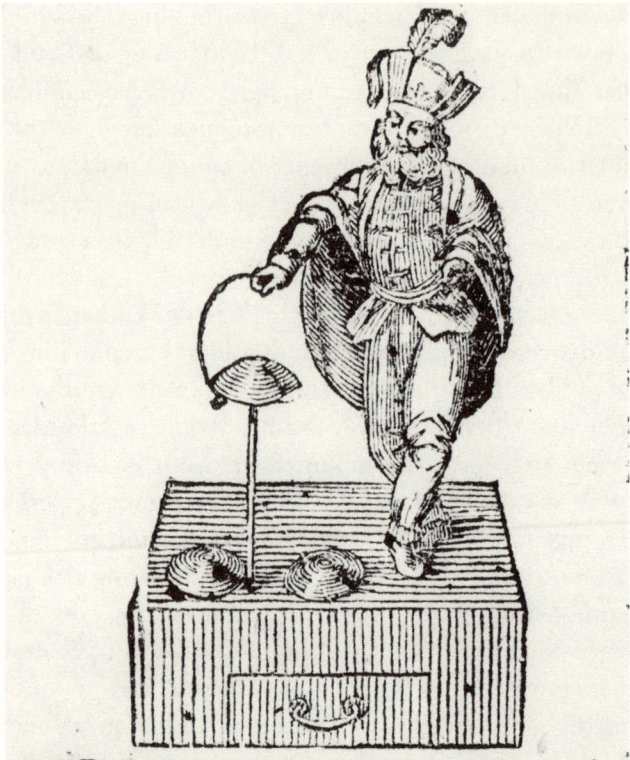

Figure 19.6. "MR. PACKARD, respectfully informs the Ladies and Gentlemen of Portland, and its vicinity, that the *Philosophical and Mechanical MUSEUM,* is open for their reception, at the Columbian Hall." Detail of advertisement with woodcut taken by Charles Packard (fl. 1802–1805) illustrating an automaton, "The little Magician, . . . a foreign philosopher, holding in one hand a magic wan[d]." Portland, Maine. Woodcut. Portland *Eastern Argus,* 15 March 1805. Courtesy, American Antiquarian Society.

devices projected voices from speaking horns, glass boxes, and suspended miniature figures. Audiences posed questions and received answers from what appeared to be a variety of inanimate objects. English balloonist Joseph Deeker introduced this entertainment into America with the "Wax Speaking Figure" shown at his balloon manufacturing workshop at 14 William Street, New York City, in 1789. Deeker's installation was visited that year by Ezra Stiles, who observed that it was "not Ventriloquism but by Tubes." When Deeker left New York City after his balloon failure, the device was taken to Albany by his colleague Samuel Prince, who exhibited it along with wax figures and a "brilliant diamond beetle."[47] Prince then brought it back to New York (where it was seen by George Washington's grandchildren and their friends) and to Providence. At least one speaking figure reached Daniel Bowen's museum in Philadelphia in 1791 where it was shown as a "beautiful Figure of a young lady, suspended by a ribbon."[48]

By 1795 showmen traveling to New York City, New Haven, Charleston, Baltimore, and Boston were demonstrating similar installations, differing only in their names, the gender of the voice that issued from them, and the manner of their promotion. Mr. Robertson's "Wonderful Speaking Automaton" was hung by a string in the middle of the room; Edward Savage's version was a "tiny being five inches high" that danced, laughed, and sang; Joseph Falconi's was a figure thirty inches high suspended by two silken strings.[49] The most widely toured of these acoustical devices was the "Astonishing Invisible Lady," also known as the "Invisible Conversant," the "Acoustic Temple," and the "Incomprehensible Crystal," whose original and subsequent imitations reached Charleston, Richmond, Easton, Wilmington, and Alexandria in the southern states, as well as

Figure 19.7. Detail of the activating mechanism for the writing automaton attributed to Henri Maillardet (1745–1830) of Geneva, Switzerland, working in London, showing the cams (rotating disks), mainspring, winding mechanism, and frame. One of the memory disks still writes: "Ecrit par L'Automate de Maillardet." London, circa 1800. An earlier writing automaton (c. 1767–1774) attributed to Pierre and Henri-Louis Jaquet-Droz is housed at the Musée d'Art et d'Histoire de Neuchâtel, Switzerland. Courtesy, Historical and Interpretive Collections of the Franklin Institute, Philadelphia.

Portland and Newburyport in New England. Charles Packard took along an "Invisible Lady" when he toured his waxworks in New England and Canada in 1805. Dubiously claiming he was the "original inventor of this curiosity . . . and the only one who has brought it to perfection," Packard brought it to eastern New England, New Haven, and New York City.[50] At least one of these acoustical shows involved a moving automaton with its vocalizations surreptitiously piped in. Calling himself a "gentleman from Europe," this entertainer displayed a "Young Lady" in Charleston in 1803 that stood "erect on a richly carved and gilt pedestal, adorned with sundry ornaments—with an elegant green Parrot at her feet." Its voice came in whispers through the customary hidden tubes.[51]

In time more advantage was to be gained from exposing the installations than in selling tickets to them, a tactic that had already been tried by several English publishers who unmasked a French machine at the Capuchin Convent in Paris. It was Packard's former partner and colleague William F. Pinchbeck (possibly the very same mechanic that installed them) who divulged their secrets in his 1805 book on conjuring. He described the usual centerpiece (glass caskets, miniature wax figures, and trumpets), the emblematic devices designed to divert attention from the real source of the voice, and the system of sound-carrying ducts and tubes concealed within a surrounding handrail that led to the actual speaker who was stationed out of sight (fig. 19.8).[52]

Pinchbeck's exposé led to some awkward moments. At Dartmouth's 1805 commencement, a local paper reported "that the deceptions of the 'Magical Temple,' as practiced by Mr. [Philip] Wood, and Co. in this town, during the last commencement, are detected. The singing, conversation, &c of 'The Invisible,' were effected by a young girl concealed in an adjoining room, who spoke through a tube running under the floor, through which it was continued into one of the posts of the frame."[53]

But at least one museum proprietor was prepared. Shortly after Packard returned from his tour of New England and the eastern United States, Daniel Bowen publicized the "Magical Temple *Improved.* Or the Invisible Lady made Visible," which enabled audiences to see the sources of the hidden voice.[54] The refinement added the element of optics to what was now not so much a deception as a scientific demonstration. But once the ruse was known, this approach did not last. John Mix of New Haven attempted to dispose of his "elegant Machine, known by the name of the Invisible Lady and the Invisible Lady made Visible" along with a "complete profile Phisiognotrace Machine."[55] And Charles Packard had in the meantime taken his Astonishing Invisible Lady to Montreal where he exhibited it to what were presumably naive, French-speaking audiences.[56]

More than any other occupation in the postrevolutionary period, exhibiting automatons was a field dominated by foreign craftsmen with English, French, German, Swiss, and Italian backgrounds. All fifty showmen circulating with automatons in the United States between 1788 and 1825 relied on European-built machines or were themselves Europeans, like Pinchbeck and Blanchard, with extensive technical training. (The only exception was a North Carolina exhibitor wanted for horse stealing whose "Automaton Figure" was never identified.)[57] By far the majority of showmen cited previous engagements at European capitals and major cities such as Edinburgh, London, Dublin, Vienna, Paris, and Hamburg. Other had just come from the courts of Spain and Portugal. Many simply claimed their machine had just come "from the chief Courts of Europe."[58]

The length of time automatons took in crossing from Europe to the New World, however, remained long. Mr. Perrette's self-moving carriage came to Boston with Blanchard's group after touring France and England for ten years. Pinchbeck's "Fair Arithmetician" and "Indian Oracle" came after years of being shown at the family's workshop and at Astley's circus in London. Mr. Martin's automaton dancer and

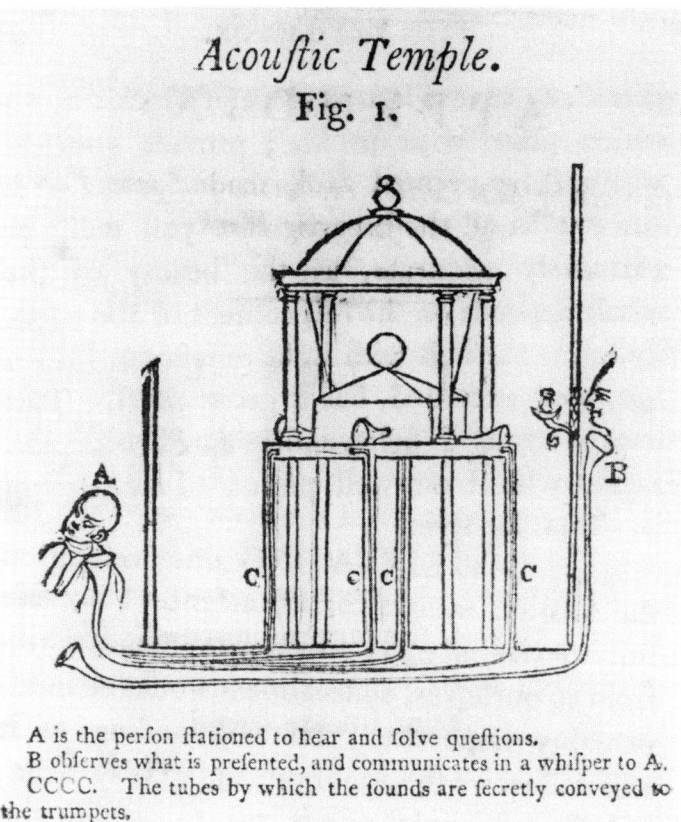

Figure 19.8. "*Acoustic Temple*. Fig. 1." Diagrammatic view of the "temple" showing the hidden sound ducts used to convey whispers from the observer (B) to the speaker (A) and from the speaker to the audience. From William F. Pinchbeck (fl. 1795–1819), *Expositor* (Boston, 1805), figure 1. Woodcut. Courtesy, American Antiquarian Society.

balancer came years following its being exhibited in European capitals. Maillardet's collection stayed in London from 1801 to 1820 before his apprentice, G. Vogel, finally displayed it in New York City. Maelzel's "Conflagration of Moscow," conceived shortly after the 1812 disaster, entertained the English metropolis and other European capitals for sixteen years before it arrived in Providence in 1828. And some machines stayed abroad in private or state collections. Vaucanson's fabled 1739 grain-digesting duck remained in Europe and Russia touring until it apparently ended up many years later as payment for a workman's wages.[59] The full-size mechanical elephant (it ate and drank on command and circulated in Paris in 1810 with "mechanical persons" on its back playing various instruments) never made it to North America.[60] No doubt as exciting as Captain Crowninshield's real one, this automaton may have been too cumbersome to move. But there was one exception to this rule. After a delay of fifty-five years, von Kempelen's chess-playing "automaton" finally toured North America in 1826—though in this case at least part of the wait was caused by the difficulty of finding chess masters who were small enough to fit inside the machine.[61]

Chapter 20

Penmanship Schools

THE EXPLOSION of popular culture released its full force in the movement to improve American penmanship in the early nineteenth century. These schools flourished under the direction of itinerant writing-masters active between 1805 and 1825—a period of time roughly comparable to the rise and dominance of the physiognotrace. Although this movement was late in starting and remained in its prime for a relatively short period of time, when measured by the number of its teachers and pupils, it grew at an astonishing rate. Using mass-marketing and system-oriented promotional methods, founders of penmanship schools set in motion a process in which students taking lessons one week were passing themselves off as "Professors of Chirography" and "Writing Masters" the next. Beginning with a single itinerant penmanship teacher in America in the 1790s, the field mushroomed to at least 179 full-time teachers in the American East before 1826, many of them working in large urban centers. They attracted thousands of aspiring students from undereducated but ambitious segments of the population, who came to believe that by improving their penmanship they would find an opportunity to advance themselves socially and professionally.

By most accounts, the founder of simplified or rapid penmanship instruction in America was John Jenkins (1755–1823; fig. 20.1), who devised a teaching procedure using six basic pen strokes to form all letters rather than twenty-six complete letters of the alphabet.[1] Little is known about Jenkins's background. A family record written by him in 1803 documents that he was married to Abigail Hall and was the father of six children, four of whom survived infancy. The family apparently lived in Westchester County, New York. His widow's application for a spouse's pension attests to his service in the Revolutionary War.[2]

Jenkins began as a teacher of penmanship in Bennington, Vermont, in 1789.[3] Shortly thereafter, he published *The Art of Writing, Reduced to a Plain and Easy System,* a manual containing thirty-two pages of instruction as well as copperplate engravings of writing samples (fig. 20.2). Printed in Boston by Isaiah

Thomas in 1791, the volume was immediately endorsed by educators. Booksellers put it on sale in Connecticut with certifications from Reverend Ezra Stiles and Noah Webster; booksellers in Rhode Island claimed over fifty recommendations including the president of Providence College.[4] In August 1794, John Jenkins and Daniel Hall (possibly a brother-in-law) opened a school in New York City "for the sole purpose of instructing youth and others in the art of penmanship agreeable to Jenkins's system lately published in Boston." This is the earliest known subscription school for systematic penmanship in America, and it may have been the only one of its kind for almost a decade. Before long, Jenkins took his school to other locations, beginning the "itinerant and moving course of life" later noted by his critics. One was advertised in 1797 in Berlin, Connecticut; a second in 1797 in nearby New London; and a third in 1799 in

Figure 20.1. *Jenkins,* by Peter Maverick (1780–1831). Inscribed below: "P. Maverick." New Jersey, circa 1810. John Jenkins (1755–1823), the founder of systematic penmanship, issued the third edition of his book at a time when he was still struggling for professional recognition. Engraved plate from John Jenkins, *Art of Writing* (Andover, Mass.: Flagg and Gould, 1813). Courtesy, Houghton Library, Harvard University, 005806991.

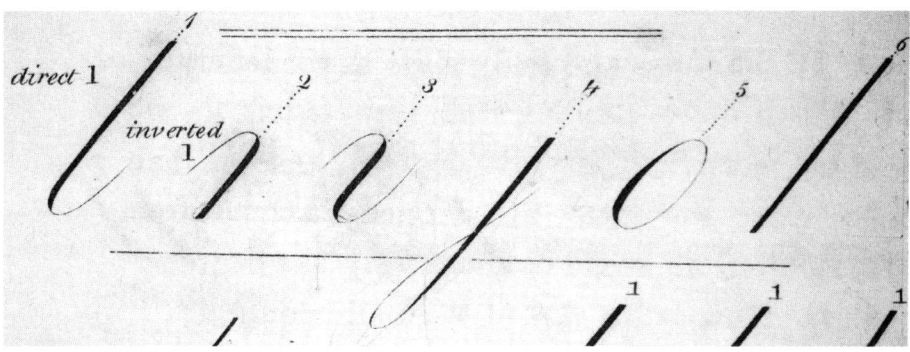

Figure 20.2. "THE PRINCIPAL STROKES." The six strokes of John Jenkins's writing system were copied and adapted by so many American penmanship teachers that Jenkins was nearly driven out of business. Only one teacher credited him for his discovery. From John Jenkins, *Art of Writing* (Andover, Mass.: Flagg and Gould, 1813). Courtesy, Houghton Library, Harvard University, 005806991.

Salem. The schools did well, and Jenkins had every expectation of a promising and profitable career.[5]

It was at that point that competitors attracted to Jenkins's methods began imitating him. One was Henry Dean, a copperplate engraver based in Salem, Massachusetts. On 15 April 1803, Dean advertised a school in Salem citing "Master Jenkins's 'entirely new plan,' which has been publicly patronized by upward of one hundred and fifty respectable characters." This attracted so many pupils Dean was obliged to recruit an assistant. Two years later Dean published his own 110-page *Analytical Guide to the Art of Penmanship,* which was based on "sections of fundamental letters." Most of it was taken without attribution from Jenkins's manual. In 1807, Dean moved to New York City where he established a permanent school and called himself a "Professor of Penmanship."[6]

The real impetus to popularizing Jenkins's style of penmanship teaching, however, was triggered by Allison (Abel) Wrifford (1779–1844), a man who apparently possessed the charisma ostensibly lacking in Jenkins—especially the gift of converting his pupils into teachers like himself.[7] Wrifford taught for a longer period and entered into more partnerships than Jenkins or any of Jenkins's followers. Like Jenkins, Wrifford rose rapidly to prominence by attracting endorsements from public figures. Raised in Strafford, Vermont, he began his teaching career in nearby Royalton but moved to Boston where he announced on 29 June 1805 that he was giving penmanship lessons to the children of three prominent families there and was willing to instruct other students. Wrifford was still young—in his mid-twenties—but he cited his previous experience, perhaps fictitious, of having taught for a "long time" in Canada.[8]

After a year in Boston, it was Wrifford's turn to take his penmanship course on the road. Calling himself a professor of "chirography," he let a room in a Portland tavern where he promised to teach pupils "a fair and legible hand" in under four weeks. The school thrived. A month later Wrifford set up a similar school in Portsmouth and taught a circuit that included, among other locations, Newburyport, Salem, Washington, D.C., and Providence. His classes were sometimes dogged by controversy over his plagiarism of Jenkins's methods, but he overcame doubts by projecting a confident tone. He persuaded the publisher of the *New-Hampshire Gazette* to herald his arrival with a short puff signed by "A Friend to Merit," which glowingly praised his abilities. He also perfected his ability to communicate to people what they most wanted to hear. He told parents that rote practice in itself would never improve handwriting—children needed experienced instruction. He told young men that penmanship was "an elegant accomplishment, which is becoming all the fashion, taste, and style"; he told female pupils they would learn a style that was "inimitably delicate, soft, and beautiful." Storekeepers, merchants, clerks, and apprentices were assured they would acquire a "good mercantile hand."[9]

Like Jenkins, Wrifford depended on letters of recommendation from well-known clergymen, teachers, and lawyers. His classes in Boston were backed by certificates from "Gentlemen in Cambridge." Those in Portland, Newburyport, Salem, Roxbury, and Providence were endorsed by the governor of New Hampshire.[10] But he may also have used less scrupulous methods to advance his career. When introducing himself in Boston in 1805, he seems to have fabricated a "penmanship teacher" named E. Rowse who announced an evening school to teach "Mr. Wrifford's new method of writing," pointing out his experience in the "first houses of London." After waiting a few days, Wrifford himself responded: "I cannot help noticing an advertisement I saw in Wednesday's *Centinel*. . . . There seems to be an essential point wanting, which Mr. R. may find would be of real use to him, viz a knowledge of the method himself." Keeping in mind Wrifford's own gift for language and dramatic prose, he may have invented "E. Rowse" [arouse] to elicit the attention of Boston newspaper readers.[11]

Once having established himself, Wrifford founded semipermanent schools in Boston, Salem, and Newburyport. He then published the first of five penmanship manuals, a step that enabled other teachers to base their teachings on his "principles." Wrifford is known to have made at least two southern trips, visiting Baltimore in 1819 and Charleston in 1824. In Baltimore he addressed other teachers, specifically stating that "Instructors, who may wish to acquire a *Systematic Knowledge of Chirography*—and particularly how to teach it to the best advantage in their schools, can be accommodated, on terms as may be agreed."[12] Wrifford also went on the lecture circuit. In Norfolk, Virginia, in 1819, he encountered northerner William Dunlap, who wrote in his diary that Wrifford had lectured to an almost empty hall but characterized him as shrewd and eccentric. Dunlap seemed to like him: "He is a singer & has a noble voice."[13]

Wrifford's influence was enhanced by his former pupils who entered the field as teachers. Amos Perley implemented "Mr. Wrifford's method of writing" in Salem in 1810.[14] George Dean held a "Wrifford Writing School" in Salem in 1811.[15] "A. Brown, a pupil of Wrifford," began teaching at the Deerfield Academy in Deerfield, Massachusetts, in 1812.[16] George Allen offered a school in penmanship based on the "systems of either Towne or Wrifford" in New Haven in 1813.[17] Altogether, at least fourteen penmanship teachers before 1820 in New England were citing Wrifford's methods, adopting his texts, or traveling with him as partners or assistants. Like Wrifford, these assistants published their own manuals—as did their assistants and pupils. They seem to have divided themselves into two camps. One, led by "Professor of Penmanship" Nathan Towne (1787–1812) of New York City, published a manual titled *A New Set of Round and Running Hand Copies* (1811), used by at least three teachers traveling within the Hudson River region and western and central Connecticut.[18] A second group were followers of Benjamin H. Rand (1792–1862), who eventually settled in Philadelphia. They relied on Rand's publication—*A New and Complete System of Mercantile Penmanship and New Invention of Running Hand* (1814)—to teach an "improved method" of cursive writing.[19] In the years from 1818 to 1823, no fewer than ten penmanship teachers utilizing Rand's texts were circulating in the areas where Rand had worked with Wrifford.[20]

In some instances the training of new teachers was measured in hours. James Guild, who worked about two years as a penmanship teacher in New York and Vermont, said he had received only thirty hours of instruction before he advertised his first school in Middlebury in a local paper where he called himself a "professor." As soon as he ended one school, Guild headed to a new community to start another. If he learned that a writing-master had recently been there, he moved on. He stayed ahead of his students by studying systems promoted by "Towns, Ginkens, Rans, Rifford, and Dean"; by committing key sections to memory; and by reciting verbatim the "rules" and correct nomenclature of chirography.[21] Guild's admission allows us to separate the "active bearers"—meaning those whose efforts focused primarily on creating writing-masters—from those who simply taught penmanship. To Guild's list of Nathan Towne, John Jenkins, Benjamin H. Rand, Allison Wrifford, and Henry Dean we can add Daniel H. Leonard and Leader Dam, who are both known to have repeatedly teamed with partners and apprentices. These seven, representing under 4 percent of the 179 known American writing-masters, all published instruction manuals and were the creative fulcrum in the field (see tables 1.1 and 1.2).

All but forgotten in this process, John Jenkins was left to pick up what scraps he could. When Jenkins came to Salem in 1808, he requested help from Reverend William Bentley to begin a class in penmanship: "Mr. Jenkins with me about his practice of Penmanship. I signed a recommendation. This man hit upon some expedients which in substance have been printed by Dean & many years ago published his first part which fell into obscurity. Dean has made his work profitable."[22]

In 1809, Jenkins was in Boston advertising "upwards of twenty-six years of his experience in different parts of the Union." In 1811, he was back again in Boston, and this time he was reduced to informing readers that his method had received "Mr. Wrifford's acknowledgement."[23] As a dearth of paying students closed in on him, Jenkins attempted to fight back. In the 1813 edition to his *Art of Writing*, he cited a letter from a student who had been taught by Allison Wrifford. This student had "critically" examined Jenkins's system and declared it his "conviction, that A. Wrifford has purloined and adopted every important and essential principle of Mr. Jenkins' system, and that his deviations have been made apparently to evade the direct charge of plagiarism."[24] Wrifford, for his part, repeatedly denied Jenkins's claim that he had plagiarized Jenkins's teaching methods and found himself locked in a long and bitter rivalry. Finally Wrifford asserted that the only reason anyone gave Jenkins credence was that he "had been extremely efficacious" in spreading his system during "an itinerant and moving course of life in the Northern States."[25] Wrifford assured the public he had never met Jenkins or read his book—adding that Jenkins "was no more the author of our mode of instruction, than he is of Christianity, or Methodism."[26]

In the ever-growing competition for students, penmanship and shorthand instructors left few promotional methods untried. Teachers of a vertical style advocated an "anti-angular system." Teachers of a cursive writing hand promised their pupils they would never again have to "take off the pen in the turns or curves." J. Sheffield, who called himself a "Finishing Writing Master," published a sample of a pupil's improvements in a newspaper advertisement, filling the center portion of an eight-inch column with illegible handwriting and displaying below it a legible sample by the same hand after ten lessons.[27]

Like all carriers of popular culture, penmanship teachers undertook their vocation possessing skills in other areas, some closely allied to penmanship but others entirely unrelated. Henry Dean had a background in copperplate printing. James Guild, Justus Da Lee, and John James Trumbull Arnold were competent miniature painters and eventually became well known in the field. J. Sheffield taught theorem painting on velvet, a technique that used stencils to make images. C. R. B. Claflin of Southborough, Massachusetts, was a calligrapher. E. Cobb was a teacher of English grammar, and Leader Dam became a Boston pharmaceutical merchant. A Mr. Holyroyd taught stenography, while E. Darling instructed his students in how to write inscriptions on paintings and maps. N. D. Gould combined penmanship lessons with a music school as William Tilley offered to inscribe satin mourning pieces and paper family registers. Jerveys C. Smyth, who opened stenography schools in Salem, Newburyport, and Portland in 1806 and 1807, was an accomplished fencing-master. Phinehas Bailey (1787–1861; see fig. 5.4) taught shorthand in northern New England and simultaneously served as a Congregational minister in the towns of East Berkshire and Charleston, Vermont. (Bailey also issued a stenographic text in Montpelier, Vermont, in 1820, which went through four editions.)[28]

But, as with other itinerants, it is hard to know now whether a given penmanship teacher was a gifted instructor or simply a well-traveled trickster. The case of Mr. and Mrs. Daniel Hewett provides conflicting data but serves as an indication that some itinerants were operating close to the legal edge. A native of Massachusetts and possibly a graduate of Brown University, Daniel Hewett (d. 1856) was the author of two penmanship manuals, a shorthand manual, an innovative compilation of early American newspapers, and a textbook on American geography.[29] Beginning in Charleston in 1818, Hewett ran a series of penmanship schools in about a dozen major eastern cities, serving several hundred to a thousand pupils at each location.[30] He collaborated closely with his wife, who held separate classes for women. The Hewetts initially charged one dollar for a course of fourteen lessons, which they later raised to two dollars. They almost always advised the public they would remain in each city only a few months while also insisting that it was "customary to receive the small amount of tuition when a Scholar commences writing."[31]

As they neared New England, however, the couple revealed signs that they had taken on more responsibilities than they could handle. Having completed a writing school located opposite St. Paul's Church in New York City in April 1820 (where they claimed they had left seven hundred satisfied scholars in Baltimore and eight hundred in Philadelphia), they continued to Albany, Boston, Portsmouth, and Newburyport. But when they got to Providence in October 1820, the couple apparently changed their names to "J. Hammond and Mrs. Hammond." Three weeks later they were in New Haven again as "D. Hewett," then back in Providence as "J. Hammond" or "John Hammond" on 2 November. In Albany they were "I. I. Harmon" on 14 November, and in Newport, Rhode Island, on 25 November they advertised as "Samuel Hall." Their final New England stop was in Hartford (as "I. Hammond") in December 1820 where they declared that their pupils now numbered "four thousand." While it is reasonable to assume that the Hewetts sometimes hired subordinates to help them teach, it is unlikely that their names all began with the letters "Ha—." In each locale the advertising copy was identical, which makes it likely they were assuming new names to allow them the liberty—if they chose to do so—of leaving town with impunity after collecting the first round of their tuition.[32]

The Hewetts' ethical standards notwithstanding, most penmanship teachers worked diligently. A former pupil and assistant of Allison Wrifford, Daniel H. Leonard made extended forays into southern Connecticut and southeastern

Massachusetts, sometimes revisiting a community after a decade. In 1810 and again in 1811, he boarded at a Mr. Otis's in New London while giving a course of fifteen two-hour lessons in a "convenient" nearby room. He also proposed holding a class at the upper end of the street provided a sufficient number of scholars applied. Like Wrifford, he set up franchises and profited handsomely from them. And like Wrifford, he turned his pupils into teachers of his method. A few weeks after Leonard left New Bedford in 1810, Cephas Cushman conducted a penmanship school "upon the principles of Mr. Jenkins, as lately taught in this town by Mr. Leonard."[33]

Leonard's class roster reflects a highly concentrated schedule. In 1820, he taught six classes of twenty-four lessons in running hand on Nantucket Island (fig. 20.3a and b). Each lesson was two hours long. His first class began at 5 a.m., and its students consisted of a sea captain, three other men, and a woman. Leonard's second two-hour class started at 8 a.m. and was attended by two women and six men. A third class of six men and one woman convened at 10 a.m. After lunch, at 1 p.m., Leonard taught a fourth class of nine women and one man. At 4 p.m. he met his fifth class of six men and three women. After dinner, at 7 p.m., he gave a final evening class to seven men. In all, Leonard instructed forty-six scholars, each one six times a week for four weeks. He charged a fee of $5.00 from those who took the entire twenty-four lessons; $2.50 from those who took twelve. He received a vest from one student named J. Averell in lieu of the money; Leonard himself contracted to pay Jethro Macy three dollars for the use of the writing room. The course finished, and Leonard left Nantucket Island and resumed his travels in southeastern New England. In time, Leonard's efforts paid off. About two decades after his visit to Nantucket he removed from Sharon to Royalton, Vermont, where he retired and purchased surrounding farms for his children.[34]

Penmanship instruction differed from most other itinerated employments practiced in America before 1826. Nearly all of its teachers, including the founder of the six-stroke system, were American-born. In other words, its entire history was a distinctively American phenomenon like psalmody, only a little more so. The only two exceptions were William Milns (1761–1801), an English graduate of Oxford University, and Godfrey Dorfeuille, a Frenchman teaching German and English penmanship in Philadelphia in 1796, both of whom began their American careers seven years after Jenkins and Hall had initiated the movement.[35] This American exclusiveness can be juxtaposed against a stratified English society where schooling included writing skills for both young men and women. The phenomenon flourished in the heady and political atmosphere of postrevolutionary life. The claims that Wrifford offered to his students—that rote practice in itself would never improve handwriting, that female pupils would learn a style that was soft and beautiful, that apprentices would acquire a "good mercantile hand"—spoke to a society that was in transition and looking for anything to help pull itself up by its bootstraps.

In the end, "systematized" penmanship was probably more significant as a method of transmitting popular culture than as a way of improving handwriting. A movement that began with John Jenkins's orthographic discovery soon turned

Figures 20.3a and b. "Nantucket 2nd Course Commenced Sept 4, 1820." Names of subscribers to Daniel H. Leonard's school of penmanship, Nantucket, Massachusetts. Leonard's classes began at 5 a.m. and concluded at 9 p.m. He had forty-six scholars. Manuscripts, two sheets, each 8 by 12 inches. Courtesy, Dartmouth College Library.

his students and imitators into penmanship teachers, who in turn instructed others to do the same. Aspiring pupils, young and old, latched onto Jenkins's ideas during the first two and a half decades of the nineteenth century—gathering temporary schools of up to eight hundred or a thousand pupils—numbers almost equal to those who lined up to have their profiles cut by physiognotrace operators. This generated a process in which penmanship teachers were constantly moving into rooms just left by a competitor, continually forming and dissolving assistantships and partnerships, and repeatedly using or abusing each other's systems, texts, and names in confusing and sometimes circular chains of promotion aimed at attracting new students. At varying points in their careers Henry Dean taught a penmanship school "using Jenkins's method"; John Jenkins established his on a technique which received "Mr. Wrifford's acknowledgement"; Allison Wrifford used a system based "on the same principles [as]" a Mr. Parkhurst and Augustus G. P. Colburn; Colburn founded his on the methodology of Benjamin H. Rand; and Rand implemented a program "as practiced by Mr. Wrifford."[36] Within months Leader Dam and Enoch Noyes were following "Rockwell's System," and Edmund Colburn was basing his classes on "Rand's system."[37] Things got so confusing that a Providence teacher preparing to open a new school in 1819 promised to teach penmanship "on Wrifford's, Dam's, Jenkins', Randall's, or the common method."[38] The self-replicating process of American popular culture was running amok.

Conclusion: America Comes of Age

Part 1: Fading Carnival Texts in American Popular Culture

THE WHOLESALE Eurocentrism of strolling and itinerant life in Boston described by English actor John Bernard in 1811 provides a starting point for understanding the emergence of American-style popular culture. Whatever else early itinerants in North America may have done to attract patrons and clients, most remained traffickers of traditional European entertainments and practices, or the latest in European arts and innovations. Itinerant portrait painters, tavern entertainers, French language teachers, dancing-masters, and even prizefighters introduced into an American setting many of the European conventions that had been left behind during the transfer of a European presence to North America or had arrived but atrophied. Working a network of Atlantic ports of call, these individuals reconstituted European perspectives where time and distance had weakened them. What was "curious" or "in the newest style" or "moving" or "historical" was described as just having crossed the Atlantic from London, Edinburgh, Dublin, Paris, Amsterdam, Hamburg, Rome, or Vienna—and even from the eastern portions of the Mediterranean.[1] And more than merely being indebted to Europe, the artists, teachers, and entertainers who endured the risks and discomforts of an Atlantic passage to reach American audiences were in most cases trying to recreate a Europe for themselves in the New World—seeking in American towns and villages the patronage they had formerly enjoyed at traditional fairs and during carnival days. Some had exhausted their drawing power among Europe's aristocracy; others, who had previously been near the tops of their professions in the European capitals, came to revive their careers. But once in America, all took calculated advantage of their transatlantic origins, holding Europe out as a cultural model by which they discouraged competitors and attracted clients and audiences.

By 1820, however, a European background was no longer essential or even preferable for success. As urban-oriented itinerancy began to wane in Jacksonian and antebellum America, show people, teachers, and artists alike moved westward away from the Atlantic ports of entry and came into contact with the remote valleys and uplands of rural America, the adjacent areas of the Louisiana Purchase, and the trans-Appalachian West. Here Europe was held in much less esteem than in the eastern cities, and as a result, traveling entrepreneurs gradually discarded their European aura and assumed what might be called "American" characteristics. Portrait painters and profile artists working in South Carolina and Georgia—who earlier had called themselves "Italian" or from "several European countries"—now promoted themselves as coming from Baltimore, New York, or Boston.[2] One painter in Charleston blithely maintained he was lately "from Martinique."[3] Another painter told people in Columbia, South Carolina, he was from Virginia.[4] A third, profilist Frederick Spencer, informed residents of Augusta, Georgia, that he would devote a week to them "on his return from Louisville."[5] Some midwestern painters even publicized the local communities where their paintings had been welcomed (for example, the Kentucky townships of Washington, Frankfort, and Lexington).[6] These were catchphrases previously unheard of in early American portrait advertising. This homebred perspective also permeated forms of entertainment. Mr. Dwyer's humorous "Lecture on Heads"—given from memory at Philadelphia's Pavilion Theatre in 1819—was "rendered suitable to an American Audience."[7]

The conversion of Europe's popular culture into an "indigenous" American one had been going on for some time. Since the early 1770s, equestrians and trick riders—both men and women—featured themselves as "Americans." Christopher H. Gardner, a trick rider who entertained in Providence in 1774, liked to posture himself as the "original *American* Rider."[8] Thomas Pool made similar claims in 1786, saying he was the "first American that ever exhibited the following Equestrian Feats of Horsemanship."[9] A Mr. Langley, who variously joined Ricketts's and Lailson's circus troupes in the period 1796 to 1799 called himself "the only American Equestrian."[10] A Mrs. Redon identified herself in 1812 as "a native of New York" and "the first American lady that has attempted the art of Horsemanship."[11] Other performers were just as persistent. Acrobat Mr. Bennett, who alternately designated himself as being "from London and Italy" or "from Canada," sometimes—if the circumstances called for it—termed himself an American. (William Bentley took him to task on that account in the privacy of his diary.)[12] Acrobat Sieur Carli's apprentice was always stereotyped as "the Young American"—as were some theatrical actors, stage dancers, and children skilled in oratory (such as Master Barrett, "the young American Roscius").[13]

In some instances an itinerant's American identity was superimposed on an existing European one. According to the two men who discovered him in 1786, the reputed 228-year-old hermit found in a cave in the Allegheny Mountains claimed he had been a commoner involved with a nobleman's daughter in

Figure 21.1. "An Account of the Wonderful *Old Hermit's Death,* and Burial." The woodcut shows the self-appointed investigator Dr. Samuel Brake reading the hermit's writing as the latter drinks the rum that later killed him. The hermit was reputedly aged 228. Broadside. Boston?: Ezekiel Russell? 1787? Courtesy, American Antiquarian Society.

London. Forced to leave England, he sailed for Italy in 1580 and was shipwrecked and ended up in a cave in Virginia. The hermit's story was first published in 1787 as a broadside with a colored cut of the moment of discovery (fig. 21.1). That same year, Isaiah Thomas issued his twelve-page chapbook history of the "American" hermit that was followed by at least five reprints in Boston, Portsmouth, Middletown, Norwich, and New Haven. Daniel Bowen, the printer of the New Haven edition, went on to create the first wax statue of the hermit, which he installed in his Philadelphia museum in 1789. Later entrepreneurs followed suit, one staging the hermit being "shaved" by a barber in 1796.[14]

In another case, the "Famous American Game Chicken," a prizefighter who challenged Boston-area opponents in 1810, followed a style that reverberates to this day. His match against an Irish pugilist named Thomas Ryan had to be postponed because Boston's selectmen forced a last-minute change in venue by informing the town's inn holders that any house of entertainment extending the use of its premises for the fight would immediately lose its license. The host, a Colonel Delacroix, hastily relocated the match to his own boxing school, and according to his detailed 27 February 1810 advertisement in the *New-England Palladium,* he promised it would prove to be "the handsomest set-to ever exhibited." The combatants were "to be gloved" and "wear armlets to prevent the possibility of danger." Both were permitted seconds and bottle holders, but the judges were not to allow more than sixty seconds between each round. The posting concluded by stating that the Game Chicken was prepared to spar with any gentleman wishing to do so, that songs and music were to be played as usual, and that after the fight a formal fencing exhibition would take place between two masters.[15]

But who actually was the "Famous American Game Chicken"? Newspapers in Philadelphia and London indicate he had taken the name of an English prizefighter from Bristol called Henry or "Hen" Pearce (1777–1809), who referred to himself as "Pearce, the Game Chicken" in an extended English career as a walkabout pugilist working a circuit of taverns, fighting rings, and sparring schools. Pearce's namesake—perhaps an expatriate English- or Irishman or even an American—appropriated his predecessor's epithet but added "Famous" and "American" to it.[16] He is now remembered for his imaginative burlesque of other prizefighters and the likelihood his attire, or "colors," mimicked the appearance and attitude of a fighting bird.[17] After one or two bouts the "Famous American Game Chicken" subsequently fell into the anonymity that characterized street culture in the early nineteenth century.

But the recharacterization of popular culture as American went much further than name changes and shifting advertising texts. To understand the heart of American acceptance or rejection of a European state of mind, it is necessary to go back to Carl W. von Sydow's concept of the selective movement of culture. Old European assumptions about society and culture—including ones that underlay collective memory and medieval healing practices—had been eroding for a long time in the English-speaking American colonies and were no longer current in the second half of the eighteenth century. This reinforces our initial premise that some European folkloric, carnivalesque, and healing customs either did not accompany early European immigrants or came but did not endure.

Once again, the American response to Dr. Anthony Yeldall is revealing. This mountebank found that local authorities and legislatures in four British colonies had enacted laws restricting his medical activities. In 1771, New York City kept him from entering. In 1772, New Jersey and Massachusetts suppressed all mountebanks and unlicensed medical hawkers. In October 1773, the Connecticut legislature stipulated that any pharmaceutical supplier erecting a stage "to declaim to and harangue the people on the virtue or efficacy of their medicines" would be fined twenty pounds, the money going to the county.[18] Just two weeks after that legislation was enacted, Yeldall's party was arrested in Preston, Connecticut, on 14 October 1773 and charged as "strollers and idlers." Yeldall hired a lawyer, and after a short trial, Yeldall and his apprentice Handley were acquitted, but the journeyman McDonald was sentenced to fifteen days' confinement in the workhouse. Yeldall's lawyer argued to no avail that any imprisonment as a delinquent was illegal, especially "as sufficient bail was offered." McDonald served his time while Yeldall and Handley waited for their assistant to be freed.[19]

But as soon as McDonald was able to rejoin them, the three stopped in Canterbury, Connecticut—a town located just north of Preston—and again set up their stage. Here a local clergyman, "imagining he could outshine the Doctor in oratory, mounted the rostrum and began his own oration with great volubility." No doubt this cleric had heard of Yeldall's trial and thought he could gain some standing by engaging him in a debate. What they discussed is not recorded. But, according to the newspaper's account, after the physician had "recovered from the surprise that this extraordinary event put him in, he attacked the Minister, and after a warm and learned contest, victory declared in favour of the Doctor."[20]

A corresponding development began to impact the careers of tooth-puller/puppeteers and tooth-puller/acrobats who were just beginning (or resuming) their tours of the new United States in the 1780s in the postrevolutionary period. According to Peter Burke, the traditional folkloric practice of combining showmanship and dental surgery was still observed in Dublin and rural England (as well as in Russia, France, and Germany), where entertainers attracted the notice of audiences that could not afford (or who mistrusted) trained physicians and then stepped up to provide the services themselves.[21] One American tooth-puller was Mr. Bayly, also known as the "Old Artist" or "Doctor Bailey," who attempted to revive his puppeteering career in Baltimore in 1781 and 1782. To help pay his bills, he continued to "extract teeth with a *touch* as usual," as he had done earlier in New York City. His health failing, however, he relinquished the show to Jacob Henninger who made no mention of tooth-drawing.[22] Another was John Templeman, who had probably learned both wirewalking and surgical dentistry as part of his European training as an acrobat. When permission for an acrobatic exhibition was denied him by Boston's selectmen in 1782, Templeman decided to focus his career on "setting" teeth rather than on performing "balancing" acts. This was no easy choice for an ambitious man who could expect to make money in both fields.[23] A few years later Irish showman and wire dancer John Brenon seems to have faced the same decision when he appeared in Philadelphia and New York City in 1786 and 1787. In his initial advertisements at Duplessis's Long Room and Corre's City Tavern, Brenon promised spectators his services as a dental-surgeon: "Said Brenon cures the Toothache without drawing.—No Cure no Pay. For the Poor Gratis." But like Bayly and Templeman before him, Brenon soon abandoned this dual vocation, making no further mention of curing toothache after leaving New York City even in several lengthy advertisements in Litchfield, Middletown, and Boston.[24] American audiences were not of a mind to accept medical services from acrobats any more than they were from conjurers.

Concurrently, other traditional links tying popular culture to medical skills began to break down. Dr. Isaac Calcott, the German-trained physician who spent four years in the British colonies, based his entire American career on a centuries-old medical belief that his birth as a seventh son of a seventh son could effect miraculous cures. This conviction still held some currency in the eighteenth-century Western world, especially in England, France, and Germany, but it was not generally taken seriously in North America—"Seventh Son" more commonly appeared as the name of an American-built sailing vessel than a type of medical practitioner.[25] Memories of it did persist, however. Boston schoolteacher John Tileston (1735–1826), for example, noted in his diary in 1765 that "Mrs. Leach [was] del[ivere]d of the 7th son, successively."[26] In 1773, the concept came under fire; two editorial pieces published in Connecticut attacked it at the time Calcott was beginning to advertise in Hartford. One satirically called Calcott a "hero" descended from the great Paracelsus; a second flatly stated he was "poorly acquainted with the machinery of the human body."[27] By the next decade the concept of seventh sons as healers had been ethnically and racially stereotyped in North America and passed along to African American household slaves and to French-Canadian immigrants in northern New England. In 1782, Elizabeth Porter Phelps twice took her African American slave Phillis to Dr. Eliakim Arms: "Thursday [7 February] my husband and I up to Mr. Arams's at Muddy Brook, he is a seventh son—we took Phyllis with us—think she has a Kings evil. . . . Thursday [28 February] . . . This day my Husband carried Phillis up to a part of Deerfield to Dr. Arams to be stroked for her Kings evil. . . . Thursday [7 March] . . . Phillis brought home. . . . Wednesday [7 May 1783] about 2 in the after-noon our Little Negro Girl Phillis expired—she was a very prety Child." Neither Phelps nor her husband, however, ever used him as their own personal physician and only consulted him for Phillis.[28]

Alternative healers were still addressing these issues well into the early decades of the nineteenth century. When wax sculptor and mountebank doctor Joseph Chiappi, established the New Roman Museum in a New York City commercial building in 1812, he carried with him "near *One Hundred and Fifty*" wax statues for exhibitions, later taking them to Philadelphia and Boston. (The Chiappi family, recently from Rome, identified themselves under a variety of names, and they may have arrived in America as a group, but the "family" may also have been simply a father and son who used aliases.)[29] Their exhibitions typically featured biblical scenes, blood-stained soldiers from recent European engagements, and an effigy of the "celebrated" Italian wax artist who made the effigies—as well as a band of musicians, a living tiger, and a mammoth turtle. But after Joseph Chiappi was sued by his Philadelphia landlord for defamation (Chiappi had made a ludicrous waxwork of the landlord, also an Italian immigrant, playing a hand organ), he was forced into bankruptcy and had to forfeit his museum. He fought back by taking out a two-column advertisement in the *New York Mercantile Advertiser* stating that he cured diseases of the eyes and calling himself "Doctor Joseph Chiappi, from Rome, professor of Anatomy, in the College of Ferarra, and of obstetrics, in the Royal Charity Hospital of Carthagena, in

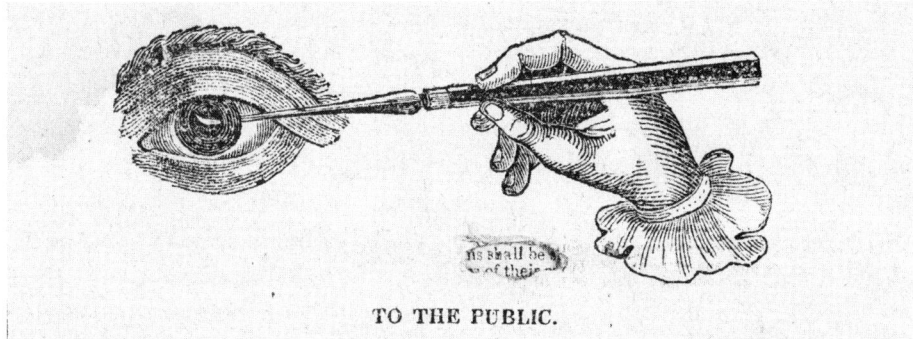

Figure 21.2. "TO THE PUBLIC. DOCTOR JOSEPH CHIAPPI, from Rome, professor of Anatomy." Advertisement by Dr. Joseph Chiappi offering obstetrical and ophthalmological services in New York City after a court verdict took away his livelihood as a waxwork maker and museum entrepreneur. Chiappi and his son later made anatomical wax sculptures for medical students, physicians, and hospitals in eastern cities. *New York Mercantile Advertiser,* 21 September 1813. Courtesy, American Antiquarian Society.

Spain." The advertisement illustrated a handheld lancet removing a cataract from a patient's eye (fig. 21.2), one of the earliest of such prints in an American paper and a bold, unconventional announcement. First seen on 21 September 1813, the advertisement remained in place until January 1815 when the Chiappi family regained their collection and opened their new Washington Museum in Philadelphia. While details are not available, it is likely that Joseph Chiappi's surgical expertise as an obstetrician and cataract surgeon allowed the family to recover its losses. In 1816, "Dr. Joseph Chiappi & Son" moved to Baltimore and began to supply medical students, physicians, and hospitals with anatomical wax models.[30]

America's reluctance to assimilate elements of Europe's traditional folklore was not confined to medical practices. Richard Brickell's lantern shows in the 1740s and 1750s featured characters like Friar Bacon, Dr. Faustus, and the Blind Beggar of Bednal Green—traditional characters from sixteenth- and seventeenth-century dramatic lore that included plays by Robert Greene and Christopher Marlowe.[31] Several variants of the Faust narrative became the plotlines of popular harlequinades in the London theaters. In America, however, when a translation of *Historia von Doctor Johann Fausten* was advertised by a Cornhill publisher in Boston in 1733, the volume targeted an educated, adult audience, not ordinary Americans. "Adorned with cuts," the translation contained biographies of the thirteenth-century English conjurers Friar Roger Bacon and Friar Thomas Bungay and the German conjurer Vandermast, but it was not likely to have been read by anyone in Brickell's audience.[32] Much the same is true of *The Blind Beggar's Daughter of Bednal-Green*—mentioned twelve times in Sybil M. Rosenfeld's 1960 study of eighteenth-century fairground theaters—a story of an English soldier whose eyesight is injured on a French battlefield during the reign of Henry III (1207–72) who amasses a fortune by mendicancy but does not reveal it to his daughter's suitors. Disseminated through ballads and English chapbooks of the seventeenth and eighteenth centuries, the story was first printed in England in 1635, and John Day published a version of *The Blind Beggar* "as it was divers times publickly acted by the Princes Servants" in 1659. Samuel Pepys visited Bednal Green in 1663 to see if anything was left of the blind beggar's house, and Martin Powell, Jr., showed a puppet play version of it in 1726.[33] By contrast, most Americans in the eighteenth century were removed from this tradition. A stage edition of the story was published by Robert Dodsley in Philadelphia in 1777, but again it was intended for intellectuals, not for general readers or children.[34]

James Wyatt's puppet plays and lantern stories may also have been unfamiliar to Americans. In New York, in 1749, Wyatt's puppet show *Maudlin, the Merchant's Daughter of Bristol,* dramatized a pre-Elizabethan legend about a young woman who dresses herself in men's attire to follow her lover into Italy.[35] After being shipwrecked in Algiers, she meets him as he is about to be burned at the stake but turns down a proposal to marry his Algerine captor because she wishes to share her lover's fate and not renounce the Christian religion. The story was printed in London as a ballad in the seventeenth and early eighteenth centuries. Rosenfeld's study indicates the piece was performed repeatedly as a "droll" or puppet play in the 1730s at London's Southwark Fair. But *Maudlin* was never published in America, and few children (or adults) attending Wyatt's production were likely to have heard of it.[36]

The public may also have been unacquainted with Wyatt's *Tragedy of Fair Rosamond*. Loosely based on the life of Rosamond Clifford, a twelfth-century English beauty and mistress of Henry II, fictitiously poisoned by his jealous queen, the story was almost six hundred years old in the 1740s when Wyatt exhibited it in New York City. Known to generations of English storytellers and readers, it had evolved through a succession of folk tales, epic poems, ballads, plays, and fictional chronicles. In the puppet version some of the characters doubled as commedia dell'arte players. (For example, Henry II played Punch, and his wife portrayed Judy.) But *Fair Rosamond,* too, essentially was unpublished in America and appeared only twice in print—as a short ballad in Newport, Rhode Island, in 1746, and as part of a formal history of English concubines printed in Boston, New York City, and Wilmington, Delaware, in 1796.[37]

In some instances, popular English pieces faltered in America until they were resurrected through unusual changes. "The Children in the Wood" also called "The Norfolk Tragedy" had been circulated for several centuries in England as a ballad, entering in the Stationers' Register in 1595 and collected by Thomas Percy in his *Reliques of Ancient English Poetry* before 1765. The ballad was published as a broadside in London in 1695, and prose versions were reproduced extensively in seventeenth- and eighteenth-century English, Irish, and Scottish chapbook histories.[38] In America, however, "The Children in the Wood" was essentially unknown during the seventeenth and the first half of the eighteenth centuries, and the story required rejuvenated publications for it to come to life. Enacted with puppets or magic-lantern "representations" by James Wyatt in New York in 1749, by Joseph Gibbes in Boston in 1768, and by James Maginnis in Portsmouth in 1795 and 1798, each performance was either preceded or followed by published ballad editions.[39]

By this time, however, the story had taken a new direction. Two English arrangers and composers, Thomas Morton (1764–1838) and Samuel Arnold (1740–1802), created a two-act opera in which the children survive, find their parents, and live happily ever after. This operatic version, first offered in Philadelphia in 1794, became a sellout in America and a favorite of theatrical producers.[40] Written variations of the musical script were published in Connecticut, Massachusetts, and New Hampshire. Before long the American promoters of the piece had debased it into a comedy, presenting it as the "much admired Musical Farce" or "new Musical Piece," versions that generated considerable popular appeal. Two "Babes in the Wood" wax figures formed part of Reuben Moulthrop and Nicholas and Elnathan Street's traveling exhibition of waxworks in Baltimore in 1800.[41]

The decline of European carnival traditions in America—and the failure to resurrect or reinvent them—reveals itself in other ways. According to the scholar Terry Castle, masquerade balls were common in London during much of the eighteenth century.[42] These events were promoted by theatrical impresarios, actors, and operatic singers, and were held in public halls and gardens. Costuming based on Harlequin's, Punchinello's, and clergymen's theatrical dress was taken directly from pantomime productions; other favorite costumes included those of the huntress Diana, the devil with his red cape and pitchfork, and anonymous characters wearing the hooded domino. But evidence for these types of public events in America is sparse. Masks or precious-metal mask components were sometimes inventoried as part of a personal estate or included in a shopkeeper's goods. The earliest such citation in the probate records of Suffolk County, Massachusetts, is the "gold mouth ps [piece] for a Mask" listed with the contents of a worked silk purse in the household of John Legg, a Boston merchant and member of the First Church who died in 1733.[43] (Mouthpieces were affixed to masks presumably because they protected wearers from injury from paper or papier-mâché but also because they hid the wearer's lips.) A second mention occurs in the 1757 inventory of Madam Elizabeth Shrimpton Stoddard, whose personal jewels included a "Gold Locket & mask Nob."[44] Both may be linked to the custom of masking at balls, but both are separated from their original purpose in these inventories; they were apparently kept because of the value of gold or because of sentiment. Masks were also for sale. The "17 Masks @ 8d" recorded in Boston shopkeeper John Smith's trade inventory taken in 1768 were listed with decorative arts and jewelry (two London dolls, eighteen paste or garnet pins, and six gross of stringed French beads).[45] Smith's seventeen masks were likely intended for theatrical use or possibly even for masquerades.

Does this suggest that masquerade assemblies were actually held in Boston? Sometime after the British evacuation of that town in March 1776, a New York City newspaper requested that a "Mr. Partridge [Patridge], who was employed last year at Boston, in making masks, is desired to leave word with the printer where he may be found."[46] No further notices appeared, but antipathy against masking was so strong in Boston that even as late as 1809, the town's selectmen voted unanimously against the staging of a masquerade ball, which they deemed "an Amusement so uncongenial to the habits & manners of the Citizens of this place, and so immediately dangerous to the Younger part of the Community."[47] George Labottiere, the French dancing-master who advertised the event in the *New-England Palladium* on 22 December 1809, tried to sell tickets at three dollars per person; no arms, canes, or walking sticks were to be allowed. When the selectmen objected, Labottiere canceled the event and issued a public apology in the newspaper on 3 January 1810, acknowledging that he was "a foreigner and almost a stranger to the stern morality of New England citizens."[48]

Another sign of the ebbing carnival atmosphere in America was the dwindling number of puppeteers after 1800 carrying "Punch comedians"—those bawdy and irreverent characters mocking English life and royalty. After decades of celebrating "Seignior Punchinello and his artificial Company of Comedians," "Mr. Punch and his Merry Family," and "the pleasant tricks of Polichinel," traditional puppeteers like William Patridge, Mr. Bayly, Jacob Henninger, and Domenic Jonoty gave way to showmen with different puppets. James Maginnis introduced his "Magical Lady" and "Old Jonathan"; Peter Blancan, his "American Jockey" and "Spanish Beau"; Mr. Maffey, his "pantomime machinery" whose "inert wood" danced in the style and costumes of nine nations.[49] The last masquerade showman playing in America was a Mr. Green, whose Punch interrogated the royal family in 1807 before allowing Jack Tar to dance a hornpipe and a "drunken Husband" to be scolded by his wife.[50] There the tradition ends. In 1829—after an absence of more than two decades—Mr. Punch did resurface in the United States, but this time with a difference. Whereas earlier commedia dell'arte puppet stories had addressed adult audiences, the unidentified showman who "extended" his "Punch and Judy" show in Providence on 10 February 1829 was touring a children's theater. He termed it "Great Fun" and invited guests to bring their families.[51] The satirically misbehaving and aggressively bawdy old Punchinello, like the stage Harlequin himself, was now largely a memory.

These trends paralleled a weakening in carnival-themed street culture. Frances Trollope noticed it in 1832 when she commented that Americans were burdened with a population entirely "divested of gaiety": "There is no trace of this feeling from one end of the Union to the other. They have no fetes, no fairs, no merry-makings, no music in the streets, no Punch, no puppet-shows."[52] Nathaniel Hawthorne captured this decline when he encountered several rural street entertainers during his tour of the Berkshires in western Massachusetts in 1838. In one instance he watched a street musician at a tavern in western Massachusetts. "After supper," wrote Hawthorne,

> as the sun was setting, a man passed the door with a hand organ, connected with which was a row of figures, such as dancers, pirouetting and twining, a lady playing on a piano, soldiers, a Negro wench dancing and opening and shutting a huge red mouth,—all these keeping time to the lively or slow tunes of the organ. The man had a pleasant but sly dark face; he carried his whole establishment on his shoulder, it being fastened to a staff which he rested on the ground when he performed. . . . He had come over the high solitary mountains where for miles there could hardly be a soul to hear his music.[53]

On another occasion Hawthorne ran into "the old Dutchman," actually German by birth, a peepshow operator who was on his way to central Massachusetts from Saratoga Springs. The old Dutchman called his show a "Diorama," and he addressed everyone in his audience as "Captain." Hawthorne continued,

> We looked through the glass orifice of his machine, while he exhibited a succession of the very worst scratches and daubings that can be imagined, dimmed with tobacco smoke, and every other wise dilapidated. There were none in the later fashion than thirty years since, except some figures that had been cut from tailor's show-bills. There were views of cities and edifices in Europe, of Napoleon's battles and Nelson's sea-fights, in the midst of which would be seen as a gigantic, brown hairy hand (the Hand of Destiny) pointing at the principal points of the conflict, while the old Dutchman explained.[54]

The lack of "gaiety" was echoed a decade later by Charles Dickens, visiting New York City in 1842, who observed that there were no itinerant bands, no wind or stringed instruments. Dickens's words almost duplicated Trollope's: There were "no Punches, Fantocinni, Dancing Dogs, Jugglers, Conjurers, Orchestrinas, or even Barrel-organs. No not one."[55]

Part 2: Itinerancy in the Antebellum Period

Carnivalesque themes aside, the itinerants active in America after the European influence began to recede were evidently more determined, numerous, and influential than ever. With the medieval connections between healing and entertainment finally severed, and the last memories of sixteenth-century traditions and historic British lore fading, itinerancy became a full-blown "industry," which expanded as the country forged its path westward. Circus companies, staffed by performers with American, European, and Mediterranean backgrounds, thrived from New Orleans to New England, with many traveling together. Some circuses turned to the Caribbean: Mr. and Mrs. Victor Pépin closed their show in Newburyport on 29 October 1819, and the entire group of seventeen equestrian performers and their families, one clerk, and eight servants, doorkeepers, and grooms—and their horses and equipment—climbed aboard Captain Swasey's brig *Nancy* to travel to Martinique for a "winter campaign in the West-Indies."[56] Wild and exotic animals were toured as organized menageries that covered distances on foot, in wagons, and on trains throughout the eastern states and the new Midwest.

Penmanship schools, specializing in mercantile and epistolary writing, emerged in every large city and virtually every small town and hamlet. Cut profiles were commonly sold at inns, taverns, hotels, theaters, glazing shops, museums, panorama exhibitions, coffeehouses, and drawing academies. Dancing-masters taught the "modern Polka," the "new Hop Waltz," and the "Sylphide Step." A lyceum movement sprang up out of nowhere served by scores of speakers. Camp meetings that had attracted a thousand people in 1805 drew ten thousand in 1822. Large-scale paintings proliferated. A "Transparent Panorama" of sacred lands in Egypt and Nubia executed by six London artists was displayed in Boston, the grand religious picture of the "Opening of the Sixth Seal" was shown in Baltimore, and the "Largest Painting in the World" (literally three miles of canvas) was exhibited in New York City.[57] An estimated forty touring waxwork partnerships—the majority of them formed by young men from three or four enterprising families in East Haven, Connecticut—combed every state of the union, some accompanying traveling circuses and menageries. In 1831, a "floating theater" made stops downstream along the Ohio and Mississippi Rivers and was sold for firewood in New Orleans at the end of the season.[58] A floating "canal museum" equipped with wax figures and a band worked its way along the Erie Canal under a Vermont proprietor.[59] Charles S. Durant (c. 1805–1873) became the first American-born aeronaut to make an ascension. The American Ruth Wheeler made herself available for cancer patients two days a week in Providence citing the testimonials of cured patients in Sutton, Uxbridge, Sturbridge, and Lexington, Massachusetts.[60] (The next year she opened rooms at Canton and Medway, and beginning in 1841 she was listed in Boston directories as a "doctress.")[61] Miss Hayden, "the Accomplished American Sybil," performed her deceptions and magic shows at Boston's Amory Hall. Another American, Miss Wyman, "The Young Sybil," demonstrated her "polite" conjuring tricks at Concert Hall in New Bedford, and Miss A. R. Mills, the "Enchantress," presented her Théâtre des illusions at Salem's Lyceum Hall.[62]

That was just the beginning. The optimism engendered by "systematic" teaching was seemingly unquenchable and served as a thinly disguised version of the alchemist's golden specific or philosopher's stone. Americans were persuaded to cure stammering under Mr. and Mrs. Chapman's newly discovered systematic methods, to teach bass viol under "the approved system of Gemaniani," to learn "Scientific Music [under] the Paddonian System," to teach string and wind instruments through "a scientific" and "a ready method," and to improve vocal singing under the "Italian system of Solmization singing."[63] Founded on the premise that education and self-improvement should be made available to all free members of society, regardless of class or background, these methods posed a direct challenge to Eurocentric values even as they most actively promoted them. As American as immigration and democracy, they were fueled by a national sense of self-improvement and six generations of social leveling. There was almost nothing that the machines and systems could not do.

The innovator in language teaching was Nicholas Gouin Dufief (1776?–1834), a French immigrant who founded a school in Philadelphia for teaching French by the repetition of familiar phrases. Arriving in the United States in 1793 at the age of seventeen, he taught himself English in an unusually short time by disregarding grammar and concentrating on everyday vocabulary and expressions—apparently getting the notion when working as a tutor in the family of attorney William Rawle of Philadelphia. But when he articulated his new system in a book, *Nature Displayed, in Her Mode of Teaching Language to Man* (first published in 1804), Dufief was immediately accused by Rawle of stealing ideas he had communicated to Dufief in conversations about the educational progress of his two sons. Dufief countered that "Mr. Rawle's notion of converting me to my own principles respecting language, is as ridiculous as if he took it into his head to go to Rome, to convert the Pope to the Roman Catholic faith."[64] Dufief won many converts (including President Thomas Jefferson in 1804) and was able to franchise his system with other teachers in Charleston, New York, and the District of Columbia. He published a Spanish-language adaptation of his method in 1811. By 1816 his name had become a standard against which other language teaching programs were measured, some typically packaging and marketing their teaching units in convenient multiples to promote larger classes.[65] In the space of seven years, J. Hamilton's French in forty-eight lessons (1819) became Nicholas Dufief's French in thirty-six lessons (1825) and Hilarian Abadie's French in twenty-four lessons (1826). J. Hamilton claimed his first lecture would teach anyone from "six years [old] to seventy" to read six verses in French from the New Testament; they would be able to make their way through the entire text after only six lessons.⁶⁶ In his own advertisement in May 1825, Dufief offered to teach Boston residents to read French texts and solemnly pledged to give "a French Ear" to every attentive learner without exception.⁶⁷

The newly fashionable arts of theorem and flower painting afforded similar opportunities. George Sugden proposed in the 1796 *Providence Gazette* holding a class in the "esteemed science of painting on silk" at the house of a Mrs. Cole. Sugden acknowledged that not all persons could draw well but vowed to "furnish his Scholars (methodically) with an easy unerring Method . . . capable of copying any Device without further instruction"—evidently through the use of stencils.⁶⁸ Decorative arts teachers Mr. and Mrs. Honfleure, citing their accomplishments in London and Paris and "innumerable references to New York, Boston, and Philadelphia," introduced in New Haven a method of painting flowers "from Nature" that reduced instruction to a few hours. In a notice they took while staying at a Mr. Pease's boardinghouse in Hartford in 1828, they promised to impart their style of painting in six lessons of one hour each. In Baltimore in 1833, they asserted their method could instruct "five times more rapidly . . . than those who practice upon the old system." To promote their technique they displayed specimens of their pupils' work before taking lessons and those painted after completing their course. The Honfleures' system was so fashionable, it was rapidly franchised, but by 1842 the pair had become daguerreotypists.⁶⁹

In the meantime, New European obsessions and inventions continued to influence popular culture. The moving panorama in America was spearheaded in 1828 by William Dunlap at the time he wrote and produced *A Trip to Niagara*, a play whose action is set on board a steamboat. Shown in the background were eighteen painted views of the Hudson River, the Erie Canal, and Lake Erie, with the final scene displaying a "sublime" view of Niagara Falls. New York City audiences "went wild" according to contemporary sources. Other artists created moving backdrops (without the accompanying plays) that were scrolled before the seated audience by means of large vertical rollers. Narrative sea voyages (especially whaling trips) and journeys on rivers (in particular the Mississippi) were the favorites. These became a staple of public amusements in America and Europe by the mid-nineteenth century.⁷⁰ Twenty thousand square feet of canvas chronicling the decline and fall of Napoleon and his arrival at St. Helena opened at Niblo's Gardens in New York City in 1833, where it was visited by "upwards of 24,000 persons."⁷¹ John Banvard produced a panorama of the Mississippi, which he worked on for seven years. He presented it to 400,000 viewers in New York and Boston in 1848, and took it to London where it was seen by 600,000 more.⁷² His rival John R. Smith painted a "Gigantic Moving Panorama of the Mississippi River" that captured almost four thousand miles of American scenery; a written description in 1849 alleges it was "one-third Longer than Any Other Pictorial Work in Existence, Four Miles in Length."⁷³

Moving panoramas by George St. P. Brewer (1814–1852) and his brother John of the Mammoth Cave, Niagara Falls, and the Ohio and Mississippi Rivers were featured at Peale's Athenaeum in Baltimore in 1849. In Boston a hundred "acres" of canvas were unrolled in "Burr's Seven Mile Mirror" of the Great Lakes and Niagara Falls in 1850.[74]

Itinerants soon began marketing phrenology. Beginning with the publication of George Combe's *The Constitution of Man* (Edinburgh, 1828) and the formation of professional societies in Portland, Washington, and Baltimore, a host of American adherents of his system became practicing phrenologists. Orson Squire Fowler in Brattleboro, Vermont, in 1834 described how easy it was: "I lay awake till 'broad daylight' . . . bought paper, hired a printer, and got out a thousand copies, along with my handbill; ordered a bust, and thirty-two dollars worth of works on Phrenology, opened by lectures, threw out my card, charged men twelve and a half cents for a phrenological chart, marked, and ladies and children six and a quarter cents; cleared forty dollars in the place, and started for Saratoga."[75]

The daguerreotype, an invention by Louis-Jacques Daguerre (1787–1851) in the late 1830s, supplanted machine-based profiles. Not long after Francis Fauvel Gouraud's 1839 lectures in New York City, a local firm began to manufacture the apparatus. "Daguerrean" artists, many with prior training as miniaturists and portrait painters, circuited the country setting up temporary "rooms," "studios," or "galleries" to produce likenesses. By 1846 their carts had become "saloons." "There is a chap traveling in Connecticut," reported one New York City paper, "who has fitted up a large double wagon into a sort of saloon, with a daguerreotype apparatus, and is going about like a tin pedlar calling at houses and taking pictures here and there, as he finds customers."[76] In Barre, Massachusetts, the editor of the *Patriot* urged everyone to come to the "Traveling Daguerreian Saloon," which was to remain on the Common for several days.[77] Many daguerrean artists supplied instruction as well as materials. According to a checklist compiled by Floyd and Marion Rinhart, approximately 1,800 daguerreotypists were active in the United States between 1839 and 1900.[78] Itinerancy in America had reached new heights.

Part 3: The Itinerant Legacy

The opening premise of this study has been that broad elements of European popular culture remained behind as English settlers arrived in Maine, Virginia, and Massachusetts Bay in the early and mid-seventeenth century. This created a "cultural silence" for a majority of the non-elite colonial population (an estimated three-quarters of those who immigrated). Over time, however, itinerant carriers working the Atlantic world—despite their pejorative role as transients—

gradually reintroduced old and brought new practices using techniques that were not significantly different from those that Peter Burke has described for early modern Europe. There were changes both in their methods and their timing, however. Appearing intermittently in the early eighteenth century, strolling practitioners got their message out primarily through newspapers and broadsides (rather than assembled crowds or street criers), and many waited decades before making their American move. Most came just before and after the American Revolution—expanding their activities as conditions permitted, many remaining only as long as they found work. The act of itinerancy was the medium through which cultural carriers disseminated their practices and ideas. The same attractions and beguilements they initiated in one section of the country they repeated elsewhere, usually with similar results. What previously had been the pervasive credulity of the seventeenth- and early eighteenth-century mentality was gradually supplanted by a more cosmopolitan awareness fostered in part by these professional and semiprofessional entrepreneurs. Although they continued to breed distrust and suspicion, itinerants collectively dispersed traditional entertainments, medical knowledge, singing expertise, portraiture, language skills, the arts of politeness, and some scientific innovations in a society just beginning to emerge from its colonial status. With them came a new intermingling of popular, schooled, and mannered culture that diffused throughout the eastern cities and into the Midwest and the South, broadening the country's horizons and helping to integrate it into the larger Atlantic community.

The later lives of the itinerants themselves provide additional perspectives on this process. Judging from their tenacity in pursuing wandering lives, most were resolute in their initial purpose. Out of a dozen representative itinerants closely examined in this study, four eventually gave up their wandering lifestyles, but eight kept it up seemingly to the very end. We can begin with those that gave it up. First was the handicapped, Connecticut-born Edward Burlesson, who had retired from showing puppets and exotic animals in 1746 when the town of Suffield, Connecticut, voted to hire him and one other person "to teach children in the Remote Parts of the Town." Burlesson was then sixty years of age, and it may be that his medical condition—whatever its nature—had at last slowed him down. He chose to serve the town that perhaps had played some role in helping him manage it.[79] Next was William F. Pinchbeck, the animal trainer and mechanic who ran a carving and gilding shop in Boston in 1803 where he created the only known surviving artifact bearing his name—a reverse-painted glass panel (fig. 21.3) now in private ownership. Pinchbeck reappeared in New York City operating a similar shop until he was declared bankrupt and his assets seized in 1812. A year later he opened the City Hall Tavern opposite the Dutch church in New York, inviting his friends and the "gentlemen of this metropolis" to partake of a collation of welcome. Pinchbeck may have later moved to Phila-

Figure 21.3. Eglomisé or reverse-painted panel for a looking glass. William Frederick Pinchbeck. Marked "Wm. Pinchbeck Del.t" and "1803." Made at a time when metallurgy and gilding work were gradually taking over Pinchbeck's career as a showman and animal handler and trainer. Height: 7½ inches; width 18¾ inches. Boston, 1803. Private collection.

delphia because he was receiving mail in that city in 1819; he was presumably then in his fifties.[80] Third was Daniel Bowen, the Rehoboth-born waxwork entrepreneur who lost his equity in the Columbian Museum to colleague William Doyle in 1813, and who partnered with panorama painter James Kidder in 1816 to establish the Phenix Museum, eventually taking it to Philadelphia. Although this new museum did not last, Bowen became a permanent resident of that city as a merchant and historian, living into his ninety-sixth year.[81] The last was John C. Devero, the well-born Irish dancing-master who gave up his itinerant career when he settled down in Utica, New York, and married Eleanor Barry, daughter of the importer Thomas Barry of Albany. Devero opened a dry-goods store in November 1802 while still a relatively young man; an avid speculator in land, he became Utica's third mayor.[82]

For the remaining eight, however, little changed over time, and we find these strollers healing, teaching, performing, and consulting many miles from "home," even at a relatively advanced age, seemingly committed to their itinerant vocations. London newspapers inform us that English-born Dr. Anthony Yeldall and his wife returned to that metropolis where he resumed his old medical treatments based on "natural" (meaning mountebank) principles—selling his "Patent Acromatic Belt" at his home on 43 Leicesterfields between 1789 and 1799. He continued to issue reports of "surprising Cures" while also engaging in debates at the King's Arms Hall on the subject of "Animal Magnetism." On 11 July 1799 he finally announced he was retiring from public business.[83] Another innovator was Scottish-born puppeteer Samuel Jameson Maginnis, who not only lent his "apparatus" to other showmen but was increasingly giving slack-wire performers and tumblers such as Donegani and Othello equal billing on his highly successful programs. Before his unexpected death in Maryland on

9 October 1805, Maginnis was on the way to Williamsburg, Richmond, and Charleston where he hoped to resume his career.[84]

Dancing-master John Griffiths, who had last taught in New York City in 1796, apparently became a rooming house proprietor in Baltimore and helped host a succession of dancing teachers traveling through that area. In June 1800, however, he resumed his former life's work as a dance instructor in Charleston, visiting inland towns such as Columbia, South Carolina, and Milledgeville, Georgia, where he proclaimed himself ready to start teaching with only "12 scholars"—no doubt far fewer pupils than he had enjoyed in Boston and Salem. Griffiths was still advertising as late as 1810, actively traveling in his fifties and sixties.[85] William King, the Salem turner, cabinetmaker, and electrician, was believed in 1819 by his estranged wife to be living in "the southern states." She was right: he was lecturing on electricity and galvanism in Charleston as "Dr. King" in 1824.[86] The next year he was in New Bern, North Carolina, where he published an eighty-three-page manual on electricity and the construction of metallic conductors, "with instructions for applying their influence in the aid of medicine and in restoring suspended animation." He designated himself a "Medical Electrician, and Lecturer on Electricity and Galvanism."[87]

John Templeman, the acrobatic dental surgeon who had spent about a decade in Boston as a securities broker, resurfaced in Washington, D.C., where he was again seen by William Wirt as a "well-dressed gentleman-like person, somewhat corpulent" working as a land dealer. But he was still active and moving about. Long after his careers as an acrobat, surgeon, and land agent had ended, he returned to work in 1811—this time in Newburyport, Massachusetts, as a superintendent for bridge-builder Timothy Palmer, who was erecting the first chain bridge in North America. Templeman was then aged between sixty-five and seventy.[88] Joseph Falconi, the Italian-born conjurer who had disappeared from the American record after performing in Providence in 1808, reemerged nine years later in 1817 in New York City where he demonstrated his usual optical and magnetic experiments (including his old "Indian" figure) at Tammany Hall. Two years later Falconi was in Hamilton, Bermuda, taking likenesses using a physiognotrace—"No resemblance, no payment."[89]

Maryland-born Ralph Letton continued his profile-taking and touring museums in New Hampshire, Rhode Island, Connecticut, upstate New York, Canada, and Kentucky; he finally relocated in 1818 to Cincinnati, Ohio, where he established still another museum and stayed at least until 1836. In 1839, he was granted permission to run a ferry over the Mississippi River in Iowa Territory. His son Van Wyck Letton became a portrait painter.[90] Finally there was Allison Wrifford, the penmanship teacher who was thought by historians to have retired in 1828. He was still active, however. A Bridgewater, Vermont, schoolteacher's diary reveals that "Mr. Wrifford an old teacher" was conducting a penmanship school in Woodstock in 1840, a town located fifty-three miles southwest of Newbury, Vermont, his residence at the time. Wrifford was then sixty-one years old. He died four years later in 1844, in Hopkinton, New Hampshire.[91]

What do these extended biographies tell us? For one thing, they confirm Peter Burke's assertion that the tie between itinerancy and popular culture was close. To be precise, in North America the two were virtually conjoined. The rapid dispersal of popular culture taking place in America not only required receptive or entertainment-hungry audiences but scores of ambitious "carriers" with a predisposition for travel and making money. Although itinerancy destroyed some families like William King's and occasioned some relatively early deaths (notably William King, Jr., James Rannie, James Guild, James Maginnis, and Miss Hervey), it was a highly successful form of cultural dissemination and served as one of several paths toward self-improvement that enhanced the lives of generations of Americans. Three-quarters of these twelve individuals were "active bearers" in Carl W. von Sydow's sense of the term, meaning they got others to follow in their footsteps, thus generating a self-perpetuating tradition.

Equally important, these biographies also remind us that most of the itinerants circulating in North America were imbedded in the larger northern Atlantic world. This was an area that comprised about one-eighth of the globe and included the eastern African coastline, the Mediterranean Sea, the Baltic Sea, the West Indian islands, eastern parts of North America itself, and portions of Mexico and Canada, all connected by maritime trading lanes. Eight of the twelve itinerants cited here were either born in Europe or had extensive European training; three had permanent ties to the Caribbean and Central America; and two spent extended periods of time in Canada. The connection of itinerants to the West Indies and Canada was especially strong. The mountebank Dr. Sharp arrived in Boston on his way to London from Jamaica in 1720; puppeteer James Wyatt told New York audiences in 1749 that "My Time in this Place is but short, I being bound to the *West-Indies*"[92]; eye-surgeon Dr. William Stork came to North America from Jamaica in 1761; entertainer Hyman Saunders played in Jamaica in 1775; acrobat Joseph Doctor left Philadelphia in 1800 to go to Havana; and John Bill Ricketts made a trip to Canada and performed in Cuba prior to his ill-fated return to England. Others included James Rannie, who entertained both in Quebec and the West Indian islands—later retiring in that region and dying in Puerto Rico. The Albiness was passing through Havana when she succumbed to fever in 1819. It was no coincidence that the first puppet theaters were found in Barbados and the Leeward Islands at the opening decade of the eighteenth-century, that the area later became a haven for theatrical companies during the American Revolution, or that early nineteenth-century circuses wintered in the West Indies.

Other prominent "northern Atlantic" source points were the British Isles, France, and the northern European ports. At least fourteen show people or entertainment companies performing in America between 1767 and 1812 cited their previous experience in London's Sadler's Wells Theatre. Ten alternative physicians were recently from London; six others could look back on experience in European capital cities of Dublin, Edinburg, Hamburg, Rome, and Paris. The mountebank Dr. Louis not only had traveled through Germany, Spain, France, Italy, and England but was described as multilingual—that he understood some German, Spanish, and Italian but spoke Latin very well. Dr. Ben Ali came from the Muslim world of the Mediterranean. Dr. Hornby (among the first to advertise electrical cures in Maryland 1786) spoke of the "general approbation he has met with from all ranks of people in Great Britain, Ireland, Holland, Germany, the West-India Islands, and most Towns on this continent." Equestrian Jacob Bates noted in 1773 that he had performed before "the Emperor of Germany, the Empress of Russia, the King of Great-Britain, the French King, the Kings of Prussia, Portugal, Sweden, Denmark, and Poland, and the Prince of Orange."[93]

In this array of colonies and countries, perhaps the greatest surprise is how much of this talent came by way of French sources rather than English. Of the estimated two thousand European strollers or itinerants who introduced popular culture into the United States, approximately one-third were expatriate French "citoyens" and "citoyennes" as well as French Caribbean exiles (see table 1.2). This figure is well above the actual ratio of French immigrants to British-speaking portions of North America, which was relatively low before the Louisiana Purchase. And if we narrow our focus to the postrevolutionary period, especially after 1790 when expatriate French-speakers had transferred their loyalties to the "new" America, the numbers jump much higher. Approximately 70 percent of new dancing-masters had French names after that date; many others offered Parisian contacts and taught the French language. It was an expatriate Frenchman who introduced the first balloon ascension in America. It was an expatriate Frenchman who first coined the term *physiognotrace,* setting off a two-decade publicity campaign of machine-made profile taking. French names overwhelmed the circus and fireworks industries. The most common foreign language taught in America was French; the most common dance was the quadrille; the most commonly taught form of defense was the French rapier.

In terms of time, the transfer of European popular culture to America was uneven and sporadic, characterized by delay rather than rapidity. Much depended on who came, when they came, and how long they stayed. Much also was contingent on those who chose not to come. The movement of show culture, street entertainments, theatrical tradition, and medical lore—all based on collective memory and local practice—probably experienced the greatest delay. Six decades passed before the first "jester" began touring in 1685 in northern

Virginia. It took four decades or more before the first ropedancers performed in Philadelphia in 1724 or the first "educated" horse was shown in New York in 1739, five decades before the first full-sized waxwork figures from Mrs. Salmon's shop were advertised at John Dyer's house in colonial Boston in 1733, six decades or more before the first English puppet show ("Punch and Joan his Wife") reached the sign of the Coach-and-Horses in Philadelphia in 1742, and more than seven decades before the first magic lanterns began to entertain patrons in a Philadelphia tavern in 1743. The theater and alternative medicine took even longer: fourteen decades passed before the first touring theater companies from the English stage began playing in Virginia in the 1750s, and eighteen decades before the first mountebank physicians and oculists began routinely practicing (or attempting to practice) in Massachusetts, Maryland, Pennsylvania, and New York City in the 1760s and the 1770s.[94]

Once imbedded in North America, however, some practices circulated quickly while others atrophied or became extinct. Itinerant practices that involved visual or game-like templates—optical machines, waxworks, lantern images, fireworks, machine-made profiles, public painting, and panoramas—disseminated easily. Waxwork museums, for example, which characteristically exhibited effigies of murderers dressed in articles of clothing worn at their executions, generated an aggressive appeal to America's elite and non-elite populations. An image of a sea monster thirty feet long and marked with the imprimatur of a leading biologist drew immediate attention. Exhibitions by performing animals and small-scale showmen, such as puppeteers, conjurers, and electrical demonstrators, spread quickly—especially those that could be readily accommodated in a tavern or barn. By contrast were the "slow movers," such as balloonists, who did not circulate readily because few could pay for them regardless of whether they were French, English, or American. Peddling dispersed slowly too because it was dangerous and provoked local opposition. Automatons took time because Europeans kept them for their own enjoyment, and perpetual motion machines because they failed to work. And the old medieval connections between showmen and dentistry quickly atrophied—as did most alternative medical schemes—because Americans saw their proponents as "quacks" and "imposters."

In terms of geographic movement, popular culture seems to have been drawn to the cities. Initially, itinerant performances and occupations were heavily concentrated in Philadelphia, New York City, and Boston, with occasional forays to Annapolis, Savannah, Charleston, and Williamsburg. These locations for years stood out as enjoying aspects of European popular or street culture not seen anywhere else. The earliest dancing teachers came to Virginia in the 1670s. The earliest "picture machines" reached Boston after 1715. The earliest professional conjurers came to New York City in the 1730s. The first "diagonal mirrors" turned up in New York City and Philadelphia in 1748 and 1749. The earliest clockwork music machines surfaced in Williamsburg and Philadelphia in 1755. After a point, however, as itinerants made incursions beyond the immediate coastal periphery into the rural uplands, popular culture began to spread to more remote locations. Towns situated miles from transit points and ports of entry—among them Hanover, New Hampshire; Middlebury, Vermont; and Milledgeville, Georgia—witnessed the arrival of physiognotrace operators, waxwork exhibitions, and subscription dancing schools. A French dancing-master who had spent about a decade in Albany, New York, founded a dancing school and finishing academy in Kentucky. Waxwork entrepreneurs like Daniel Bowen and Reuben Moulthrop traveled the entire eastern seaboard from Savannah, Georgia, all the way north to Montreal in Lower Canada, with scores of stopping places in between. An unknown showman—perhaps Pinchbeck himself—performed with a learned pig in Frankfort, Kentucky, in January 1802. Ventriloquists John and James Rannie (performing singly or together) followed a path that led from Boston to Salem to New York City to Baltimore to Philadelphia to Canada to the West Indies and thence to Kentucky, Charleston, Natchez, and New Orleans.

In terms of the psychology of cultural movement, imitation was at the heart of itinerant behavior. Beginning with Jacob Henninger, who purchased or inherited Mr. Bayly's conjuring equipment in 1783 (and who tried to resell it once he realized how much work it was), there was Hannah Brenon learning slack-wire tricks from her new husband in 1790, J. Manly selling off his "colours" and "glasses" to prospective miniature makers in 1794, Mr. Brigshaw purchasing and showing Pinchbeck's Pig of Knowledge in 1798, Mr. Robinson bringing Rossignol's bird imitations to Boston in 1800, Mr. Banks purchasing Maginnis's puppets to show them in Charleston in 1804, William Jennys purchasing the rights (and advertising language) of William King's profile machine in 1805, Mr. Barton purchasing the same Maginnis puppets from Banks to show them in Charleston in 1811, Mr. Martin selling off his tools and in 1811, six artists "simultaneously" depicting a Gloucester sea monster in 1817, James Guild staying ahead of his penmanship pupils by reading copybooks by five teachers in 1820, and Ethan Allen Greenwood passing off his newly acquired waxworks to anonymous buyers in 1822. There was even a new "Learned Pig"—which did everything that Pinchbeck's old one did—exhibited in a stone house opposite a Colonel Easton's former residence in St. Louis, Missouri, in 1823.

All of this suggests that the innovations in popular and everyday culture that were taking place in America in this period originated and dispersed through the bottom stratum of society. From a larger perspective it appears that popular "Opinions" began in the seventeenth and early eighteenth centuries in the limited scenario postulated by Jonathan Swift. The "great culture"—based on literacy and classical learning—was largely restricted to those who knew Latin, Greek, or Hebrew, attended college, or had private tutors. In this scenario the great culture flourished in its scholarship, academic debates, and intimate knowledge of English and European aristocratic life but did not readily descend to the common people, who in many instances had acquired only rudimentary schooling. As time went on, however, the "little culture" of fairground amusements and performances, which had been left behind in England and elsewhere, began to reassert itself through itinerancy operating within the ambiance of American exceptionalism. Arriving through strollers disembarking in eighteenth-century port communities, the old popular traditions, drolls, entertainments, and specialty services began to be enjoyed by increasingly large portions of the populace. While the European tradition of "blind singers," passion plays, and topical or religious card games, cited by Peter Burke and Philip Butterworth and others, did not come to the New World, other diversions that characterized Elizabethan and early Stuart popular life in England did. But this time they followed the pattern described by the Grimm brothers, who claimed their tales first originated among anonymous storytellers.

In the end it was rank-and-file Americans—sidewalk crowds, tavern patrons, boardinghouse residents, dockworkers, servants, agricultural workers, seamen, and patrons of commercial retail establishments—who provided the first audiences for most popular entertainments. An estimated eight out of every ten performers whose occupations later became part of traveling circuses started their American careers on the "street," meaning in an animal shed, on a rope strung between two chimneys, inside a back lane, or even in a prison yard. These included the unidentified female ropedancer and her seven-year-old boy who gave performances in the Northern Liberties of Philadelphia in 1724; John Bradley, the "Protestant dissenter" who was denied permission to perform in Boston in 1734; and John Childs, who "flew" off Reverend Timothy Cutler's Episcopal church in Boston in 1757. This pattern extended to dozens of outdoor or semi-outdoor performers such as trick riders, posture-masters, wire-walkers, animal showmen, firework exhibitors, and balloonists. An estimated eight out of every ten performers who later became independent showmen and -women—conjurers, lanternists, puppeteers, model-makers, and waxwork proprietors—started their American careers in tavern long rooms, inns, store lofts, stables, barns, theaters, market halls, commercial outbuildings, and schools of self-defense. These locations were mostly dispersed along established channels of communication made up of packet boats, ferries, high roads, and turnpikes running between Boston, New York City, Philadelphia, Baltimore, Williamsburg, and Charleston. We think of the "tricks" shown at John Wing's waterfront tavern in Boston in 1687, Joseph Broome's "Wonders of the World" at the home of a New York City baker in 1734, Richard Brickell's use of the magic lantern in Philadelphia in 1743, Mr. Bayly's "dexterity" at the dockside Orange Tree Tavern in New York City in 1767, and prizefighters like "The American Game Chicken" in Boston in 1810.[95]

While people of education and social status were clearly in attendance, the major part of itinerants' audiences were America's disenfranchised classes, including large numbers of household servants and at least some slaves (according to the notices banning them). The aspirations of these classes were exposed in the runaway notices posted by their owners or superiors, which like a regional accent made them identifiable and subject to arrest. Runaways were described as "bred to tumbling," "has a good Notion of Slight of Hand," or "tell fortunes by the cards."[96] This may explain the rapid imitation of "active bearers" by these audiences—a pattern amply documented in this study—who eventually helped undermine and replace the "genteel" English tastes that had accompanied the initial migrations. Populism and antiestablishment attitudes tended to define many aspects of eighteenth-century itinerants: alternative and "Indian" healers who defied medical protocols; wax workers who advertised themselves as accomplished eye surgeons; electrical healers who sold tickets for spectators; and penmanship instructors, drawing teachers, grammarians, and French-language teachers who promised mastery of their subject matter through truncated and "systematized" courses.

Shifting audience patterns are also found in theatrical venues. The showmen who in John Bonnin's time in the 1740s had offered delicate views of European gardens and palaces to "*insensible*" New York City ladies, fifty years later were promoting a "MONSTER; A Calf with Two Heads" at George Esterly's Harrowgate Springs in Philadelphia.[97] (Esterly also featured the off-color "Broken Bridge" skit.) A review of the play *George Barnwell* appearing in a 1795 New York City paper revealed that refined theatergoers were watching circuses and that common people were attending plays. One critic reported that the "pit and Gallery" at the John Street Theatre were full, "but the *genteel* part of the community were with Mr. Ricketts, therefore empty Boxes."[98] Then there is James Rannie's "Notice to Colored People" in June 1802 in Philadelphia. Not wanting to "overlook the many polite solicitaions he has received," Rannie decided to gratify their curiosity and "informs them, that Tuesday evening, the 15th inst. and every Tuesday during his stay in this city, will be set apart for their private accomodation."[99] Granted, not everything is known about the elder Rannie's motives or even whether or not he followed through on his promise. At one dollar per ticket he may have been willing to do anything to increase his take. But of two things we can be sure: First, Rannie, like most itinerants, seldom entertained in the homes of merchants and power brokers, and, second, most itinerants sought audiences in everyday locations that provided a populist backdrop for their activities. How else to explain the mutual attraction between itinerants and the slave or nonwhite communities? An 1801 Virginia advertisement ("100 Dollars Reward") by a slave owner indicates how easily runaways fit into itinerants' constantly moving world. "A few days after his elopement," it reads, Harry, a seventeen-year-old "genius" on the fiddle, "was seen at the Red House races on the 21st of May last, acting in the capacity of fiddler to Messrs. Hackley and Landy, slight of hand performers—perhaps he imposed himself on them as a free man, and continued with them; if not, no doubt he has gone for Maryland or Pennsylvania, with a forged certificate of his freedom."[100] This attraction continued. In 1809, puppeteer Mr. Blancan advised newspaper readers in New York City that "a gallery will be provided for people of Colour." And about a decade later, in 1821, we are told that a black runaway from Raleigh, Virginia, left the town "with the Proprietors of the Wax Figures which were lately exhibited there."[101]

The increasingly dominant role played by popular culture in early America is best exemplified in public experiments with laughing gas. Nitrous oxide was first synthesized by Englishman Joseph Priestley working with decaying vegetable matter in 1772; it was first isolated for breathing by Humphrey Davy in Cornwall in 1800. Description of these experiments were published in scientific studies by English university educators, but nitrous oxide's entertainment value as a stimulant (inducing high tones of voice, laughter, and giddiness) was not publicly recognized in England until 1824, when a Mr. Charles administered it to members of his audience in Liverpool. In America, however, this recognition was realized decades earlier and led the way to "respirations" involving itinerant chemists or physicians and dozens of audience members. None of these groups was strictly scientific. On 30 March 1809 the *New-York Gazette* announced that G. Chilton would "prepare a quantity of Nitrous Oxide for respiration . . . at No. 38 Dey Street [a private home]." Tickets were fifty cents. To avoid any misunderstandings, he later inserted an accompanying cut showing a profile of a man inhaling the gas from a small balloon (fig. 21.4). In October 1809, he and other physicians were producing twenty gallons per night for the same purpose in Newark. These exhibitions lasted for many decades. One of Chilton's imitators manufactured another "quantity of it" at the request of several gentlemen in Albany; another, a Dr. Jones, prepared a "quantity" for those who wished to inhale it in Philadelphia in 1814. John Griscom (1774–1852), an educator and chemist (and son of a prominent clergyman), gave public demonstrations of the substance in his course in New York City in 1817; at the time Griscom was on the medical faculty of Queens College, and he assured newspaper readers that three-quarters of all profits would benefit the Orphan Asylum in New York City.[102] Music was sometimes played during these occasions, and special nights were reserved for women. Not surprisingly, a number of the old, self-serving weaknesses soon manifested themselves. An inn keeper in Reading, Pennsylvania, took out an advertisement saying a strolling chemist demonstrating exhilarating

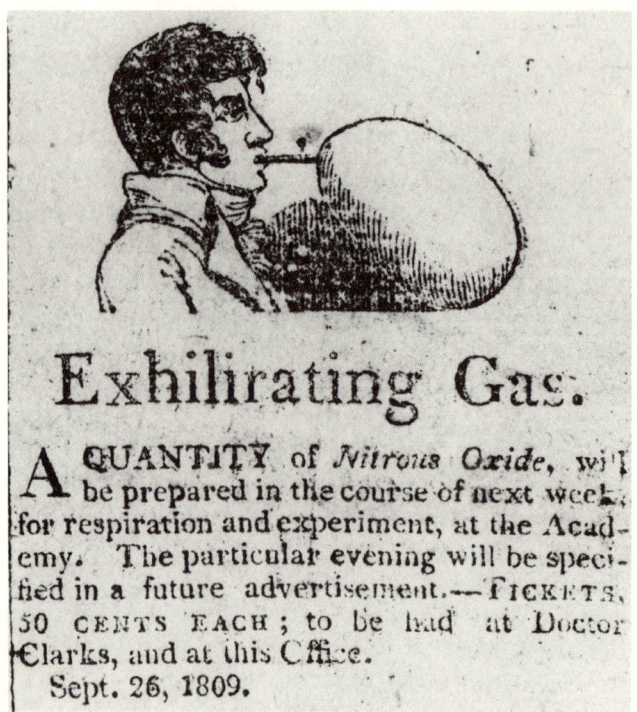

Figure 21.4. "Exhilirating Gas." Quantities of Nitrous Oxide Gas were prepared by G. Chilton, for "respiration & experiment" for evening meetings at his academy in New York City. An "Astronomical Lecturer, from London," Chilton kept a school in New York City for teaching natural philosophy and the use of globes. He later took his school to New Jersey. New York *American Citizen,* 26 September 1809. Courtesy, American Antiquarian Society.

gas in that town in 1831 "absconded from his boarding-house, without paying his bill," and warned other inn keepers not to trust him, "unless he has something more tangible than *gas* to pay his just debts."[103] But in the end there was a positive outcome. "Grand exhibitions" of laughing gas were still at the height of popularity when Gardner Q. Colton (b. 1814) gave one at a lecture in Hartford, Connecticut, on 10 December 1844 attended by Dr. Horace Wells, a dentist. The following day Wells had it administered to himself while a fellow dentist extracted a tooth—one of the earliest applications of anesthetics to medical practice.[104]

THIS BOOK began with a scene in John Wing's Castle Tavern in 1687 Boston where Judge Samuel Sewall and other members of the Third Church dissuaded the proprietor from allowing the performance of a conjurer in a room "fitted with Seats." Sewall then led the group through several verses of Psalm 90. It ends with two incidents involving touring elephants, each with its own story to tell. One is tied to the enchantment David D. Hall describes as residually prevalent in the seventeenth and early eighteenth centuries.[105] The other marks the mentality of resistance to popular culture. Together they attest to the complexity of the itinerant presence in the New World.

The first episode concerns the unnamed female elephant imported in 1796 by Captain Jacob Crowninshield and sold to a Mr. Owen of Philadelphia.[106] After visiting Philadelphia, Baltimore, and the southern states, the animal returned to New York City before beginning a tour of New England in 1797 that took her to coastal communities like Providence, Salem, Marblehead, and Newburyport (fig. 21.5).[107] In a private record kept in the years 1797 to 1799, Lydia Hill Almy of Smithfield marked the important events in her life while her husband was away on an eighteen-month whaling voyage. One of these was the brief stopover of the Crowninshield elephant in Rhode Island. The animal had finished her circuit of the southern states and was now headed northward through Woonsocket (and then to Attleboro and Dedham) to reach Cambridge, where she was scheduled to make an appearance at Harvard's July commencement. On 19 April 1798, or about nine and a half months after the animal had spent a week at Judge Peleg Arnold's tavern in Woonsocket, Lydia Almy described an event as unusual as the elephant herself: "[I had] herd of somthing very remarkable as closely engaged my mind said to be true that within nine months after the Elefant was shone at peleg arnolds there were five children born of women in the nabour hood which resembled it very much eaven to its trunk."[108] She evidently subscribed to the gossip regarding Woonsocket women who had seen the elephant in the first few weeks of their pregnancies, believing the old wives' tale that pregnant mothers who had witnessed extraordinary objects would bear children that in part resembled those objects—a belief that seemed to have accompanied the Albiness's visits to North America. According to Almy, five such "Elefant" children were born in that Rhode Island neighborhood, each one serving as a prime example of American credulity.

The second elephant episode pertains to "Old Bett," who had been purchased in 1804 by New York City museum proprietor Edward Savage as a two-year-old measuring approximately eight feet high. In 1808, she was acquired by animal entrepreneur Hackaliah Bailey of Somers, New York, who leased her to Nathan Howes, his uncle. Howes took Old Bett throughout the eastern United States in the period from 1812 to 1816. In New York City she was cast in the opera *Forty Thieves,* staged at the Olympic Theatre in 1812.[109] From there Old Bett began a walking trip through the Hudson River Valley, twice wintering in Albany and gradually heading eastward. Her tour was sensational. The animal was often moved at night to prevent free showings, but excited residents responded by lining the roads with bonfires.[110] In Lebanon, New Hampshire, she was remembered as having "brought together more people than had ever collected at any time before on any occasion, estimated at 5000 [and] they came from all adjoining towns."[111] Advertisements and diary entries place the elephant

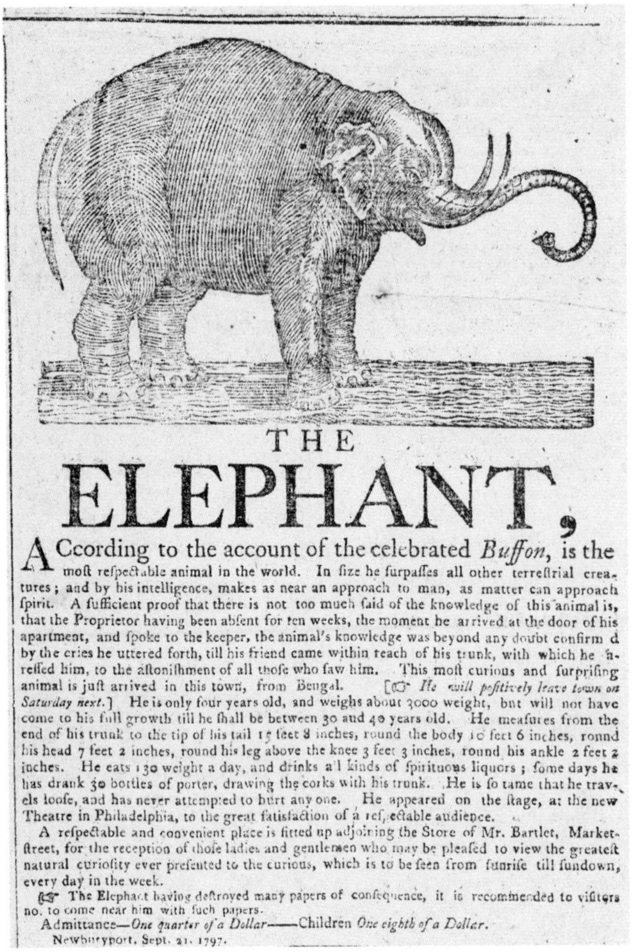

THE

ELEPHANT,

ACcording to the account of the celebrated *Buffon*, is the moſt reſpectable animal in the world. In ſize he ſurpaſſes all other terreſtrial creatures; and by his intelligence, makes as near an approach to man, as matter can approach ſpirit. A ſufficient proof that there is not too much ſaid of the knowledge of this animal is, that the Proprietor having been abſent for ten weeks, the moment he arrived at the door of his apartment, and ſpoke to the keeper, the animal's knowledge was beyond any doubt confirm d by the cries he uttered forth, till his friend came within teach of his trunk, with which he careſſed him, to the aſtoniſhment of all thoſe who ſaw him. This moſt curious and ſurpriſing animal is juſt arrived in this town, from Bengal. [☞ *He will poſitively leave town on Saturday next.*] He is only four years old, and weighs about 3000 weight, but will not have come to his full growth till he ſhall be between 30 and 40 years old. He meaſures from the end of his trunk to the tip of his tail 15 feet 8 inches, round the body 10 feet 6 inches, ronnd his head 7 feet 2 inches, round his leg above the knee 3 feet 3 inches, round his ankle 2 feet 2 inches. He eats 130 weight a day, and drinks all kinds of ſpirituous liquors; ſome days he has drank 30 bottles of porter, drawing the corks with his trunk. He is ſo tame that he travels looſe, and has never attempted to hurt any one. He appeared on the ſtage, at the new Theatre in Philadelphia, to the great ſatisfaction of a reſpectable audience.

A reſpectable and convenient place is fitted up adjoining the Store of Mr. Bartlet, Market-ſtreet, for the reception of thoſe ladies and gentlemen who may be pleaſed to view the greateſt natural curioſity ever preſented to the curious, which is to be ſeen from ſunriſe till ſundown, every day in the week.

☞ The Elephant having deſtroyed many papers of conſequence, it is recommended to viſitors not to come near him with ſuch papers.

Admittance—*One quarter of a Dollar*——Children *One eighth of a Dollar.*

Newburyport, Sept. 21, 1797.

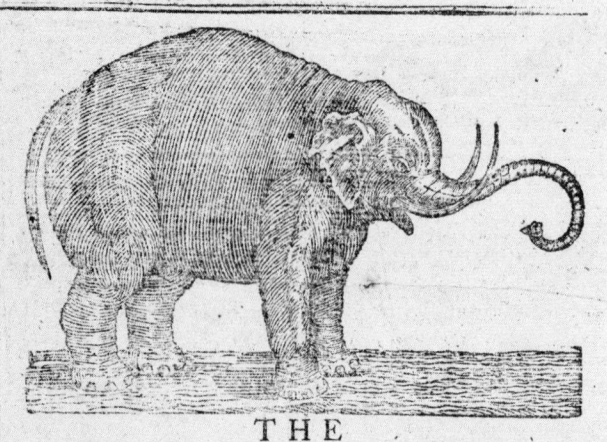

Figure 21.5. "THE ELEPHANT." Illustrated broadside announcing the arrival of the first elephant (a female) imported into America by Captain Jacob Crowninshield. During her tour of New England in 1797 and 1798, she was exhibited at the store of a Mr. Bartlett, Newburyport, Massachusetts. Woodcut, 11 by 8 inches. Newburyport: William Barrett, 1797. Courtesy, Newburyport Archival Center at the Newburyport Public Library.

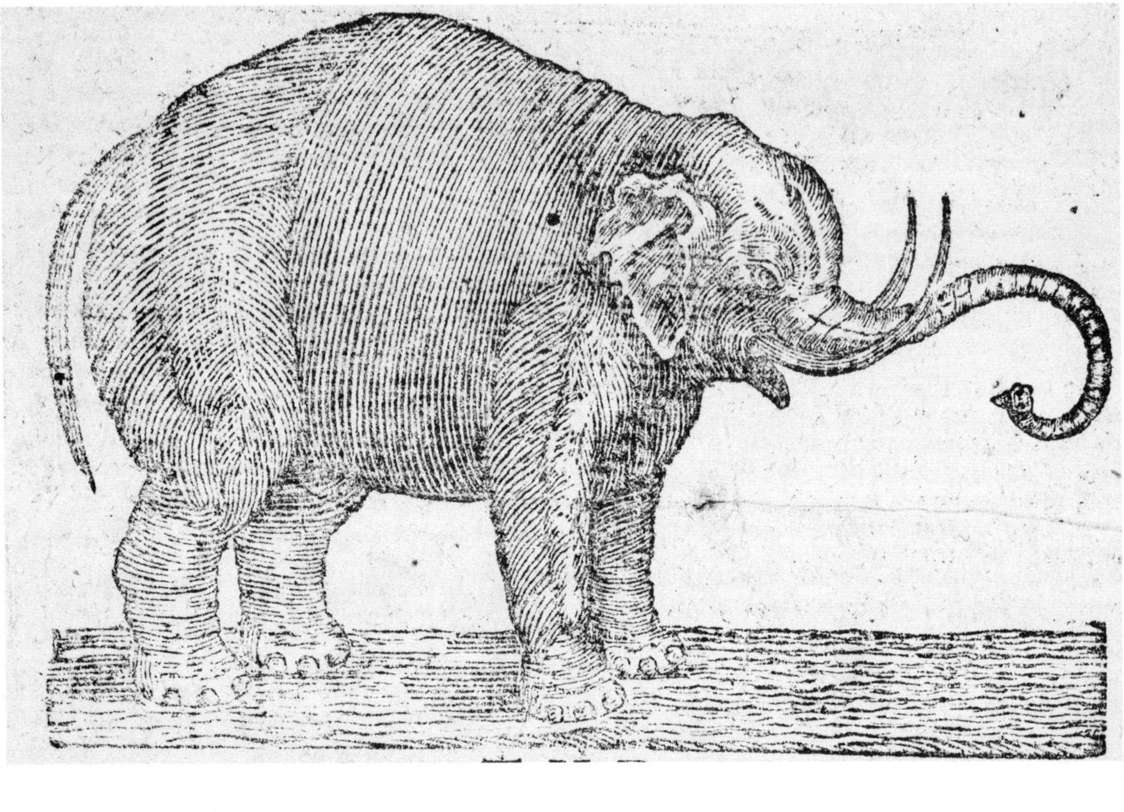

Conclusion: America Comes of Age 383

traveling southeast from Keene in 1815, thence to Dover, Portsmouth, and Newburyport, and wintering in Boston from November 1815 to April 1816.[112]

Old Bett resumed her tour in the spring, visiting Salem in April 1816. There, on the 29th, fifty-two-year-old Margaret Holyoke recorded that she "went to see an Elephant weighd 6000, 8 feet high." William Bentley, who saw her on the same day, took the time to calculate that she was "13 feet round the body." The animal then trekked northeast into the district of Maine, arriving in Portland on 22 May, Hallowell on 28 May, Readville on 6 July, and Winthrop on 8 July; she subsequently turned south to reach Monmouth on 10 July.[113] A 29 July 1816 entry in Reverend William Bentley's diary completes the story: "We learn that the Elephant exhibited as a Curiosity in this town lately, was shot in open day by a villain in Alfred, Maine. We have such wretches in our country who have all the lawlessness of our Savages & a full share of them in Maine."

Figure 21.6. "NOTICE. The Skeleton of that unfortunate Elephant that was shot the 26th of July last, in District of Maine . . . may be seen at No. 301 Broadway." Purchased in 1804 in New York City, Old Bett toured the eastern United States until 26 July 1816 when she was shot and killed in Alfred, Maine. Advertisement with woodcut taken by proprietor Nathan Howes and published in New York City. *New-York Evening Post*, 16 April 1817. Courtesy, American Antiquarian Society.

It is said the pretence was that money should not be raised in that way in that neighborhood."[114]

William Bentley provided one final reference to the animal, relating that "the poor Elephant was destroyed in Maine because he took money from those who could not afford to spend it."[115] But other investigators narrowed the culprit down to a "miserable vagabond" called Davis, a local resident who apparently owned little or no property in Alfred. As a flood of editorials condemned the deed, the elephant continued to make news. After expressing his indignation over the viciousness of human nature, proprietor Nathan Howes carried the skin and bones of the elephant to Boston, and the animal's skeleton was assembled and exhibited in New York City the following year (fig. 21.6).[116] Old Bett's unhappy fate is a reminder that in 1816, American provincialism—possibly at its most militant—was still riding high in the countryside.

Notes

Introduction

1. Morley, *Memoirs of Bartholomew Fair;* Frost, *Old Showmen,* chaps. 1–3; Rosenfeld, *Theatre of the London Fairs,* chaps. 1–7.

2. Speaight, *English Puppet Theatre,* 151. Friar Bungay and Friar Bacon were thirteenth-century English alchemists and sorcerers best known from an Elizabethan stage play by Robert Greene.

3. *The Chapmans and Travellers Almanack; The Traveller's and Chapman's Daily Instructor;* Weiss, *A Catalogue of the Chapbooks,* frontispiece.

4. Marlow, *Life and Times of George I;* Smith, *The Cries of London;* Shesgreen, *Criers and Hawkers of London.*

5. Burke, *Popular Culture in Early Modern Europe,* 99–115.

6. See, for example, *Rivington's New-York Gazetteer,* 2 September 1772 (Dr. Graham); *Salem Mercury,* 21 July 1789 (Donegani); Charleston *City Gazette,* 11 June 1798 (Salenka); Alexandria *Columbian Advertiser,* 22 October 1802 (Rannie); Salem *Essex Register,* 11 January 1809 (Leopard); and Philadelphia *Poulson's,* 21 October 1812 (portraits).

7. Cosentino, *The Paintings of Charles Bird King,* 87; Hoopes, *American Narrative Painting,* 59; Williams, *Mirror to the American Past,* 74, pl. 118; *The Working American,* 21.

8. Twain, *The Adventures of Huckleberry Finn,* chap. 19, "The Duke and the Dauphin Come Aboard," 346.

9. Twain, *Life on the Mississippi,* 409. Elsewhere in this volume, Twain remembered that river-borne itinerants were common in the antebellum period: "Formerly . . . we should have passed acres of lumber-rafts and dozens of big coal-barges; also occasional little trading-scows, peddling along from farm to farm, with the peddler's family on board; possibly a random scow, bearing a humble Hamlet & Co. on an itinerant dramatic trip" (231).

10. "This is to give Notice That there will be a Bar and a Number of Turkeys set up as a Mark next Thursday Before noon at the Punch Bowl Tavern in Brookline." *Boston Evening Post,* 11 January 1773.

11. Rowe, *Letters and Diary,* 26 October 1764, 13 March 1765, 23 March 1770, 67, 77, 200.

12. Tony Bennett, "Popular Culture: A Teaching Object," cited in Storey, *An Introductory Guide,* 1; Stuart Hall, quoted in Reay, *Popular Cultures in England,* 1.

13. Burke, *Popular Culture in Early Modern Europe,* i; Harris, "Problematizing Popular Culture," 10.

14. Barry, "Springfield Mountain," 4–6.

15. Benes, "Night Processions"; Bell, "Du Simitère's Sketches."

16. Sydow, "On the Spread of Tradition," *Selected Papers on Folklore*, 12–16; Burke, *Popular Culture in Early Modern Europe*, 91: "In short, it is useful to distinguish what the Swedish folklorist Carl von Sydow called the 'active bearers' of popular traditions from the rest, who were relatively passive. It is with this minority of active tradition-bearers or 'carriers' that this chapter is mainly concerned."

17. William Penkethman, an English showman, called himself a "Comedian" in the London *Daily Courant,* 4 September 1714.

18. Lawrence W. Levine's statement that popular culture was "the folklore of industrial society" not only colors Jim Cullen's opening essay in his *Popular Culture in American History* but James W. Cook and colleague's opening propositions in *The Cultural Turn in U. S. History.* Cullen, *Popular Culture in American History,* 4; Cook, Glickman, and O'Malley, eds., *The Cultural Turn in U.S. History,* 3–57.

19. Ashby, *With Amusement for All,* 4–9.

20. Burke, *Popular Culture in Early Modern Europe,* 23–25, 29, 58, 63, 91–115; Malcolmson, *Popular Recreations,* 21.

21. Swift, "An Argument against Abolishing Christianity in England," quoted in Burke, *Popular Culture in Early Modern Europe,* 58.

22. Burke, *Popular Culture in Early Modern Europe,* 4, 113.

23. McGlathery, *Grimm's Fairy Tales,* 40: "With the provision of this information, it had become clear that the Grimms' immediate informants were generally not common folk, but indeed cultured friends of theirs."

24. Deetz, *In Small Things Forgotten,* 5, 39.

25. Hall, *Worlds of Wonder,* 71.

26. Burke, "Popular Culture in Seventeenth-Century London," 45; Griffin, *England's Revelry,* 99–103, 114–41; Sewall, *Diary,* 2 March 1690, 1:252—this, despite Sewall's warning against "Skailing or throwing at Cocks."

27. Sydow, "On the Spread of Tradition," 36–37.

28. For example, the earliest entry in Readex's "Early American Newspapers" for Charleston's *South Carolina Weekly Gazette* is 1783, whereas the paper was founded in 1732.

1. Itinerants and Popular Culture

1. Sewall, *Diary,* 22, 28 April, 4 December 1687, 1:137–38, 154. Verse 12 begins, "Teach us to count our days." *The Whole Booke of Psalmes Faithfully Translated into English Metre* (Cambridge, Mass.: Stephen Daye, 1640).

2. Burke, *Popular Culture in Early Modern Europe,* 214–15.

3. Durand, *A Huguenot Exile,* 158, cited in Keller, *Dance and Its Music,* 218.

4. In his study of English vagrancy between 1598 and 1664, Paul Slack notes that a "fortune teller, a minstrel, a morris-dancer and two conjurors" were included among the vagrants recorded at Salisbury in the early seventeenth century. Slack, "Vagrants and Vagrancy in England," 364. In London in 1702, "the incomparable German" turned sixty "Balls" into sixty "little live Birds, which whistle upon the Table"; he traveled with a "Tall Woman, between 7 and 8 Foot high"—an Italian who weighed over four hundred pounds. London *Flying Post,* 26 May 1702.

5. Butterworth, *Magic on the Early English Stage,* 37, 43, 46–47; London *Flying Post,* 20 August 1698.

6. *Boston Records,* 20:111.

7. For example, natural philosophy lecturer Henry Moyes was blind from the age of eighteen months; organists John L. Birkenhead and Oliver Shaw were blind since birth; profile artist Sally Rogers was born without arms; and painter John Brewster, Jr., was "deaf and dumb."

8. William Powers, who juggled pennies with his feet, appeared in Portsmouth and Boston taverns in 1789. Portsmouth *New Hampshire Spy,* 28 January 1789; Boston *Massachusetts Centinel,* 3 January–18 February 1789.

9. Bentley, *Diary,* 25 May 1798, 2:269–70.

10. Parkman, "Diary," 1, 27, 28 June 1777.

11. Albany *New York Gazetteer,* 20 October 1783. Little is known of Griffiths's background. He may have been the son of a Boston schoolteacher of the same name, but if so, there is no record of his birth, marriage, or death in that town. *Boston Gazette,* 9 October, 18 December 1769. John Griffiths kept an evening school on Queen Street "opposite William Vassals, Esq." *Boston Gazette,* 22 April 1771, 20 March 1775; *Boston Weekly News-Letter,* 3 February 1774.

12. A newspaper publisher, Bowen advertised the sale of "A Collection of Figures of the Newest and Most Fashionable Country-Dances" in the *New Haven Chronicle,* 12 September 1786. Keller, "John Griffiths"; Trumbull, ed., *Memorial History of Hartford County,* 1:585–86; New York *Independent Journal,* 25 November, 15 December 1784, 1 January 1785; *New Haven Gazette,* 28 April, 5, 19 May, 31 August 1785; *New York Packet,* 21 March, 11 April, 7 August, 26 October 1786; Hartford *Connecticut Courant,* 7 May, 13 August 1787; *Norwich Packet,* 18 October 1787; *Providence Gazette,* 22 February, 30 August 1788, 19 November 1791, 4 February 1792; Boston *Independent Chronicle,* 11 December 1788; Boston *Massachusetts Centinel,* 19 July 1788, 11 September 1789; *Salem Gazette,* 13 November 1792; Northampton *Hampshire Gazette,* 19 March 1794; *New York Diary,* 8 September 1796. Griffiths returned to New York City for the winter season 1796–97 and to Connecticut in the fall of 1797: *Litchfield Monitor,* 22 November, 13, 22, 29 December 1797.

13. In the *Providence Gazette,* 30 August 1788, Griffiths expressed his appreciation for the "great Hospitality and Politeness experienced by himself and Family, since his Residence here." Keller, "John Griffiths," 94n17; Keller, *Dance and Its Music,* 403n83; *New York Daily Advertiser,* 20 November 1786.

14. "Monday [7 April 1794] the girls attended the dancing school for the first time. . . . Satt[urday]. [19 April 1794] Mr. Griffith the dancing Master drank tea here. . . . Monday [21 July 1794] . . . in the Eve we all went to the ball which closes the dancing school." Phelps, "Diary," 120 (July 1966): 210–12.

15. Dunlap, *Diary,* 18 November 1819, 1 December 1819, 2:488, 493.

16. Dunlap, *Diary,* 20 October 1819, 2:475.

17. Dunlap, *History of the Rise and Progress,* 1:273, cited in Hill, "New England Itinerant Portraitists," 150.

18. *Boston Gazette,* 7 November 1768, 9 February 1770; *Boston Evening Post,* 11 March 1771; Rowe, *Letters and Diary,* 23 March 1770, 200; *Journal of the Times* (published in *New-York Journal*), 26 January 1769; Sonneck, *Early Concert-Life,* 260; Lambert, comp., "Music Masters in Colonial Boston," 2:1079. For Maginnis's itinerary, see table 9.1 at http://scholarworks.umass.edu/umpress_short_time_only/ and *New York Morning Chronicle,* 18 April 1804.

19. Wirt, *Memoirs,* 26, cited in Keller, *Dance and Its Music,* 277. Wirt later served as attorney general of the United States.

20. "The first wire dancer I ever saw was one Templeman who was the most compleat in

the art. He performed in the old Theatre South Street; the house was crowded every night." Durang, *Memoir,* 11. Templeman performed on the slack wire and flying rope at the new playhouse in Southwark, Philadelphia, and at the Rhode Island State House in Providence. Philadelphia *Pennsylvania Evening Post,* 6 March 1780; Providence *American Journal,* 7 February 1781. He had previously in 1779 received a license to perform in Maryland. *Journal and Correspondence of the Council of Maryland,* 43:33.

21. *Boston Records,* 25:167–68; Burke, *Popular Culture in Early Modern Europe,* 95.

22. *Salem Gazette,* 27 June, 4 July 1782, 9 January 1783. For other Templeman references, see Guerra, *American Medical Bibliography,* s.v. "J. Templeman"; Brigham, *Paul Revere's Engravings,* 148; *Newport Mercury,* 23 November 1780; *Providence Gazette,* 3 January 1781; Providence *American Journal,* 3 May 1781; *Boston Evening Post,* 11 May 1782; *Boston Gazette,* 23 April 1781, and 7 January 1782; Portsmouth *New-Hampshire Gazette,* 19 April 1783. See also *Boston Records,* 25:167–68.

23. Dow, ed., *Holyoke Diaries,* Diary of Mary (Vial) Holyoke, 23 July 1782, 22 March 1783, 107–8. Templeman's first name was John, not William as has been suggested in the index by Alan S. Downer, editor of John Durang's *Memoir.*

24. Boston, *Herald of Freedom,* 6 February 1789: "Publick Securities Bought, [and] sold . . . also Brokers Business done for very reasonable Commissions."

25. Boston *Massachusetts Centinel,* 16 August 1786; *Boston Directory* (1789); Durang, *Memoir,* 100, 144n8.

26. Ballantine, "Journal," 10 August 1773.

27. Ballantine, "Journal," 10, 17, 34, 31 August, 7 September 1773.

28. Phelps, "Diary," week of 29 August 1773, 118 (April 1964): 125.

29. Breen, "An Empire of Goods"; Breen, "The Meaning of 'Likeness': Portrait-Painting in an Eighteenth-Century Consumer Society," 43. Full details of Yeldall's itinerary for the years 1770–1797 are listed in table 1.3 at http://scholarworks.umass.edu/umpress_short_time_only/.

30. *New London Gazette,* 15 October, 12 November 1773; Philadelphia *Pennsylvania Journal,* 30 March 1774; Philadelphia *Pennsylvania Gazette,* 13 March 1780.

31. Philadelphia *Pennsylvania Evening Post,* 23 May 1776.

32. To *couch* a cataract is to turn down or displace the opaque lens of the eye. Philadelphia *Pennsylvania Ledger,* 23 November 1776; Philadelphia *Pennsylvania Evening Post,* 23 May 1776, 23 January 1780; Philadelphia *Pennsylvania Gazette,* 13 September 1770; Philadelphia *Pennsylvania Packet,* 9 October 1775.

33. Philadelphia *Pennsylvania Packet,* 27 January 1780.

34. Since the reward was only five pounds, Prince was probably an indentured servant. Philadelphia *Pennsylvania Packet,* 15 August 1774. The cup now belongs to Berkeley Divinity School, Middletown, Conn.

35. Dunlap, *History of New York for Schools,* 148–49. Dunlap's source was probably an old copy of a New York newspaper. An English paper, however, says in 1775 that John McDonald was shot and seriously wounded in White Plains, N.Y., by a Tory farmer who refused to pay him for pulling an acre of flax. London *Morning Chronicle,* 14 September 1775.

36. Philadelphia *Pennsylvania Packet,* 17 June 1778.

37. Philadelphia *Pennsylvania Packet,* 12 December 1778, 1, 27 January, 3 October 1780; New York *Royal Gazette,* 17 March 1781; Philadelphia *Freeman's Journal,* 27 February, 6 November 1782; Philadelphia *Independent Gazetteer,* 8, 10 October 1789.

38. Philadelphia *Porcupine's Gazette,* 20, 30 June 1797; New York *American Minerva,* 24 August 1797; Boston *Massachusetts Mercury,* 9 January–1 April, 17 April, 21 December 1798, 11 January 1799, 11 July 1800; *Salem Gazette,* 4 May 1798, 24 March 1807; *Newburyport Herald,*

25 May 1798, 7 April 1807; Portsmouth *New-Hampshire Gazette*, 3, 8 June 1798; *Providence Gazette*, 8 September 1798; *New-York Evening Post*, 17 February 1802; *Newburyport Herald*, 11, 15 March 1803, 4 May 1802, quoted in Barriskill, "Newburyport Theatre," 43:5–6; Boston *New-England Palladium*, 11 August, 1 September 1807; *New York Diary*, 13 September 1796. Full details of Pinchbeck's itinerary for the years 1795–1819 are listed in table 1.4 at http://scholarworks.umass.edu/umpress_short_time_only/.

39. *Philadelphia Gazette*, 14 August 1795; *Philadelphia Aurora*, 12 December 1796; *New York Daily Advertiser*, 31 August 1797; Boston *Massachusetts Mercury*, 9 January 1798.

40. *Portland Gazette*, 6 August 1798.

41. Philadelphia *Porcupine's Gazette*, 30 June 1797; New York *American Minerva*, 24 August 1797; *Newburyport Herald*, 4 May 1802, 11 March 1803, 7 April 1807; Boston *New-England Palladium*, 11 August, 1 September 1807.

42. Boston *Massachusetts Mercury*, 5 October 1798.

43. Boston *Columbian Centinel*, 24 July 1805.

44. Boston *New-England Palladium*, 4, 11 September 1807.

45. Butterworth, *Magic on the Early English Stage*, 59.

46. *London Gazette*, 1 January 1715, 10 September 1720. These were directed to suppress "Stage-Players, Mountebanks, Rope-dancers, Prize Players, Poppet Shewers, . . . Shew keepers of wild beasts, moving Pictures, Musical Clocks, Horse-Docters, . . . [those who] make show of Motions and strange Sights, as Activity of Body, Dexterity of Hand, Spinning of Glass."

47. Bernard, *Retrospections of America*, 29–30: "They wore the same clothes, spoke the same language, and seemed to glow with the same affable and hospitable feelings. In walking along their mall I could scarcely believe I had not been whisked over to St. James Park; and in their houses the last modes of London were observable in nearly every article of ornament or utility."

2. Travel Routes and Circuits

1. Hamilton, *Itinerarium*, 10.
2. Rice, *Early American Taverns*, 105–6.
3. Parkman, "Diary," 17 June 1773.
4. Ballantine, "Journal," 24 August 1763.
5. Rowe, *Letters and Diary*, 54–55. The date of the arrival was 20 October 1764.
6. Kornhauser, *Ralph Earl*, 32; Priest, *Travels in the United States of America*. Hempstead, *Diary*, 1 October 1727, 189: "Cheesbrough Arived from Antegua 30 days al well."
7. *New-York Evening Post*, 10 March 1821.
8. *New London Gazette*, 26 April, 19 May 1767.
9. Smith, *Tour of Four Great Rivers*, 4.
10. Read kept a log of his trip; quoted in Bushnell, "Daniel Read of New Haven," 192–93.
11. Breck, *Recollections*, 90; Kendall, *Travels through the Northern Parts of the United States*, 2:9–10.
12. *Newport Mercury*, 2 October 1769.
13. Durang, *Memoir*, 41.
14. New Haven *Connecticut Journal*, 25 April 1786.
15. Hagerstown *Maryland Herald*, 24 January 1799.
16. Dunlap, *Diary*, 14–20 December 1797, 1:195–99.
17. Guild, "Journal," 289–96; Andrew Law to William Law, Alexandria, Va., 11 November 1791, cited in Crawford, *Andrew Law*, 60.

18. Knox, *The Sharples*, 12.

19. Durang, *Memoir*, 47–93. The path was the same one taken by General John Burgoyne in the 1770s.

20. Bernard, *Retrospections of America*, 345–56.

21. Hudson, N.Y., *Northern Whig*, 24 October 1815; *Albany Argus*, 26 October, 15 July 1815; *Providence Gazette*, 23 July 1815.

22. Providence *Rhode-Island American*, 16 July 1811; Boston *Columbian Centinel*, 29 April 1815; *Boston Evening Transcript*, 1 April 1839.

23. Providence *United States Chronicle*, 29 December 1791. Full details of Griffiths's itinerary for the years 1783–1810 are listed in table 2.1 at http://scholarworks.umass.edu/umpress_short_time_only/.

24. John C. Devero was born in Enniscorthy, County Wexford, son of Thomas and Catherine Cornish Devereux, owners of "The Leap," a landed estate named after the width of the foss, or ditch, that surrounded the principal mansion; most of their children and numerous relatives sympathized with the Irish rebellion of 1798. One Devereux family member was killed in battle; another was condemned to be hanged by an English court-martial. *Trial of John Devereux*; see also *Out of Ireland*, a documentary broadcast by WGBH, Boston, Mass., 16 June 1995.

25. Hartford *Connecticut Courant*, 24 December 1796; Hartford *American Mercury*, 17 October 1796; *Norwich Packet*, 8 June, 22 August 1797; *Newport Mercury*, 5 March, 5 July 1799, 17 March, 6 August 1800, 16 March 1802; New London *Connecticut Gazette*, 8 June 1797, 27 February, 2 March 1798, 7, 21 August, 11 December 1799, 23 July 1800, 28 January 1802; *Litchfield Monitor*, 20 July 1801; *Providence Gazette*, 8 June 1799, 19 March, 8 July 1800, 21 March 1801, 12 June 1802; Trumbull, *Memorial History of Hartford County*, 1:586.

26. *Newport Mercury*, 3 July 1798, 31 March 1801; *Providence Journal*, 6 March 1799; *Providence Phoenix*, 22 January 1803; *Norwich Packet*, 22 June 1797; *Norwich Courier*, 11 September 1799; New London *Connecticut Gazette*, 4 December 1799, 6 August 1800.

27. *Providence Gazette*, 24 December 1802.

28. Bernard, *Retrospections of America*, 304–7. "Mr. Bernard, on his return from Portland, will offer a course of Lectures, Moral & Entertaining, under the title of Variety, Or, Pictures from real Life." Haverhill *Merrimack Intelligencer*, 24 June 1809.

29. Barriskill, "The Newburyport Theatre," 43:14; Salem *Essex Register*, 14 June 1819; Haverhill *Essex Patriot*, 14 August 1819.

30. New London *Connecticut Gazette*, 19 August, 26 November 1806, 14 April 1807; Middletown, Conn., *Middlesex Gazette*, 13 March 1807; New Haven *Connecticut Journal*, 5 February 1807; Providence *Columbian Phenix*, 21 May 1808, 29 December 1810, 2 February 1811; *Providence Gazette*, 21 May 1808, 24 December 1810, 2 February 1811; Albany *Balance and New York State Journal*, 4 January 1809; Providence *Rhode-Island American*, 7 February 1812: "Dr. Hall, who has charge of it [the Providence Museum] . . . Mr. Letton, being occupied with other concerns in the State of New York." Letton handbill, fig. 4.1, is at the Connecticut Historical Society and is reproduced in Carrick, *Shades of Our Ancestors*, opp. 118; *Quebec Mercury*, 4 November 1805, courtesy of Lydia Foy.

31. Charleston *City Gazette*, 12 December 1795.

32. Georgetown *Centinel of Liberty*, 13 October 1797; *Charleston Gazette*, 12 November 1802.

33. Alexandria *Virginia Journal*, 7 July 1785; *Charleston Gazette*, 18 March 1791.

34. *Charleston Times*, 18 July 1805.

35. Baltimore *Federal Gazette*, 21 November 1798.

36. Charleston *City Gazette*, 17 December 1803, 3 February 1804; *Charleston Courier*, 27 July 1803, cited in Rutledge, "Artists in the Life of Charleston," 128.

37. Annapolis *Maryland Gazette*, 17 May 1792; Baltimore *Maryland Journal*, 13 June 1786; Charleston *City Gazette*, 13 September 1790; Philadelphia *Claypoole's*, 4 December 1797; Philadelphia *Porcupine's Gazette*, 2 December 1797; Savannah *Georgia Gazette*, 6 November 1800.

38. *Portland Gazette*, 4 August 1806; *Boston Patriot*, 21 June 1809; Boston *Columbian Centinel*, 24 June 1809; Portsmouth *New-Hampshire Gazette*, 20 April 1810; *Newburyport Herald*, 14 August 1810; Exeter, N.H., *Constitutionalist*, 22 October–26 November 1810.

39. *Norwich Packet*, 11 December 1794; Providence *Rhode-Island Museum*, 29 December 1794; *New Bedford Medley*, 15 January 1795.

40. "Cuff . . . talks high and low Dutch and English." *Hudson Balance*, 6 July 1801. "Har . . . speaks English and low Dutch." *Hudson Balance*, 23 August 1802. Smith, *Tour of Four Great Rivers*, 3–18.

41. Webster, *Autobiographies*, Diary, 1–27 May 1786, 227–28.

42. Worcester *Massachusetts Spy*, 1 August 1804; *Albany Centinel*, 8 January 1805.

43. Hudson, N.Y., *Northern Whig*, 25 January 1814.

44. Savannah *Columbian Museum*, 14 May 1799; *Albany Balance*, 13 September, 4 December 1810; *Albany Advertiser*, 26 October 1815, 6 January, 12 February 1816; *Albany Argus*, 26 October 1815; Hudson, N.Y., *Northern Whig*, 28 September, 5 October 1812, 2 March 1813, 19 January 1814, 24 October 1815, 27 February 1816, 23 November 1818, 15 February 1820; *Pittsfield Sun*, 29 August 1810, 23 December 1818. J. Johnson may have been Joseph H. Johnson, who advertised a dancing academy in Newburyport in 1799.

3. A Legacy of Diversity, a Reputation for Distrust

1. *Boston Gazette*, 10, 24 October 1720; *Boston News-Letter*, 10 October 1720; *Providence Gazette*, 24 June 1769.

2. Philadelphia *Pennsylvania Gazette*, 1 November 1775, 4 July 1765, 5 January 1748, 5 April 1750; Philadelphia *Pennsylvania Packet*, 17 June 1776; Philadelphia *American Weekly*, 17 August 1727, 22 December 1733.

3. Hempstead, *Diary*, 14 December 1739, 355.

4. Butterworth, *Magic on the Early English Stage*, 59–73.

5. Boston *Massachusetts Centinel*, 16 August 1786; *New York Morning Post*, 25 November 1786, 29 November 1788; Wright, *Revels in Jamaica*, 284–85.

6. Georgetown *Centinel of Liberty*, 11 April 1797.

7. *Boston Evening Post*, 18 September 1769.

8. *New York Columbian*, 14 March 1817.

9. *Providence Gazette*, 9, 16 July 1768; Keller, *Dance and Its Music in America*, 137, 202, 214–16.

10. *Portsmouth Oracle*, 22 May 1809.

11. Boston *Herald of Freedom*, 11 May 1790.

12. New London *Connecticut Gazette*, 21 July 1780; *Richmond and Manchester Advertiser*, 9 May 1795; *New-York Gazette*, 16 January 1775; Philadelphia *Pennsylvania Packet*, 18 April 1774; New Haven *Connecticut Journal*, 30 August 1775; New York *Constitutional Gazette*, 18 October 1775; *New-York Journal*, 30 November 1775.

13. Boston *Columbian Centinel*, 7 February 1795, 7 July 1799; Boston *Russell's Gazette*,

24 June 1799; *Salem Gazette,* 12 July 1799; Harrisburg *Oracle of Dauphin,* 17 April 1799; *New-York Commercial Advertiser,* 21 February 1799; *Carlisle Gazette,* 3 September 1800; *Philadelphia Gazette,* 3 June 1800; Philadelphia *Aurora General Advertiser,* 7 March 1805.

14. *Boston News-Letter,* 7 January, 4 February, 18 March, 28 October 1773.

15. Keller, *Dance and Its Music in America,* index, "Musicians, black, by name," 691; Boston *Massachusetts Mercury,* 21 July 1795.

16. *New York Mercury,* 13 August 1753.

17. Baltimore *Maryland Journal,* 4 December 1787.

18. *New-York Morning Post,* 11 April 1788.

19. Baltimore *Federal Intelligencer,* 12 April 1794.

20. Charleston *City Gazette,* 12 February 1803.

21. Boston *Massachusetts Mercury,* 23 December 1800; *Boston Gazette,* 29 December 1800; *New York Morning Chronicle,* 19 April 1804.

22. Dow, ed., *Holyoke Diaries,* Diary of Mary (Vial) Holyoke, 22, 24, 27 July 1789, 121; Boston *Massachusetts Centinel,* 30 May–15 July, 22 August–16 September 1789; *Salem Mercury,* 21, 28 July 1789; *New-York Daily Advertiser,* 8 January 1791; *Salem Gazette,* 20 August 1794; *Norwich Packet,* 29 May 1794; New London *Connecticut Gazette,* 18 June 1794; Portsmouth *New-Hampshire Gazette,* 8 August 1796; Newburyport *Political Gazette,* 18 August 1796, cited in Barriskill, "Newburyport Theatre," 41:242–45; Portland *Oriental Trumpet,* 16 January 1797; *Portland Gazette,* 9 March–11 May 1801. See also Felt, *Annals of Salem,* 2:84; Vail, "Random Notes," 155–56; and Cloris, "This Evening, January 1st, 1801."

23. *Portland Gazette,* 5 August 1801.

24. Knox, *The Sharples,* 12–13.

25. Durang, *Memoir,* 43.

26. Philadelphia *American Weekly Mercury,* 7 May 1724.

27. Boston *Massachusetts Centinel,* 2 June 1787; *New-York Commercial Advertiser,* 20 October 1801; *New York Morning Chronicle,* 28 February 1804; *New-York Columbian,* 6 January 1812; *New-York Evening Post,* 3 February 1818; Charleston *City Gazette,* 12 January 1819; *Augusta Chronicle,* 10 June 1826.

28. Philadelphia *American Weekly Mercury,* 7 May 1724; *New-York Commercial Advertiser,* 20 October 1801; *New York Morning Chronicle,* 5 March 1804; *Albany Gazette,* 23 August 1805; *New-York Evening Post,* 21 February 1812, 3 February 1818; Middletown, Conn., *Middlesex Gazette,* 28 June 1810; *Portland Gazette,* 2 December 1826; Providence *Rhode-Island American,* 17 April 1827.

29. Salem *Essex Gazette,* 10 July 1769, quoted in the *Boston Evening Post,* 7 August 1769. The full text reads,

> I Attended an association of all the ministers of this county (Lincoln): One of the gentlemen intimated, that a certain Squaw, now residing in the bounds of Brunswick, (about 24 miles below Case Bay) had lately extracted several raging running Cancers, of some years standing, within his own knowledge: I rested not till I had enquired of Mr. Miller, the minister of that place, concerning her; he confirmed all I had heard, with these additions, that she uses no charm: Herbs and roots, manufactured in her own way, are her only remedies: She draws out the Cancer, however far and wide it has spread, without injuring the parts circumjacent, or even affecting them in the least. She never undertakes any cure without four Dollars in hand: If she fails of effecting it, she voluntarily returns the Fee; she has been known to come and offer so to do, when none but herself was apprehensive her medicines would miscarry.—To convince her patient she designs no harm, she always herself takes part of what she prescribes.* She

has obtained a great name in these parts, and gains reputation daily. *It seems she uses an inward as well as outward Application.

30. *Boston Directory* (1798, 1800, 1803); Boston *Massachusetts Mercury,* 23 January 1798; Boston *New-England Palladium,* 12 March 1805; Boston *Columbian Centinel,* 13 March 1805.

31. Boston *New-England Palladium,* 12 March 1805; Pope, "Cancers."

32. Bentley, *Diary,* 8 May 1799, 2:302; Benes, "Fortunetellers, Wise-Men, and Magical Healers," 134–36. An unlocated portrait of Deb Saco depicting her in the costume of a fortune-teller was seen by Alice M. Earle in the collection of the Peabody Museum of Salem: Earle, *Stage Coach and Tavern Days,* 96.

33. Hempstead, *Diary,* 12 June 1758, 685.

34. Hempstead, *Diary,* 6 December 1729, 26 August 1742, 18 June 1728, 7, 19 June 1753, 29 August 1758, 214, 392, 197, 594, 689; Schaefer, *Useful Friend,* index, "stranger," 245; *Hudson Balance,* 17 May 1808.

35. Stiles, *Literary Diary,* 9 June 1786, 3:222–25.

36. Child, *Soldier, Engraver, Forger,* 52–67; Sonneck, *Early Concert-Life,* 36; Seilhamer, *History of the American Theatre,* 3:45. The author thanks Richard M. Candee and Deborah Childs for the correct dating of the Brunton image.

37. Shaw, *Exhibition,* entry 3. Martin was with Placide's company in New York City in February 1792. Seilhamer, *History of the American Theatre,* 2:345. See also Durang, *Memoir,* 148n47; Odell, *Annals of the New York Stage,* 2:210; Boston *New-England Palladium,* 24 July 1804; and Boston *Repertory,* 13 January 1807. It is possible that the actor/acrobat "Mr. Martin" and the "Mr. Martin—Artist from Paris" cited here were two different individuals. If so, we are sure the latter was responsible for causing museum proprietor Daniel Bowen's second fire in Boston in January 1807 because Martin alluded to the event in a Providence newspaper: "This artist will be very grateful for the patronage he shall receive in his new career, from those persons who are sensible of the misfortunes by fire which he encountered last year in Boston." Providence *Columbian Phenix,* 5 March 1808. For a description of the fire, see Richmond *Impartial Observer,* 2 February 1807; Bentley, *Diary,* January 1807, 3:272; Benes, "'A Few Monstrous Great Snakes,'" 36; and Clapp, *Record of the Boston Stage,* 88: "On the 15th of January, 1807, the Museum again took fire, from the explosion of a preparation which Mr. Martin used in the exhibition of the Phantasmagoria, then occupying the upper hall."

38. Portsmouth *New-Hampshire Gazette,* 13, 23 August 1773.

39. *New-Hampshire Gazette,* 13, 27 August, 10 September 1773.

40. Williamsburg *Virginia Gazette,* 9 August 1774.

41. Salem *Essex Gazette,* 5 July 1774; New Haven *Connecticut Journal,* 30 August 1775; *New-York Journal,* 7 December 1775; Philadelphia *Pennsylvania Gazette,* 6 April 1774; Philadelphia *Pennsylvania Packet,* 18, 25 April 1774.

42. *Newport Mercury,* 25 April 1774; *Boston Post-Boy,* 30 May, 11 July 1774; Salem *Essex Gazette,* 21–28 June 1774; New Haven *Connecticut Journal,* 30 August, 6 September 1775.

43. *Wochentliche Pennsylvania Staatbote,* 18 January 1774; *Newport Mercury,* 25 April, 9 May 1774; *Providence Gazette,* 14 May 1774; Felt, *Annals of Salem,* 2:437; Salem *Essex Gazette,* 21 June 1774; New York *Constitutional Gazette,* 9 September, 14 October 1775, 9 March 1776; *Rivington's New-York Gazetteer,* 26 October 1775; *Rivington's New-York Loyal Gazette,* 8 November 1777; *New-York Daily Advertiser,* 4 January 1776; *New-York Journal,* 4 January 1776; *New-York Gazette,* 26 February 1776; *New York Royal Gazette,* 12 June 1777, 20 January 1781, 11 February 1783.

44. *New-York Journal,* 15 February 1776.

45. Nashville *Tennessee Gazette*, 14 June 1820; *Providence Patriot*, 14 January 1824; *New-York Spectator*, 12 March 1824; Dedham *Village Register*, 19 March 1824; *Haverhill Gazette*, 20 March 1824; Cooperstown *Watch-Tower*, 22 March 1824; *Baltimore Patriot*, 2 April 1824; Easton *Republican Star*, 5 April 1824. Bennington *Vermont Gazette*, 6 April 1824; Boston *New-England Galaxy*, April 1824.

46. Bentley, *Diary*, 13 November 1787, 6 June 1796, 6 February 1807, 26 November 1809, 1:81, 2:191, 3:275–76, 479. See also Perley, *History of Salem*, 328–29. According to Perley, *History of Salem*, 2:329, William King married Rebecca Phippen when he was thirty-one. Keyes, "William King"; Carrick, *Shades of Our Ancestors*, 45–52; New York *American Minerva*, 16 December 1794–28 July 1795.

47. Bentley, *Diary*, 13 November 1787, 1:81; *Salem Mercury*, 14 July 1789; *Salem Gazette*, 22 May 1793; Keyes, "William King."

48. New York *American Minerva*, 4 June 1795; Bentley, *Diary*, 6 June 1796, 2:191.

49. *Newburyport Herald*, 14 December 1804; Portsmouth *New-Hampshire Gazette*, 19 March 1805; Portland *Eastern Argus*, 2 August 1805; Hanover *Dartmouth Gazette*, 28 March 1806; *Salem Register*, 9 December 1805. Full details of King's itinerary for the years 1783–1825 are listed in table 3.1 at http://scholarworks.umass.edu/umpress_short_time_only/.

50. Bentley, *Diary*, 6 February 1807, 3:275–76.

51. William King, Jr., also made profiles in Bermuda. *Bermuda Gazette*, 12 November 1808.

52. Bentley, *Diary*, 26 November 1809, 3:479.

53. New London *Connecticut Gazette*, 5 April 1809; *Norwich Courier*, 3 May 1809.

54. Criminality even extended into families. Charles and Rebecca Windsor, originally from Quebec but later residents of Paris, worked in Rhode Island and southeastern Massachusetts and the outer islands in 1825 and 1826 teaching French and lace-making. At the start of their fourth year in Newport, the couple was obliged to temporarily suspend their school when they learned from Canada that Rebecca's parents were ill in Quebec. The couple rushed to their side. In 1832, word came to Newport that they had relocated to Montreal and that Charles had unexpectedly died there "of cholera," preventing Rebecca's return and settlement of their numerous outstanding debts. Nothing further was learned of the couple until the *Newport Mercury* disclosed in 1833 that, contrary to the earlier news, Charles Windsor, "whose death was reported in this paper," was still alive and had been living in Le Havre, France. The *Mercury* stated that Windsor had recently absconded from Le Havre "after having been guilty of many acts of swindling." *Providence Patriot*, 3 August 1825; *New Bedford Mercury*, 16 September, 2 December 1825; *Newport Mercury*, 13 May 1826; Mason, "Newport Lace School"; Candee, "Lace Schools and Lace Factories," 116–23; Keyes, "William King," 203.

55. *Albany Argus*, 24 February, 16, 23 December 1814.

56. Greenwood, "'Extracts,'" 159–60.

57. Harding, *My Egotistigraphy*, 40.

58. *Boston Gazette*, 24 December 1792; Philadelphia *Aurora General Advertiser*, 1 April 1796.

59. *Newburyport Herald*, 14 March 1797.

60. Hartford *Connecticut Mirror*, 1 October 1827.

4. Establishing a Public Presence

1. *New-York Gazette*, 14 November 1748.
2. Lathem, *Chronological Tables*, 2–43.
3. Hempstead, *Diary*, 21 November 1753, 604.

4. Tudor, *Deacon Tudor's Diary*, 17 June 1786, 102–3.

5. Francesco, *Power of the Charlatan*, 110–18; Burke, *Popular Culture in Early Modern Europe*, chap. 4; Brand, *Popular Antiquities of Great Britain*, vol. 1.

6. See Brand, *Popular Antiquities of Great Britain*, 2:348–60, and Walker, *Essex Markets and Fairs*, 8, 24–26. See also "Fun and Games at the Fairlop Fair in 1815" by Thomas Rowlandson, illustrated in Walker, *Essex Markets and Fairs*, 24–25. For the London events, see Speaight, *English Puppet Theatre*, 148, and Speaight, *Punch and Judy*, 60.

7. Leeds, *American Almanack*. John Durang described similar fairs and harvest frolics in Pennsylvania: Durang, *Memoir*, 5. *New-York Journal*, 26 March 1767; Webster, *Autobiographies*, Diary, 27 October 1785, 219.

8. Sewall, *Diary*, 4 December 1687, 1:196; *Boston News-Letter*, 2 March 1712; Boston *New-England Weekly Journal*, 25 December 1732.

9. *Boston Gazette*, 14 May 1739; *Boston Post-Boy*, 18 November 1765.

10. Boston *New-England Weekly Journal*, 19 November 1733; Boston *Federal Orrery*, 16 April 1795; Boston *Constitutional Telegraphe*, 2 April 1800.

11. *New-York Gazette*, 1 August 1768; Charleston *South Carolina Gazette*, 10 May 1783; Elizabethtown *New-Jersey Journal*, 3, 31 January 1787.

12. Middletown, Conn., *Middlesex Gazette*, 10 October 1789; Hartford *American Mercury*, 26 October 1789; *Litchfield Monitor*, 24 November 1789.

13. *Boston News-Letter*, 16 February 1712; Lambert, comp., "Music Masters in Colonial Boston," 2:1077; Keller, *Dance and Its Music*, 324; *New-York Morning Post*, 21 June, 16 August 1787.

14. Philadelphia *Pennsylvania Chronicle*, 6 November 1769; Philadelphia *Pennsylvania Packet*, 26 October 1772, 5 August 1790; *Baltimore Daily Intelligencer*, 2 November 1795; Charleston *City Gazette*, 5 October 1796; Savannah *Georgia Gazette*, 22 February 1769; Savannah *Royal Georgia Gazette*, 15 March 1781.

15. Daniels, *Puritans at Play*, 146; Struna, *People of Prowess*, 145.

16. *Newport Mercury*, 19 December 1763; 24 September, 1 October 1764; 28 October 1765; 21 July 1766; 26 September, 17 October 1768; 4, 11 September 1769; 2 November 1772; 28 June, 26 July, 2 August, 15 November 1773.

17. *Newport Mercury*, 26 July 1783, 30 September 1785, 5 August 1799; Brooks, *Olden-Time Music*, 61.

18. *Newport Mercury*, 2, 22 May 1797; 3 July 1798; 5 March, 25 June, 5 August 1799; 17 March, 11 April 1800; 16 March, 21 December 1801.

19. *Boston Chronicle*, 7 March 1768.

20. *Charleston Gazette*, 28 November 1793.

21. Boston *Massachusetts Mercury*, 25 August 1795.

22. Boston *Columbian Centinel*, 22 November 1809.

23. *Salem Gazette*, 10 January 1809; Bentley, *Diary*, 11 January 1809, 3:408; *Salem Gazette*, 4 May 1809, cited in Belknap, *Artists and Craftsmen of Essex County*, 6.

24. Baltimore *Federal Gazette*, 23 May 1793; Philadelphia *Gazette of the United States*, 3 July 1797.

25. Cast members of the Boston Theatre, Federal Street, as taken from the Boston *Massachusetts Mercury*, 17 June 1796: The band: Leaumont, Stone, Austin, Anderson, Granger, L'Espouse, Ives, Labarre, Nicholas Jr., Relain, Henri, Graupner, Muck, Priest, Daugel, Gardie, Schetky. Players: Chalmers, Mr. and Mrs. Whitlock, Mr. and Mrs. Marshall, Bates, Hipworth, Mr. and Mrs. Hogg, Mr. and Mrs. Rowson, Beete, Weston, Dixon, Mr. and Mrs. Solomon, Mrs. Graupner (late Miss Heslyer), Mme. Gardie, Mme Lege, Mons.

Lege, Mons. Sala, Villers, Hailton, Kenny, Ashton, Miss Ashton, Ratcliffe, Clark, Mrs. Baker, Miss Green; Mr. Campbell, prompter.

26. Boston *Massachusetts Mercury,* 17 June 1796. See also Alden, "A Season in Federal Street"; Winsor, *Memorial History of Boston,* 4:363–65; Clapp, *Record of the Boston Stage,* chap. 3; and Boston *Columbian Centinel,* 27 March 1797.

27. *New York Packet,* 17 September 1785, cited in Moore, "John Durang," 20.

28. Mates, *American Musical Stage,* 11, 83, 89; *New-York Gazette,* 24 September 1759; *Rivington's New-York Gazetteer,* 12 January 1775.

29. Alden, "A Season in Federal Street," 32–35.

30. *New-York Journal,* 26 March 1767.

31. Philadelphia *Pennsylvania Chronicle,* 28 October, 11 November 1771.

32. New York *Independent Journal,* 29 December 1784.

33. *Boston Records,* 27:185–86; Boston *Massachusetts Mercury,* 7 January 1803.

34. Philadelphia *American Weekly Mercury,* 7 May 1724.

35. Philadelphia *Pennsylvania Gazette,* 24 February 1743, 14, 21 September 1752; *New-York Gazette,* 16 May 1748, 27 April, 4 May 1752; *New-York Mercury,* 12 January 1756.

36. Philadelphia *Pennsylvania Gazette,* 25 December 1755; Philadelphia *American Weekly Mercury,* 7 May 1724; *New-York Mercury,* 8 March 1756.

37. Trenton *New Jersey Gazette,* 5 January 1784; Keene *New Hampshire Sentinel,* 15 March 1806; *New Bedford Mercury,* 26 May 1815.

38. *New-York Daily Advertiser,* 15 June 1793; New York *Mercantile Advertiser,* 18 May 1802, cited in Gottesman, *Arts and Crafts,* 3:14–15; Letton, "Wax Exhibition . . . Wethersfield."

39. Microcosm, "Boston, May 13, 1756"; *Boston Post-Boy,* 26 January 1767.

40. Boston *Massachusetts Centinel,* 30 May–15 July, 22 August–16 September 1789; *Salem Mercury,* 21, 28 July 1789; Dow, ed., *Holyoke Diaries,* Diary of Mary (Vial) Holyoke, 23 April 1784, 110.

41. *Boston Evening-Post,* 7 August 1769.

42. *Providence Gazette,* 22 February 1794; Pope, "Cancers."

43. Sonneck, *Early Opera in America,* 31; Willard, *History of the Providence Stage,* 5; *Newport Mercury,* 11 August 1761.

44. Boston *Massachusetts Mercury,* 11 July 1800.

45. Boston *Columbian Centinel,* 9 January 1808; *Newport Mercury,* 17 June 1809: "Ladies taught the whole art of Flower Making Drawing and Painting, as above, and every attention paid the pupils, by Mr. and Mrs. White. . . . Terms, each pupil; for each different Flower when Perfect, 75 cents, twelve different Flowers, 7 dollars. . . . Ladies, at the expiration of their engagement, will have the privilege of receiving the last Flower of each sort they might have made, so as to form a handsome cabinet." An ornamental and sign painter, japanner, and decorator of dressing boxes and fire screens, a J. White had recently come from England and India. *New York Public Advertiser,* 30 March 1810.

46. Philadelphia *Poulson's,* 30 September 1808.

47. Philadelphia *Pennsylvania Packet,* 13 July 1772; *New-York Gazette,* 29 June 1748. Dr. Lawrence Storch, for example, offered to cure venereal disease in Baltimore for "No Cure, No Pay." Baltimore *Maryland Journal,* 6 May 1787. Likewise, Dr. William Rowan (from London) in Richmond advertised as "No cure no money." Williamsburg *Virginia Gazette,* 7 April 1768.

48. *Philadelphia Gazette,* 29 April 1799.

49. Pittsfield, Mass., *Berkshire Gazette,* 25 July 1798.

50. Leonard, "Writing."

51. Portsmouth *New-Hampshire Gazette,* 22 November 1797, quoted in Pichierri, *Music in New Hampshire,* 236; *Brattleboro Reporter,* 21 February 1816; *Newburyport Herald,* 13 October 1801; Haverhill *Merrimack Intelligencer,* 27 April 1816.

52. *New-York Daily Advertiser,* 11 August, 16, 23 September 1789, 12 January 1793; *Salem Gazette,* 15 December 1795; Charleston *City Gazette,* 8 January 1795; Boston *Columbian Centinel,* 25 July 1795; Boston *Massachusetts Mercury,* 3, 6, 20 November 1795; *Providence Gazette,* 9 April 1796; *Newport Mercury,* 17 May 1796; *New York Herald,* 18 June 1796; *New York Argus,* 26 August 1796.

53. *Nantucket Gazette,* 17, 24 June 1816. John Warner Barber reported of Nantucket that "South-east of this island is Tuckernuck, an island containing about 1,000 acres of land and which affords pasture for 1,000 sheep and 50 head of horned cattle." Barber, *Historical Collections,* 445.

54. Timothy Dwight noted that commencement will take place "at the usual time, viz on the 2nd Wednesday in September." New Haven *Connecticut Journal,* 2 September 1805.

55. *Providence Gazette,* 30 August 1788; New Haven *Connecticut Journal,* 4 September 1793.

56. Broadside, 27 June 1797, Rhode Island Historical Society, Providence, cited in Kihn, "The Circus in Connecticut," 13. The "dwarf child" was shown "at Mrs. Kidders, in Cambridge, opposite the college." Boston *Columbian Centinel,* 15 July 1797. William Bentley gave a long description of the "perfect miniature" Calvin Phillips, contrasting him favorably with his predecessor, Emma Leach, of Beverly, Massachusetts. Barriskill, "Newburyport Theatre," 41:213–14; Bentley, *Diary,* 26 July 1797, 2:229.

57. Bentley, *Diary,* 17 July 1800, 2:344: "We dined at Mrs. Hilliard's after having visited the public rooms, & having seen a Curious Bird, the Cassaway, whose admeasurement we did not take." New Haven *Connecticut Journal,* 9 October 1800; Bentley, *Diary,* 24 August 1804, 3:106–8.

58. *Newburyport Herald,* 7 April 1807, 14 August 1810; Providence *United States Chronicle,* 25 August 1803; Philadelphia *Pennsylvania Packet,* 13 July 1772; *New-York Daily Advertiser,* 13 January 1789; Boston *Columbian Centinel,* 29 June, 30 September 1805, 1 June 1825; *Norwich Courier,* 27 February 1811; Philadelphia *Freeman's Journal,* 29 March 1786; Philadelphia *American Weekly Mercury,* 7 May 1724; *New-York Journal,* 30 November 1775; *Boston Gazette,* 2 September 1757; *New-York Gazette,* 12 July 1773; *Boston Evening-Post,* 18 September 1769.

59. Quoted from an oration by James Sloan, a former member of Congress from New Jersey. *Otsego Herald,* 27 September 1819: "The ventriloquists, mountebanks, rope dancers, slight of hand deceivers, those who carry about wax figures paintings and other deceptive likenesses to draw from children and other weak minds, the product of their labor giving them in return no intrinsic value."

60. Boston *Columbian Centinel,* 21 February, 5, 26 August 1818; Salem *Essex Register,* 5 June 1819. J. Thomas Scharf and Thompson Westcott reported she was in Philadelphia in 1811. *History of Philadelphia,* 2:954. The earliest European reference to the Albiness is found in Zerah Colburn's *Memoir;* he found her in Belfast, Ireland, in 1813: "An English woman named Harvey, remarkable for a fair skin, red eyes, and hair glistening like polished metal, nearly white: she had a brother possessing similar peculiarities" (63). See also Wilson and Caulfield, *Book of Wonderful Characters,* 378–79.

61. Jackson, *Silhouette,* 115; McKechnie, *British Silhouette Artists,* 233, 317–18, 769–70; Groce and Wallace, *Dictionary of Artists in America,* s.v. "Herve, Henry"; Rutledge, "Artists in the Life of Charleston," 201; Mayne, *British Profile Miniaturists,* 71; Hand, *Signed Miniatures,* 19.

62. *Quebec Gazette*, 21 August, 4 September 1817, courtesy of Lydia Foy, National Archives of Canada, Ottawa; *Albany Gazette*, 13 December 1817; *Albany Argus*, 16, 19 December 1817; Norfolk *American Beacon*, 13, 15, 17 June 1818; Boston *Columbian Centinel*, 5 August 1818, 24 September–9 October 1819; *Boston Daily Advertiser*, 5, 8 September 1818; Portland *Eastern Argus*, 27 October 1818; *Boston Gazette*, 9 September 1819; *Boston Recorder*, 30 October 1819; Felt, *Annals of Salem*, 2:96; *Charleston Courier*, 5 January 1820, cited in Rutledge, "Artists in the Life of Charleston," 201.

63. *Albany Gazette*, 10 December 1817.

64. The miniature has not been located but was listed in a catalogue in 1828. Swan, *The Athenaeum Gallery*, 181–82.

65. Charleston *Southern Patriot*, 13 January 1820, cited in Rutledge, "Artists in the Life of Charleston," 201. An obituary reports that "Mrs. Eliza Herve—better known in this town by the appellation of *Albiness*"—died of the "prevailing sickness" in February 1820 on reaching Havana. Boston *Christian Watchman*, 22 April 1820.

5. Acquiring Skills

1. Charleston *City Gazette*, 5 February 1801.
2. Seybolt, *Apprenticeship and Apprenticeship Education*, chap. 7.
3. *New-York Gazette*, 18 May 1772.
4. Northampton, Mass., *Hampshire Gazette*, 12 March 1800; Northampton, Mass., *Republican Spy*, 15 July 1806.
5. *Newburyport Herald*, 26 May, 2, 5, 9, 16, 23 June 1807.
6. *New-York Journal*, 29 August 1771; Philadelphia *Pennsylvania Chronicle*, 1 November 1773; Dunlap, *History of New York for Schools*, 146; *New-York Commercial Advertiser*, 16 May, 6 June 1801. For other master/apprentice relationships, see Bennington *Epitome of the World*, 21 September 1807, and *Philadelphia Aurora*, 16 April 1796.
7. *Oxford Dictionary of National Biography*, s.v. "Pinchbeck, Christopher (1669/70–1732), Edward Pinchbeck (1713?–1766?), and Christopher (1709/10–1783)," 44:346–47; Britten, *Old Clocks and Watches and Their Makers*, 333–36; *Dictionary of National Biography*, s.v. "Pinchbeck," 1193–94; Jay, *Learned Pigs*, 8–15; Jay, *Many Mysteries Unravelled*; Speaight, *English Puppet Theatre*, 106, 156; Frost, *Old Showmen*, 110, 123–24.
8. Macmichael, *Story of Charing Cross*, 284; London *Gazetteer and New Daily Advertiser*, 13 July 1771.
9. London *Public Advertiser*, 25 January 1772; *Oxford Dictionary of National Biography*, s.v. "Pinchbeck Family (per. c. 1720–1783)"; Frost, *Old Showmen*, 176–78; Jay, *Learned Pigs*, 8–9. Other pig showmen included J. Fawkes with an "amazing Pig of Knowledge" (*Northampton Mercury* [England], 24 June 1786) and a Mr. Nicholson with "the Learned Pig" (London *Morning Herald*, 16 February 1785). Nicholson's appearance on the stage at Sadler's Wells was followed by mass resignations among other performers and acrobats, who felt belittled by having to share the stage with an animal.
10. Philadelphia *Pennsylvania Gazette*, 20 February 1753. This may well have been the same John McDonald that Yeldall hired as a journeyman in the 1770s.
11. Savannah *Georgia Gazette*, 22 April 1790.
12. Charleston *Columbian Herald*, 9 February 1796.
13. *Philadelphia Gazette*, 24 June 1797.
14. Boston *Repertory*, 1 February 1814.

15. *Augusta Chronicle*, 21 March 1828.

16. *Boston Daily Advertiser*, 21 February 1814, 1 July 1818; Boston *Columbian Centinel*, 15, 25 July, 14–17 August 1818; *Albany Argus*, 15 October 1818; *Providence Patriot*, 7 March–9 April 1827; *Augusta Chronicle*, 21 March, 15 April 1828; *Saratoga Sentinel*, 14 July 1829; Charleston *City Gazette*, 8 February 1830. See also Wright, "James Warrell," 15; Vail, "Random Notes," 158; and Chindahl, *History of the Circus*, 13.

17. Salem *Essex Register*, 4 August 1821; *Boston Commercial Gazette*, 7 June 1821.

18. *Boston Directory* (1803); Wheatland, "Notice of Some of the Descendants of Joseph Pope," 115; John Pope, Inventory, 26 July 1796, Suffolk County Probate Records, 95:251–52; *Providence Gazette*, 2 January, 3 December 1790, 17 February 1794, 2 June 1802, 9 April 1808, 7 January 1809; Providence *Columbian Phenix*, 2 August 1806; Boston *Columbian Centinel*, 8 July 1809; *Providence Patriot*, 27 December 1826–3 January 1827.

19. Stiles, *Literary Diary*, 11 January 1773, 1:332–33; Pope, "Cancers." See also Boston *Massachusetts Centinel*, 15 September 1785, 4 October 1786, 10 October 1790.

20. *Boston Directory* (1789); Administrative File, 1796, "John Pope late of Boston Physician deceased," Suffolk County Probate Records, 94:691; Boston *Massachusetts Centinel*, 15 September 1785, 10 October 1790. Gregory H. Laing kindly identified John Pope and his sons.

21. Tufts, *Autobiography of a Criminal*, 56.

22. Tufts, *Autobiography of a Criminal*, 66. See "Molly Ockett and Her World," www.bethelhistorical.org, based on an exhibition at the Bethel Historical Society, Bethel, Maine, from July 2004 to May 2007.

23. Tufts, *Autobiography of a Criminal*, chap. 8.

24. Tufts, *Autobiography of a Criminal*, 273.

25. Tufts, *Autobiography of a Criminal*, 66; Day, "Henry Tufts as a Source on the Eighteenth-Century Abenakis." Eventually, Tufts was accused of stealing silverware from a household in Salem, Massachusetts, and sentenced to be hanged. He spent several years in prison before finally winning a reprieve and moving to Limington, Maine.

26. Durang, *Memoir*, 11. For Durang's early life, see his *Memoir*, 3–46.

27. "Theatre—Federal-Street . . . The Dwarf Dance by Mr. Durang." Boston *Massachusetts Mercury*, 17 November 1795; Charleston *City Gazette*, 8 May 1816; *Alexandria Herald*, 7 January 1818.

28. *Appletons' Cyclopædia*, s.v. "Durang, Charles," 2:269; Durang, *Memoir*, xviii.

29. Harding, *My Egotistigraphy*, 26–31.

30. Guild, "Journal," 250–60, 275, 277–79, 288.

31. Guild, "Journal," 261, 263–64, 268.

32. Guild, "Journal," 298–99, 299, 301, 303–6; *Albany Argus*, 20 May 1817; Howell, *Bicentennial History*, 1:705; Kern and Kern, "James Guild."

33. *Providence Gazette*, 24 June 1769.

34. Boston *Massachusetts Mercury*, 20 April 1798.

35. Pinchbeck offered to dispose of a trained pig at a low rate in the Boston *Massachusetts Mercury*, 20 April 1798, at about the same time that Brigshaw made his first appearance in Newport. *Newport Mercury*, 10 April, 8 May 1798; *Providence Gazette*, 28 April, 12 May, 8 September 1798; *Norwich Packet*, 14 May 1798, *Newburyport Herald*, 29 May 1798; Dover, N.H., *Sun*, 4 July 1798; *Portland Gazette*, 30 July 1798.

36. Boston *New-England Palladium*, 12 June, 28 August 1810.

37. *Boston Post-Boy*, 11 December 1749.

38. Baltimore *Maryland Journal,* 13 May 1783.

39. *New-York Gazette,* 7 August 1793; *Philadelphia Gazette,* 22 December 1794.

40. Greenwood, "'Extracts,'" 157.

41. Baltimore *Federal Gazette,* 16 November 1796.

42. "The Articles of Agreement Made between Daniel H. Leonard and James Brown Junr, Both of Sharon Vermont, Witnesseth," 5 March 1813, Rauner Special Collections, Dartmouth College Library. The text is as follows:

> First—I, Daniel H. Leonard agree to teach James Brown Junr what I can now in three days in the principles of teaching the art of Writing in the manner in which I have been teaching for several years past—and at some convenient time, this Spring or Summer to teach him further on said principles.
>
> I James Brown Junr agree to use all reasonable exertions to render myself thoroughly Competent to the business of teaching the Art of Writing on said System. Also I engage to devote my whole time to said business from this date till the 1st of June 1814. To keep an exact account of the number of persons I teach in every place and prices for which I teach them, and faithfully to pay to said Leonard or his heirs every four months one fourth part of all the money (or property of any kind) which I shall receive for teaching during said term, of one year and three months—I also engage to confine myself to Windsor County Vt during this Spring, and afterwards to teach in such part of the Country as Said Danl. H. Leonard shall direct—
>
> We both engage to strive to render the business respectable and useful where ever we introduce it—To preserve specimens of improvement and Recommendations . . . Witness our hands
>
>   Sharon March 5th 1813 Daniel H. Leonard / James Brown Jr.

43. Hall, *Worlds of Wonder,* 83.

44. London *Daily Courant,* 1 February 1705, 2 May 1711. For a closer look at English mimicking practices, see Aspin, *Picture of the Manners,* 280–81.

45. *London Daily Post,* 25, 27 July 1743.

46. Highfill, Burnim, and Langhans, *Biographical Dictionary,* s.v "Rossignol, Gaetano," 13:115–17.

47. "Sieur Gaetana a la Rossignol"; a "New Rossignol" who played at Breslaw's theater; the "original English Rossignol" (Mr. Adams); a "New Venetian" who sang "à la Rossignol"; "Infant Rossignol"; and the English Rossignol. London *Public Advertiser,* 12 January 1775, 3 May, 24 September 1777; London *Morning Herald,* 15 February 1793; London *World,* 20 August 1785; London *Morning Post,* 11 July 1796, London *Times,* 29 May 1797; *London Gazette,* 13 January 1783; London *Parker's General Advertiser,* 4 November 1782.

48. Hamilton, *Itinerarium,* 102–3.

49. *New-York Daily Advertiser,* 19 November 1793.

50. Portland *Eastern Herald,* 23 January 1797.

51. *Boston Gazette,* 9 December 1800; *New-York Daily Advertiser,* 28 June 1802.

52. *Albany Gazette,* 10 October 1803.

53. London *Morning Herald,* 15 February 1793; *London Gazette,* 13 January 1783; London *Parker's General Advertiser,* 4 November 1782; London *World,* 20 August 1787; London *Morning Post,* 11 July 1796; London *Times,* 29 May 1797; *Portland Gazette,* 27 April 1801; Strutt, *Sports and Pastimes,* xlv, 204.

54. *New-York Commercial Advertiser,* 18 January 1803; *New-York Evening Post,* 2 July 1802; Boston *Commercial Gazette,* 15 December 1800; Boston *Massachusetts Mercury,* 9 December 1800; Portland *Eastern Herald,* 23 January 1797.

6. The Impact of Images

1. *New-York Gazette,* 1 August 1768.

2. The earliest known advertising relief cut printed in an American paper was a provincial copy of an image that had already been seen in London and Dublin. The so-called Microcosm, a music machine designed and built by London clockmaker Henry Bridges, was published as a woodcut in a London paper beginning in July 1734, and it remained there for almost a year and a half. It later surfaced in a Dublin newspaper in 1745 when Bridges and the machine visited that country. Similar copies appeared in New York City, Philadelphia, and Boston in 1755 and 1756 at the time Bridges's son took the Microcosm to the American colonies. London *Daily Journal,* 17 July 1734; *London Daily Post,* 13 January 1737; *Dublin Journal,* 31 December 1745.

3. Boston *New-England Palladium,* 6 May 1803; *New-York Daily Advertiser,* 30 December 1795.

4. Garvin and Garvin, *On the Road North of Boston,* 100; Flint, "Early-Nineteenth-Century Circus," 133. See also Charles E. Culver, "The History of the Town of Somers," in Scharf, *History of Westchester County,* 2:480. Culver, a descendant of early town residents, described Hachaliah Bailey and his elephant, Bailey's Elephant Hotel, the elephant monument in front of the hotel, and the early animal business conducted by farmers from Somers and surrounding towns: "About the year 1815 he [Bailey] imported the first elephant into this country. This was the celebrated 'Old Bet[t],' and for a long time she constituted the sole 'show.'" While the Crowninshield elephant of 1796 preceded Old Bett, Culver remembered the second animal's name. Richard Flint kindly provided the Culver information.

5. Easton *Republican Star,* 30 June 1807; Philadelphia *Poulson's,* 1 September 1807; *Alexandria Advertiser,* 11 December 1807; Richmond *Enquirer,* 29 April 1808; Lexington *Reporter,* 15 December 1808; New Bern *Carolina Federal Republican,* 8 February 1812; *Alexandria Gazette,* 17 April 1812.

6. Easton *Republican Star,* 30 June 1807; *Pittsfield Sun,* 24 September 1812; Boston *Independent Chronicle,* 27 November 1815. Full details of Old Bett's itinerary for the years 1804–1816, including her age and measurements at various times, are listed in table 6.1 at http://scholarworks.umass.edu/umpress_short_time_only/. As is noted there, Old Bett (a female) apparently walked everywhere she went, and an estimated 90 percent of her overnight stays were unannounced.

7. Peter Maverick was the son of engraver Peter Rushton Maverick (1755–1811). See Stephens, *The Mavericks.*

8. McPharlin, *Puppet Theatre in America,* 93.

9. Philadelphia *Independent Gazetteer,* 1 April 1788; *Providence Gazette,* 20 February 1796.

10. *Boston Daily Advertiser,* 4 March 1813; 26 September, 26 November 1818; 13 January 1820; 10 December 1821.

11. New London *Connecticut Gazette,* 15 April 1807.

12. New London *Connecticut Gazette,* 3 June 1789; Middletown, Conn., *Middlesex Gazette,* 23 May 1798; Hartford *Connecticut Courant,* 22 June 1788; "To the Curious. . . . Two Camels, Male and Female." The author thanks Joel S. Berson for pointing out that Leavenworth's stable was located in New Haven and not in Boston as is suggested by Vail, "Random Notes."

13. New York *American Minerva,* 2 March 1796; "Gabriel Salenka, Lately Arrived from Europe."

14. *Providence Gazette,* 27 June 1794; Boston *Columbian Centinel,* 6 August 1794, 25

February 1795; Boston *American Apollo,* 2 October–13 November 1794; *Salem Gazette,* 14 April 1795; Newburyport *Impartial Herald,* 19 May 1795, 27 April 1802; Portsmouth *Oracle of the Day,* 20 June 1795; Hartford *Connecticut Courant,* 28 March 1796; Hartford *American Mercury,* 4 April–9 May 1796, 21 May 1801; New Haven *Connecticut Journal,* 22 June 1796, 14 September 1802; New York *American Minerva,* 31 August 1796; *New-York Gazette,* February 1797, April 1800; *Albany Register,* 2 September 1800; New London *Connecticut Gazette,* 10 June 1801; *Boston Gazette,* 13 August 1801; *Salem Register,* 25 March 1802; Portsmouth *New-Hampshire Gazette,* 11 May 1802; *New York Mercantile Advertiser,* 13 November 1802. Full details of the itinerary of this "beautiful African Lion" for the years 1791–1807 are listed in table 6.2 at http://scholarworks.umass.edu/umpress_short_time_only/.

15. Philadelphia *Claypoole's,* 26, 28 March, 2 April 1792.

16. Windsor *Vermont Republican,* 6 July 1818; New York *National Advocate,* 27 March 1817; New Haven *Connecticut Journal,* 27 October 1818; *Pittsfield Sun,* 15 May 1822.

17. Charleston *City Gazette,* 17 April 1798.

18. John Hodgson, Manchester, N.H., to Haverhill, Mass., Public Library, 23 March 1994, author's collection; Hodgson, "An Other Voice." While ventriloquy was not widely publicized until the beginning of the nineteenth century, it was well known before then. A Mr. Rayner and his daughter, a tightrope walker, performed at Hussey's booth at Bartholomew Fair in 1746. Frost, *Old Showmen,* 147–49. Frost described a man at Bartholomew Fair in 1751 "who talks in his belly and can fling his voice into any part of the room" (171).

19. Pinchbeck, *Expositor,* 54–55: "The performer provides himself with a doll, which he calls Tommy, from whom the feigned voice appears to proceed. Placing Tommy on his knee, a conversation apparently takes place between him and Tommy, in which the Exhibitor contrives to make correction necessary: Then punishes him by placing him under his coat, where Tommy is heard speaking in a smothered tone of voice." "Tommy" had been the traditional name of a ventriloquist's respondent voice since the 1790s. John A. Hodgson, personal communication, 2015. See also Conners, *Dumbstruck,* 276–77.

20. Fredericktown *Republican Gazette,* 10, 12 December 1802; Georgetown *Olio,* 19 May 1803; *New York Morning Chronicle,* 4 May 1804.

21. *Natchez Gazette,* 28 January 1806.

22. Butterworth, *Magic on the Early English Stage,* 41, 159.

23. Boston *Independent Chronicle,* 10 December 1789.

24. London *Daily Journal,* 8 November 1729.

25. New York *Weekly Museum,* 18 April 1795.

7. Street Performers

1. *New-York Weekly Journal,* 15 April 1734; *Boston Evening-Post,* 18 September 1769; *Boston Patriot,* 7 March 1810.

2. For an alternative perspective on the North American "success" with animals, see Mizelle, "'Man Cannot Behold It without Contemplating Himself.'"

3. Eliot, *Diary,* 19 December 1726, 31; Earle, *Customs and Fashions in Old New England,* 242; Kihn, "The Circus in Connecticut," 1; Vail, "Random Notes," 119–20. See also *Boston Gazette,* 26 September 1720, 16–23 October 1721, 4 March 1723, 22 December 1726; Philadelphia *American Weekly Mercury,* 31 August 1727; *New-York Gazette,* 6 May 1728, cited in Vail, "Random Notes," 120; Hempstead, *Diary,* 18, 19 April 1729, 208. Lions for public exhibition were imported into the American colonies as early as 1716 (*Boston Weekly News-Letter,*

26 November 1716, 7 April 1718, 15 December 1726). A "Lyoness," however, was brought to Portsmouth, New Hampshire, by Capt. Archibald Macphederis in 1715 (*Boston Weekly News-Letter*, 11 July 1715). The author is grateful to Sandra Rux for this information.

4. Winsor, *Memorial History of Boston*, 2:480n3; *New-York Gazette*, 16 April 1733, cited in Vail, "Random Notes," 123; *Boston Weekly News-Letter*, 19 April 1733.

5. Winsor, *Memorial History of Boston*, 2:480n3. That the Lanechtskipt may have been *Langnekschip* was kindly suggested by Joel S. Berson.

6. *Boston Weekly Rehearsal*, 1733–1734, quoted in Earle, *Customs and Fashions in Old New England*, 243; *Boston Evening Post*, 23 May 1737; *Boston Gazette*, 13 April 1741, 10 October 1749; Boston *Independent Chronicle*, 30 April 1802; Boston *Columbian Centinel*, 3 November 1798, 4 April 1805; *Albany Balance*, 27 July 1810; *Providence Patriot*, 17 September 1825; Boston *Massachusetts Mercury*, 16 December 1800.

7. Camels were exhibited in Boston in 1721 and 1739. *Boston Gazette*, 2 October 1721, 23 September 1739; Parkman, "Diary," 28 February 1739; Hempstead, *Diary*, 13 July 1739, 349.

8. Vail, "Random Notes," 122; *Boston Gazette*, 2, 9, 23 October 1721; Parkman, *Diary*, 28 February 1739, 61; Hempstead, *Diary*, 13 July 1739, 353 (courtesy of Luis Mendes, Bristol, R.I.); *New-York Gazette*, 19 November 1739, cited in Vail, "Random Notes," 122; *Boston Post-Boy*, 11 April 1743.

9. Philadelphia *Pennsylvania Gazette*, 16 November 1743; *New-York Gazette*, 1 August 1768; *Newburyport Herald*, 19 August 1800; Portland *Eastern Argus*, 24 May 1805.

10. *New-York Daily Advertiser*, 17, 18 August 1787.

11. Stiles, *Literary Diary*, 2 June 1789, 3:355: "Viewed two Camels in To[wn] a Male aet. 10. Nineteen hands high on the Bunch, and a Female aet 4. They were bro't from the African shore on the Mediterranean last year via West Ind. To N York. The owner gave 200 Half Joes or 1600 Doll. For them. He shewed them into Vermont as high as L. Champlain last Fall—at Boston all last Winter obliged to Warm the stables with a Stove."

12. Ames, *Diary*, 6 July 1789, 1:477. Now in the collection of Historic New England, the hair sample was labeled "This Hair was taken from the neck of a Camel in Hingham in the spring of 1789" and came from the estate of Susan Norton, granddaughter of historian Charles Eliot Norton, whose family originally came from Hingham, Massachusetts. Nancy C. Carlisle kindly provided this information.

13. *New-York Daily Advertiser*, 7 September 1787; Boston *Massachusetts Centinel*, 13 November, 20 December 1788, 18 July 1789, 13 January 1790; Middletown, Conn., *Middlesex Gazette*, 23 May 1789; New Haven *Connecticut Journal*, 3 June 1789, 30 June 1790; Hartford *Connecticut Courant*, 15, 22 June 1789, 24 May 1790; *Salem Mercury*, 4 August 1789, 6 October 1789; Portsmouth *New Hampshire Spy*, 8 September 1789; *Litchfield Monitor*, 16 February 1791; New London *Connecticut Gazette*, 1 April 1791. See also Vail, "Random Notes," 122–23; Kihn, "The Circus in Connecticut," 5–6; Brooks, *Quaint and Curious Advertisements*, 112–13; and Trumbull, *Memorial History of Hartford County*, 2:578–79.

14. *Boston Democrat*, 3 March 1804; *Charleston Courier*, 11 March 1807, 27 January 1808; *New-York Columbian*, 1, 2 June 1812; Philadelphia *Poulson's*, 19 December 1812.

15. Stiles, *Literary Diary*, 2 June 1789, 3:355; Hartford *Connecticut Courant*, 24 May 1790.

16. Flint, "Early-Nineteenth-Century Circus," 133; Kihn, "The Circus in Connecticut," 12–13.

17. Bentley, *Diary*, 30 September 1797, 2:235; *New York Argus*, 25 April 1795; Baltimore *Federal Gazette*, 8, 10, 11 October 1796; Dunlap, *History of the American Theatre*, 182–83.

18. *Salem Gazette*, 10 January 1809; *Newburyport Herald*, 30 January–6 February 1809;

Portsmouth *New-Hampshire Gazette,* 4 April 1809; Portland *Eastern Argus,* 25 May 1809; Bentley, *Diary,* 11 January 1809, 3:408, cited in Vail, "Random Notes," 134; Boston *New-England Palladium,* 12 June, 28 August 1810.

19. *Newport Mercury,* 9 June 1795; *Providence Gazette,* 20 June 1795. See also Bentley, *Diary,* 1 August 1795, 2:156: "A Bison in Town. It confirms Buffon's opinion that it is the Cow in a state of nature, & that the difference is accidental. In the afternoon it was carried through the Town, & such persons gave as pleased to compensate the man for his Trouble."

20. "But to prevent all disputes with the Negro at the Gate who constantly attends, each Person (whether seen him before or not) is desired to pay to the said Negro six pence a piece." *Boston Weekly News-Letter,* 7 April 1718. Sharper was inventoried in Savage's westernmost garret. Arthur Savage, Probate Inventory, 1735, Suffolk County Probate Records, 32:206.

21. Baltimore *Federal Gazette,* 8, 11 November 1800; Boston *Independent Chronicle,* 8 February 1802; Boston *Columbian Centinel,* 26 May 1802, 19 January 1803, 28 April 1810; Boston *New-England Palladium,* 25 May 1802; *Newburyport Herald,* 18 January 1803; Worcester *Massachusetts Spy,* 26 September 1804; *Boston Records,* 30:152: "Pollard Othello (blk) Eupha Brown (blk)." Thwing, *Inhabitants,* 34,619, 34,620.

22. *Providence Gazette,* 9 November 1771; *New-York Journal,* 12 December 1771.

23. *Newport Mercury,* 1 November 1773.

24. *Boston Post-Boy,* 30 August 1773; Philadelphia *Independent Gazette,* 17 March 1789; Philadelphia *Federal Gazette,* 2 February 1791.

25. Durand, *A Huguenot Exile,* 158; Sewall, *Diary,* 2 July 1712, 2:693: "Saw a man playing Tricks on a Rope on board the Man of War."

26. Byrd, *Secret Diary,* 15 August 1712, 570.

27. Pepys, *Diary,* 21 September 1668, 4:25.

28. Philadelphia *American Weekly Mercury,* 7 May 1724; *Boston Records,* 13:259–60; Winsor, *Memorial History of Boston,* 2:480.

29. Williamsburg *Virginia Gazette,* 17–24 March 1738, cited in Keller, *Dance and Its Music,* 201.

30. Dow, *Arts and Crafts,* 117; *Boston Gazette,* 12, 19 September 1757; Wilson, "The Old North Church." For a description of rope flying in England, see Aspin, *Picture of the Manners,* 266–68.

31. Snow, "America's First Flyer," 111–13.

32. *Boston Gazette,* 12, 19 September 1757; *Boston News-Letter,* 15 September 1757.

33. Drake, *Life and Correspondence of Henry Knox,* 100; Manning-Sanders, *The English Circus,* 252–54; Breck, *Recollections,* 41–42. J. L. Bell of Newton, Mass., kindly provided these references.

34. Charleston *City Gazette,* 8 March 1808; *Charleston Courier,* 8 February 1808; Philadelphia *Poulson's,* 8 June 1808; *New-York Evening Post,* 17 July 1809; Boston *New-England Palladium,* 27 February 1810; *Boston Patriot,* 7 March 1810; Salem *Essex Register,* 28 March 1810; *Salem Gazette,* 7 April 1810; Barriskill, "Newburyport Theatre," 43:28–29; Boston *Columbian Centinel,* 14 April 1810; Providence *Rhode-Island American,* 30 November 1810; Emery, ed., *Reminiscences of a Nonagenarian,* 230: "Here, when I was a child, a man walked across State street on a tight rope, stretched from one of the chimneys to that of the 'Wolfe Tavern,' an event which made no little sensation in the staid town."

35. New York *American,* 20 June 1820; *Baltimore Patriot,* 27 November 1820; Boston *Repertory,* 28 April 1821; Camden, S.C., *Chronicle,* 1 January 1823.

36. *Baltimore Patriot,* 27 April 1822; Hartford *American Mercury,* 8 July 1823.

37. *New-York Journal*, 14 May 1768, 22 June 1769; *New-York Gazette*, 27 June 1768; Odell, *Annals of the New York Stage*, 1:143.

38. *Boston Gazette*, 18 September, 9, 23 October 1769.

39. Philadelphia *Porcupine's Gazette*, 7 July 1798; *New-York Daily Advertiser*, 21 May 1799; Fredericksburg *Virginia Herald*, 18 November 1797; *Alexandria Times*, 30 November 1797; *New-York Evening Post*, 2 October 1802.

40. Boston *Columbian Centinel*, 13 August 1796.

41. *Portsmouth Oracle*, 26 August 1797; Boston *Columbian Centinel*, 5, 26 August, 28 October 1797, 13 June 1798; Boston *Massachusetts Mercury*, 1 May 1798.

42. *New-York Evening Post*, 19 August 1809; *Salem Gazette*, 18 June 1811; Brock, *A History of Fireworks*, s.v. "Ruggieri family"; *Boston Gazette*, 6 September 1819, 17 January 1820.

43. *New-York Evening Post*, 16 October 1820; *Providence Gazette*, 1, 5 September, 10, 20, 31 October 1821; *Newport Mercury*, 6 October 1822.

44. *Newport Mercury*, 16 July 1808; *Providence Gazette*, 13 August, 16, 24 September 1808; Boston *Columbian Centinel*, 5 November 1808.

45. Philadelphia *Pennsylvania Packet*, 20 July 1784.

46. New York *Independent Journal*, 24 July 1784, 8 January 1785; *New York Packet*, 10 October 1785. Busselot may have been active in Boston; see Felt, *Annals of Salem*, 2:88; *Providence Gazette*, 2 April 1785, cited in Crouch, *Eagle Aloft*, 97; and New York *Independent Journal*, 1 January 1784.

47. Deeker, "Air Balloon"; Stiles, *Literary Diary*, 22, 23 September 1789, 3:367; *New-York Daily Advertiser*, 11 June–23 September 1789; Crouch, *Eagle Aloft*, 100–101; *New York Packet*, 23 September 1789, and *New-York Journal*, 24 September 1789, both cited in Crouch, *Eagle Aloft*, 102.

48. Crouch, *Eagle Aloft*, chap. 4; Blanchard, *Journal of My Forty-Fifth Ascension*; Blanchard, *The Principles, History and Use of Air-Balloons*, 37–38. John Durang of Philadelphia witnessed this event: "He rose out of sight waving a flag, cross'd the Deleware 16 miles in the Jerseys." Durang, *Memoir*, 9–10.

49. Boston *Massachusetts Mercury*, 29 May–2 June, 3 July–7 August, 23 October, 3–20 November 1795: "Aerostatic experiment . . . in lieu of his 46th ascension." *New-York Daily Advertiser*, 12 January 1793; New York *American Minerva*, 21 August 1794; *Salem Gazette*, 15 December 1795; Portsmouth *New-Hampshire Gazette*, 6 February 1796; *Providence Gazette*, 9 April 1796; *Newport Mercury*, 17 May 1796; *New York Herald*, 18 June 1796; *New York Argus*, 11 January, 12 July 1796. See also Felt, *Annals of Salem*, 2:88; Goler, "'Here the Book of Nature,'" 16–17; Rolt, *The Aeronauts*, 88–90; and Crouch, *Eagle Aloft*, chap. 4. Blanchard returned to Europe in 1798 and did not complete his forty-sixth ascension until 12 August 1798 at Rouen, France.

50. Crouch, *Eagle Aloft*, 102; *Providence Gazette*, 30 September 1803; Boston *New-England Palladium*, 24 February, 11 April 1809; Providence *Columbian Phenix*, November 1809.

51. Ames, *Diary*, 15, 17 July 1797, 1:623.

52. Elizabethtown *New-Jersey Journal*, 4 November 1795. Mizelle, "'Man Cannot Behold It without Contemplating Himself,'" offers a persuasive discussion of Cressin and his performing animals.

53. George Washington's Philadelphia Household Account Book, 16 November 1796, cited by Mary V. Thompson, research historian, Mount Vernon Estate and Gardens, Fred W. Smith National Library for the Study of George Washington.

54. Dow, ed., *Holyoke Diaries*, Diary of Mary (Vial) Holyoke [Margaret's diary], 20 July 1797, 135.

55. Bentley, *Diary,* 30 August 1797, 2:235. Bentley first spoke of "his tail" and "his Tusks" but then corrected himself: "We say *his* because of the common language. It is a female & teats appeared just behind the forelegs."

56. *Providence Gazette,* 1 July 1797.

57. Bentley, *Diary,* 29 April 1816, 4:384.

58. Sanger, *Journal,* 14 August 1821, 557.

59. "N.B. Mr. Jeremiah Fowler and Captain Maynard here. The former brought a Jackal, an Entertaining Sight. How wondrously are the Works of God diversify'd! How manifest are thy Works, O Lord! in wisdom has thou made them all!" Parkman, "Diary," 25, 26 April 1750.

60. Ballantine, Journal, quoted in Lockwood, *Westfield and Its Historic Influences,* 1:408: "Apr. 9 [1764] Saw a She Lyon at Landlord Fowlers."

61. Dow, ed., *Holyoke Diaries,* Diary of Mary (Vial) Holyoke [Margaret's diary], 15 July 1793, 129; Samuel Adams, Ipswich, Mass., Diary, 4 December 1793, cited in Rice, *Early American Taverns,* 115.

62. Quoted in Barriskill, "Newburyport Theatre," 41:350.

63. *New-York Gazette,* 4 July 1768.

64. Portsmouth *New-Hampshire Mercury,* 7 January 1785; *Salem Gazette,* 4 January 1785; Newburyport *Essex Journal,* 26 January 1785; Charleston *South-Carolina State-Gazette,* 16 March 1785; Windsor *Spooner's Vermont Journal,* 7 June 1785; Charleston *Columbian Herald,* 16 March 1796.

65. Boston *Massachusetts Mercury,* 26 April, 10 May 1796; Philadelphia *Claypoole's,* 7 June 1797; Philadelphia *Porcupine's Gazette,* 18 July 1797; Washington's Philadelphia Household Account Book, 17 November 1795, Mount Vernon Estate and Garden. Washington paid three dollars to a "man who had a very sagacious Dog."

66. Philadelphia *Pennsylvania Gazette,* 21 August 1740.

67. New York *Minerva,* 28 July 1797.

68. Bentley, *Diary,* 31 July 1792, 27 March 1810, 1:384, 3:507.

69. Webster, *Autobiographies,* 1 May 1785, 211.

70. Webster, *Autobiographies,* 13 August 1790, 279.

71. Pynchon, *Diary,* 13 April 1785, 211.

72. Dow, ed., *Holyoke Diaries,* Diary of Mary (Vial) Holyoke [Margaret's diary], 22 November 1790, 123.

73. Bentley, *Diary,* 5 January 1788, 22 November 1790, 1:113, 214; Felt, *Annals of Salem,* 2:84.

74. Bentley, *Diary,* 19 December 1795, 2:168; Hazard, *Nailer Tom's Diary,* 19 May 1796, 187; the event was advertised in the *Newport Mercury,* 17 May 1796.

75. Charleston *City Gazette,* 24 August 1795.

76. Philadelphia *Pennsylvania Packet,* 20 July 1784; New York *Independent Journal,* 24 July 1784; Philadelphia *Federal Gazette,* 9 January 1793; Philadelphia *Dunlap's,* 10 January 1793.

77. Boston *Columbian Centinel,* 7 September 1796; Boston *Massachusetts Mercury,* 17 July 1798.

78. Durang, *Memoir,* 49.

79. Barriskill, "Newburyport Theatre," 43:29; Emery, ed., *Reminiscences of a Nonagenarian,* 230.

80. Philadelphia *Pennsylvania Gazette,* 15 January 1745.

81. Rowe, *Letters and Diary,* 1 November 1771, 221.

82. Rowe, *Letters and Diary*, 5 October 1773, 251; Ames, *Diary*, 5 October 1773, 1:255: "Went Boston saw Bates perform."

83. Chindahl, *History of the Circus*, 6; Vail, "Random Notes," 172; Greenwood, *The Circus*, 15–17; *Boston Weekly News-Letter*, 23 September, 7 October 1773; *Boston Post-Boy*, 4 October 1773: "Mr. Bates and his Horses Weighed in the Balance. In which it is shewn with great brevity, that his Exhibitions in Boston, are impoverishing, disgraceful to human Nature, and downright Breaches of the 6th Commandment." Bates, "Horsemanship, by Mr. Bates"; Rowe, *Letters and Diary*, 8 September, 5 October 1773, 249, 251. *Boston Post-Boy*, 4 October 1773.

84. *Newport Mercury*, 1 November 1773.

85. Boston *Federal Orrery*, 29 August 1796.

86. Philadelphia *Constitutional Diary*, 21 December 1799.

87. Philadelphia *Pennsylvania Packet*, 4 March 1780.

88. *New-York Chronicle*, 13, 20 July 1769.

89. Milbank, *First Century*, 34; Washington, Pa., *Reporter*, 20 September 1819.

90. New York *Columbian Gazette*, 9 October 1794; Flint, "Early-Nineteenth-Century Circus," 134–36, 139.

91. Augusta *Southern Centinel*, 6 February 1794; *Salem Gazette*, 22 June 1827; *Baltimore Patriot*, 15 January 1822; *Charleston Courier*, 4 March 1806; *New-York Columbian*, 2 August 1810; *Philadelphia Aurora*, 7 February 1806; Washington *National Intelligencer*, 17 November 1806; *Alexandria Herald*, 24 December 1819; Philadelphia *Dunlap's*, 18 January 1792.

92. *Charleston Evening Gazette*, 19 April 1786.

93. Philadelphia *Federal Gazette*, 23 October 1792; *New-York Daily Advertiser*, 7 August 1793; Boston *Massachusetts Mercury*, 15 May 1795, 12 August 1796; Boston *Columbian Centinel*, 13 August, 29 September 1796; Boston *Federal Orrery*, 29 August, 5 September 1796; Hartford *Connecticut Courant*, 17 August 1795; *Providence Gazette*, 18 August 1795. For Ricketts's early career in Edinburgh, see Baston, "Transatlantic Journeys."

94. *Albany Chronicle*, 28 July, 7 August 1797; New York *Weekly Museum*, 18 December 1798. See also Chindahl, *History of the Circus*, 7–8; Kihn, "The Circus in Connecticut," 8; Thayer, *Annals of the American Circus*, 4ff; Mates, *American Musical Stage*, 162; and *New-York Gazette*, 18 February 1800.

95. Dow, ed., *Holyoke Diaries*, Diary of Mary (Vial) Holyoke [Margaret's diary], 22 August 1796, 135.

8. Tavern Entertainers I: Magic Lanternists

1. *New-York Mercury*, 8 December 1755.

2. Bentley, *Diary*, 14 September 1801, 2:392.

3. Bentley, *Diary*, 1 July 1813, 4:176.

4. Samuel Adams, Diary, 4, 19 December 1793, cited in Rice, *Early American Taverns*, 115–16.

5. *New-York Evening Post*, 18 July 1743, quoted in Odell, *Annals of the New York Stage*, 1:24. An unidentified sleight-of-hand showman, again possibly Richard Brickell, advertised in the *New-York Weekly Journal*, 18 July 1743. *New-York Evening Post*, 8, 14, 22 September 1746; "Punch's Opera, Bateman or the Unhappy Marriage," *New-York Gazette, and Weekly Post-Boy*, 31 August, 7 September 1747, cited in Odell, *Annals of the New York Stage*, 1:27. See also Sonneck, *Early Opera in America*, 14; *New-York Weekly Journal*, 9 May 1748; *New-York Gazette*, 27 April 1752; Philadelphia *Pennsylvania Gazette*, 20 August, 21, 24 September

1752; Charleston *South-Carolina Gazette*, 2 July 1753; and *New-York Mercury*, 29 December 1755, 5, 12 January 1756. For Bateman as a chapbook title, see Neuburg, *Chapbooks*, 37. See also Wilson, *Memorial History of the City of New York*, 2:460. Howard, *Punch and Judy in Nineteenth-Century America*, 13, agrees with the theater historian Paul McPharlin that Mosely was probably the puppeteer and Brickell did mechanical entertainments.

6. *New-York Weekly Journal*, 14 August 1749; *Boston Chronicle*, 22 February 1768; Philadelphia *Federal Gazette*, 25 July 1791. Full details of Brickell's itinerary for the years 1742–1756 are listed in table 8.1 at http://scholarworks.umass.edu/umpress_short_time_only/.

7. *New-York Daily Advertiser*, 11 December 1794; Hartford *American Mercury*, 5 January 1828; Barre, Mass., *Farmer's Gazette*, 4 July 1834.

8. Henry Clark operated the Sign of the Coach-and-Horses Tavern on Chestnut Street: Philadelphia *Pennsylvania Gazette*, 30 December 1742, 4, 13 January, 24 February, 10 March 1743. Joseph Barber operated the Temple Bar on Second Street: Philadelphia *Pennsylvania Gazette*, 27 January, 2, 17, 24 February 1743.

9. Philadelphia *Pennsylvania Gazette*, 27 January 1743. Brickell posted a similar notice in New York City and described the "30 humorous and entertaining Figures, larger than Men or Women," listing them in some detail. *New-York Evening Post*, 15 September 1746, 31 August, 7 September 1747.

10. *Boston Evening-Post*, 12, 26 December 1743.

11. Rising received permission from the selectmen to show his microscope and "other Curious Instruments" on 26 December 1743. *Boston Records*, 17:45; *Boston Gazette*, 27 December 1743, 10 January 1744; *Boston Evening-Post*, 5 March 1744.

12. See Stafford and Terpak, *Devices of Wonder*, 297–305, and Hankins and Silverman, *Instruments and the Imagination*, 37–71. Additional information can be obtained in Musée d'Orsay, *Lanternes Magiques;* Barber, "Evenings of Wonders"; Robinson, *The Lantern Image;* and Hoffmann, *Lanterna Magica*.

13. New York *Ladies' Weekly Museum*, 17 May 1817; "Tablet of Memory," *Encyclopedia Britannica*, 11th edn. (New York: Encyclopedia Britannica Company, 1911), 16:661.

14. Musée d'Orsay, *Lanternes Magiques*, 17–21; Robinson, *The Lantern Image*, 6–10; Stafford and Terpak, *Devices of Wonder*, 297.

15. Pepys, *Diary*, 19 August 1666, 2:434.

16. *Boston Evening-Post*, 12, 26 December 1743; Philadelphia *Pennsylvania Gazette*, 27 January, 24 February 1743; *New-York Evening Post*, 20 September 1746; *New-York Gazette*, 31 August, 7 September 1747.

17. *New-York Evening Post*, 20 September 1746.

18. *New-York Gazette*, 30 October 1749; *New-York Weekly Journal*, 8 August, 18, 15 September, 16 October 1749.

19. Patricia Crain, "'*Babes in the Wood*': Print, Orality, and Children's Literature in the Nineteenth-Century United States," paper delivered at "Home, School, Play, Work: The Visual and Textual Worlds of Children" Conference, Worcester, Mass., 14–15 November 2008.

20. *Boston Gazette*, 27 December 1743.

21. Philadelphia *Pennsylvania Gazette*, 2 August 1744; *London Daily Advertiser*, 20 July 1743; *London Daily Post*, 27 July, 5, 8 September 1743. Other "representations" were shown in London theaters of the "terrible Battles that were fought between the Saxons and the ancient Britains" (*London Daily Post*, 5 September 1724), a recent sea battle in the Mediterranean (London *General Advertiser*, 4 May 1744), and the siege and capture of Cape Breton "with the procession of colours and standards" (London *Public Advertiser*, 16 September 1759). See

Rosenfeld, *Theater of the London Fairs,* 52, 85, 105, 115, 167, which notes that the "famous Dettingen victory was celebrated in all five booths" at Bartholomew Fair in 1743. Rosenfeld, however, identified these as "scenery," not projections.

22. Philadelphia *Pennsylvania Gazette,* 4 September 1755.

23. Philadelphia *Pennsylvania Chronicle,* 3 April 1769.

24. "Also curious Italian machinery which presents against the wall." *Newport Mercury,* 31 August 1767; *New-York Mercury,* 13 April 1767; *Boston Post-Boy,* 21 September 1767.

25. *New-York Weekly Journal,* 3 July 1749; Newburyport *Political Gazette,* 1 October 1795; Providence *United States Chronicle,* 28 April 1796; Baltimore *Federal Gazette,* 26 July 1797; Newburyport *Impartial Herald,* 11 June 1796; Newark *Centinel of Freedom,* 12 November 1805.

26. *New-York Weekly Journal,* 14 August 1749; Portland *Eastern Herald,* 12 October 1796; *New-York Daily Advertiser,* 21 November 1794; Philadelphia *Pennsylvania Chronicle,* 3 April 1769; *Boston Post-Boy,* 21 September 1767.

27. Hartford *Connecticut Courant,* 18 March 1807; *Newport Mercury,* 4 May 1802; Fredericktown, Md., *Political Intelligencer,* 1 February 1806; *New-York Weekly Journal,* 7 July 1749.

28. *Newport Mercury,* 1 May 1798; Savannah *Georgia Gazette,* 22 June 1798; *Charleston Courier,* 9 April 1809.

29. Philadelphia *Dunlap's,* 22 August 1791; *New-York Gazette,* 4 June 1790; Newburyport *Political Gazette,* 1 October, 1 November 1795.

30. Charleston *Columbian Herald,* 17 July, 12 August 1786; *New-York Morning Post,* 20 November 1789; *Philadelphia Packet,* 3 July 1790; Philadelphia *Federal Gazette,* 7 July 1790, 1 June, 1 August 1791; *New-York Gazette,* 4 January 1790; Philadelphia *Mail,* 11 July 1792; Norfolk *Virginia Chronicle,* 28 July 1794; *New-York Daily Advertiser,* 13 July 1795, 21, 31 January 1809; *Salem Gazette,* 22 September 1795; Newburyport *Political Gazette,* 1, 8 October, 1 November 1795; Portsmouth *New-Hampshire Gazette,* 27 October 1795, 29 March 1803; Philadelphia *Claypoole's,* 4 February 1797; Providence *United States Chronicle,* 27 April 1797; Baltimore *Federal Gazette,* 7 September 1797; *Alexandria Expositor,* 25 February 1805; *New York Diary,* 27 November 1797; Providence *Rhode-Island American,* 1 February 1811.

31. Newburyport *Political Gazette,* 1 October 1795; "To the Curious! . . . Mr. Maginnis"; *Massachusetts Mercury,* 21 November 1797; *Newport Mercury,* 16 October 1799; Charleston *Columbian Herald,* 17 July 1786; *The Favourite Airs . . . in the Ombres Chinoises,* cited and illustrated in Speaight, *Puppet Theatre,* 145–46.

32. Philadelphia *Dunlap's,* 22 August 1791.

33. Philadelphia *Federal Gazette,* 5 August 1791; Philadelphia *Dunlap's,* 5 September 1791, 15 August 1792; Stubbs, *Cultivating National Identity,* 12.

34. Charleston *City Gazette,* 17 February 1797.

35. Savannah *Georgia Gazette,* 22 June 1798.

36. Providence *United States Chronicle,* 28 April 1796; Portsmouth *New-Hampshire Gazette,* 21 March 1798.

37. *Newport Mercury,* 4 May 1802.

38. Easton *Republican Star,* 28 February 1804.

39. New York *Royal Gazette,* 29 April 1780. The English fleet took over Havana in 1762.

40. Charleston *City Gazette,* 9 April 1796.

41. Philadelphia *Aurora General Advertiser,* 20 March 1797; Baltimore *Federal Gazette,* June 1797; Charleston *City Gazette,* 19 June 1798.

42. Walpole, N.H., *Farmer's Weekly Journal,* 2 October 1797.

43. Charleston *City Gazette,* 19 November 1807.

44. *Salem Gazette,* 19 April 1816.

45. *New-York Evening Post,* 20 September 1746; Savannah *Georgia Gazette,* 22 June 1798.

46. Philadelphia *Pennsylvania Gazette,* 8 January 1767; Wheatland, *The Apparatus of Science at Harvard,* 129–30; Sara J. Schechner, senior curator of the Historical Scientific Instrument Collection at Harvard University, personal communication, 25 March 2009.

47. The Atkinson Academy in Atkinson, N.H., employed a "Magic Lantern and Illuminated Diagrams" in an advertisement in 1831. *Haverhill Gazette,* 19 January 1831.

48. Keene *New-Hampshire Sentinel,* 25 May 1837; Portsmouth *Journal,* 31 March 1838.

49. *Boston Gazette,* 21 May 1754.

50. *New-York Gazette,* 1 February 1762.

51. New York *Royal Gazette,* 18 June 1779.

52. Boston *Columbian Centinel,* 5 December 1798.

53. Boston *Columbian Centinel,* 13 September 1817.

54. *New-York Daily Advertiser,* 24 December 1817.

55. McClintock and McClintock, *Toys in America,* cite the advertisement from the *New-York Commercial Advertiser,* 1819, 95. This information was kindly provided by Linda Lapides, Baltimore, Md.

56. Newburyport *Impartial Herald,* 11 June 1796; *Boston Gazette,* 5 July 1802.

57. Pepys, *Diary,* 19 August 1666, 2:434.

58. Georgetown *Washington Federalist,* 26 November 1804.

59. Georgetown *Washington Federalist,* 28 November 1804; Fredericktown *Political Intelligencer,* 1 February 1805; Newark *Centinel of Freedom,* December 11, 1805; New Haven *Connecticut Herald,* 10 February, 14 April 1807; Hartford *Connecticut Courant,* 18 March 1807.

9. Tavern Entertainers II: Puppeteers, Ropedancers, Conjurers

1. *Boston Weekly Rehearsal,* 30 October 1732; Boston *New-England Weekly Journal,* 23 December 1734.

2. Oldmixon, *British Empire in America,* 2:137–38; Parkman, "Diary," 14, 17 August 1739; DeForest, *History of Westborough,* 53–55. That Burlesson's "Cabbin" housed a bed and bedding for overnight accommodations is suggested by contemporary usage to describe slave sleeping quarters in eighteenth-century Boston household inventories. Suffolk County Probate Records, Inventory nos. 7650 (12 October 1741), 8357 (7 January 1745). Ross W. Beales, Jr., kindly provided the Parkman quotation.

3. Winsor, *Memorial History of Boston,* 2:480n3.

4. Sheldon, *Documentary History of Suffield,* 134, 136, 146.

5. Edward Burlesson to Thomas and John King, 14 May 1736; Edward Burlesson to Thomas King, 25 January 1733, both Kent Memorial Library, Suffield, Conn. Edward Burlesson's and Elizabeth Jesse's marriage intentions were published on 25 June 1720. The banns were forbidden by Mrs. King, mother of Elizabeth, on 28 June 1720 and by her stepfather, Joseph King, on 4 July 1720. *Suffield Vital Records,* 1:132; *Burleson v. King,* Hampshire Co., Massachusetts Bay Colony, 29 August 1721, Hampshire County, Massachusetts, Court of Common Pleas, LDS G.S. microfilm roll no. 905340, book 2, p. 56, Special Collections and University Archives, University of Massachusetts, Amherst; E. Burlesson, "A Lamentation in Memory," 1725, cited in Guerra, *American Medical Bibliography,* 63, reproduced at 44.

6. Lynde, *Diaries,* 136.

7. Edward Burlesson to Thomas King, 25 January 1733, Kent Memorial Library, Suffield, Conn.

8. Winsor, *Memorial History of Boston,* 2:480n3; Sheldon, *Documentary History of Suffield,* 134, 136, 146, 302. The unidentified proprietor of a Greenland bear in Boston in 1733, assumed to be Burleson, advertised by means of a "farewell speech" given by "Ursa Major, or the great White Bear" from his "den" in Boston before leaving for London. Earle, *Customs and Fashions in Old New England,* 243; Vail, "Random Notes," 123–24; *Boston Weekly News-Letter,* 19 April 1733. See also Edward Burleson to Thomas and John King of Suffield, Hartford, Conn., 14 May 1736, Kent Memorial Library, Suffield, Conn. Lester Smith of Suffield kindly assisted with this research.

9. Philadelphia *Pennsylvania Gazette,* 30 August 1764. Philips was one of the six inmates sought by the prison warden who had broken out of the York jail on 8 August 1764 and mentioned in the *Pennsylvania Gazette* want advertisement.

10. Philadelphia *Pennsylvania Gazette,* 25 January 1770.

11. Speaight, *English Puppet Theatre,* 109.

12. Speaight, *History of the English Puppet Theatre,* 92–108, 155–56.

13. Speaight, *History of the English Puppet Theatre,* 150.

14. Burnet, *A Second Tale of a Tub,* frontispiece; Pepys, *Diary,* 4 September 1668, 4:16; Frost, *Old Showmen,* 97–98.

15. Speaight, *English Puppet Theatre,* 97, 150; Speaight, *Punch and Judy,* 20.

16. Philadelphia *Pennsylvania Gazette,* 30 December 1742, cited in Sonneck, *Early Opera in America,* 14.

17. *New-York Gazette,* 31 August, 7 September 1747.

18. Speaight, "Punch's Opera at Bartholomew Fair."

19. London *Daily Post,* 23 August 1740.

20. Shershow, "'Punch and Judy' and Cultural Appropriation"; Battestin, "Fielding and 'Master Punch' in Panton Street"; *New-York Journal,* 3 July–16 October 1749; Sonneck, *Early Opera in America,* 14; *The Unfortunate Concubines; the History of Fair Rosamond, Mistress to Henry II, and Jane Shore, Concubine to Edward IV* (London: R. Ware, C. Hitch, and J. Hodges, 1748), cited in Heltzel, *Fair Rosamond,* 44; Speaight, *English Puppet Theatre,* 94–95, 108–9, 150–55; Pepys, *Diary,* 24 September 1668, 4:25.

21. *New-York Weekly Journal,* 24, 30 July, 21, 28 August, 18 September, 16 October 1749; *New-York Evening Post,* 23, 26 October 1749; *New-York Gazette,* 9, 30 October 1749; London *Daily Post,* 28 August 1727.

22. Wyatt, *Life and Surprizing Adventures,* 8–9.

23. *New-York Journal,* 26 March 1767.

24. *New-York Journal,* 30 April 1767; *New-York Gazette,* 24 December 1770; New York *Royal Gazette,* 29 April 1780.

25. Philadelphia *Pennsylvania Gazette,* 25 January 1770.

26. Philadelphia *Pennsylvania Chronicle,* 27 May 1771. A notice in London's *Public Advertiser* on 12 June 1759 publicizes that "Mr. Saunders's Company Tumblers and Dancers from Bristol, Bath, and Hot Wells" was to appear at the races at Ascot-Heath and at the playhouse in Windsor to show his skill as an acrobat "without a Pole."

27. *New-York Journal,* 8 November 1770; *New-York Gazette,* 7 January 1771; Philadelphia *Pennsylvania Packet,* 19 October 1772; Charleston *South-Carolina Gazette,* 31 December 1772, 19 April 1773.

28. *Boston Chronicle,* 22 February 1768; *Boston Post-Boy,* 16 January 1764.

29. *Boston Chronicle,* 14 March 1768; Rowe, *Letters and Diary,* 22 January 1767, 120.

30. Christopher, *Illustrated History of Magic,* 53.

31. Harrower, "Diary of John Harrower," 8 October 1774, 87.

32. Christopher, *Illustrated History of Magic*, 54; Bayly, "[By Permission]. At the Sign of St. Patrick"; Henninger, "By Authority. At the Next Door."

33. New Haven *Connecticut Journal*, 8 July 1795; *Salem Gazette*, 14, 21 April 1797; Newburyport *Political Gazette*, 10, 17, August 1797; Portland *Eastern Herald*, 31 May, 3, 7 June 1797.

34. Maginnis called himself "from Edinburgh" in Charleston *State Gazette*, 29 January 1800. Durang, *Memoir*, 40: "About this time [December 1795] arrived a James McGinnis and three more with him, all musicians belonging to Prince Henry's Band, deserted from Canada. McGinnis got up a grand exhibition next to the theatre, as there was no prospect to get anything by a benefit in the theater. The managers gave me permission to perform with McGinnis on the off play nights of the theater, which answered a good purpose to me. I got up, in machinery, The Storming and Destruction of the Bastile, with great praise." The obituary of Maginnis, "the celebrated puppet-show-man," was published in the *New-York Spectator*, 23 September 1805.

35. Newburyport *Political Gazette*, 1 October 1795; Boston *Columbian Centinel*, 23 December 1795, 6, 27 January 1796; *Newburyport Herald*, 2 March 1798; *Newport Mercury*, 25 September, 9 October 1799; Boston *Massachusetts Mercury*, 18 March, 10, 21 November 1797, 9, 23, 29, 30 December 1800, 6 January 1801; *New-York Evening Post*, 19, 25 April 1804; *New-York Herald*, 26 December 1804. See also "To the Curious," 1795, transcribed in Winslow, ed., *Harper's Literary Museum*, 390–91; "Pleasing Entertainments"; Cloris, "This Evening, January 1st, 1801"; Sonneck, *Early Opera in America*, 152; and Odell, *Annals of the New York Stage*, 2:67. Full details of Maginnis's itinerary for the years 1795–1805 are listed in table 9.1 at http://scholarworks.umass.edu/umpress_short_time_only/.

36. Baltimore *Federal Gazette*, 26 July 1797.

37. Washington *National Intelligencer*, 14 December 1804; *New-York Herald*, 26 October 1805. Maginnis died on 9 October 1805.

38. Charleston *City Gazette*, 19, 21, 24 November 1807; *Charleston Courier*, 21 November 1807.

39. *Charleston Courier*, 27 July 1811.

40. Philadelphia *Mail*, 1 August 1791; Baltimore *Maryland Journal*, 10 March 1786; *New-York Morning Post*, 17 July 1787; *Albany Register*, 26 July 1790; *Newport Mercury*, 3 August 1790.

41. *Norwich Packet*, 23 January 1794; *Newport Mercury*, 3 August 1796; Charleston *South-Carolina State-Gazette*, 8 November 1800; *Providence Phoenix*, 18 June 1803; *Newburyport Herald*, 2 October 1807.

42. Charleston *City Gazette*, 6 August 1808; *New-York Commercial Advertiser*, 11 January 1809.

43. Williamsburg *Virginia Gazette*, 15 April 1773.

44. *New-York Gazette*, 14 March 1774; Philadelphia *Pennsylvania Evening Herald*, 27 September 1786; *New-York Daily Advertiser*, 21, 27 July 1787; *New-York Morning Post*, 17 July 1787.

45. *New-York Daily Advertiser*, 31 August 1787, cited in Odell, *Annals of the New York Stage*, 1:262. A caricature sketch written for the 24 July 1787 *New-York Daily Advertiser* termed Brenon "John Patrick M'Donnough O'Shagnesse."

46. *New-York Journal*, 19 July 1787; *New-York Daily Advertiser*, 18 July–3 August 1787; Middletown *Middlesex Gazette*, 18 August 1788, 19 December 1789; Hartford *American Mercury*, 26 October 1789; *Litchfield Monitor*, 24 November 1789. See also Trumbull, *Memorial History of Hartford*, 1:579, and Vail, "Random Notes," 155–58.

47. Boston *Herald of Freedom*, 3 November, 8 December 1788; Bentley, *Diary*, 22 November 1790, 1:214. The complete entry reads, "22. A Baloon Driver, Wire dancer, & Legerdemain Irishman and wife are to exhibit this day at 1/6, & /9 for children. The Baloon passed overhead at three o'clock towards the Harbour into which it dropped."

48. *New-York Morning Post*, 19 June 1788: "Eloped from her husband, on Friday the 13th instant, MARY BRENON, supposed to have gone off with another man; this is to forewarn all persons not to harbour or trust the said MARY, my wife, on any account; as I am determined to pay no debts of her contracting from the date hereof, as witness my hand, JOHN BRENON, Performer on the Slack Wire. New-York, June 14, 1788." Boston *Massachusetts Centinel*, 13 September 1788, dated Hartford, 8 September 1788: "Married, on Thursday evening last, JOHN BRENON, Esq. the celebrated Wire-dancer, to the very amiable Miss Hannah Etridge; a young lady possessed of every accomplishment to make the marriage bed agreeable." See also *American Herald and Worcester Recorder*, 16 October 1788.

49. *New-York Morning Post*, 19 June 1788, 11, 16 April 1790; Boston *Massachusetts Centinel*, 13 September 1788.

50. *Windham Herald*, 9 August 1792.

51. Conners, *Dumbstruck*, 266.

52. *Philadelphia Gazette*, 23 May 1801.

53. *Aberdeen Journal*, 12 May 1800.

54. The two leading sources for following the Rannies' American sojourn are Charles J. Pecor, *Ten Year Tour*, and John Hodgson, "An Other Voice," who both investigated the subject thoroughly just after newspapers became available on microfilm and online. Pecor, however, was unaware that James was John's older brother, and it was Hodgson who correctly first saw the occasional conflict between the two entertainers. See also Wright, *Revels in Jamaica*, 310–11; Gottesman, *Arts and Crafts*, 3:374–78; Barriskill, "Newburyport Theatre," 43:8; Boston *Columbian Centinel*, 20 March 1813, 5, 9 December 1801; *New-York Commercial Advertiser*, 8 December 1801; and Boston *Massachusetts Mercury*, 9 December 1801. Their appearance as "Messrs. Rannie" took place in Boston on 22 January 1802 at the Haymarket Theatre. See also Rannie, "Ventriloquism." Full details of the Rannies' itinerary for the years 1801–1811 are listed in table 9.2 at http://scholarworks.umass.edu/umpress_short_time_only/.

55. *New-York Commercial Advertiser*, 25 February, 16 March 1802; Philadelphia *Poulson's*, 27 April 1802.

56. *Alexandria Expositor*, 6 May 1803; Lexington, Ky., *Palladium*, 11 May 1805; *Portland Gazette*, 20 May 1805; *New-York Commercial Advertiser*, 25 February 1802; *New-York Daily Advertiser*, 1 April 1804; *Philadelphia Gazette*, 7 June 1802.

57. *New-York Daily Advertiser*, 1, 18 April 1804; *New-York Chronicle*, 19 March 1804; New York *American Citizen*, 21 April 1804; *New-York Commercial Advertiser*, 28 April, 24 May 1804; *New-York Evening Post*, 17 April, 25 May 1804; New York *Morning Chronicle*, 4, 24, 25 May 1804; *Salem Gazette*, 25 September 1804; Newburyport *Political Calendar*, 1 October 1804; Portsmouth *Political Star*, 25 October, 1 November 1804; *Orleans Gazette*, 19 March 1806; *Natchez Gazette*, 27, 28 January 1806; Charleston *City Gazette*, 3 March 1807; Rannie, "The European Ventriloquist's Exhibition"; Boston *Columbian Centinel*, 20 March 1813. Other relevant Rannie references include *New-York Commercial Advertiser*, 8 December 1801; Boston *Columbian Centinel*, 5, 13 December 1801, 28 July 1804, 6 January 1808, 26 December 1810; *Salem Register*, 11 January 1802; Boston *Massachusetts Mercury*, 22 January 1802; Philadelphia *Aurora General Advertiser*, 13 May 1802; Newark *Centinel of Freedom*, 6 October 1802; *Newport Mercury*, 4 June 1804, 18 February 1811; *Providence Gazette*, 23 June 1804; Boston

New-England Palladium, 13 July 1804; *Portland Gazette,* 27 May 1805; *Newburyport Herald,* 25 March 1808; *Salem Gazette,* 12 October 1810; Providence *Columbian Phenix,* 9 March 1811; *Boston Gazette,* 18 April 1811.

58. "Ventriloquism, for One Night and Positively No Longer"; *Newport Mercury,* 18 February 1811; Providence *Columbian Phenix,* 9 March 1811; *Boston Gazette,* 18 April 1811. Herman Boaz was a German conjurer living in Britain after 1788. Gustavus Katterfelto was a Prussian conjurer who found notoriety in England from 1792 to 1799. Philip Breslaw was the author of *Breslaw's Last Legacy* (1795).

59. Parkman, "Diary," 14, 17 August 1739.

60. Lynde, *Diaries,* 20 March 1732, 9 December 1763, 136, 188.

61. Philadelphia *Pennsylvania Gazette,* 30 December 1742; *New-York Gazette,* 27 April 1752; *New-York Mercury,* 12 January 1756; Charleston *South-Carolina Gazette,* 16 July 1753.

62. *New-York Weekly Journal,* 7 August 1749; *New-York Journal,* 26 March 1767; *New-York Gazette,* 24 December 1770.

63. Mabel L. Webber, ed., "Extracts from the Journal of Mrs. Ann Manigault, 1754–1781," *South Carolina Historical and Geological Magazine,* 58–59, cited in Keller, *Dance and Its Music,* 88.

64. Rowe, *Diary,* 22 January 1767, 29.

65. *Boston Post-Boy,* 21 September 1767; Rowe, *Letters and Diary,* 15 September 1767, 142. See also Vail, "Random Notes," 152–54.

66. Dow, ed., *Holyoke Diaries,* Diary of Mary (Vial) Holyoke, 2, 4 September 1783, 109; emphasis added.

67. New York *Royal Gazette,* 29 April 1780; McPharlin, *Puppet Theatre in America,* 50; *Boston Records,* 25:285–86.

68. Bentley, *Diary,* 22 November 1790, 1:212; *New-York Morning Post,* 5 April 1788; Webster, *Autobiographies,* 5 April 1788, 252.

69. Dow, ed., *Holyoke Diaries,* Diary of Susanna (Holyoke) Ward, 31 April 1795, 175.

70. Dow, ed., *Holyoke Diaries,* Diary of Mary (Vial) Holyoke, 15 December 1795, 133.

71. Dow, ed., *Holyoke Diaries,* Diary of Mary (Vial) Holyoke, 7 September 1796, 135.

72. Dow, ed., *Holyoke Diaries,* Diary of Margaret Holyoke, 13 January 1802, 141; Bentley, *Diary,* 22 January 1802, 2:409.

73. Dickerson, "Diary," 5 May 1802, 2:678.

74. The ten taverns were Punch Bowl, Brookline; George Tavern, Boston Neck; Fenno's Tavern, Middletown; Nichol's Long Room, Middletown; Vandewater's Long Room, New York; Corre's City Tavern, New York; Hunt's on Coenties Dock, New York; Major Aorson's Tavern, New York; Duplessis's Long Room, Philadelphia; and Woart's Free Mason's Hall (Green Dragon), Boston. The three halls were Hampden Hall, New York; Assembly Room, Portsmouth; and Assembly Room, Salem, and the one storefront was the store on Mease's Wharf, Philadelphia.

75. *New-York Journal,* 8 April 1767.

76. Philadelphia *Pennsylvania Packet,* 10 February 1772. The best description of *conveyance* and the related term *confederacy* (teaming with another hidden conjurer) is given in Butterworth, *Magic on the Early English Stage,* chap 3.

77. *Boston News-Letter,* 6 December 1733; *New-York Gazette,* 9 October 1749; *New-York Mercury,* 10 December 1753; *Charleston Morning Post,* 1 December 1786; Philadelphia *Gazette of the United States,* 6, 23 January 1796; Philadelphia *Aurora General Advertiser,* 4 April 1796.

78. Philadelphia *Pennsylvania Gazette,* 1 December 1748.

79. Philadelphia *Pennsylvania Gazette*, 30 July 1752.
80. *New-York Journal*, 16 March 1769.
81. Philadelphia *Pennsylvania Gazette*, 10 April 1745.
82. Philadelphia *Pennsylvania Gazette*, 11 June 1772.
83. Hartford *Connecticut Courant*, 7 March 1777.
84. New London *Connecticut Gazette*, 29 May 1778.
85. Butterworth, *Magic on the Early English Stage*, 178–79.

10. Art of Psalmody

1. Sewall, *Diary*, 23 February 1718, 2:885–86.
2. Sewall, *Diary*, 2 February 1718, 2:881.
3. Sewall, *Diary*, 25 October 1691, 17 October 1700, 28 December 1705, 5 July 1713, 1:283, 436, 538, 2:720.
4. *Psalms, Hymns, and Spiritual Songs;* Foote, *American Hymnody*, 15–16, 31, 53–54.
5. Thomas Walter, *The Grounds and Rules of Musick Explained*, cited in Winslow, *Meetinghouse Hill*, 152; Walter, *The Sweet Psalmist of Israel;* Buechner, "Thomas Walter"; Cotton Mather, *The Accomplished Singer;* Mather Byles, "To Mr. Smibert, on Viewing His Pictures"; and John Adams, all cited in Foote, *American Hymnody*, 72, 96, 106, 155.
6. Foote, *American Hymnody*, 97–100, 103–5; Winslow, *Meetinghouse Hill*, chap. 10; Buechner, *Yankee Singing Schools*, 9.
7. Sewall, *Diary*, 16 March 1721, 2:976; Mather, *Diary*, 16 March 1721, 2:608; Boston *New-England Courant*, 11 December 1721, quoted in Buechner, *Yankee Singing Schools*, 29.
8. Boston *New-England Courant*, 19 March 1722; "Church Records of the Old Town of Reading," 52.
9. Buechner, "Thomas Walter," 53–54.
10. Boston, Roxbury, Cambridge, Charlestown, Reading, Dorchester, Weston, Bridgewater, Ipswich, Newbury, and Taunton. From Peter Thacher, *Cases of Conscience*, cited in Buechner, "Thomas Walter," 59.
11. Trayser, *Barnstable*, 47; Deyo, *History of Barnstable County*, 385; Stone, *History of Beverly*, 265–66; Winslow, *Meetinghouse Hill*, 166.
12. Chauncey, *Regular Singing Defended;* Walker, *First Church in Hartford*, 226.
13. Gay, *Farmington Papers*, 23–39. Prickt notes adopted in Franklin, Mass., 1739 (Hurd, *History of Norfolk County*, 162); Beverly, Mass., 1730 (Stone, *History of Beverly*, 266); Halifax, Mass., 1740 (Massachusetts Society of Mayflower Descendants, "Halifax, Mass., Church Records"). Limited tunes adopted by Weston, Mass., 1723 (Peirce, comp., *Town of Weston*, 529).
14. Excerpts from the diary of Timothy Edwards appear in Stoughton, *"Windsor Farms,"* 96–97. Stiles, *History of Ancient Windsor*, 1:273–75; and *Records of the Services*, 96–100. See also Kenyon, "George and Mathew Beale," cited in Cooke, "Itinerant Yankee Singing Masters," 28n5.
15. Cooke, "Itinerant Yankee Singing Masters," 18–19.
16. Newark *Centinel of Freedom*, 23 October 1809; Amos Holbrook to Andrew Law, Bloomfield, N.J., 10 March 1809, cited in Crawford, *Andrew Law*, 192; Amzi Chapin, Journal, cited in Thomas and Benes, "Amzi Chapin," 77, 83, 87, 89, 91.
17. When psalmodist Andrew Law found that his school in New York City was losing momentum, he printed up handbills and forwarded them to his brother in Connecticut: "I send you 200 advertisements. . . . I wish you to send the adv. to Country Towns to be set

up in the public houses, and send some to . . . the Country round Boston and some fewer eastward. I shall send on some more as soon as I can. I will send some up the North River and the West part of Connecticut and southern states." Andrew Law to William Law, New York City, 1 October 1786, quoted in Crawford, *Andrew Law,* 54.

18. An unidentified "Person who has taught the various Branches of Psalmody in the Provinces of New-York, Massachusetts-Bay, and Connecticut" advertised a school in 1770; Elias Gilbert, a "singing school," in 1770 and 1772; and Andrew Van North, a "Singing-School," in 1771. *Newport Mercury,* 1 January, 4 June, 10 October 1770, 28 September 1772.

19. Benjamin Williams, Samuel Wadsworth, Mr. Munson, and Mr. Ripley. Salem *Essex Gazette,* 24 November 1772, 14 September 1773, quoted in Brooks, *Olden-Time Music,* 110; Buechner, *Yankee Singing Schools,* 63, 78–79; Salem *Essex Gazette,* 19–26 April 1774.

20. William Billings and John Barry in 1769, John Barry and a Mr. Crane in 1772, and Moses Deshon in 1773. *Boston Gazette,* 2 October 1769, 6 January 1772, 13 December 1773.

21. Newark *Centinel of Freedom,* 16 August 1797; Hagerstown *Maryland Herald,* 26 October 1803.

22. Another example of a tunebook is Hezekiah Moors, *The Province Harmony* (1809), cited in Cooke, "Itinerant Yankee Singing Masters," 34.

23. *Boston Gazette,* 2 October 1769; Stephen Peabody, Diary, 7 March 1771, Adams Family Papers, Massachusetts Historical Society, Boston, quoted in Nathan, *William Billings,* 25. Billings taught school in Stoughton in 1774 where he also met his wife. *New England Historical and Genealogical Register* 14 (1860): 251–52; *Providence Gazette,* 28 May 1774. See also Metcalf, *American Writers and Compilers,* 51–64, and Bentley, *Diary,* 28 September 1800, 2:350–51.

24. Parkman, "Singing Book"; Ebenezer Parkman, Diary, and Anna Sophia Parkman, Diary, 12, 13–15, 17, 20, 21, 25, 27, 28–31 January, 1, 2, 4–9, 11 February 1788, quoted in Buechner, *Yankee Singing Schools,* 116–18. Badcock, a resident of Wrentham, was married and the father of a daughter, Sarah, born 1777; his son, Lemuel, born 1775, had died in August 1777. *Vital Records of Wrentham,* 15, 408.

25. Sampsel, "Samuel Babcock," 52, 70.

26. Parkman, "Diary," 30 January, 8 February 1778. Anna Sophia Parkman wrote on 11 February that "I spin. pm. this day Mr. Badcock finish his school and we settled with him. My part of School expenses is 18/10." Cited in Forbes, *Hundredth Town,* 86–87. See also Buechner, *Yankee Singing Schools,* 116–18.

27. Parkman, "Diary," 27 February, 1, 2 April 1778.

28. Parkman, *Diary,* 27 October, 1 November, 1 December 1778, 18 January, 4, 10 February 1779, 11 June 1780, 52, 72, 86, 96–97, 243.

29. Parkman, "Diary," 24 March 1766; 12 May 1771 ("N.B. Ensign [Jeduthan] Fay, his Wife and Daughter, went out at the first Mention of it"); 8 March 1778 ("but Mr. Ebenezer Chamberlain sat otherwise and did not stand as the rest. I fear he is disgusted"); 31 March 1778 ("N.B. Old Mr. Hardy fell into an unhappy Frame about the Singers—Said their Behavior was abominable!"); 3, 14 March 1779.

30. *Rivington's New-York Gazetteer,* 1 December 1774; Wilson and Keller, *Connecticut's Music,* 53–54; Trumbull, *Memorial History of Hartford County,* 1:578; Hartford *Connecticut Courant,* 21 September 1808. A Hartford historian states that Amos Bull was teaching psalmody "on the south side" of Hartford as late as 1808, and a series of advertisements in the *American Mercury* for that year indicates he also owned a hardware and dry goods store in that city. Hartford *American Mercury,* 22 September, 6, 24, 27 October 1808.

31. New York *Independent Journal,* 7 July 1784.

32. Webster, *Autobiographies,* 1785, 215. "The Thanksgivings of New England progress Southward. Governor Jay has appointed a Thanksgiving in New York on the 26th inst." Bentley, *Diary,* 21 November 1795, 2:166.

33. "Mr. Spicer, respectfully informs the inhabitants of Hudson, that he again proposes teaching a Singing School in this City, if sufficient encouragement is given." *Hudson Balance,* 28 November 1808. See also New London *Connecticut Gazette,* 5 October 1803; Cooke, "Itinerant Yankee Singing Masters," 29–30; Meech and Meech, comps., *History of the Descendants of Peter Spicer,* 83; and Crawford, *Andrew Law,* 62n.

34. Buechner, *Yankee Singing Schools,* 48; Redfield, *A Succinct Account,* 11–12.

35. Cooke, "Itinerant Yankee Singing Masters," 22; *Newburyport Herald,* 8 December 1797; *Salem Gazette,* 17 February 1804.

36. *Portsmouth Oracle,* 26 September 1795; Bentley, *Diary,* 14 July 1796, 2:191. On a later occasion Bentley complained of "A Mr. [Isaac] Lane with our singers. Great disturbance around the Singing School. Such is the insensibility characteristic of some young men, that they will venture into places from which they are utterly prohibited." Bentley, *Diary,* 23 September 1796, 2:199.

37. *Alexandria Gazette,* 26 September 1815; Charles Town, Va., *Farmer Repository,* 22 June 1815; Hudson, N.Y., *Northern Whig,* 26 February 1814; *Baltimore Patriot,* 30 January 1815.

38. *Hallowell Gazette,* 26 April 1820; Middlebury, Conn., *National Standard,* 18 March 1820.

39. Mason, *Reminiscences of Newport,* 158; Bartlett, *The Story of the Negro in Rhode Island,* 12; Millar, "Newport's Early Composers"; Piersen, *Black Yankees,* 104; Southern, *Music of Black Americans,* 72–73.

40. Millar, "Newport's Early Composers," 73.

41. *Boston Repertory,* 6 December 1805.

11. Musical Life

1. New Haven *Connecticut Journal,* 16 July 1794, cited in Bushnell, "Daniel Read of New Haven," 169–70. See also Kelly, *Early Connecticut Meetinghouses,* 2:25, and *Norwich Packet,* 16 February 1797.

2. New Haven *Connecticut Journal,* 16 July 1794, 4 April 1799.

3. Atwater, *History of the City of New Haven,* 211; Bushnell, "Daniel Read of New Haven," 169. Read had already published five teaching manuals and collections. Kroeger and Crawford, "Daniel Read," xiii–xxii.

4. New Haven *Connecticut Journal,* 23 December 1795.

5. New Haven *Connecticut Journal,* 7 January 1796; Middletown *Middlesex Gazette,* 22 January 1796, quoted in "Reuben Moulthrop," 46; Hartford *Connecticut Courant,* 15 February 1796.

6. "For the benefit of Mr. Salter . . . A Concert at Booth's Assembly Hall late Mix's . . . To conclude with a beautiful view of a sea engagement between two fleets." New Haven *Connecticut Journal,* 23 December 1796.

7. New London *Connecticut Gazette,* 2 February 1797.

8. *Norwich Packet,* 16 February 1797; *Newark State Gazette,* 18 December 1798; *Guardian, or New Brunswick Advertiser,* 11 December 1798; Fredericksburg *Virginia Herald,* 9 May 1800; Richmond *Virginia Federalist,* 10 May 1800; Charleston *City Gazette,* 1 March 1800, all cited in Sonneck, *Early Concert-Life,* 40, 59, 62, 248, 362.

9. *Georgetown Gazette,* 15 March 1800.

10. New Haven *Connecticut Journal,* 10 May 1802.

11. Byles, *A Short History of the Organs.*

12. Schetky (1776–1831) was a member of the Federal-Street Theater band; he was a son of cellist Johann G. Christoff Schetky and arranged František Koczwara's "The Battle of Prague" for a military band. Pachelbel taught in Boston, Newport, New York, and Charleston. Lambert, comp., "Music Masters in Colonial Boston," 2:1021–26. Pelham, the son of engraver and artist Peter Pelham, was a student of Pachelbel. *Boston Evening-Post,* 30 May 1743.

13. *Newport Mercury,* 17 June 1771. The effort apparently failed and the society began advertising in South Carolina on 11 April 1772.

14. *New-York Gazette,* 6–13 January 1736, quoted in Sonneck, *Early Concert-Life,* 159. "Ev'g attended ma chere and Ed'd and Mary to a concert by Mr. Graupener, his daughter, a child of only 9 years, assisted by the amateurs of the town." Rodman, *Diary,* 29 August 1833, 119. The nine-year-old was Harriet Hills Graupner (b. 1823), the first child of Graupner's second wife, Mary Hills Graupner. See Nason, *A Memoir of Mrs. Susanna Rowson,* 102–3n2.

15. Johnson, "The Musical Van Hagens"; Hoover, "Epilog to Secular Music," 785. He was described as leader of the band at the Haymarket Theatre in the Boston *Columbian Centinel,* 21 January 1797. Van Hagen and the "Principal Musicians from Boston" regularly toured the eastern corridor towns of Portland, Portsmouth, Newburyport, and Salem. Portland *Oriental Trumpet,* 21 May 1800; Portsmouth *New-Hampshire Gazette,* 3 June 1800; Newburyport *Impartial Herald,* 9, 13 June 1800, cited in Barriskill, "Newburyport Theatre," 43:1–3.

16. Boston *Massachusetts Mercury,* 25 January 1798; Boston *Columbian Centinel,* 14, 24 August 1799.

17. Boston *Massachusetts Mercury,* 12 December 1797; *Salem Gazette,* 8 May 1798.

18. Johnson, *Musical Interludes,* 291; Nason, *Memoir of Mrs. Susanna Rowson,* 102–3n2.

19. Boston *Columbian Centinel,* 21 December 1799.

20. *New-York Daily Gazette,* 27 September 1792: "J. Hewitt, Professor of Music, from New York respectfully informs the Ladies and Gentlemen of Providence he intends to reside here during the summer months . . . at Mr. Aldrich's." *Providence Gazette,* 14 July 1804, 20 July 1805; Boston *New-England Palladium,* 27 December 1810, 4 October 1811; *Salem Gazette,* 5 March 1811, 24 January 1824; Boston *New-England Galaxy,* 30 April 1824.

21. "Agree with Mr. Hewitt, who is to lead my Orchestra next season." Dunlap, *Diary,* 26 June 1798, 1:302.

22. New York *American Minerva,* 5 February, 30 May 1795; *New-York Evening Post,* 10 March 1802, 22 November 1804, 17 March, 21 April 1817; Boston *Columbian Centinel,* 11 September 1805, 26 December 1810; Boston *New-England Palladium,* 16 May 1809. See also Lowens, *Music and Musicians in Early America,* 103, 194–202; *New Grove Dictionary of Music and Musicians,* s.v. "James Hewitt." For the Hewitt family, see *Boston Daily Advertiser,* 28 March, 9 August 1817; Boston *Columbian Centinel,* 26 December 1810, 20 August 1817; and Wagner, "James Hewitt."

23. New York *American Minerva,* 5 February, 30 May 1795; Boston *Columbian Centinel,* 26 December 1810; *New-York Evening Post,* 22 November 1804.

24. *Salem Gazette,* 8, 15 May 1798.

25. Alden, "A Season in Federal Street," 33; Boston *Massachusetts Mercury,* 8 November 1793; Newburyport *Impartial Herald,* 20 January 1795.

26. Portsmouth *New-Hampshire Gazette,* 24 September 1789; Hartford *American Mercury,* 27 April 1798.

27. Boston *Columbian Centinel,* 24 January, 22 February 1798; Boston *Massachusetts Mercury,* 25 November 1796, 29 December 1797, 1 October 1814; *Salem Gazette,* 27 December 1809. "Caroline Dolliver, executrix estate of Peter Dolliver late of Boston, gentleman deceased." Boston *New-England Palladium,* 8 July 1816; Thwing, *Inhabitants,* 29165; Hehr, "Theatrical Life in Salem," 32.

28. *New-York Journal,* 28 April 1768.

29. John Anderson, Diary, New-York Historical Society, cited in McPharlin, *Puppet Theatre in America,* 62.

30. *Boston Post-Boy,* 21 September 1767: "with good Music to entertain the Company"; *New-York Journal,* 30 April 1767: "Different Performances every Evening, and good Musick"; Baltimore *Maryland Journal,* 10 March 1786: "Supplied with good Music."

31. *New-York Daily Advertiser,* 26 June 1795; Portsmouth *New-Hampshire Gazette,* 21 March 1798; *Newport Mercury,* 24 September 1794.

32. Shepard, "Chester and Westfield Diaries," 24 August 1797, 116; Priest, *Travels in the United States of America,* 47.

33. Dow, ed., *Holyoke Diaries,* Diary of Mary (Vial) Holyoke, 28 April 1783, 110; *Salem Gazette,* 16 April, 17 May 1784; Pichierri, *Music in New Hampshire,* 141.

34. New London *Connecticut Gazette,* 1 April 1799.

35. Pynchon, *Diary,* 29 November, 2 December 1787, 29 March 1788, 16 February 1789, 293, 302, 328. For Garnet, see Portsmouth *New-Hampshire Gazette,* 24 September 1789; Portsmouth *New Hampshire Spy,* 23 June 1788, 17 March 1789; and Barriskill, "Newburyport Theatre," 41:218.

36. *Boston Evening-Post,* 24 December 1750.

37. Williamsburg *Virginia Gazette,* 14 September 1769, cited in Keller, *Dance and Its Music,* 240.

38. Keller, *Dance and Its Music,* 115–16, 144, 170, 239–45, 285–88, 358–60, 414–15, 459–62, 536–38, 555–57, 641–42, 651.

39. Keller, *Dance and Its Music,* 241.

40. Easton, Md., *Republican Star,* 16 August 1814.

41. *Boston Evening Post,* 23 January 1738; *Boston Post-Boy,* 23 June 1740; *Boston Gazette,* 13 November 1757.

42. *Hudson Balance,* 6 July 1801, 23 August 1802; *New-York Gazette,* 29 August 1768.

43. Pynchon, *Diary,* 30 May 1788, 308–9; Bentley, *Diary,* 3 April 1791, 1:242.

44. Pynchon, *Diary,* 13 August 1781, 103.

45. Boston *Massachusetts Mercury,* 21 July 1795.

46. *Boston Evening-Post,* 14 January 1740.

47. *New-York Daily Advertiser,* 7 May 1799.

48. Bentley, *Diary,* 24 June 1806, 3:237.

49. Baldwin, *Diary,* 8 December 1831, 149–50.

50. *Newport Mercury,* 31 August 1767; *Charleston Evening Gazette,* 18 October 1785.

51. *Newport Mercury,* 13 August 1792.

52. Dickinson, Diary, 26 April 1795, (219); *Salem Gazette,* 3 February 1803. The Dickinson quotation has been punctuated for meaning; Kevin M. Sweeney kindly provided this reference.

53. Quoted in Wagner, "James Hewitt," 270.

12. Pantomime Entertainment

1. *New-York Weekly Journal*, 19 February 1738; Shapiro, "Action Music," 50–51; Keller, *Dance and Its Music*, 85–88.

2. Only Massachusetts specifically banned theatrical performances by law, but a majority of residents in Connecticut, New Hampshire, and Rhode Island were against them. Seilhamer, *History of the American Theatre*, 1:28–29, cited in Mates, *American Musical Stage*, 160n119; *New-York Mercury*, 1 October 1753–25 March 1754; Willard, *History of the Providence Stage*, 3–11.

3. Theater companies traveling in rural New England continued to use this language well into the nineteenth century; see, for example, the "Moral Lectures" given at C. Munn's Room in Greenfield, Massachusetts, and announced in the Greenfield, Mass., *Franklin Herald*, 8 September 1812. Sonneck, *Early Opera in America*, 31; Willard, *History of the Providence Stage*, 5; *Newport Mercury*, 12 August 1762.

4. "Boston People flock up to Newport to see the Plays by the English Actors"; "Tom Palmer here bound to Newport to see Plays"; "The distress'd Mother acted this Evening." Ames, *Diary*, 9, 10, 14 September 1761, 23, 24 August 1762, 1:63, 69, 90.

5. Part of a three-week engagement in Providence; see *Boston Gazette*, *Boston Post-Boy*, and *Boston Evening-Post*, all 23 August 1762.

6. Sonneck, *Early Opera in America*, 12; *New-York Weekly Journal*, 5 February 1739. See Odell, *Annals of the New York Stage*, 1:38, for "Harlequin Dance at end of 1st act of Beggar's Opera . . . Pierot Dance after 2nd act" (1751).

7. "Harlequin Dance," *New-York Gazette*, 7 January 1751; "At the New Theatre in Nassau-Street . . . Harlequin Skeleton," *New-York Mercury*, 4 March 1754; "At the new School House in Providence, . . . To which will be added (*Gratis*) a Pantomime Entertainment in Grotesque Characters, call'd Harlequin Collector, or the Miller Deceived," *Boston Evening-Post*, 23 August 1762.

8. Portsmouth *New-Hampshire Gazette*, 2 October 1772–1 January 1773.

9. Wells, "Some Notes on the Early Eighteenth-Century Pantomime"; Wells, "Spectacular Scenic Effects." Few descriptions of pantomimes exist. English composers and songwriters such as John Rich, John Thurmond, Charles Dibdin (1745–1814), Thomas John Dibdin (1771–1841), and William Reeve (1757–1815) published prompt copies of their most successful compositions—sometimes compiling detailed directions or descriptions for the mimed action. Fiske, *English Theatre Music*, 67ff.

10. In 1762, an English newspaper called the title of James Love's *The Witches; or, Harlequin Cherokee* "an absolute misnomer; with so little about Cherokees and so much about witches and cauldrons the pantomime should have been called Harlequin Macbeth." Fiske, *English Theatre Music*, 407. For a new perspective on John Rich and additional details on his 1753 image, see Joncus and Barlow, eds., *"The Stage's Glory,"* especially "Picturing Rich," by Marcus Risdell, 266–72, and fig. 17.3 in this volume.

11. Ames, *Diary*, 23 August 1762, 1:90.

12. The steps and head and arm motions characteristic of a Harlequin dance were recorded by G. Le Rousseau in *Chacoon for a Harlequin* (London, 1730) and reproduced in Chapman, "English Pantomime and Its Music," 57–59. Wilson, *Christmas Pantomime*, 56; Fiske, *English Theatre Music*, 83–84, 238–39. "Birth of Harlequin" was published in 1732 as part of a ballad opera. See also Keller, *Dance and Its Music*, 85–87.

13. Lambranzi, *New and Curious School*, nos. 32, 26, 27.

14. This arrangement is described in a hypothetical conversation among "Sullen," "Rambler," and "Critic" in *A Comparison between the Two Stages* (London, 1702), 45–48, cited in Chapman, "English Pantomime and Its Music," 45–46.

15. Cited in Fiske, *English Theatre Music*, 82. This episode is also known from references in Alexander Pope's *Dunciad* and from Henry Fielding's *Tumble-down Dick*, a Harlequin satire dating to the 1740s.

16. *New-York Daily Advertiser*, 3 June 1786; *Loudon's New-York Packet*, 5 June 1786; *New-York Daily Gazette*, 4 July 1789; Philadelphia *Independent Gazetteer*, 19 June 1790; Philadelphia *Gazette of the United States*, 23 January 1796; Boston *Polar Star*, 14 December 1796; Charleston *City Gazette*, 2 March 1795; Philadelphia *Aurora*, 19 January 1796; New York *Diary*, 18 November 1797; *Philadelphia Gazette*, 27 March 1799; *New-York Commercial Advertiser*, 10 June 1799; Boston *Columbian Centinel*, 25 April 1801.

17. Reeve and Bates, *Harlequin Mungo*. The description was printed for J. Griffith, prompter, in 1788. Reeve composed the music and lyrics, Bates arranged the pantomime, and Dixon (who called himself Dickinson in America) designed the scenery and machinery.

18. For example, *Harlequin Balloonist* (Boston *Columbian Centinel*, 6 October 1792), *Harlequin Fisherman* (New York *Diary*, 17 May 1793), *Harlequin Gardener* (Hartford *Connecticut Courant*, 28 September 1795), and *Harlequin's Wishing Cap* (Boston *Constitutional Telegraphe*, 15 January 1800).

19. *Portland Gazette*, 30 May 1803.

20. *New-York Mercury*, 8 March 1762; Philadelphia *Pennsylvania Gazette*, 2 April 1767; Portsmouth *New-Hampshire Gazette*, 2 October 1772; New York *Independent Journal*, 14, 21 September 1785; *Charleston Morning Post*, 20 November 1786; Philadelphia *Federal Gazette*, 7 July 1790, 17 May 1791, 4 June 1792; *New-York Daily Gazette*, 11 October 1791; New York *Daily Advertiser*, 24 February 1792, 22 May 1801; Boston *Independent Chronicle*, 20 September 1792; Charleston *City Gazette*, 23 May 1795; Hartford *American Mercury*, 21 September 1795; Philadelphia *Gazette of the United States*, 22 April 1797; Boston *Columbian Centinel*, 25 October 1797, 4 January 1800; Philadelphia *Claypoole's*, 29 April 1799.

21. *Newport Mercury*, 3 August 1796; Boston *Columbian Centinel*, 15 June 1799; *Providence Gazette*, 19 September 1807; Seilhamer, *History of the American Theatre*, 2:322.

22. Rosenfeld, *The Theatre of the London Fairs*, 45; Philadelphia *Federal Gazette*, 7 July 1790; Boston *Columbian Centinel*, 12 April 1800.

23. Boston *Federal Orrery*, 12 November 1795; Boston *Columbian Centinel*, 5 March 1800. For example, "Animated pictures by the Portrait turned Painter," *Providence Gazette*, 29 August 1802; "The painter's Gallery of Animated Pictures," Boston *Massachusetts Mercury*, 5 March 1800.

24. Boston *Federal Orrery*, 12 November 1795; Boston *Columbian Centinel*, 5 March 1800; Hartford *American Mercury*, 31 August 1795.

25. *The Elopement; or, Harlequin's Tour through the Continent of North America* (New York, 31 May 1787), cited in Porter, *With an Air Debonair*, checklist, 447; *Plymouth Rock; or, Harlequin Released from Bondage* (Portsmouth, 11 June 1796), cited in Porter, *With an Air Debonair*, checklist, 479; *The Landing of Our Forefathers at Plymouth Rock; or, Harlequin Indian*, cited in Portsmouth *New-Hampshire Gazette*, 10 June 1800; Boston *Russell's Gazette*, 30 April 1802.

26. Boston *New-England Palladium*, 4 May 1804, 19 April 1806, 6 April 1810.

27. Philadelphia *Aurora*, 2 January 1795; Baltimore *Federal Intelligencer*, 19 November 1795; Boston *Federal Orrery*, 7 January 1796; Boston *Massachusetts Mercury*, 5 January 1796;

Philadelphia *Claypoole's,* 29 August 1800; Philadelphia *Gazette of the United States,* 6 January 1796; Philadelphia *Poulson's,* 18 March 1805.

28. For example, *The Four Seasons* and *Hurry-Scurry:* Boston *New-England Palladium,* 1 February, 27 December 1811.

29. *Charleston City Gazette,* 11 June 1795.

30. *American Volunteers; or Virtue Triumphant:* Boston *Columbian Centinel,* 5, 12 March 1800; Boston *Massachusetts Mercury,* 4 July 1800; Boston *Commercial Gazette,* 3 May 1804.

31. Boston *New-England Palladium,* 25 March, 1 July 1808, 5, 31 May 1809; *Boston Gazette,* 6 April 1810; Boston *Columbian Centinel,* 2 July 1808, 6 March 1809, 28 April 1810; *Four Seasons; or, Harlequin's Vagaries: Boston Gazette,* 5 April 1810.

32. Charleston *South-Carolina State-Gazette,* 9 June 1794.

33. Charleston *Columbian Herald,* 9 February 1796.

34. *Alexandria Times,* 4 September 1799.

35. *Death of Harlequin* and *Harlequin Robbers* were presented at Roulstone's amphitheater. Boston *New-England Palladium,* 22 August, 26 September 1809. Acrobats Mr. Robinson and Samuel Maginnis presented *Death of Harlequin* at their exhibition at the Haymarket Theatre. Boston *Massachusetts Mercury,* 16 December 1800, 6 January 1801. "Punch's Opera": *Salem Gazette,* 19 November 1807. "A dance called Les Chacons by a Harlequin": Boston *Columbian Centinel,* 10 September 1808. "Harlequin creeping into a bottle": Newburyport *Impartial Herald,* 11 June 1796.

36. Wax figures of Harlequin and Columbine were exhibited at Fraunces Tavern. *New-York Gazette,* 3 August 1772, cited in Odell, *Annals of the New York Stage,* 1:158.

37. Boston *New-England Palladium,* 25 March 1808, 17 March 1812. "New Scenery, designed & executed by Mr. Worrall." Boston *Independent Chronicle,* 11 May 1812.

38. Niklaus, *Harlequin Phoenix,* 148; Wilson, *Christmas Pantomime,* 65–69; Mayer, *Harlequin in His Element;* Boston *New-England Palladium* and Boston *Columbian Centinel,* both 28 April 1812.

39. Dunlap, *History of the American Theatre,* 142, 147, 171–72.

40. Boston *New-England Courant,* 31 July 1725.

41. Boston *New-England Palladium,* 2 October, 15 December 1812; Boston *Columbian Centinel,* 12 October 1814.

42. "Pavillion of Pleasure," *Boston Gazette,* 6 April 1810; "Torrents of Real Water," *Boston Daily Advertiser,* 3 June 1814.

13. A Time to Dance

1. Benson, "Itinerant Dancing and Music Masters," 324; *Boston Records,* 10:57; Lambert, comp., "Music Masters in Colonial Boston," 2:943–46.

2. Lambert, comp., "Music Masters in Colonial Boston," 2:944–46.

3. Benson, "Itinerant Dancing and Music Masters," 270–72; *Boston Records,* 10:61; Lambert, comp., "Music Masters in Colonial Boston," 2:946–54; Sewall, *Diary,* 17 December 1685, 4 February 1686, 1:88, 96; Mather, *An Arrow against Profane and Promiscuous Dancing.*

4. *Boston Weekly News-Letter,* 23 April 1715; Sewall, *Diary,* 29 November 1716, 2:838; *Boston Gazette,* 29 February–7 March 1719.

5. Benson, "Itinerant Dancing and Music Masters," 289; Lambert, comp., "Music Masters in Colonial Boston," 2:954–69; Foote, *American Hymnody,* 80–81, 97.

6. Lambert, comp., "Music Masters in Colonial Boston," 2:739.

7. *Providence Gazette,* 15, 22, 29 January, 5, 12 February 1763; Kimball, *Providence in Colonial Times,* 311–13; Stiles, *Literary Diary,* 7, 12 March 1782, 3:10–11; Webster, *Autobiographies,* Diary, 10 September 1788, 258.

8. Lipman, *Rufus Porter,* 5; Kihn, "The Value Family in Connecticut"; New London *Connecticut Gazette,* 21 November 1798; *Salem Gazette,* 18 May 1802, 3 September 1803, 4 March 1805; Bentley, *Diary,* 5 September 1811, 4:46–47. "S. Hemenway came to Salem to study with Dr. Holyoke & had been educated at Cambridge. He maintained himself by a Dancing School." Pomp, a slave of William Bucknam of Malden, Massachusetts, was a fiddler and caller whose lyrics were preserved in the town's history. Corey, *History of Malden,* 419n.

9. *New-York Evening Post,* 17 October 1809, 2 January 1812; New York *L'Oracle and Daily Advertiser,* 1 January 1808; Hartford *Connecticut Mirror,* 9 July 1810; *Providence Gazette,* 23 November 1811; Trollope, *Domestic Manners of the Americans,* 301.

10. Dow, ed., *Holyoke Diaries,* Diary of Rev. Edward Holyoke, 24 July 1742, 7; Ames, *Diary,* 7 April, 11, 17 October 1760, 1:45, 53, 56. Ephraim Turner's inventory lists a horse, a chaise, and two "negro men" named Tom and Cato. Ephraim Turner, Will, 23 September 1765, Suffolk County Probate Records, 64:553.

11. William Turner, Sr., and Ann Dumaresq marked their 1767 nuptials by sitting for companion pastel portraits by John Singleton Copley. Boston *Massachusetts Centinel,* 29 March 1788. William Pynchon's diary records Mr. Turner's schools in Salem on Friday, 5 September 1783, 160; Monday, 16 August 1784, 191; and Monday, 20 September 1784, 194. By 1785 Turner may have reversed the days, working in Salem on Tuesdays and Thursdays; see Pynchon, *Diary,* 31 May 1785, 4 September 1788, 213, 316. For Griffiths, see Boston *Massachusetts Centinel,* 22 October 1788.

12. *Boston Gazette,* 20 March 1775; Portsmouth *New-Hampshire Gazette,* 28 July 1801, 30 March 1802; *Newburyport Herald,* 28 July 1801, 21 May 1802; Lambert, comp., "Music Masters in Colonial Boston," 2:1146–47.

13. Boston *New-England Palladium,* 4 September 1810; Dow, ed., *Holyoke Diaries,* Diary of Susanna (Holyoke) Ward, 5 November, 5, 12 December 1821, 177. According to Ward's diary, Turner was "carried away crazy" to the hospital in Salem in 1821 and died there seven years later.

14. Foster, *The Coquette,* 51; Boston *Columbian Centinel,* 9 September 1797; Boston *Russell's Gazette,* 29 October 1798; Boston *Massachusetts Mercury,* 3 May 1799. Frazier was author of a dance manual entitled *Scholar's Companion,* printed in Boston by Daniel Bowen in 1796. Trumbull, *Memorial History of Hartford County,* 1:586; New London *Connecticut Gazette,* 2 January 1805; *New-York Evening Post,* 13 October 1807.

15. Boston *Columbian Centinel,* 5 December 1795, 10 February, 16 March 1796; *Providence Gazette,* 21 May 1796, 3 June 1797; *Newport Mercury,* 10 October 1796; Bennington, Vt., *Tablet of the Times,* 6 April 1797; Worcester *Massachusetts Spy,* 4 September 1797, 14 May 1813; Staples, *The History of Pioneer Lexington,* 226.

16. *Baltimore Evening Post,* 2 November 1792; Fredericktown *Maryland Gazette,* 22 August 1793; Georgetown *Columbian Chronicle,* 13 March 1795; *New-York Daily Advertiser,* 26 January 1803; *Albany Centinel,* 4 September 1804; *Orleans Gazette,* 18 September 1805.

17. *New Haven Gazette,* 28 April 1785; Hartford *American Mercury,* 13 August 1787; *Norwich Packet,* 18 October 1787; Providence *United Sates Chronicle,* 29 December 1791; Northampton *Hampshire Gazette,* 12 March 1794. For example, Griffiths held schools in Concert-Hall (Boston *Massachusetts Centinel,* 22 October 1788) and Dearborn's Academy (Boston *Argus,* 24 April 1792).

18. *New Haven Gazette,* 18 November 1784, 5 May 1785; *Litchfield Monitor,* 9 August 1785, 24 February 1786; *Albany Journal,* 13 March 1788; *New-York Daily Advertiser,* 22 September 1789; *Baltimore Evening Post,* 17 April 1793; *Baltimore Daily Intelligencer,* 8 September 1794; Moore, "The Duport Mystery," 29; Easton *Maryland Herald,* 1 June 1803; Charles Town, Va., *Farmer's Repository,* 1 June 1810, 15 May 1812.

19. *Providence Gazette,* 20 October 1822; *Providence Phoenix,* 4 March 1809; Hartford *Connecticut Courant,* 3 November 1800; *Pittsfield Sun,* 17 December 1804, 18 February 1808.

20. Boston *Independent Chronicle,* 23 July 1789; New York *Greenleaf's New Daily Advertiser,* 15 November 1796.

21. New York *Weekly Museum,* 29 December 1798; Hartford *American Mercury,* 27 October 1794; Boston *Massachusetts Mercury,* 17 April 1798; Boston *Massachusetts Centinel,* 4 October 1788, and *Boston Gazette,* 5 January 1789, quoted in Lambert, comp., "Music Masters in Colonial Boston," 2:1148–49; Keller, "John Griffiths," 102.

22. *Albany Argus,* 29 November 1814; Boston *Columbian Centinel,* 13 November 1805.

23. Benson, "Itinerant Dancing and Music Masters," 291–93; *New-York Mercury,* 29 October 1753; Portsmouth *New-Hampshire Gazette,* 30 July 1773. Giardini was probably Felice Giardini (1716–1796), a London composer of comic opera. *Rivington's New-York Gazetteer,* 19 January 1775. John Essex (d. 1744) was one of the English translators of the choreographic system of the French dancing-master Raoul-Auger Feuillet (1659–1710); *Oxford Dictionary of National Biography,* s.v. "John Essex."

24. *New-York Daily Advertiser,* 5 January 1786.

25. Boston *Massachusetts Centinel,* 3 January 1789; Boston *New-England Palladium,* 4 April 1809, 20 March 1810; Hartford *Connecticut Mirror,* 22 July 1811.

26. *New-York Evening Post,* 13 November 1807.

27. Bancroft, Diary, 20 July 1794.

28. Webster, *Autobiographies,* 15 January 1788, 250.

29. See, for instance, Mr. Carter in Charlestown and Cambridgeport, Boston *Columbian Centinel,* 29 April 1815; Mr. Nadau in Roxbury, Boston *Massachusetts Mercury,* 6 March 1795; and Lovet Stimson in Dedham, Taunton, and Providence, Providence *Rhode-Island American,* 16 July 1811.

30. *Augusta Herald,* 13, 20 May 1801.

31. Boston *New-England Palladium,* 7 June, 16 July, 2, 13 August 1811.

32. A copy of Francis Nichols's *A Guide to Politeness* at the Harvard University Theater Collection, Houghton Library, has the title of this tune written by an early user on the inside of the back wrapper. Theater Collection, Harvard Depository, 2010TW-6.

14. Confronting the Professions

1. The number of listeners at Whitefield's farewell sermon in Boston on 12 October 1740 was estimated by him at 30,000; a Boston newspaper reported 23,000. See Gaustad, *Great Awakening in New England,* 26–27n8. Ethan Allen Greenwood reported that more than 20,000 spectators witnessed the execution of four pirates in Boston on 18 February 1819. Greenwood, "'Extracts,'" 141.

2. Philadelphia *Pennsylvania Gazette,* 20 August 1761.

3. *London Evening Post,* 6 August 1747; *London Gazette,* 11 April 1749.

4. Partridge, "William Claggett"; Chapin, "Was Claggett, the Clock Maker"; Champlin, "William Claggett." "I innoculated Thomas Claggett of Newport Clockmaker who informed me that his Father was the first Person in America that ever made an Electric Machine &

that Dr. B. Franklin only improv'd upon his Father &c: with many other curious affairs." Ames, *Diary,* 6 November 1776, 1:302.

5. Owen, "Eighteenth-Century Organs."

6. Extract from an article from Newport, 29 December 1746, reprinted in a Boston newspaper, quoted in Partridge, "William Claggett," 113.

7. *Boston Evening-Post,* 7 September 1747, reproduced in Winslow, *Harper's Literary Museum,* 387.

8. *Boston Evening-Post,* 28 September, 12 October 1747, 8 December 1748.

9. Capt. John Williams, Inventory, April 1748, Suffolk County Probate Records, docket 8963 (reel 16, 41:202).

10. Odell, *Annals of the New York Stage,* 1:28; *New-York Weekly Journal,* 9 May 1748, transcribed in Gottesman, *Arts and Crafts in New York,* 1:376–77; *New-York Gazette,* 16 May 1748.

11. *New-York Gazette,* 16 May 1748, 27 April 1752.

12. *Boston Evening-Post,* 7, 14, 21 October 1751; Lemay, *Ebenezer Kinnersley,* 74–79; Odell, *Annals of the New York Stage,* 1:47; Kinnersley, "A Course of Experiments."

13. Bates, "Notice Is Hereby Given to the Curious." See also Evans, *American Bibliography,* 3:6816, and Rink, *Technical Americana,* 743.

14. *Boston Gazette,* 7 May 1751, 5, 12 March 1754, 26 February 1756, 12 September 1757. "Electrical Experiments, that were exhibited by Mr. Ebenezer Kinnersley, in Faneuil-Hall, are now exhibited near the Old North meetinghouse by Joseph Hiller." *Boston Gazette,* 5 March 1754. See also Dow, *Arts and Crafts,* 302.

15. *New-York Gazette,* 31 October 1763, cited in Gottesman, *Arts and Crafts in New York,* 1:387; *New-York Gazette,* 24 October, 26 December 1763, 2, 9 January 1764; *Newport Mercury,* 13, 20 February 1764; *Providence Gazette,* 3 March 1764; *Boston Records,* 20:171. See also Johnson, *A Course of Experiments.* Johnson's death was reported in the *Boston Post-Boy,* 13 February 1769, cited in Morse, "Lectures on Electricity," 373.

16. *Boston Gazette,* 7 January 1765; *Boston Post-Boy,* 4 February 1765; Garvin and Garvin, *On the Road North of Boston,* 13; Portsmouth *New-Hampshire Gazette,* 21 November 1766; Dow, ed., *Holyoke Diaries,* Diary of Mary (Vial) Holyoke, 2 January 1771, 75 ("At Mason's Lecture"); Mason, *A Course of Experiments.*

17. New York *National Advocate,* 15 May 1817.

18. Alexander Anderson, M.D., "Diarum Commentarium Vitae," New York, 1793–98, cited in Goler, "'Here the Book of Nature,'" 17n16.

19. *New-York Gazette,* 8 August 1768; *New-York Commercial Advertiser,* 22 January 1798; Charles Town, Va., *Farmer's Repository,* 10 June 1808.

20. Portland *Eastern Argus,* 18 August 1808.

21. Philadelphia *Pennsylvania Gazette,* 5 August 1762.

22. Prime, *History of Long Island,* 173.

23. See, for example, *Boston Evening-Post,* 30 May 1739; *New-York Mercury,* 31 October 1757; *New-York Gazette,* 9 April 1767, 9 December 1806; Philadelphia *Pennsylvania Gazette,* 20 December 1770, 30 September 1772; Boston *Massachusetts Spy,* 17 February 1774; Charleston *City Gazette,* 7 May 1813; *Baltimore Patriot,* 12 June, 14 December 1821; and New Haven *Connecticut Herald,* 24 September 1822.

24. Parkman, "Diary," 17 October 1760: "N.B. an ugly drunken, Swearing, raging Pedler here."

25. Philadelphia *Pennsylvania Packet,* 10 June 1772; New York *Royal Gazette,* 26 February 1776; Parker, "Extracts from the Diary," 25 March 1771, 14; *Boston Post-Boy,* 26 February 1739.

26. On 7 February 1765, the Philadelphia *Pennsylvania Packet* noted of a missing peddler that "his hat and budget have been found."

27. Breen, "An Empire of Goods," 467–68; *Province and Court Records of Maine,* 6:xxix–xxx, 72–88.

28. Philadelphia *Pennsylvania Gazette,* 19 August 1762; Samuel Lane, "An Account of Things I Give My Daughter Sarah Thompson toward Her Portion," cited in Nylander, "Provision for Daughters," 26.

29. Murphy, "Entrepreneurship in the Establishment of the American Clock Industry," 183.

30. Dwight, *Travels in New-England,* 2:33–34.

31. Kline, "New Light on the Yankee Peddler," 91. Hamilton, *Men and Manners,* 126.

32. New Haven *Connecticut Journal,* 15 February 1775, 6 July 1780; New Bedford *Columbian Courier,* 26 June 1799.

33. *New-York Weekly Journal,* 22 May 1738, 3 December 1739.

34. *Boston News-Letter,* 2 November 1753; *New-York Gazette,* 8 October 1756; New Haven *Connecticut Gazette,* 9 July 1757; *South-Carolina Gazette,* 8 November 1783; *Newport Mercury,* 8 July 1800; New York *Weekly Argus,* 30 August 1804; *Philadelphia Aurora,* 16 March 1805; *Richmond Enquirer,* 6 February 1806; Frankfurt, Ky., *Palladium,* 15 January 1807; Washington *National Intelligencer,* 31 October 1811.

35. Boston *Columbian Centinel,* 5 March 1800.

36. "To the Honorable the Senate and House of Representatives of NewHampshire, Now in General Court Convened," Petitions, 1816, New Hampshire Archives, Concord, courtesy of Richard M. Candee.

37. Eliot, *Diary,* 24 March 1726.

38. *Boston News-Letter,* 25 September 1740, quoted in Gaustad, *Great Awakening in New England,* 26.

39. Nathan Bowen, almanac diary, Marblehead, Mass., transcribed in Bentley, *Diary,* 12 November 1809, 3:477.

40. Wheelock, "Diary," 19 October 1741, 238.

41. Reverend Benjamin Colman in a 1744 letter to a colleague, quoted in Goen, *Revivalism and Separatism in New England,* 30, 31.

42. Nathan Bowen, almanac diary, in Bentley, *Diary,* 12 November 1809, 3:475.

43. Cited in Gaustad, *Great Awakening in New England,* 71–72.

44. Beales, "The Ecstasy of Sarah Prentice," 107n29; Brekus, *Strangers and Pilgrims,* 23.

45. Lambert, "'I Saw the Book Talk.'"

46. *Boston Post-Boy,* 23 June 1740.

47. Eliot, *Diary,* 28 March–5 June 1742, 33–34.

48. Seeman, "'Justice Must Take Plase.'"

49. Eliot, *Diary,* 28 March–23 April 1742, 51.

50. Ichabod Jones material in this and the following two paragraphs is derived from, Parkman, "Diary," 3–13 January, 8, 25 March 1774. Parkman sometimes called him "Isaac Jones." On 3 January 1774, Parkman wrote, "At Eve came an old, miserable man *Ichabod Jones,* he says, of Dorchester. He lyes by the Fire. A poor distempered, rheumatic, [———] Object. I keep his Horse also." On 4 January 1774, he continued, "at the Vendue of Miss *Mary Bradish's* House yesterday at *Deacon Woods,* there was one Mr. Jones, who goes about as a Vagrant, Sings, makes Verses and is sometime Crazy."

51. Weis, *Colonial Clergy,* 66.

52. Ballantine, "Journal," excerpted in Lockwood, *Westfield and Its Historic Influences*, 1:424: "20 [December 1770] One Ichabod Jones lodged here—he is said to have a considerable estate but makes no use of it. Rides about the country, lives on the charity of the people, says he is sick but travels in all weather, in all ways, there is an appearance of religion."

53. Salem *Essex Gazette*, 28 November 1769; Boston *Evening-Post*, 11 December 1769, reprinted in New London *Connecticut Gazette*, 15 December 1769. An announcement in the *Boston Post-Boy* of 23 January 1770 says that "Friday last John Jones, for Burglary, was Branded with the Letter B in his Forehead, in King Street, before a great Number of Spectators."

54. *Boston Democrat*, 14 November 1804; New London *Connecticut Gazette*, 22 May 1805; Stinchfield, *Some Memoirs*. See also Marini, "Evangelical Itinerancy in Rural New England," 52, 61. On a visit to New York State in 1814, Ethan Allen Greenwood encountered a Baptist itinerant that he did not like: "There is great attention paid to religion in Troy by most of the people who are very pious & sincere. Attended Church & in the eve. We had a baptist itinerant preacher who presented Zeal without knowledge." Greenwood, "'Extracts,'" between 18 October and 12 November 1814, 120.

55. *New Bedford Mercury*, 6 August 1824.

56. Trollope, *Domestic Manners of the Americans*, 170, 172; Marini, "Evangelical Itinerancy in Rural New England," 50.

57. Trollope, *Domestic Manners of the Americans*, 77.

58. Trollope, *Domestic Manners of the Americans*, 276–77.

59. Francesco, *Power of the Charlatan*, 73–98.

60. *London Evening Post*, 28 April 1719. Among Sharp's associates was a Dr. Needham, one of several inventors of the "celebrated necklace"—an amulet for children designed to ward off diseases.

61. *Boston Weekly News-Letter*, 3 October 1720; *Boston Gazette*, 3 October, 14 November 1720, 13 January, 13 March 1721.

62. *Boston Gazette*, 13 March 1721.

63. Boston *New-England Courant*, 11–18 December 1721.

64. Philadelphia *Pennsylvania Gazette*, 16 July 1752.

65. Philadelphia *Pennsylvania Gazette*, 27 February 1753. Kate Keller describes this individual as a dancing-mistress, citing an advertisement in the Baltimore *Maryland Gazette*, 25 January 1753: "Earlier in the 1750s, a woman named Sarah Knox circulated in the area [Williamsburg, Va.] teaching dancing, changing her name from Knox to Howard to Wilson. She was reported as a run-away in 1752 near the Carter holdings at Corotoman in Lancaster County." Keller, *Dance and Its Music*, 214. See also Williamsburg *Virginia Gazette*, 17 July 1752.

66. *Kingston Journal* (Jamaica), 29 November 1760.

67. Leffler et al., "The First Cataract Surgeons in Anglo-America," cites *The English Registry, for the Year of Our Lord, 1752* (Dublin: Exshaw, 1752), 50–51.

68. Guerra, *American Medical Bibliography*; Ames, *Diary*, 17–18, 23, 25 June, 30 July 1764, 1:113–14; Philadelphia *Pennsylvania Gazette*, 20 August 1761, 21 January, 25 February 1762; *New-York Gazette*, 21 March 1763; New London *Connecticut Gazette*, 2 December 1763; *Boston Post-Boy*, 6 August 1764; Portsmouth *New-Hampshire Gazette*, 16 November 1764.

69. Leffler et al., "The First Cataract Surgeons in Anglo-America." See also Robert Olwell, who postulated that the same Dr. Stork who had performed eye surgery in colonial America in the 1760s later returned as a dealer in Florida real estate and published *An Account*

of East-Florida: With Remarks on Its Future Importance to Trade and Commerce. Olwell, "The Eye of the Beholder: Advertising, Promotion, and Self-Fashioning in the Peripatetic Career of a Mid-Eighteenth-Century 'Oculist' and Colonial Author," conference paper at "Before Madison Avenue: Advertising in Early America," American Antiquarian Society, Worcester, Mass., 4–5 November 2011.

70. *Newport Mercury,* 17 April 1769; *Providence Gazette,* 17, 24 June 1769; New London *Connecticut Gazette,* 18, 25 August 1769; Hartford *Connecticut Courant,* 18 September, 2 October 1769; *New York Journal,* 7, 25 July 1771; New Haven *Connecticut Journal,* 3 March, 18 June 1773; Boston *Massachusetts Spy,* 25 March 1773; Portsmouth *New-Hampshire Gazette,* 6 August 1773; Guerra, *American Medical Bibliography.*

71. Stiles, *Literary Diary,* 8 June 1786, 3:222–25.

72. *New-York Gazette,* 20 May 1771; Philadelphia *Pennsylvania Chronicle,* 28 October 1771, 28 August 1772; Philadelphia *Pennsylvania Packet,* 7 June, 20 September 1773; *Rivington's New-York Gazetteer,* 15 July 1773. See also, for example, "The Eye, in Three Parts," *New-York Journal,* 28 August 1773.

73. King, *Medical World of the Eighteenth Century,* 53; Francesco, *Power of the Charlatan,* 202–5; Graham, *The General State of Medical and Chirurgical Practice;* Porter, *Quacks,* 140–60.

74. "Doct. Perkins and Son, *Now at Wendell's hotel, Albany.*" *Albany Gazette,* 31 July 1797.

75. *Dictionary of American Biography,* 466–67; *Appletons' Cyclopædia,* s.v. "Elisha Perkins," 4:728. "Dr. Perkins and Son . . . will use their metallic instruments gratis for a few days": Hartford *American Minerva,* 3 July 1797. "Dr. Perkins, Author of the Metallic Points, has taken lodgings": Boston *Columbian Centinel,* 14 October 1797. Boston *Massachusetts Mercury,* 18 September 1798. See also Heslip and Kellogg, "The Beardsley Limner Identified as Sarah Perkins."

76. Philadelphia *Pennsylvania Gazette,* 26 October 1749. *New-York Gazette,* 9 May 1748: "Electricity became all the Subject in Vogue; Princes were willing to see this new Fire which a Man Produced from himself: And is tho't to be of Service in many Ailments."

77. Parkman, "Diary," 24 February, 8 June 1779.

78. Gale, *Brief Instructions,* 19–20; *New-York Daily Advertiser,* 6 April 1787; Boston *Massachusetts Centinel,* 3 May 1788.

79. Boston *Independent Chronicle,* 31 October 1805; Boston *Democrat,* 4 July 1806; Newark *Centinel of Freedom,* 19 May 1807, 9 August 1808.

80. *Baltimore Patriot,* 11 January 1826.

81. Boston *New-England Palladium,* 14 September 1806; "Doct. Griffin, the Celebrated Indian Doctor!" Broadside, Newport, R.I., n.d., Countway Library, Harvard Medical School, Boston; New Haven *Connecticut Journal,* 6 September 1804; Wolfe, "Peter Smith's Indian Doctor's Dispensatory."

82. Philadelphia *Pennsylvania Packet,* 7 June 1773; Boston *Massachusetts Centinel,* 24 October 1787; Hartford *Connecticut Mirror,* 29 March 1813; Amherst, N.H., *Farmer's Cabinet,* 6 August 1823.

83. Hamilton, *Itinerarium,* 160; *Boston Gazette,* 10 January 1774.

84. Philadelphia *Pennsylvania Gazette,* 15 June 1758. Contemporary folklorists have observed the same occupational unity among itinerants in twentieth-century America and in Medieval Europe. See Dargan and Zeitlin, "American Talkers," 30, who cite Mikhail Bakhtin's observation that the "actor of a popular spectacle and the hawker of popular medicine were often the same person." Bakhtin, *Rabelais and His World,* 153.

85. "For sale an elegant Electrical machine, mounted in a strong manner, so as to act with power sufficient to perform any experiment either Medical or divertive, such as dancing images, dancing balls; a set of balls, chains, discharges, &c all enclosed in a Box, together with a 3 gallon Jar and insulating stool." New Haven *Connecticut Journal,* 2 February 1802.

86. Electrical healers included nine museum proprietors (William Doyle; Philip Woods; Gardiner Baker; C. W. Peale; E. Savage; and unidentified proprietors in Amherst, N.H., Philadelphia, and two in Baltimore), seven showmen (Richard Brickell, Joseph Falconi, William King, William F. Pinchbeck, Cesar Cossa, Thaddeus Gale, and unidentified Salem magic lanternist), four profile takers or miniature makers (Martin Howe, Henry Williams, John Carman, and John Carman, Jr), four electrical mechanics (Dr. Hamilton, J. Shecut, Benjamin Tucker, and Isaac Greenwood), three waxwork proprietors (Mr. Vail, John A. Friedle, and an unidentified proprietor in Easton, Md.), one painter (Cephas Thompson), and one pharmaceutical seller (Hervey Frink).

87. Portland *Eastern Argus,* 28 July 1808; Nairne, *Nairne's Patent Electrical Machine;* Boston *New-England Palladium,* 26 March 1811. Nairne machines are held at the Huntington Library, San Marino, Calif., and the Smithsonian Institution.

88. *Newport Mercury,* 17 November, 8 December 1795: "Signior Falconi will exhibit his Natural and Philosophical Experiments. . . . A small automaton in Turkish dress will answer, by Signs, any Question put to it. . . . Also, Weather Permitting, The electrical and Perpetual Lamp; This singular Piece is actuated by the ingenious Philosophical Discovery of Mr. Volta, fully described in Cavello's Treatise on Electricity, viz. The Electophorus, or Perpetual Electricity." For the contributions by Allesandro Volta (1745–1827) and Tiberius Cavallo (1749–1809), see Dibner, *Galvani-Volta,* 32.

89. "I finished my Electrising mashene. . . . Electrified Lucy meadically for the first time. Abigail Alden called and was Electrified through the shoulders for rheumatism." Thompson and Thompson, Journal, 20, 22 August 1822, vol. 1.

90. *Richmond Argus,* 2 January 1801.

91. Boston *Columbian Centinel,* 20 April 1814.

92. *Portland Gazette,* 24 December 1804; Boston *Columbian Centinel,* 28 September 1803; *New-York Evening Post,* 4 April 1803.

15. Waxwork Museums

1. In his *Letters from an American Farmer,* J. Hector St. John de Crèvecoeur asked, "What then is this American, this new man? . . . He is an American, who leaving behind him all his ancient prejudices and manners, receives new ones from the new mode of life he has embraced, the new government he obeys, and the new rank he holds. . . . Here individuals of all nations are melted into a new race of men, whose labours and posterity will one day cause great changes in the world" (54–55).

2. "The above Figures are new, and allowed to be striking Likenesses." Advertisement for a four-day waxwork exhibition by N. and E. Street, Newark *Centinel of Freedom,* 8 January 1805.

3. A rhymed verse accompanied a 1761 Boston waxwork show suggesting that audiences liked to touch them:

> All you that come this curious Art to see
> From Handling any Thing must cautious be:
> Lest by a slight Touch e'er you are aware,

That Mischeif may be done you can't Repair,
Lo! This Advice we give to every Stranger,
Look on, and welcom, but to touch ther's Danger;
And if this Art be pleasing to your Eye
Then let the Artists find your Generosity.

See Evans, *Early American Imprints,* ser. 1, no. 41182.

4. Blease, *Suvorof,* frontispiece; *Storia della campagna,* 1:frontispiece; Anthing, *History of the Campaigns,* 1:frontispiece; Boston *Columbian Centinel,* 18 December 1799; Dedham, Mass., *Columbian Minerva,* 23 January 1800.

5. "Wax Exhibition. / R. Letton," Broadside (see fig. 4.1). "Suwarrow boot legs for sale . . . at the subscriber's Suwarrow Boot Leg Manufactory": *New-York Evening Post,* 3 November 1803, 23 October 1804.

6. Trollope, *Domestic Manners of the Americans,* 62.

7. Altick, *Shows of London,* chap. 4; Wall, "Wax Portraiture." The Bordentown Historical Society in Bordentown, N.J., has a miniature figure attributed to Patience Wright; one life-size figure by her of William Pitt stands in Westminster Abbey.

8. *Boston News-Letter,* 6 December 1733; *New-York Weekly Journal,* 3 July 1749; *New-York Gazette,* 9 October 1749; Philadelphia *Pennsylvania Gazette,* 11 Sept 1752; *South-Carolina Gazette,* 25 June 1753.

9. Hempstead, *Diary,* 23 July 1751, 558.

10. *South-Carolina Gazette,* 16 July 1753.

11. Dunlap, *History of the Rise and Progress,* 1:150–56; Silverman, *Cultural History of the American Revolution,* 179–80; Sellers, *Patience Wright,* 34–35, 41; Haberly, "The Long Life of Daniel Bowen"; Greenwood, "'Extracts.'" Museum professional Philip Woods (whose career in many ways paralleled Ralph Letton's) gave up his Boston and Portland museums and founded a new establishment in Cincinnati; later his extensive wax collection was consumed in a fire in 1851. Columbus *Daily Ohio Statesman,* 16 July 1851.

12. New Haven *Connecticut Journal,* 4 September 1793.

13. New Haven *Connecticut Journal,* 14 June 1814; Stivers, "Wax Figures," 42; New York *Commercial Advertiser,* 13 December 1803, cited in Gottesman, *Arts and Crafts,* 3:88–89.

14. New Haven *Connecticut Journal,* 23 December 1795; Philadelphia *Poulson's,* 11 October 1811; Providence *Rhode-Island American,* 5 July 1811.

15. *New-York Gazette,* 25 May 1812; New Haven *Connecticut Journal,* 2 May 1820.

16. Stiles, *Literary Diary,* 21, 22, 28, 31 August 1793, 3:503; Boston *New-England Palladium,* 22 December 1813, 8, 22 February 1814; Boston *Daily Advertiser,* 22 February 1814; *Salem Gazette,* 29 November 1799; Boston *Massachusetts Mercury,* 29 May 1801.

17. Boston *Independent Chronicle,* 4 January 1798: "The Queen appears in a rage of distraction—the King's Sister deeply affected—the young Princess is fainting—and the Dauphin is embracing his unhappy father—the Queen's Maid of Honor also appears in great distress. A guard of Soldiers are waiting to conduct him to the place of execution." See also Boston *Massachusetts Mercury,* 5 December 1797; Bentley, *Diary,* 12 March 1798, 2:261; and Boston *Columbian Centinel,* 6 February 1799. For print sources, see Chiappe, *Louis XVI,* and "French Revolution Digital Archive."

18. Portland *Eastern Argus,* 10 February 1812; New York *Weekly Museum,* 3 March 1804.

19. *New-York Gazette,* 22 May 1812; New Haven *Connecticut Herald,* 8 September 1807; *New-York Daily Gazette,* 9 September 1789.

20. For more on Fairbanks, see Connecticut *Norwich Packet,* 19 August, 22 September 1801; Ames, *Diary,* Ames's undated postmortem examination notes with commentary on the

case by Robert B. Hanson, 18, 20–22 May, 17, 18 December 1801, 2:725–39, 746–49, 754–55; Fairbanks, *Solemn Declaration;* Thacher, *Danger of Despising the Divine Counsel;* New Haven *Connecticut Journal,* 12 September 1802; and *Salem Gazette,* 17 November 1801. See also Freeman, "'Melancholy Catastrophe!'"

21. New Haven *Connecticut Journal,* 6 September 1804; Northampton *Hive,* 25 December 1804.

22. New Haven *Connecticut Journal,* 27 August 1812, 1 June 1813; Boston *Columbian Centinel,* 28 November 1812.

23. *Carlisle Gazette,* 11 May 1803.

24. Hartford *Connecticut Courant,* 5 January 1801; *New-York Daily Advertiser,* 2 September 1789; New York *Columbian Gazetteer,* 17 October 1793; Boston *Columbian Centinel,* 25 January 1805.

25. *Newburyport Herald,* 12 November 1799; *New-York Daily Advertiser,* 2 September 1789; *Boston Gazette,* 19 September 1796.

26. Portland *Eastern Argus,* 10 February 1812; Savage, *John Winthrop's History of New England,* 2:162; Trumbull, *Complete History of Connecticut,* 1:135.

27. Keller, "Purveyor to the Peddlers."

28. *Account of the Extraordinary Abstinence of Ann Moor,* ii: "A likeness in wax, of this wonderful woman is to be seen at the Columbian Museum, Tremont-Street, next the Stone Chapel, Boston." A later announcement printed in New Bedford, Mass., reported that Ann Moore was residing with her daughter in an English "property" in Macclesfield, Cheshire, which "she acquired by her long practiced fraud." *New Bedford Mercury,* 9 June 1815.

29. Boston *Columbian Centinel,* 29 October 1796. Gardiner Baker's "The Celebrated Aeronaut M. Blanchard" is cited in Baker, "Museum & Wax-Work." *Harlequin Balloonist; or, Pierrot in the Clouds* was advertised in the *New-York Morning Post,* 4 May 1792, and in the Boston *American Apollo,* 5 April 1793. See also Seilhamer, *History of the American Theatre,* 2:344, 3:22.

30. Burke, *Popular Culture in Early Modern Europe,* 23–25; Thwing, *Inhabitants,* 17336.

31. Dow, *Arts and Crafts,* 287, which cites *Boston Gazette,* 10 February 1747; Boston *New-England Weekly Journal,* 22 May 1739; *Boston Gazette,* 27 August 1745. Sarah Briggs and Thomas Brooks were married in 1716 and had five children. Thwing, *Inhabitants,* 7208.

32. *Boston Gazette,* 30 April 1751; *Boston Evening-Post,* 22 April 1751.

33. Adams, *Works,* 2:34: "These wax-works are all of the Doctor's own hands."

34. New Haven *Connecticut Journal,* 23 September 1789; Haberly, "The Long Life of Daniel Bowen," 321. See also Decatur, *Private Affairs,* 62, 318–19, 321–22.

35. Dow, ed., *Holyoke Diaries,* Diary of Mary (Vial) Holyoke, 26 July 1791, 125: "26. Tea at Madm Jeffrys. Eveng at the Wax Works." Bentley, *Diary,* 13 June, 12 November 1791, 7 October 1803, 1:265, 322, 3:52.

36. *Litchfield Monitor,* 11 January 1797; Stockbridge *Western Star,* 30 January 1797. Full details of the itinerary of Moulthrop and his various partners for the years 1793–1803 are listed in table 15.1 at http://scholarworks.umass.edu/umpress_short_time_only/.

37. Diary of Sally Ripley, Greenfield, Mass., 1799–1801, 1805–9, American Antiquarian Society, Worcester, Mass.

38. Carlyle, *French Revolution,* 2:266–67.

39. *Boston News-Letter,* 6 December 1733; Boston *New-England Palladium,* 2 December 1808.

40. Altick, *The Shows of London,* 52; Boston *New-England Palladium,* 29 November 1808; Scharf and Westcott, *History of Philadelphia,* 2:950.

41. Altick, *The Shows of London*, 254–55; New Haven *Connecticut Journal*, 23 June 1807; *New-York Evening Post*, 20 April 1810, 4 July 1811, 10 June 1812; Boston *New-England Palladium*, 16 August 1808, 7 October 1809; Portland *Eastern Argus*, 28 July 1808, 10 December 1816; Boston *Columbian Centinel*, 28 August 1809; *Boston Daily Advertiser*, 24 June 1809; *Nantucket Gazette*, 17 June 1816; *Newburyport Herald*, 25 April 1817; *Providence Gazette*, 2 October 1824.

42. Koke, *American Landscape and Genre Paintings*, 2:188–208 (entries 1438 and 1439).

16. Public Painters

1. Silverman, *Cultural History of the American Revolution*, 95–96. A general description of transparencies in England is found in Orme, *Essay on Transparent Prints*.

2. Boston *Columbian Centinel*, 10 November 1821; *Paul Revere's Boston*, entry 152; Rowe, *Letters and Diary*, 21 April 1766, 91, 95.

3. Drake, *History and Antiquities of Boston*, 724.

4. Philadelphia *Aurora General Advertiser*, 15 February 1797.

5. *Boston Gazette*, 15 February 1802. Phillips died in North Andover on 10 February 1802. *Appletons' Cyclopædia*, s.v. "Samuel Phillips Jr.," 4:762; *Boston Democrat*, 1 January 1806; Boston *Columbian Centinel*, 3 May 1815.

6. *Boston Daily Advertiser*, 13 April 1814; Boston *Repertory*, 12 April 1814; Boston *Columbian Centinel*, 3 November 1819; Ames, *Diary*, 3 November 1818, 2:1120. The light of the conflagration was also noticed in Pomfret, Connecticut; Amherst and Portsmouth, New Hampshire; and Saco, Maine. Boston *Columbian Centinel*, 13 November 1818.

7. *Providence Gazette*, 6 August 1818; *Boston Gazette*, 1 May 1820.

8. Charleston *City Gazette*, 12 November 1799; Worcester *Massachusetts Spy*, 20 November 1799; Northampton *Hampshire Gazette*, 12 March 1800; Boston *Columbian Centinel*, 12 March 1800; Hartford *Connecticut Courant*, 17 March 1800; Peacham, Vt., *Green Mountain Patriot*, 26 March 1800; New Haven *Connecticut Journal*, 25 June 1800; *New-York Daily Advertiser*, 18 March 1800; *Albany Gazette*, 20 March 1800; Philadelphia *Gazette*, 5 May 1800; *Worcester Palladium*, 30 April 1856. Earl's view apparently was not the first of Niagara exhibited in New England; a version was reported by an English merchant visiting Boston in 1785: "In the afternoon went to see some paintings, amongst the rest an attempt to describe the Falls of Niagara. I can only say that the picture and artist are on a part, there being no merit in either." Hadfield, *An Englishman in America*, 191.

9. In 1832, Worrall's view of Providence was purchased by a local church that in turn donated it to the Rhode Island Historical Society where it remains. Goodyear, *American Paintings at the Rhode Island Historical Society*, entry 37; "Notes on Landscapes in the Picture Gallery," *Providence Journal*, 5 November 1883; "Key to the Drop-Scene," 1812.

10. For example, *View of Boston*, "painted by Mr. Worrall." Boston *Columbian Centinel*, 26 September 1818; Portland *Eastern Argus*, 7 August 1820.

11. Boston *New-England Palladium*, 18 September 1810; "A Panorama of Boston." A rival view of Boston was shown in New York City in 1811; the work of an unknown artist, it was taken "from a steeple, corner of Park and Common streets" and displayed in a large building erected for the purpose. *New-York Evening Post*, 28 June 1811.

12. Little, "Michele Felice Corné"; Mason, *Reminiscences of Newport*, chap. 44. Corné's installations are found in the Boston *Columbian Centinel*, 13 January, 20 December 1806; *Boston Patriot*, 3 December 1806, 1 July 1815; *Salem Gazette*, 30 November 1809, 4 December 1812; New Haven *Connecticut Journal*, 13 October 1813; Boston *New-England Palladium*,

1 October 1813; *Albany Argus,* 30 November 1813; and *Boston Daily Advertiser,* 22 February 1814.

13. *Boston Democrat,* 26 November 1806; Boston *Columbian Centinel,* 29 November 1806; Bentley, *Diary,* 6 February 1807, 3:275.

14. Portsmouth *New-Hampshire Gazette,* 3 March 1807; Providence *Columbian Phenix,* 16 May 1807; Portland *Eastern Argus,* 4 August 1808.

15. Charleston *City Gazette,* 20 July 1809.

16. *Nantucket Gazette,* 24 June 1816.

17. *Alexandria Gazette,* 17 April 1818; Washington *National Messenger,* 18 May 1818.

18. *Boston Democrat,* 3 December 1806, 13 January 1807; *Salem Gazette,* 23 January 1807; Salem *Essex Register,* 2 February 1807; Portsmouth *New-Hampshire Gazette,* 3 March 1807; *Providence Gazette,* 9 May 1807; Boston *New-England Palladium,* 19 May 1807, 24 April 1812; Bristol, R.I., *Mt. Hope Eagle,* 30 June 1807; Portland *Eastern Argus,* 28 July, 21 August 1808; *Nantucket Gazette,* 24 June 1816; *New Bedford Mercury,* 28 June 1816; Goodyear, *American Paintings at the Rhode Island Historical Society,* entry 35.

19. *New-York Mercury,* 8 March 1810; *Boston Repertory,* 2 January 1815; *Boston Daily Advertiser,* 22 April 1818; *Boston Intelligencer,* 10 June 1820; New Haven *Connecticut Herald,* 13 October 1897; Philadelphia *Aurora General Advertiser,* 24 October 1805; *Charleston Courier,* 10 March 1807; Boston *Commercial Gazette,* 24 May 1810, October 1813, 14 March 1814; Philadelphia *Franklin Gazette,* 21 October 1819; Charleston *City Gazette,* 16 February 1808, 20 January 1817; New York *National Advocate,* 1 June 1820; Baltimore *Federal Republican,* 16 March 1810; Providence *Rhode-Island American,* 6 October 1818, 27 August 1824; Boston *Evening-Post,* 8 October 1811; Washington *National Intelligencer.*

20. *Boston Daily Advertiser,* 11 June 1816.

21. *Boston Daily Advertiser,* 13 June 1816; Providence *Rhode-Island American,* 6 July 1812, 1 November 1816; *Providence Gazette,* 2 November 1816.

22. Boston *New-England Palladium,* 14 June, 26 July 1816; *Providence Gazette,* 2 November 1816, 13 October 1818.

23. Boston *Columbian Centinel,* 12 April 1815.

24. New York *National Advocate,* 24 April 1817; Philadelphia *Poulson's,* 23 October 1817.

25. Boston *Columbian Centinel,* 10 October 1817; Boston *Commercial Gazette,* 15 June 1818.

26. *New-York Daily Advertiser,* 25, 29 September 1817.

27. New Haven *Connecticut Journal,* 21 October 1817.

28. Philadelphia *Poulson's,* 24 November 1817.

29. Philadelphia *Poulson's,* 10 March 1818.

30. *City of Washington Gazette,* 12 June 1818; Norfolk, Va., *American Beacon,* 2 March 1818.

31. *Boston Daily Advertiser,* 7 October 1817.

32. Philadelphia *Poulson's,* 17 January 1818; *Alexandria Gazette,* 23 February 1818.

33. Ames, *Diary,* 26 August 1817, "Memoranda 1818," 4 September 1818, 2:1086, 1105, 1118.

34. Thoreau, *Journal,* 14 January 1858, 10:243–44.

35. Boston *Columbian Centinel,* 22 November 1794, 25, 17 March 1795; Pragnell, *The London Panoramas.* For the Westminster panorama at 222 Greenwich Street, see New York *American Minerva,* 21 August 1795, and New York *Weekly Museum,* 2 December 1797, both cited in Gottesman, *Arts and Crafts,* 2:29, 33. Philadelphia *Aurora General Advertiser,* 19 February 1797; Baltimore *Federal Gazette,* 25 October 1796; Charleston *City Gazette,* 13 February 1798.

36. Dow, ed., *Holyoke Diaries,* Diary of Mary (Vial) Holyoke, 28 April 1795, 132.
37. Dow, ed., *Holyoke Diaries,* Diary of Margaret Holyoke, 16 March 1814, 158.
38. Bentley, *Diary,* 4 February 1795, 2:126.
39. Bentley, *Diary,* 6 February 1807, 3:276.
40. Bentley, *Diary,* 1 December 1809, 3:481.
41. "Theatre. The Managers . . . Immortal Washington"; *Boston Gazette,* 27 March 1820; *Boston Evening Gazette,* 28 September 1822; Boston *Dramatic Mirror,* 29 February 1829.
42. *New-York Daily Advertiser,* 11 July 1800. William Winstanley was an English copyist and panorama maker then living in New York City.
43. *New York Mercantile Advertiser,* 18 November 1818; Philadelphia *Franklin Gazette,* 14 December 1819.

17. Taking Faces I: The Itinerant Portraitist

1. Corné's painting and Perry's wax figure were originally shown at the Exchange Coffee House: Boston *New-England Palladium,* 22 December 1813. Later they were transferred to the Columbian Museum: Boston *New-England Palladium,* 8, 22 February 1814; *Boston Daily Advertiser,* 21 February 1814; *Boston Repertory,* 22 February 1814. The panorama traveled to New York City in June: *New-York Evening Post,* 21 June 1814. See also "A Key to the Grand Panorama"; *New-York Evening Post,* 21, 29 June 1814. Philip Woods later toured a waxwork of Perry: *Nantucket Gazette,* 17 June 1816.
2. Boston *New-England Palladium,* 1 March 1814.
3. Portland, *Eastern Argus,* 25 November, 9 December 1803, 7 October 1813; Boston *New-England Palladium,* 6 May, 16 June 1806; Boston *Columbian Centinel,* 11 October 1806, 8 October 1808, 12 January 1811; "Anatomical Wax-Works," *New-York. Evening Post,* 19 May 1817. For additional background on Williams, see Dunlap, *History of the Rise and Progress,* 3:30.
4. Pierpont, *Ode; Appleton's Cyclopædia,* s.v. "John Pierpont," 5:14; Clapp, *Record of the Boston Stage,* chap. 4.
5. *Boston Daily Advertiser,* 4 June 1814; Boston *New-England Palladium,* 1 March 1814.
6. Quoted in Bumgardner, "Early Career of Ethan Allen Greenwood," 220.
7. Trollope, *Domestic Manners of the Americans,* 282.
8. Paine, *Roses and Thorns,* 99.
9. Kellogg, "Found"; "Boarding Ralph Earl and his wife" and "Washing for Mr. and Mrs. Earl," Jared Lane account book, 23 May–28 July 1796, cited in Kornhauser, "Ralph Earl as an Itinerant Artist," 180.
10. Dunlap, *History of the Rise and Progress,* 2:205–7; Warren, "Connecticut Pastels"; Boston *Colombian Centinel,* 31 August 1796; Boston *Massachusetts Mercury,* 6 September 1796; *New-York Daily Advertiser,* 17 July 1798; New York *Greenleaf's New Daily Advertiser,* 19 June 1799; Knox, *The Sharples,* 120; *Catalogue of American Portraits in the New-York Historical Society,* 29.
11. John S. Blunt and William P. Codman advertised "Persons wishing portraits, can (if preferr'd) be waited on at their houses": quoted from the Concord *New Hampshire Patriot* in Garvin and Garvin, *On the Road North of Boston,* 98. Trigant de Beaumont offered fencing and dancing for those "who may wish to be taught at their lodgings": *New-York Evening Post,* 28 November 1804. Mr. Cressin "will also perform for private parties at any time," broadside illustrated in Barriskill, "Newburyport Theatre," 41:331.

12. George Washington Johnson, "My Father's Annals, begun by George Washington Johnson Ap. '67," quoted in Jones, "The Portraits of Richard and William Jennys," 86–87. Jones notes that Donna-Belle Garvin kindly provided this quotation.

13. Bumgardner, "Early Career of Ethan Allen Greenwood," 221–22; Black, "Two Painters," 228.

14. Diary of Dr. Samuel Adams, Bath, Maine, 21 November 1816, cited in Kern and Kern, "Benjamin Greenleaf," 40; Merrill, "Diary," 24 March 1831 (which notes that Jordan was painting M. F. Peaslee and his wife). Gregory H. Laing kindly provided the Merrill information.

15. Boston *Columbian Centinel,* 29 December 1802, 5, 12 January, 2 November 1803, 14, 24 October 1804; Boston *Gazetteer,* 21, 22 October, 2, 9, 30 November 1803; *Portland Gazette,* 23 December 1805, 4, 18 August 1806, cited in Hill, "New England Itinerant Portraitists," 159; *Portland Gazette,* 12 May 1821, 2 December 1823. Brewster advertised at "Dr. Stearns" in Salem, 4 May 1809, cited in Belknap, *Artists and Craftsmen of Essex County,* 6; *Newburyport Herald,* 25 December 1801, 22 January 1802, 17 November 1809. John Brewster, Jr., also advertised in 1797 and 1798 in the *Windham Herald* and the *Chelsea Courier* in eastern Connecticut, cited in Little, "John Brewster, Jr.," 99; Portland *Eastern Argus,* 13 March 1821.

16. *Poughkeepsie Journal,* 31 December 1799 (communicated by Joyce Hill to the author in 1985); *Hallowell Gazette,* 10 September 1823; New Orleans *Louisiana Advertiser,* 25 July 1820.

17. Diary of Rev. James Cogswell, 13 December 1790, cited in Little, "John Brewster, Jr.," 97–98. Stearns (1754–1819) is cited in Van Wagenen, *Genealogy and Memoirs of Isaac Stearns,* 146–47. Farnam (1771–after 1823) was listed at 17 Summer Street in the *Boston Directory* (1825). Boston *Columbian Centinel,* 14, 24 October 1804. Brewster stayed "for the winter" at Mr. Moore's, 53 Middle Street; cited in Hill, "New England Itinerant Portraitists," 158.

18. Boston *New-England Palladium,* 13 May 1806; *Portsmouth Oracle,* 14 January 1809.

19. Dunlap, *History of the Rise and Progress;* Trollope, *Domestic Manners of the Americans,* 282.

20. Table 17.1 at http://scholarworks.umass.edu/umpress_short_time_only/ lists all advantages advertised by portraitists, miniaturists, and profilists in American newspapers during the years 1765–1825, ranked by frequency.

21. Boston *Columbian Centinel,* 18 September 1805.

22. Wright and Brooks, "Medals."

23. *Newburyport Herald,* 22 September 1815. See, for example, the inventory of Mehitable Bowdoin, Boston, January 1750: "Four Family Pictures and a Coat of Arms which according to Custom are not prized." Suffolk County Probate Records, 44:476–77. See also inventory of Paul Dudley, Roxbury, 1 January 1750, Suffolk County Probate Records, 44:492.

24. *Boston Post-Boy,* 18 November 1765; *New-York Daily Advertiser,* 30 September 1793; *Charleston Courier,* 21 November 1804.

25. *Newburyport Herald,* 25 December 1801; *New-York Evening Post,* 9 September 1805; New Haven *Connecticut Journal,* 21 July 1808; *Providence Journal,* 15 February 1799.

26. *Newport Mercury,* 28 April 1810. In New Bedford, the two artists "engage to give a speaking Likeness, in Miniature style, for the sum of *two dollars and twenty five cents,* and require but half an hour's sitting." *New Bedford Mercury,* 15 June 1810. The opera was performed by Alexandre and Madam Placide, a Mr. Mallet, and a Mr. Douvillier: *Newport Mercury,* 23 August 1793.

27. Portsmouth *New-Hampshire Gazette,* 31 March 1801.

28. Portsmouth *New-Hampshire Gazette,* 1825, cited in Little, "Itinerant Painting in America," 212.

29. *Salem Gazette,* 24 January 1809. The text reads: "His productions in the point of resemblance shall . . . excell any other executed in this place, or no payment will be expected."

30. *Newburyport Herald,* 10 October 1800.

31. "To the paynter's, and sat and had some more of my picture done, but it do not please me for I fear it will not be like me." Pepys, *Diary,* 3 December 1661, 3 February 1666, 1:239, 2:359.

32. Quoted in "The Hancock House and Its Founders," *Atlantic Monthly* 11 (1863): 707. See also Saunders, *John Smibert,* 76–77. Hancock used language remarkably similar to the caricature drawn by playwright Richard Sheridan when urging a potential buyer to put a high value on selling a family's portraits. The "merit of these [portraits] is the inveterate likeness—all stiff and awkward as the originals." Richard Sheridan, *The School for Scandal,* Act 4, scene 1, lines 11–14.

33. Riley, "John Smibert and the Business of Portrait Painting."

34. Quoted in Aiken, "The Emergence of the Portrait Miniature," 36.

35. Trollope, *Domestic Manners of the Americans,* 268.

36. Green, "English Origins of Seventeenth-Century Painting in New England," 17; Silverman, *Cultural History of the American Revolution,* 636.

37. Benjamin West used the term "liney" in 1766 when discussing a painting that John Singleton Copley had sent him. Adams, Jones, and Ford, eds., *Letters and Papers of John Singleton Copley,* 44.

38. Merrill, "Diary," 11 April–12 June 1831.

39. On Peckham, Merrill wrote, "I spent the evening at Mr. Peckham. His brother is there taking their portraits" (8 March 1832); "Sat today at Mr. Peckhams" (13 March 1832); "Lois sat again at Mr. Peckham to have her portrait taken" (22 March 1832); "Paid for our portraits $20.00" (31 March 1832). Hill, "In Search of Early Massachusetts Itinerant Artists," 6. See also Johnson, "Deacon Robert Peckham." Baldwin, *Diary,* 24 March 1834, 282–83: "I had a visit today from Robert Peckham, a portrait painter. He now lives in Westminster, where he has resided for the [last] twelve years. He has also lived in Boston and in various other places. He was born in Petersham in 1785. . . . Robert, the painter, never received any instruction in his art. He is not distinguished in his profession, tho' he succeeds tolerably well in obtaining likenesses and has always gained his living by the art. His portraits are badly colored and, sometimes, are laughable caricatures. His price is ten dollars, and his business is almost wholly in the country. I have in some instances seen the name of the person intended to be painted written upon the picture, which was the surest way of identifying it. He is, notwithstanding, a very worthy and devout man."

40. John Vanderlyn to John Vanderlyn, Jr., 9 September 1825, quoted in Black, "Two Painters," 232; Trollope, *Domestic Manners of the Americans,* 394–95.

41. Tatham, *Abraham Tuthill,* 6.

42. For portraits of Perry by Stuart and Jarvis, see Dutton, *Oliver Hazard Perry,* frontispiece and opp. 160.

43. Boston *New-England Palladium,* 29 November 1808. See also Boston *Columbian Centinel,* 4 February 1809.

44. Doyle, "Miniatures and Portraits." See also Boston *Columbian Centinel,* 9 April 1808.

45. Boston *New-England Palladium,* 2 July 1811; "The Columbian Museum."

46. "Profiles of every description executed by Doyle or Williams, at the house fronting

the late Columbian Museum . . . excellent profile likenesses of the late Rev. Dr. Stillman, may be had at the above place." Boston *New-England Palladium,* 24 April 1807.

47. Boston *Independent Chronicle,* 12 February 1825; *Boston Evening Transcript,* 2 July 1832. See also *Boston Liberator,* 17 November 1832, and *Salem Gazette,* 16 November 1832, where Mrs. Williams advertised casts made from a "face of Dr. Spurzheim," the well-known lecturer on phrenology.

48. Pepys, *Diary,* 15 February 1669, 4:103.

49. Rowe, *Diary,* 23 August, 12 September 1766, 108, 130. "Mr. Copeland" has not been identified.

50. Baltimore *Federal Gazette,* 12 April 1800.

51. *Salem Gazette,* 15 October 1792; *Providence Gazette,* 5 November 1808. Reuben Moulthrop of New Haven also worked with wax portrait making, possibly making full-size replicas like Henry Williams and William Doyle. In 1793, he offered visitors to his first wax museum an "exact likenesses in Wax, taken by Mr. Moulthrop." That he made casts is suggested by his offer to do so "at short Notice." New Haven *Connecticut Journal,* 3 September 1793.

52. See, for example, the portrait of Eunice Spafford, oil on wood by Noah North (1809–1880), at the Shelburne Museum, Shelburne, Vt., where stencil designs are applied to the subject's chair. Other examples are in Little, "John Brewster, Jr.," 122; Fouratt, "Ruth Henshaw Bascom," 204; and Kellogg, "Ruth W. and Samuel A. Shute."

18. Taking Faces II: The Physiognotrace

1. Stiles, *Literary Diary,* 11 August 1790, 3:400.

2. *Providence Gazette,* 21 August 1790; Boston *Independent Chronicle,* 30 September 1790, cited in Jackson, *Silhouette,* 84; Wright and Brooks, "Medals." Stiles's unnamed artist may also have been a drawing teacher, Mr. Lacour, who left New York City and went through New Haven in January 1790. New Haven *Connecticut Journal,* 16 January 1790. Lacour is not known to have used a delineator, however.

3. Pepys, *Diary,* 21 May 1666, 27 October 1668, 2:355, 4:41.

4. Inventory of Bethesda Bordman, Boston widow, taken July 1756, Suffolk County Probate Records, 51:706; *Boston Gazette,* 2 August 1790. The contents of Daniel Bowen's Print Warehouse, auctioned in 1802, included "complete microscope and Camera Glasses with sets of elegant painted views." Boston *Columbian Centinel,* 26 May 1802.

5. Kemp, *Science of Art,* 167–203.

6. Boston *Massachusetts Mercury,* 24 May 1796; Boston *Columbian Centinel,* 9 July 1796. New York *Time-Piece, and Literary Companion,* 26 May 1797: "Apply to Mr. John Benson at the Lapidary and optical store." John Durang, the Philadelphia-born stage dancer who painted scenery and made and operated puppets, installed a camera obscura in the window of his bedroom. Durang, *Memoir,* 25.

7. *New York Weekly Mercury,* 9 November 1778; *New-York Gazette,* 23 November 1778; *New York Royal Gazette,* 10 May 1780, quoted in Jackson, *Silhouette,* 91; Philadelphia *Pennsylvania Packet,* 22 April 1783.

8. *Boston Gazette,* 11 June 1792.

9. *New-York Daily Gazette,* 7 August 1793.

10. Boston *Columbian Centinel,* 9 June 1792; *New-York Daily Advertiser,* 15 June 1793.

11. Hazard, *Nailer Tom's Diary,* 7 March 1796, 185.

12. Bryant, Diary, 23, 26 May 1798; 8 May 1799.
13. Fouratt, "Ruth Henshaw Bascom," 191.
14. Philadelphia *Aurora General Advertiser*, 7 November, 12 December 1796.
15. *New-York Daily Advertiser*, 28 January 1797.
16. In 1814, Saint-Mémin returned to France where he took a position as director of a museum. Mayne, *British Profile Miniaturists*, 30–31; Jackson, *Silhouette*, 63–65, 69; Miles, "1803—The Year of the Physiognotrace," 127–33; Miles, "Saint-Mémin, Valdenuit, Lemet."
17. *Albany Balance*, 10 March 1809; *New-York Evening Post*, 5 April 1805. See also Jackson, *Silhouette*, 120.
18. Philadelphia *Repository*, 1 January 1803; Philadelphia *Poulson's*, 2 July 1803.
19. Philadelphia *Aurora General Advertiser*, 1 June 1803.
20. *New-York Evening Post*, 4 January 1803; Jackson, *Silhouette*, 64; Peale, *Charles Willson Peale and His World*, 153; Sellers, *Charles Willson Peale*, 192. Hawkins received a patent for his physiognotrace in July 1803; see *Charleston Courier*, 27 July 1803, cited in Rutledge, "Artists in the Life of Charleston," 128; and *New York Morning Chronicle*, 11 December 1804.
21. Boston *Commercial Gazette*, 13 September 1804.
22. Boston *Columbian Centinel*, 22 September 1804; Miles, "1803—The Year of the Physiognotrace," 130, 136nn40, 47; *Boston Democrat*, 18 December 1805; *Boston Gazette*, 13 March 1806; Metcalf, *American Psalmody*, 27; Lowens, *Music and Musicians in Early America*, 170. Hawkins's patented machines did not go out of style; Henry Hervé, who toured with the Albiness in eastern America, may have been using one as late as 1819. See Jackson, *Silhouettes*, s.v. "Henry Hervé," 115; Mayne, *British Profile Miniaturists*, 71, and McKechnie, *British Silhouette Artists*, 235–36.
23. New York *Chronicle Express*, 23 June 1803; *New-York Evening Post*, 10 August 1803; New York *Morning Chronicle*, 27 June 1803; Boston *New-England Palladium*, 29 July, 23 September, 30 December 1803, 6 March 1804; Boston *Columbian Centinel*, 1, 19 October 1803. "A Complete Physiognotrace of the best workmanship, for sale, price 50 dollars. Apply to Joseph Thebaud, 12 Beekman street." *New York Mercantile Advertiser*, 27 November 1804.
24. Amherst, N.H., *Farmer's Cabinet*, 13 August 1805; *Portsmouth Oracle*, 9 February 1811; Charleston *City Gazette*, 7 December 1803.
25. Boston *New-England Palladium*, 23, 26 July 1805, 6 May 1806; Boston *Columbian Centinel*, 13 April 1805, 11 October, 12 November 1806; Jackson, *Silhouette*, 152–53; *Boston Recorder*, 11 September 1819.
26. Pinchbeck, *Witchcraft*, 81.
27. Portsmouth *New-Hampshire Gazette*, 26 February 1805.
28. *Portland Gazette*, 27 April 1805.
29. *Haverhill Museum*, 11 June–6 August 1805; Amherst, N.H., *Farmer's Cabinet*, 13 August 1805. "As he invented and used the same delineating Pencil some years ago which Mr. King uses it will be in his power to produce as accurate an Outline." *Newburyport Herald*, 19 February 1805.
30. *New Bedford Mercury*, 4 December 1807; Salem *Essex Register*, 23 January 1808; *Salem Gazette*, 4, 15 March 1808. See also Belknap, *Artists and Craftsmen of Essex County*, and Jackson, *Silhouette*, s.v. "Moses Chapman," 89, and plate 67. Chapman's physiognotrace is illustrated in Carrick, *Shades of Our Ancestors*, opp. 6.
31. Bumgardner, "Early Career of Ethan Allen Greenwood," 216. "On Dec. 14th [1808] cut 32 profiles." Greenwood, "'Extracts,'" 104, 110.
32. New London *Connecticut Gazette*, 6 September 1808; Boston *Columbian Centinel*, 18 September 1805, 26 October–5 November 1808; *Portsmouth Oracle*, 14 January 1809;

Newburyport Herald, 3 January 1809; *Richmond Argus,* 1 August 1807; *Norwich Olive Branch,* 17 September 1808. Samples of Chamberlain's profiles can be seen at the American Antiquarian Society, Worcester, Mass.

33. Concord *Courier of New Hampshire,* 12 June 1805.

34. *Newburyport Herald,* 19 February 1805.

35. *Boston Democrat,* 18 December 1805; *Boston Gazette,* 13 March 1806; *Newport Mercury,* 26 April 1805, 13 November 1806.

36. New Haven *Connecticut Journal,* 19 October 1809; *Newport Mercury,* 27 April 1810; *Salem Gazette,* 10 July 1810; Salem *Essex Register,* 11 July 1810; *Newburyport Herald,* 7 September, 5, 26 October, 29 November 1810; *Portsmouth Oracle,* 9 February 1811; Portland *Eastern Argus,* 21 February 1811; Carrick, *Shades of Our Ancestors,* opp. 70; Belknap, *Artists and Craftsmen of Essex County,* 21; Jackson, *Silhouette,* 79, 133, plate 55; Richmond *Virginia Gazette,* 28 January 1804, and *Richmond Argus,* 14 March 1804, both cited in Catterall, *Richmond Portraits,* 241.

37. King reported he had taken "above twenty thousand [profiles] in Salem, Newburyport, Portsmouth, Portland, and their adjoining towns." Hanover *Dartmouth Gazette,* 24 March 1806, reproduced in Garvin and Garvin, *On the Road North of Boston,* 99. King's itinerary can be traced through *Newburyport Herald,* 11 December 1804; Portsmouth *New-Hampshire Gazette,* 15 October 1805; Portland *Eastern Argus,* 31 May 1805, 26 June 1806; Bentley, *Diary,* 6 February 1807, 3:275–76; *Salem Gazette,* 3 February 1807; and Providence *Columbian Phenix,* 21 May 1808.

38. Boston *Columbian Centinel,* 22 September 1804.

39. Boston *Columbian Centinel,* 1, 8, 19 October 1803; Boston *Independent Chronicle,* 28 November 1803, 2 January 1804.

40. Allodi, "Appendix B: Pastel Profiles"; Belknap, *Artists and Craftsmen of Essex County,* 13; *New York Mercantile Advertiser,* 18 May 1802; *Charleston Times,* 23 April 1803, quoted in Rutledge, "Artists in the Life of Charleston," 129; Boston *Columbian Centinel,* 19 October 1803, 28 April, 18, 28 July 1804; Boston *New-England Palladium,* 6 January, 20 July, 3 August 1804; *Salem Gazette,* 1 June 1804; *Montreal Gazette,* 31 October 1808–9 January 1809, and *Quebec Gazette,* 16 April 1810, both cited in Allodi, "Appendix B: Pastel Profiles," 305–7.

41. Boston *Columbian Centinel,* 14 January 1804.

42. Weitenkampf, *Sketch of the Life Charles Balthazar Julien Fevret de Saint-Mémin,* 9; *Alexandria Gazette,* 28 March 1812; Hawkins, "The History and Resuscitation of the Claviole"; Providence *Columbian Phenix,* 21 May 1808.

43. Boston *Columbian Centinel,* 19 October 1803; Boston *New-England Palladium,* 6 January 1804; *New-York Evening Post,* 9 September 1805.

44. *Folk Art in America,* entry 95; Blumenthal, "Martha Ann Honeywell Cut-Outs"; Bentley, *Diary,* 27 January 1809, 3:41; Jackson, *Silhouettes,* 116. For sample announcements, see New Haven *Connecticut Journal,* 20 September 1808; Providence *Columbian Phenix,* 15 October 1808; *Newburyport Herald,* 21, 24 March 1809, cited in Barriskill, "Newburyport Theatre," 43:24–25; *Portsmouth Oracle,* 28 April 1809; Hudson, N.Y., *Northern Whig,* 29 August 1809; Jackson, *Silhouette,* s.v. "Master Hankes," "William Hubard," and "Sally Rogers," 113, 117–18, 139; *Boston Gazette,* 8 December 1808; Boston *New-England Palladium,* 21 November 1806; *New York Post,* 28 May 1807.

45. Jackson, *Silhouette,* s.v. "Wm. Henry Brown," 86; Carrick, *Shades of Our Ancestors,* 153, 157; Belknap, *Artists and Craftsmen of Essex County,* 21. "In my way to my lodgings in Boston I saw the sign of a person who cut full-length profiles. I went into his room, where I found my friend Fowle. He introduced me to the profile cutter, whose name is Brown,

from Charleston, S.C. and I was amazed to find that he completed the profile in about four minutes." Baldwin, *Diary,* 8 August 1834, 325.

46. Shaw, "'Moses Williams,'" 37–38.

47. *New-York Evening Post,* 5 April 1805; *Albany Centinel,* 3 May 1805; Concord *Courier of New Hampshire,* 21 August 1805; "The Astonishing Invisible Lady . . . [and] Patent Physiognomy Trace," *Montreal Gazette,* 7 October 1805 (courtesy of Lydia Foy, National Archives of Canada, Ottawa); Pinchbeck, *The Expositor,* fig. 1, 37.

48. Boston *Columbian Centinel,* 8, 21 June, 24 July 1805; *New York Diary,* 18 August 1796.

49. For example, Edward Savage: Boston *New-England Palladium,* 23 September 1803; Martin Howe: Boston *Columbian Centinel,* 13 April 1805; William Doyle: Boston *New-England Palladium,* 24 April 1807.

50. London *Morning Post,* 16 November 1803.

51. London *Parker's General Advertiser,* 25 March 1784; London *Morning Chronicle,* 22 September 1781, 1 January 1801, 20 July 1820.

52. *Newburyport Herald,* 7 September 1810; Portland *Eastern Argus,* 21 February 1811; *Quebec Gazette,* 21 August 1817 (courtesy of Lydia Foy, National Archives of Canada, Ottawa); *Albany Argus,* 19 December 1817; *Boston Daily Advertiser,* 8 September 1819. For Jennys, see Jones, "The Portraits of Richard and William Jennys."

19. The World of Automatons

1. Beyer, *Faszinierende Welt der Automaten,* 56–60; Pyke, *Biographical Dictionary of Wax Modellers,* 152.

2. *Boston Post-Boy,* 21 April 1735.

3. *New-York Mercury,* 24 June 1754; Philadelphia *Pennsylvania Gazette,* 4 July 1754.

4. Philadelphia *Pennsylvania Chronicle,* 30 October 1769.

5. Portsmouth *New-Hampshire Gazette,* 16 August 1771.

6. Christopher, "Magic in Early Baltimore," 299–300; "Extract of a Letter from a Gentlemen in Kingston to His Friend in Spanish-Town," Charleston *South-Carolina Gazette,* 17 July 1785; Jamaica *Savanna-la-Mar Gazette,* 19 August 1788. Full details of Falconi's itinerary for the years 1785–1819 are listed in table 19.1 at http://scholarworks.umass.edu/umpress_short_time_only/.

7. *New-York Weekly Journal,* 21 June 1787. The Indian was first illustrated in the Philadelphia *Independent Gazetteer,* 2 May 1788. The name was cited in an editorial discussing a local judge: "But like Mr. Maccabee (the automaton of Signior Falconi) he waited the instruction of his master." Philadelphia *Independent Gazetteer,* 2 May 1788.

8. Providence *United States Chronicle,* 18 February 1796.

9. *New-York Weekly Journal,* 12 July 1787; Boston *Massachusetts Centinel,* 25 July 1787; New London *Connecticut Gazette,* 5, 12 November 1795; *Newport Mercury,* 8 December 1795; *Providence Gazette,* 27 February 1796, 16, 23 January 1808; Boston *Columbian Centinel,* 15, 20, 25 June 1796; Providence *Columbian Phenix,* 4 February 1808; *New-York Evening Post,* 19, 26 May 1817. For Falconi's advertisements in New York City and Philadelphia, see *New-York Weekly Journal,* 12 July 1787; *New-York Journal,* 19 July 1787; and Philadelphia *Pennsylvania Packet,* 27 February 1788.

10. Baltimore *Maryland Journal,* 14 November 1787; Norfolk *Virginia Chronicle,* 14 July 1794.

11. Baltimore *Federal Gazette,* 23 January 1801; *Augusta Herald,* 11 December 1799; *Albany*

Gazette, 29 May 1797; Providence *United States Chronicle,* 11, 18 February 1796; Charleston *City Gazette,* 10 October 1799.

12. Boston *Federal Orrery,* 2 June 1796.

13. *New-York Journal,* 28 June 1787. Falconi was also seen as a "wizzard." Mount Pleasant *New Jersey Chronicle,* 27 June 1795.

14. Boston *Columbian Centinel,* 6, 9, 15, 17, 20 June 1796.

15. Figures compiled from table 19.1 at http://scholarworks.umass.edu/umpress_short_time_only/.

16. Philadelphia *Independent Gazetteer,* 24 August 1793; Philadelphia *Dunlap's,* 24 August 1793.

17. Boston *Massachusetts Mercury,* 2 June 1795; Boston *Columbian Centinel,* 30 September 1795.

18. Newburyport *Impartial Herald,* 10 November 1795; *Portsmouth Oracle,* 18 November 1795; New York *American Minerva,* 13 January 1796.

19. Portsmouth *New-Hampshire Gazette,* 30 January 1796.

20. Boston *Columbian Centinel,* 30 September 1795.

21. *Boston Courier,* 3 October 1795; *Providence State Gazette,* 28 March 1796.

22. Philadelphia *Aurora General Advertiser,* 19 May 1797; *Philadelphia Gazette,* 27 May 1797; *New-York Daily Advertiser,* 11 June 1796. Archytas was a Greek mathematician and astronomer. Jacques de Vaucanson was an eighteenth-century French inventor known for mechanical representations of a duck, a flute player, and a drum player. "Kempelon" was Wolfgang von Kempelen, a Hungarian who invented what appeared to be an automaton chess player. See Altick, *Shows of London,* 64–65.

23. Boston *Massachusetts Mercury,* 29 September, 2, 9, 16 October 1795.

24. *Philadelphia Gazette,* 21 August 1795. Pinchbeck may have manufactured them himself after studying models made by his grandfather Christopher Pinchbeck, Sr. (1669–1732), a skilled metallurgist and automaton maker. He may also have copied models by Pierre (1721–1790) and Henri-Louis Jaquet-Droz (1752–1791) of Neuchâtel and Geneva, Switzerland, which were brought to London in 1776, or those by Jean-Henri Maillardet (1745–1830), another Swiss clock and automaton maker. Maillardet managed the London branch of the Swiss clockmaking firm of Jaquet-Droz and Leschot.

25. Philadelphia *Aurora General Advertiser,* 12, 13 December 1796.

26. Boston *Independent Chronicle,* 28 November 1803.

27. *Montreal Gazette,* 7 October 1805.

28. *New York Diary,* 27 May, 12 June 1797.

29. Savannah *Columbian Museum,* 22 January 1799; *New-York Commercial Advertiser,* 15 May 1801; *New-York Daily Advertiser,* 6 June 1801.

30. Boston *Repertory,* 30 December 1806; Philadelphia *Poulson's,* 9 September 1808; Boston *Columbian Centinel,* 25 July 1810; New York *Political Bulletin,* 30 March 1811. Full details of Martin's itinerary for the years 1806–1811 are listed in table 19.2 at http://scholarworks.umass.edu/umpress_short_time_only/.

31. Charleston *City Gazette,* 20 November 1799; *Newburyport Herald,* 2 March 1798.

32. Trenton *True American,* 29 December 1801. See also *Philadelphia Repository,* 23 May 1801; Charleston *City Gazette,* 10 February 1803. For references to Rannie's claim they were in the Encyclopedia, see *Albany Gazette,* 1 November 1802, and Charleston *City Gazette,* 14 December 1802. In "An Other Voice," John Hodgson has identified the volume as the *Encyclopedia; or, Dictionary of Arts, Sciences and Miscellaneous Literature,* published in 1798.

33. *New-York Daily Advertiser* 2 April 1804; *New-York Commercial Advertiser*, 10 April 1804; *New-York Evening Post*, 16–21 April 1804. See also Newburyport *Political Calendar*, 1 October 1804: "A Philosophical Fish, Will also perform many wonderful deceptions, by drawing several cards from the pack which had been thought of by the company, and also writing down, with a pen, any words or numbers desired."

34. Boston *Columbian Centinel*, 9 December 1801.

35. Richmond *Virginia Patriot*, 26 June 1818.

36. Charleston *City Gazette*, 1 February 1820.

37. *New-York Gazette*, 1 December 1820; *New-York Evening Post* 3 January 1821.

38. *Baltimore Patriot*, 14 April 1823.

39. Dow, ed., *Holyoke Diaries*, Diary of Susanna Holyoke Ward, 27 November 1833, 181; *Portsmouth Journal*, 22 February 1834.

40. See, for example, Philadelphia *Independent Gazetteer*, 31 March 1788; Norfolk *Virginia Chronicle*, 9 October 1794; Providence *United States Chronicle*, 18 February 1796; and *Salem Gazette*, 13 September 1796.

41. Conners, *Dumbstruck*, 351; Flanagan, *Speech Analysis*, 166–67.

42. *Boston Democrat*, 29 August, 12 September 1804.

43. Charles Packard, "At Washington Hall . . . the Invisible Lady, Acoustic Temple, Writing Figure, Automaton Tumbler . . . Little Magician," Broadside, Salem, 1804, Harvard Theatre Collection, Cambridge, Mass.

44. Beyer, *Faszinierende Welt der Automaten*, 82–83; Penniman, "Maillardet's Automaton."

45. Bogger, *Norfolk*, 139–40, cites the *Norfolk Herald*, 27 June 1807, 31 May 1811, 31 August 1812; Bigler, *Schloss Hellbrunn*, 66–69. For a discussion of early powered garden amusements, see LaGrandeur, *Androides and Intelligent Networks*, 36–47.

46. See, for example, the discussion in Butterworth, *Magic on the Early English Stage*, chap. 5.

47. *New-York Daily Advertiser*, 18 August 1789; *New-York Journal*, 24 September 1789; Deeker, "Air Balloon"; Stiles, *Literary Diary*, 12 September 1789, 3:367.

48. New York *Weekly Museum*, 22 May 1790; *Providence Gazette*, 13 October 1790; Boston *Massachusetts Centinel*, 16 October 1790; *New-York Daily Advertiser*, 21 March 1791; Philadelphia *Freeman's Journal*, 9 March 1791; Decatur, *Private Affairs*, 89.

49. New York *American Citizen*, 5 December 1803; *New-York Evening Post*, 5 April 1805; Saco, Maine, *Freeman's Friend*, 16 October 1805.

50. New York *American Citizen*, 5 December 1803; Boston *New-England Palladium*, 4 July 1804; Portland *Eastern Argus*, 27 September 1804, 15 March 1805; Salem *Essex Register*, 8 October, 6 December 1804; *Newburyport Herald*, 5 November 1804, cited in Barriskill, "Newburyport Theatre," 43:12–14; *Portland Gazette*, 13 February–20 March 1805; *Providence Gazette*, 20 July 1805; *Newport Mercury*, 28 September 1805; New Haven *Connecticut Journal*, 11 July 1805; *New-York Evening Post*, 5 April 1805; Odell, *Annals of the New York Stage*, 2:204, 209; "Astonishing Invisible Lady."

51. Charleston *City Gazette*, 18 July 1803.

52. Thicknesse, *The Speaking Figure*; E. J. Ingennato, *The Invisible Lady and Her Secret Unveiled*, cited in Charney, *Magic*, 128–29; Pinchbeck, *Expositor*, fig. 1, 31.

53. Saco, Maine, *Freeman's Friend*, 16 October 1805.

54. Boston *Columbian Centinel*, 31 August 1805; Pinchbeck, *Witchcraft*, 81; Pinchbeck, "Expounder."

55. New Haven *Connecticut Herald*, 6 January 1807.

56. *Montreal Gazette,* 7 October 1805.
57. Raleigh, N.C., *Star,* 13 November 1812.
58. Charleston *City Gazette,* 8 November 1809.
59. Boston *Columbian Centinel,* 14 October 1795; *Philadelphia Gazette,* 21 August 1795; Philadelphia *Aurora General Advertiser,* 12, 13 December 1796; *New-York Evening Post,* 26 March 1808; *New-York Gazette,* 1 December 1820; *Providence Patriot,* 29 October 1828; Droz, "From Jointed Doll to Talking Robot," 38.
60. Boston *New-England Palladium,* 31 July 1810.
61. Standage, *The Turk,* chap. 11.

20. Penmanship Schools

1. Nash, *Some Early American Writing Books,* 11–15; Boston *Columbian Centinel,* 30 September 1809; Boston *New-England Palladium,* 10 October 1809, 26 July 1811.
2. "John Jenkins born Nov. 20th In the Year 1755, Abigail Hall, born March [ ] 1765. And were Married March 19th 17[ ]." National Archives, Washington, D.C. This document was submitted to the U.S. government to qualify Abigail Hall Jenkins to obtain her husband's Revolutionary War pension. See Allen, *Family Record,* 25.
3. Jenkins, *Art of Writing,* ix. Jamie Franklin kindly provided this information.
4. *Providence Gazette,* 22 January 1791; *Boston Gazette,* 24 January 1791.
5. New York *American Minerva,* 15 August 1794; New London *Connecticut Gazette,* 29 November 1797; *Salem Gazette,* 21 October 1799.
6. *Salem Gazette,* 15 April 1803; Nash, *Some Early American Writing Books,* 13–14; *New York Evening Post,* 6 November 1804; New York *Commercial Advertiser,* 11 June 1807.
7. Born on 15 February 1779 in Strafford, Vt., Abel Wrifford called himself Allison and acquired that name legally in 1821. He married Ellen Elizabeth Green in 1821. *Boston Daily Advertiser,* 28 March 1821.
8. Nash, *Some Early American Writing Books,* 14–15; Nash, "Early Writing Masters in Vermont"; Lyford, *History of Concord,* 2:1262; Boston *New-England Palladium,* 18 June 1805; Boston *Columbian Centinel,* 29 June 1805. The Boston families included those of Harrison Gray Otis, General Henry Knox, and Rufus Amory. Full details of Wrifford's itinerary for the years 1805–1840 are listed in table 20.1 at http://scholarworks.umass.edu/umpress_short_time_only/.
9. Portland *Eastern Argus,* 14 August 1806; Portsmouth *New-Hampshire Gazette,* 19 August 1806, 30 June 1810; *Salem Gazette,* 23 January 1810; *Newburyport Herald,* 28 November 1809.
10. Portland *Eastern Argus,* 8 July 1806; *Portland Gazette,* 18 August 1806; Boston *Independent Chronicle,* 14 December 1809.
11. Boston *Columbian Centinel,* 5 October 1805.
12. *Baltimore Patriot,* 18 March 1819.
13. Wrifford's first manual was *A New Plan of Writing Copies* (Boston, 1810). This was followed by a second edition (Boston, 1813) retitled *A New System of Penmanship.* Boston *New-England Palladium,* 17 March 1812. "We have in the house Mr. Wrifford a teacher of writing, a New England man, a character, he affords me entertainment by shrewd remarks & eccentric manners. He is a singer & has a noble voice. . . . Wrifford attempts to give a lecture on teaching but no one comes to hear him but myself and two others." Dunlap, *Diary,* 18 November, 1 December 1819, 2:488, 493.

14. *Salem Gazette,* 11 September 1810.

15. *Salem Gazette,* 27 September 1811.

16. Greenfield, Mass., *Franklin Herald,* 27 October 1812.

17. New Haven *Connecticut Herald,* 30 March 1813.

18. A "running" hand allowed no separation between individual letters. Nash, *American Penmanship,* 23; New Haven *Connecticut Journal,* 5 December 1816. Metcalf Horace and I. Johnson gave instructions patterned after "the celebrated System introduced by Messrs. Wrifford and Towne" in Hudson, New York, in 1812. Hudson, N.Y., *Northern Whig,* 21 September 1812.

19. Portsmouth *New-Hampshire Gazette,* 4 September 1810; Salem *Essex Register,* 5, 11 January 1811; *Newport Mercury,* 22 June 1811; *Albany Argus,* 25 July 1816; Nash, *Some Early American Writing Books,* 18.

20. Among them were Mr. Shepard: Portsmouth *New-Hampshire Gazette,* 2 August 1820; Freeman Page: Belfast, Maine, *Hancock Gazette and Penobscot Patriot,* 26 December 1821, quoted in Nash, *American Penmanship,* 20–21; J. H. Bugbee: *Providence Gazette,* 25 October 1823; Edmund Colburn: Boston *Columbian Centinel,* 28 November 1818, and Haverhill *Essex Patriot,* 4 July 1818; and Augustus G. P. Colburn: *Newburyport Herald,* 9 June 1818, and *Newport Mercury,* 10 May 1822.

21. Guild, "Journal," 277–79.

22. Bentley, *Diary,* 19 October 1808, 3:389–90.

23. Boston *New-England Palladium,* 10 October 1809, 26 July 1811.

24. Jenkins, *Art of Writing* (1813 edn.), xiv.

25. Boston *New-England Palladium,* 17 March 1812.

26. Boston *Columbian Centinel,* 10 January 1816.

27. *Boston Evening Transcript,* 12 July 1832; Salem *Essex Register,* 11 January 1811; *New-York Evening Post,* 6 June 1807; Belfast, Maine, *Hancock Gazette and Penobscot Patriot,* 26 December 1821, quoted in Nash, *American Penmanship,* 20–21; *Newport Mercury,* 16 June, 21 July 1821.

28. *Salem Gazette,* 17 September 1825, quoted in Brooks, *Olden-Time Music,* 114; Nash, *American Penmanship,* 54; *Providence Gazette,* 3, 17 July 1820; *Salem Gazette,* 29 May 1807; *Newburyport Herald,* 21, 31 October 1806; *Portland Gazette,* 19 January 1807; Lovejoy, *History of Royalton,* 627; Bailey, *A System of Stenography.*

29. *The Self Taught Penman* (1818), *The Writing Master* (1830), *The Traveler's Guide through the United States* (1822), and *The Traveller and Monthly Gazetteer* (1828). "Daniel Hewett's List of Newspapers and Periodicals."

30. Charleston *City Gazette,* 31 March 1818; *Alexandria Herald,* 12 May 1819.

31. *Baltimore Patriot,* 9, 21 April 1823; Wilmington *American Watchman,* 24 November 1819.

32. *New-York Evening Post,* 26 February, 13 March, 7 April 1820; *Albany Argus,* 8 May 1820; Albany *New-York Statesman,* 19 May 1820; Boston *New-England Galaxy,* 31 July, 11 August 1820; *Boston Patriot,* 1 September 1820; Portsmouth *New-Hampshire Gazette,* 27 September 1820; *Newburyport Herald,* 29 September 1820; *Providence Gazette,* 2 October, 2 November 1820; New Haven *Connecticut Journal,* 24 October, 7 November 1820; *Newport Mercury,* 25 November 1820; Hartford *Connecticut Mirror,* 11, 24 December 1820; Hartford *American Mercury,* 12 December 1820.

33. New London *Connecticut Gazette,* 19, 26 December 1810, 2 January, 31 July 1811; *New Bedford Mercury,* 9 July 1810.

34. *New Bedford Mercury,* 2 March, 13 April 1810; New London *Connecticut Gazette,* 19 December 1810, 31 July 1811; Nash, *Some Early American Writing Books,* 15–16; Nash, *American Penmanship,* 17–20.

35. Milns published a writing manual titled *Penman's Repository: Containing Twenty Correct Alphabets* (1787) in London, and he may have emigrated to America in 1789, but his manual became available in the United States only after Milns started a business education school specializing in bookkeeping and writing improvement in New York in 1796. *New York Argus,* 10 October 1796; Philadelphia *Aurora General Advertiser,* 8 June 1796. For Dorfeuille, see *Philadelphia General Advertiser,* 24 December 1793.

36. *Salem Gazette,* 19 April 1803; Boston *New-England Palladium,* 26 July 1811; *Providence American,* 22 May 1828; Haverhill *Merrimack Intelligencer,* 9 September 1815; *Newburyport Herald,* 9 June 1818; *Newport Mercury,* 10 May 1822, 22 June 1811.

37. *Newport Mercury,* 19 December 1818; Haverhill *Merrimack Intelligencer,* 9 September 1815; Boston *Columbian Centinel,* 28 November 1818.

38. *Providence Patriot,* 7 April 1819.

21. Conclusion: America Comes of Age

1. Philadelphia *Claypoole's,* 16 February 1797.
2. Charleston *City Gazette,* 5 November 1795, 24 January 1797; *Charleston Courier,* 21 November 1804; Lexington, Ky., *Park West Monitor,* 24 January 1817.
3. *Charleston Courier,* 23 August 1806.
4. Columbia, S.C., *State Gazette,* 28 April 1827.
5. Georgia *Augusta Herald,* 16 May 1804.
6. Lexington, Ky., *Reporter,* 6 May 1809.
7. Philadelphia *Franklin Gazette,* 26 May 1819.
8. *Providence Gazette,* 30 July 1774.
9. *Providence Gazette,* 26 August 1786.
10. Boston *Polar-Star,* 25 October 1796.
11. *New-York Public Advertiser,* 15 June 1812.
12. *Salem Gazette,* 5 January 1790; Portsmouth *New-Hampshire Spy,* 3 February 1790; *New-York Daily Advertiser,* 25 February 1792. Bentley, *Diary,* 8 January 1790, 1:135: "Last evening one Bennet pretending to be the first American Wire Dancer appeared & exhibited in this Town."
13. Philadelphia *Independent Gazette,* 31 January, 14 March 1788; Baltimore *North American and Mercantile Daily Advertiser,* 19 October 1808.
14. "An Account of the . . . Death"; *New-Hampshire Spy,* 23 March 1787.
15. Boston *New-England Palladium,* 27 February, 6, 13 March 1810; *Boston Records,* 33:428.
16. *Boston Repertory,* 15 May 1804; *New-York Commercial Advertiser,* 29 February 1808.
17. Cook, "Cockfighting in North American and New England"; Boston *Columbian Centinel,* 27 October 1806.
18. New London *Connecticut Gazette,* 8 October 1773; McNamara, *Step Right Up,* 8–10; Salem *Essex Gazette,* 4 August 1772; *Connecticut Public Records,* 14:208–9.
19. Philadelphia *Pennsylvania Chronicle,* 1 November 1773, which quotes a Norwich, Conn., dispatch of 14 October 1773.
20. Philadelphia *Pennsylvania Chronicle,* 1 November 1773. The "parson" who interrupted Yeldall has not been identified. Neither the first church in Canterbury, Connecticut, nor

its separatist counterpart supported professional clergymen—a long-term circumstance described by historian Richard M. Bayles in his 1889 *History of Windham, County, Connecticut*, 491, who quotes from the *Boston Gazette*, 16 December 1742 of the considerable doctrinal "confusion" in the town that persisted well into the 1770s.

21. Burke, *Popular Culture in Early Modern Europe*, 94–95: "This combination of healer and entertainer is in fact an extremely old one. Healing was, and in some parts of the world still is, a social drama, a public performance involving elaborate rituals."

22. Baltimore *Maryland Journal*, 26 November, 31 December 1782, 1, 6 May 1783.

23. *Boston Records*, 25:167–68; Hartford *Connecticut Journal*, 21 October 1794; Providence *American Journal*, 7 February 1781; *Salem Gazette*, 23 January 1783.

24. *New-York Morning Post*, 17 July 1787; *New-York Journal*, 19 July 1787; *New-York Daily Advertiser*, 18 July–3 August 1787; Boston *Herald of Freedom*, 6 November 1788; Litchfield *Weekly Monitor*, 24 November 1789; Middletown, Conn., *Middlesex Gazette*, 19 December 1789; Francesco, *Power of the Charlatan*, chap. 3.

25. "Isaac Calcott, a seventh son of a seventh son": *Providence Gazette*, 24 June 1769. "Dr. Calcott, a seventh son of a seventh son": Boston *Massachusetts Spy*, 25 March 1773. Beck, "Traditional Folk Medicine in Vermont," 41–42. For a history of English "seventh sons" in the sixteenth and seventeenth centuries, see Thomas, *Decline of Magic*, 200–204. As the name of a sailing vessel, see *New-York Gazette*, 11 September 1758.

26. John Tileston, Diary, 8 April 1765, quoted in Colesworthy, *John Tileston's School*, 77.

27. New Haven *Connecticut Journal*, 19 March, 18 June 1773.

28. Phelps, "Diary," 7, 28 February, 7 March 1782, 119:127–28. See also Sheldon, *History of Deerfield*, 2:35: "Eliakim, son of William b. 1737; being the seventh son, he was always called 'Doctor' . . . d. April 16, 1810." Seeking medical help from seventh sons was still practiced in twentieth-century northern New England and Canada though it seems to have been limited to rural people of French-Canadian origins. Beck, "Traditional Folk Medicine in Vermont," 41–42.

29. These names included Louis Chiappi, Luigi Chiappi and Co., and Don Louiso Chiappi; John Chiappi; Joseph Chiappi and Son; Don Joseph Chiappi; and Dr. Don Joseph Cheape.

30. *New-York Gazette*, 22 May 1812; *New York Mercantile Advertiser*, 21 September 1813, 10 December 1814; Philadelphia *Poulson's*, 28 December 1813, 4 January 1815; Boston *Independent Chronicle*, 5 September 1814; *Baltimore Patriot*, 31 May 1816.

31. *New-York Evening Post*, 8 September 1746; "The Famous Historie of Fryer Bacon"; Greene, *The Honorable Historie of Frier Bacon and Frier Bongay*; Marlowe, *Doctor Faustus*; Vale, *The Legend of the Blind Beggar's Daughter*.

32. Boston *New-England Courant*, 18 June 1733; *History of Dr. John Faustus*.

33. Speaight, *English Puppet Theatre*, 56–57; Ashton, *Chap-Books*, 38, 53, 360; Neuberg, *Chapbooks*, 38; Weiss, *A Catalogue of the Chapbooks*, 28, 34; Pepys, *Diary*, 26 June 1663, 2:13.

34. Philadelphia *Pennsylvania Evening Post*, 15 July 1777.

35. *New-York Gazette*, 9 October 1749.

36. *New-York Journal*, 3 July–16 October 1749; Frost, *Old Showmen*, 122.

37. Heltzel, *Fair Rosamond*, 44; Philadelphia *Aurora General Advertiser*, 11 May 1796; Evans, *Early American Imprints*, ser. 1, 40395, 47944, 30563.

38. Neuberg, *Chapbooks*, 37; Philpott, *Dictionary of Puppetry*, s.v. "Babes"; Ashton, *Chap-Books*, 369–75; Laws, *American Balladry from British Broadsides*, 289–91; Porter, *British Opera in America*.

39. *New-York Evening Post,* 23 October 1749; *New-York Gazette,* 30 October 1749. "Widow Franklin" printed a version in Newport in 1746. ("Widow Franklin" was Ann Franklin, wife of Benjamin Franklin's half-brother James.). A second ballad edition came out in Providence in 1768. Evans, *Early American Imprints,* ser. 1, 41808. A third appeared in Boston circa 1776 to 1805: "The Children in the Woods: Being a True Relation of the Inhuman Murder of Two Children of a Deceased Gentleman in Norfolk," Broadside, Evans, *Early American Imprints,* 1st ser., 19401. Other copies of the ballad were presumably in circulation when Maginnis made it part of his program in the 1790s. Smith, "Broadsides and Their Music," 311–14.

40. Philadelphia *Aurora General Advertiser,* 22 November 1794.

41. Hagerstown *Maryland Herald,* 3 April 1800. The full list of "dormant" English popular literature titles is much larger than these examples suggest. *Bateman's Tragedy; or, The Perjur'd Bride Justly Rewarded,* the history of the unfortunate love of a German for his prospective wife, was presented by Richard Brickell and Richard Mosely in New York in 1747 but never printed in America, nor was *The Enchanted Lady of the Grove* (performed in New York City by Bayly and Tea in 1767) or *Princess Elizabeth; or, The Rise of Judge Punch* (staged by James Wyatt). *Whittington and His Cat* (produced by Wyatt in 1749) appeared in America only in 1770 for adult readers. *The World Turned Upside Down* was sold in Boston bookstores as early as 1780, but while addressed to children, it consisted of thirty-four "curious" copperplates designed to provoke laughter and did not in any way reflect the historical European significance of this medieval practice of upending social and ideological values. Boston *Independent Chronicle,* 30 November 1780. *The Adventures of Grimalkin,* the story of a female cat, was not available in America until 1815.

42. Castle, *Masquerade and Civilization.* In the early part of the century, Swiss-born John James Heidegger (1659?–1749), also called Count Heidegger, who was appointed manager of the Haymarket Theatre in 1713, began staging weekly masked assemblies by 1717. He gained a reputation as "Master of the Revels" for George II. Later, Venetian-born Theresa Cornelys (1723–1797), opera singer and friend of Giovanni Casanova (1725–1798), began managing masquerades in 1760 and remained active through 1772.

43. John Legg, merchant, Inventory, 24 May 1733, Suffolk County Probate Records, 35:122.

44. Madam Elizabeth Stoddard, Inventory, 15 July 1757, Suffolk County Probate Records, 52:641. The total of her inventory was £305.10.7.

45. John Smith, Boston merchant, Inventory, 1 September 1768, Suffolk County Probate Records, 67:199. John Smith was a shopkeeper on the corner of Newbury (now Washington) and West Streets.

46. *New-York Gazette,* 16 February 1777, cited in Gottesman, *Arts and Crafts,* 2:308.

47. *Boston Records,* 33:423.

48. *Boston Patriot,* 3 January 1810; Boston *New-England Palladium,* 2, 5 January 1810.

49. New York *Chronicle Express,* 14 March 1803; Charleston *City Gazette,* 6 August 1808; *Baltimore Patriot,* 3 November 1818.

50. *Newburyport Herald,* 2 October 1807.

51. Providence *Rhode-Island American,* 10 February 1829.

52. Trollope, *Domestic Manners of the Americans,* 209.

53. Hawthorne, *Passages from the American Note-Books,* 173–74.

54. Hawthorne, *Passages from the American Note-Books,* 179–80.

55. Charles Dickens, *American Notes* (1842), quoted in Speaight, *Punch and Judy,* 128.

56. Philadelphia *Franklin Gazette,* 3 November 1819.

57. Boston *Daily Evening Transcript,* 3 April 1850; *Baltimore Gazette,* 10 May 1833; *New-York Herald,* 17 February 1848.

58. Hémard, "The Floating Palace"; Claeren, "Pittsburg and the First Showboat."

59. Philadelphia *National Gazette,* 29 September 1825.

60. *Providence Patriot,* February–May, 1825; Dedham, Mass., *Village Register,* 17 March 1825, 14 September 1826.

61. "Wheeler Ruth, doctress, h. 13 Leveret." *Stimpson's Boston Directory,* 1841, 461.

62. Boston *Liberator,* 15 November 1839; *New Bedford Mercury,* 13 December 1839; *Salem Register,* 7 January 1841.

63. Concord *New Hampshire Repository,* 5 August 1824; *Baltimore Patriot,* 10 February 1826; Portland *Eastern Argus,* 5 May 1826; *Augusta Chronicle,* 10 January 1827; Hudson, N.Y., *Northern Whig,* 28 September 1813; Hartford *Connecticut Mirror,* 8 October 1827; *New Bedford Mercury,* 3 September 1824.

64. [N. G. Dufief], *The Logic of Facts; or, The Conduct of W. Rawle, Esq. . . . toward N. G. Dufief* (Philadelphia: A. Dickenson, 1806), 6, 22–23; Boston *New-England Galaxy,* 30 May 1825; Philadelphia *Poulson's,* 31 December 1811. Dufief's work was offered in a Newport bookstore in 1811: *Newport Mercury,* 10 August 1811.

65. *New-York Evening Post,* 12 November 1804; Boston *New-England Palladium,* 29 March 1811; Boston *Columbian Centinel,* 26 June 1816. For other itinerant French teachers advertising Dufief's methods, see Madame Grandval, *Portsmouth Oracle,* 19 April 1817; Salem *Essex Register,* 20 November 1818; Miss M. Yvonnet, Boston *Columbian Centinel,* 21 March 1818, 1 May 1819; and Boston *New-England Galaxy,* 20 May 1825.

66. *Salem Gazette,* 13 September 1825; Hartford *Connecticut Mirror,* 21 July 1828; *Providence Patriot,* 6 June 1827; Abadie and Sons, *A French Grammar.*

67. Boston *Columbian Centinel,* 1 June 1825.

68. *Providence Gazette,* 5 February 1796.

69. Hartford *Connecticut Mirror,* 1, 29 September 1828; New Haven *Columbian Register,* 6 December 1828; *Richmond Compiler,* 8 October 1829; *Baltimore Gazette,* 12 November 1833; Drepperd, *American Pioneer Arts,* 121; Palmquist and Kailbourn, *Pioneer Photographers,* 331.

70. Willard, "Panoramas," 67; Coad, *William Dunlap,* 107. For an early New York City version of a moving panorama, see *A Description of Sinclair's Grand Peristrephic.*

71. *Baltimore Gazette,* 10 May 1833.

72. Willard, "Panoramas."

73. Smith and Risley, *Professor Risley and Mr. J. R. Smith's Original Gigantic Moving Panorama.*

74. *Baltimore Sun,* 15 March 1849; *Boston Evening Transcript,* 11 June 1850.

75. Fowler, *Human Science,* 213.

76. *New York Mirror,* 31 October 1846.

77. Barre, Mass., *Patriot,* 30 July 1852.

78. Rinhart and Rinhart, *The American Daguerreotype,* 380–416.

79. Sheldon, *Documentary History of Suffield,* 302.

80. Boston *Gazetteer,* 15 October 1803; Boston *New-England Palladium,* 9 May 1809; New York *Columbian,* 29 January 1812; *New-York Evening Post,* 25 May 1813.

81. Haberly, "The Long Life of Daniel Bowen," 320; Philadelphia *Poulson's,* 14 November 1817; Philadelphia *Franklin Gazette,* 19 March 1819.

82. *Albany Gazette,* 1 March 1813; Bagg, ed., *Memorial History of Utica,* 68.

83. London *World*, 22 June 1789; London *Public Advertiser*, 20 April 1791; London *Oracle and Daily Advertiser*, 13 December 1797, 11 July 1799.

84. *Alexandria Daily Advertiser*, 16 October 1805.

85. Baltimore *Democratic Republican*, 6 May 1802; Charleston *South-Carolina State-Gazette*, 29 August 1800; South Carolina *Columbia Gazette*, 29 August 1800; Milledgeville *Georgia Journal*, 22 August 1810; Keller, *Dance and Its Music*, 403n83.

86. Charleston *City Gazette*, 11 February 1824.

87. *Providence Gazette*, 26 November 1808, 14 July 1810; Providence *Columbian Phenix*, 21 May 1808; *Newport Mercury*, 17 February 1809; "Electrical Exhibition at the House of Joseph Wheeler, in Kingston, William King, Electrician," Broadside, Kingston, N.Y., 1810, American Antiquarian Society, Worcester, Mass., and Library of the Yale University Medical School, New Haven, Conn.; "Rational Amusements, at [———] William King, Philosophical and Medical Electrician," Broadside, c. 1810, Library of the Yale University Medical School; King, *A Manual of Electricity*.

88. Wirt, *Memoirs*, 26; *Lancaster Journal*, 8 February 1811; *Newburyport Herald*, 1 January 1811. A note in Boston's *Columbian Centinel* of 11 October 1817 reported that "Mr. John Templeton, formerly of this town, has published in the Washington papers a very useful article on the subject of the construction of bridges."

89. New York *National Advocate*, 15, 22 May 1817; *Bermuda Gazette*, 6, 13 November 1819; Christopher, *Illustrated History of Magic*, 56.

90. Haverstock, comp., "Ralph Letton b. 1778."

91. Montague, "Memorandum Book," 21 November 1840: "Went after Charles who has been to writing school to Mr. Wrifford an old teacher, went with waggon." Concord *New Hampshire Patriot*, 10 October 1844; *Boston Evening Transcript*, 10 October 1844.

92. *New-York Evening Post*, 23 October 1749.

93. Baltimore *Maryland Journal*, 1 August 1786; *New-York Journal*, 1 July 1773.

94. A few cultural curiosities came to the New World rapidly, however. The so-called solar microscope, demonstrated first in London in 1743, reached Boston in a matter of weeks, requiring only the time it took to make a sea passage (two months). Edmund Rising, who introduced it, also brought over a "Camera Obscura" depicting the Battle of Dettingen just a few months after England's important victory over a combined French and Prussian force. London *Daily Advertiser*, 20 July 1743.

95. Sewall, *Diary*, 4 December 1687, 1:154; *New-York Weekly Journal*, 15 April 1734; *New-York Journal*, 8 April 1767.

96. Philadelphia *Pennsylvania Gazette*, 20 February 1753, 11 June 1772; New London *Connecticut Gazette*, 29 May 1778.

97. *New-York Gazette*, 14 November 1748; Philadelphia *General Advertiser*, 3 August 1791.

98. Review dated 21 March 1795 cited in Moy, "Entertainments at John B. Ricketts's Circus," 201.

99. *Philadelphia Gazette*, 10 June 1802.

100. Baltimore *Federal Gazette*, 27 August 1801.

101. *New York Mercantile Advertiser*, 4 January 1809; *Raleigh Register*, 16 February 1821.

102. Other examples include a Dr. Preston, who displayed "Exhilarating Gas" at the circus in New York City in 1820 and then in Massachusetts at the amphitheater in Boston, and an unidentified chemist who gave lectures (and respirations) at the theater in Washington and at the Carolina Coffee-House in Charleston in 1822. *New-York Evening Post*, 29 May 1809, 18 February 1817, 14 April 1820; Newark *Centinel of Freedom*, 26 September, 2, 3, 24

October 1809; *Albany Balance,* 6 April 1810; Philadelphia *Poulson's,* 2 February 1814; *Appletons' Cyclopædia,* s.v. "John Griscom," 3:2; *New-York Daily Advertiser,* 29 February 1820; *Boston Intelligencer,* 14 October 1820; Washington *National Intelligencer,* 8 April 1820; Charleston *City Gazette,* 7 January 1822.

103. Reading, Penn., *Berks Journal,* 15 January 1831.

104. *New-York Evening Post,* 30 May 1820; *Boston Daily Advertiser,* 3, 12, 17 October 1820, cited in Barriskill, "Newburyport Theatre," 43:305; *Appletons' Cyclopædia,* s.v. "Gardner Q. Colton," 2:696.

105. Sewall, *Diary,* 4 December 1687, 1:154; Hall, *Worlds of Wonder,* 71.

106. McClung and McClung, "Capt. Crowninshield Brings Home an Elephant."

107. *Massachusetts Broadsides,* entries 2815–2817. See also *New-York Journal,* 13 April 1796, 23 August 1796, 25 April 1797; Philadelphia *Aurora General Advertiser,* 12 August 1796; Hartford *Connecticut Mirror,* 7 May 1797; *Providence Gazette,* 1, 8 July 1797; Boston *Massachusetts Mercury,* 25 July, 24 October 1797, 12 January 1798; Boston *Columbian Centinel,* 26 July 1797; *Salem Gazette,* 1, 12 September 1797; Portsmouth *New-Hampshire Gazette,* 2 October 1797; Baltimore *Federal Gazette,* 12 February 1798; Hartford *Connecticut Courant,* 10 May 1798; New Haven *Connecticut Journal,* 23, 30 May 1798; Ames, *Diary,* 15 July 1797, 1:623.

108. *Providence Gazette,* 1, 8 July 1797; Lydia Hill Almy, Diary, 1797–99, 27, Peabody Essex Museum Library, Salem, Mass. Mary Beaudry generously contributed this item.

109. "Last night of the elephant . . . will appear before the public, draw a cork from a bottle, take an apple from his keeper's mouth." *New-York Evening Post,* 5, 10 June 1812. "40 Thieves . . . in Act I the procession of the caravan with the living elephant." *New-York Evening Post,* 8 June 1812.

110. *New-York Evening Post,* 5 June 1812; Hudson, N.Y., *Northern Whig,* 21 September 1812; Greenfield, Mass., *Franklin Herald,* 17 October 1812; *Albany Argus,* 1 November 1813, 27 October 1814; Middlebury *Vermont Mirror,* 17 May 1815; New Hampshire *Dover Sun,* 7 October 1815; *Portsmouth Oracle,* 14 October 1815; *Newburyport Herald,* 24 October 1815; Boston *Columbian Centinel,* 8 November 1815; Boston *The Yankee,* 10 November 1815; *Salem Gazette,* 23 April 1816; Portland *Eastern Argus,* 29 May 1816; Hallowell, Maine, *American Advocate,* 29 June, 6 July 1816.

111. Sarah Lathrop Truman, "Reminiscences of Lebanon, N.H.," quoted in Garvin and Garvin, *On the Road North of Boston,* 100.

112. Jacob Wendell to Abraham and George Wendell, Portsmouth, 13 October 1815, Abraham Wendell Papers, Portsmouth Athenaeum, Portsmouth, N.H.; interleaved almanac diary at the Peabody-Essex Museum, Salem, Mass., cited in Barriskill, "Newburyport Theatre," 43:280; *Newburyport Herald,* 22 October 1815; Bentley, *Diary,* 9 January 1816, 4:369. See also table 6.1 (Old Bett's itinerary, 1804–1816) at http://scholarworks.umass.edu/umpress_short_time_only/.

113. Dow, ed., *Holyoke Diaries,* Diary of Margaret Holyoke, 29 April 1816, 164; Bentley, *Diary,* 29 April 1816, 4:384; "Now or Never—A Female Elephant," Portland *Eastern Argus,* 22 May 1816; Hallowell, Maine, *American Advocate,* 6 July 1816.

114. Bentley, *Diary,* 29 July 1816, 4:400–401. Other accounts are in the Portland *Eastern Argus,* 31 July 1816, and *Salem Register,* 27, 31 July 1816, cited in Flint, "Early-Nineteenth-Century Circus," 133.

115. Bentley, *Diary,* 6 August 1816, 4:402; Middlebury *Vermont Mirror,* 28 August 1816.

116. *New-York Evening Post,* 16 April 1817: "Skeleton of the elephant that was shot the 26th July last, in the District of Maine, so well known to the public, is got up for inspec-

tion." See also *Concord Gazette,* 6 August 1816: "The skin and bones of the Elephant which has fallen victim to some villains rancour at the Eastward have been carried to Boston. It is reported that the person who shot this noble and lamented animal, was hired by some one worse than himself to perpetrate the villainous act." In another sense, however, Old Bett continued to live on. Of the four images advertising the animal, three continued to be used by later animal handlers. A fourth image, whose engraver minutely duplicated M's distinctive initial with the letter "B," may have been made by Abel Bowen. *Boston Daily Advertiser,* 27 December 1817, 18 February 1818; Charleston *City Gazette,* 14 December 1821; *Providence Patriot,* 4 September 1822

Bibliography

Abadie, Hilarian, and Sons. *A French Grammar; or, Theoretical and Practical Lessons in the French Language.* Philadelphia: Privately printed, 1823.

An Account of the Extraordinary Abstinence of Ann Moor, of Tutbury, Staffordshire. Boston: True, 1811.

"An Account of the Wonderful *Old Hermit's Death,* and Burial." Boston?: Ezekiel Russell? 1787? Broadside. American Antiquarian Society, Worcester, Mass.

Adams, C. F., Guernsey Jones, and W. Chauncey Ford, eds. *Letters and Papers of John Singleton Copley and Henry Pelham.* New York: Kennedy Graphics, 1970.

Adams, John. *The Works of John Adams, Second President of the United States.* Edited by Charles F. Adams. 10 vols. Boston: Little and Brown, 1850.

Aiken, Carol. "The Emergence of the Portrait Miniature in New England." In *Painting and Portrait Making in the American Northeast: 1994 Annual Proceedings of the Dublin Seminar for New England Folklife,* 30–45. Boston: Boston University Scholarly Publications, 1996.

Alden, John. "A Season in Federal Street: J. B. Williamson and the Boston Theatre, 1796–1797." *Proceedings of the American Antiquarian Society* 65, pt. 1 (1955): 9–74.

Allen, Gloria Seaman. *Family Record: Genealogical Watercolors and Needlework.* Washington, D.C.: DAR Museum, 1989.

Allodi, Mary M. "Appendix B: Pastel Profiles." In *Berczy,* edited by Mary M. Allodi, Peter N. Moogk, and Beate Stock, 304–7. Ottawa: National Gallery of Canada, 1991.

Altick, Richard D. *The Shows of London.* Cambridge, Mass.: Harvard University Press, 1978.

Ames, Nathaniel. *The Diary of Dr. Nathaniel Ames of Dedham, Massachusetts, 1758–1822.* Edited by Robert B. Hanson. 2 vols. Camden, Maine: Picton Press, 1998.

Anthing, Frederick. *History of the Campaigns of Count Alexander Suworow Rymnikski.* 2 vols. London: J. Wright, 1799.

Appletons' Cyclopædia of American Biography. Edited by James G. Wilson and John Fiske. 6 vols. New York: D. Appleton, 1888.

Ashby, LeRoy. *With Amusement for All: A History of American Popular Culture since 1830.* Lexington: University Press of Kentucky, 2006.

Ashton, John. *Chap-Books of the Eighteenth Century.* 1882. Reprint, New York: Blom, 1966.

Aspin, Jehoshaphat. *A Picture of the Manners, Customs, Sports, and Pastimes, of the Inhabitants of England.* London: J. Harris, 1825.

"Astonishing Invisible Lady, the Acoustic Temple, and Incomprehensible Crystal, Now

Exhibiting at Mr. Craig's, Sign of the Queen of Otaheite, Wilmington, [Delaware]." N.p.: N.p., 1804. Broadside. American Antiquarian Society, Worcester, Mass.

Atwater, Edward E. *History of the City of New Haven to the Present Time.* New York: W. W. Munsell, 1887.

Bagg, M. M., ed. *Memorial History of Utica, N.Y.* Syracuse, N.Y.: Mason, 1892.

Bailey, Phinehas. *A System of Stenography or Shorthand Writing Selected from the Most Approved Authors.* Haverhill, Mass.: Burrill and Hersey, 1821.

Baker, Gardiner. "Museum & Wax-Work, at the Exchange, New-York, the Public Are Informed." New York: N.p., 25 November 1793. Broadside. Massachusetts Historical Society, Boston. Early American Imprints, ser. 1, no. 25908.

Bakhtin, Mikhail. *Rabelais and His World.* Translated by Hélène Iswolsky. Bloomington: Indiana University Press, 1984.

Baldwin, Christopher Columbus. *Diary of Christopher Columbus Baldwin, Librarian of the American Antiquarian Society, 1829–1835.* Worcester, Mass.: American Antiquarian Society, 1901.

Ballantine, Rev. John. "Journal of the Reverend John Ballantine, 1737–1774." Transcribed and annotated by Joseph D. Bartlett, 1886. Original at the Westfield Athenaeum; typescript copy at the American Antiquarian Society.

———. "Diary." Portions of Ballantine's diary are excerpted in John Lockwood, *Westfield and Its Historic Influences,* 1:379–441.

Balzer, Richard. *Optical Amusement: Magic Lanterns and Other Transforming Images.* Watertown, Mass.: Privately printed, 1987.

Bancroft, Elizabeth. Diary, 1793–1795, Pepperell, Mass. Typescript copy at the American Antiquarian Society, Worcester, Mass.

Barber, John Warner. *Historical Collections . . . Relating to the History and Antiquities of Every Town in Massachusetts.* Worcester, Mass.: Dorr, Howland, 1839.

Barber, Theodore X. "Evenings of Wonders: A History of the Magic Lantern Show in America." Ph.D. diss., New York University, 1993.

Barriskill, James W. "The Newburyport Theatre." *Essex Institute Historical Collections* 41 (July 1955): 211–45; 41 (October 1955): 329–52; 43 (January 1957): 1–35; 43 (October 1957): 279–314.

Barry, Phillips. "Springfield Mountain: Materials for a Critical Study." *Bulletin of the Folk-Song Society of the Northeast* 7 (January 1934): 4–6, 10–14.

Bartlett, Irving H. *From Slave to Citizen: The Story of the Negro in Rhode Island.* Providence, R.I.: Urban League, 1954.

Baston, Kim. "Transatlantic Journeys: John Bill Ricketts and the Edinburgh Equestrian Circus." *Popular Entertainment Studies* 4, no. 2 (2013): 5–28.

Bates, Benjamin. "Notice Is Hereby Given to the Curious . . . A Course of Experiments on the Newly Discovered Electrical Fire." Newport, R.I.: James Franklin, 1752. Broadside. Evans, *American Bibliography,* 3:6816; Rink, *Technical Americana,* 743.

Bates, Jacob. "Horsemanship, by Mr. Bates, the Original, Who Has Had the Honor of Performing before the Emperor of Germany." [Boston]: N.p., [1773]. Broadside. American Antiquarian Society, Worcester, Mass.

Battestin, Martin C. "Fielding and 'Master Punch' in Panton Street." *Philological Quarterly* 45 (1968): 191–208.

Bayles, Richard M., ed. *History of Windham County, Connecticut.* New York: W. W. Preston, 1889.

Bayly, Mr. "[By Permission] At the Sign of St. Patrick, Fell's Point . . . the Noted Old Artist Will Exhibit His Grand Medley of Entertainments." Baltimore: M. K. Goddard, 1783. Broadside. Early American Imprints, ser. 1, no. 44384.

Beales, Ross W., Jr. "The Ecstasy of Sarah Prentice: Death, Re-Birth, and the Great Awakening in Grafton, Massachusetts." *Historical Journal of Massachusetts* 25 no. 2 (Summer 1991): 101–23.

Beck, Jane C. "Traditional Folk Medicine in Vermont." In *Medicine and Healing: 1990 Annual Proceedings of the Dublin Seminar for New England Folklife*, 34–43. Boston: Boston University Scholarly Publications, 1992.

Belknap, Henry W. *Artists and Craftsmen of Essex County, Massachusetts.* Salem, Mass.: Essex Institute, 1927.

Bell, J. L. "Du Simitère's Sketches of Pope Day in Boston, 1767." In *The Worlds of Children, 1620–1920: 2002 Annual Proceedings of the Dublin Seminar for New England Folklife*, 209–17. Boston: Boston University Scholarly Publications, 2004.

Benes, Peter. "The American Death of Harlequin: Musical Pantomimes in Boston before 1815." In *New England Music: The Public Sphere, 1600–1900: 1996 Annual Proceedings of the Dublin Seminar for New England Folklife*, 30–47. Boston: Boston University Scholarly Publications, 1998.

———. "Dr. Anthony Yeldall: A Philadelphia Pharmacist Navigates the American Northeast," 109–15. In *Waterways and Byways, 1600–1890: 2009 Annual Proceedings of the Dublin Seminar for New England Folklife.* Concord, Mass.: Dublin Seminar for New England Folklife, 2014.

———. "'A Few Monstrous Great Snakes': Daniel Bowen and the Columbian Museum, 1789–1816." In *New England Collectors and Collections: 2004 Annual Proceedings of the Dublin Seminar for New England Folklife*, 22–39. Boston: Boston University Scholarly Publications, 2006.

———. "Fortunetellers, Wise Men, and Magical Healers in New England." In *Wonders of the Invisible World: 1993 Annual Proceedings of the Dublin Seminar for New England Folklife*, 127–48. Boston: Boston University Scholarly Publications, 1995.

———. "Night Processions: Celebrating the Gunpowder Plot in England and New England." In *New England Celebrates: Spectacle, Commemoration, and Festivity: 2000 Annual Proceedings of the Dublin Seminar for New England Folklife*, 9–28. Boston: Boston: University Scholarly Publications, 2002.

———. "'Peddlers in Divinity': Street Religion in Massachusetts and Rhode Island before 1830." In *Life on the Streets and Commons, 1600 to the Present: 2005 Annual Proceedings of the Dublin Seminar for New England Folklife*, 27–40. Boston: Boston University Scholarly Publications, 2008.

Benson, Norman A. "The Itinerant Dancing and Music Masters of Eighteenth-Century America." Ph.D. diss., University of Minnesota, 1963.

Bentley, William. *The Diary of William Bentley, D.D., Pastor of the East Church, Salem, Massachusetts.* 4 vols. 1905–1914. Reprint, Gloucester, Mass.: Peter Smith, 1962.

Bernard, John. *Retrospections of America, 1797–1811.* Edited from the manuscript by Mrs. Bayle Bernard. New York: Harper and Brothers, 1887.

Beyer, Annette. *Faszinierende Welt der Automaten: Uhren, Puppen, Spielereien.* Munich: Callway Verlag, 1983.

Bickford, Christopher P. "The Dark Days of Hartford Theatre, 1800–1853." Typescript copy at the Connecticut Historical Society, Hartford.

Bigler, Robert R. *Schloss Hellbrunn: Wunderkammer der Gartenarchitektur.* Vienna: Böhlau, 1996.

Billings, William. *The New-England Psalm-Singer; or, American Chorister: Containing a Number of Psalm-Tunes, Anthems and Canons, in Four and Five Parts.* Boston: Edes and Gill, [1770].

———. *The Psalm-Singer's Amusement: Containing a Number of Fuging Pieces and Anthems Composed by William Billings Author of the Singing Master's Assistant.* [Boston]: Printed by the Author, 1781.

Black, Mary C. "Contributions toward a History of Early Eighteenth-Century New York Portraiture: The Identification of the Aetatis Suae and Wendell Limners." *American Art Journal* 12 (1980): 4–32.

———. "Two Painters: Itinerants in New York and New England." In *Itinerancy in New England and New York: 1984 Annual Proceedings of the Dublin Seminar for New England Folklife,* 226–43. Boston: Boston University Scholarly Publications, 1986.

Blanchard, Jean-Pierre. *Journal of My Forty-Fifth Ascension.* 1793. Reprint, *Magazine of History with Notes and Queries* 64 (1918): 261–82.

———. *The Principles, History and Use of Air-Balloons. Also a Prospectus of Messrs. Blanchard and Baker's Intended Aerial Voyage from the City of New-York 1796.* New York: Fellows, 1796.

Blease, W. Lyon. *Suvorof.* London: Constable, 1920.

Blumenthal, M. L. "Martha Ann Honeywell Cut-Outs." *Magazine Antiques* 19 (May 1931): 379.

Bogger, Thomas L. *Norfolk: The First Four Centuries.* Charlottesville: University Press of Virginia, 1994.

Bolton, Ethel S. *Wax Portraits and Silhouettes.* Boston: Colonial Dames, 1915.

The Boston Directory. Boston: John Norman, 1789.

The Boston Directory. Boston: Rhoades and Laughton, 1798.

The Boston Directory. Boston: John West, 1800.

The Boston Directory Containing the Names of the Inhabitants. Boston: John West, 1803.

The Boston Directory; Containing Names of the Inhabitants; Their Occupations, Places of Business and Dwelling Houses. Boston: John H. A. Frost and Charles Stimpson, Jr., 1825.

Boston, Massachusetts, Registry Department. *Reports of the Records Commissioners.* 39 vols. Boston: Rockwell and Churchill, 1876–1909. Cited as *Boston Records.*

Bourne, Henry. *Antiquitates Vulgaress; or, The Antiquities of the Common People.* 1725. Reprint, New York: Arno Press, 1977.

Brand, John. *Popular Antiquities of Great Britain.* 3 vols. London: J. R. Smith, 1870.

Breck, Samuel. *Recollections of Samuel Breck.* Edited by H. E. Scudder. Philadelphia: Porter and Coates, 1877.

Breen, T. H. "An Empire of Goods: The Anglicization of Colonial America, 1690–1776." *Journal of British Studies* 25 (October 1986): 457–99.

———. "The Meaning of 'Likeness': American Portrait Painting in an Eighteenth-Century Consumer Society." *Word and Image* 6, no. 4 (October–December 1990): 325–50.

———. "The Meaning of 'Likeness': Portrait-Painting in an Eighteenth-Century Consumer Society." In *The Portrait in Eighteenth-Century America,* edited by Ellen G. Miles, 37–60. Newark: University of Delaware Press, 1993.

Brekus, Catherine A. *Strangers and Pilgrims: Female Preaching in America, 1740–1845.* Chapel Hill: University of North Carolina Press, 1998.

Breslaw, Philip. *Breslaw's Last Legacy; or, The Magical Companion.* London: W. Lane, 1795.
Brigham, Clarence S. *Paul Revere's Engravings.* New York: Atheneum, 1969.
Britten, F. J. *Old Clocks and Watches and Their Makers.* London: Batsford, 1911.
Brock, Alan St. H. *A History of Fireworks.* London: Harrap, 1949.
Brooks, Henry M. *Olden-Time Music: A Compilation from Newspapers and Books.* Boston: Ticknor, 1888.
———. *Quaint and Curious Advertisements.* Boston: Ticknor, 1886.
Brooks, Lynn M. *John Durang: Man of the American Stage.* Amherst, N.Y.: Cambria Press, 2011.
Brown, James. *A Treatise on the Nature and Reasons of the English Grammar: Illustrated by a Machine Constructed for That Purpose.* Boston: W. W. Clapp, 1815.
Bryant, Sarah Snell. Diary, 1795–1835, Cummington, Mass. Houghton Library, Harvard University.
Buechner, Alan C. "Thomas Walter and the Society for Promoting Regular Singing in the Worship of God: Boston, 1720–1723." In *New England Music: The Public Sphere, 1600–1900: 1996 Annual Proceedings of the Dublin Seminar for New England Folklife,* 48–60. Boston: Boston University Scholarly Publications, 1998.
———. *Yankee Singing Schools and the Golden Age of Choral Music in New England, 1760–1800.* Boston: Boston University for the Dublin Seminar for New England Folklife, 2003.
Bumgardner, Georgia B. "The Early Career of Ethan Allen Greenwood." In *Itinerancy in New England and New York: 1984 Annual Proceedings of the Dublin Seminar for New England Folklife,* 212–25. Boston: Boston University Scholarly Publications, 1986.
Burke, Peter. *Popular Culture in Early Modern Europe.* New York: Harper and Row, 1978.
———. "Popular Culture in Seventeenth-Century London." In *Popular Culture in Seventeenth-Century England,* edited by Barry Reay, 31–58. London: Croom Helm, 1985.
Burnet, Thomas. *A Second Tale of a Tub; or, The History of Robert Powell, the Puppet-Show-Man.* London: J. Roberts, 1715.
Bushnell, Vinson C. "Daniel Read of New Haven (1757–1836): The Man and His Musical Activities." Ph.D. diss., Harvard University, 1978.
Butterworth, Philip. *Magic on the Early English Stage.* Cambridge: Cambridge University Press, 2005.
Byles, G. Huntington. *A Short History of the Organs and Music of Trinity Church, New Haven, Connecticut.* New Haven, Conn.: N.p., 1952. http://anglicanhistory.org.
Byrd, William. *The Secret Diary of William Byrd of Westover, 1709–1712.* Richmond: Dietz Press, 1941.
Candee, Richard M. "Lace Schools and Lace Factories: Female Outwork in New England's Machine-Lace Industry, 1818–1838." In *Textiles in New England: Designing, Production, and Consumption: 1997 Annual Proceedings of the Dublin Seminar for New England Folklife,* 100–126. Boston: Boston University Scholarly Publications, 1999.
Carlyle, Thomas. *The French Revolution: A History.* 2 vols. New York: Dutton, 1906.
Carrick, Alice Van Leer. "Novelties in Old American Profiles." *Magazine Antiques* 14 (1928): 322–27.
———. *Shades of Our Ancestors: American Profiles and Profilists.* Boston: Little, Brown, 1928.
Castle, Terry. *Masquerade and Civilization: The Carnivalesque in Eighteenth-Century English Culture and Fiction.* Stanford, Calif.: Stanford University Press, 1986.
Catalogue of American Portraits in the New-York Historical Society. New York: New-York Historical Society, 1941.

Catalogue of an Exhibition of Miniatures Painted in America, 1720–1850. New York: Metropolitan Museum of Art, 1927.

Catterall, Louise F. *Richmond Portraits.* Richmond: Valentine Museum, 1949.

Champlin, Richard L. "William Claggett: A Printer Confirmed." *Newport History: Journal of the Newport Historical Society* 67, pt. 4, no. 233 (Spring 1996): 197–99.

Chapin, Howard M. "Was Claggett, the Clock Maker, an Engraver?" *Rhode Island Historical Society Collections* 22, no. 2 (April 1929): 41–45.

Chapman, Clive G. "English Pantomime and Its Music, 1700–1730 (with transcriptions and appendices)." Ph.D. diss., Royal Holloway College, University of London, 1981.

The Chapmans and Travellers Almanack for the Year of Christ 1694 Wherein All the Post Roads, with Their Several Branches and Distances, the Marts, Fairs, and Markets in England and Wales, Are Alphabetically Disposed in Every Month. London: Thomas James, 1694.

Charney, David F. *Magic: The Great Illusions Revealed and Explained.* New York: Quadrangle/New York Times Book Company, 1975.

Chater, John. *Another High Road to Hell.* London: Ezekiel Russell, 1768.

Chauncey, Nathaniel. *Regular Singing Defended . . . by Arguments . . . Approved of, by the General Association of Hartford, May the 12th. 1727.* New London, Conn.: T. Green, 1728.

Chiappe, Jean-François. *Louis XVI: III. L'Otage.* Paris: Librairie académique Perrin, 1989.

Child, Deborah M. *Soldier, Engraver, Forger: Richard Brunton's Life on the Fringe in America's New Republic.* Boston: New England Historic Genealogical Society, 2015.

Chindahl, George L. *A History of the Circus in America.* Caldwell, Idaho: Caxton, 1959.

Christopher, Milbourne. *The Illustrated History of Magic.* Portsmouth, N.H.: Heinemann, 1996.

———. "Magic in Early Baltimore." *Maryland Historical Magazine* 38 (December 1943): 299–330.

"Church Records of the Old Town of Reading, Massachusetts and of the First Parish of Reading and South Reading from 1648 to 1846." Bound typescript. 1934. Reading Public Library, Reading, Massachusetts.

Claeren, Wayne H. "Historical Society Notes and Documents: Pittsburg and the First Showboat: A New Angle on the Chapmans." *Western Pennsylvania Historical Magazine* 59, no. 2 (April 1976): 231–39.

Clapp, William W. *A Record of the Boston Stage.* Boston: James Munroe, 1853.

Clay, Reginald S., and Thomas H. Court. *The History of the Microscope.* 1932. Reprint, Tortola, British Virgin Islands: Longwood Press, 1978.

Cloris, Pedro. "This Evening, January 1st, 1801. At Washington Hall: Part 1st. The Celebrated Don Pedro Cloris, Will Perform His Graceful and Manly Feats of Activity, on the Slack Wire. . . . Part 2d. A Curious Philosophical Apparatus, above 100 Figures, as Large as Life, in Brilliant Colours." Salem, Mass.: N.p., 1801. Broadside. Peabody-Essex Museum, Salem, Mass.

Coad, Oral Sumner. *William Dunlap.* New York: Dunlap Society, 1917.

Colburn, Zerah. *A Memoir of Zerah Colburn; Written by Himself.* Springfield, Mass.: G. and C. Merriam, 1833.

Colesworthy, D. C. *John Tileston's School.* Boston: Antiquarian Book Store, 1887.

"The Columbian Museum . . . Contains Upward of Over 20,000 Curiosities. . . . Doyle & Williams, Miniature and Portrait Painters, at the Museum; Where Profiles Are Correctly Cut." Brighton, Mass.: D. and A. Bowen, 1812. Broadside. American Antiquarian Society, Worcester, Mass.

Connecticut Public Records (1772–1775). Vol. 14. Edited by Charles T. Hoadley. Hartford, Conn.: Case Lockwood, 1887.

Conners, Steven. *Dumbstruck: A Cultural History of Ventriloquism.* New York: Oxford University Press, 2000.

Cook, James W., Lawrence B. Glickman, and Michael O'Malley, eds. *The Cultural Turn in U. S. History: Past, Present, and Future.* Chicago: University of Chicago Press, 2008.

Cook, Peter W. "Cockfighting in North America and New England, 1680–1900." In *New England's Creatures: 1993 Annual Proceedings of the Dublin Seminar for New England Folklife,* 164–82. Boston: Boston University Scholarly Publications, 1995.

Cooke, Nym. "Itinerant Yankee Singing Masters in the Eighteenth Century." In *Itinerancy in New England and New York: 1984 Annual Proceedings of the Dublin Seminar for New England Folklife,* 16–36. Boston: Boston University Scholarly Publications, 1986.

Corey, Deloraine P. *The History of Malden, Massachusetts, 1633–1785.* Malden, Mass.: Privately printed, 1899.

Corry, Mary Jane, Kate Van Winkle Keller, and Robert M. Keller. "The Performing Arts in Colonial American Newspapers, 1690–1783: Text Database and Index." CD-ROM. New York: University Music Editions, 1997.

Cosentino, Andrew J. *The Paintings of Charles Bird King (1785–1862).* Washington, D.C.: Smithsonian Institution Press, 1977.

Crawford, Richard A. "'Ancient Music' and the Europeanizing of American Psalmody, 1800–1810." In *A Celebration of American Music,* edited by Richard A. Crawford, R. Allen Lott, and Carol J. Oja, 225–55. Ann Arbor: University of Michigan Press, 1990.

———. *Andrew Law, American Psalmodist.* Evanston, Ill.: Northwestern University Press, 1968.

Crouch, Tom D. *The Eagle Aloft: Two Centuries of the Balloon in America.* Washington, D.C.: Smithsonian Institution Press, 1983.

Cullen, Jim. *Popular Culture in American History.* Malden, Mass.: Blackwell, 2001.

Currier, John J. *History of Newburyport, Massachusetts.* 2 vols. Somersworth, N.H.: New Hampshire Publishing, 1977–1978.

Daniel, George. *Merrie England in the Olden Time.* 2 vols. London: Richard Bentley, 1842.

"Daniel Hewett's List of Newspapers and Periodicals in the United States in 1818." *Proceedings of the American Antiquarian Society* 44 (October 1934): 365–96.

Daniels, Bruce C. *Puritans at Play: Leisure and Recreation in Colonial New England.* New York: St. Martin's Press, 1995.

Dargan, Amanda, and Steve Zeitlin. "American Talkers: Expressive Styles and Occupational Choice." *Journal of American Folklore* 96, no. 379 (January–March 1983): 3–33.

Day, Gordon M. "Henry Tufts as a Source on the Eighteenth-Century Abenakis." *Ethnohistory* 21 (1974): 189–97.

Dean, Henry. *Hocus Pocus; or, The Whole Art of Legerdemain, in Perfection. By Which the Meanest Capacity May Perform the Whole without the Help of a Teacher.* Philadelphia: Mathew Carey, 1795.

Decatur, Stephen, Jr. *Private Affairs of George Washington.* Boston: Houghton Mifflin, 1933.

Deeker, Joseph. "Air Balloon. The Subscriber, Who Is the Proprietor of the Speaking Image, Begs Leave to Inform the Public, That He Is Perfectly Acquainted with the Nature and Construction of Air Balloons." New York: N.p., 10 June 1789. Broadside. Early American Imprints, ser. 1, no. 45463.

Deetz, James. *In Small Things Forgotten: The Archeology of Early American Life.* Garden City, N.Y.: Anchor Press / Doubleday, 1977.

DeForest, Heman P. *The History of Westborough, Massachusetts.* Westborough, Mass.: Town of Westborough, 1891.
"Description of Dunlap's Painting of Christ Rejected by the High Priest, Elders and People." Norfolk, Va.: Shields, Ashburn, 1822. Broadside. Library Company of Philadelphia.
A Description of Sinclair's Grand Peristrephic or Moving Panorama of the Battle of Navarino. New York: Craighead and Allen, 1835.
Deyo, Simeon L. *History of Barnstable County, Massachusetts.* New York: Blake, 1890.
Dibner, Bern. *Galvani-Volta: A Controversy That Led to the Discovery of Useful Electricity.* Norwalk, Conn.: Burndy Library, 1952.
Dickerson, Mahlon. "Diary." In *Letters of the Lewis and Clark Expedition: With Related Documents, 1783–1854,* 2nd edn., 2 vols., edited by Donald D. Jackson, 2:677–79. Urbana: University of Illinois Press, 1978.
Dickinson, Rebecca. Diary, 1787–1802. Microfilm copy at the Henry N. Flynt Library, Historic Deerfield, Deerfield, Mass.
Dictionary of American Biography. Edited by Edward T. James and Robert Livingston Schuyler. 20 vols. New York: Scribner's, 1928–36.
Dictionary of National Biography, 1912–1921. Edited by George Smith. London: Oxford University Press, 1927.
Douglass, William. *A Summary, Historical and Political, of the First Planting, Progressive Improvement and Present State of British Settlements in North America.* Boston: Rogers and Fowle, 1749.
Dow, George F. *The Arts and Crafts in New England, 1705–1775: Gleanings from Boston Newspapers.* Topsfield, Mass.: Wayside Press, 1927.
———, ed. *The Holyoke Diaries, 1709–1856.* Salem, Mass.: Essex Institute, 1911.
Doyle, William M. S. "Miniatures & Portraits. . . . Doyle Takes Likenesses of the Dead in His Own Peculiar Way, by Means of a Mask." Boston: Columbian Museum, 1808. Broadside. Old Sturbridge Village Library, Sturbridge, Mass.
Drake, Francis S. *Life and Correspondence of Henry Knox.* Boston: Samuel G. Drake, 1873.
Drake, Samuel G. *The History and Antiquities of Boston.* Boston: L. Stevens, 1856.
Drepperd, Carl W. *American Pioneer Arts and Artists.* Springfield, Mass.: Pond Ekberg, 1942.
Droz, Edmond. "From Jointed Doll to Talking Robot." *New Scientist* 14, no. 282 (12 April 1962): 37–40.
Dufief, Nicolas Gouin. *Nature Displayed in Her Mode of Teaching Language to Man; or, A New and Infallible Method of Acquiring a Language.* Philadelphia: Thomas Watts, 1804.
Dunkle, Robert J., and Ann S. Lainhart. *Records of the Churches of Boston.* CD-ROM. Boston: New England Historic Genealogical Society, 2002.
Dunlap, William. *Diary of William Dunlap (1766–1839).* 3 vols. New York: New-York Historical Society, 1930.
———. *History of New York for Schools.* New York: Collins, Kesse, 1837.
———. *The History of the American Theatre.* New York: Harper, 1832.
———. *History of the Rise and Progress of the Arts of Design in the United States.* 2 vols. 1834. Reprint, New York: Dover Publications, 1969.
———. *Memoirs of the Life of George Frederick Cooke, Late of the Theatre Royal.* New York: Longworth, 1813.
Durand, of Dauphiné. *A Huguenot Exile in Virginia; or, Voyages of a Frenchman exiled for his Religion with a description of Virginia & Maryland.* Edited by Gilbert Chinard. New York: Press of the Pioneers, 1934.

Durang, John. *The Memoir of John Durang, American Actor, 1785–1816.* Edited by Alan S. Downer. Pittsburgh: University of Pittsburgh Press for the Historical Society of York County, 1966.
Dutton, Charles S. *Oliver Hazard Perry.* New York: Longmans, Green, 1935.
Dwight, Timothy. *Travels in New-England and New York.* 4 vols. New Haven, Conn.: T. Dwight, 1821.
Earle, Alice M. *Customs and Fashions in Old New England.* 1893. Reprint, Rutland, Vt.: Charles Tuttle, 1973.
———. *Stage-Coach and Tavern Days.* 1900. Reprint, New York: Dover Publications, 1966.
"Early American Newspapers, 1690–1922." Digital edition. New York: Readex, 1968–2014.
Eliot, Jacob. "Diary." *Historical Magazine,* 2nd ser., 5 (January 1869): 33–34.
———. *Diary of the Rev. Jacob Eliot, M.A., 1716–1764.* Edited by William I. Morse. Cambridge, Mass.: Morse, 1944.
Emery, Sarah Anna, ed. *Reminiscences of a Nonagenarian.* Newburyport, Mass.: W. H. Huse, 1879.
Emlen, Robert P. "The Great Gale of 1815: Artifactual Evidence of Rhode Island's First Hurricane." *Rhode Island History* 48, no. 2 (1990): 51–60.
Encyclopedia; or, Dictionary of Arts, Sciences and Miscellaneous Literature. 21 vols. Philadelphia: Thomas Dobson, 1798.
Evans, Charles. *American Bibliography: A Chronological Dictionary of All Books . . . Printed in the United States of America.* 14 vols. New York: P. Smith, 1941–1959.
———. *Early American Imprints, Series I (1639–1800).* Digital edition. New Canaan, Conn.: Readex and American Antiquarian Society, 2002.
Fairbanks, Jason. *Solemn Declaration of the Late Unfortunate Jason Fairbanks.* Dedham, Mass.: Ebenezer Fairbanks Jr., 1801.
"The Famous Historie of Fryer Bacon." In *Miscellanea Antiqua Anglicana; or, A Select Collection of Curious Tracts.* London: Triphook, 1816.
Felt, Joseph B. *Annals of Salem, Massachusetts.* 2 vols. Salem, Mass.: Ives, 1845–1849.
Fiske, Roger. *English Theatre Music in the Eighteenth Century.* 2nd ed. New York: Oxford University Press, 1986.
Flanagan, James L. *Speech Analysis, Synthesis, and Perception.* Berlin: Springer, 1965.
Flint, Richard W. "Entrepreneurial and Cultural Aspects of the Early-Nineteenth-Century Circus and Menagerie Business." In *Itinerancy in New England and New York: 1984 Annual Proceedings of the Dublin Seminar for New England Folklife,* 131–49. Boston: Boston University Scholarly Publications, 1986.
Folk Art in America. Williamsburg, Va.: A. A. Rockefeller Folk Art Collection, 1974.
Fontaine, Laurence. *History of Pedlars in Europe.* Translated by Vicki Whittaker. Durham, N.C.: Duke University Press, 1966.
Foote, Henry Wilder. *Three Centuries of American Hymnody.* 1940. Reprint, Hamden, Conn.: Archon, 1968.
Forbes, Harriette M. *The Hundredth Town: Glimpses of Life in Westborough, 1717–1817.* Boston: Rockwell and Churchill, 1889.
Foster, Hannah Webster. *The Coquette; or, The History of Eliza Wharton.* 1797. Reprint, Boston: William P. Fetridge, 1855.
Fouratt, Mary Eileen. "Ruth Henshaw Bascom: Itinerant Portraitist." In *Itinerancy in New England and New York: 1984 Annual Proceedings of the Dublin Seminar for New England Folklife,* 190–211. Boston: Boston University Scholarly Publications, 1986.

Fowble, E. McSherry. *Two Centuries of Prints in America, 1680–1880.* Charlottesville: University Press of Virginia, 1987.

Fowler, Orson Squire. *Human Science; or, Phrenology.* Philadelphia: National, 1873.

Francesco, Grete de. *The Power of the Charlatan.* Translated by Miriam Beard. New Haven, Conn.: Yale University Press, 1939.

Fraser, Antonia. *Faith and Treason: The Story of the Gunpowder Plot.* New York: Doubleday, 1996.

Freeman, Dale H. "'Melancholy Catastrophe!' The Story of Jason Fairbanks and Elizabeth Fales (1801)." *Historical Journal of Massachusetts* 26, no. 1 (Winter 1998): 1–25.

"French Revolution Digital Archive." Stanford University Libraries and Bibliothèque Nationale de France. frda.stanford.edu.

Frost, Thomas. *The Old Showmen and the Old London Fairs.* 1881. Reprint, Ann Arbor, Mich.: Gryphon Books, 1971.

"Gabriel Salenka, Lately Arrived from Europe, Has the Honour to Inform the Public That He Has Brought with Him a Dog." [Philadelphia]: W. W. Woodward, [1796?]. Broadside. American Antiquarian Society, Worcester, Mass.

Gale, T. *Brief Instructions for Administering Medical Electricity.* Harford, Conn.: Privately printed, 1805.

Gardiner, John. *The Speech of John Gardiner . . . to Consider the Expediency of Repealing the Law against Theatrical Exhibitions.* Boston: Joseph Bumstead, 1792.

Garvin, Donna-Belle, and James L. Garvin. *On the Road North of Boston: New Hampshire Taverns and Turnpikes, 1700–1900.* Concord: New Hampshire Historical Society, 1988.

Gaustad, Edwin S. *The Great Awakening in New England.* New York: Harper, 1957.

Gay, Julius. *Farmington Papers.* Hartford: Privately printed, 1929.

Gentilcore, David. *Medical Charlatanism in Early Modern Italy.* Oxford: Oxford University Press, 2006.

Gilmore, William J. "Peddlers and the Dissemination of Printed Materials in Northern New England, 1780–1840." In *Itinerancy in New England and New York: Annual Proceedings of the Dublin Seminar for New England Folklife,* 76–89. Boston: Boston University Scholarly Publications, 1984.

Ginzburg, Carlo. *The Night Battles: Witchcraft and Agrarian Cults in the Sixteenth and Seventeenth Centuries.* Translated by John and Anne Tedeschi. 1966. Reprint, Baltimore: Johns Hopkins University Press, 1992.

Goen, C. C. *Revivalism and Separatism in New England, 1740–1800.* New Haven, Conn.: Yale University Press, 1962.

Goler, Robert I. "'Here the Book of Nature Is Unfolded': The American Museum and the Diffusion of Scientific Knowledge in the Early Republic." *Museum Studies Journal* 2 (Spring 1986): 10–21.

Goodyear, Frank H. *American Paintings at the Rhode Island Historical Society.* Providence: Rhode Island Historical Society, 1974.

Gottesman, Rita S. *The Arts and Crafts in New York, 1777–1804.* 3 vols. New York: New-York Historical Society, 1936–1954.

Graham, James. *The General State of Medical and Chirurgical Practice.* Bath, England: R. Crutwell, 1778.

Green, Samuel M. "English Origins of Seventeenth-Century Painting in New England." In *American Painting to 1776: A Reappraisal,* edited by Ian M. G. Quimby, 15–70. Winterthur, Del.: Winterthur, 1971.

Greene, Robert. *The Honorable Historie of Frier Bacon and Frier Bongay.* 1594. Reprint, [Amersham, Buckinghamshire?]: Tudor Facsimile Text, 1916.

Greenwood, Ethan A. "'Extracts from the Journals of Ethan A. Greenwood': Portrait Painter and Museum Proprietor." Edited by Georgia Brady Barnhill. *Proceedings of the American Antiquarian Society* 103 (April 1993): 91–178.

Greenwood, Isaac J. *The Circus: Its Origin and Growth Prior to 1835.* New York: Dunlap Society, 1898.

Greve, Charles T. *Centennial History of Cincinnati.* Chicago: Biographical Publications, 1904.

Griffin, Emma. *England's Revelry: A History of Popular Sports and Pastimes, 1660–1830.* London: Oxford University Press, 2005.

Groce, George C., and David H. Wallace. *The New-York Historical Society's Dictionary of Artists in America.* New Haven, Conn.: Yale University Press, 1957.

Guerra, Francisco. *American Medical Bibliography, 1639–1783.* New Haven, Conn.: Yale University and Lathrop C. Harper, 1962.

Guild, James. "From Tunbridge, Vermont, to London, England: The Journal of James Guild, Peddler, Tinker, Schoolmaster, Portrait Painter, from 1818 to 1824." Edited by Arthur W. Peach. *Proceedings of the Vermont Historical Society* 5, no. 3 (1937): 249–313.

Haberly, Loyd. "The Long Life of Daniel Bowen." *New England Quarterly* 32 (1959): 320–32.

Hadfield, Joseph. *An Englishman in America.* 1785. Reprint, Toronto: Hunter-Rose, 1933.

Haliburton, William. *Effects of the Stage on the Manners of a People; and the Propriety of Encouraging and Establishing a Virtuous Theater. By a Bostonian.* Boston: Young and Etheridge, 1792.

Hall, David D. *Worlds of Wonders, Days of Judgment: Popular Religious Belief in Early New England.* New York: Knopf, 1989.

Hamilton, Alexander. *Hamilton's Itinerarium: Being a Narrative of a Journey from Annapolis, Maryland . . . from May to September, 1744.* Edited by Albert B. Hart. St. Louis: Bixby, 1907.

Hamilton, Thomas. *Men and Manners in America.* Philadelphia: Carey, Lea and Blanchard, 1833.

Hand, Sidney. *Signed Miniatures.* London: S. Hand, 1924.

Hankins, Thomas L., and Robert J. Silverman. *Instruments and the Imagination.* Princeton, N.J.: Princeton University Press, 1995.

Harding, Chester. *My Egotistigraphy.* Cambridge, Mass.: Wilson, 1866.

Harris, Tim. "Problematizing Popular Culture." In *Popular Culture in England, ca. 1500–1850,* edited by Tim Harris, 1–27. London: Macmillan, 1995.

Harrower, John. "Diary of John Harrower, 1773–1776," *American Historical Review* 6 (1 October 1990): 65–107.

Haverstock, Mary S., comp. "Ralph Letton b. 1778 MD son of Michael b. 1740." Kent State, Ohio: Kent State University Press, 2000. rootsweb.ancestry.com.

Hawkins, John Isaac. "The History and Resuscitation of the Claviole, or Finger-Keyed Viol." In *Mechanic's Magazine, Museum, Register, Journal, and Gazette,* edited by J. C. Robertson, 122–31. London: Robertson and Company, 1845.

Hawthorne, Nathaniel. *Passages from the American Note-Books of Nathaniel Hawthorne.* Boston: Houghton, Mifflin, 1886.

Hazard, Thomas Benjamin. *Nailer Tom's Diary: Otherwise the Journal of Thomas B. Hazard of Kingstown, Rhode Island, 1788 to 1840.* Boston: Merrymount Press, 1930.

Hehr, Milton G. "Theatrical Life in Salem, 1783–1823." *Essex Institute Historical Collections* 100 (January 1964): 3–37.

Heltzel, Virgil B. *Fair Rosamond: A Study in the Development of a Literary Theme.* Evanston, Ill.: Northwestern University Studies, 1947.

Hémard, Ned. "The Floating Palace." *New Orleans Nostalgia.* 2009. neworleansbar.org/uploads/files/TheFloatingPalaceArticle_000.pdf.

Hempstead, Joshua. *The Diary of Joshua Hempstead.* New London, Conn.: New London Historical Society, 1999.

Henninger, Jacob. "By Authority. At the Next Door to the New-England Coffee-House, in Fell's-Point, Baltimore, on [blank] Evening, the [blank] the Noted Jacob Henniger Will Exhibit His Grand Medley of Entertainments." Baltimore: M. K. Goddard, 1783. Broadside. Early American Imprints, ser. 1, no. 44383.

Heslip, Colleen C., and Mary Kellogg. "The Beardsley Limner Identified as Sarah Perkins." *Magazine Antiques* 126 (September 1984): 548–65.

Highfill, Philip H., Kalman A. Burnim, and Edward A. Langhans. *A Biographical Dictionary of Actors, Actresses, Musicians, Dancers, Managers and Other Stage Personnel in London, 1660–1800.* 16 vols. Carbondale: Southern Illinois University Press, 1973.

Hill, Joyce. "In Search of Early Massachusetts Itinerant Artists." *Bay State Historical League Bulletin* 8 (1982): 1–6, 21–24.

———. "New England Itinerant Portraitists." In *Itinerancy in New England and New York: 1984 Annual Proceedings of the Dublin Seminar for New England Folklife,* 150–71. Boston: Boston University Scholarly Publications, 1986.

Hill, Uri I. *The Sacred Minstrel, No. 1: Containing an Introduction to Psalmody.* Boston: Manning and Loring, 1806.

History of Dr. John Faustus. Boston: John and Thomas Fleet, [1798?].

Hodgson, John A. "An Other Voice: Ventriloquism in the Romantic Period." 1999. www.erudit.org/revue/ron/1999/v/n16/005878ar.html.

———. Personal communication with the author. 26 February–23 March 2015.

Hoffmann, Detlief. *Lanterna Magica: Lichtbilder aus Menschenwelt under Gotterwelt.* Berlin: Frolich and Kaufmann, 1982.

Hoopes, Donelson F. *American Narrative Painting.* Los Angeles: Los Angeles County Museum of Art, 1974.

Hoover, Cynthia A. "Epilog to Secular Music in Early Massachusetts." In *Music in Colonial Massachusetts, 1630–1820: II. Music in Homes and in Churches,* edited by Barbara Lambert, 715–868. Boston: Colonial Society of Massachusetts, 1985.

Hornblow, Arthur. *History of the Theater in America.* Philadelphia: Lippincott, 1919.

Howard, Ryan. *Punch and Judy in Nineteenth-Century America: A History and Biographical Dictionary.* Jefferson, N.C.: McFarland, 2013.

Howell, George R. *Bi-Centennial History of Albany: History of the County of Albany, N.Y., 1609–1886.* 4 vols. New York: Munsell, 1886.

Hurd, D. Hamilton. *History of Norfolk County, Massachusetts.* Philadelphia: J. W. Lewis, 1884.

Jackson, E. Neville. *Silhouette: Notes and Dictionary.* New York: Scribner's, 1938. Reprint, New York: Dover Publications, 1981, under the title *Silhouettes: A History and Dictionary of Artists.*

Jaffee, David. *A New Nation of Goods: The Material Culture of Early America.* Philadelphia: University of Pennsylvania Press, 2010.

———. "Peddlers of Progress and the Transformation of the Rural North, 1760–1860." *Journal of American History* 78, no. 2 (September 1991): 511–35.
Jay, Ricky. *Learned Pigs and Fireproof Women*. New York: Villard Books, 1986.
———. *Many Mysteries Unravelled; or, Conjuring Literature in America, 1786–1874*. Worcester, Mass.: American Antiquarian Society and Mulholland Library of Conjuring Arts, 1990.
Jenkins, John. *The Art of Writing, Reduced to a Plain and Easy System, on a Plan Entirely New*. Boston: Isaiah Thomas and Ebenezer Andrews, 1791.
———. *The Art of Writing, Reduced to a Plain and Easy System, on a Plan Entirely New, in Seven Books*. New edn. Cambridge: Printed for the author, 1813.
Johnson, Dale T. "Deacon Robert Peckham: 'Delineator of the Human Face Divine.'" *American Art Journal* 11 (January 1979): 27–36.
Johnson, H. Earle. *Musical Interludes in Boston, 1795–1830*. New York: Columbia University Press, 1943.
———. "The Musical Von Hagens." *New England Quarterly* 16 (1943): 110–17.
Johnson, Odai, and William J. Burling. *The Colonial American Stage, 1665–1774: A Documentary Calendar*. Cranbury, N.J.: Associated University Presses, 2001.
Johnson, William. *A Course of Experiments in That Curious and Entertaining Branch of Natural Philosophy, Called Electricity*. New York: H. Gaine, 1964.
Joncus, Berta, and Jeremy Barlow, eds. *"The Stage's Glory": John Rich, 1692–1761*. Newark: University of Delaware Press, 2011.
Jones, William Bright. "The Portraits of Richard and William Jennys and the Story of Their Wayfaring Lives." In *Painting and Portrait Making in the American Northeast: 1994 Annual Proceedings of the Dublin Seminar for New England Folklife*, 64–97. Boston: Boston University Scholarly Publications, 1995.
Journal and Correspondence of the Council of Maryland, 1779–1780. Volume 43 of the Maryland State Archives. Archives of Maryland Online, aomol.msa.maryland.gov.
Katritzky, M. A. "Marketing Medicine: The Image of the Early Modern Mountebank." *Renaissance Studies* 15 (2001): 121–53.
———. *Women, Medicine, and Theatre, 1500–1750: Literary Mountebanks and Performing Quacks*. Aldershot, U.K.: Ashgate, 2007.
Keller, Kate Van Winkle. *Dance and Its Music in America, 1528–1789*. Hillside, N.Y.: Pendragon Press, 2007.
———. "Early American Social Dance: A Bibliography of Sources to 1820." 2001. www.colonialmusic.org/Resource/DanceBibl.htm.
———. "John Griffiths, Eighteenth-Century Itinerant Dancing Master." In *Itinerancy in New England and New York: 1984 Annual Proceedings of the Dublin Seminar for New England Folklife*, 90–111. Boston: Boston University Scholarly Publications, 1986.
———. "Purveyor to the Peddlers: Nathaniel Coverly Jr., Printer of Songs for the Streets of Boston." In *Life on the Streets and Commons: 2005 Annual Proceedings of the Dublin Seminar for New England Folklife*, 11–26. Boston: Boston University Scholarly Publications, 2007.
Kellogg, Helen. "Found: Two Lost American Painters." *Antiques World* 1, no. 2 (December 1978): 6–47.
———. "Ruth W. and Samuel A. Shute." In *American Folk Painters of Three Centuries*, edited by Jean Lipman and Tom Armstrong, 164–70. New York: Hudson Hills Press, 1980.
Kelly, J. Frederick. *Early Connecticut Meetinghouses*. New York: Columbia University Press, 1948.

Kemp, Martin. *The Science of Art: Optical Themes in Western Art from Brunelleschi to Seurat.* New Haven, Conn.: Yale University Press, 1990.

Kendall, Edward A. *Travels through the Northern Parts of the United States.* 3 vols. New York: Riley, 1809.

Kenyon, Mary Beale. "George and Matthew Beale: English Singing Masters in Connecticut, 1727–1773." MS 79491. Connecticut Historical Society, Hartford.

Kern, Arthur B., and Sybil B. Kern. "Benjamin Greenleaf: Nineteenth-Century Portrait Painter." *Clarion* 10 (Spring–Summer 1985): 40–47.

———. "James Guild: Quintessential Itinerant Portrait Painter." *Clarion* 17 (Summer 1992): 48–57.

———. "The Pastel Portraits of William M. S. Doyle." *Clarion* 13 (Fall 1988): 41–47.

"A Key to the Grand Panorama Painting of the Victory on Lake Erie." Boston: N.p., 1814. Broadside. American Antiquarian Society, Worcester, Mass.

"Key to the Drop-Scene." *Rhode Island Historical Publications,* new ser., 6, no. 4 (January 1899): 231–32.

"Key to the Drop-Scene": "Theatre . . . End of the Play, Will Be Exhibited a Grand Panorama View of Providence (R.I.) from a Correct Drawing Taken on the Spot. The Drawing and Painting by Mr. Worrall." N.p.: N.p., 6 August 1812. Broadside. Rhode Island Historical Society, Providence.

Keyes, Homer E. "The Editor's Attic: William King Tames the Serpent; The Serpent Bests William King; William King Repents; The Serpent Triumphs; The Fruit of the Weed." *Magazine Antiques* 12, no. 3 (September 1927): 201–3.

Kihn, Phyllis. "The Circus in Connecticut." *Connecticut Historical Society Bulletin* 22 (1957): 1–17.

———. "The Value Family in Connecticut." *Connecticut Historical Society Bulletin* 34, no. 3 (July 1969): 79–93.

Kimball, Gertrude S. *Providence in Colonial Times.* Boston: Houghton Mifflin, 1912.

King, Lester S. *The Medical World of the Eighteenth Century.* 1958. Reprint, Huntington, N.Y.: Krieger, 1971.

King, William. *A Manual of Electricity: Containing Observations on the Electrical Phenomena, and Directions for the Construction of Metallic Conductors.* Newbern, N.C.: N.p., 1825.

Kinnersley, Ebenezer. "A Course of Experiments, on the Newly-Discovered Electrical Fire." Newport, R.I.: N.p, 16 March 1752. Broadside. John Hay Library, Brown University.

Kircher, Athanasius. *Ars Magna Lucis et Umbrae.* Amsterdam: Janssonium and Weyerstraet, 1671.

Kline, Priscilla C. "New Light on the Yankee Peddler." *New England Quarterly* 12, no. 1 (March 1939): 80–98.

Knapp, Samuel L. *Life of Lord Timothy Dexter.* Newburyport, Mass.: Tilton, 1848.

Knox, Katharine McCook. *The Sharples: Their Portraits of George Washington and His Contemporaries.* 1930. Reprint, New York: Da Capo, 1972.

Koke, Richard J. *American Landscape and Genre Paintings in the New-York Historical Society.* 2 vols. New York: New-York Historical Society, 1982.

Kornhauser, Elizabeth M. "Ralph Earl as an Itinerant Artist: Patterns of Patronage." In *Itinerancy in New England and New York: 1984 Annual Proceedings of the Dublin Seminar for New England Folklife,* 172–90. Boston: Boston University Scholarly Publications, 1986.

———. *Ralph Earl: The Face of the Young Republic.* New Haven, Conn.: Yale University Press, 1991.

Kroeger, Karl, and Richard Crawford. "Daniel Read and American Psalmody." In *Daniel Read Collected Works,* edited by Karl Kroeger, xiii–xxxviii. Madison, Wis.: A-R Editions for the American Musicological Society, 1995.

LaGrandeur, Kevin. *Androides and Intelligent Networks in Early Modern Literature and Culture: Artificial Slaves.* New York: Routledge, 2013.

Lambert, Barbara, comp. "Music Masters in Colonial Boston." In *Music in Colonial Massachusetts, 1630–1820: II. Music in Homes and in Churches,* edited by Barbara Lambert, 935–1158. Boston: Colonial Society of Massachusetts, 1985.

Lambert, Frank. "'I Saw the Book Talk': Slave Readings of the First Great Awakening." *Journal of Negro History* 77, no. 4 (1992): 185–98.

Lambranzi, Gregorio. *New and Curious School of Theatrical Dancing.* Nuremberg, 1716. Reprint, edited by C. W. Beaumont, London: Imperial Society 1928.

Lane, William C., ed. *Catalogue of English and American Chap-Books and Broadside Ballads in Harvard College Library.* Cambridge, Mass.: Library of Harvard University, 1905.

Lathem, Edward C. *Chronological Tables of American Newspapers, 1690–1820.* Barre, Mass.: American Antiquarian Society and Barre Publishers, 1972.

Laws, G. Malcolm. *American Balladry from British Broadsides.* Philadelphia: American Folklore Society, 1957.

Leeds, Titan. *American Almanack for the Year of Christian Account, 1722.* New York: Bradford, 1721.

Leffler, Christopher T., et al. "The First Cataract Surgeons in Anglo-America." *Survey of Ophthalmology* 60 (2015): 86–92.

Lemay, J. A. Leo. *Ebenezer Kinnersley: Franklin's Friend.* Philadelphia: University of Pennsylvania Press, 1964.

Leonard, Daniel H. "Writing D. H. Leonard Will Give a Course of Lessons Wholy on Running Hand for $1.00 Per Scholar." Subscription blank. Dartmouth College Library, Hanover, N.H.

Letton, Ralph. "Wax Exhibition. R. Letton, Informs the Ladies and Gentlemen of the Vicinity of Hartford, That He Has Completed His Wax Museum . . . for Exhibition, at the House Where He Lives, the West End of Maj. J. Hart's House. . . . Hartford, 5th April, 1808." [Hartford, Conn.?]: N.p., 1808. Broadside. Connecticut Historical Society, Hartford, 1808 L651w.

———. "Wax Exhibition. R. Letton, Informs the Ladies and Gentlemen of the Vicinity of Wethersfield That He Has an Elegant Collection of New Wax Figures . . . for Exhibition, at the House of Eleazer Porter, Where He Will Continue for 5 Days Only . . . April 11, 1808." [Hartford, Conn.?]: N.p., 1808. Broadside. Connecticut Historical Society, Hartford, 1808 L651wa.

Lieberkühn, Johann Nathanael. *Dissertationes quatuor. . . . Description d'un microscope anatomique.* London: T. Cadell, 1782.

Lipman, Jean T. *Rufus Porter: Yankee Pioneer.* New York: Potter, 1968.

"A List of Portraits Painted by Ethan Allen Greenwood." *Proceedings of the American Antiquarian Society* 56 (April 1946): 129–53.

Little, Nina F. *American Decorative Wall Painting, 1700–1850.* Sturbridge, Mass.: Old Sturbridge Village, 1952.

———. "Itinerant Painting in America, 1750–1850." *New York History* 30 (April 1949): 204–16.

———. "John Brewster, Jr.: 1766–1854. Deaf-Mute Portrait Painter of Connecticut and Maine." *Bulletin of the Connecticut Historical Society* 25 (October 1960): 97–129.

———. "Michele Felice Corné, 1752–1845." *Magazine Antiques* 102, no. 2 (August 1972): 262–69.

———. *Paintings by New England Provincial Artists, 1775–1800.* Boston: Museum of Fine Arts, 1976.

Lockwood, John H. *Westfield and Its Historic Influences.* 2 vols. Springfield, Mass.: Privately printed, 1922.

Lovejoy, Mary Evelyn Wood. *History of Royalton, Vermont.* Burlington, Vt.: Free Press, 1911.

Lowens, Irving. *Music and Musicians in Early America.* New York: Norton, 1964.

Lyford, James O. *History of Concord, New Hampshire.* 2 vols. Concord, N.H.: Rumford, 1903.

Lynde, Benjamin, and Benjamin Lynde, Jr. *The Diaries of Benjamin Lynde and of Benjamin Lynde Jr.* Edited by F. E. Oliver. Boston: Riverside Press, 1880.

Macmichael, J. Holden. *The Story of Charing Cross and Its Immediate Neighborhood.* London: Chatto and Winds, 1906.

Malcolmson, Robert. *Popular Recreations in English Society, 1700–1850.* Cambridge: Cambridge University Press, 1973.

Manning-Sanders, Ruth. *The English Circus.* London: T. Werner Laurie, 1952.

Marini, Stephen A. "Evangelical Itinerancy in Rural New England: New Gloucester, Maine, 1754–1807." In *Itinerancy in New England and New York: 1984 Proceedings of the Dublin Seminar for New England Folklife,* 49–64. Boston: Boston University Scholarly Publications, 1986.

Marks, Joseph E. *The Mathers on Dancing.* Brooklyn: Dance Horizons, 1975.

Marlow, Joyce. *The Life and Times of George I.* London: Weidenfeld and Nicolson, 1973.

Marlowe, Christopher. *Doctor Faustus.* Edited by John D. Jump. Cambridge, Mass.: Harvard University Press, 1962.

Mason, David. *A Course of Experiments in That Instructive and Entertaining Branch of Natural Philosophy, Called Electricity.* Boston: N.p., 1765.

Mason, George C. *Reminiscences of Newport.* Newport, R.I.: C. E. Hammett, Jr., 1884.

———. "Newport Lace School." *Rhode Island Historical Magazine* 6, no. 1 (July 1885): 75–76.

Massachusetts Broadsides. Boston: Massachusetts Historical Society, 1929.

Massachusetts Society of Mayflower Descendants. "Halifax, Mass., Church Records." *Mayflower Descendant* 27, no. 1 (January 1925): 26.

Mates, Julian. *The American Musical Stage before 1800.* New Brunswick, N.J.: Rutgers University Press, 1962.

Mather, Cotton. *Diary of Cotton Mather.* Edited by Worthington C. Ford. 2 vols. New York: Ungar, 1911.

Mather, Increase. *An Arrow against Profane and Promiscuous Dancing: Drawn out of the Quiver of the Scriptures.* Boston: Samuel Green, 1684. Early American Imprints, ser. 1, no. 370.

Mayer, David. *Harlequin in His Element: The English Pantomime, 1806–1836.* Cambridge, Mass.: Harvard University Press, 1969.

Mayne, Arthur. *British Profile Miniaturists.* London: Faber and Faber, 1970.

McClintock, Inez Bertail, and Marshall McClintock. *Toys in America.* Washington, D.C: Public Affairs Press, 1961.

McClung, Robert M., and Gale S. McClung. "Capt. Crowninshield Brings Home an Elephant." *American Neptune* 18 (April 1958): 137–41.

McGlathery, James M. *Grimm's Fairy Tales: A History of Criticism on a Popular Classic.* Columbia, S.C.: Camden House, 1993.

McKay, David P. "Opera in Colonial Boston." *American Music* 3, no. 2 (1985): 133–42.

McKechnie, Sue. *British Silhouette Artists and Their Work, 1760–1860.* London: P. Wilson for Sotheby Parke Bernet, 1978.

McNamara, Brooks. *Step Right Up: An Illustrated History of the American Medicine Show.* Garden City, N.Y.: Doubleday, 1976.

McPharlin, Paul. *Puppet Theatre in America: A History, 1524 to Now.* New York: Harper, 1949.

McSparran, James. *Letter Book and Abstract of Out Services.* Boston: Merrymount Press, 1899.

Meech, Susan Spicer, and Susan Billings Meech, comps. *History of the Descendants of Peter Spicer.* Boston: Stanhope Press, 1911.

Merrill, Isaac W. "Diary of Isaac W. Merrill of Haverhill, 1828–1875." Typescript copy at the Haverhill Public Library, Haverhill, Mass.

Metcalf, Frank J. *American Psalmody: Titles of Books containing Tunes Printed in America from 1721 to 1820.* 1917. Reprint, New York: Da Capo Press, 1968.

———. *American Writers and Compilers of Sacred Music.* New York: Abingdon, 1925.

Microcosm. "Boston, May 13, 1756. To Be Seen (for a Short Time) at the House of Mr. William Fletcher: Merchant, New-Boston; that Elaborate and Matchless Pile of Art, Called, the Microcosm, or, The World in Miniature." N.p.: N.p., 1756. Broadside. American Antiquarian Society, Worcester, Mass.

Milbank, Jeremiah. *First Century of Flight in America.* Princeton, N.J.: Princeton University Press, 1943.

Miles, Ellen G. "1803—The Year of the Physiognotrace." In *Painting and Portrait Making in the American Northeast: 1994 Annual Proceedings of the Dublin Seminar for New England Folklife,* 118–37. Boston: Boston University Scholarly Publications, 1995.

———. "Saint-Memin, Valdenuit, Lemet: Federal Profiles." In *American Portrait Prints,* edited by Wendy W. Reaves, 1–28. Charlottesville: University Press of Virginia for the National Portrait Gallery, 1980.

Millar, John F. "Newport's Early Composers." *Newport History* 53 (Spring 1980): 67–76.

Mizelle, Brett. "'Man Cannot Behold It without Contemplating Himself': Monkeys, Apes and Human Identity in the Early American Republic." *Explorations in Early American Culture: A Supplemental Issue of Pennsylvania History* 66 (1999): 144–73.

Montague, Justin Selah. "Memorandum Book No. 5." Bridgewater, Vt., 1840–1842. Private collection.

Moore, Lillian. "The Duport Mystery." *Dance Perspectives* 7 (1960): 5–103.

———. "John Durang—The First American Dancer." In *Chronicles of the American Dance,* edited by P. Magriel, 15–37. New York: Henry Holt, 1948.

Morley, Henry. *Memoirs of Bartholomew Fair.* London: Chapman and Hall, 1859.

Morse, William N. "Lectures on Electricity in Colonial Times." *New England Quarterly* 7 (June 1934): 364–74.

Moy, James S. "Entertainments at John B. Ricketts's Circus, 1793–1800." *Educational Theatre Journal* 30 (1978): 186–202.

Mudd, A. I. "Early Theatres in Washington City." *Records of the Columbia Historical Society* 5 (1901): 64–86.

Murphy, John J. "Entrepreneurship in the Establishment of the American Clock Industry." *Journal of Economic History* 26, no. 2 (June 1966): 169–86.

Musée d'Orsay. *Lanternes Magiques, Tableaux Transparents.* Paris: Réunion des Musées Nationaux, 1995.

Nairne, Edward. *The Description and Use of Nairne's Patent Electrical Machine.* London: Nairne and Blunt, 1793.

Nash, Ray. *American Penmanship, 1800–1850: A History of Writing and a Bibliography of Copybooks from Jenkins to Spencer.* Worcester, Mass.: American Antiquarian Society, 1969.

———. "Early Writing Masters in Vermont." *Proceedings of the Vermont Historical Society* 9, no. 1 (March 1941): 27–37.

———. *Some Early American Writing Books and Masters.* Hanover, N.H.: Privately printed, 1943.

Nason, Elias. *A Memoir of Mrs. Susanna Rowson.* Albany: Munsell, 1870.

Nathan, Hans. *William Billings: Data and Documents.* Detroit: College Music Society, 1976.

Neuburg, Victor E. *Chapbooks. A Bibliography of References to English and American Chapbook Literature of the Eighteenth and Nineteenth Centuries.* London: Vine Press, 1964.

New-England Galaxy (weekly serial), vols. 4–13. Boston: J. T. Buckingham, 1820–1830. Houghton Library, Harvard University.

New Grove Dictionary of Music and Musicians. Edited by Stanley Sadie. London: Macmillan, 1995.

Nichols, Francis D. *A Guide to Politeness; or, A System of Directions for the Acquirement of Ease, Propriety and Elegance of Manners.* Boston: Privately printed, 1810.

Niklaus, Thelma. *Harlequin Phoenix; or, the Rise and Fall of a Bergamask Rogue.* London: Bodley Head, 1956.

Niles, John M. *The Life of Oliver Hazard Perry.* Hartford, Conn.: W. S. Marsh, 1820.

"Nineteenth-Century British Newspapers." Digital edition. London: British Library and Gale Cengage Learning, 2014.

"Nineteenth-Century U.S. Newspapers." Digital edition. Gale Cengage Learning, 2014.

Nylander, Jane C. "Provision for Daughters: The Accounts of Samuel Lane." In *House and Home: 1988 Proceedings of the Dublin Seminar for New England Folklife,* 11–27. Boston: Boston University Scholarly Publications, 1990.

Odell, George C. D. *Annals of the New York Stage.* 14 vols. New York: Columbia University Press, 1917–1945.

Oldmixon, J. *The British Empire in America.* Rev. edn. 2 vols. London: J. J. Brotherton et al., 1741.

Orme, Edward. *An Essay on Transparent Prints, and on Transparencies in General.* London: J. G. Barnard, 1807.

Owen, Barbara. "Eighteenth-Century Organs and Organ Building in New England." In *Music in Colonial Massachusetts, 1630–1820: II. Music in Homes and in Churches,* edited by Barbara Lambert, 667–68. Boston: Colonial Society of Massachusetts, 1985.

Oxford Dictionary of National Biography. 60 vols. Oxford: Oxford University Press, 2004.

Paine, Susanna. *Roses and Thorns; or, Recollections of an Artist.* Providence, R.I.: Albro, 1854.

Palmquist, Peter E., and Thomas R. Kailbourn. *Pioneer Photographers of the Far West: A Biographical Dictionary.* Stanford, Calif.: Stanford University Press, 2000.

"A Panorama of Boston, and Its Vicinity. Painted by Messrs Smith & Worrall." Boston: N.p., c. 1810 or 1811. Broadside. American Antiquarian Society, Worcester, Mass.

Parker, James. "Extracts from the Diary of James Parker of Shirley." *New England Historic Genealogical Register* 69 (January 1915): 9–24.

Parkman, Ebenezer. "The Diary of Ebenezer Parkman." Typescript copy transcribed by Ross W. Beales, Jr., in the possession of the author.

———. *The Diary of Ebenezer Parkman, 1703–1782.* Edited by Francis G. Walett. Worcester, Mass.: American Antiquarian Society, 1974.

———. "Singing Book Made by Rev. Ebenr. Parkman of Westboro Mass July 17, 1721." Commonplace book, Cambridge, Mass., 1721. Massachusetts Historical Society, Boston.

Partridge, Albert L. "William Claggett of Newport, R.I., Clockmaker." *Old-Time New England* 27, no. 3 (1937): 110–15.

Peale, Charles Willson. *Charles Willson Peale and His World.* Edited by J. Greenspun. New York: Abrams, 1982.

Paul Revere's Boston, 1735–1816. Boston: Museum of Fine Arts, 1975.

Pecor, Charles J. *The Ten Year Tour of John Rannie: A Magician-Ventriloquist in Early America.* Glenwood, Ill.: Magic Books, 1998.

Peirce, Mary Frances, comp. *Town of Weston: Births, Deaths, and Marriages . . . Church Records, 1709–1825.* Boston: McIndoe Brothers, 1901.

Penniman, Charles F., Jr. "Maillardet's Automaton." Undated typescript. Franklin Institute Science Museum, Philadelphia.

Pepys, Samuel. *Diary and Correspondence of Samuel Pepys, F. R. S.* 4 vols. New York: Davos Press, n.d.

Perley, Sidney. *The History of Salem, Massachusetts. Volume II: 1638–1670.* Salem, Mass.: Sidney Perley, 1926.

Phelps, Elizabeth Porter. "The Diary of Elizabeth (Porter) Phelps (1747–1817)." Edited by Thomas E. Andrews. *New England Historical and Genealogical Register* 118–22 (January 1964–October 1968).

Phillips, John. *Familiar Dialogues on Dancing, between a Minister and a Dancer.* New York: T. Kirk, 1798.

Philpott, A. R. *Dictionary of Puppetry.* Boston: Plays, Inc., 1969.

Pichierri, Louis. *Music in New Hampshire, 1623–1800.* New York: Columbia University Press, 1960.

Pierpont, John. "Ode, Written by John Pierpont, Esq. For the Dinner in Honour of Commodore Perry." [Boston]: N.p., [1814?]. Broadside. Houghton Library, Harvard University, Cambridge, Mass.

Piersen, William D. *Black Yankees: The Development of an Afro-American Subculture in Eighteenth-Century New England.* Amherst: University of Massachusetts Press, 1988.

Pinchbeck, William F. *The Expositor; or, Many Mysteries Unravelled.* Boston: Privately printed, 1805.

———. "Expounder, the Mystery of the Invisible Lady Unfolded and Explained." Salem: N.p., 1805. Broadside. American Antiquarian Society, Worcester, Mass.

———. *Witchcraft; or, The Art of Fortune-Telling Unveiled.* Boston: Privately printed, 1805.

"Pleasing Entertainments: At [blank] on [blank] 1798, Will Be Performed a Favorite Tragic Piece, Called, the Babes in the Wood." N.p.: N.p., [1798]. Filled out in manuscript: "Mr. Stowe's hall, Monday August 13." Broadside. Windham County Historical Society, Newfane, Vt.

Pope, John. "Cancers. The Following Is a Small Specimen of What Is Likely Will Soon Be Exhibited to the Public View of the Like Kind Done within Twenty-Six Years Past . . . Feb. 6, 1793." Boston: N.p., [1793]. Broadside. Massachusetts Historical Society, Boston.

———. "Certificates of Cures in Cancerous Cases, Performed by John Pope, of Providence, in the State of Rhode-Island, &c." Providence: Bennett Wheeler, 1800. Broadside. Early American Imprints, ser. 1, no. 38342.

Porter, Roy. *Quacks: Fakers and Charlatans in English Medicine.* London: Tempus, 2000.

Porter, Susan C. *British Opera in America: Children in the Wood (1795) and Blue Beard (1811)*. New York: Garland, 1994.

———. *With an Air Debonair: Musical Theatre in America, 1785–1815*. Washington, D.C.: Smithsonian Institution, 1991.

Pragnell, Hubert J. *The London Panoramas of Robert Barker and Thomas Girtin*. London: Topograpical Society, 1968.

Priest, William. *Travels in the United States of America Commencing in the Year 1793 and Ending in the Year 1797*. London: J. Johnson, 1802.

Prime, Nathaniel S. *A History of Long Island*. New York: R. Carter, 1845.

Province and Court Records of Maine. 6 vols. Portland: Maine Historical Society, 1928.

The Psalms, Hymns, and Spiritual Songs, of the Old and New-Testament, Faithfully Translated into English Metre. Boston: John Allen and Vavasour Harris, 1695.

Pyke, E. J. *A Biographical Dictionary of Wax Modellers*. Oxford: Clarendon Press, 1973.

Pynchon, William. *The Diary of William Pynchon of Salem*. Edited by Fitch E. Oliver. Boston: Houghton, Mifflin, 1890.

Rand, Benjamin H. *A New and Complete System of Mercantile Penmanship and New Invention of Running Hand*. Philadelphia: N.p., 1814.

Rannie, James or John. "The European Ventriloquist's Exhibition." Portsmouth, N.H.: S. Whidden, [1811]. Broadside. New York Public Library, Ford Collection.

Rannie, James or John. "Ventriloquism. The Ladies and Gentlemen of Boston Are Respectfully Informed, That on Wednesday Evening, Dec. 9, 1801, Will Be Displayed . . . the Inimitable Powers of the European Ventriloquist. Being His First Appearance in America." [Boston]: N.p., 1801. Broadside. Massachusetts Historical Society, Boston.

Rapoza, Andrew V. "The Trials of Phillip Reade, Seventeenth-Century Itinerant Physician." In *Medicine and Healing: 1990 Annual Proceedings of the Dublin Seminar for New England Folklife*, 82–94. Boston: Boston University Scholarly Publications, 1992.

Reay, Barry. *Popular Cultures in England, 1550–1750*. London and New York: Longman, 1998.

Records of the Services of the Two Hundred and Fiftieth Anniversary of the Congregational Church at Windsor, Connecticut. Windsor, Conn.: Congregational Church at Windsor, 1880.

Redfield, Levi. *A Succinct Account of Some Memorable Events . . . in the Life of Levi Redfield, Late of Connecticut*. Brattleboro, Vt.: B. Smead, 1798.

Redfield, Robert. *Peasant Society and Culture: An Anthropological Approach to Civilization*. Chicago: University of Chicago Press, 1956.

Reeve, William, and William Bates. *Harlequin Mungo; or, A Peep into the Tower*. London: J. Skirven for J. Griffith, 1788.

"Reuben Moulthrop, 1763–1814." *Connecticut Historical Society Bulletin* 20 (April 1955): 44–51.

Rice, Kym S. *Early American Taverns: For the Entertainment of Friends and Strangers*. New York: Fraunces Tavern Museum, 1983.

Riley, Stephen T. "John Smibert and the Business of Portrait Painting." In *American Painting to 1776: A Reappraisal*, edited by Ian M. G. Quimby, 159–80. Charlottesville: University Press of Virginia for the Winterthur Museum, 1971.

Rinhart, Floyd, and Marion Rinhart. *The American Daguerreotype*. Athens: University of Georgia Press, 1981.

Rink, Evald. *Technical Americana: A Checklist of Technical Publications Printed before 1831*. Millwood, N.J.: Kraus, 1981.

Ripley, Sally. Diary, 1799–1801, 1805–1809. American Antiquarian Society, Worcester, Mass.

Robinson, David. *The Lantern Image: Iconography of the Magic Lantern, 1420–1880.* East Sussex: Magic Lantern Society of Great Britain, 1993.

Rodman, Samuel. *The Diary of Samuel Rodman: A New Bedford Chronicle of Thirty-Seven Years, 1821–1859.* New Bedford, Mass.: Reynolds Printing, 1927.

Rolt, L. T. C. *The Aeronauts: A History of Ballooning, 1783–1903.* London: Longmans, 1966.

Rosenfeld, Roslyn M. "An Index of Miniaturists and Silhouettists Who Worked in Montreal." *Journal of Canadian Art History* 5, no. 2 (1981): 111–21.

———. "Miniatures and Silhouettes in Montreal, 1760–1860." Master's thesis, Concordia University, Montreal, Quebec, 1981.

Rosenfeld, Sybil M. *The Theatre of the London Fairs in the Eighteenth Century.* Cambridge: Cambridge University Press, 1960.

Rowe, John. *The Diary of John Rowe, A Boston Merchant, 1764–1779.* Edited by Edward L. Pierce. Cambridge, Mass.: John Wilson and Son, 1895.

———. *Letters and Diary of John Rowe, Boston Merchant, 1759–1762, 1764–1779.* Edited by Anne Rowe Cunningham. Boston: W. B. Clarke, 1903.

Rutledge, Anna W. "Artists in the Life of Charleston through Colony and State from Restoration to Reconstruction." *Transactions of the American Philosophical Society* 39, pt. 2 (1949): 101–236.

St. John de Crèvecoeur, J. Hector. *Letters from an American Farmer.* 1782. Reprint, New York: Duffield, 1908.

Sampsel, Laurie J. "Samuel Babcock (1760–1813), Archetypal Psalmodist of the First New England School of Composers." Ph.D. diss., University of Pittsburg, 2009.

Sandham, Elizabeth. *The Magic Lantern.* Philadelphia: Benjamin Johnson, 1807.

Sanger, Abner. *Very Poor and of a Lo Make: The Journal of Abner Sanger (1774–1821).* Edited by Lois K. Stabler. Portsmouth, N.H.: Peter E. Randall for the Historical Society of Cheshire County, 1986.

Saunders, Richard H. *John Smibert: Colonial America's First Portrait Painter.* New Haven, Conn.: Yale University Press, 1995.

Savage, James. *John Winthrop's History of New England.* 2 vols. Boston: Phelps and Farnham, 1825–1826.

Schaefer, Patricia M. *A Useful Friend: A Companion to the Joshua Hempstead Diary, 1711–1758.* New London, Conn.: New London County Historical Society, 2008.

Scharf, J. Thomas. *History of Westchester County, New York.* 2 vols. Philadelphia, L. E. Preston, 1886.

Scharf, J. Thomas, and Thompson Westcott. *History of Philadelphia, 1609–1884.* 2 vols. Philadelphia: Everts, 1884.

Schechner, Sara J. "John Prince and Early American Instrument Making." In *Sibley's Heir: A Volume in Memory of Clifford Kenyon Shipman,* edited by Frederick Allis and Philip Smith, 431–503. Boston: Colonial Society of Massachusetts, 1982.

Seeman, Erik R. "'Justice Must Take Plase': Three African Americans Speak of Religion in Eighteenth-Century New England." *William and Mary Quarterly,* 3rd ser., 66, no. 2 (1999): 393–414.

Seilhamer, George O. *History of the American Theatre, 1888–1891.* 3 vols. 1888–1891. Reprint, New York: Blom, 1968.

Sellers, Charles C. *Charles Willson Peale.* New York: Scribner's, 1969.

———. *Patience Wright: American Artist and Spy in George III's London.* Middletown, Conn.: Wesleyan University Press, 1976.

"Seventeenth and Eighteenth Century English Newspapers from the Collection of the Reverend Charles Burney, 1619 to 1800." Digital edition. London: British Library and Gale Cengage Learning, 2014. Sewall, Samuel. *The Diary of Samuel Sewall, 1674–1729*. Edited by M. Halsey Thomas. 2 vols. New York: Farrar, Straus and Giroux, 1973.

Seybolt, Robert F. *Apprenticeship and Apprenticeship Education in Colonial New England and New York*. New York: Columbia University Press, 1917.

Shapiro, Anne Dhu. "Action Music in American Pantomime and Melodrama, 1730–1913." *American Music* 2 (1984): 49–72.

Shaw, Gwendolyn DuBois. "'Moses Williams, Cutter of Profiles': Silhouettes and African American Identity in the Early Republic." *Proceedings of the American Philosophical Society* 149, no. 1 (March 2005): 22–39.

Shaw, Robert Gould. *Exhibition—Prints, Playbills, Advertisements, and Autograph Letters to Illustrate the History of the Boston Stage from 1791 to 1825 from the Collection of Mr. Robert Gould Shaw*. Boston: Club of Odd Volumes, 1914.

Sheldon, George. *A History of Deerfield, Massachusetts*. 2 vols. Greenfield, Mass.: E. A. Hall, 1895.

Sheldon, Hezekiah S. *Documentary History of Suffield . . . 1660–1749*. Springfield, Mass.: Bryan, 1929.

Shepard, David F., Jr. "The Chester and Westfield, Mass., Diaries (1795–1798) of David Shepard Jr. (1777–1828)." Baltimore: Privately printed, 1975.

Sherman, Frederick F. "Attribution of Unsigned American Miniatures." *Art in America* 28 (July 1940): 124–25.

Shershow, Scott C. "'Punch and Judy' and Cultural Appropriation." *Cultural Studies* 8, no. 3 (1994): 527–55.

Shesgreen, Sean. *The Criers and Hawkers of London: Engravings and Drawings by Marcellus Laroon*. Stanford, Calif.: Stanford University Press, 1990.

Silverman, Kenneth. *A Cultural History of the American Revolution*. New York: Crowell, 1976.

Slack, Paul A. "Vagrants and Vagrancy in England, 1598–1664." *Economic History Review* 27, no. 3 (1974): 360–79.

Smith, Carleton S. "Broadsides and Their Music." In *Music in Colonial Massachusetts, 1630–1820: I. Music in Public Places*, edited by Barbara Lambert, 157–328. Boston: Colonial Society of Massachusetts, 1985.

Smith, John Rowson, and Richard Risley. *Professor Risley and Mr. J. R. Smith's Original Moving Panorama of the Mississippi River*. London: John K. Chapman, 1849.

Smith, John Thomas. *The Cries of London: Itinerant Traders of Antient and Modern Times*. London: Nichols, 1839.

Smith, Richard. *A Tour of Four Great Rivers . . . in 1769 Being the Journal of Richard Smith of Burlington, New Jersey*. New York: Scribner's, 1906.

Snow, Edward R. "America's First Flyer." In *Pirates, Shipwrecks, and Historic Chronicles*, 111–14. New York: Dodd, Mead, 1981.

Sonneck, Oscar G. T. *Early Concert-Life in America (1731–1800)*. Leipzig: Breitkopf and Hartel, 1907.

———. *Early Opera in America*. Boston: Boston Music Company, 1915.

Southern, Eileen. *Music of Black Americans: A History*. New York: Norton, 1971.

Speaight, George. *The History of the English Puppet Theatre*. 2nd ed. London: Hale, 1990.

———. *Punch and Judy: A History*. London: Plays, Inc., 1970.

———. "Punch's Opera at Bartholomew Fair." *Theater Notebook* 7, no. 4 (Summer 1953): 73–94.
Stafford, Barbara M., and Frances Terpak. *Devices of Wonder: From the World in a Box to Images on a Screen*. Los Angeles: Getty Research Institute, 2002.
The Stage: The High Road to Hell. Being an Essay on the Pernicious Nature of Theatrical Entertainments. London: W. Nicoll, 1767.
Standage, Tom. *The Turk: The Life and Times of the Famous Eighteenth-Century Chess-Playing Machine*. New York: Walker, 2002.
Staples, Charles R. *The History of Pioneer Lexington, 1779–1806*. 1939. Reprint, Lexington: University of Kentucky Press, 1996.
Stephens, Stephen D. *The Mavericks, American Engravers*. New Brunswick, N.J.: Rutgers University Press, 1950.
Stiles, Ezra. *The Literary Diary of Ezra Stiles, D.D., LL.D*. Edited by Franklin B. Dexter. 3 vols. New York: Charles Scribner's Sons, 1901.
Stiles, Henry R. *History of Ancient Windsor*. 2 vols. New York: Norton, 1859.
Stimpson's Boston Directory. Boston: Charles Stimpson, 1841.
Stinchfield, Ephraim. *Some Memoirs of the Life, Experience, and Travels of Elder Ephraim Stinchfield*. Portland, Maine: F. Douglas, 1819.
Stivers, Mabel P. "Wax Figures in Old Museums." *Old-Time New England* 17 (July 1926): 42–46.
Stone, Edwin M. *History of Beverly, Civil and Ecclesiastical*. Boston: J. Munroe, 1843.
Storer, Malcolm. "The Manly Washington Medal." *Proceedings of the Massachusetts Historical Society*, 3rd ser., 52 (1919): 5–8.
Storey, John. *An Introductory Guide to Cultural Theory and Popular Culture*. Athens: University of Georgia Press, 1993.
Storia della campagna fatta in Italia da S. A. il' generale feld-maresciallo principe Suwarow. 5 vols. Firenze: Presso Giovacchino Pagani, 1799–1800.
Stoughton, John A. *"Windsor Farms": A Glimpse of an Old Parish*. Hartford, Conn.: Clark and Smith, 1883.
Strickler, Susan E. *American Portrait Miniatures: The Worcester Art Museum Collection*. Worcester, Mass.: Worcester Art Museum, 1989.
Struna, Nancy L. *People of Prowess: Sport, Leisure, and Labor in Early Anglo-America*. Urbana: University of Illinois Press, 1996.
Strutt, Joseph. *The Sports and Pastimes of the People of England*. London: Methuen, 1801.
Stubbs, Naomi J. *Cultivating National Identity through Performance: American Pleasure Gardens and Entertainment*. New York: Palgrave Macmillan, 2014.
Suffield Vital Records. 3 vols. Hartford, Conn.: Connecticut State Library, 1928.
Suffolk County Probate Records, Suffolk County, Mass. Microfilm copy at the Boston Public Library.
Swan, Mabel M. *The Athenæum Gallery, 1827–1873*. Boston: Boston Athenæum, 1940.
Sydow, Carl W. von. *Selected Papers on Folklore*. New York: Arno Press, 1977.
Tanaka, Yuko. "Preservation of French-speaking Automatons and Their Pronunciations in Eighteenth-Century France, Focusing on l'Abbé Mical's *Têtes Parlantes* (Speaking Heads) and A. Rivarol's *Lettre* of 1783." *Journal Aesthetics*, no. 18 (March 2014): 13–27. http://www.bigakukai.jp/aesthetics_online/aesthetics_18/no.18_top.html
Tatham, David. *Abraham Tuthill: Portrait Painter in the Young Republic*. Watertown, N.Y.: Jefferson County Historical Society, 1983.

Thacher, Thomas. *The Danger of Despising the Divine Counsel, Exhibited in a Discourse, Delivered at Dedham Third Precinct, Sept. 13, 1801, the Lord's Day after the Execution of Jason Fairbanks.* Dedham, Mass.: H. Mann, 1802.

"Theatre. The Managers Have the Pleasure, Respectfully, of Informing the Public . . . the Much Admired Patriotic, Grand Transparency, Delineating the Important Events in the Military and Civil Life of the Immortal Washington." Boston: Russell and Gardner, 28 September 1822. Broadside. American Antiquarian Society, Worcester, Mass.

Thicknesse, Philip. *The Speaking Figure and the Automaton Chess-Player, Exposed and Detected.* London: J. Stockdale, 1784.

Thayer, Stuart. *Annals of the American Circus, 1793–1829.* Manchester, Mich.: Privately printed, 1976.

Thomas, David C., and Peter Benes. "Amzi Chapin: A New England Cabinetmaker Singing and Working in the South and Trans-Appalachian West." In *Rural New England Furniture: People, Place and Production: 1998 Annual Proceedings of the Dublin Seminar for New England Folklife,* 76–99. Boston: Boston University Scholarly Publications, 2000.

Thomas, Keith. *Religion and the Decline of Magic.* New York: Scribner, 1971.

Thompson, Cephas, and Lucy Thompson. Journal. Middleborough, Mass., 1822–1856. 2 vols. Boston Athenæum.

Thoreau, Henry D. *The Journal of Henry D. Thoreau.* Edited by Bradford Torrey. 14 vols. Boston: Houghton Mifflin, 1949.

Thwing, Annie Haven. *Inhabitants and Estates of the Town of Boston, 1630–1822.* CD-ROM. Boston: New England Historic Genealogical Society and Massachusetts Historical Society, 2001.

"To the Curious! . . . Mr. Maginnis, From Saddler's Wells, London." Boston: Alexander Martin, c. 1795 or 1796. Broadside. Massachusetts Historical Society, Boston.

"To the Curious. To Be Seen at Major Leavenworth's Stable, Opposite Mr. Lothrop's, State-Street, Two Camels, Male and Female, Lately Imported from Arabia." [New Haven]: Thomas and Samuel Green, [1789]. Broadside. American Antiquarian Society, Worcester, Mass.

Towne, Nathan. *A New Set of Round and Running Hand Copies, with Rules for Writing.* [Connecticut]: N.p., [1811].

The Traveller's and Chapman's Daily Instructor. London: G. Sawbridge, 1705.

Trayser, Donald G. *Barnstable: Three Centuries of a Cape Cod Town.* Hyannis: F. B. and F. P. Goss, 1939.

The Trial of John Devereux, Jun. of Shelbeggan, in the County of Wexford, before a Court-Martial Held in the City of Cork, on the Twenty-Seventh of November 1799. Dublin: John Jones, 1800.

Trollope, Frances M. *Domestic Manners of the Americans.* 1832. Edited by Donald Smalley. New York: Vintage Books, 1949.

Trumbull, Benjamin. *A Complete History of Connecticut.* 2 vols. 1797. Reprint, New Haven, Conn.: Maltby, Goldsmith, 1818.

Trumbull, J. Hammond, ed. *Memorial History of Hartford County.* 2 vols. Boston: Edward L. Osgood, 1886.

Tucker, Louis Leonard. "'Ohio Show-Shop': The Western Museum of Cincinnati, 1820–1867." In *A Cabinet of Curiosities,* edited by Whitfield J. Bell, Jr., et al., 73–105. Charlottesville: University Press of Virginia, 1967.

Tudor, John. *Deacon Tudor's Diary; or, "Memorandoms of 1709, &c. . . ."* Boston: W. Spooner, 1896.

Tufts, Henry. *The Autobiography of a Criminal.* Edited by Edmund Pearson. New York: Duffield and Company, 1930.

Twain, Mark. *The Adventures of Huckleberry Finn.* In *The Portable Mark Twain,* edited by Bernard De Voto, 193–540. New York: Penguin Books, 1968.

———. *Life on the Mississippi.* 1883. Reprint, New York: Collier, 1917.

Vail, R. W. G. "Random Notes on the Early American Circus." *American Antiquarian Society Proceedings* 43 (1933): 116–83.

Vale, George F. *The Legend of the Blind Beggar's Daughter of Bednal-Green.* London: Blythenhale Press, 1933.

Van Wagenen, Avis S. *Genealogy and Memoirs of Isaac Stearns and His Descendants.* Syracuse, N.Y.: Courier, 1901.

"Ventriloquism, for One Night and Positively No Longer." Portsmouth, N.H.: S. Whidden, 12 February 1811. Broadside. Ford Collection, New York Public Library.

Vital Records of Salem, Massachusetts. 6 vols. Salem, Mass.: Essex Institute, 1918.

Vital Records of Wrentham, Massachusetts, to the Year 1850. Boston: Stanhope, 1910.

Wagner, John W. "James Hewitt, 1770–1827." *Musical Quarterly* 58, no. 2 (April 1972): 259–70.

Walker, George L. *The First Church in Hartford.* Hartford, Conn.: Brown and Gross, 1884.

Walker, Wendy. *Essex Markets and Fairs.* Chelmsford, England: Essex Record Office, 1981.

Wall, A. J. "Wax Portraiture." *New-York Historical Society Quarterly* 9 (April 1925): 3–26.

Walter, Thomas. *The Sweet Psalmist of Israel, a Sermon Preach'd at the Lecture Held in Boston, by the Society for Promoting Regular and Good Singing, and for Reforming the Depravations and Debasements Our Psalmody Labours Under.* Boston: J. Franklin for S. Gerrish, 1722.

Warren, William L. "A Checklist of Jennys Portraits." *Connecticut Historical Society Bulletin* 21 (April 1956): 33–64.

———. "Connecticut Pastels, 1775–1820." *Connecticut Historical Society Bulletin* 24, no. 4 (1959): 97–128.

Webster, Noah. *The Autobiographies of Noah Webster from the Letters and Essays, Memoir, and Diary.* Edited by Richard M. Rollins. Columbia: University of South Carolina Press, 1989.

Wehle, Harry B. *American Miniatures, 1730–1850.* Garden City, N.Y.: Garden City Publishing, 1937.

Weis, Frederick L. *The Colonial Clergy and the Colonial Churches of New England.* Lancaster, Mass.: Descendants of the Colonial Clergy, 1936.

Weiss, Harry B. *A Catalogue of the Chapbooks in the New York Public Library.* New York: New York Public Library, 1936.

Weitenkampf, Frank. *Sketch of the Life of Charles Balthazar Julien Fevret de Saint-Mémin: Issued to Accompany an Exhibition of His Engraved Portraits at the Grolier Club, March 9–25, 1899.* [New York]: [The Club], [1899].

Wells, Mitchell P. "Some Notes on the Early Eighteenth-Century Pantomime." *Studies in Philology* 32 (1935): 598–607.

———. "Spectacular Scenic Effects of the Eighteenth-Century Pantomime." *Philological Quarterly* 17 (January 1938): 67–81.

Wheatland, David P. *The Apparatus of Science at Harvard, 1765–1800.* Cambridge, Mass.: Harvard University Press, 1968.

Wheatland, Henry. "Notice of Some of the Descendants of Joseph Pope of Salem." *Essex Institute Historical Collections* 8 (1866): 104–18.

Wheelock, Eleazar. "Diary of Eleazar Wheelock, D.D., during his Visit to Boston." *Historical Magazine,* 2nd ser., 5 (1869): 237–40.

Whitmore, William Henry. "Abel Bowen." *Bostonian Society Publications* 1, no. 2 (1887): 1–32.

Willard, Charlotte. "Panoramas: The First Movies." *Art in America* 47 (1959): 64–69.

Willard, George O. *History of the Providence Stage, 1762–1891.* Providence: Rhode Island News, 1891.

Williams, Hermann, Jr. *Mirror to the American Past.* New York: New York Graphic Society, 1973.

Wilson, A. E. *Christmas Pantomime: The Story of an English Institution.* London: Allen and Unwin, 1934.

Wilson, Henry, and James Caulfield. *The Book of Wonderful Characters.* London: J. C. Hotten, 1869.

Wilson, James G. *Memorial History of the City of New York from Its First Settlement to the Year 1892.* 4 vols. New York: New York History Company, 1892–1893.

Wilson, Ruth M., and Kate Van Winkle Keller. *Connecticut's Music in the Revolutionary Era.* Hartford, Conn.: Bicentennial Commission, 1979.

Wilson, Susan. "The Old North Church." *Boston Globe,* 11 April 1991, 10–11.

Winslow, Ola E, ed. *Harper's Literary Museum: A Compendium of Instructive, Entertaining, and Amusing Material.* New York: Harper, 1927.

———. *Meetinghouse Hill, 1630–1783.* New York: Macmillan 1952.

Winsor, Justin. *The Memorial History of Boston.* 4 vols. Boston: Osgood, 1881–1883.

Wirt, William. *Memoirs of the Life of William Wirt.* Edited by John P. Kennedy. Philadelphia: Blanchard and Lea, 1856.

Wolfe, Richard J. "A Footnote to the Publication of Peter Smith's Indian Doctor's Dispensatory (1813)." *Harvard Library Bulletin* 27, no. 2 (April 1979): 209–22.

The Working American. Smithsonian Institution Traveling Exhibition. Washington, D.C.: Smithsonian Institution, 1979.

Wrifford, Allison. *A New Plan of Writing Copies: With Accompanying Explanations and Remarks.* Boston: W. Hooker, 1810.

———. *A New System of Penmanship: With Accompanying Explanations and Remarks.* Boston: N.p., 1813.

Wright, Joseph, and Samuel Brooks (attributed). "Medals, Miniature and Profile Painting and Shades." N.p.: N.p., 23 September 1790. Broadside. Reprinted in *Massachusetts Historical Society Proceedings* 52 (1910): 5.

Wright, R. Lewis. "James Warrell: Artist and Entrepreneur." *Virginia Cavalcade* 22 (1973): 5–19.

Wright, Richardson L. *Grandfather Was Queer: Early American Wags and Eccentrics from Colonial Times to the Civil War.* Philadelphia and New York: J. B. Lippincott, 1939.

———. *Hawkers and Walkers in Early America.* Philadelphia: Lippincott, 1927.

———. *Revels in Jamaica, 1682–1838.* New York: Dodd, Mead, 1937.

Wyatt, James. *The Life and Surprizing Adventures of James Wyatt.* London: E. Duncomb, 1748.

Acknowledgments

THIS TOPIC of this book was the subject of a conference titled "Itinerancy in New England and New York," sponsored by the Dublin Seminar for New England Folklife and held at the Essex Institute (now the Peabody Essex Museum) on 16 and 17 June 1984. The participants included Georgia Brady Barnhill, Mary C. Black, Nym Cooke, Barbara R. Dailey, Richard W. Flint, Mary Eileen Fouratt, William J. Gilmore, Joyce Hill, Kate Van Winkle Keller, Elizabeth M. Kornhauser, Stephen A. Marini, Bettina A. Norton, Marius B. Peladeau, Donald M. Scott, Robert F. Trent, and Ruth M. Wilson. Advisors included Nina Fletcher Little, Jonathan K. Fairbanks, and William Lamson Warren. To them the author will always be grateful.

Individuals who read all or a portion of the manuscript prior to publication include Georgia Brady Barnhill, Ross W. Beales, Jr., Jane Montague Benes, Kveta Emilie Benes, Milena Armsby Benes-Rosecan, Joel S. Berson, Richard M. Candee, Richard W. Flint, John A. Hodgson, Kate Van Winkle Keller, Gregory H. Laing, and Kevin M. Sweeney. The chief support for locating, coordinating, and scanning images came from the American Antiquarian Society, especially from Jaclyn Penny, graphic arts assistant. Robert Delap and Mariam Touba of the New-York Historical Society were also extremely helpful. In addition, the following people and institutions have helped shape the ideas that were incorporated into the work: Andrea Anderson, James I. Armstrong, Jr., Andrew H. Baker, Mary C. Beaudry, John L. Bell, Philip Bergen, Christopher P. Bickford, Michael Birtwistle, Roderick H. Blackburn, Ruth M. Blair, David Bosse, Harry Breger, David S. Brooke, Deborah G. Bruneau, Alan C. Buechner, Wanda Burch, Joyce Butler, Nancy C. Carlisle, Elizabeth Carroll-Horrocks, Richard Champlin, Deborah Childs, Edward S. Cooke, Jr., Patricia Crain, Abbott L. Cummings, Susan Danforth, Jackie Donovan, Robert M. Doty, Peter Drummey, Brooke Elkan-Moore, Robert P. Emlen, Linda Eppich, J. Worth Estes, Anne Farnam, Annette Fern, J. Sheldon Fisher, Lydia Foy,

Jamie Franklin, Donald R. Friary, Sarah Galligan, Donna Belle Garvin, James L. Garvin, William H. Gerdts, Robert I. Goler, Katherine H. Griffin, David D. Hall, Dominic W. Hall, Marilyn F. Hoffman, William N. Hosley, William B. Jones, Helen Kellogg, Arthur B. Kern, Sybil B. Kern, Phyllis Kihn, Barbara Lambert, Linda F. Lapides, Christopher T. Leffler, Sylvia Lunt, Wilhelmina V. Lunt, Luis Mendes, Ellen G. Miles, Brett Mizelle, Robert Olson, Robert Olwell, Thomas W. Parker, Thomas B. Payne, Jaclyn Penny, Sumpter Priddy, Andrew V. Rapoza, Kym S. Rice, Sandra Rux, Sara J. Schechner, Caroline F. Sloat, Lester Smith, David C. Thomas, Amy L. Trout, Ruth Wilbur, Richard J. Wolfe, Nan Wolverton, Philip Zea, and Philip D. Zimmerman. *Institutions and libraries:* Abby Aldrich Rockefeller Folk Art Museum at Colonial Williamsburg, American Antiquarian Society, Bibliotèque nationale de France, Boston Athenæum, Boston Public Library, Boston University Scholarly Publications, Bostonian Society, British Library, Charleston Library Society, Collection of Historical and Scientific Instruments (Harvard), Connecticut Historical Society, Cotsen Children's Library (Princeton), Countway Library of Medicine (Harvard), Currier Gallery of Art, Dartmouth College Library, Dublin Seminar for New England Folklife, Fenimore Art Museum, Fine Arts Library (Harvard), Henry N. Flynt Library at Historic Deerfield, Franklin Institute, Golden Ball Tavern, Harvard Art Museums/Fogg Museum, Harvard Theatre Collection, Houghton Library (Harvard), Historic Northampton, Huntington Library, Lamont Library (Harvard), Library Company of Philadelphia, Library of Congress, Loeb Music Library (Harvard), Los Angeles County Museum of Art, Maine Historical Society, Massachusetts Historical Society, Metropolitan Museum of Art, National Endowment for the Humanities, National Gallery of Art, New Bedford Whaling Museum, Newburyport Public Library, New England Historic Genealogical Society, New Hampshire Historical Society, New Haven Museum, New-York Historical Society, New York Public Library, Old Sturbridge Village, Peabody Essex Museum, Redwood Library and Athenaeum, Rhode Island Historical Society, Sudbury Historical Society, Westfield Athenaeum, Widener Library (Harvard), Wilton (New Hampshire) Historical Society, Winterthur Museum, and York County Heritage Trust.

At the University of Massachusetts Press I am grateful for the work of Dennis Anderson, Carol Betsch, Yvonne Crevier, Clark Dougan, Mary V. Dougherty, Karen Fisk, Jack Harrison, Margaret A. Hogan, and Bruce Wilcox.

Photo Credits

Frontispiece and figs. 1.1, 1.3, 1.4, 3.4, 4.2, 6.2, 6.3, 6.4, 6.5, 6.6, 6.8, 6.12, 6.13, 6.14, 6.18, 6.19, 6.21, 6.23, 6.24, 6.26, 6.27, 7.1, 7.3, 7.4, 7.8, 7.9, 7.10, 7.12, 8.1, 9.5, 9.7, 18.3, 19.1, 19.2, 19.3, 19.4, 19.5, 19.6, 19.8, 21.1, 21.2, 21.3, 21.5: Jaclyn Penny at the American Antiquarian Society
Fig. I.1: Richard Walker, Fenimore Art Museum, Cooperstown
Figs. 1.2, 18.5: Library Company of Philadelphia
Figs. 2.1, 3.3, 9.1, 14.2: Connecticut Historical Society
Fig. 3.1: Northampton Historical Society
Figs. 3.2, 10.1: Peabody Essex Museum, 15,027 and 32,011
Figs. 4.1, 6.1, 8.3, 9.3, 15.1, 16.2, 16.6, 16.7, 17.1, 17.2, 18.1, 18.4, 20.1, 20.2, 21.4: Peter Benes
Fig. 5.1: New Hampshire Historical Society
Figs. 5.2, 5.3, 12.2: York County Heritage Trust
Figs. 5.4, 5.5: Arthur B. Kern
Fig. 5.6: Nina Fletcher Little
Figs. 6.7, 6.17, 6.20, 6.22, 9.6, 9.9, 15.5, 15.8, 15.9, 17.3, 17.4, 17.5: ©New-York Historical Society, neg. nos. 90793d, 90792d, 90791d, 90793d, 90794d, 90789d, 233503, 23503, 51427, 8517, 8510A, 27991
Figs. 6.9, 6.25, 7.7, 18.2: Library of Congress
Figs. 6.10, 6.11, 6.28: Rick Rhodes, Charleston, S.C.
Fig. 6.16: Maine Historical Society
Fig. 7.2: The New Haven Museum

Figs. 7.5, 7.6, 9.3: Metropolitan Museum of Art
Figs. 7.11, 8.2: New York Public Library
Fig. 7.13: The National Gallery of Art
Figs. 7.14, 8.4, 9.2: Harvard Theatre Collection, Harvard University
Fig. 8.5: Collection of Historical Scientific Instruments, Harvard University, Rendition A20918
Fig. 9.4: Los Angeles County Museum of Art
Fig. 9.8: The Whaling Museum, New Bedford, Mass.
Figs. 11.1, 16.3, 16.4, 16.5: Rhode Island Historical Society, RHi X3 1399, RHi X3 2570, RHi X3 3035, RHi X3 116
Fig. 11.2: British Library Board, Evan 9205
Fig. 13.1: New England Historic Genealogical Society
Fig. 14.1: Imaging Department ©President and Fellows of Harvard College
Fig. 14.3: Huntington Library, San Marino, California
Fig. 15.2: Winterthur Museum
Figs. 15.3, 15.4: Bostonian Society
Fig. 15.6: Redwood Library
Fig. 15.7: Bibliothèque nationale de France
Fig. 16.1: The Boston Athenaeum
Fig. 17.6: Colonial Williamsburg, image # TC1982-1554
Fig. 19.7: Charles Penniman, Franklin Institute
Fig. 20.3: Dartmouth College Library
Fig. 21.3: Anonymous photographer

Index

Abadie, Hilarian (French language teacher), 367
Abbot, Sarah (c. 1649–1739) (peddler), 253
Abenaki, 52, 59, 89–90
Aberdeen, Scotland, 186
Académie de Musique, 54
acrobatic theaters: composition of, 187–88; growth of, 153
acrobats: 1–2, 6–8, 12, 20, 32; audiences of, 7, 148–50; black, 35, 56–58; circus, 87–88; ethnicity of, 35, 52, 55–56; individual, 138–39; multiple careers of, 23–24; numbers of, 34; runaways as, 194; teams of, 18–19, 58, 135–36, 138, 151, 153. *See also individual acrobats, ropedancers, wirewalkers, slack-wire and tightrope performers*
"active bearers," 8, 10, 298, 325, 349, 373, 378, 386n16
actors and actresses: 8, 12, 32, 54, 73–74, 199; couples and groups of, 19, 58, 158; ethnicity of, 35, 54, 73; London companies of, 226, 420n4; numbers of, 34; references for, 78. *See also individual actors and actresses*
Adams, Martha (animal exhibitor), 128
Adams, Dr. Samuel (1745–1819) (physician, Ipswich inn holder, diarist): 156; on Greenleaf in Bath, Maine, 305; on Harrington, 157–58; on puppeteers, 158;
admission, costs of, 78, 100, 130, 132, 134, 139, 141, 144, 147, 159–60, 186, 188, 191–92, 274
Adolphe, Mademoiselle (ropedancer), 139
Adventures of Harlequin and Scaramouch; Or, the Spaniard Trick'd, The (pantomime), 225
advertisements: 2, 19, 69, 112, 284; directed at children, 161, 146, 169–70, 247, 312, 348; influence of, 112; jargon of, 123; marketing strategies of, 2, 132, 284; postures of, 81–82;

promises in, 68, 75–76, 78–79, 122–23, 306; as sources of data, 34–35, 302, 306–7; for tracking itinerants, 7, 12, 20, 381, 383; want, 220–21, 257; written appeals in, 68–69. *See also* images; woodcuts; *individual entrepreneurs*
aerial excursions, 29–30. *See also* balloon flights
affidavits, 21, 78, 119
"Africana, Signora" (black acrobat), 56
African American congregations, 20
African Americans: 19, 52, 133–35, 220–22, 360; exclusion of, 58; named, 11, 52–53, 55, 59–60, 134–35, 166, 326–27; numbers of, 35, 55–56; venues for, 378–79
African animals, 107, 110–11, 113–16, 119, 123, 146, 152, 232, 402n14. *See also* table 6.2
Africans, 4, 19, 52, 57, 76, 133, 138, 221, 373; numbers of, 35, 55–56
afterpieces, 194, 225–26, 235–36
Ainsworth, Henry (1571–1622) (psalm translator), 201
Akin, James (1773–1846) (profilist, engraver, book illustrator), 28, 30–31, 105, 322–23
Albany Museum, 46, 93
Albares, Francisco (street musician), 222
Albiness. *See* Hervey, Elizabeth
Aldrich's Hall, Providence, 42, 295, 418n20
Alexander the Great (play), 119
Alexandria, Va., 36, 45, 47, 73, 90, 101–2, 107, 109, 140–41, 166, 179, 208–9, 214, 226, 233, 247, 293–94, 296, 336, 341
Alfred, Maine, 383–84
Ali, Ibrahim Adam Ben (alternative healer), 20, 55, 79, 374
Allegheny Mountains, 356
Allen, Andrew (actor), 144

483

Allen, George (penmanship teacher), 349
Almy, Lydia Hill (1769–1837) (diarist), 381
Amboy, N.J., 70
American Company (theater company), 226
American Company of Comedians (theater company), 165
American Museum, New York City, 252, 283
American Revolution, 8, 20, 24, 26, 33, 71, 139, 164, 180, 184, 191, 194, 237, 245, 248, 253, 283, 370, 373
American Tars; Or Huzza for the Navy (play), 235
American Volunteers (play), 231–32
Ames, Nathaniel (1741–1822) (physician, diarist): 12, 130, 241; on Bates, 150; on Crowninshield elephant, 145–46; on Exchange Coffee House fire, 290; on Newport plays, 226; on sea monsters, 296; on Dr. Stork, 262
Amesbury, Mass., 45
Amory Hall, Boston, 366
amphitheaters, 90, 141–42, 149, 151, 153, 449n102
Anaconda, Attacking a Horse and Its Rider [Ward] (painting), 295
Analytical Guide to the Art of Penmanship [Dean], 347
Ancora, Pietro (c. 1780–1844) (artist, drawing-master), 78–79
Anderson, Alexander (1775–1870) (physician, engraver, diarist), 106, 184, 252
Angelis, Dr. (alternative healer), 56
animal acts: 123, 146–48, 151, 217–18; accompanied by music, 215; English, 87, 148
animal handlers: 2, 34–35, 76, 87, 95, 122, 128–29, 146, 151, 170, 173, 248, 371, 451; acceptance of, 127; of color, 102, 133–34, 404n20; ethnicity of, 35; numbers of, 34; routes traveled by, 129, 133; schedules of, 132–33, 135
animal proprietors, 34–35, 95, 100–101, 103–4, 107, 128–29, 135, 174, 188, 381, 383–84; of color, 133–34; schedules of, 132–33; tours of, 110–12
animals: admission prices for, 78, 100, 130, 132, 134, 147; caged, 73, 100, 128, 132, 135; cost of, 132; exotic, 5, 11, 71, 100, 127, 129, 134, 145, 151, 193, 366, 370; financial risk of, 132; popular names of, 152; travel of, 21, 41, 135, 151, 154–55, 175, 366, 377, 382–83
animal showmen: 52, 398n9; ethnicity of, 35; numbers of, 34. *See also* animal handlers; animal proprietors
animals, trained, 21, 27, 28, 31–32, 36, 39, 78, 96, 105, 107–8, 122–23, 334, 376
animal trainers, 18, 27, 52, 73, 87, 148, 370–71
Annapolis, Md., 12, 45, 47, 179, 194–95, 226, 262, 318, 375

Anthem Suitable to be Performed at an Ordination . . . , *An* [Lane], 208
Anthony Street Theatre, New York City, 139
anti-foreign sentiment, 74, 235
Antiquities of the Common People [Bourne], 11
apothecaries, 20, 73
apprentices, 25, 86–87, 127, 175, 181, 199, 245, 274, 337, 344
apprenticeships, 85–87, 92, 96, 176
Archytas (428–347 B.C.) (Greek mathematician, philosopher, scientist), 334, 441n22
Armour, Monsieur (dancing-master), 246
Arms, Dr. Eliakim (1737–1810) (alternative healer), 360, 446n28
Arnal, Louis (dancing-master), 245–46
Arnold, John James Trumbull (1812–1865) (painter, penmanship teacher), 350
Arnold, Judge Peleg (1751–1820), 381
Arnold, Samuel (1740–1802) (English arranger, composer), 363
Arrow Against Profane and Promiscuous Dancing [Mather, I., et al.], 238
artificial comedians (puppets), 95, 165, 178, 180–82
"artificial figures" (puppets), 158, 179
"Artificial Wax-work Commedians," 23
artists: ethnicity of, 35; with handicaps, 19, 305, 326, 387n7; numbers of, 34; reasons for preferment by, 305–6, table 17.1. *See also* painters; pastel artists; *individual artists*
Art of Writing, Reduced to a Plain and Easy System, The [Jenkins], 345–47, 350
Ashburnham, Mass., 258
Aspin, Jehoshaphat [pseudonym] (author), 11
Assembly Hall, Salem, Mass., 205, 251
Astley's circus, London, 216, 343
"Astonishing Invisible Lady" (acoustical device), 341–42, 440n47
Attleboro, Mass., 40, 381
audiences: at agricultural events, 80; characterization of, 4, 8, 49, 70, 150, 273, 378; of color: 21, 58, 221, 378–79; at commencements, 80; misconduct of, 142, 149, 151; outdoor, 138–39, 143–50; for professional musicians, 212, 223–24; for puppeteers, 190–91; sought by itinerants, 2, 18, 36, 45, 47, 68–69, 85; tavern and assembly hall, 189–91, 194; for theater professionals, 225–26
Augusta, Ga., 58, 88, 214, 216, 223, 247, 324, 356
Augusta, Maine, 45
aurists, 74, 262–63
automaton, chess playing, 329–30, 334, 337, 344, 441n22

automaton proprietors: Baker, 335; Blanchard, 145, 191, 221, 332–33, 338, 343; Bowen, 342; Brickell, 158; Deeker, 340; Duboise, 337; Falconi, 4, 106, 115, 191, 330–32, 334, 338, 341, 372; Haddock, 337; Kallanback, 337; Maelzel, 337, 344; Maginnis, 181, 335; Maison, 333–34, 338; Martin, 335, 343–44; Meyere, 335; Mix, 342; Packard, 334–35, 339–40, 342; Paff, 335; Pinchbeck, 86–87, 334, 342–43; Prince, 340–41; Rannies, 188, 335–37, 339; Robertson, 341; Savage, 341; Vogel, 337, 344; von Kempelen, 337, 339, 344; Wood, 342. *See also* tables 1.4, 8.1, 9.1, 9.2, 19.1, and 19.2

automatons: 327, 335–37; American exhibition of, 329, 343–44; European: 87, 328–30, 333–34, 343–44; makers of, 23, 27, 145, 329, 334, 344; mechanisms of, 338–39, 341; musical, 87; North American introduction of, 329–33; numbers of showmen of, 34–35, 343; speaking, 333–34, 339–42; water driven, 339. *See also individual automatons*

Avvakum (c. 1620–1681) (Russian archpriest), 18

"Babes in the Wood" (English ballad), 163; wax figures of, 181, 363

Babes in the Wood (puppet show), 179

Babcock, Samuel (1760–1813) (singing master, composer), 206

Bache, William (physiognotrist), 321, 325, 328

backdrops: 233, 299; moving, 368

Bacon, Roger (c. 1214–1292) (English philosopher, Franciscan friar, conjurer), 160, 361

Baconais, Mr. (dancing-master), 40

Badcock, Lemuel (1748–1835) (singing master), 206–7, 210, 416n24

Badger, Joseph (1708–1765) (artist), 266, 308

Bailey, Doctor (puppeteer). *See* Bayly, Mr.

Bailey, Hackaliah (1774–1845) (animal proprietor), 381, 401n4

Bailey, Janette McArthur (1791–1839), 94

Bailey Phinehas (1787–1861) (shorthand teacher, minister), 94, 351

Baker, Gardiner (d. 1798) (museum, waxworks, and automaton proprietor): 297, 335; American Museum of, 252, 283; automatons of, 335; with Bowen, D., 151; and menage of animals, 151; waxworks of 283

Baldwin, Christopher C. (1800–1835) (librarian, editor, diarist), 221–22, 309–10, 436n39

balladeers, 7

ballads, 6, 9, 159, 162–63, 178, 254, 274, 362–63s

Ballantine, Rev. John (1716–1776) (minister, diarist): 12; on catamount/lion, 147–48; on Jones, I., 258; on razor grinder, 37; on Yeldall, 13, 24–25, 30

balloonists: 2, 73, 137, 142, 375, 377; ethnicity of, 35; numbers of, 34, 54, 327. *See also individual balloonists*

balloons, hot air: 6–7, 20, 153, 155; advertisements for, 100, 105; cost of admission to, 144; launches of, 142–45, 149, 151, 193, 199, 326, 374; making of, 72; as publicity, 184; subscriptions for, 27, 30, 54, 80, 143–44, 221, 283, 332. *See also individual balloonists*

"Baltimorean Boy" (black musician, acrobat), 56

Bancroft, Elizabeth (1773–1867) (school teacher, diarist), 246

band, black, 12, 56, 221

band members, 37, 73–74, 181, 215–16, 245, 395n25, 412n34, 418n12

bands, for entertainments, 141, 144, 153, 179, 360, 366

Banks, Mr. (puppeteer, lantern performer), 167–68, 181–82, 376

Banks, William (equestrian), 52

Banton, T. S. (profilist), 307

Banvard, John (1815–1891) (painter), 368

Barbados, 172, 373

Barbary, Africa, 129, 292

Barker, Henry Aston (1774–1856) (son of Robert, Edinburgh artist), 296–98

Barker, Robert (1739–1806) (Edinburgh artist), 96, 296–98

barns, 18, 24, 37, 129, 132–33, 143, 156, 158, 250, 292, 375, 377

Barnstable, Mass., 59, 202

Barre, Mass., 369

Barrell, Peter (reputed thief), 222

Barriskill, James W. (theater historian), 11

Barry, John (singing master), 205

Barry, Phillips (1880–1937) (folklorist), 6

Bartholomew Fair, London, 1, 69, 87, 175, 177, 228, 230, 402n18

Barton, Mr. (puppeteer), 182, 376

Baschia, Nicholas (Italian fireworks artist), 54

Bascom, Ruth Henshaw (1772–1848) (profilist), 313, 317

Bateman and His Ghost (puppet show), 179

"Bateman, or the Unhappy Marriage" (German folktale, puppet show), 176

Bates, Benjamin (electrical demonstrator), 250

Bates, Jacob (equestrian), 82, 135, 150, 374

Bates, William (actor), 74, 229, 232

Bath, England, 73, 411n26

Bath, Maine, 45–46, 305

Battle of Dettingen, 163, 409n21

"Battle of Prague" (sonata), 213, 217, 418n12

Bayly Mr. [Doctor Bailey, the Old Artist, the Old Man] (puppeteer, toothpuller, conjurer, lanternist, singer): 74, 170, 180, 190–91, 364, 377–78; conjuring equipment of, 95, 193, 376; as lanternist, 95, 218; as "Old Artist," 180, 359; puppets of 95, 178, 359; as toothpuller, 359
Bay Psalm Book, 201
Beacon Hill, Boston, 153
Beale, George (1675–1760) (psalmodist), 203–4, 210
Beale, Matthew (1715–after 1797) (son of George, psalmodist), 203–4, 210
Beales, Ross W., Jr. (historian), 13, 479
bears, 5, 18, 128, 135, 151–52, 166–67, 411n8
Beekman's tavern, New York City, 190
beggars, 37, 189
Beggar's Opera, 5, 227
Bellisarius, Mr. (actor), 183
Benazech, Charles (1767–1794) (English painter), 280–81
Bengal, India, 100, 132, 134, 166, 295
Benjamin, Abraham (balancer), 193
Bennett, Mr. (acrobat, slack-wire performer, conjurer): 55, 71, 191–92, 356
Bennington, Vt., 243, 266, 345
Benson, Norman A. (dance historian), 11
Bentley, Rev. William (1759–1819) (minister, diarist): 12, 183; on African Society, 221; on alternative healers, 156; on Barkers' panorama, 298; on Bennett, 356; on Billings, 205–6; on Blanchard, 149; on Brenon, J., 149, 184, 190, 413n47; and college commencements, 81, 82, 122; on Corné, 298; on elephants, 132, 146–47, 406n55; on entertainments, 20, 27, 81, 148, 397n57, 404n19; on Hancock, [N.], 156; on Jenkins, 349–50; on King, W., Sr., 64–66, 292, 325; on Lane, 208, 417n36; on mixed race families, 59; on Old Bett, 383–84; on Phillips, C., 397n56; on Rannie, 191; and "Sweating Doctor," 156; on waxworks, 283–84
Berault, Charles (dancing-master, musician), 216–17, 243
Bernard, John (1756–1828) (English actor, author), 12, 33, 41, 46, 355, 389n47
Berry, Messr. (acrobat, pantomimist), 138
Beverly, Mass., 168–69, 202, 397n56
Beze, Mademoiselle (miniature painter), 58
Bigelow, Horatio (1790–1824) (newspaper editor, publisher), 106
Billings, William (1746–1800) (psalmodist), 205–6, 208, 210
Bills of the Day, 99. *See also* advertisements
Birth of Harlequin; or, the Enchanted Cauldron (pantomime), 62, 230

"Birth of Harlequin, The" (comic tune), 228, 420n12
Bishop, James (waxworks exhibitor), 276, 278, 280, 282, 285
bison, 93, 129, 133, 404n19
Bisset, Samuel (1721–1783) (English animal trainer), 87, 148
Blake, Lemuel and William P. (bookstore owners), 169–70
Blancan, Miss (puppeteer), 183
Blancan, Peter (puppeteer), 106, 166, 183–84, 364, 379
Blanchard, Elizabeth (b. c. 1815) (daughter of William, singer, slack-wire performer), 88
Blanchard, George (b. c. 1813) (son of William, balancer, circus performer), 88
Blanchard, Jean-Pierre (1753–1809) (French balloonist, automaton exhibitor): 52, 54, 106, 149, 405n49; automatons of, 144–45, 191, 221, 332–33, 338, 343; black band of, 12, 56, 221; "Curious Carriage" of, 332–33; fundraising of, 73, 80, 144–45, 221, 283, 332–33; manned flight in North America of, 143–44, 405n48; waxwork figure of, 283
Blanchard, Mr. W[illiam]. (circus proprietor), 88
Bleecker, Johanna Abeel (1764–1810) (wife of Leonard), 303–4
Bleecker, Leonard (c. 1755–1844) (merchant), 303–4
Blind Beggar's Daughter of Bednal-Green, The (puppet play), 161–62, 361–62
Blodget's tavern [Samuel], Boston, 190
Blouin, Dr. (alternative healer), 55, 63
Blue Beard (play), 119, 132
boarding houses, 18, 70, 80
Boduin, Dr. L. (alternative healer), 55, 63
Bonnin, John (optical machine and diagonal mirror operator), 68, 378
Book of Psalmes [Ainsworth], 201
Boquet, Louis (French language and flageolet teacher), 72
Boston Athenæum Gallery, 84
Boston Common, 27, 144, 255, 289, 316
Boston Harbor, 135, 296
Boston Medical Society, 24
Boston Museum, 96, 267–68, 272, 300, 321
Boston selectmen: 75; and acrobats, 24, 149–50, 359; and animal handlers, 173; and Bradley, 136, 149–50, 377; and Burlesson, 173; and Childs, 150; and Clete, 237–38; and dancing instruction, 237–38; and 1810 prizefight, 357; and electrical experiments, 251; and Johnson, W., 251; and masquerades, 364; and puppeteers, 179, 190; and Rannie,

James, 186, 188; and ropedancing, tightrope performances, 136, 149–50, 377; and rope flying 150; and Sherlot, 238; and Stepney, 238; and Templeman, 24, 359; and ventriloquists, 186, 188
Boston Theatre, 144, 234, 290, 299, 332, 395n25. *See also* Federal Street Theatre
Boston waterfront, 70, 128, 377
Bouchardon, Edmé (1698–1762) (French artist, engraver), 161
Boucherie, L. (fireworks artist, musical instrument teacher and repairer), 142
Boudier, J. J. (engraver, physiognotrist), 317–18, 325–26, 328
Bourne, Henry (clergyman, author), 11
Bowen, Abel (1790–1850) (nephew of Daniel, engraver, publisher, author), 29, 291
Bowen, Daniel (c. 1760–1856) (printer, museum proprietor): 29, 82, 151, 276, 290, 294–96, 298, 301, 316, 321, 341–42, 437n4; Columbian Museum of, 75, 77, 134–35, 218, 272, 300, 320, 393n37; later life of, 371; waxworks of, 71, 76–77, 81, 156, 267, 272–74, 280–85, 300, 357, 376
Bowen, Nathan (diarist), 255–56
Boylston Hall Museum, Boston, 290
Bozrah, Conn., 207
Bradford, Mass., 201
Bradley, John (acrobat, tightrope performer, ropedancer), 136, 149–50, 377
Brady, Nicholas (1659–1726) (Anglican divine, poet), 201–2, 217
Brattleboro, Vt., 80, 181, 208, 369
Brattle Square Meetinghouse, 200, 205
Breck, Hannah Andrews (1747–1830), 136, 138, 148
Breck, Samuel (1771–1862) (son of Hannah, author), 138
Brenon, Hannah Etridge (second wife of John, acrobat, slack-wire performer), 71, 185, 376
Brenon, John (fl. 1773–1790) (acrobat, slack-wire performer, singer, actor, conjurer): 55, 199, 412n45; as acrobat, 71, 183–84, 359; cost of admission to, 186; as wirewalker, ropedancer, 186, 190–91, 193; as toothdrawer, 23, 359
Brenon, Mary (first wife of John, singer, actor, conjurer), 183–85, 413n48
Breschard, Jean-Baptiste (circus proprietor, equestrian), 142, 154
Breslaw, H. C. (circus proprietor), 37
Breslaw, Philip (London conjurer), 87, 98, 183, 400n47, 414n58
Brewer, George St. P. (1814–1852) (painter), 369

Brewer, John (b. 1824) (brother of George St. P., painter), 369
Brewster, John, Jr. (1766–1854) (portrait painter), 73, 305, 313, 387n7, 413nn15, 17
Brewster, Royal (1770–1835) (brother of John, Jr., physician), 305
Brickell, Richard (fl. 1742–1756) (showman, musician): 12, 75, 159, 178, 190–91, 193, 199, 251, 274; and electrical presentations, 250, 265, 429n86; itinerary of, table 8.1; as lantern showman, 160–62, 158, 168, 170, 218, 361, 377, 407n5, 408n9
Brickell and Mosely, 159–60, 176–78, 190, 407–8n5, 447n41
Bridges, Henry (1697–1754) (English mechanic, clockmaker), 75, 222–23, 401n2
Bridges, James (b. c. 1725) (son of Henry, music machine exhibitor), 222–23
Brigshaw, Mr. (animal proprietor), 95, 376, 399n35
Bristol, England, 51, 143, 358, 362
Bristol, R.I., 48, 77
British Empire in America [Oldmixon], 172
British Isles, 37, 51, 374
Broadbent, Samuel, Jr. (1810–1880) (artist, daguerreotypist), 308
broadsides: 7, 9, 12, 68, 99–100, 107, 130, 254, 271, 274, 370; and Burlesson, 174; and Coverly, Jr., 283; and King, W., Sr., 322; and Packard, 339; and peddlers, 254
Broadway, New York City, 70, 99, 117, 183, 296, 383
"Broken Bridge, The" (song, shadow play, lantern show, skit), 164–66, 170, 183, 378
Bromfield, Edward, Jr. (Boston selectman, 1732–1735), 128
Brooklyn, N.Y., 26
Brooks, Samuel (fl. 1780-1790) (miniature painter, profilist), 314–16
Brooks, Sarah Briggs (wife of Thomas, waxworks exhibitor, shopkeeper), 70, 283, 431n31
Brooks, Thomas (shopkeeper, waxworks exhibitor), 70, 283, 431n31
Broome, Joseph (German conjurer), 127, 377
Brown, A. (penmanship teacher), 349
Brown, James, Jr. (penmanship teacher), 96, 400n42
Brown, Mr. (fireworks artist), 142
Brown, Rev. Richard, Jr. (1675–1732) (minister, diarist), 202
Brown, William H. (1808–1883) (profilist), 326, 439n45
Brownell, George (fl. 1703–after 1750) (musician, dancing and manners teacher), 70, 239, 241

Brownell, Thomas (dancing-master), 240–41
Bruce, Captain (mariner), 37
Brunton, Richard (d. 1832) (engraver), 61
Brunswick, Maine, 46, 59, 77, 392
Bryant, Sarah Snell (1768–1847) (mother of William C. Bryant, profilist), 317
Buechner, Alan Clark (music historian), 12
Buell, Rev. Samuel (1716–1789) (minister), 311
Bull, Amos (1745–1825) (singing teacher), 207, 416n30
Bull, Capt. Frederick (tavern keeper), 71
bull-baiting, 69
Bunch of Grapes Tavern, Philadelphia, 71
Burke, Peter (cultural historian): 5–6, 18, 68, 377; on healing and entertainment, 24, 359, 446n21; and itinerancy and popular culture, 9, 370, 373; and Redfield's "great" and "little culture," 9, 211, 283; and "tradition bearers," 8
Burlesson, Edward, Jr. (1686–after 1746) (animal and puppet showman, teacher): 13, 173–74, 191; as animal proprietor, 128–29, 174; broadside by, 174; "cabbin" of, 40, 173, 175; handicap of, 52, 173, 370; as puppeteer, 9, 52, 54, 128, 173–76, 189, 193, 248; as schoolteacher, 8, 370
burlettas, 58, 178
Burlington, N.J., 76
Burr, Aaron (1756–1836) (U.S. vice president), waxworks of, 281–82
Burton, Charles (showman, singer), 170
Busselot, Charles (French balloonist, fencing teacher, showman), 142–43, 405n46
Butterworth, Philip (historian), 10, 19, 119, 194–95, 377
Byrd, William (1674–1744) (diarist, planter, surveyor), 12, 135
Byrne, Mr. (dancing-master), 247

Cabot, Mrs. John (owner of Titus), 221
Cabot, Titus (slave, violinist), 221
Cadete, Dr. F. (alternative healer, mountebank), 55, 70
Cadusch, Mr. (dancing-master), 247
Calcott, Dr. Isaac (alternative healer, mountebank): 61, 93, 95; medical career of, 51, 262–63, 267, 359–60, 446n25; travel circuit of, 263
Calcutta, India, 132
Cambridge, Mass., 42, 60, 63, 81, 97, 135, 146, 216, 246, 348, 381
Cambridgeport, Mass., 246, 424n29
camels and dromedaries, 71, 100, 101, 107, 128–32, 151, 292, 401n12, 403nn7, 11, 12

camera obscura, 160, 164, 167, 314, 316, 321, 325, 437n6, 449n94
camp meetings, 259, 266, 366
Canada: 41, 46, 56, 89, 181, 356, 394n54, 412n34, 446n28; itinerants' travel to, 65, 139, 149, 154, 192, 259, 271, 274, 284, 322, 326, 342, 372–73, 376
Canadaigua, N.Y., 93
cancer-curers: 59, 77, 88–89, 366, 392; treatments by, 55, 261
Cannata, Antonio (fencing teacher), 106
Canterbury, Conn., 43, 358, 445
Cape Cod, Mass., 38, 45–46, 259
caravans, 151–52, 450n109
cards, 4, 23, 27–28, 31, 52, 86, 339
Carli, Sieur (acrobat), 56–57, 356
carnival traditions, European, decline in America of, 355–56, 358–59, 361–65
Carolinas, 18, 46–47, 179
carriages, 36, 39, 62, 69, 326, 332–33, 343
Casanova, N.Y., 93
cassowaries, 81, 122, 130
Castine, Maine, 252
Castle, Terry (English scholar), 373
Castle Tavern, Boston, 17–18, 239, 377, 380
casts, use in portraiture of, 311–12, 437nn47, 51
catamounts, 129, 147, 157–58
Catawissa, Penn., 252
Caulfield, Thomas (actor), 46
Cavenough's Inn, Albany, 183
Cayetano troupe [Cayetano Mariotini, d. 1818], 142
Caylus, Anne Claude Philippe de Tubières, comte de (1692–1765) (French engraver), 161
Cenas, Gaspard (dancer, dancing-master), 47, 71, 247
Central America, 18, 373
Champion, Mr. (street musician), 222
chapbooks, 7–9, 107, 162, 170, 178, 271, 274, 282–83, 357, 362–63
Chapin, Amzi (1768–1835) (singing master, composer, instrument maker), 204, 210
Chapman, Mary (puppeteer), 179
Chapman, Moses (1783–1821) (African American profilist), 322–24
Chapman, Mr. and Mrs. (speech teachers), 367
Charlestown, Mass. 42, 136, 138, 241, 246, 255–56, 265–66
Charlestown, Md., 87
Charles Town, Va., 209, 244
Chauncy, Rev. Charles (1705–1787) (minister), 256
Cheapside, London, 83, 328

Chesapeake River Valley, 1
Chester, England, 148
Chester, Penn., 70, 179, 261
Chester, Vt., 208
Chevalier, Charles F. (dancing-master), 247
Chiappi, Joseph (d. 1834) (wax sculptor, mountebank, physician), 23, 360–61, 446n29
Chiappi family, 360
"Children in the Wood, The" (folktale), 163, 182, 362–63, 447n39
Childs, John (rope flyer), 81, 136–38, 148, 150, 377
Chilton, G. (nitrous oxide exhibitor, lecturer, educator), 379–80
Chinese shades (shadow puppets), 158, 165, 180, 218. *See also* Ombres Chinoises
chirography, 22, 345, 347–48
Chodowiecki, L. Wilhelm (1765–1805) (engraver), 165, 218
Choice, Peter (hairdresser, bootblack, profilist), 23
Chrétien, Gilles-Louis (1754–1811) (musician, engraver, inventor), 318, 321
Christ Church, Boston, 136–37
Christian, Francis (dancing-master), 55
Christopher, Milbourne (historian), 11–12
Church, Mr. ("Aboriginal" acrobat), 56
Churchill, James (English puppeteer), 178
Church of England, 26, 238, 255
Church-Street Theatre, Charleston, 183
circus: 6, 19, 24, 32, 87, 90, 164, 266, 374, 449n102; in England, 216, 343; professionals, 34–35; in Scotland, 153; troupes, 37, 88, 142, 153, 155, 290, 356, 366
"Citizen Sans Culottes" ["Citizen Democrat"] (automaton), 333
City Hall Tavern, New York City, 370
City Hotel, New York City, 216
City Hotel, Trenton, N.J., 214
civet cat, 81–82
Claflin, C. R. B. (penmanship teacher), 350
Claggett, Rebecca (wife of William), 95
Claggett, William (1696–1749) (clockmaker, organ mechanic, instrument maker, electrical demonstrator), 95, 249–50
Clark, Captain (conjurer), 190
Clark, Dr. William (physician), 70
Clements, Bernard (equestrian), 52
Clete, Charles (dancing-master), 220, 237–38
Clinch [Clench], Mr. (London mimic), 97–98
clocks, astronomical, 87, 333
clocks, musical, 32, 75, 87, 158, 222, 376, 389n46, 401n2

clockwork figures, 72, 181–82, 329, 335, 337, 339
Cloris, Peter. *See* Donegani
Clown (commedia dell'arte character), 234
clowns, 6, 18, 30, 36, 97, 136, 230, 232–34
Cobb, E. (penmanship, grammar teacher), 350
Coburn, A. (singing master), 205
Coco and Gibonne (monkeys), 146–47
Codet, Mr. (fireworks artist), 54, 138, 141–42
Colburn, Augustus G. P. (penmanship teacher), 354
Colburn, Edmund (penmanship teacher), 354
Cole, Moses Dupre (1783–1849) (painter), 86, 122–23
college commencements: 36, 69, 76, 80; at College of Rhode Island, 81, 283; at Dartmouth College, 342; at Harvard College, 81–82, 95, 122, 381; at Yale College, 81, 145, 239, 281, 283, 397n54
College of William and Mary, 9–10
Colles, John (fl. North America, 1778–1783) (artist, profilist), 316, 326
Colton, Gardner Q. (b. 1814) (lecturer), 380
Columbia, S.C., 356, 372
Columbian Museum: 27, 134, 276, 371; fire, 62, 75; live animals at, 82; paintings at, 300, 311, 434n1; physiognotrace at, 320; transparency at, 290; waxworks at, 77, 83, 218, 272, 285, 431n28, 434n1
Columbine (commedia dell'arte character), 168, 184, 194, 226, 229–30, 233–34, 422n36
Combe, George (1788–1858) (phrenologist, author), 369
comedians: 18, 233, 386n17; company of, 78, 162, 165, 177–78, 226, 274; company of artificial, 95, 165, 175, 180–81, 298, 364
Comédie-Française, 54
commedia dell'arte, 175, 179, 194, 226, 230, 232, 234, 262, 364
composers: 21, 54, 214, 218, 225; Italian, 216; named, 74, 205–6, 213, 215–17, 228–29, 363, 420n9, 424n23; numbers of, 204
Concert-Hall, Boston, 5, 21, 76, 186, 188–89, 241–42, 423n17
Concert Hall, New Bedford, Mass., 367
Concert-Hall, Salem, 57
concert life, 32, 199, 215–17
concerts: with fireworks, 139; subscription, 216–17, 223
Concord, Mass., 259, 283, 292
Concord, N.H., 323
"Conflagration of Moscow" (automaton), 337, 344
Congregational singing, state of, 200–202

conjurers: 5, 13, 18, 73, 85, 122, 158, 166, 183, 359, 361, 365, 375, 380; costume of, 119; ethnicity of, 35, 55; named, 23, 68, 86–87, 108, 127, 178, 181, 184, 251, 267, 335, 372, 414n58; numbers of, 9, 34, 377
Connecticut River, 38, 43–45, 203
Connecticut River Valley, 13, 21, 25, 203, 222, 255, 257, 284
Constantinople, 55, 140, 294
Constitution (frigate), 141
Constitution and Guerriere (patriotic effusion), 235
Constitution of Man, The [Combe], 369
Cooke, Nym (musicologist), 11, 489
Cooper, Thomas Apthorpe (1776–1849) (actor), 132
Cooperstown, N.Y., 3, 103
Copley, John Singleton (1738–1815) (American painter), 291, 308, 423n11, 436n37
Coquette; or, the History of Eliza Wharton, The [Foster], 242
Corday, Charlotte (1768–93) (French assassin), waxworks of, 278, 285
Corné, Michele Felice (1752–1845) (painter), 66, 267, 292–94, 298, 300, 434n1
Corre's Assembly Room, New York City, 71, 330
Corre's City Tavern, New York City, 56, 183–84, 332, 359, 414n74
Cory, Barney, coffeehouse of, 76
Cossa, Cesar (lanternist, glassblower, electrical healer, optician), 170–71, 429n86
costumes, of showmen, 24, 33, 90, 117–21, 144, 187
cotillions, 50, 80, 213–14, 245–46
Covent Garden, London, 54, 73, 97, 225, 227, 245
Coventry, Conn., 259
Coverly, Nathaniel, Jr. (1775?–1824) (printer), 283
Cowley, Mary (dancing academy, boardinghouse, coffeehouse proprietess), 43, 72
Creation of the World (puppet play), 177
credulity, American, 370, 381
Cressin, Mr. (animal showman), 106, 123, 146–47, 170, 218–19
Crighton's Tavern, Savannah, Ga., 71
criminality, of itinerants, 60–62, 64, 222, 253, 380, 394n54
Cronin, Timothy (dancing-master), 247
"Crook'd Shanks" (melody), 210
Crosby, William (musician, dancing and fencing teacher), 62
Cross, Anthony (electrical healer), 268
Crowninshield, Capt. Jacob (1770–1808) (shipper), 107, 132, 381–82

Crowninshield elephant: 81, 107, 109, 145–46, 344, 381–82, 401n4; cost of admission to, 132
Cryder, Susanna (innkeeper), 63
"cultural memory," 193, 358–64, 374
cultural transmission, 9, 19, 98, 199, 245, 369–70, 374, 380
culture: appeal to rank and file, 377–79; division between popular and mannered, 212–13, 224, 247, 271; mannered or schooled, 6, 10, 200, 212, 225, 248, 283; merging of mannered and popular, 210–11, 237, 271, 283, 370
culture "carriers," 8, 10, 52, 66, 70, 85, 99, 172–73, 247, 267, 350, 369–70, 373, 386n16
Cummington, Mass., 317
"cunning" trades, 59, 95
Curtis, Joseph (acrobat), 153
Cushing, Rev. John (1744–1823) (minister), 258
Cushing, Seth (animal exhibitor), 130
Cushman, Cephas (penmanship teacher), 352
Cutler, Rev. Timothy (1684–1765) (minister), 136, 377

Dabney, John (mathematical instrument maker, lanternist, optician), 160–61, 170
Daguerre, Louis-Jacques (1787–1851) (French artist, inventor), 369
daguerreotypists, 2, 40, 368–69
Da Lee, Justus (1793–1878) (penmanship teacher, miniature painter), 350
Dam, Leader (penmanship teacher), 349–50, 354
Dance and Its Music in America, 1528–1789 [Keller], 11, 13
dances: 215, 240; contra, 50; cotillions, 213, 245–46; country, 80, 87, 90, 218, 244–46; flag, 153, 245, "mixt," 237–38; names of, 21, 221, 235, 237, 244–46; popular, 246; in taverns, 6
dancing instruction, 237, 247; beginnings in America of, 237; competition in, 242–43; for middle-class citizens, 247; music for, 56, 218–20; venues for, 71–72, 163, 186
dancing-masters: 2, 8, 11–13; advertisements of, 41, 44, 75, 80, 245; concurrent schools of, 207; criminality of, 64; curriculum of, 244–46; ethnicity of, 35, 54–55, 240, 246; and European connections, 245–46; and Harlequin pantomimes, 225–26; lengths of stay of, 44, 50, 76, 243–44; and manners, 244; numbers of, 19–29, 34, 54, 237, 240, 247; opposition to, 5, 237–39, 242; references for, 78; travel of, 40–42, 44, 47, 49–50, 242–44, 247. *See also* manners, schools of; *individual dancing-masters*
dancing parties and balls, 152, 217, 240, 242, 246

dancing schools: 22, 64, 71–72, 74, 80, 214, 217, 239–43, 245–46, 376; arguments regarding, 239, 242; in Boston, 237, 246; lengths of stay of, 44, 50, 76, 243–44; subscriptions for, 72, 79–80, 243, 246, 376
Dandy Jack (trained monkey), 152
Daniels, Bruce C. (historian), 70–71
Darling, E. (penmanship teacher), 350
Dartmouth, Mass., 48
Dartmouth College, 322, 342
Dastuge, Dr. (alternative healer), 55, 63
Davenport, Rev. James (1716–55) (minister), 255
Davenport, Mr. (waxworks exhibitor), 282
Day, Augustus (painter, profile taker), 47
Day, John (peddler), 267
Dean, George (penmanship teacher), 349
Dean, Henry (penmanship teacher, engraver), 347, 349–50, 354
Dean, Samuel (animal proprietor), 133
Dearborn, Benjamin, academy of, 243, 423n17
Dearborn's long room, Boston, 181
Deblois, Gilbert and Lewis (shopkeepers, retailers of magic lanterns), 169
Deblois family, 70
decorative arts, 20, 326, 364, 368
Dedham, Mass.: 42, 216; camels at, 130–31; dancing instruction at, 246; elephants at, 145–46, 381; and Exchange Coffee House fire, 290; and Fairbanks, 280–82
Deeker, Joseph (balloonist, acoustical device exhibitor), 80, 143, 199, 340–41
Deerfield, Mass., 42, 360, 446n28
Deerfield Academy, Deerfield, Mass., 349
Deetz, James (historian), 10
De Florat, J. A. (fl. 1784 in N.J.) (miniature painter), 76
De Francesco, Grete (historian), 260
deGraffenried, Christopher (dancing-master), 55
deGraffenried, Tscharner (son of Christopher, dancing-master), 55
Delacroix, Colonel (boxing school proprietor), 357–58
delineator (physiognotrace), 314, 317, 321, 327–28, 437n2
Dench, James (fireworks artist), 142
Denmark, 73–74, 374
dental surgeons, 23–24, 359, 372
deserters, 52, 89, 194, 208
de St. Pry, Mr. (dancing-master), 54
Devero, Francis (brother of John), 44
Devero, John C. (1774–after 1840) (dancing-master), 43–45, 240, 242, 244, 246, 371, 390n24

Devero, Walter (brother of John), 44
Dexter, Timothy (1748–1806) (merchant), waxworks of, 282
"Dexterity of Hand," 32, 127, 194, 389n46
"diagonal mirror" (viewing device), 68, 139–40, 164, 375
dialects, 51, 175
Dibdin, Charles (1745–1814) (British musician, dramatist, actor), 229, 420n9
Dickens, Charles (1812–1870) (author), 365
Dickerson, Mahlon (1770–1853) (N.J. governor, Secretary of Navy, diarist), 191
Dickinson [Dixon, Dickson], James A. (theater manager, actor), 74, 217, 229, 233, 421n17
Dickinson, Rebecca (1738–1815?) (seamstress, diarist), 222
Dickinson's tavern, Brattleboro, Vt., 80
Dick Wittington and His Cat (puppet show, traditional English story), 179
Distressed Mother, The [Philips] (play), 226
D'Obleville, Lawrence (dancing-master), 54
Dock Square, Boston, 17, 129, 239
Dodsley, Robert (1704–1814) (English author, publisher, playwright), 362
dogs, trained, 21, 28–32, 36, 52, 57, 105, 107–8, 115, 119, 147, 166, 406n65
Dolliver, Amelia (b. 1784) (sister of Peter, musician), 218
Dolliver, Caroline (b. 1783) (sister of Peter, musician), 218, 419n27
Dolliver, Charles Saunders (b. 1779) (brother of Peter, musician), 218
Dolliver, Peter (1777–1816) (musician), 218, 419n27
Donegani [Don Carlos, Don Pedro, Peter Cloris] (black acrobat, slack-wire performer, balance master, musician, singer), 56–58, 62, 86, 97, 235, 371
Don Pistole (puppet, Spanish pirate), 177–78
Doolittle, Abel B. (1786–1809) (engraver), 322
Doolittle, Amos (1754–1832) (engraver), 291–92
Dorchester, Mass., 216, 258, 426n50
Dorfeuille, Godfrey (language, penmanship teacher), 352
Doughty's long room, Charleston, 190
Douglas [Home] (play), 226
Douglass, David (1720–1786) (stage singer, actor), 72, 78, 226–27
Dover, England, 144, 149
Dover, N.H., 95, 103, 383
Dow, Lorenzo (1777–1834) (itinerant preacher), 249, 259, 266, 278
Doyle, Margaret G. (fl. 1820–1830) (daughter of William, miniaturist), 83–84

Doyle, William M. S. (1769–1828) (museum proprietor, artist): advertising by, 301, 305–6, 311, 325; casting in wax by, 302, 311, 313, 437n51; and Columbian Museum, 83, 371, 218, 276, 285, 300; as electrical healer, 429; self-portrait of, 277; sketch of Phillips's death by, 290; transparencies by, 290; waxworks of, 83, 218, 274, 276–77, 285, 300

Dozol, John (dancing-master), 247

drop curtains, 290, 292

Drury Lane, London, 54, 73, 227, 245

Dublin, Ireland, 18, 55, 153, 184–85, 343, 355, 359, 374, 401n2

Duboise, Charles Ame (automaton proprietor), 337–38

Dubuke, Dr. (alternative healer), 55, 63

Ducoing's long room, Norfolk, Va., 339

Duff, Mr. (slack-wire dancer, actor, lanternist), 167, 170

Dufief, Nicholas Gouin (1776?–1834) (language teacher), 367–68

Dugee, Anthony Joseph (acrobat), 56

Duhigg, O. (fl. 1792–1804) (dancing-master), 52, 243

"Duke" and "Dauphin" (characters in *Huckleberry Finn*), 3–4, 266

dulcimers, 87, 148, 158, 162, 274

Dumoulain, Mr. (acrobat), 153, 235

Dunlap, William (1766–1839) (historian, diarist, playwright, theater manager, painter): on artists, 306; panorama by, 368; as portrait painter, 22, 66; on theater, 132; travel of, 40; on Wrifford, 22, 348; on Yeldall, 26, 86

Duplessis's long room, Philadelphia, 184, 359, 414n74

Du Poke, Mr. (dancing, French, and fencing teacher), 54

Duport, Mr. (dancing-master), 246

Durand, of Dauphiné (Huguenot refugee, diarist), 18, 135

Durand, John (1731–1805) (artist), 308–9

Durang, Catharine (sister of John, wife of Charles Busselot), 143

Durang, Charles (1796–1870) (son of John, actor, dancing-master, theater historian), 92

Durang, Ferdinand (c. 1785–1831) (son of John, actor), 92

Durang, John (1768–1822) (stage dancer, equestrian, artist, diarist): 12, 23–24, 143, 166, 170, 183, 234; on Albany crowds, 148; on Blanchard, 405n48; camera obscura of, 437n6; early career of, 90; on Maginnis, 181, 412n34; ombres chinoises of, 143; on Roussell, 90; self-portraits, 90–91, 231; on Templeman, 24, 387–88n20; travel of, 39, 41

Durang, Mary McEwen (wife of John, actress), 58, 92

"Durang's Hornpipe" (dance), 90–91, 231

Durant, Charles S. (c. 1805–1873) (balloonist), 366

Dusolla, Mr. (fireworks artist), 54, 142

Dutch: 32, 49–51, 85, 128, 160, 200, 266, 274, 336; church, 240, 370; culture, 47–48; rope-dancers, 19

Duval, Mr. (balloonist), 144–45

Duvivier, F., and Son (profilists), 47

Dwight, Timothy (1752–1817) (college president), 254, 397n54

Dwyer, Mr. (actor), 356

Dyer, John (cloth-dresser, waxworks exhibitor), 274, 283, 285, 375

Eager's Tavern, Boston, 265

Eagle Tavern [Baird's], Albany 42

Eagle Tavern, Richmond, Va., 139

Earl, Ralph (1751–1801) (artist): 37, 44, 86, 291–92, 303, 432n8, 434n9; admission charged by, 291–92

Earle, Alice M. (1851–1911) (antiquarian), 11, 393n32

East Berkshire, Vt., 351

East Hampton, N.Y., 253, 311

East Haven, Conn., 64, 274, 281, 366

Easton, Md., 64, 102, 341

East Windsor, Conn., 138, 263

Edwards, Rev. Timothy (1669–1758) (minister, diarist), 203

Edwards, William (bookseller), 252

electrical cures, 5, 374

electrical demonstrators: 6, 64, 75, 156, 158, 250–51, 298, 328, 332, 375; multitalented, 267–68; reception of, 248; venues for, 156. *See also individual electrical demonstrators*

electrical experiments, 32, 66, 71, 171, 251–52

"electrical fire," 248–51, 267, 428n76

electrical healers: 23, 44, 66, 171, 265–68, 298, 321, 372, 374, 378, 429n86; ethnicity of, 35; numbers of, 34, 267. *See also individual electrical healers*

electrical lecturers: 44–45, 95, 168, 250–51, 325, 372; ethnicity of, 35; numbers of, 34, 251, 267. *See also individual electrical lecturers*

electrical machines, 7, 95, 249–50, 267–68, 285, 424–25n4, 429nn85, 88

elephants, 129, 151, 295, 380. *See also* Crowninshield elephant; Old Bett

Eliot, Rev. Jacob (1700–1766) (minister, diarist), 128, 255, 257
Elizabethtown, Md., 205
Elizabethtown, N.J., 70, 146
elk, 129
Elliott, Mr. (conjurer), 183
Emery, Sarah Smith (1787–1879) (author), 138, 150
employment, difficulties of, 22, 199, 217, 306
English grammar instruction, 49, 67, 81, 204, 210–11, 350, 367, 378
English language, 10, 48–49, 51, 67
Enstone, Edward (organist, dancing-master), 238–39
entertainers: imitations by servants and children of, 138, 148, 194–95; language and jargon of, 193; married, 19, 84, 92, 135, 183–85, 303, 413n48
entertainments: Italian, 226–27; miniaturizing of, 158–59
"Equestrian Pantheon," 153
equestrians: 20, 73, 150, 153, 233; ethnicity of, 35; named, 41, 135, 142, 149, 153–55, 234, 356, 366; numbers of, 34. *See also individual equestrians*
Erie Canal, 366, 368
Essex County, England, 69
Essex County, Mass., 221
Essom, Thomas (singing master), 209
Esterly, George (concert garden manager), 166, 388
Exchange Coffee House, Boston (coffeehouse, hotel), 290–91, 295, 434n1
Exchange Coffee House, Providence, 183
Exeter, England 73
Exeter, N.H., 43, 45, 47, 156, 221, 246
Expositor; or Many Mysteries Unraveled, The [Pinchbeck], 28, 116, 343, 402n19

"Fair Arithmetician" (automaton), 334, 343
Fairbanks, Jason (1780–1801) (murderer), waxworks of, 280–82
fairgrounds: 9–10, 377; London, 1, 54, 172, 186, 225, 283, 362; Scottish, 186
"Fair Rosamond," 1. *See also Tragedy of Fair Rosamond, The*
fairs: American, 69–70, 179, 365; European, 25, 80, 355. *See also* street fairs; *individual fairs*
Falconi, Joseph (fl. 1785–1819) (showman, automaton exhibitor, conjurer, electrical demonstrator): advertisements by, 86; automatons of, frontispiece, 106, 115, 330–32, 338, 429n88, 440n7; electrical demonstrations of, 71, 251, 267, 332, 429nn 86, 88, 441n13; and "Le Pont Cassé," 166; ombres chinoises of, 218; optical machines of, 171, 372; rhetoric of, 68; science lectures of, 23; speaking figure of, 341; tour of, 330–32, 372, 440n6, table 19.1; venues of, 191; woodcuts of, 106, 115
Fales, Elizabeth (1782–1801) (murder victim), waxworks of, 280–82
"Famous American Game Chicken" (prizefighter), 357–58
Faneuil Hall, Boston, 250, 425n14
"Fantoccini" (marionettes), 181, 183–84
Farmer's Inn [Lewis], 29
Faulks, Mr. (equestrian), 135, 148
Fawkes, Guy (1570–1606) (Gunpowder Plot conspirator), 288–89
Fawkes, Pinchbeck, and Terwin's Great Theatrical Booth, 177
Federal Street Theatre, Boston, 73, 74, 90, 233
fencing, 54, 62, 101, 106
fencing-masters: 8, 48, 74, 106, 143, 156, 161, 239–40, 351, 358; ethnicity of, 35; numbers of, 34, 54, 62. *See also individual fencing-masters*
Fenton, Jotham (optical lens maker, museum operator), 316
fiddlers: 4, 18, 215, 218, 220, 223; servant, 237, 379, 423n8. *See also* violinists
Field, John (multiracial ventriloquist, musician), 222
Fielding, Henry (1707–1754) (novelist, playwright), 178. *See also* Nash, Madame de la
finishing schools, 74, 215, 283
fireworks: 6, 20, 32, 127, 180, 193, 375; advertisements for, 82; cost of admission to, 139, 141–42; music accompaniment for, 218; programs of, 5, 127, 139–42; subscriptions for, 139, 141; suppliers of 54, 140; venues for, 71, 139, 141–42, 149
fireworks artists: 8, 74, 108, 139, 141–42, 335; ethnicity of, 35, 54, 139, 374; numbers of, 34, 54; and other entertainments, 23, 62, 142, 153, 155, 217, 336. *See also individual fireworks artists*
First Baptist Church, Boston, 311
Fissour, Felix (fireworks artist), 54, 82, 127, 139, 151
flower-making, 5, 78, 396n45
flower painting, 368
Folhaber, Jost (peddler), 252
folklore, 159, 284, 298, 361
Folwell, Samuel (1764–1813) (artist), 47
Fontaine, F. (fireworks artist, musician), 142
Forbes, Harriette Merrifield (1856–1951) (author, photographer), 11

foreign language: lessons, 6, 72, 374; methods of teaching, 367–68; subscriptions for instruction, 79; teachers, 34–35. *See also* individual languages
"Fortunate Lady" (automaton), 337–38
fortune-tellers, 32, 59, 67, 93, 393n32
Forty Thieves (opera), 119, 132, 381
Foss's tavern, Portsmouth, N.H., 251
Foster, Hannah Webster (1759–1840) (author), 242
Fowler, Orson Squire (1809–87) (phrenologist), 369
franchises, 96, 204, 264, 318, 322, 353, 367–68
Francis, Mr. (dancing-master), 186, 247
Francisquy, Signior [Francisqui, Jean-Baptist] (equestrian, dancer, pantomimist), 154, 234
Franconi, Mr. [Antonio] (1737–1836) (equestrian acrobat), 138
Frankfort, Ky., 36, 356
Franklin Institute, Philadelphia, 339, 351
Fraunces Tavern, New York City, 244, 422n36
Frazier, Ignatius Curley (fl. 1797–1814) (dancing-master), 242, 423n14
Freake limner (seventeenth-century artist), 308
Fredericksburg, Va., 12, 62, 140, 179, 243
Fredericktown, Md., 118, 171, 337–38
French language, 48, 51, 72, 74, 216, 242–43, 355, 367–68, 374, 378
French Revolution, 20, 48, 167, 170, 280, 285. *See also* Louis XVI
Fretzel, Johannes H. (runaway servant, alternative healer, preacher), 266
Frye's Tavern, Salem, Mass., 138
Fuller, J. (physiognotrist, inventor), 321–23
Fuller, Mr. (singing master), 207

Galliard, Johann Ernst (c. 1687–1749) (composer), 226, 228
Gamble, Richard (runaway, conjurer), 150
Gardie, Anna (stage dancer, ballerina), 243, 395n25
Gardiner, Maine, 45
Gardiner, Peter (puppeteer), 179
Gardner, Christopher H. (equestrian), 54, 356
Garnet, Horatio (musician, teacher), 217, 220
Garrick, David (1717–1779) (actor, playwright), 229
Garvin, Donna-Belle (historian), 11, 70, 435n12
Garvin, James (historian), 12, 70
Gatty, Signior (fireworks artist), 54
Genius of America (afterpiece), 235
Gentilcore, David (historian), 10
Georgetown, Md., 24, 47, 118, 214, 243, 292, 320
German language, 9, 51

Germany, 18, 20, 49, 52, 55, 63, 82, 335, 339, 359–60, 374
Gervaise, Louise (dancing-mistress), 58
Gibbes, Joseph (English puppeteer), 72, 179, 227, 363
Gilley, W. B. (publisher), 170
Ginzburg, Carlo (historian), 10
Glasgow, Scotland, 55, 186
Glastonbury, Conn., 43
Gloucester, Mass., 183, 220, 296, 376
Godeau, Monsieur (rope dancer), 139, 153
Godeau and Blanchard's Circus, 88
Godfrey, Ezra (sculptor), 312
Godwin, James (theater company manager), 165
Golden Ball Inn [Ammidon's, Snow's], Providence, 43, 292
Goodwin, Edwin Weyburn (1800–1845) (painter), 93
Gorée Island, Senegal, 110, 113, 232
Goshen, Conn., 71, 284
Goudal, Miss (miniature painter), 58
Gould, N. D. (penmanship and music school teacher), 350
Gouraud, Francis Fauvel (1808–1847) (daguerreotype expert), 369
Graffam's tavern, Portland, 132
Graham, Dr. James (1745–1794) (alternative healer, medical imposter), 68, 74–75, 263, 266–67
Grainger, Samuel (dancing-master, school teacher), 239
Granary, Boston, 129
"Grand Caravan of Living Animals," 151–52
Grandfather Was Queer: Early American Wags and Eccentrics [Wright], 11
"Grand Panorama View of the Town of Providence" [Worrall] (painting), 292
Grant, Primus (servant or slave, musician), 221
Grant's Tavern, Baltimore, 71
Gras, Mr. (fencing teacher), 106
Graupner, Catherine Comerford Hillier (1773–1821) (wife of Johann, musician), 216–17, 232
Graupner, Gottlieb (1767–1836) (musician, composer, educator, music store proprietor): 215, 217, 395n25, 418n14; music store of, 74, 142, 216
Graupner, Johann (c. 1767–1836) (musician), 216
Great Awakening revival, 255–56
"great culture," 9, 283, 376–77
Greek language, 10
Green, Dr. (English mountebank), 261–62
Green, Mr. (puppeteer), 193, 364
Greene, Robert (1558?–1592) (English author), 361, 385n2

Greene's Lane, Boston, 144
Greenfield, Mass., 284, 420n35
Greenleaf, Benjamin (1769–1821) (portrait painter), 305
Greenwood, Ethan Allen (1779–1856) (painter, museum proprietor, physiognotrist, diarist): 44, 424n1; on a Baptist itinerant, 427n54; circuit of, 44; on painting the dead, 303; as physiognotrist, 322; as portrait painter, 304–5; waxworks museums of, 67, 96, 275, 376
Greenwood, Isaac (1730–1803) (entertainer, surgeon-dentist, electrical mechanic), 251, 265, 429n86
Greenwood's Gallery of Fine Arts, 290
Griffiths, John (fl. 1783–1810) (dancing-master): 21, 387n11; advertising by, 54, 75, 245; circuit of, 21–22, 42–45, 240, 242–44, 372, 387n12, 390n23, table 2.1; later career of, 372; tenures of, 243–44
"Grimacer" (an entertainment), 27, 334
Grimaldi, Joseph (1778–1837) (English actor, dancer), 234
Grimm, Jacob Ludwig Carl (1785–1863) (German folklorist, philologist, author), 9, 377
Grimm, Wilhelm Karl (1786–1859) (German folklorist, philologist, author), 9, 377
Griscom, John (1774–1852) (physician, educator, chemist; nitrous oxide exhibitor), 379
Groton, Mass., 208, 246
Guey, Louis J. (fl. 1800–1808) (dancing-master), 244
Guide to Politeness, A [Nichols], 240, 424n32
Guild, James (1797–1844) (penmanship teacher, painter, diarist): 12, 373; early career of, 92–94, 349; as painter, 92–94, 350; as penmanship teacher, 18–19, 93–94, 349, 376
Guille, Louis Charles (French balloonist), 54, 151

Hacker's Assembly Room, Providence, 239
Hackley, Mr. [possibly Hackley, W.] (puppeteer), 181
Hackley, W. (conjurer, lanternist), 181, 183, 379
Haddock, Mr. (automaton exhibitor), 337
Hadley, Mass., 21, 25, 173, 194
Hagerstown, Md., 40, 131, 244
Hale, Moses (alternative healer), 266
Hale, Robert (1702–1767) (physician), 168–69
Halifax, Nova Scotia, 22, 45, 65, 129, 325
Hall, Daniel (penmanship teacher), 346
Hall, David D. (historian), 10, 96–97, 380, 480
Hall, Dr. (male midwife, museum proprietor), 46, 390n30
Hall, J. P., and Charity Shaw (pharmaceutical dispensers), 266

Hallam, Lewis (1714–1756) (actor, theater manager), 74, 90, 226
Hallowell, Maine, 45, 123, 209, 305, 383
Hamburg, Germany, 343, 355, 374
Hamilton, Dr. Alexander (1712–1756) (physician, author, diarist), 36, 97
Hamilton, Alexander (1755–1804) (U.S. Secretary of Treasury), 281
Hamilton, Bermuda, 372
Hamilton, "Charles" [alias Charlotte, Sarah Knox] (felon, indentured servant, imposter, mountebank), 261–62
Hamilton, J. (French language teacher), 367–68
Hamilton, James [alias John R. Bedford, G. Gallop] (imposter), 266–67
Hamilton, Thomas (1789–1842) (English writer), 254
Hampden Hall, New York City, 71, 183, 414n74
Hampton, Conn., 305
Hampton, N.H., 254
Hampton, Va., 265
Hancock, Rev. John (1671–1752) (minister), 318
Hancock, Mr. [Nathaniel] (c. 1785–1809) (miniature painter), 156
Hancock, Thomas (1703–1764) (son of Rev. John, merchant), 307–8, 436n32
handbills: 7, 12, 99, 107, 123, 143, 186, 230, 306, 415n17; Cressin, 219; Fowler, 369; King, 65; Letton, 86; Newel, 100; Salenka, 112, 115; Woods, 285; Wright and Brooks, 314–15
Handley, Michael (entertainer, apprentice), 25, 86, 358
Harding, Chester (1792–1866) (portrait painter, writer), 12, 67, 92, 310
Harlequin: actors, 62, 90, 92, 154, 227–29; appearance in America of, 225–26; birth stories of, 62, 229, 230; choreographed movements of, 228; costume of, 119, 228; pantomimes, 6, 92, 194, 227, 229–30, 232; tradition, English, 227–29; tunes, 228
harlequinades: 5, 58, 90, 225; American emphasis in, 232; decline of, 234; delay in arrival of, 245; dying and restoration scenes in, 230; growth in popularity of, 233; plots of, 230–32; stage tricks in, 226
"Harlequin and Columbine," 168, 194
Harlequin Balloonist; or, Pierrot in the Clouds (pantomime), 232
Harlequin Dr. Faustus (pantomime), 232
Harlequin genre, American disappearance of, 235–36
Harlequin Mungo; or, a Peep into the Tower (pantomime), 229, 231, 421n17

Harlequin Ranger (pantomime), 229–30
Harlequin Restored (pantomime), 231–32
Harlequin Salamander; or, the Humors of the Clown (pantomime), 234
Harlequin's Choice (pantomime), 234
Harlequin Shipwreck'd; or The Grateful Lion (pantomime), 232
Harlequin's Invasion [Garrick] (speaking pantomime), 229
Harlequin Skeleton: Or, the Miller Deceived (pantomime), 227
Harlequin's Release (pantomime), 232
Harlequin's Tour through the Continent of North America (pantomime), 232
Harmonia Evangelica [Wood], 208
Harper, Joseph (1759–1811) (theater manager, actor), 75, 144, 332
Harrington, E. (dancing-master), 80
Harrington, Mr. (acrobat, slack-wire performer, lanternist), 148, 157–58, 167, 179
Harris, John (fl. 1700–1726) (London puppeteer), 1, 175,
Harris, Mrs. (miniature painter), 58
Harris, Tim (historian), 6
Harrisburg, Penn., 55
Harrowgate Springs, Philadelphia (concert garden), 166, 378
Harvard College: 9, 97, 127, 202, 206, 241, 247; commencements, 81–82, 95, 122, 381; magic lantern at, 168–69
Hatfield, Mass., 222
Havana, Cuba, 110, 167, 373, 398n65, 409n39
Haven, Gilbert (profilist), 306, 323
Haverhill, Mass., 43, 45, 64, 80, 305, 309
Haverhill, N.H., 322
hawkers, 1, 252–55, 358
Hawkers and Walkers in Early America, 11
Hawkins, John Isaac (1772–1855) (physiognotrist, inventor): 212, 318; patent holders, 47, 318–20, 322, 325–28, 438n22; physiognotrace of, 211, 318–19, 321–22, 438n20
Hawthorne, Nathaniel (1804–1864) (writer), 365
Hayden, Miss (conjurer, magician), 366
Haymarket Theatre, Boston, 74, 140, 233, 413n54, 418n15
Hazard, Thomas Benjamin [Nailer Tom] (1756–1845) (carpenter, diarist), 149, 317
Hazard's Hotel, Albany, 83
healers, alternative: 1, 8, 18, 20–21, 25, 52, 260–68, 446n21; advertising by, 68, 77–79, 122, 267, 360–61; African American, 21, 31, 55; distrust of, 61, 85, 265; diversity of, 55–56; ethnicity of, 35; Native American: 52, 59, 76–77, 89–90, 265–66, 378; numbers of, 34, 55, 59; women, 59–60, 76–77, 89–90. *See also* electrical healers; mountebanks; seventh sons; *individual alternative healers*
Hebron, Conn., 43
Hempstead, Joshua (1678–1758) (diarist, carpenter, farmer, gravestone cutter, surveyor), 12, 60, 52, 69, 128–29, 274
Henninger, Jacob (puppeteer), 95, 180, 359, 364, 376
Henri, Peter [Pierre] (c. 1760–1822) (miniature painter), 72
hermit, 228 years of age, 356–57
Hervé, Henry (husband of Hervey, E., miniaturist, profilist), 82–85, 328
Hervey, Elizabeth (d. 1820) (wife of Hervé, H., albiness), 82, 83, 373, 381, 397n60, 398n65, 438n22
Hewes, George (tanner, animal exhibitor), 129
Hewett, Daniel (d. 1856) (penmanship teacher, author), 351
Hewett, Mrs. Daniel (writing teacher), 351
Hewitt, James (1770–1827) (musician, composer, publisher), 215–17, 223, 418n20
Hewitt, John Hill (1801–90) (son of James, musician, songwriter), 223–25
Hickox and Page, waxwork museum of, 296
Hidden's Tavern [James], Providence, 43, 100
Hill, Uri K. (1780–1844) (musician, engraver, music compiler, profilist), 210–12, 320, 324
Hiller, Abigail (wife of Joseph, school proprietress, waxworks exhibitor), 251, 283
Hiller, Joseph (jeweler, electrical exhibitor, waxworks exhibitor), 250–51, 425n14
Hilliard's tavern, Cambridge, Mass., 81, 397n57
Hingham, Mass., 131, 403n12
Historia von Doctor Johann Fausten [anonymous], 361
History of New York for Schools [Dunlap], 26
Hobart's tavern, Stonington, Conn., 129
Hodgson, John A. (historian), 11, 116, 413n54, 441n32
Hoechstaetter, John David [Johann] (carver, portrait painter), 312
Hogarth, William (1697–1764) (English artist), 136–37, 172, 177
Holbrook, Amos (grammar and singing teacher), 204
Holland, 20, 49, 52, 139, 285, 374. *See also* Netherlands, Kingdom of the
Holt, Henry (dancing-master), 225–26, 245
Holyoke, Rev. Edward (1689–1767) (minister, college president, diarist), 241
Holyoke, Edward Augustus (1728–1829) (son of Rev. Edward, physician, diarist), 24, 191, 242

Holyoke, Elizabeth [Betsy] (1771–1789) (daughter of Edward A., diarist), 190
Holyoke, Judith [Judy]. *See* Turner, Judith Holyoke
Holyoke, Margaret ["Peggy"] (1763–1825) (daughter of Edward A., diarist), 146–49, 155, 190–91, 241, 298, 383
Holyoke, Mary Vial (1737–1802) (wife of Edward A., diarist), 24, 190–91, 218, 298
Holyoke, Samuel Adams (1762–1820) (singing teacher), 80, 208–10
Holyoke, Susanna ["Sukey"]. *See* Ward, Susanna Holyoke
Holyoke family, 12, 149, 190, 283
Holyroyd, Mr. (penmanship and stenography teacher), 350
Home, John (1722–1808) (Scottish minister, playwright), 226
Honfleure, Mr. and Mrs. (decorative arts teachers), 368
Hopkins, John (d. 1570) (schoolteacher, rector, author), 201
Hopkinton, Mass., 52
Hopkinton, N.H., 373
Hornby, Dr. (surgeon-dentist, electrical healer), 265, 374
hornpipe (dance), 23, 30, 90–91, 153, 181–82, 184, 245, 335, 337
horse of knowledge (trained horse), 122–23
horseracing, 5, 11, 69, 71, 150
hotels, 18, 20, 49, 129, 139, 188, 192, 284, 335–36. *See also individual hotels*
Howard, John (alternative healer), 55–56
Howe, Dr. Martin (profilist, electrical healer, museum proprietor), 23, 321, 429n86
Howes, Nathan (elephant proprietor), 381, 383–84
Hoyt, Richard (puppeteer), 179
Hubbard's tavern, New Haven, 46
Hubbardston, Mass., 44, 303
Huckleberry Finn [Twain], 2–4, 266
Hudson, N.Y., 61, 103, 105, 207, 209, 221, 417n33, 444n18
Hudson River, 38, 42, 45, 48–49, 281, 349, 368
Hudson River Valley, 1, 19, 207, 244, 284, 381
Hulett, David D. (son of William, dancing-master), 240
Hulett, John Hamilton (d. c. 1811) (son of William, dancing-master), 240, 245–46,
Hulett, William C. (d. 1785) (musician and dancing-master), 74, 245
Huletts, 49
hurdy-gurdies, 222
Hurry-Scurry (pantomime), 234

Hutchens, Hezekiah (cotton dealer, amateur artist, panorama proprietor), 291
Hutchins, Master (acrobat, equestrian), 153
Huygens, Christiaan (1629–1695) (Dutch mathematician, scientist), 160
Hyde de Neuville, Anne-Marguerite-Henriette Rouillé de Marigny, baroness (d. 1849) (French artist), 286–87
Hymes, Henry (showman, lanternist), 74, 163–64, 170, 190, 218, 222

ichneumon (mongoose), 81–82, 152
images: accuracy of, 112–19; as advertising, 2, 99; deterioration of, 107, 109, 112; early, 99–100, 101–2, 401n2; English, 119, 122, 177, 401n2; engravers of, 105–6, 110; as "huckster" stratagems, 122; individualized, 106; owned by showmen, 106; as persuasion, 119, 123; placement of, 107, 110–12, 131; realism of, 112, 115–19; reuse of, 112; stock, 106–7, 115. *See also* woodcuts
imitations: of artwork, 298–99; of automatons, 341–43; chains of, 97–98, 376; and cultural movement, 166, 298, 376–78; as entertainment form, 97–98, 376; of woodcuts, 113–15
"impromptu fiddlers," 216
Indian Doctor's Dispensatory [Smith], 266
"Indian Oracle" (automaton), 343
"Infant Roscius, The" (stage artist), 218
information zones, 43–44
Inman, Henry (1801–1846) (artist), 93–94
inns, 70, 132, 156, 192, 284, 366, 377. *See also individual inns*
Introduction to the Singing of Psalm-Tunes [Tufts], 201
"Invisible Lady" ["Acoustic Temple," "Astonishing Invisible Lady," "Invisible Conversant," "Incomprehensible Crystal," "Invisible Woman"] (acoustical device), 28, 81, 86, 341–42, 442n43
Ipswich, Mass., 18, 156, 253, 255, 257, 328
Ireland, 20, 52, 55, 148, 195, 238, 259, 316, 374, 397n60
Irishmen, 32, 149, 190, 253, 413n47
Italian artists, 160–61, 280, 356, 360
Italian court society, 237
Italian language, 63, 374
Italian performers: 19, 22, 32–33, 42, 55–57, 64, 78, 86, 106, 127, 138–39, 141, 162, 180, 222, 234, 239, 247, 330, 372, 386n4; numbers of, 35, 54–55, 251, 272, 343
Italian Renaissance, 235
Italian shades ["Ombres Italianes"], 5, 158, 164, 166

Italy: itinerants' prior experience in, 56, 63, 192, 225, 308, 356, 374; as origin of some itinerants, 18, 20, 35, 52, 55, 127, 222. *See also individual itinerants*
itinerancy: and cultural dissemination, 369–70; liabilities of, 62; negative connotations of, 66–67; risks of, 22, 252
Itinerant Artist, The [King] (painting), 3
itinerants: American born, 52, 204, 362; antiestablishment aspects of some, 377–80; assumption of "American" characteristics by, 355–58; attitudes by tavern keepers toward, 70–72; as bearers of European arts, entertainments, and innovations, 32–33, 355; connection to Atlantic world of, 52, 373; criminal reputations of, 60–67; difficulty in finding acceptance of, 69–70, 364; diversity of, 22, 35, 52, 54–60; families of, 64–66; gifts of aid by, 74–75, 81, 151, 263–64, 359; handicapped, 19, 133, 212, 387n7; imitators of, 194–95; influx of, 20–21; and intersection with other cultural practices, 10, 199–200; later lives of, 370–73; laws suppressing, 32, 186, 254–55, 358, 389n46; lengths of stay of, 2, 75–76, 243–44; multiple callings of, 22–24, 64, 158, 170, 214, 217, 267, 359, 429n86; movement westward of, 2, 356, 366; national origins of, 35, 52–58, 374; nostalgic memories of, 2–3; numbers in early America of, 1–2, 34; professional language of, 193, 267; professional links of, 72–73; public distrust of, 61–62; reliance on broadsides and advertisements by, 99–102; reliance on printed words by, 68–70; and reluctance to teach their crafts, 85–86; repeat visits by, 42–43; stereotypes of, 24–32; strategies of, 74–80; and transfer of popular culture, 85–88, 96–98, 194–95, 373, 375–76; use of American nationality by, 356–58; use of Europe as cultural model by, 355; use of multiple names by, 56, 63, 261, 266–67; verbal fluency of, 193, 267; versatility of, 22–24; women, 58–60, 75, 76–79, 88, 183–86, 257, 261–62, 266, 366–67
itinerant vocations, English, 1, 389n46
itineraries. *See* tables 1.3, 1.4, 2.1, 3.1, 6.l, 6.2, 8.1, 9.1, 9.2, 15.1, 19.l, 19.2, and 20.1 on ScholarWorks website. *See also individual itinerants*
Ives, John H. (musician, music and dancing teacher), 74, 213–14, 217, 395n25
ivory turners, 64–65

jackals, 147, 406n59
Jackson, John (peddler), 267
Jacobs, Isaac (peddler), 253
Jacobs's long room [Jacob], Charleston, 70
Jacot, Madame (painter), 58
Jaffee, David (historian), 11
Jamaica, 52, 60, 188, 260, 262, 330, 335, 373
James River, 45
japanners, 20, 249, 396n45
Jaquet-Droz, Henri-Louis (1752–1791) (Swiss clock and automaton maker), 329, 341, 441n24
Jaquet-Droz, Pierre (1721–1790) (Swiss clock and automaton maker), 329, 341, 441n24
Jarvis, John Wesley (1780–1840) (painter, profilist), 311, 320
Jefferson Hall, Portsmouth, N.H., 392
Jeffries, John (1745–1819) (physician, balloonist), 144, 149
Jenkins, John (1755–1823) (penmanship teacher, author): circuit of, 346, 349–50; declining business of, 349–50; early career of, 345–46; imitators of, 347, 350, 352, 354; instruction manual by, 345–46, 350; personal life of, 345, 443n2; and rivalry with Wrifford, 347–48; teaching method of, 345, 350, 354
Jennys, Richard (c. 1734–after 1809) (father of William, painter), 308
Jennys, William (1774–1859) (painter, profilist), 304, 308, 323, 328, 376
jesters, 18, 135, 374
Joan [Judy] (Punch's wife), 159, 175, 177, 226, 362, 364, 375
Joan, James [Juhan] (d. 1797) (singer, musician, dancing and French teacher, instrument salesman), 5, 22
John Sheppard, or Harlequin in Newgate (pantomime), 235
Johnson, Ben (1572–1637) (playwright), 1
Johnson, C. (London engraver), 275
Johnson, George Washington (diarist), 304
Johnson, J. [or Johnston] (fl. 1799–1818) (dancing-master), 41–42, 49–51, 391n44
Johnson, Jesse and Elizabeth (parents of George W., Jenny's sitters), 304
Johnson, Miss (drawing and embroidery teacher), 49
Johnson, William (electrical demonstrator, author), 251, 425n15
Johnston, Mr. (acrobat, high-wire acts), 184
John Street Theatre, New York City, 378
Jones, Dr. (nitrous oxide exhibitor), 379
Jones, F. P. (profilist), 318
Jones, Ichabod (itinerant preacher, vagrant), 258–59, 267, 427n52
Jones, J. (acrobat, singer, actor), 87, 233, 235

Jones, Dr. John (itinerant preacher, vagrant), 259
Jones, Master (son of Jones, J., singer), 87
Jones's Tavern, New Bern, N.C., 102
Jonotty, Dominic (puppeteer, acrobat, Chinese shades exhibitor), 180, 218
Jordan, Samuel (1803–after 1835) (painter), 305, 308–9, 310, 435n14
jugglers, 1, 8, 19, 55, 67–68, 97, 119, 148, 365
juggling, 86, 98, 195

Kallanbach, F. H. (automaton exhibitor), 337
kangaroos, 130
Katritzky, M. A. (British historian), 10
Kearney, F[rancis]. (1785–1837) (artist, engraver), 300
Keene, N.H., 46, 76, 147, 383
Keisselbach, George (physician, oculist), 72
Keller, Kate van Winkle (dance historian), 11, 13, 56, 220
Kendall, Edward Augustus (1776?–1842) (English author), 38
Kentucky, 36, 92, 204, 255, 259, 356, 372, 376
Keyes, Homer Eaton (1875–1938) (antiquarian, writer, professor), 65
Kidd, Mr. (actor, theater manager), 165
Kidder, James (1776–1852) (artist, museum proprietor), 294–95, 298, 371
Kilby, Christopher (1705–1771) (colony agent), 307–8
Kimberly, Mr. (dancing-master), 79
King, Charles Bird (1785–1862) (artist), 2–3
King, Daniel (electrical demonstrator), 249
King, Nathaniel Phippen (1796–1819) (son of William, Sr., cabinetmaker), 66
King, Rebecca Phippen (wife of William, Sr.), 64, 66, 394n46
King, Thomas (tenant of Burlesson), 174
King, William, Jr. (c. 1788–1809) (son of William, Sr., profilist), 65–66, 373
King, William, Sr. (1754–after 1825) (profilist, cabinetmaker, ivory turner, electrical lecturer and demonstrator): advertising of, 123, 322, 325; as cabinetmaker, 64, 322, 372; career of, 64–65; circuit of, 65–66, table 3.1; and Corné's panorama, 66, 292–93, 298; marriage of, 64, 394n46; as medical electrician, 66, 267, 328, 372, 449n87; as profilist, 52, 65, 322–23, 376, 438n29, 439n37
King's Arms Tavern, Boston, 135
King's Chapel, Boston, 238
Kingsley, Bathsheba (d. 1748) (itinerant preacher), 257
King's Theatre, London, 54

Kingston, Jamaica, 262, 330
Kingston, New York, 66, 207, 449n87
Kinnersley, Ebenezer (1711–1778) (electrical lecturer, researcher), 168, 248, 250–51
Kircher, Athanasius (1602–1680) (Jesuit polymath, inventor), 160, 162
Kreutzinger Joseph (1757–1829) (Austrian artist, engraver), 272–73, 280
Kyle, Joseph (1815–1863) (artist), 276

Labarre, Trille (1758–1797) (music academy teacher, composer), 74, 217
Lablond's tavern [Anne], 260–61
Labottiere, George (dancing and fencing teacher), 240, 245–46, 364
Lailson, Philip (equestrian, circus proprietor), 87, 140, 149, 154–55, 356
Lake Champlain, 41, 130, 403n11
Lambert, Barbara (music historian), 11
Lambert, Daniel (1770-1809) (animal breeder, jail keeper, celebrity), 278, 285–87
Lancaster, Mass., 243
Lancaster, Penn., 131
Lancon, Mr. (dancing-master), 47
Lane, Isaac (1766–1803) (singing master, psalmodist, composer), 208, 210, 417n36
"Lanechtskipt," 128, 173, 403n5
Lang, Mr. (panorama proprietor), 96
Langdon, John (shopkeeper, retailer of magic lanterns), 170
Langley, Mr. (equestrian), 154, 356
Lansingburgh, N.Y., 49, 244
lanternists. *See* magic lanternists; *individual magic lantern performers*
Large, Mr. (dancing-master), 243
Latin, 9
Law, Andrew (1749–1821) (psalmodist, publisher), 40, 204, 210, 415–16n17
"Learned Pig, The" (song), 148
Learned Pig, The (trained pig), 29, 31, 78, 95, 105, 334, 376
Leaumont, R. (pianist, French language and dancing teacher), 74, 217, 395n25
Leavenworth, Major, stable of, 107, 130-31
Lebanon, Conn., 257
Lebanon, N.H., 381
Lebanon, N.Y., 284
lecturers: with magic lanterns, 159-60, 164, 168; on science, 2, 19, 380, 387, 437n47. *See also individual lecturers and electrical lecturers*
Lee, N.H., 89
Leeds, Titan (1699-1738) (almanac publisher), 69
Leeward Islands, 172, 373

Leffler, Christopher (surgeon), 262
Legé, Mr. (ballet master, dancing school proprietor), 74, 234, 395–96n25
legerdemain, 8, 149–50, 158, 175, 183, 190, 193, 413n47. *See also* sleight of hand
Legg, John (d. 1733) (merchant), 363
Leicester, England, 285
Leicester, Mass., 317
Lemet, Louis (c. 1779–1832) (profilist), 318
Lenox, Mass., 284
Leonard, Daniel H. (1783–1837) (penmanship teacher, pharmaceutical merchant), 96, 351–53, 400n42
leopards: 95, 99–100, 129–30, 132, 134
letters of reference, 19, 76, 78
Letton, Ralph (1778–c. 1836) (profile taker, waxworks and museum proprietor): advertisements of, 76, 107; circuit of, 46, 372, 390n30; waxworks of, 77, 272, 274
Lewis, Capt. Meriwether (1774–1809) (American explorer), 191
Lexington, Ky., 92, 102, 188, 233, 243, 356
Lexington, Mass., 292, 366
Life and Death of Harlequin (pantomime), 230, 422n35
Life and Surprizing Adventures of James Wyatt, The [Wyatt], 178
likenesses, wax, 302, 311–13
"Lilliputian Cobler" (automaton), 334
limners, 12, 47, 70, 75, 308, 312
lion, African: 107, 119, 152, 232; images of, 110–15; itinerary of, 401–2n14, table 6.2
lions, 82, 128–29, 134, 147, 167, 173, 402–3n3, 406n60
Litchfield, Conn., 67, 71, 131, 213, 244, 284, 359
Little African Theatre, 146
Little Compton, R.I., 262
"little culture," 9–10, 211, 377
"Little Magician . . . of the Turkish type" (automaton), 339–40
llama, 152
Lockwood, Edward (alternative healer), 266
Long Island, 38, 128, 253, 255, 262, 311
Long Island Sound, 38, 43–44, 60, 284
long rooms, 71, 156, 159, 183. *See also individual long rooms*
Louis, Dr. (alternative healer, mountebank), 55, 63, 374
Louisburgh, S.C., 165
Louisiana, 19, 305
Louisiana Purchase, 356, 374
Louis XVI (1754–1793) (King of France), 81, 142, 213, 276, 278, 280–81
Lovet's Hotel, New York City, 186

Lowell, Mass., 42
Lun, Mr. *See* Rich, John
Luscombe, Capt. Humphrey (d. 1688) (a founder of King's Chapel, Boston), 238
Lyceum Hall, Salem, Mass., 367
lyceum movement, 366
lyceums, 335
Lynde, Benjamin, Jr. (1700–1781) (justice, diarist), 189
Lyon, Emanuel (peddler), 253

MacDonald, Master (actor, acrobat, slack-wire performer), 153
Madeira, 130
"Mademoiselle Moderate" ["Wonderful Woman"] (automaton), 333
Maelzel, John [Johann N.] (1772–1838) (musician, inventor, automaton exhibitor), 337, 344
magic, 19, 23, 194–95, 232–33, 340, 366
"magic inkhorn" (a deception), 86
magic lanternists: ethnicity of, 35; numbers of, 34, 164. *See also individual lanternists*
magic lanterns: academic uses of, 159–60, 168, 410n47; for children and juveniles, 169; for entertainment, 159–64, 166–68; in Europe, 160, 408n21; influence of, 170; invention of, 160; names of, 160, 163–64; North American use of, 158–60, 170; retail sales of, 169–70; subjects shown by, 161–68; with other entertainments, 159, 170–71
magic lantern shows: cost of admission to, 159–60; duration of, 159; historical subjects of, 163, 167; musical accompaniment for, 162–63, 165–66, 218; in theaters, 166
magic lantern slides: for children and juveniles, 161; of current events, 163, 167–68; Italian, 160, 161, 163, 168; maritime scenes of, 167; packaged sets of, 167; religious subjects of, 163, 167
Magic on the Early English Stage [Butterworth], 19
Maginnis, Mrs. James (wife of Samuel, puppeteer, actress, singer), 58
Maginnis, Samuel Jameson [James] (c. 1772–1805) (puppeteer, magic lanternist, actor, singer): 18, 22–23, 52, 56, 97, 166, 412n34, 422n35; automatons of, 181, 335; and "Children in the Wood," 182, 362–63, 447n39; death of, 181, 371–73; itinerary of 387n18, table 9.1; lantern shows of, 167, 218; puppetry of, 28, 181–82, 364, 371–72, 376
Magos, Sal (b. c. 1778) (biracial herb seller, fortune-teller), 59
Maillardet, Henri (1745–1830) (Swiss clock and automaton maker), 329, 337, 341, 344, 441n24

Maine, 112, 186, 222, 254, 303, 369, 383–84. *See also* Maine cities and towns
Maison, John (automaton showman), 68, 81, 191, 333–34, 348
Mallet, François (d. 1834) (musician, teacher, vocalist), 216–17, 435n26
mammoth hog, 122, 124
Manfredi, Catherina (daughter of Manfredi, acrobat), 153
Manfredi, Luisa (daughter of Manfredi, acrobat), 153
Manfredi, Mr. [Signior] (ropedancer, acrobat), 138, 153–54, 235
Manfredi, Mrs. (wife of Manfredi, acrobat), 153
Manhattan, N.Y., 80
Manigault, Ann Ashby (d. 1782) (wife of Gabriel, diarist), 190
Manly, J. (miniature painter, profilist, engraver), 95–96, 316–17, 376
Mann, Dr. (physician, naturalist, antiquarian, profilist), 317
manners, schools of, 49, 64, 237, 239, 244, 364. *See also* polite arts, schools of
Marat, Jean-Paul (1743–1793) (physician, politician), 285
Marlowe, Christopher (1564–1593) (English playwright, poet), 361
Martin, Mr. (acrobat, conjurer, fireworks artist, automaton exhibitor): 57–58, 62, 97; automatons of, 336, 343–44; as "Little Devil," 57; sale of equipment by, 376, 393n37; tour of, 335, table 19.2
Martinique, 66, 86, 356, 366
Martling's long room, New York City, 334
Marycoo, Occramer [Newport Gardner] (1746–1826) (singing master, composer), 210
Maryland City, Md., 36
masks, 226, 311–12, 363–64
Mason, David, Jr. (1726–1794) (son of David, Sr., japanner, painter, electrical demonstrator, lecturer), 249, 251
Mason, David, Sr. (1703–1746) (upholsterer), 251
Mason, George (d. 1773) (pastelist), 70, 307, 312
Mason, N.H., 208
Masons, Brotherhood of, 64, 184–85, 192, 247, 312
masquerade: assemblies and balls, 363–64, 447n42; characters, 179, 227, 235; entertainments, 225, 233
Mather, Rev. Cotton (1663–1728) (minister, author), 201–2
Mather, Rev. Increase (1639–1723) (minister, author, college president), 238
Maudlin, the Merchant's Daughter of Bristol (English legend, ballad, puppet show), 362

Maverick, Peter (1780–1831) (engraver), 105–6, 346, 401n7
May, Mrs. (puppeteer), 167, 178
Mayfair, London, annual fair at, 69
Mayhew, Frederick (1785–1854) (portraitist), 76
Maynard's tavern [John], Westborough, Mass., 173, 189
McClure, Rev. David (1748–1820) (minister, diarist), 138
McDonald, John (acrobat, journeyman), 25–26, 86, 358, 388n35, 398n10
McDonald, John (runaway apprentice), 87, 398n10
McIntire, James (peddler), 267
McLean, John (watchmaker), 56
McPharlin, Paul (puppeteer, author), 11
Medford, Mass., 42, 60, 216
Medical Charlatanism in Early Modern Italy [Gentilcore], 10
medical electricians. *See* electrical healers
medieval period, 7, 10, 12, 22, 25, 138, 266, 358, 365–66, 428n84, 447n41
Meigs, Josiah (1757–1822) (city clerk, publisher, college president, balloonist), 149
memory: collective, 358, 374; common, 11, 360; cultural, 193–94, 358–64, 366, 374; living, 162
menageries: 116, 129, 151, 366; proprietors of, 34–35, 151, 284
Mera, Lewis (glass spinner, magic lanternist), 170
Merchants' Hall, Boston, 106, 296
Merrill, Isaac W. (1803–1879) (diarist), 304–5, 308–10, 435n14, 436n39
Merrimack River, 45
Merry-Andrews, 6, 26, 78, 81
"Metallic Points" ["Metallic Tractors"], 67, 263–64, 428n75
Mexico, 106, 278, 330, 373
Meyere, Camou (automaton proprietor), 86, 335
Michel, M. (balloonist), 151
"Microcosm," 75, 222–23
microscopes, 5, 11
Middlebury, Vt., 94, 209, 349, 376
Middletown, Conn., 38, 43, 46, 58, 61, 185, 263, 357, 359
Milledgeville, Ga., 372, 376
Mills, Miss A. R. (conjurer), 367
Milns, William (1761–1801) (penmanship teacher), 372, 376
Milton, Mass., 216, 246
mimics: 11, 34–35, 87, 97–98; automaton, 329
Minasi, James Anthony (1776–1865) (engraver), 272–73
ministers, itinerant, 255–60
Mississippi, 19, 67

Mississippi River, 2, 4, 366, 368–69, 372, 385n9
Mix, John (museum and automaton proprietor), 144–45, 280, 282, 285–87, 296, 298, 342
models, scale, 5, 71, 156
Magos, Sal (biracial herb seller, fortune-teller), 59
monkeys, 123, 146–47, 152, 160, 218–19
Monstrous Sea Serpent (panorama), 296
Montaes, John [Jerome or J. Montas] (dancing-master), 64
Montpelier, Vt., 351
Montreal, Canada, 41, 96, 139, 156, 294, 328, 342, 376, 394n54
Moodey, Rev. Joshua (1633–1697) (minister), 238
Moody's Tavern, Albany, 245
Moore, Ann (1761–1813) ("Fasting Woman," imposter), 283, 431n28
Moore, John (wine merchant), 72, 179
Moore, William (peddler), 254
moose, 129
Morgan, William Sampson (dancing-master, musical entrepreneur, actor), 62, 227, 245
Moscow in Flames (transparency), 290
Mosely, Richard (puppeteer), 159–60, 176–78, 190, 407–8n5, 447n41
Mother Goose; or, The Birth and Adventures of Harlequin (pantomime), 230
Moulthrop, Reuben (1763–1814) (artist, wax-work modeler and proprietor): as artist, 279, 437n51; itinerary of, 284, 431n36, table 15.1; waxworks of, 81, 156, 213, 274–76, 279, 281–82, 284–85, 293, 363, 376
mountebanks: 1, 2, 6, 8, 10, 68–69, 79, 81, 119, 138, 150, 161–62, 168, 266, 375, 397n59; ethnicity of, 35, 55; laws restricting, 32, 358, 389n46; numbers of, 34; specialized, 262. *See also* healers, alternative; *individual mountebanks*
moving pictures ["tableaux animes"], 32, 183, 389n46
"Mr. Aristocrat" (automaton), 333
"Mr. Maccabee" (automaton), 115, 330–32, 338, 372, 440n7
Mullert, L. (German acoustical device entrepreneur), 339
Mungo (theatrical character), 229
music, American appreciation of, 214, 222–24
musicians: of color, 220–22; for dances, 210, 218, 220–21, 224; for dancing academies, 218, 220; and music-machine operators, 222; part-time, 215; range of, 215, 218, 220; reliance on itinerancy of, 215–16; self-taught, 205, 212. *See also* dancing instruction: music for; *individual musicians*

musicians, professional: dependence on popular entertainments by, 213–15, 217–18; in early America, 215–18. *See also individual musicians*
music machines: 160–61, 222, 249, 360, 365; operators of, 34–35, 222

Nadau, Monsieur (dancing teacher), 72, 242–43
Nairne patent device, 267–68, 429n87
Nanterre, France, 18
Nantucket, Mass., 80, 278, 293, 352–53, 397n53
Naples, Italy, 66, 97, 298, 330
Narragansett Bay, 43
Narragansett Sound, 284
Narrative of the Life, Adventures, Travels and Sufferings of Henry Tufts [Tufts], 89
Nash, Madame de la (English puppeteer), 175, 178. *See also* Fielding, Henry
Nashua, N.H., 42
Nashville, Tenn., 64
Natchez, Miss., 188, 376
Native American: acrobats, 56; animal handlers, 133–34; healers and medical remedies, 59, 76, 89–90, 265–66, 378, 428n81; instrumentalists, 220–21; itinerant ministers, 257; peddlers, 253. *See also individual Native Americans*
Native Americans: 19, 35, 52, 267; as pantomime characters, 232, 421n25; waxworks of, 213, 279, 289
Natural History of Norway [Pontopiddan], 296–97
Nature Displayed, in Her Mode of Teaching Language to Man [Dufief], 367
Needham, Dr. (English transient healer), 427n60
Negro, Flora (b. 1723) (slave, itinerant minister), 257
"Negro Boy, The" (minstrel melody), 216
Nelson, Mr. (sign, ornamental, and portrait painter), 92
Nesbet, William (black acrobat), 56
Netherlands, Kingdom of the, 52, 215, 325
networks, informal, welcoming itinerants, 70–73
Neuchâtel, Switzerland, 58, 337, 341, 441n24
Newark, N.J., 71, 171, 205, 214, 266, 379
New Assembly Room, New York City, 216
New Assembly Room, Portland, 58
New Assembly Room, Salem, 242
New Bedford, Mass., 48, 76, 118, 187, 215, 259, 293, 322–23, 352, 367
New Bern, N.C., 47, 102, 372, 401n5
"New Booth," Society Hill, Philadelphia, 58, 136
New Brunswick, N.J., 71, 214
Newbury, Mass., 10, 148, 201

Newbury, Vt., 373
Newburyport, Mass., selectmen, 138, 150
New Castle, Penn., 70
Newel, Christopher (animal proprietor), 100
New England Psalm Singer: or, American Chorister, The [Billings], 205
New Exchange, New York City, 156
New Exhibition Room, Boston, 75
Newfane, Vt., 181
New Haven selectmen, 239
New Lebanon, N.Y., 49, 284
Newman, Margaret (importer, retailer of toys), 170
New Milford, Conn., 204
New Orleans, La., 88, 110, 139, 188, 243, 266, 305, 366, 376
New Roman Museum, New York City, 360
New South Church, Boston, 205
newspaper editors, on itinerants, 63–64, 67, 148, 248, 253, 332, 360
New Version of the Psalms of David [Tate and Brady], 201
New York City waterfront, 190, 194
Niagara Falls, 86, 291, 368–69
Niblo's Gardens, New York City, 368
Nichols, Francis D. (dancing-master, author), 240, 247, 424n32
Nichols, Jonathan (singing master), 205
Nichol's Long Room, Middletown, Conn., 185, 414n74
nitrous oxide, 379–80
Nixon, T. (physiognotrist, watercolorist), 321, 325
Noble, Enoch [Constant] (runaway slave, black healer), 21
Norcross, Elisha (animal proprietor), 95, 132–33
Norfolk, Va., 22, 45, 83, 85, 106, 139, 166, 265, 296–97, 339, 348
"Norfolk Tragedy, The" (ballad), 163, 182, 362
North, Noah (1809–1880) (portrait, sign, ornamental painter), 313
Northampton, Mass., 21, 42, 44, 53, 210, 243, 281, 291
North Carolina, 37, 102, 195, 204, 220, 343, 372
Northwest Territory, 133–34
Norway, 11, 31, 297
Norwich, Conn., 40, 42–44, 48, 60, 66, 183, 207, 213, 243–44, 357
November fifth. *See* Pope Night
Noyes, Enoch (penmanship teacher), 364
Nugent, Henry Paul (fl. 1795–1813) (theatrical dancer, French and dancing teacher), 242–43
Number of Original Airs, Duetto's and Trio's, A [Hill]

obelisk, 288–89
Occut, Molly [Ockett] (c. 1740–1816) (Abenaki healer, herbalist), 89
oculists, 8, 55, 63, 72, 74, 262–63, 375, 378. *See also individual oculists*
"Ode on Masonry" (musical composition), 166
Old American Company, 39, 73, 97, 166, 283
Old Bett (elephant): cost of admission to, 147; images of, 102–5, 109, 383; owners of, 381; tours of, 102–3, 132, 147, 381, 383–84, 401n6, table 6.1
Oldmixon John (1673–1742) (English historian), 172–73
Old Newgate Prison, East Granby, Conn., 61
Old South Meetinghouse, Boston, 205, 292
Oleves, Mr. (dancing-master), 246
olios, 158
Olympic Theatre, New York City, 381
Ombres Chinoises (shadow puppets), 143, 165, 183, 218. *See also* Chinese shades
"Ombres Italianes Grandes, Les" (lantern show). *See* Italian shades
operas, 225, 232, 307, 363, 424n23, 435n26. *See also individual operas*
"optic tragedies" (magic lantern slides), 158, 162, 164
Orange Tree Tavern, New York City. *See* Sign of the Orange Tree
organs: 97, 212, 214, 239, 249; barrel or hand, 160–61, 222, 360, 365; pedal, 213, 218, 271, 273
Ostinelli, Sophia Hewitt (b. 1799) (daughter of Hewitt, James, singer, musician), 216
ostriches, 81–82
Othello (black acrobat, slack-wire performer), 56, 371
outdoor audiences, composition of, 145–51
outdoor venues: 127, 130, 132, 134–36, 139, 141–46, 153; covered seating at, 142; preventing free admissions at, 149; women's seating at, 135
Owen, Mr. (Crowninshield elephant proprietor), 56, 371
Oyster Pond, Long Island, 38

Pachelbel, Charles Theodore (1690–1750) (composer, instrumentalist), 215, 418n12
Packard, Charles (fl. 1802–1805) (waxworks, museum, and automaton proprietor, profilist): 106; automatons of, 334–35, 339–40; "Invisible Lady" of, 81, 342; profiles of, 320, 325; waxworks of, 218, 274–75
packet boats, 18, 36–39, 41, 43, 46–48, 65, 101, 252, 288, 377
Padlock, The [Dibdin] (play), 229

Paff, John (automaton proprietor), 335
Paillolet's tavern, Baltimore, 183
Paine, Elisha (1693–1775) (Baptist preacher, diarist), 257
Paine, Susanna (1792–1862) (portrait painter, author), 58–59, 303
painters: 280, 302–4; ethnicity of, 35; landscape, 86; large-scale, 288, 290–99, 432nn8, 22; miniature, 7, 56, 58, 75–76, 78, 95–96, 190, 199–200, 267, 306–7, 313–14, 429n86; numbers of, 34; portrait, 2, 12, 19–20, 44, 46, 58, 66, 75, 86, 93, 190, 267, 303–13, 355–56; stage, 73–74, 144, 235, 288. *See also individual painters*
Palmer, Timothy (1751–1821) (bridge builder), 372
panharmonicon, 339
panthers, 134, 151, 157
pantographs, 316, 318, 321–22, 324
pantomimes: 6, 92, 20, 62, 153–54, 225–36, 420n9; decline of, 235; laws regarding, 420n2; locally inspired, 232–33
"Parachute or Falling Screen" (parachute), 73
parades, 69, 312
Paris, France, 18, 50, 54–55, 58, 63–64, 83, 139, 141, 161, 172, 212, 217, 226–27, 242, 245–46, 279, 294, 318, 326, 333, 342–44, 355, 368, 374, 393n37, 394n54
Parkman, Rev. Ebenezer (1703–1782) (minister, diarist): 12–13; on Badcock and singing, 206–7; on Burlesson, 173–74, 189; on camel, 129; on electrical machines, 265; on jackal, 147; on Jones, I., 257–58, 426n50; on Noble, 21; on peddlers, 37, 253, 425n24
Parkman, Hannah (d. 1777) (daughter of Rev. Ebenezer), 21
Park Theatre, New York City, 216
Parmelee, Ebenezer: large hall of, 213; New Haven tavern of, 279
Parsons, Nathan (naturalist), 296
Parsons, T. (dentist), 72
partnerships: and acquisition of skills, 93–95; acrobatic, 56; of dancing-masters, 240; of penmanship teachers, 437–48; of profilists, 316, 318; of puppeteers, 180; of waxwork proprietors, 271–72, 282, 366
Partridge, John (equestrian, amphitheater proprietor), 153
Partridge, Mr. [Patridge, William?] (mask maker), 364
Passamaquoddy, 59
pastel artists, 40, 49, 58, 264, 277, 307, 313, 423n11. *See also* artists; *individual pastelists*
Patch, Sam (1807–1829) (daredevil), 8–9
Patrick, T. (fireworks artist), 142

Patridge, William (puppeteer, conjurer, lanternist, singer, mimic), 97–98, 170, 178, 190
patronage zones, 43–50
Paul, Jeremiah, Jr. (c. 1761–1820) (painter, profile artist), 47, 318, 321
Pavilion Theatre, Philadelphia, 356
Peale, Charles Willson (1741–1827) (artist, museum proprietor, electrical healer), 47, 110, 318–20, 326
Peale, Raphaelle (1774–1825) (son of Charles W., profilist, artist): 46, 307; as profilist, 319–20, 322–23, 325, 327
Peale, Rembrandt (1778–1860) (son of Charles W., artist, museum keeper), 46
Peale's Museum [Philadelphia Museum, Peale's American Museum], 47, 296, 320–21
Pearce, Henry ["Hen," "Game Chicken"] (1777–1809) (English pugilist), 358
Peckham, Robert (1785–1877) (artist), 309–10, 439n39
peddlers: 2, 18, 37, 122, 156, 248–49, 252, 266–67, 385n9; crimes by, 253; dangers to, 252–53, 426n26; ethnicity of, 35, 253; goods of, 253–54; laws against, 254–55, 358; numbers of, 34; transportation of, 254. *See also individual peddlers*
"Peddlers in Divinity," 257–59
Pelham, Peter (1721–1805) (musician, composer), 215, 418n12
penmanship, 5–6, 210
penmanship schools, 345–54s
penmanship teachers: 8, 76, 78, 156, 347; advertising of, 81; ethnicity of, 35, 352–53; franchising agreements of, 96; numbers of, 34, 345; and other skills, 350–51; and popular culture, 353–54; promotional methods of, 350; schedules of, 352–52. *See also individual penmanship teachers*
Penniman, John Ritto [Pennyman, R.] (1782–1841) (painter, portraitist), 290
Penrose's assembly room, Newport, R.I., 43, 72
Pépin, Martha Townes (1788–1863) (wife of Victor, equestrienne), 366
Pépin, Victor (1780–1845) (equestrian, circus performer, owner), 366
Pepys, Samuel (1633–1703) (London diarist, Member of Parliament, naval administrator): 1, 12, 135; on "blind beggar," 362; and drawing pictures, 315; face mold of, 312; and magic lanterns, 160, 170; and portraits, 307, 436n31; and puppets, 175; telescope of, 160
Percy, Thomas (1729–1811) (Bishop of Dromore, Ireland, author), 362–63

Perkins, Benjamin D. (1774–1810) (son of Elisha, bookseller, salesman), 67
Perkins, Dr. Elisha (1741–1799) (physician, inventor), 263–65, 428n75
Perkins, John D. (1769–1847) (son of Elisha, minister, salesman), 67
Perkins, Sarah (1771–1831) (daughter of Elisha, artist), 264
Perley, Amos (penmanship teacher), 349
Perrette, Mr. (automaton exhibitor), 333, 343
Perry, Oliver Hazard (1785–1819) (naval commander), 300–302, 311–12, 333, 343, 434n1
Perseus and Andromeda [Theobald and Galliard] (pantomime), 226
Perspective View of the Falls of Niagara [Earl] (painting), 291–92
Perth Amboy, N.J., 26, 70
pharmacists, 24, 73, 79, 305. *See also* Stearns, W.
Phelps, Elizabeth Porter (1747–1817) (diarist), 13, 21, 25, 30, 358, 360, 387n14
Phenix Museum, Boston, 294, 371
Philadelphia (frigate), 290
Philips, Ambrose (1674–1749) (English poet, playwright), 226
Philips, William (escaped inmate, Welch showman), 175
Phillips, Ammi (1788–1865) (portraitist, diarist), 304–5, 308
Phillips, Calvin (child with dwarfism), 81, 397n56
Phillips, Mr. (legerdemain performer), 183
Phillips, Mr. (London lanternist), 163
Phillips, Lt. Gov. Samuel, Jr. (1752–1802) (Lt. Gov. of Mass., merchant, academy founder), 290
"Philosophical Fish" (automaton), 336–37, 442n33
phrenology, 2, 3, 8, 326, 369, 437n47
physicians, 2, 19, 24–25, 31, 51, 59, 72, 77, 88–89, 130, 190, 242, 260, 262, 285, 305, 317, 359–61. *See also* healers, alternative; mountebanks; *individual physicians*
physiognotraces: 47, 211, 314–28
Picture of the Manners, Customs, Sports and Pastimes . . . of England, A [Aspin], 11
Pierpont, Rev. John (1785–1866) (poet, minister), 301
Pierrot (commedia dell'arte character), 106, 232, 283
Pig of Knowledge, The (trained pig), 21, 27, 28, 32, 36, 105, 398n9
Pinchbeck, Christopher, Jr. (1709–1783) (son of Christopher, Sr., English clock, automaton maker), 87, 329

Pinchbeck, Christopher, Sr. (1669–1732) (English clockmaker, jeweler, automaton maker), 87, 177, 329
Pinchbeck, Edward (1713?–1766) (son of Christopher, Sr., English clock and automaton maker, conjurer, puppeteer), 87, 329
Pinchbeck, William Frederick (fl. 1795–1819) (son of Christopher, Jr., automaton exhibitor, animal proprietor, carver, gilder, inventor, balloonist, conjurer, author): 27, 68, 85, 87, 335; advertising of, 27–28, 78, 105; aerial excursion of, 29–30, 105; animal training by, 81, 87, 248; automatons of, 27, 86–87, 334, 339, 343; carving and gilding shop of, 370; conjuring manuals by, 28–29, 116, 157, 321, 342; as electrical healer, 429n86; itinerary of, 389n38, table 1.4; lantern exhibit of, 30; later career of, 370–71; Pig of Knowledge of, 27–29, 148, 334, 376, 399n35; purchase agreement of, 95; sapient dog of, 30–31, 105, 119, 148, 334; and transference of popular culture, 31–32
Pittsburgh, Penn., 92
Pittsfield, Mass., 41, 46, 50, 79, 103
Placide, Alexandre (fl. 1791–1812) (1750–1812) (acrobat, mime, tightrope dancer, choreographer), 58, 61–62, 75, 232, 234, 393n37, 435n26
Placide, Charlotte Sophia Wrighten (1780–1823) (wife of Alexandre, actress), 62
Placide, Madame (partner of Alexandre, dancer, choreographer), 58, 435n26
Plaisted, Maj. Ichabod (militia officer, representative) (1700–1762), 189
Plant, Thomas (conjurer), 175
Planter's Hotel, Charleston, 293
plaster casts, 311–12
plays, passion, 195, 377
Plymouth, Mass., 129
Plymouth Rock; or, Harlequin Released from Bondage (pantomime), 232
Polichinelle [Punch], 106, 180
polite arts, 20, 370; schools of, 42, 49, 239, 251. *See also* manners, schools of
Polk, Charles Peale (artist) (1767–1822), 47
Pollard, Eupha Brown (wife of Othello), 135, 404n21
Pollard, Othello (African American acrobat, leopard proprietor, entrepreneur), 134–35, 404n21
"Pont Cassé, Le" (French folksong, entertainment), 165–66. *See also* "Broken Bridge, The"
Pontopiddan, Erich (1698–1764) (author, bishop, historian), 296

Pool, Thomas (equestrian), 54, 356
Pool's coffeehouse [Thomas], Keene, N.H., 46
Pope, Benjamin (1783–1811) (son of John, cancer curer), 88
Pope, Hannah Raymer (1743–1805) (wife of John, cancer curer), 59
Pope, John (1740–96) (cancer curer), 59, 77–78, 88–89, 264
Pope, John, Jr. (1769–1806) (son of John, cancer curer), 88
Pope, Samuel (1781–after 1831) (son of John, cancer curer), 88
Pope Night, 4, 7, 11
popular culture: adaptability of, 22, 199–200; American opposition to, 239, 248–49; channels of dissemination of, 194, 195, 377–79; definitions of, 5–8; delayed transmission of European, 98, 170, 172, 332, 344, 374–75; early audiences for, 2, 18–19, 70–71, 377; elements of excluded in this study, 7–8; explosion of, 271, 345; geographic movement of, 375–76; imitation in dissemination of, 97–98, 376; meaning in early America of, 5–6; newspapers as method of reintroduction for, 12–13, 43–44, 78, 99; North Atlantic, Caribbean, and French influences, 372; practices of that atrophied, 31–32, 358–66; practices of that dispersed slowly, 375; practices of that succeeded, 375; recharacterization of as "American," 355–58; role of itinerants in, 6–7, 18–20, 32, 85–87, 193–95, 370–74; self-replicating process of, 348–49, 373; shifting audience patterns of, 378–79; source of, 1–5; tavern-oriented axis of, 71–72, 156–58, 191; traditional practices of, 1, 7, 30–31, 266, 311, 359; traditional versus innovative practices of, 24; uneven transfer of, 374–75
popular culture, bearers of. *See* "active bearers"; culture "carriers"
Popular Culture in Early Modern Europe [Burke], 5, 8–9, 18, 24, 68, 221, 283, 359, 370, 373, 377, 390
Poree, Michael (surgeon-dentist), 72
portraitists, itinerant: 300–13; advertisements by, 75–76, 306–7; ethnicity of, 35; numbers of, 34; and residence with sitters, 303–5; scarcity of work for, 303, 306; and travel with families, 303. *See also* painters
portraiture, machine aided, 316–27
portraiture, public expectations for, 300, 302, 305, 307–13
Portugal, 56, 330, 343, 374

posture-masters, 9, 75, 135–36, 158, 377
Potomoc River, 18, 45
Potter, Richard (1783–1835) (African American ventriloquist, singer, conjurer), 11, 52–53, 55, 166
Potter, Sally Harris (c. 1785–1836) (wife of Richard, singer), 53
Poughkeepsie, N.Y., 207, 305
Pouyard, Joseph (lanternist), 183, 218
Powell, Martin (d. 1725) (English puppeteer), 175–76
Powell, Martin, Jr. (fl. 1725–1726) (son of Martin, puppeteer), 175, 362
Powers, Asahel Lynde (1813–1843) (artist), 38
Pownall, Mary Ann Wrighten (d. 1796) (actress, singer), 62
Preston, Conn., 358
Priest, William (English bassoonist, author), 37, 218
Prince, James (sea captain), 297
Prince, James (collector of customs), 305
Prince, Rev. John (1751–1836) (minister, instrument designer and repairer), 168
Prince, Samuel (automaton and waxworks exhibitor), 340–41
Prince, Rev. Thomas (1687–1758) (minister), 201
prints, 280, 288, 295, 316, 318, 361
prizefighters: 18, 32, 355, 357–58, 378; ethnicity of, 35; numbers of, 34
profile takers: 122, 156, 356; additional careers of, 23, 28, 64, 211, 274, 292, 317, 328; advertisements by, 47, 86, 107, 306–7, 312; ethnicity of, 35; numbers of, 34; travel of, 40, 44, 46, 303; warranties by, 123. *See also individual profilists*
Promise (anthem), 210
Providence River, 138
Providence Theatre, 106
provincialism, 4, 5, 20, 21, 25, 61, 81, 119, 128, 173, 200, 202, 210, 212, 214, 227, 280, 302, 309, 384
psalmody: 199–211; growth of, 201–4; New England as regional center of, 207
psalmody teachers: and Congregational singing, 200–201, 210; ethnicity of, 35, 210; numbers of, 34, 204–5; schools of, 202–3, 205, 207–9; supplementary work of, 208, 211; travel to South and Midwest of, 208–9. *See also individual psalmodists*
public buildings, as locations for entertainments, 191, 193
Pucci, Signor (musician, singer), 42
Puerto Rico, 188, 373

Punch (commedia dell'arte character): 106; entertainments, 74, 159, 178–79; in pantomimes, 226, 228, 233, 335; puppets, 175–80, 364–65; puppet shows, 158, 362, 375

Punchinello [Punch], 11, 182, 190, 236, 242, 373

Punch's Company of Comedians (puppets), 162, 178, 274

"Punch's Opera," 11, 176–77, 183

puppeteers: 1, 74, 95, 176–82; beginnings in America of, 173, 178; ethnicity of, 35; numbers of, 9, 34, 54, 175; travel of, 179; venues of 18, 40, 72, 156, 179, 189–90, 218, 377. *See also individual puppeteers*

puppetry: 6–7, 11, 69, 72, 137, 172; London circuit of, 175

puppets: descriptions of, 177–82; Italian, 181–82, 184; voice of, 175

puppet shows, 5, 11, 72, 106, 164–65, 167, 173, 178, 181–83, 189–90, 194, 274, 363, 365, 375; accompanied by music, 218; in Barbados and Leeward Islands, 172; in England, 1, 69, 87, 137, 172, 175, 362

purchase agreements, 95

Putnam, John (physiognotrist), 321–22

Pynchon, William (1723–1789) (lawyer, diarist), 12, 149, 220–21, 242

Quebec, 41

Quebec City, 41, 83, 294, 298, 328, 373, 394n54

Quesnay, Alexandre (dancer, dancing-master), 42, 49

Quesnay's Academy of Polite Arts, New York City, 42

railway lines, 42

Ranelagh Gardens, New York City, 139

Rannie, James [Mr. Rannie, Sr.] (1772–1812) (brother of John, ventriloquist; automaton proprietor, conjurer, slack-wire performer): 117, 119–21, 186–87, 191, 335–36, 373, 378; cost of admission to, 188, 191; death of, 188–89

Rannie, John [Mr. Rannie, Jr.] (c. 1775–after 1811) (brother of James, ventriloquist, automaton proprietor, conjurer slack-wire performer), 117–20, 186, 188–89

Rannie brothers: 186–89; arguments between, 188; arrival in North America of, 186; automatons of, 188, 335–39; circuit of, 376, 423n54, table 9.2; costumes worn by, 117–21, 187; dummy used by, 116–18; and Pinchbeck, 28; publicity of, 188; relief cuts of, 106, 117–21, 188; retirement of, 187–89

rattlesnakes, 59, 122, 129, 151

Rauschner, John Christian (1760–after 1812) (German wax modeler), 274, 277

Read, Daniel (1757–1836) (singing master, composer), 38, 208, 213–14, 417n3

Reading, Mass., 156, 202

Reading, Penn., 85, 379

Reasonableness of Regular Singing: or, Singing by Note, The [Symmes], 201

Redfield, Levi (1745–1838) (singing master, author), 208, 210

Redfield, Robert (1897–1958) (anthropologist), 9

Redon, Mrs. (equestrienne), 356

Reeve, William (1757–1815) (actor, composer), 229, 420n9, 421n17

Reeves, Richard (fl. 1641–1679) (London instrument maker), 160

references, personal, 19, 76, 78

"regular singing," 201–3, 210. *See also* psalmody

religious proselytizers, 248, 255–60. *See also* Great Awakening revival; *individual revivalists*

Reliques of Ancient English Poetry [Percy], 363

Representation of the Great Storm at Providence, A [Kidder] (painting), 295

Restoration of Harlequin (pantomime), 62

Retrospections of America [Bernard], 33, 389n47

Revear, John (dancing-master), 247

Revels in Jamaica [Wright], 11

Revere, Paul (1735–1818) (silversmith, engraver), 6, 289

Rice, Kym S. (historian), 36–37, 70

Rice's long room, Providence, 42

Rich, John [Mr. Lun] (1692–1761) (English theater producer, actor, manager, performer), 227–30, 235, 420n9

Richardson, Calvin (dancing-master), 244

Richardson, Mr. (musician), 274

Richmond, Mass., 284

Ricketts, John Bill (c. 1767–1800) (English equestrian, circus proprietor): amphitheaters of, 141, 151, 154; with Blanchard, 73; with Church, 56; circus troupe of, 155; and combination of entertainments, 153; with Durang, 90, 149; genteel audience of, 378; with Hutchins, 153; with Langley, 356; lost at sea, 154; Philadelphia riding school of, 153; portrait of, 154; with Spinacuta, 140, 153; with Sully, 153–54; training of, 153; transparencies of, 290; travel of, 41, 149, 373

Ricketts, Master [Francis] (brother of John Bill, equestrian, tumbler), 153–54

riders, trick, 73, 150, 153, 199, 356, 377. *See also* equestrians; *individual equestrians*

Rinhart, Floyd and Marion (collectors), 369

Ripley, Sally [Sarah] (1785–1871) (diarist), 284
Rising, Edmund (optical specialist, lanternist, solar microscope exhibitor), 4, 23, 163, 170, 408n11, 449n94
Riviere, Madame (portraitist, miniaturist, art teacher), 58
Rivington, James (bookseller, stationer), 169
Robardet, James (fl. 1784–1812) (dancing-master), 47, 240, 244
Roberts, John (miniature and pastel artist), 307
Robertson, Mr. (automaton exhibitor), 341
Robinson, Mr. [or Robertson] (mimic, acrobat), 97–98, 376
Rockingham, Vt., 208, 305
Rollinson, William (1762–1842) (English engraver, artist, profilist), 316–17
Rome, Italy, 18, 78, 167, 181–82, 212, 294, 355, 360, 374
ropedancers: 1, 19, 73, 135–36, 138, 153, 156, 183–86, 192, 375; ethnicity of, 35; numbers of, 9, 34; unidentified, 58, 136, 377. *See also individual ropedancers and slack-wire performers*
rope flyers, 8, 127, 135–38, 148
Rosee, Riyt [Rose] (miniature painter, French language, and fencing teacher), 48
Rosenfeld, Sybil M. (theatrical historian), 225, 362
Roses and Thorns [Paine], 59
Rosier, Mr. and Mrs. (instrumentalists, singers), 20, 217
Rossetti, Signior (portraitist), 307
Rossignol, Gaetano (fl. 1774–1800) (mimic), 97–98, 376, 400n47
Roussell, Louis (dancing-master), 56, 90
Rowe, John (1715–1787) (English merchant, diarist): on Boston obelisk, 289; on Boston stage, 5; on entertainers, 190; on equestrians, 150; on face mold, 312; on Jerusalem model, 5; on sailing times, 37
Rowse, E. (penmanship teacher, possibly fabricated), 348
Rowson, Susanna (1762–1824) (writer, actress, educator), 74, 216, 395n25
Roxbury, Mass., 129, 246, 312, 348
Royalton, Vt., 93, 347, 352
royalty, wax effigies of, 16, 81, 178, 213, 274, 276, 278
Ruggieri, Gaetano [Mr. Rudgery], 141–42
Ruggles, Mr. (dancing-master), 245
runaways: 6, 19, 194, 220, 257; advertisements for, 6, 48, 51, 101, 148, 150, 194–95, 220–21, 266, 378–79
Russia, 18, 166, 344, 359, 374

Rutland, Vt., 41
Ryan, Thomas (pugilist), 357
Rye, N.Y., 40

Sabbath culture, 69
Sabbe, Dr. Joseph (alternative healer), 55
Sabin, Thomas, house of, Providence, 81
Saco, Maine, 305, 432n6
Sadler's Wells, London, 163, 172, 181, 192
Sadler's Wells Theatre, London, 374, 398n9
"Sagacious Mermaid" (automaton), 191, 331–32, 338
sailors, 90, 127, 135, 153, 213–14, 290, 298
Saint Mémin, Balthazar Julien Fevret de (1770–1852) (artist, profilist), 317–18, 325–26, 438n16
Salem, Maine, 83
Salenka, Gabriel (conjurer, musician, fireworks artist, animal trainer, lanternist): as animal trainer, 52, 107–8, 112, 115, 148; as lanternist, 164, 166, 168
Salisbury, Conn., 284
Salmon, Mrs. (1670–1760) (English waxworks exhibitor, modeler), 193–94, 375
Sals, Dr. John (alternative healer), 55
Salter, Cleaveland (b. c. 1787) (son of Daniel, musician, singer, dancer), 213–14
Salter, Daniel (fl. 1791–1818) (organist, lanternist, music teacher), 212–14, 223
Salter, Rebecca (b. c. 1791) (daughter of Daniel, musician, singer, dancer), 213–14
Sandford, John (profilist), 319
Sanford, Isaac (d. 1842) (engraver), 301–2
Sanger, Abner (1739–1822) (farmer, diarist), 157
Santo Domingo, 52
Saratoga, N.Y., 88, 369
Saratoga Springs, N.Y., 365
Saunders, Hyman (conjurer, ropedancer, juggler), 71, 179, 191, 193, 373, 441n26
Sauvages en cire [Hyde de Neuville], 286
Savage, Arthur (d. 1735) (merchant mariner, lion proprietor), 134, 138, 404n20
Savage, Edward (1761–1817) (painter, inventor, profilist, museum, elephant, and automaton proprietor, medical electrician), 290, 296–98, 320–21, 325, 341, 381, 429n86
Sawco, Cuffe (father of Deborah), 60
Sawco, Deborah [Saco] (d. 1839) (African American fortune-teller), 59–60
Saxon, Monsieur (wire and ropedancer), 87
Saxon, "the young" (son of Saxon, Monsieur, acrobat), 87
Saybrook, Conn., 38, 128
Scaramouch (commedia dell'arte character), 177, 181–82, 225–26, 228

Schaffer, John (deserter), 85
Schenectady, N.Y., 41, 48–49, 244
Schetky, John George (1776–1831) (composer, musician), 215, 395n25, 418n12
Schiavonetti, Luigi (1765–1810) (Italian engraver), 280–81
Schipper, Gerrit (1775–c. 1830) (profilist, pastelist), 49, 325, 328
schools, concurrent: dancing, 42–44, 207, 241–43; singing, 204, 210
Schuylkill River, 45
Scituate, R.I., 40
Scotland, 52, 55, 158, 186, 195, 308
Scudder, John (d. 1821) (museum proprietor, panorama promoter), 297–98
Seabury, Rev. Samuel (1729–1796) (Episcopal bishop), 26
sea captains, 73, 128–29, 352
sea lions, 129, 138
sea monsters, 288, 296–98, 375–76
Seilhamer, George (1836–1916) (theater historian), 62
servants, 10, 127, 148, 150, 195, 257, 262–63, 326, 366, 377–78. See also runaways
Sewall, Samuel (1652–1730) (jurist, merchant, printer, diarist): 12; on a conjurer, 17, 70, 380; on sailor's rope tricks, 135; on singing, 200–202; on Stepney's dancing school, 238
Seven Stars coffeehouse [Mrs. Coffin's], Boston, 70
seventh sons (alternative healers), 8, 51, 359–60, 446nn25, 28
"shades" (movable shadow puppets), 165–66
shades (profiles), 314–15, 317, 328
shadowgraph (physiognotrace), 324
shadow puppets, 158, 165–66, 182, 218. See also Chinese shades; Ombres Chinoises
Sharon, Conn., 284
Sharon, Vt., 96, 352, 400n42
Sharp, Dr. (mountebank, physician, alternative healer), 51, 55, 260–61, 373, 427n60
Sharp, John (equestrian), 148
Sharper (slave, possible animal keeper), 134, 404n20
Sharples, Ellen Wallace (1769–1849) (third wife of James, portraitist, diarist), 58, 303–4
Sharples, Felix (c. 1786–1830) (son of James, portraitist), 58, 303–4
Sharples, James (c. 1751–1811) (portraitist, pastel artist), 40–41, 58, 303–4
Sharples, James, Jr. (c. 1788–1839) (son of James, portraitist), 58, 303–4
Sharples, Rolinda (1793–1838) (daughter of James, portraitist), 58, 303–4

Shaw, Charity [Long, Mrs. C.] (dispensary owner), 266
Shaw, James (diagonal mirror entrepreneur), 139–40
Sheffield, Conn., 284
Sheffield, J. (penmanship and theorem painting teacher), 350
Sherlot, Henry (dancing-master), 238
shipwrecks, 19, 45, 139, 230, 357, 362
Shirley, Mass., 208, 253
Shrimpton, Lt. Col. Samuel (1643–1697) (Boston merchant), 238
Shute, Ruth Whittier (1803–1882) (wife of Samuel A., portraitist), 303, 308, 313
Shute, Gov. Samuel (1662–1742) (royal governor, army officer), 238–39
Shute, Samuel A. (1803–1836) (physician, portraitist), 303
Sicard, Mr. (dancing-master), 47, 247
Sign of Lord John Murray, New York City, 190
Sign of the Blue-Anchor, New York City, 190
Sign of the Coach-and-Horses, Philadelphia, 190, 408n8
Sign of the Connestoga Wagon, Philadelphia, 29
Sign of the Dolphin Privateer, New York City, 178, 190
Sign of the Green Dragon, Boston, 71
Sign of the Orange Tree, New York City, 178, 190, 193, 377
Sign of the Spread-Eagle, New York City, 190
Simonds, Ezekiel (singing master), 209
Skinner, Richard C. (surgeon-dentist, author), 66
slack-wire performers, 32, 55, 100, 178, 217. See also ropedancers; wire dancers; wirewalkers; *individual performers*
Slater's Tavern, Baltimore, 56
slaves: 10, 19, 100–101, 156, 360, 378; as itinerant ministers, 257; as musicians, 6, 56, 220–21. See also runaways
sleight of hand, 9, 156, 158, 181, 182, 234. See also legerdemain; "slight of hand"
"slight of hand," 52, 87, 183, 190, 194, 221, 378–79, 397n59. See also legerdemain; sleight of hand
sloops, 38, 41, 46, 101
Smibert, John (1688–1751) (painter), 307–8
Smith, J. H. (keyboardist, violinist), 217
Smith, John R[owson]. (1810–1864) (painter), 368
Smith, John Rubens (1755–1849) (painter), 302
Smith, Mr. (language and English grammar teacher), 49

Smith, Rev. Peter (1753–1816) (minister, physician), 266
Smith, Richard (1735–1803) (attorney, N.J. Continental Congressman, author), 38
Smith, William H. (dancing-master), 44
Smithfield, R.I., 381
Smyth, Jerveys C. (penmanship and fencing teacher, stenography school proprietor), 350–51
Snow, Edward Rowe (1902–1982) (author, storyteller, historian), 136
Society for Promoting Regular Singing, Boston, 202
Society Hill, Philadelphia, 58, 75, 136
Society of Friends, 59
Sollee's "theatre" [Sollee, John Joseph Stephen Leger], Charleston, 138
Solomon, Miss (vocalist), 217
Solomon, Mrs. (actress, vocalist), 20, 74, 217, 395n25
South America, 18
Southbury, Mass., 202
Southold, N.Y., 255
Southwark Fair [Hogarth] (engraved print), 137
Southwark Fair, London, 1, 69, 87, 135–37, 148, 175, 177, 228, 362
South Windsor, Conn., 203
Spanish fandango, 56
Spencer, Frederick (profilist), 356
Spicer, Ishmael (1760–1832) (singing master, composer, publisher), 207, 210, 417n33
Spinacuta, Laurent (fireworks artist, equestrian, dancer, slack-wire and tightrope walker), 54, 58, 140–41, 149, 153, 232
Spinacuta, Signora (wife of Laurent, equestrienne, dancer, tightrope walker), 58
Sports and Pastimes of the People of England [Strutt], 11, 98
Spottee (trained horse), 122–23
Springfield, Mass., 174, 203–4
Springfield, N.J., 70
"Springfield Mountain" (ballad), 6
stagecoaches, 42
stage lines, 43
stage professionals: 2, 19–20, 62, 73, 78; changing careers of, 74; ethnicity of, 35, 54, 73; numbers of, 34, 225
stage singers, 156, 212, 216
stage wagons, 18, 40
Standish, Maine, 305
Starr, Eli (pharmaceuticals agent), 265–66
St. Bartholomew district, London, 1
St. Cecilia Society, Charleston, 214–15

Stearns, William (fl. 1781–1829) (pharmacist, state legislator, animal exhibitor), 73, 132, 305, 435n15
Stephens, Mr. (innkeeper, animal exhibitor), 130
Stepney, Francis (fl. 1685–1686) (dancing-master), 238
Sternhold, Thomas (1500–1549) (psalm translator), 201
Steward, Joseph (1753–1822) (painter, profilist, museum proprietor, clergyman), 282, 305
Stiles, Rev. Ezra (1727–1795) (educator, minister, author, college president, diarist): on Dr. Calcott, 263; on camels, 130, 132, 403n11; on dancing schools, 239; on Deeker's balloon, 143; on Deeker's "speaking figure," 340; on Jenkins's manual, 346; and Moulthrop, 279; on Pope, Sr., 88; profile of, 314–15, 326; waxworks of, 213
Stillman, Rev. Dr. Samuel (1737–1807) (minister), 311, 436–37n46
Stimson, Lovet (dancing-master), 42, 424n29
St. James's, London, annual fair at, 11
St. John, New Brunswick, 45
St. John de Crèvecoeur, J. Hector (1735–1813) (writer), 271, 288, 428n1
St. John's, Quebec, 41
St. Laurence's, Paris, annual fair at, 172
St. Lawrence River, 41
St. Louis, Missouri, 67, 376
Stockbridge, Mass., 42, 204, 284
Stoddard, Elizabeth Shrimpton (d. 1757) (wife of Samuel Shrimpton, Jr., and David Stoddard), 239, 363, 447n44
Stoneham, Mass., 265
Stonington, Conn., 60, 129
stories, traditional, 10, 162–63, 178–79, 193–94, 274, 362
Stork, Dr. Lawrence (oculist), 55
Stork, Dr. William (d. 1768) (oculist, mountebank, real estate agent), 249, 262–63, 266, 373, 427–28n69
Stoughton, Mass., 205, 416n23
Strafford, Vt., 347, 443n7
strangers: 61, 74, 76; itinerants as, 52, 68, 70, 81; in Hempstead's diary, 60
Street, Elnathan (b. 1774) and Nicholas (b. 1772) (brothers, brothers-in-law of Moulthrop, waxworks proprietors), 280–81, 363
street fairs, London, 1, 11, 21, 69, 87, 136, 175, 177, 228, 230, 402n18. *See also individual fairs*
street musicians, 2, 7, 12, 215
street performers, 135–55
strollers, English, 32, 62, 73, 159, 172–73, 179

Struna, Nancy L. (American Studies professor), 71–72
Strutt, Joseph (engraver, artist, writer), 98
Stuart, Gilbert (1755–1828) (portrait artist), 22, 154, 311
Stupendous Falls of Niagara, The [Earl] (painting), 291
Sturbridge, Mass., 366
Sturgess, Mr. (slack-wire performer), 190
Suffield, Conn., 8, 173–74, 189, 246
Suffolk, Va., 265
Suffolk County, Mass., 363
Sugden, George (d. 1800) (ornamental and fabric painter, teacher), 368
Sullivan, Mr. (dancer, bagpiper), 184
Sullivan's Island, Charleston, 182
Sully, Matthew, Jr. (d. 1812) (son of Matthew, Sr., actor, acrobat, equestrian), 87, 90, 153–54, 233, 235
Sully, Matthew, Sr. (d. 1815) (English comedian, actor, tumbler, singer), 90, 233
surgeon-dentists, 12, 24, 66–67, 72, 265
surgery, cataract, 23, 25, 249, 262, 361, 388n32
Susap, Polly (Abenaki partner of Tufts, H.), 90
Susquehanna River, 45
Sutton, Mass., 265, 366
Sutton's tavern, New Brunswick, N.J., 214
Suvorov-Rymnikski, Gen. Alexander (1730–1800) (Imperial Russian Army general), 272–73, 278, 280
Sweden, 8, 32, 374
Swift, Jonathan (1667–1745) (Irish author, clergyman), 9, 376
Switzerland, 55, 58, 329, 337, 341
Sydow, Carl Wilhelm von (1878–1952) (Swedish folklorist), 8, 11, 31, 358, 373, 386n16
Symmes, Rev. Thomas (1678–1725) (minister, composer), 201
systematized instruction: 345, 353; of language, 367–68; of music, 367; of penmanship, 96, 345–51, 353–54, 400n42, 443n13; of phrenology, 369; of theorem and flower painting, 368

table 1.1, thirty-five itinerant occupations, 34
table 1.2, national origins of thirty-five itinerant occupations, 35
tables, on ScholarWorks website, http://scholarworks.umass.edu/umpress_short_time_only/: 1.3 Yeldall, Anthony; 1.4 Pinchbeck, William F.; 2.1 Griffiths, John; 3.1 King, William; 6.1 Old Bett; 6.2 African lion; 8.1 Brickell, Richard; 9.1 Maginnis, Samuel Jameson; 9.2 Rannic, James and John; 15.1 Moulthrop, Reuben; 17.1 portrait advertisements; 19.1 Falconi, Joseph; 19.2 Martin, Mr.; 20.1 Wrifford, Allison
Tammany Hall, New York City, 372
Tammany Museum, 335
Tate, Nahum (1652–1715) (Irish poet, playwright), 201–2, 206–7
Taunton, Mass., 42, 415n10, 424n29
tavern entertainers, diversity of, 35, 55
tavern life, richness of, 156–58
tavern musicians, black, 56
tavern proprietors, importance for itinerants, 71–72, 159
taverns: limited space of, 158–59; numbers of, 71–72; waterfront, 70, 190, 194, 377
Taylor, Edward (1642–1729) (poet, clergyman, diarist), 96–97
Tea, Mr. (puppeteer), 218, 447n41
Teel's tavern, Norwich, Conn., 183
Templeman, John (c. 1750–c. 1817) (slack-wire dancer, dental surgeon, securities broker, land agent, construction superintendent): 12, 52, 151, 388n23; as dental surgeon, 24, 359; description of, 23–24, 119; later career of, 372; as slack-wire dancer, 23–24, 387–88n20
Tessie and Goichon (puppeteers), 180
testimonials, 68, 77–78, 262, 302, 366
Tetley, William Birchall (artist, dancing and art teacher), 245
theater, floating, 366
theater companies, traveling, 2, 20, 62, 78, 148, 166, 226, 375, 420n3
theatergoers, American, 194, 225–26, 378, 420n4
theater managers, 74, 90, 165–66, 216, 225, 228, 230, 232, 234–35, 332, 412n34, 447n42
Theatre of London Fairs in the Eighteenth Century, The [Rosenfeld], 225, 408–9n21
Theatre Pitoresque & Mechanique (puppet theater), 106, 183–84
theatrical troupes, laws pertaining to, 75, 78, 186
Theobald, Lewis (1688–1744) (author), 226
theorem painting, 350, 368
Third Church, Boston, 17, 172, 200–201, 380
Third Church, Salem, Mass., 20
Thomas, Isaiah (1749–1831) (printer, publisher, author), 345–46, 357
Thomas, Keith (historian), 10
Thomas, Miss (puppeteer, lanternist), 183
Thompson, Cephas (1775–1856) (painter, electerizer, inventor), 267–68, 429n86
Thoreau, Henry David (1817–1862) (diarist, author, naturalist, philosopher), 296

tiger-lyons, 167, 249
tigers, 112, 116, 152, 166–67, 295, 360
tightrope performers, 18, 30, 33, 73, 135–36, 138, 140, 153, 402n18. *See also individual tightrope walkers and dancers*
Tileston, John (1735–1826) (Boston educator, diarist), 360
Tioli, Jonn [John] Baptist (theatrical dancer, dancing-master), 55, 239
Todd, J. [Isaac] (profilist), 318
Todd, Mr. (lanternist?), 158
Tommy (ventriloquist dummy), 116–20, 402n19
Tontine Assembly Room, New York City, 188
Tontine Building, Northampton, Mass., 291
Tontine Coffeehouse, New York City, 299
Tottenham Court, London, annual fair at, 1, 69
Towne, Nathan (1787–1812) (penmanship teacher), 349, 444n18
"tradition bearers," 7, 8, 11, 19, 22, 199, 225, 386n16
Tragedy of Fair Rosamond (legend, puppet show), 194, 362. *See also* "Fair Rosamond"
Trajetta, Filippo (1777–1854) (Italian composer, music teacher, academy founder), 216
translators, 156
transparencies, 288–90
"transparent pantomime[s]" (possible lantern exhibitions), 166
transportation, types of, 36–42
travel: circuits, 44–47; corridors, 45–46; dangers of, 36, 41, 252–53; transatlantic, 37
Trenton, N.J., 45, 214
Trinity Church, Boston, 215, 241
Trinity Church, New Haven, 212–14
Trinity Church, New York City, 216
Tripoli panoramas, exhibition of, 292–98
Triumph of Mirth (pantomime), 231
Trollope, Frances M. (1779–1863) (English writer): on American painters' patronage, 303; on American painting, 308; on camp meetings, 259–60; on Harding, 310; on dancing-masters, 240; on lack of American gaiety, 365; on waxworks, 272, 284–85, 287
Trott, Benjamin (d. 1843) (miniaturist), 22
Tucker, Alice (1751–1808) (diarist), 148
Tudor, John (1709–1795) (merchant, church deacon, diarist), 69
Tufts, Henry (1748–1831) (thief, preacher, alternative healer, author), 89–90, 265, 399n25
Tufts, Rev. John (1689–1750) (minister, music educator), 201, 239
tumblers: 8, 55, 73, 138, 148, 153, 199–200, 371; in England, 19, 411n26; ethnicity of, 35; numbers of, 9, 34

Tunbridge, Vt., 92
Turin, Italy, 127, 139
Turner, Ann Dumaresq (b. 1747) (wife of William, Sr.), 241
Turner, Ephraim (1709–1765) (father of William, Sr., and Thomas, dancing-master), 240–41
Turner, Judith Holyoke (1774–1841) (daughter of Holyoke, E. A., wife of William, Jr.), 190, 242
Turner, Thomas (1754–1809) (half-brother of William, Sr., dancing-master, musician), 47, 71, 241–42
Turner, William, Jr. (1769–1828) (son of William, Sr., dancing-master), 241–42, 298
Turner, William, Sr. (1745–1792) (dancing-master), 21, 241–42
Tuthill, Abraham G. D. (1776–1843) (painter), 310–11
Twain, Mark [Samuel L. Clemens] (1835–1910) (author), 2–4, 266

Ugly Club, Savannah, 71
Union Hall, Newburyport, Mass., 120, 183
"Ursa Major, or the great White Bear," 128, 411n8
Utica, N.Y., 102, 266, 371
Uxbridge, Mass., 376

Vagaries, or Harlequin Triumphant, The (pantomime), 184
Vail, R. W. G. (1890–1966) (author, librarian), 11
Val, Mr. and Mrs. (stage dancers), 234
Valdenuit, Thomas Bluget de (1763–1846) (military officer, profilist, artist), 317–18, 326
Van Antwarp, Mr. (acrobat, slack-wire walker), 153
Vanderlyn, John (1775–1852) (artist, panorama exhibitor), 297–98, 310
Vandewater's long room, New York City, 71, 414n74
Van Dyck, Abraham (innkeeper, animal exhibitor), 70, 99–100, 119
Van Hagen, Elizabeth (1750–c. 1809) (wife of Peter, Sr., voice, pianoforte teacher), 215–16
Van Hagen, Peter Albertus, Jr. (1781–1837) (son of Peter, Sr., instrument and vocal music teacher), 215–17
Van Hagen, Peter Albrecht, Sr. (c. 1755–1803) (music teacher, retailer, publisher, organist), 215–16, 418n15
Van Wizenfeltz, "speaking figure" by, 334
Varinot, Ambroise (fireworks artist and factory owner), 54, 140–41
Vaucanson, Jacques de (1709–1782) (French automaton inventor), 329, 334, 344, 441n22

Vauxhall Garden, Charleston, 183
Vauxhall Gardens, New York City, 139
Venetian Globe (magic lantern), 163–64
"Venetian Moor" [Othello], 56
ventriloquists: 5, 8, 52, 76, 397n59, 402n19; ethnicities of, 35, 55; numbers of, 34. *See also individual ventriloquists*
ventriloquy, 20, 28, 118, 188, 402n18
Ver Beck, Mr. (dancing-master), 49, 51
Victorani, Mr. [Victorian] (acrobat), 127, 138, 150
Vienna, Austria, 212, 273–74, 343, 355
View of the Tyger Hunt, The [anonymous] (painting), 295
Vilallave, Don José [Joseph] (acrobat, circus proprietor), and family, 87–88, 153
violinists: 135, 210, 215, 218, 220, 239, 246; black, 56, 215, 220–22. *See also individual musicians and violinists*
vocational combinations, 22–24, 359. *See also itinerants: multiple callings of*
Vogel, G. (automaton exhibitor), 337, 344
Volta, Alessandro (1745–1827) (Italian physicist, chemist, inventor), 32, 171, 251, 267, 332, 429n88
Von Eeckenberg, Herr (fl. 1743) (German performer, mimic), 97
Von Haegen, P. A., Jr. *See* Van Hagen, Peter Albertus, Jr.
Von Kempelen, M. Wolfgang (1734–1804) (Hungarian inventor, author, artist), 330, 337, 339, 344, 441n22

Waldo, Samuel Lovett (1783–1861) (painter), 307
Walgenstein, Thomas (1622–1701) (Danish mathematician, inventor), 160
Walter, Rev. Thomas (1696–1725) (clergyman, musician, choirmaster), 201–2
Ward, James (1769–1859) (English painter), 295
Ward, Susanna Holyoke (1779–1860) (daughter of Holyoke, E. A., diarist), 191, 337
Ware, Thomas (1803–1836) (portrait painter), 308
warranties and guarantees, 47, 78–79, 81, 123, 267, 302, 359, 396n47
Warrell, James (actor, painter, dancing-master, museum proprietor), 233, 235
Warren, Dr. John (1753–1815) (physician, army surgeon), 77–78
Washington, D.C., 12, 296, 367
Washington, George (1732–1799): 72, 336–37, 341; moving tableaux of, 141; New England tour of, 32, 76, 312; transparent portraits of, 290, 299; and waxworks, 278, 283
Washington Hall, New York City, 296

Washington Hall, Salem, Mass., 58, 122, 188, 217, 281, 442n43
Washington Museum, Boston, 320, 334
Washington Museum, Philadelphia, 361
Washington Tavern, Richmond, Va., 102
Watertown, Mass., 216, 246
waxworks exhibitions: American "founders" of, 274; audiences of, 76, 298; beginnings in North America of, 274, 375; at college commencements, 81; connections to musical pantomimes of, 283; cost of admission to, 274; influence on popular art of, 288; and lantern shows, 162–63, 167–68; music for, 213, 215, 217–18; venues for, 71, 156, 178, 251, 296, 377
waxworks figures: authenticity of, 273, 275–77, 281–82, 284–87; dispersal of, 284, 375–76, 431n36; and mannered and popular culture, 283–87; modeled from prints, 280; numbers of displays of, 273; numbers of sculptors of, 272; numbers of traveling exhibitions of, 271–72; and pantomimes, 283; for scientific use, 27; subjects of, 81, 193, 213, 234, 277–79, 285–87, 301, 360, 363, 430n17; timeliness of, 272–73, 280–81
waxworks proprietors: business acumen of, 277; combination of careers of, 23, 46, 70, 190, 267, 327, 342, 429n86; ethnicity of, 35; numbers of, 34; partnerships of, 40, 366. *See also individual proprietors*
Way, Mary (1769–1833) (artist, teacher), 58
Weaver, William J. (1759–1817) (artist), 307
Webster, Noah (1758–1843) (lexicographer, author, teacher, singing master, grammarian, diarist): on ball of Hulett, J. H., 246; on balloon ascensions, 149; on horseraces, 70; and Jenkins's manual, 346; and philology lectures, 49; singing schools of, 207; and slack-wire dancing, 190–91; on Yale's commencement ball, 239
Weigh House, New York City, 190
Wells, H. A. (circus proprietor), 37
Wells, Dr. Horace (1815–1848) (dentist), 380
Wells, Rachel Lovell (1735–1796) (sister of Wright, P. L., waxworks modeler), 274–75
Wendall, Mr. (amateur mimic and musician), 97
West, James (actor, balloonist), 144
Westborough, Mass.: as location for Badcock, 206–7; for Burlesson, 18, 40, 173, 175, 189; for camel, 129; for jackal, 147; for Jones, I., 257–58; for Noble, E., 21; for Parkman, E., 12
Westchester County, N.Y., 345
Westfield, Mass., 24–25, 37, 147–48, 257–59, 427n52

West Indies: 18, 20, 273; and camels, 130; and lion, 128; and specific itinerants, 27–28, 64, 106, 179, 240, 243, 250–51; and theater companies, 226; travel time to, 37
Westover, Va., 135
Wethersfield, Conn., 42, 46, 77, 246, 263
Weymouth, Mass., 205
Wheeler, Ceaser (servant, violinist), 237–38
Wheeler, N[athan]. (1789–1849) (painter, profilist), 47–48
Wheeler, Ruth (alternative healer), 366, 448n61
Whidden's Assembly Room, Portsmouth, N.H., 242
"whispering Fairy" (automaton), 334
White, D. (wife of White, J., flower-making teacher), 78
White, J. (ornamental and sign painter, japanner, decorator, flower-making teacher), 78
White, John (dancing-master), 218
Whitefield, Rev. George (1714–1770) (Methodist preacher, revivalist), 249, 255–56, 424n1
Whitehall, N.Y., 41, 280
White Horse Tavern, Boston, 148
Whole Booke of Psalmes, The [Sternhold and Hopkins], 201
Wicker, Jacob (ornamental painter), 86, 291
Williams, Henry (1787–1830) (miniaturist, wax artist, profilist, electrical healer), 267, 301–2, 306, 311, 321, 429n86, 437n51
Williams, Capt. John (d. 1748) (merchant, importer), 249–51
Williams, Moses (1777–c. 1825) (African American profilist, freed slave), 326–27
Williams, William (painter, art teacher), 47
Williams's long room, Charleston, 71
Williamstown, Mass., 44, 243
Willington, Conn., 213
Willman, Mr. (bird trainer), 52
Wilson, Robert ["Whistling Bor"] (animal proprietor), 134
Winchester, Mass., 309
Windsor, Charles and Rebecca (French and lace-making teachers), 394n54
Windsor, Conn., 203–4
Windsor County, Vt., 96, 400n42
Windsor Falls, Conn., 45
Wing, John (tavern keeper, artillery captain), 1, 17–18, 239, 377, 380
Wing's Lane, Boston, 1, 70, 249, 283
Winsor, Justin (1831–1897) (historian, author, librarian), 128
wire dancers, 8, 186. *See also* slack-wire performers

wirewalkers, 122, 135, 150, 153
Wirt, William (1772–1834) (author, U.S. Attorney General), 12, 23, 372, 387n19
Wiscasset, Maine, 46
Wolfe Tavern [Davenport's], Newburyport, Mass., 242
Wolton, Mr. (English equestrian), 148
Women, Medicine, and Theatre [Katritzky], 10
"Wonderful Woman" (automaton), 10, 333
Wood, Joseph (1778–1830) (miniaturist, profilist, inventor), 321
Wood, William (singing master), 208–9
Woodbury, Conn., 204
Woodbury, N.J., 144
woodcuts: as advertising, 2, 99–100, 188, 401n2; English, 177, 401n2; misleading, 119; as source of information, 115. *See also* images; *individual itinerants*
Woodruff's tavern [Isaac], Springfield, N.J., 70
Woods, Philip (1774–1828) (museum proprietor, waxworks exhibitor, electrical healer): and Boston Museum, 96, 267, 278, 285, 321, 430n11; and Corné's panoramas, 267, 293, 300; as medical electrician, 267–68, 298, 429n86; and waxworks, 80, 218, 267, 275, 278–79, 282, 285, 301, 434n1
Woodside, John (peddler), 252
Wood's long room, Charleston, 182
Woodstock, Vt., 373
Woonsocket, R.I., 381
Worcester, Mass., 96, 185, 189, 221, 243, 257, 291, 309
Worrall, John (c. 1783–1825) (actor, painter): as Harlequin actor, 233–34; large-scale paintings of, 292; as stage painter, 233–35, 293, 432n9; transparency by, 299
Worlds of Wonder, Days of Judgment [Hall], 10
Wrifford, Allison [Abel] (1779–1844) (penmanship teacher, author): 52, 443n7; advertising by, 68, 348; circuit of, 22, 347–38, table 20.1; early career of, 347; later career of, 372–73, 449n91; manuals by, 348; pupils of as teachers, 349, 351; recommendations for, 348; and rivalry with Jenkins, 347–48, 350, 354
Wright, Joseph (1756–1793) (painter, profilist), 314–15, 326
Wright, Patience Lovell (1725–1786) (sister of Wells, R. L., waxworks modeler), 81, 274–77, 314, 430n7
Wright, Richardson L. (1887–1961) (magazine editor, author, historian), 11
Wyatt, James (fl. 1749 in New York) (puppeteer, waxworks proprietor, lanternist): and "The

Children in the Wood," 163, 362–63; lantern stories of, 162–63, 362–63; puppet plays of, 163, 178–79, 190, 194, 362–63, 447n41; travel to West Indies of, 373; venues of, 190–91; as waxworks proprietor, 162, 190, 274;
Wyman, Miss (conjurer), 366–67

Yale College, 81, 143, 239, 254, 263, 281, 283, 314
Yeates, Mr. (active after 1725) (London puppeteer), 175, 178
Yeates, Mr., Jr., 178
Yeldall, Dr. Anthony (fl. 1770–1799) (alternative healer, mountebank, pharmaceutical peddler): 13; and apprentice, 86; arrest of, 358–59; as culture carrier, 30–32; early career in America of, 25–26; itinerary of, 26, 36, 388n29, table 1.3; as mountebank, 24–25, 31, 55, 74; in New York City, 27; as pharmaceutical peddler, 26, 266; return to London of, 371
yellow fever, 274
York, Va., 265
Yorkshire County, England: 51, 54; trick riders, 73, 150
Yorktown, Va., 20, 226, 278
"young Negro Boy" (black acrobat), 56

zebra, 130

Born in Geneva, Switzerland, Peter Benes received his education at the Mill Hill School in London, Berkeley (California) High School, Harvard College, Harvard University Graduate School of Education, and Boston University's American and New England Studies Program. He is the cofounder (1976), director, and editor of the The Dublin Seminar for New England Folklife, a continuing series of conferences, exhibitions, and publications exploring everyday life, work, and culture in New England's past formerly published by Boston University but now affiliated with Historic Deerfield, Inc. Benes's first book, *The Masks of Orthodoxy: Folk Gravestone Carving in Plymouth County, Massachusetts, 1689–1805* (University of Massachusetts Press, 1977), received the Chicago Folklore Prize. His second book, *Meetinghouses of Early New England* (University of Massachusetts Press, 2012), was the winner of the Abbott Lowell Cummings Prize of the Vernacular Architecture Forum and the Fred B. Kniffen Book Award from the Pioneer America Society for excellence in material culture studies. His other publications include four exhibition catalogues, two coedited volumes, and numerous articles on New England history, cartography, art, and culture. In 2011 he and his wife, Jane Montague Benes, received the Bay State Legacy Award for their contributions to Massachusetts history; in 2014 an Award of Merit from the American Association for State and Local History; and in 2015 a Preservation Award from Historic Deerfield. Jane and Peter have two daughters and five grandchildren; they live in Concord, Massachusetts.

MAY 04 2017

14

HEWLETT-WOODMERE PUBLIC LIBRARY
3 1327 00630 6823

28 Day Loan

Hewlett-Woodmere Public Library
Hewlett, New York 11557

Business Phone 516-374-1967
Recorded Announcements 516-374-1667
Website www.hwpl.org